Generative AI Security

IEEE Press
445 Hoes Lane
Piscataway, NJ 08854

Generative AI Security

Defense, Threats, and Vulnerabilities

Shaila Rana and Rhonda Chicone
ACT Research Institute

IEEE Press
WILEY

Published by John Wiley & Sons, Inc., Hoboken, New Jersey.

Library of Congress Cataloging-in-Publication Data Applied for:

Hardback ISBN: 9781394368488

Cover Design: Wiley
Cover Image: © Sergey Nivens/stock.adobe.com

Set in 9.5/12.5pt STIXTwoText by Straive, Chennai, India

To the pioneers of cybersecurity and the next generation of innovators, may this work inspire a safer, more secure digital future. And to our family, friends, and colleagues whose support and encouragement made this journey possible, this book is as much yours as it is ours.

Contents

About the Authors

Dr. Shaila Rana is the Founder of CyberSecure, a cybersecurity consulting firm, and a Professor of Cybersecurity and IT. She is also the co-founder of the ACT Research Institute, which is an AI, cybersecurity, and technology-focused think tank. Dr. Rana is also the chair of an IEEE Standards Association (SA) for ZTA in Healthcare, an Author at Pluralsight, and an Instructor at O'Reilly. Her research focuses primarily on AI, cybersecurity, and VR/AR. She has authored multiple books and courses focusing on security risks associated with AI, security governance, and cybersecurity laws and regulations. She holds a PhD specializing in Information Systems Security and holds an MS in Computer Information Systems, specializing in Cybersecurity. Dr. Rana publishes and presents at multiple conferences annually and serves as a reviewer for multiple journals.

Dr. Rhonda Chicone is a dedicated academic, professor, researcher, and software engineer with dual passions for software product development and cybersecurity. Throughout her career, she has held various positions, including software engineer, software engineering manager, director of software development, CTO (Chief Technology Officer), CSO (Chief Security Officer), and Professor, primarily focusing on commercial software products. Her significant contributions to program development within academia demonstrate her strong passion for the intersection of innovation, education, and technology. She is the Co-Founder of the ACT Research Institute, an AI, cybersecurity, and technology-focused think tank. In addition to her professional achievements, she frequently publishes and presents at national conferences.

Preface

At the intersection of innovation and security lies one of the most transformative technological developments of our time: generative artificial intelligence. As we stand at this critical juncture, the need for a comprehensive understanding of how generative AI reshapes our cybersecurity landscape has never been more urgent. This book was born from a recognition that while much has been written about generative AI's capabilities and potential applications, significantly less attention has been paid to the complex security implications that accompany these powerful technologies. The relationship between generative AI and cybersecurity is not merely additive but transformative. These technologies fundamentally alter both how we defend our digital assets and how those assets can be compromised.

Our approach in this book is unique in that we examine generative AI through what we call the "Triangular Approach," exploring generative AI as a security tool that enhances our defensive capabilities, as a weapon that can be leveraged by malicious actors, and as a target that itself requires protection. This three-dimensional perspective provides security professionals, technology leaders, and organizations with a comprehensive framework for understanding and addressing the complete spectrum of generative AI security concerns. In the chapters that follow, we move from foundational concepts to practical applications, from theoretical risks to real-world defensive strategies. We've included case studies throughout that illustrate how organizations of various sizes are navigating these challenges, along with actionable guidance that readers can apply immediately to strengthen their security postures.

This book arrives at a pivotal moment. Organizations worldwide are rapidly adopting generative AI technologies, often without fully understanding the security implications. Our goal is to equip you with the knowledge needed to make informed decisions, implement effective protections, and harness the benefits of generative AI while mitigating its risks. Whether you're a CISO developing an enterprise-wide AI security strategy, a security analyst working to protect AI systems, or a business leader seeking to understand the security implications of your

AI investments, this book provides a roadmap for navigating the complex intersection of generative AI and cybersecurity.

The future of digital security will be defined by how well we understand and manage the relationship between generative AI and cybersecurity. It is my sincere hope that this book contributes meaningfully to that understanding and helps create a more secure digital ecosystem for all.

San Jose, CA
October 2025

Dr. Shaila Rana
Dr. Rhonda Chicone

Introduction

In an era where artificial intelligence is reshaping the digital landscape, generative AI stands at the forefront of both innovation and security concerns (Palo Alto Networks, n.d.). From creating synthetic media to automating complex cybersecurity tasks, generative AI is a powerful tool that can either strengthen or compromise our digital defenses. As organizations worldwide integrate these technologies into their operations, understanding their security implications has become not just advantageous but also essential.

This book explores the intricate and subtle relationship between generative AI and cybersecurity and offers a comprehensive examination of how these technologies affect our security landscape. We delve into both of the equations: how generative AI can enhance our security postures through advanced threat detection and automated response systems, and how it can be weaponized by malicious actors to create more sophisticated attacks. However, we also critically examine the unique vulnerabilities of AI models themselves, an often overlooked but critical aspect of AI security.

For security professionals, IT managers, and technology decision-makers, this knowledge is no longer optional. As generative AI becomes increasingly embedded in our digital infrastructure, the ability to harness its benefits while mitigating its risks will determine the effectiveness of any modern security strategy. Through practical examples, technical insights, and strategic guidance, this book provides the foundational knowledge needed to navigate this complex landscape. Whether you're looking to implement generative AI security solutions, defend against AI-powered threats, or simply understand the implications of these technologies for your organization's security posture, this book will serve as your comprehensive guide to securing systems in the age of generative AI!

1

Generative AI in Cybersecurity

The rapid rise of generative artificial intelligence (GAI) has fundamentally transformed the cybersecurity landscape. From crafting convincing phishing emails to detecting complex attack patterns, GAI is both an unprecedented challenge and a powerful tool in the ongoing battle to secure our digital systems. As we enter this new era, security professionals must develop a deep understanding of these technologies to effectively protect their organizations. This chapter lays the groundwork for understanding GAI and its complex relationship with cybersecurity. We begin by exploring the fundamental concepts of GAI, examining how these systems learn to create new content and the various types of models that drive this innovation.

We'll then trace the evolution of AI in cybersecurity, from its early applications in malware detection to today's sophisticated AI-driven security systems. This historical context is crucial for understanding how we arrived at our current security landscape and where we might be heading. The chapter concludes by examining the dual nature of GAI in security—its potential as both a defensive tool and a security threat—while exploring its current applications across various sectors. As we navigate through this chapter, you'll develop a foundational understanding of GAI that will serve as a basis for the more technical and strategic discussions in subsequent chapters. Whether you're a seasoned security professional or new to the field of AI security, this chapter will equip you with the essential context needed to understand the opportunities and challenges that lie ahead.

1.1 What Is Generative AI?

We've heard of ChatGPT (probably extensively at this point), we've heard of Claude, we've heard of DALL-E, and we've heard of so many GAI tools. But, what exactly is GAI? GAI encompasses a class of AI systems designed to create new content, ranging from text and images to code and synthetic data. At its core,

Generative AI Security: Defense, Threats, and Vulnerabilities, First Edition. Shaila Rana and Rhonda Chicone.

GAI learns patterns from existing data and uses these patterns to generate novel outputs that maintain the statistical properties and characteristics of the training data (Cohan, 2024). Unlike traditional AI systems that focus on classification or prediction tasks, GAI models can produce entirely new content that has never existed before, while maintaining coherence and relevance to their training (Palo Alto Networks, n.d.).

The landscape of GAI models is diverse, with several key architectures dominating the field. Large Language Models (LLMs) (Alto, 2023), like GPT-4 and Claude, specialize in text generation and understanding, while Generative Adversarial Networks (GANs) excel at creating realistic images and videos. Diffusion models, exemplified by DALL-E and Stable Diffusion, have revolutionized image generation through their ability to gradually transform random noise into coherent images (Ali et al., 2021). Variational Autoencoders (VAEs) offer another approach, focusing on learning compact representations of data that can be used to generate new samples (Doersch, 2016). Moreover, the applications of GAI span across numerous industries and use cases. In software development, AI assistants help write and debug code, potentially increasing developer productivity by 30–40% according to recent studies (Hendrich, 2024). In creative industries, GAI tools are being used for content creation, with platforms like Midjourney generating millions of images daily (Kumar, 2024). The healthcare sector employs generative models to synthesize medical images for training and research, while financial institutions use them for fraud detection and risk analysis (Avacharmal et al., 2023).

It is one of the fastest-growing consumer applications in history. The CEO of Amazon, Andy Jassy, recently said that "Generative AI may be the largest technology transformation since the cloud" (Resinger, 2024). Fortune 500 companies have already leveraged AI and are setting a new global standard, especially when it comes to AI-driven supply chain optimization (Lundberg, 2024). The global GAI market is projected to reach $200 billion by 2025, reflecting an extraordinary compound annual growth rate (Alfa People, 2024). In terms of user adoption, platforms like ChatGPT reached 100 million users within just two months of launch, making it one of the fastest-growing consumer applications in history (Mahajan, 2024).

This widespread adoption has significant implications for cybersecurity, as organizations must now consider both the opportunities and risks presented by these powerful technologies. These adoption rates and market projections paint a clear picture: GAI is not just a technological trend but a fundamental shift in how we create, process, and interact with digital content. It is not going away anytime soon and becoming a forgotten technology (like 3D televisions). For cybersecurity professionals, understanding this technology and its capabilities is crucial for protecting organizations against emerging threats while leveraging its potential for enhanced security measures. However, the rapid evolution and adoption of GAI bring us to a critical juncture where we must consider its future trajectory and implications. As we look ahead, several key trends and developments are likely to shape the landscape of GAI. First, we're seeing increasing convergence between different types of GAI models. While early systems specialized in specific domains like text or images, newer architectures are becoming more versatile, capable of handling multiple modalities simultaneously (Chen et al., 2024). This convergence suggests a future where GAI systems become more comprehensive and integrated, potentially leading to more sophisticated and nuanced applications across industries.

The role of GAI in cybersecurity reveals a triangular dynamic that reshapes our understanding of digital defense. Organizations are now navigating a three-dimensional landscape where GAI simultaneously serves as a powerful security tool, presents itself as a potential weapon in the wrong hands, and emerges as a target with its own unique vulnerabilities. As security teams deploy AI to enhance threat detection, automate response procedures, and proactively identify weaknesses, malicious actors are exploring how these same technologies can be weaponized to create increasingly sophisticated attacks. Meanwhile, the AI systems themselves harbor vulnerabilities that require protection, creating a complex security matrix where defenders must not only leverage AI capabilities but also defend the very tools they rely upon from exploitation or compromise.

Moreover, the democratization of generative AI technology presents opportunities, challenges, and a target. As these tools become more accessible, we're seeing unprecedented levels of innovation and creativity across various sectors. Small businesses and individual developers can now leverage capabilities that were previously available only to large organizations with substantial resources. However, this democratization also raises concerns about potential misuse, emphasizing the need for robust governance frameworks and security measures. Another significant trend is the increasing focus on efficiency and optimization in GAI systems. While early models required substantial computational resources, newer approaches are exploring ways to achieve similar or better results with reduced processing power and energy consumption. This trend toward "green AI" reflects growing awareness of the environmental impact of AI systems and could lead to more sustainable approaches to AI development and deployment (Bolón-Canedo et al., 2024). The integration of GAI with other emerging technologies is also shaping its evolution. The combination of GAI and quantum computing (which we will discuss in Chapter 8), for instance, could lead to breakthrough capabilities in areas like drug discovery, materials science, and complex system simulation (Kumar et al., 2024). Similarly, the intersection of GAI with edge computing could enable more sophisticated real-time applications while addressing privacy and latency concerns (Ale et al., 2024). Looking ahead, we can expect GAI to become increasingly embedded in our digital infrastructure, moving from standalone applications to integrated systems that enhance various aspects of our technological landscape.

This integration will likely lead to new challenges in security, privacy, and governance, requiring ongoing adaptation of our regulatory and ethical frameworks.

The impact of GAI on workforce dynamics and skill requirements cannot be overlooked (hence, one of the reasons for this book). As these systems become more sophisticated, there's a growing need for professionals who can effectively work alongside AI systems, understanding both their capabilities and limitations. This suggests a future where human expertise becomes even more valuable, especially in areas requiring judgment, creativity, and ethical consideration. Overall, this rapid evolution and widespread adoption of GAI technologies underscore the importance of maintaining a balanced perspective—one that recognizes both the transformative potential of these technologies and the need for responsible development and deployment.

1.2 The Evolution of AI in Cybersecurity

The integration of AI into cybersecurity has evolved dramatically over the past several decades, transforming from simple rule-based systems to today's sophisticated AI-driven security platforms. In the 1980s and early 1990s, cybersecurity relied primarily on signature-based detection methods, where systems would identify threats by matching them against databases of known malicious patterns (Alam, 2022). The first significant application of AI in cybersecurity emerged in the late 1990s with the introduction of anomaly detection systems that could identify unusual patterns in network traffic (Garcia-Teodoro et al., 2009).

An important milestone occurred in the early 2000s with the development of machine learning (ML)-based intrusion detection systems (IDS) (Secureworks, 2024). These systems marked a significant advancement by moving beyond rigid rule-based approaches to more dynamic threat detection. Now, coming to 2010, security information and event management (SIEM) platforms began incorporating AI capabilities, enabling real-time analysis of security alerts and correlation of events across multiple systems (González-Granadillo et al., 2021). The introduction of IBM Watson for Cybersecurity in 2016 was another watershed moment, demonstrating how AI could process vast amounts of unstructured security data and natural language information to enhance threat intelligence (Rashid, 2016). Between 2018 and today, several transformative developments have reshaped AI-driven security. The emergence of AI-powered endpoint detection and response (EDR) systems revolutionized endpoint security by providing continuous monitoring and automated response capabilities (The State of AI Cyber Security 2024, 2024). Security orchestration, automation, and response (SOAR) platforms integrated AI to automate incident response workflows, significantly reducing response times from hours to minutes (Express Computer,

2023). During this period, deep learning models became increasingly adept at detecting zero-day malware (Hindy et al., 2020).

In its current state, AI-driven security has become an indispensable component of modern cybersecurity architecture. Today's security operations centers (SOCs) leverage AI for everything from threat hunting and vulnerability management to automated patch prioritization and user behavior analytics (Yaseen, 2022). Security tools now incorporate advanced natural language processing (NLP) to analyze threat intelligence feeds, while ML models continuously adapt to evolving attack patterns (Balantrapu, 2024). The integration of AI has also enabled predictive security measures, allowing organizations to anticipate and prevent potential threats before they materialize. This evolution has led to a paradigm shift, where AI is no longer just a tool for security analysts but an essential partner in maintaining robust cybersecurity defenses.

The sophistication of current AI security systems is evident in their ability to process and analyze enormous volumes of security data in real time. Modern security platforms can process over 1 trillion security events per day using AI to filter out noise and identify genuine threats with unprecedented accuracy (Montasari, 2024). This capability has become crucial as 4000 new cyberattacks occur every day (Palatty, 2025). This number is quickly growing and evolving, probably different and more now as you read this. Thus, this makes manual analysis practically impossible. The current state of AI in cybersecurity represents a convergence of multiple technologies—ML, NLP, behavioral analytics, and automation—working in concert to provide comprehensive security coverage.

1.3 Overview of GAI in Security

In general, the use of GAI in security is referred to as a dual-edged sword or having a dual nature. But, there's a third side that we will address in this book, how AI itself can be compromised. This is an increasingly significant attack vector in our current landscape. But, for now, in this section, let's focus on how GAI can be both a tool and a weapon.

As a defensive tool, GAI enhances security operations by automating threat detection, generating synthetic data for training security systems, and developing robust defensive strategies (Kumar & Sinha, 2023). Security teams can leverage GAI to create realistic attack scenarios for testing defenses, automate the writing of security rules and policies, and even generate patches for newly discovered vulnerabilities (Hoang, 2024). The technology's ability to process and analyze vast amounts of security data in real time has revolutionized incident response, enabling security teams to identify and respond to threats faster than ever before. Furthermore, GAI can assist in anomaly detection by establishing baseline network behavior patterns and flagging deviations that might indicate security breaches, often identifying subtle attack patterns that human analysts might miss (NIST AI, 2024).

However, the same capabilities that make GAI valuable for defense also make it a formidable tool for attackers. Malicious actors can exploit GAI to create more sophisticated phishing campaigns, develop polymorphic malware that evades traditional detection methods, and automate the discovery of system vulnerabilities (Schmitt & Flechais, 2024). The technology's ability to generate highly convincing deepfakes and synthetic media poses new challenges for authentication and trust (Farouk & Fahmi, 2024). Moreover, attackers can use GAI to scale their operations, launching more numerous and varied attacks while requiring fewer resources and less technical expertise. GAI can be used to craft persuasive social engineering messages tailored to specific targets by mining publicly available information, significantly increasing the success rates of such attacks compared to traditional methods (Metta et al., 2024). The accessibility of powerful GAI tools has lowered barriers to entry for cybercriminals, with studies showing that even individuals with limited technical skills can now generate functional malware using LLMs (Zhang & Tenney, 2023). This "democratization" of attack capabilities has expanded the threat landscape, as attacks that previously required significant expertise can now be executed by a wider range of actors. Additionally, GAI systems have been shown to excel at identifying zero-day vulnerabilities through automated code analysis and fuzzing techniques, potentially giving attackers an edge in discovering exploitable flaws before patches are available (Kaur et al., 2024). However, we will discuss this in more detail in later chapters.

Consequently, this leads us to a complex dynamic where it is a constant cat-and-mouse game, or an AI-powered arms race. Organizations must now develop security strategies that not only leverage AI's defensive capabilities but also account for AI-enhanced threats. This includes implementing AI-powered security controls while simultaneously developing defenses against AI-generated attacks. The challenge lies in staying ahead of adversaries who are equally capable of exploiting these technologies, making it crucial for security professionals to understand both aspects of GAI's role in the security landscape. This duality underscores the importance of responsible AI development and deployment, as well as the need for continued innovation in AI security measures. Adding to this complexity, security teams must now consider model poisoning attacks, where adversaries attempt to corrupt training data or fine-tuning processes of security-focused AI systems to introduce backdoors or biases (Huckelberry et al., 2024). As organizations increasingly rely on GAI for security operations, ensuring the integrity of these systems becomes a critical concern.

An important aspect of this book is the necessity to bridge the gap between the theoretical and the practical. Thus, let's go over a hypothetical example that mirrors a real-world situation. We will first examine how traditionally we have looked at GAI in cybersecurity: through a dual-lens wherein GAI is both a tool and a weapon. Let's pretend there is an organization named Midwest Health Solutions, a regional healthcare provider with 50 employees, recently implemented GAI tools to enhance their security operations. With a small IT team of just three people, they saw AI as a way to multiply their defensive capabilities without expanding headcount. The organization began using AI to automate their security monitoring and incident response. Their AI system helped analyze patient records access patterns, flagging unusual behavior that might indicate data breaches. It also assisted in generating and updating security policies, ensuring compliance with healthcare regulations while adapting to new threats. The AI tool proved particularly valuable in creating realistic phishing simulations for employee training, significantly improving their security awareness program. However, six months into their AI implementation, Midwest Health Solutions became the target of an AI-powered attack. The attackers used GAI to create highly convincing spear-phishing emails that appeared to come from the organization's CEO. These emails contained contextually accurate information gathered from public sources and social media, making them particularly persuasive. The AI-generated messages even mimicked the CEO's writing style, having learned it from publicly available communications. Several employees received personalized emails discussing specific projects they were working on, with urgent requests for patient information or financial transfers. While most employees recognized these as suspicious thanks to their AI-enhanced security training, one administrative assistant nearly fell for the attack, stopped only by the AI-powered email filtering system that the organization had implemented.

The incident highlighted both the defensive and offensive capabilities of GAI. The same technology that helped Midwest Health Solutions create effective security training and detection systems was being used by attackers to create sophisticated social engineering attacks. The organization's AI security tools detected the attack pattern and helped prevent data loss, but the event served as a wake-up call. In response, Midwest Health Solutions expanded their use of AI defensive tools, implementing additional layers of AI-powered authentication and monitoring. They also used their AI system to analyze the attack patterns and generate new security rules to prevent similar incidents. The AI helped identify vulnerabilities in their systems that the attackers might have used to gather information for their targeted campaign.

Essentially, this scenario demonstrates how small organizations must navigate the dual nature of GAI in cybersecurity. While AI provides powerful tools for defending against attacks and automating security operations, it also enables more sophisticated and personalized attacks. Success in this environment requires understanding both aspects of the technology and implementing appropriate controls while maintaining constant vigilance against evolving AI-powered threats. Moreover, this example also shows how AI can level the playing field for smaller organizations, providing enterprise-level security capabilities with minimal staff, while simultaneously illustrating the new threats these organizations face from adversaries wielding the same technology.

1.4 Current Landscape of Generative AI Applications

The current landscape of GAI applications spans across numerous sectors, with businesses and industries leading adoption. In the corporate world, GAI is transforming operations through automated content creation, customer service chatbots, and intelligent process automation (Chakraborty et al., 2023). Major enterprises are using these technologies for everything from marketing content generation to product design and development. Financial institutions leverage GAI for fraud detection, risk assessment, and algorithmic trading (Chen et al., 2023), while manufacturing sectors employ it for design optimization and predictive maintenance (Rane et al., 2024). Healthcare organizations are using GAI to assist in drug discovery, medical imaging analysis, and personalized treatment planning (Prabhod, 2023). In government and defense, GAI applications have become increasingly sophisticated and mission-critical. Defense agencies utilize these technologies for threat analysis, intelligence processing, and military strategy simulation (National Research Council, Division on Engineering, Physical Sciences, Board on Mathematical Sciences, Their Applications, Committee on Modeling, & Simulation for Defense Transformation, 2006). Government organizations employ GAI for public service automation, policy analysis, and emergency response planning (Pandey, 2024).

The research and academic sector is a crucial innovation hub for GAI development. Universities and research institutions are pushing the boundaries of what's possible with GAI, conducting groundbreaking research in areas such as model architecture, training methodologies, and ethical AI development (Liu & Jagadish, 2024). Academic laboratories are exploring novel applications in fields ranging from climate science to particle physics, while also investigating the societal implications of widespread AI adoption (Xu et al., 2021). Collaborative research projects between academia and industry are accelerating the development of more efficient and capable AI systems.

Healthcare deserves special mention as a sector where GAI is making remarkable and important strides. Beyond traditional medical applications, GAI is being used to simulate patient scenarios for medical training, generate synthetic medical data for research while preserving privacy, and assist in surgical planning through 3D model generation (Sai et al., 2024). The technology is also revolutionizing pharmaceutical research by helping in the design of new molecular structures and predicting drug interactions (Tiwari et al., 2023).

The media and entertainment industry has emerged as another major adopter of GAI technologies. Film studios use AI for special effects generation, content editing, and even script analysis (Kavitha, 2023). Gaming companies employ GAI for creating dynamic content, realistic character behaviors, and procedurally generated environments (Karaca et al., 2023). News organizations utilize AI for automated content creation, fact-checking, and personalized news delivery (Xu et al., 2023). The creative industries, including advertising and design, are leveraging GAI for rapid prototyping, creative ideation, and automated content variation generation (Alabi, 2024).

It is also important to examine how we use GAI in our personal lives. It has become an increasingly integral part of daily life, transforming how individuals manage their homes, pursue hobbies, and handle everyday tasks. People are using AI assistants to help with everything from writing emails and crafting resumes to planning meals and generating workout routines (McGeorge, 2023). It is so easy to have ChatGPT create a grocery list for you based on your budget, allergies, and food preferences. Creative individuals are leveraging tools like Midjourney and DALL-E to create personal artwork, design home renovation concepts, or assist with hobby projects. Parents are using GAI to help their children with homework explanations, while others use it for personal budgeting, travel planning, and even drafting important personal communications (Kaplan, 2024).

Anthropic has unveiled the Model Context Protocol (MCP), an open-source standard designed to bridge the gap between AI assistants and external data sources, including content repositories, business tools, and development environments (Anthropic, 2024). This protocol tackles a fundamental limitation that has hindered even the most sophisticated AI models: their isolation from valuable data trapped behind information silos and legacy systems. By replacing fragmented, custom integrations with a universal standard, MCP offers developers a streamlined approach to connecting AI systems with the data they need, comprising three key components: the protocol specification with Software Development Kits (SDKs), local server support in Claude Desktop applications, and an open-source repository of prebuilt servers for popular enterprise systems like Google Drive, Slack, GitHub, and Postgres.

From a security perspective, MCP represents a significant evolution in how GAI functions as a tool, though the implications for its potential as a weapon or target remain largely implicit rather than explicitly addressed in Anthropic's announcement. As a tool, MCP dramatically enhances AI utility by creating standardized access channels to diverse data sources, enabling AI assistants to produce more contextually relevant and accurate responses based on previously inaccessible information. Early adopters, including Block and Apollo, have already integrated the protocol, while development tool companies such as Zed, Replit, Codeium, and Sourcegraph are leveraging MCP to help AI agents better understand coding contexts and produce more functional code with fewer attempts. The weaponization and targeting aspects of this technology, though not directly discussed in the announcement, merit consideration as the protocol creates new pathways to potentially sensitive information. The increased connectivity between AI systems and data sources could introduce novel security vulnerabilities if not properly implemented and maintained, with MCP servers potentially becoming attractive targets for threat actors seeking unauthorized access to connected systems. Despite these implicit concerns, Anthropic's emphasis remains on the protocol's collaborative, open-source nature and its potential to transform how AI interacts with real-world data ecosystems—replacing today's fragmented integration landscape with a more sustainable architecture, where AI systems maintain context as they navigate between different tools and datasets.

The integration of GAI into smart home systems and personal devices has further expanded its role in private life. Voice assistants powered by GAI can manage home automation systems, provide personalized entertainment recommendations, and even help with language learning and personal education (Soofastaei, 2024). DIY enthusiasts are using AI to generate project plans and instructions, while amateur photographers employ AI tools for image editing and enhancement. This democratization of AI technology has made sophisticated capabilities accessible to the average person, fundamentally changing how individuals approach personal productivity, creativity, and problem-solving in their daily lives. Consequently, this further highlights the importance of understanding the role that GAI plays in our current digital landscape. Moreover, applications of this technology will continue to evolve (especially with Artificial General Intelligence, or AGI, on the near horizon).

1.5 A Triangular Approach

A distinctive feature of this book's approach is its examination of GAI through a critical triangular framework—viewing AI simultaneously as a tool, a weapon, and a target in the cybersecurity landscape. This multifaceted perspective provides a comprehensive understanding of both the opportunities and challenges presented by GAI in security contexts. As a tool, GAI offers unprecedented capabilities for enhancing cybersecurity operations. From automating threat detection and response to generating synthetic data for security testing, AI systems can augment human capabilities and improve security postures. Organizations are leveraging these tools to analyze vast amounts of security telemetry, identify patterns that might escape human notice, and respond to potential threats with increased speed and accuracy. This toolset aspect of AI extends to areas like automated penetration testing, security policy generation, and incident response planning. The weapon aspect of GAI cannot be ignored—these same capabilities that enhance security operations can be weaponized by malicious actors. Adversaries can use GAI to create more sophisticated phishing attacks, develop new malware variants, or automate the discovery of system vulnerabilities. The ability of GAI to create convincing deepfakes and synthetic content adds another layer to potential attack vectors, requiring organizations to develop new approaches to authentication and verification. Probably most critically, GAI systems themselves have become high-value targets for attackers. As organizations increasingly rely on AI for critical decisions and operations, the security of these systems becomes paramount. Adversaries might attempt to poison training data, exploit model vulnerabilities, or manipulate AI outputs through adversarial attacks. Understanding AI as a target requires organizations to implement specific security measures to protect their AI systems while ensuring the integrity and reliability of AI-generated outputs.

Fundamentally, we need to have a paradigm shift in how we think of AI security: from the dual-edged lens to a triangular framework. Traditional dual-edged thinking, which focuses primarily on offensive and defensive capabilities, emerged from a time when cybersecurity primarily involved protecting systems from external threats while potentially leveraging similar tools for testing and validation. However, this perspective becomes inadequate when dealing with AI systems that can simultaneously serve as security tools, potential weapons, and vulnerable targets themselves. The dual-edged approach fails to account for the unique vulnerabilities of AI systems, potentially leaving organizations exposed to sophisticated attacks that target their AI infrastructure directly, even as they focus on using AI for defense and protecting against AI-powered attacks.

The triangular framework becomes especially important when considering the cascading effects possible in AI security incidents. Under the traditional dual-edged approach, organizations might successfully implement AI-powered security tools and develop countermeasures against AI-enabled attacks, yet remain vulnerable to attacks that compromise their AI systems themselves. This blind spot can lead to catastrophic security failures where compromised AI systems not only cease to provide defensive capabilities but potentially become weapons against their own organizations. For instance, a compromised AI security system might not only fail to detect threats but also actively help conceal malicious activity or even generate false alerts that distract from real security incidents. This interconnected nature of AI security risks and the AI supply chain demands a more comprehensive approach that explicitly recognizes and addresses the vulnerability of AI systems themselves. The triangular framework thus represents not just an evolution in security thinking but a necessary adaptation to the reality of AI-dependent security operations. Organizations must develop security strategies that simultaneously leverage AI's capabilities, defend against its malicious use, and protect their AI infrastructure—a complexity that simply cannot be captured in traditional dual-edged security models. Consequently, this triangular framework—tool, weapon, and target—provides a structured approach for organizations to assess and address the security implications of GAI. It emphasizes the need for a balanced strategy that leverages AI's benefits while protecting against its potential misuse and securing the systems themselves. Throughout this book, this framework serves as a lens through which we examine various aspects of GAI security, from technical implementations to policy considerations and future trends.

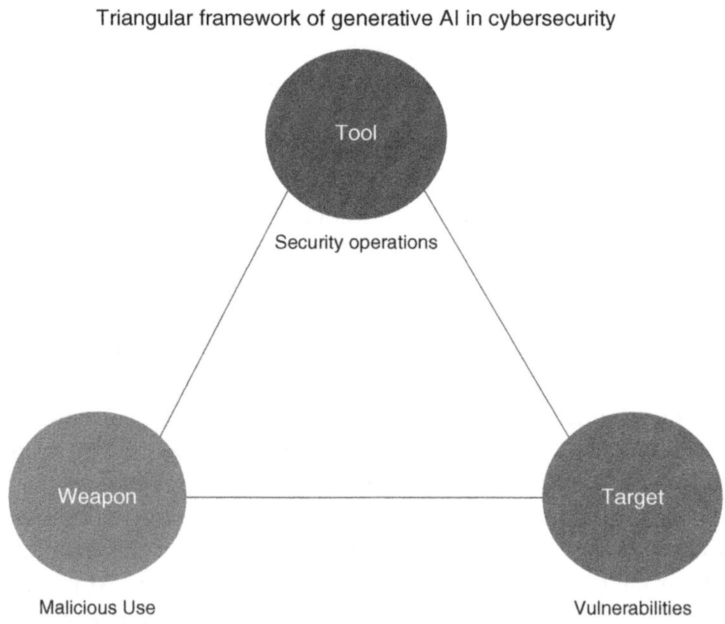

The triangular framework of GAI in cybersecurity illustrates the complex, interconnected relationship between three critical dimensions. As a TOOL, GAI enhances security operations through automation, threat detection, and incident response capabilities. However, this same technology can undergo WEAPONIZATION, where malicious actors leverage GAI for sophisticated attacks, including phishing, malware generation, and deepfakes. Simultaneously, AI systems themselves become high-value TARGETS, containing inherent VULNERABILITIES that adversaries seek to exploit through data poisoning, model manipulation, and adversarial attacks. This framework emphasizes the critical need for the

PROTECTION of AI assets while acknowledging that compromised AI tools can be turned against their owners. The relationship between weapon and target illustrates how malicious actors specifically develop EXPLOITATION techniques aimed at AI vulnerabilities, creating a complex security ecosystem where these three aspects continuously interact and influence each other.

The adoption of a triangular framework for understanding GAI security, rather than the traditional dual-lens perspective, is crucial for understanding the term "Generative AI Security." While the dual-lens view (tool vs. weapon) has dominated security discussions, this binary perspective fails to capture the full complexity of AI security challenges in today's landscape. The addition of the third dimension—AI as a target—provides a more comprehensive and nuanced understanding of the security implications of GAI systems. Moreover, the traditional dual-lens approach focuses primarily on the offensive and defensive capabilities of AI, creating a somewhat simplistic arms-race narrative. While this perspective is valuable, it overlooks the critical vulnerability of AI systems themselves. Organizations implementing AI security solutions often focus on how to use AI defensively or protect against its malicious use, without adequately considering how to secure their AI infrastructure and models. This oversight can lead to significant security gaps and potential vulnerabilities. Consider, for example, an organization that successfully implements AI-powered threat detection (tool) and develops robust defenses against AI-generated attacks (weapon). Without considering AI as a target, they might overlook vulnerabilities in their own AI systems, such as potential data poisoning attacks or model manipulation. These vulnerabilities could compromise the entire security infrastructure, rendering both defensive and offensive preparations ineffective.

The triangular framework also better reflects the interconnected nature of modern AI security challenges. An attack on an AI system (target) might compromise its defensive capabilities (tool) while simultaneously turning it into a weapon against its own organization. This cascade effect demonstrates why organizations need to consider all three aspects simultaneously rather than treating them as separate concerns. Additionally, the triangular approach helps organizations develop more comprehensive security strategies. When planning AI security implementations, they must consider not only how to use AI effectively and defend against AI-powered attacks but also how to protect their AI infrastructure itself. This includes considerations such as secure training data and model architectures, implementing robust access controls for AI systems, monitoring for signs of model manipulation or compromise, developing incident response plans specific to AI system attacks, ensuring the integrity of AI-generated outputs, and so much more. Thus, the emergence of AI-specific attack vectors, such as model extraction attacks, adversarial examples, and training data poisoning, further emphasizes the importance of this third dimension. These attacks target the AI systems themselves, potentially compromising both their defensive and offensive capabilities. Understanding and protecting against these threats requires a distinct set of skills and approaches that might be overlooked in a dual-lens framework.

A triangular framework also aligns better with emerging regulatory requirements and compliance frameworks that increasingly recognize AI systems as critical infrastructure requiring specific protection measures. As organizations face growing pressure to demonstrate responsible AI use and robust security measures, the ability to address all three aspects of AI security becomes increasingly important. Looking ahead in this book, the triangular framework provides a more sustainable approach to AI security as technology continues to evolve. New AI capabilities and threats will likely emerge, but they can be effectively categorized and addressed within this three-dimensional understanding. This comprehensive perspective helps organizations stay ahead of emerging threats while maintaining effective security postures across all aspects of their AI implementations.

In general, as aforementioned, GAI is a distinct paradigm shift in how organizations conceptualize and approach AI integration into their security architectures. Frameworks like NIST AI Risk Management Framework (RMF) provide valuable guidance for managing AI-related risks. However, this triangular approach offers a more nuanced and comprehensive perspective specifically tailored to the unique challenges and opportunities presented by GAI technologies. Unlike the NIST AI RMF, which takes a broader risk-management approach to AI implementation, the triangular framework explicitly recognizes GAI's simultaneous roles as a tool, weapon, and target. This multidimensional perspective is crucial for organizations grappling with GAI's unique characteristics and capabilities. While NIST's framework focuses on organizational processes and risk management strategies, treating AI primarily as a technology to be managed and controlled, the triangular framework acknowledges that GAI is not just a risk to be mitigated but also a powerful tool that can enhance security operations when properly leveraged. Furthermore, the triangular framework builds upon NIST AI RMF's foundation while addressing specific gaps in GAI security considerations. Where NIST broadly discusses risks like bias, transparency, and trustworthiness, this framework delves deeper into GAI-specific challenges such as prompt injection attacks, model hallucinations, synthetic media risks, and the unique vulnerabilities of LLMs. For instance, while NIST provides general guidance on AI trustworthiness, the triangular framework specifically addresses how organizations can simultaneously leverage GAI's capabilities while protecting against its potential weaponization and securing the AI systems themselves.

A key differentiation here lies in how the triangular framework approaches GAI integration into information architectures. Rather than focusing solely on risk management processes, it provides a structured approach for organizations to understand and navigate the complex interplay between GAI's various roles.

This is particularly important given the rapid evolution of GAI technologies and the growing demand for clear guidance on AI governance, risk, and compliance. The framework acknowledges that organizations need to do more than just manage risks—they need to actively leverage AI's capabilities while maintaining robust security measures. Moreover, the framework's treatment of GAI as a tool represents a significant departure from NIST's more risk-centric approach. While NIST AI RMF primarily focuses on managing AI-related risks, the triangular framework explicitly recognizes and provides guidance on how organizations can effectively leverage GAI to enhance their security operations. This includes considerations for using AI in threat detection, automated response, and security testing—aspects that may be underemphasized in more traditional risk-management frameworks.

Moreover, the triangular framework addresses emerging challenges specific to GAI that may not be fully captured in the NIST AI RMF. For example, guidance on protecting against data poisoning attacks targeting GAI models, managing the risks of AI hallucinations in security-critical applications, and addressing the ethical implications of synthetic media generation are crucial. These specific considerations are becoming increasingly important as organizations deploy GAI systems in security-sensitive environments. Another key distinction is the emphasis on the interconnected nature of GAI security. While NIST AI RMF treats different aspects of AI risk management somewhat independently, a triangular approach explicitly recognizes how compromises in one area can affect others. For instance, it helps organizations understand how a successful attack on an AI system (target) might not only compromise its defensive capabilities (tool) but also potentially turn it into a weapon against the organization. Furthermore, this book also expands on NIST's foundation by providing more specific guidance on emerging issues like copyright and intellectual property concerns in GAI, the challenges of detecting and preventing deepfake content, and the unique security implications of LLMs. These are areas where organizations need more detailed guidance than what is currently provided in broader AI RMFs.

In terms of practical implementation, a triangular approach complements NIST AI RMF by providing a more actionable approach specifically for GAI security. While NIST offers valuable high-level guidance on AI risk management, organizations often need more specific direction on how to handle the unique challenges posed by GAI technologies. The triangular framework fills this gap by providing concrete guidance on balancing the benefits and risks of GAI while ensuring robust security measures. Furthermore, the framework's recognition of GAI as both a tool and a potential vulnerability helps organizations develop more balanced security strategies. Rather than focusing primarily on risk mitigation, as many traditional frameworks do, it encourages organizations to think creatively about how they can leverage GAI's capabilities while maintaining appropriate security controls. This balanced approach is particularly important as organizations seek to remain competitive while managing the inherent risks of advanced AI technologies. Essentially, a triangular view, as proposed in this book, provides a more adaptable foundation for addressing future developments in GAI security. As new capabilities and threats emerge, organizations can continue to evaluate them through the lens of tool, weapon, and target, ensuring comprehensive coverage of security considerations. This flexibility, combined with its specific focus on GAI, makes the framework a valuable complement to broader AI risk management approaches like NIST AI RMF.

Chapter 1 Summary

This foundational chapter introduced the revolutionary impact of GAI on cybersecurity through a comprehensive triangular framework. The chapter defined GAI as a class of systems that create new content by learning patterns from existing data. It covered technologies like LLMs, GANs, and diffusion models. The chapter traced the evolution of AI in cybersecurity from simple rule-based systems in the 1980s to today's sophisticated AI-driven security platforms. It highlighted key milestones, including ML-based IDS, SIEM platforms with AI capabilities, and modern AI-powered EDR systems.

The chapter presented its central contribution: a triangular framework that moved beyond traditional dual-lens perspectives. This framework examined GAI simultaneously as a **tool** that enhances security operations, a **weapon** that can be exploited by malicious actors, and a **target** vulnerable to attacks itself. The approach acknowledged the complex interconnections between these three dimensions. It provided security professionals with a structured methodology to leverage AI's benefits while addressing its unique risks and vulnerabilities. The framework was illustrated through real-world applications across various sectors, from healthcare and finance to government and personal devices. This demonstrated AI's widespread adoption and the critical need for balanced security strategies.

The triangular framework represented a paradigm shift from traditional cybersecurity thinking. It recognized that AI systems are not merely tools to be used or threats to be defended against, but also critical assets that require protection. This multidimensional perspective was essential because compromised AI systems can cascade into catastrophic failures. Security tools can become weapons against their own organizations. The triangular framework captured the full complexity of AI security challenges, including AI-specific vulnerabilities like data poisoning, model manipulation, and adversarial attacks. Organizations needed to develop comprehensive security strategies that simultaneously leveraged AI's defensive capabilities, protected against AI-enhanced threats, and secured their AI infrastructure itself. The rapid evolution and democratization of GAI technologies created an AI-powered arms race. Thus, both defenders and attackers gained access to increasingly sophisticated tools. Success in this environment required understanding all three dimensions of the framework. Organizations needed to implement security measures that addressed the interconnected nature of modern AI security challenges.

Hypothetical Case Study: The Triangular Approach to AI Security

Global Financial Services Corp (GFSC), a mid-sized financial institution with 2000 employees, faced a critical turning point in early 2024 when it discovered their traditional dual-lens approach to AI security was insufficient. Initially viewing AI solely as a defensive tool and potential weapon, GFSC learned through experience the critical importance of considering AI systems themselves as potential targets. Their journey illustrates the essential nature of a triangular approach to AI security. GFSC's initial implementation focused heavily on AI as a tool, deploying sophisticated threat detection systems that processed over 100 million security events daily. Their AI-powered SOC demonstrated impressive early results, reducing false positives by 75% and significantly decreasing incident response times. The organization also implemented GAI for creating synthetic data, enabling more effective security testing and training scenarios. This tool-focused approach initially seemed comprehensive, with AI systems autonomously identifying and responding to potential threats while continuously learning from new attack patterns. Simultaneously, GFSC developed defenses against AI as a weapon, anticipating how adversaries might use the technology. They implemented systems to detect AI-generated phishing attempts, defend against automated vulnerability scanning, and identify synthetic media attacks. However, this dual-lens approach overlooked a critical vulnerability: their own AI systems as potential targets.

The oversight became apparent when GFSC discovered sophisticated attempts to compromise their AI security systems. Attackers had launched a three-pronged assault that perfectly illustrated the interconnected nature of the triangular framework. First, they attempted to poison the training data of GFSC's threat detection systems, demonstrating AI's vulnerability as a target. Once compromised, these same systems could be weaponized against the organization. Finally, this would diminish the effectiveness of AI as a defensive tool, creating a cascade of security failures. This incident prompted GFSC to fundamentally restructure its security approach around the triangular framework. For AI as a tool, they enhanced their systems with more sophisticated models and implemented AI-powered forensics capabilities. They developed comprehensive testing protocols to ensure their AI tools remained effective and reliable, with regular validation of outputs and performance metrics.

For AI as a weapon, GFSC implemented specialized detection systems for identifying AI-generated attacks, including advanced behavioral analysis to spot automated attack patterns. They developed AI-powered deception technology to mislead attacker's AI systems and created sophisticated authentication mechanisms to counter deepfake attempts. Most significantly, they developed robust protections for their AI systems as potential targets. This included implementing secure development practices specifically for AI systems, establishing strict access controls for training data, and deploying continuous monitoring for signs of model manipulation. They created dedicated incident response procedures for AI system attacks and established regular security assessments of their AI infrastructure.

The interconnected nature of these three aspects became clear as GFSC's new security framework took shape. They discovered that enhancements in one area often strengthened the others. For example, protecting their AI systems from being targeted improved their effectiveness as defensive tools. Similarly, understanding how AI could be weaponized helped them better protect their own AI systems from compromise.

The results proved transformative. Within a year, GFSC reported a 90% reduction in successful attacks, with no successful compromises of their AI systems. More importantly, they developed a sustainable approach to AI security that could adapt to emerging threats while maintaining effectiveness across all three aspects of the framework. The key insight from GFSC's experience was the recognition that AI security requires a holistic, triangular approach. The traditional dual-lens view of AI as either a tool or weapon creates dangerous blind spots, particularly as AI systems become more crucial to organizational operations. Their experience demonstrated that protecting AI systems as potential targets is not just a third consideration but an essential component that influences the effectiveness of AI both as a tool and as a potential weapon.

GFSC's case illustrates how the triangular framework provides a more complete and effective approach to AI security. It helps organizations understand the interconnected nature of AI security challenges while providing a structured approach to addressing them. As AI technology continues to evolve, this comprehensive perspective becomes increasingly crucial for maintaining effective security postures and protecting against emerging threats. Looking ahead, GFSC continues to refine its approach, recognizing that all three aspects of the triangular framework require continuous attention and adaptation. Their experience serves as a valuable model for organizations seeking to implement effective AI security measures in an increasingly complex threat landscape.

Quiz

Questions

1 Which of the following best describes the triangular framework for AI security?
   a) AI as a tool, AI as a weapon, AI as a solution
   b) AI as a tool, AI as a weapon, AI as a target
   c) AI as a defense, AI as an attack, AI as a system
   d) AI as a tool, AI as a threat, AI as a technology

2 According to the chapter, why is viewing AI security through just a dual-lens perspective insufficient?
   a) It's too expensive to implement
   b) It only focuses on defensive capabilities
   c) It overlooks AI systems themselves as potential targets
   d) It requires too much technical expertise

3 When did AI first become significantly integrated into cybersecurity?
   a) 1980s with rule-based systems
   b) Late 1990s with anomaly detection
   c) 2020s with generative AI
   d) 2010s with machine learning

4 What makes generative AI different from traditional AI systems?
   a) It's faster at processing data
   b) It's more expensive to implement
   c) It can create entirely new content
   d) It only works with text data

5 A key statistic mentioned in the chapter about ChatGPT's adoption was:
   a) It reached 50 million users in six months
   b) It reached 100 million users in two months
   c) It reached 1 million users in one month
   d) It reached 10 million users in three months

Answer Key

1 **Correct Answer: b) AI as a tool, AI as a weapon, AI as a target. This is correct because the chapter explicitly defines these three aspects as the triangular framework**
   - a) is incorrect because "solution" isn't part of the framework and oversimplifies the concept
   - c) is incorrect because while similar, it doesn't use the precise terminology introduced in the chapter
   - d) is incorrect because "technology" is too broad and doesn't capture the security implications

2 **Correct Answer: c) It overlooks AI systems themselves as potential targets. This is correct because the chapter emphasizes how the dual-lens perspective misses the crucial third aspect of AI systems being targets themselves**
   - a) is incorrect because cost isn't mentioned as a limitation of the dual-lens approach
   - b) is incorrect because the dual-lens approach actually considers both defensive and offensive capabilities
   - d) is incorrect because technical expertise isn't cited as a limitation of the dual-lens approach

3 **Correct Answer: b) Late 1990s with anomaly detection. This is correct, as the chapter specifically mentions this as the first significant application of AI in cybersecurity**
   - a) is incorrect because the 1980s had rule-based systems, not AI
   - c) is incorrect because it's far too recent
   - d) is incorrect because it misses the earlier applications

4 **Correct Answer: c) It can create entirely new content. This is correct, as the chapter defines this as the key distinguishing feature of generative AI**
   - a) is incorrect because processing speed isn't mentioned as a distinguishing factor
   - b) is incorrect because cost isn't mentioned as a defining characteristic
   - d) is incorrect because generative AI works with multiple types of data, not just text

5 **Correct Answer: b) It reached 100 million users in two months.**

References

Alabi, M. (2024). Generative AI and its applications in creative industries. [PhD dissertation, Ladoke Akintola University of Technology].

Alam, S. (2022). Cybersecurity: Past, present and future. arXiv preprint arXiv:2207.01227.

Ale, L., Zhang, N., King, S. A., & Chen, D. (2024). Empowering generative AI through mobile edge computing. *Nature Reviews Electrical Engineering*, *1*(7), 478–486.

Alfa People. (2024, November 2). Fresh numbers from AlfaPeople: How companies will invest in AI implementation. https://alfapeople.com/us/how-companies-will-invest-in-ai-implementation/#:~:text=For%202025%2C%2041%20percent%20of,reach%20%24200%20billion%20by%202025.

Ali, S., DiPaola, D., & Breazeal, C. (2021, May). What are GANs?: Introducing generative adversarial networks to middle school students. *Proceedings of the AAAI Conference on Artificial Intelligence* (Vol. 35, No. 17, pp. 15472–15479).

Alto, V. (2023). *Modern generative AI with ChatGPT and OpenAI models: Leverage the capabilities of OpenAI's LLM for productivity and innovation with GPT3 and GPT4.* Packt Publishing Ltd.

Anthropic. (2024, November 25). Introducing the model context protocol. https://www.anthropic.com/news/model-context-protocol.

Avacharmal, R., Pamulaparthyvenkata, S., & Gudala, L. (2023). Unveiling the Pandora's box: A multifaceted exploration of ethical considerations in generative AI for financial services and healthcare. *Hong Kong Journal of AI and Medicine*, *3*(1), 84–99.

Balantrapu, S. S. (2024). AI for predictive cyber threat intelligence. *International Journal of Management Education for Sustainable Development*, *7*(7), 1–28.

Bolón-Canedo, V., Morán-Fernández, L., Cancela, B., & Alonso-Betanzos, A. (2024). A review of green artificial intelligence: Towards a more sustainable future. *Neurocomputing*, *599*, 128096.

Chakraborty, U., Roy, S., & Kumar, S. (2023). *Rise of generative AI and ChatGPT: Understand how generative AI and ChatGPT are transforming and reshaping the business world* (English Edition). BPB Publications.

Chen, B., Wu, Z., & Zhao, R. (2023). From fiction to fact: The growing role of generative AI in business and finance. *Journal of Chinese Economic and Business Studies*, *21*(4), 471–496.

Chen, Z., Xu, L., Zheng, H., Chen, L., Tolba, A., Zhao, L., Yu, K., and Feng, H., (2024). Evolution and prospects of foundation models: From large language models to large multimodal models. *Computers, Materials & Continua*, *80*(2), 1753–1808.

Cohan, P. (2024). What is generative AI? In *Brain rush: How to invest and compete in the real world of generative AI* (pp. 9–28). Berkeley, CA: Apress.

Doersch, C. (2016). Tutorial on variational autoencoders. arXiv preprint arXiv:1606.05908.

Express Computer. (2023, July 3). Generative AI revolutionising cybersecurity and transforming SIEM, SOAR & UEBA landscape. https://www.expresscomputer.in/guest-blogs/generative-ai-revolutionising-cybersecurity-and-transforming-siem-soar-ueba-landscape/100488/#:~:text=Generative%20AI%20is%20transforming%20the,an%20increasingly%20complex%20threat%20landscape.

Farouk, M. A., & Fahmi, B. M. (2024). Deepfakes and media integrity: Navigating the new reality of synthetic content. *Journal of Media and Interdisciplinary Studies*, *3*(9), 47–94.

Garcia-Teodoro, P., Diaz-Verdejo, J., Maciá-Fernández, G., & Vázquez, E. (2009). Anomaly-based network intrusion detection: Techniques, systems and challenges. *Computers & Security*, *28*(1–2), 18–28.

González-Granadillo, G., González-Zarzosa, S., and Diaz, R. (2021). Security information and event management (SIEM): Analysis, trends, and usage in critical infrastructures. *Sensors (Basel)*, *21*(14), 4759.

Hendrich, L. (2024, May 29). Research shows AI coding assistants can improve developer productivity. Forte Group. https://fortegrp.com/insights/ai-coding-assistants.

Hindy, H., Atkinson, R., Tachtatzis, C., Colin, J. N., Bayne, E., & Bellekens, X. (2020). Utilising deep learning techniques for effective zero-day attack detection. *Electronics*, *9*(10), 1684.

Hoang, H. (2024). *Generative AI security: Why AWS for generative AI security. Internet Conference 2024.* https://internet-conference.vn/sites/default/files/2024-06/5.AWS.pdf.

Huckelberry, J., Zhang, Y., Sansone, A., Mickens, J., Beerel, P. A., & Reddi, V. J. (2024). TinyML security: Exploring vulnerabilities in resource-constrained machine learning systems. arXiv preprint arXiv:2411.07114.

Kaplan, J. (2024). *Generative artificial intelligence: What everyone needs to know*. Oxford University Press.

Karaca, Y., Derias, D., & Sarsar, G. (2023). AI-powered procedural content generation: Enhancing NPC behaviour for an immersive gaming experience. Available at SSRN 4663382.

Kaur, G., Bharathiraja, N., Singh, K. D., Veeramanickam, M. R. M., Rodriguez, C. R., & Pradeepa, K. (2024). Emerging trends in cybersecurity challenges with reference to pen testing tools in Society 5.0. In V. Khullar, V. Sharma, M. Angurala, & N. Chhabra (Eds.), *Artificial intelligence and society 5.0* (pp. 196–212). Chapman and Hall/CRC.

Kavitha, L. (2023). Copyright challenges in the artificial intelligence revolution: Transforming the film industry from script to screen. *Trinity Law Review*, *4*(1), 1–8.

Kumar, A. (2024, December 30). Fun fact: AI creates about 34 million images every single day. Medium. https://amitkumar2211.medium.com/fun-fact-ai-creates-about-34-million-images-every-single-day-99a7bbd0fd63.

Kumar, G., Yadav, S., Mukherjee, A., Hassija, V., & Guizani, M. (2024). Recent advances in quantum computing for drug discovery and development. *IEEE Access, 12*, 64491–64509.

Kumar, V., & Sinha, D. (2023). Synthetic attack data generation model applying generative adversarial network for intrusion detection. *Computers & Security, 125*, 103054.

Liu, J., & Jagadish, H. V. (2024). Institutional efforts to help academic researchers implement generative AI in research. *Harvard Data Science Review* (Special Issue 5). https://doi.org/10.1162/99608f92.2c8e7e81.

Lundberg, I. (2024, September 4). Future of business: How AI is transforming fortune 500 companies. Forbes. https://www.forbes.com/councils/forbescoachescouncil/2024/09/04/future-of-business-how-ai-is-transforming-fortune-500-companies/#:~:text=Generative%20AI%20is%20quickly%20becoming,and%20recommending%20more%20sustainable%20practices.

Mahajan, V. (2024, October 10). 100+ incredible ChatGPT statistics & facts in 2024. Notta.

McGeorge, D. (2023). *The ChatGPT revolution: How to simplify your work and life admin with AI*. John Wiley & Son.

Metta, S., Chang, I., Parker, J., Roman, M. P., & Ehuan, A. F. (2024). Generative AI in cybersecurity. arXiv preprint arXiv:2405.01674.

Montasari, R. (2024). *National security in the artificial intelligence era: Challenges and implications of advanced technologies* [Doctoral dissertation]. Cardiff Metropolitan University. Figshare. https://figshare.cardiffmet.ac.uk/articles/thesis/National_security_in_the_Artificial_Intelligence_era_Challenges_and_implications_of_advanced_technologies/26485588.

National Research Council, Division on Engineering, Physical Sciences, Board on Mathematical Sciences, Their Applications, Committee on Modeling, & Simulation for Defense Transformation. (2006). *Defense modeling, simulation, and analysis: Meeting the challenge*. National Academies Press.

National Institute of Standards and Technology. (2024, July). *Artificial Intelligence Risk Management Framework: Generative Artificial Intelligence profile (NIST AI 600-1)*. U.S. Department of Commerce. https://doi.org/10.6028/NIST.AI.600-1.

Palatty, N. (2025). How many cyber attacks per day: The latest stats and impacts in 2025. *Astra*. https://www.getastra.com/blog/security-audit/how-many-cyber-attacks-per-day/.

Palo Alto Networks (n.d.). What is Generative AI in Cybersecurity? *CyberPedia*. https://www.paloaltonetworks.com/cyberpedia/generative-ai-in-cybersecurity.

Pandey, J. K. (2024). Unlocking the power and future potential of generative AI in government transformation. *Transforming Government: People, Process and Policy*. https://doi.org/10.1108/TG-01-2024-0006.

Prabhod, K. J. (2023). Leveraging generative AI for personalized medicine: Applications in drug discovery and development. *Journal of AI-Assisted Scientific Discovery, 3*(1), 392–434.

Rane, N. L., Kaya, O., & Rane, J. (2024). Advancing industry 4.0, 5.0, and society 5.0 through generative artificial intelligence like ChatGPT. In *Artificial Intelligence, Machine Learning, and Deep Learning for Sustainable Industry 5.0* (pp. 137–161). Deep Science Publishing.

Rashid, F. (2016, December 6). IBM Watson steps into real-world cybersecurity. NYU Tandon School of Engineering. https://engineering.nyu.edu/news/ibm-watson-steps-real-world-cybersecurity.

Resinger, D. (2024, April 11). Amazon CEO: Generative AI 'may be the largest technology transformation since the cloud' ZD Net. https://www.zdnet.com/article/amazon-ceo-generative-ai-may-be-the-largest-technology-transformation-since-the-cloud/.

Sai, S., Gaur, A., Sai, R., Chamola, V., Guizani, M., & Rodrigues, J. J. (2024). Generative AI for transformative healthcare: A comprehensive study of emerging models, applications, case studies and limitations. *IEEE Access*, *12*, 31078–31106.

Schmitt, M., & Flechais, I. (2024). Digital deception: Generative artificial intelligence in social engineering and phishing. *Artificial Intelligence Review*, *57*(12), 1–23.

Secureworks. (2024, May 8). Intrusion detection vs. intrusion prevention vs. next generation IPS vs. next generation firewalls vs. NDR. https://www.secureworks.com/blog/the-evolution-of-intrusion-detection-prevention.

Soofastaei, A. (Ed.). (2024). *Advanced virtual assistants—A window to the virtual future*. BoD–Books on Demand.

The State of AI Cyber Security 2024. 2024. Darktrace. https://cdn.prod.website-files.com/626ff4d25aca2edf4325ff97/6616ac89caf4b6d08d22c3d6_State%20of%20AI%20in%20Cyber%20Security.pdf.

Tiwari, P. C., Pal, R., Chaudhary, M. J., & Nath, R. (2023). Artificial intelligence revolutionizing drug development: Exploring opportunities and challenges. *Drug Development Research*, *84*(8), 1652–1663.

Xu, J., Fan, S., & Ye, X. (2023). The application of artificial intelligence in news editing: A case study of automated news generation. *Research in Media and Communication*, *1*(1), 41–52.

Xu, Y., Liu, X., Cao, X., Huang, C., Liu, E., Qian, S., Liu, X., Wu, Y., Dong, F., Qiu, C. W., Qiu, J., Hua, K., Su, W., Wu, J., Xu, H., Han, Y., Fu, C., Yin, Z., Liu, M., … Zhang, J. (2021). Artificial intelligence: A powerful paradigm for scientific research. *The Innovation*, *2*(4), 100179.

Yaseen, A. (2022). Accelerating the SOC: Achieve greater efficiency with AI-driven automation. *International Journal of Responsible Artificial Intelligence*, *12*(1), 1–19.

Zhang, J., & Tenney, D. (2023). The evolution of integrated advance persistent threat and its defense solutions: A literature review. *Open Journal of Business and Management*, *12*(1), 293–338.

2

Understanding Generative AI Technologies

2.1 ML Fundamentals

Let's start with supervised learning. Supervised learning represents one of the fundamental approaches in machine learning, where an algorithm learns to map inputs to outputs based on a labeled dataset (Nasteski, 2017). In this paradigm, the algorithm is trained on pairs of input data and their corresponding correct outputs (labels), learning to recognize patterns that connect the features of the input to the desired output (Hastie et al., 2009). The "supervised" aspect comes from the fact that the training process is guided by these known correct answers, much like a teacher supervising a student's learning process. The learning process involves the algorithm iteratively making predictions on the training data, comparing these predictions to the actual labels, and adjusting its internal parameters to minimize the difference between predicted and actual outputs (Cunningham et al., 2008). This process continues until the algorithm achieves acceptable performance on both the training data and previously unseen validation data, indicating it has learned generalizable patterns rather than merely memorizing the training examples.

Theoretically, it makes sense. Right? But here's an example. Consider training a model to detect phishing emails. You would start with a large dataset of emails that have been labeled as either "phishing" or "legitimate." Each email in the training set would be processed to extract relevant features such as sender domain patterns, presence of urgent language, links to external domains, and header information. The supervised learning algorithm would analyze these labeled examples to learn which combinations of features are most indicative of phishing attempts. After training, when presented with a new, unlabeled email, the model can analyze its features and predict whether it's likely to be phishing based on the patterns it learned from the training data. The model's accuracy can be measured by comparing its predictions to known labels in a test dataset that wasn't used during training.

Generative AI Security: Defense, Threats, and Vulnerabilities, First Edition. Shaila Rana and Rhonda Chicone.

Then, there is unsupervised learning. Unsupervised learning is an approach to machine learning where algorithms learn patterns and structures from data without explicit labels or correct answers (Ghahramani, 2003). Unlike supervised learning, these algorithms must discover the inherent organization, groupings, or relationships within data on their own (Naeem et al., 2023). This type of learning is beneficial when dealing with large amounts of unlabeled data, where manually creating labels would be impractical or impossible. In general, the primary goal of unsupervised learning is to find hidden patterns or natural groupings within data. Common techniques include clustering (grouping similar items together), dimensionality reduction (finding simpler representations of complex data), and anomaly detection (identifying unusual patterns) (Soleimani-Babakamali et al., 2023). These methods rely on measuring similarities and differences between data points, identifying underlying data distributions, and discovering natural boundaries between different groups of data.

For example, let's consider network traffic analysis in a large enterprise environment. An unsupervised learning algorithm could analyze network traffic patterns without pre-existing labels of "normal" or "malicious." The algorithm might discover distinct clusters of network behavior—for instance, one cluster representing typical employee web browsing, another showing patterns of regular data backups, and a third representing automated system updates. If new traffic patterns emerge that don't fit into any of these established clusters, this could indicate potential security incidents like data exfiltration or botnet activity. The algorithm might also identify unusual patterns in seemingly normal traffic, such as regular HTTP requests that deviate subtly from typical human browsing patterns, potentially revealing command-and-control communications. Subsequently, this approach is really valuable in modern cybersecurity because it can detect novel threats that wouldn't be caught by traditional signature-based detection methods or supervised learning models trained on known attack patterns. It's especially effective for identifying zero-day attacks and advanced persistent threats (APTs) that don't match previously seen malicious behavior. This is essential in today's cyber and threat landscape.

Reinforcement learning (RL) is a bit different. RL in machine learning is where an agent learns optimal behavior through continuous interaction with an environment (Matsuo et al., 2022). The agent performs actions, receives feedback in the form of rewards or penalties, and adjusts its strategy to maximize long-term rewards. This approach mimics how humans and animals learn through trial and error, where successful actions are reinforced and unsuccessful ones are discouraged. The learning process in RL is driven by what's called a reward function, which provides immediate or delayed feedback about the quality of the agent's actions (Ladosz et al., 2022). The agent must balance between exploiting known successful strategies and exploring new possibilities that might lead to better outcomes. This exploration–exploitation trade-off is a fundamental challenge in RL, as the agent must decide when to stick with proven approaches and when to try something new. A key concept in RL is the policy—the strategy that determines what action the agent should take in any given state (Andrychowicz et al., 2020). Through interaction with the environment, the agent continuously updates its policy based on the outcomes of its actions. This process often involves learning value functions that estimate the long-term benefit of taking particular actions in specific states. In fact, Andrew Barto and Rich Sutton, once considered eccentric for their work on RL, have been awarded the prestigious Turing Award for pioneering a method now fundamental to modern AI systems, including ChatGPT, robotics, and programs like AlphaGo (Knight, 2025).

As done with supervised and unsupervised learning, let's address a practical example. Let's consider an autonomous incident response system based on RL. The agent (the response system) operates in an environment (the network infrastructure) where it can take various actions like isolating systems, blocking traffic, or initiating backup procedures. When it detects a potential security incident, it must decide on the most appropriate response. The agent receives positive rewards for successfully containing threats while minimizing business disruption, and penalties for both allowing security breaches and causing unnecessary operational disruption. Over time, the agent learns which responses are most effective for different types of security incidents, adapting its strategy based on the outcomes of its actions.

There's also another way that it can be put—let's compare RL to how you would train a dog. Think about teaching a dog to sit. Initially, the dog (our agent) doesn't know what behavior you want. When the dog happens to sit, you give it a treat (positive reward). When it doesn't sit after hearing the command, it gets no treat (neutral or negative reward). Over time, through this system of rewards, the dog learns to associate the sitting behavior with treats and thus learns the optimal behavior for getting rewards. Now, let's translate this to a cybersecurity context. Imagine a RL system monitoring network traffic for potential threats. Like our dog learning to sit, the AI system starts with limited knowledge of what constitutes suspicious behavior. For instance, the AI agent observes network traffic patterns (the environment). When it flags suspicious activity that turns out to be a genuine threat, it receives a positive reward. When it raises false alarms, it receives a negative reward. If it misses actual threats, it also receives a negative reward. Through this continuous process of action and feedback, the system learns to better distinguish between normal and suspicious network behavior. The exploration–exploitation trade-off comes into play when the system must decide between exploitation (using known patterns that have successfully identified threats in the past) and exploration (investigating new or unusual patterns that might represent previously unseen threats). Just as a dog might try different behaviors to see which ones earn treats, the AI system might explore different traffic patterns or characteristics to identify new types of threats while balancing this against the reliable detection methods it has already learned. This becomes especially relevant when dealing with evolving cyber threats. Traditional rule-based systems might miss new attack variants, but a RL system can adapt and learn to identify novel threats through this continuous process of observation, action, and feedback.

So, what makes RL different? Really, what makes RL distinct from supervised and unsupervised learning is its interactive nature and focus on sequential decision-making (Morales & Escalante, 2022). Unlike supervised learning, which learns from labeled examples, or unsupervised learning, which finds patterns in data, RL learns through direct interaction and feedback. The agent must learn not just to make single decisions but to consider the long-term consequences of its actions. This makes RL very suitable for dynamic environments where the optimal strategy may change over time and where immediate actions can have delayed consequences—characteristics that are particularly relevant in cybersecurity contexts.

Another fundamental important to discuss is feature engineering and selection. Feature engineering and selection are an important foundation of machine learning, often determining the success or failure of ML models before they even begin training (Dhal & Azad, 2022). At its core, feature engineering is the art and science of transforming raw data into meaningful representations that ML algorithms can effectively process. This process involves creating new features from existing data, transforming variables to better represent underlying patterns, and selecting the most relevant characteristics for the task at hand (Wang et al., 2022). In practice, feature engineering requires deep domain knowledge combined with technical expertise. For example, in cybersecurity applications, raw network traffic data might be transformed into more meaningful features like packet frequency patterns, byte distribution statistics, or timing relationships between events (Leevy et al., 2021). A security expert might know that the ratio of incoming to outgoing traffic is more informative than raw traffic volumes, or that the entropy of packet payloads can be a strong indicator of encrypted malicious content. These insights guide the creation of features that make patterns more apparent to ML algorithms.

Feature selection, meanwhile, focuses on identifying which features are most relevant and informative for the specific problem being solved (Abiodun et al., 2021). This process is crucial because including irrelevant or redundant features can introduce noise into the model, leading to poorer performance and increased computational overhead. Modern machine learning systems might deal with hundreds or thousands of potential features, making it essential to select only those that contribute meaningfully to the model's predictive power. Thus, the importance of feature engineering and selection cannot be overstated in ML fundamentals because even the most sophisticated algorithms can fail if they're working with poorly engineered or irrelevant features. The old computing adage "garbage in, garbage out" is somewhat relevant here—no amount of algorithmic sophistication can compensate for poorly chosen or badly engineered features. This is why experienced machine learning practitioners often spend more time on feature engineering and selection than on model selection and training.

2.2 Deep Learning and Neural Networks

Deep learning and neural networks are an approach to machine learning that attempts to mimic the human brain's information processing mechanisms. At their core, neural networks consist of interconnected layers of artificial neurons, each capable of processing and transforming input data through a series of mathematical operations (Thakur & Konde, 2021). These networks can automatically learn hierarchical representations of data, with each successive layer extracting increasingly complex features. The "deep" in deep learning refers to the use of multiple layers—sometimes hundreds or thousands—which enables these systems to learn intricate patterns and relationships in data that simpler ML approaches might miss (Dong et al., 2021). Modern deep learning architectures have achieved incredibly remarkable success across various domains, from image and speech recognition to natural language processing (NLP) and, notably, generative AI applications. The power of deep learning lies in its ability to automatically discover the representations needed for feature detection or classification, eliminating much of the manual feature engineering required by traditional machine learning approaches (Dargan et al., 2020). This has made it extremely valuable in cybersecurity applications where threats constantly evolve and manual feature engineering might lag behind emerging attack patterns.

ANNs are computing systems inspired by the biological neural networks found in human brains (Nwadiugwu, 2020). At their most basic level, ANNs consist of interconnected nodes (artificial neurons) organized in layers that process information through weighted connections (Qamar & Zardari, 2023). Each neuron receives inputs, applies mathematical transformations, and produces outputs that are passed to subsequent layers. This structure allows ANNs to learn complex patterns and relationships within data by adjusting the weights of connections during the training process. In general, the fundamental building block of an ANN is the artificial neuron, which takes multiple inputs, applies weights to these inputs, sums them together with a bias term, and then passes the result through an activation function (Abdolrasol et al., 2021). This activation function introduces nonlinearity into the network, enabling it to learn complex, nonlinear relationships in data. Common activation functions include ReLU (Rectified Linear Unit), sigmoid, and tanh, each serving different purposes in network design (Rahman et al., 2024). The architecture of an ANN typically includes an input layer that receives raw data, one or more hidden layers that process this information, and an output layer that produces the final result (Madhiarasan & Louzazni, 2022). The number of hidden layers and neurons in each layer, along with the connections between them, defines the network's capacity to learn and represent complex patterns. The process of training involves feeding data through the network, comparing the output with desired results, and adjusting weights through backpropagation to minimize error (Gülcü, 2022).

Consider a modern smart home security system that uses ANNs for intruder detection. The system processes inputs from multiple sources—security cameras, motion sensors, door/window sensors, and even sound detectors—much like how the human brain processes information from different senses. The input layer of the neural network receives raw data from these various sensors. Each sensor's data represents a different input node—video feeds might provide data about movement and shapes, motion sensors detect physical presence, and sound detectors capture unusual noises. Just as our brain processes visual, auditory, and tactile information simultaneously, the neural network processes all these inputs in parallel. The hidden layers of the network then process this information through complex interconnections. For example, one layer might analyze the video feed for human shapes, while another processes motion patterns, and yet another evaluates the time of day and typical household activity patterns. These layers work together, weighting different factors based on their learned importance—much like how our brain gives different weights to different sensory inputs when making decisions. The network has been trained through countless examples of both normal and suspicious activity. During training, it learned that rapid motion near a window at 3 AM, combined with unusual sounds and no prior door entry, likely indicates a break-in attempt. Conversely, it learned that similar motion during daylight hours, accompanied by familiar face recognition and normal entry patterns, probably indicates routine household activity. The output layer makes the final determination: is this situation normal or a potential security threat? If the network determines a threat is present, it triggers appropriate responses—perhaps alerting homeowners, notifying security services, or activating additional security measures. Thus, what makes this system particularly powerful is its ability to learn and adapt. If it generates false alarms, these can be marked as incorrect during system reviews, and the network adjusts its internal weights accordingly. Over time, it becomes better at distinguishing between genuine threats and harmless activities. For instance, it might learn that the neighbor's cat triggering motion sensors at night is a normal occurrence and shouldn't trigger an alarm. This example demonstrates the key components of neural networks: multiple input sources (sensors), processing layers that learn complex patterns (threat analysis), and outputs that drive actions (security responses). The system's ability to process multiple inputs simultaneously, learn from experience, and make complex decisions mirrors the biological neural networks that inspired its design. Just as our brains learn to recognize patterns and make judgments based on multiple sensory inputs, ANNs can learn to recognize and respond to complex patterns in real-world data.

In today's applications, ANNs are being deployed across numerous domains. In cybersecurity, they're used for anomaly detection in network traffic, malware classification, and user behavior analysis (Ali et al., 2024). Financial institutions employ ANNs for fraud detection, risk assessment, and algorithmic trading (Gayam, 2021). Healthcare organizations use them for disease diagnosis, medical image analysis, and patient outcome prediction (Hu et al., 2021). In autonomous vehicles, ANNs process sensor data for real-time decision-making and navigation (Stateczny et al., 2022). Tech companies leverage ANNs for recommendation systems, content moderation, and NLP tasks (Laugier, 2022; Soundarapandian, 2024). The versatility and power of ANNs have made them a cornerstone of modern AI applications, enabling systems to perform complex tasks that previously required human expertise.

Next, there are convolutional neural networks (CNNs). CNNs are specialized neural networks designed primarily for processing grid-like data, particularly images and videos (Khan et al., 2020). Unlike traditional neural networks that process data uniformly, CNNs use a mathematical operation called convolution to scan across the input data, identifying important features through specialized filters or kernels (Krichen, 2023). This approach is inspired by how the human visual cortex processes visual information, with different neurons responding to specific patterns in their field of view. The key innovation of CNNs lies in their ability to automatically learn hierarchical feature representations. In the early layers, CNNs typically detect simple features like edges, corners, and color gradients (Taye, 2023). As data moves through deeper layers, the network combines these basic features to recognize more complex patterns such as textures, shapes, and eventually entire objects. This hierarchical learning process makes CNNs effective at computer vision tasks. CNNs achieve efficiency (efficiency being the key word here) through parameter sharing and local connectivity (Alzubaidi et al., 2021). Rather than having separate weights for every input pixel (as in a fully connected neural network), CNNs use the same set of weights across different positions in the input. This dramatically reduces the number of parameters the network needs to learn while also making the network invariant to the position of features in the input—if it can recognize a pattern in one part of an image, it can recognize it anywhere.

Now, an example to understand it in a tangible way. Imagine you're a security analyst reviewing surveillance camera footage. When you look for suspicious activity, you don't analyze every pixel individually—instead, your brain automatically picks out relevant patterns: people, objects, and movements. A CNN works similarly. If trained for security surveillance, its first layer might detect basic elements like movement or changes in lighting. The next layer might combine these to identify human shapes or objects. Deeper layers could then recognize specific activities, like someone tailgating through a security door or leaving a suspicious package. The CNN doesn't need to be told exactly where in the camera frame to look—it applies its learned patterns across the entire image, just as you would scan the entire scene for suspicious activity. This makes CNNs particularly effective for automated video surveillance, facial recognition systems, and other security applications where pattern recognition in visual data is crucial. But remember, this is important to balance with ethical considerations.

There are also Recurrent Neural Networks (RNNs), which are specialized neural networks designed to handle sequential data, where the order and context of information matter (Vamosi et al., 2022). Unlike traditional neural networks that process each input independently, RNNs maintain an internal memory state that allows them to use information from previous inputs when processing current data. This "memory" enables RNNs to understand context and temporal dependencies in sequences, making them particularly well-suited for tasks involving time-series data, text, or any data where sequence matters (Oluwafemi, 2023). The key feature of RNNs is their feedback loop structure, where the output from one step becomes part of the input for the next step (Bonassi et al., 2022). This recursive nature allows the network to maintain a form of state or memory across the sequence. Modern RNN variants like Long Short-Term Memory (LSTM) and Gated Recurrent Units (GRU) have sophisticated mechanisms to control what information is remembered or forgotten, helping them capture both long-term and short-term dependencies in the data (Mienye et al., 2024).

While CNNs excel at spatial patterns (like those found in images), RNNs specialize in temporal patterns (like those found in sequences) (Wang & Karimi, 2025). However, these architectures aren't mutually exclusive—they're often combined in modern AI systems. For instance, in video analysis, CNNs might process individual frames to extract spatial features, while RNNs analyze how these features change over time. This combination is powerful for tasks that require both spatial and temporal understanding.

Let's say there is a network intrusion detection system analyzing a stream of network traffic. An RNN can be used to identify suspicious patterns in packet sequences that might indicate an attack. While a traditional system might look at each packet in isolation, an RNN can understand the context of each packet within the broader traffic flow. For instance, it could learn that a specific sequence of seemingly innocent packets, when occurring in a particular order over time, indicates a slow-and-low attack attempt. The RNN's memory allows it to recognize these temporal patterns—like a series of failed login attempts spread out over hours, or the gradual buildup of a DDoS attack—patterns that might be missed by systems that don't maintain this temporal context.

Another example may be helpful here. Think of an AI-powered email security system analyzing incoming messages for potential phishing attempts. Unlike traditional security tools that might look at each email in isolation, an RNN-based system maintains "memory" of previous emails and their patterns, much like how a human security analyst builds context over time. Now, consider a sophisticated phishing campaign targeting your organization. The attacker sends seemingly innocuous emails over several weeks, gradually building a narrative. Each individual email might appear harmless—a first email might introduce the sender as a potential client, a second discusses general business topics, and a third mentions a specific project. Traditional security systems analyzing each email independently might miss the broader pattern, but an RNN, with its ability to maintain context across the sequence, can identify suspicious patterns in this communication chain. The RNN's "memory" allows it to recognize how the conversation evolves. It might be noticed that despite different sender addresses, these emails share subtle linguistic patterns or that the communication is following a known attack progression. When the final email arrives containing a malicious link or request for sensitive information, the RNN has the full context of the previous communications to better assess the risk. This temporal understanding is particularly powerful for detecting slow-moving attacks (which is especially crucial in today's threat landscape riddled with sophisticated cybercrime groups, APTs, etc.). For instance, the RNN might learn that legitimate business communications follow certain patterns over time—regular response intervals, consistent tone, predictable escalation of requests. Deviations from these patterns, even subtle ones spread across weeks, can be flagged as potential security risks. The system's effectiveness improves over time as it learns from more examples. Each new phishing campaign it encounters adds to its understanding of how these attacks evolve. The RNN might learn that certain seemingly benign phrases, when appearing in a specific sequence across multiple emails, often precede malicious requests. It could recognize patterns like gradual trust-building attempts, subtle pressure tactics, or the strategic timing of urgent requests—patterns that emerge only when analyzing the temporal relationship between messages. This same principle applies to other security contexts. In network monitoring, RNNs can track user behavior over time, learning normal patterns of system access and flagging unusual sequences of actions. In malware detection, they can analyze the temporal patterns of system calls or network connections, identifying malicious behavior that only becomes apparent when viewed as a sequence rather than individual events. Essentially, the power of RNNs lies in this ability to maintain and learn from context over time, much like how human analysts develop intuition about threats based on patterns they've observed throughout their careers. This makes them useful for security applications where the timing and sequence of events are as important as the events themselves.

2.3 Generative Models

This leads us to talking about generative models. Generative models are a class of artificial intelligence systems designed to learn the underlying patterns in data and generate new, similar data points (Harshvardhan et al., 2020). These models have revolutionized AI's creative capabilities, enabling the generation of images, text, code, and other content that closely resembles human-created work. The three primary architectures that dominate the generative AI landscape are generative adversarial networks (GANs), variational autoencoders (VAEs), and transformer-based models, each with its unique approach to content generation. Thus, let's go through each one in a bit more detail.

GANs operate on a unique principle of adversarial training, where two neural networks compete against each other (Saxena & Cao, 2021). The generator network attempts to create realistic data, while the discriminator network tries to distinguish between real and generated data. This continuous competition drives both networks to improve—the generator becomes better at creating realistic data, while the discriminator becomes better at detecting fakes. This architecture has been shown to be effective for generating highly realistic images, synthetic data, and even network traffic patterns for security testing (Navidan et al., 2021). Recent advances in GANs have led to the development of conditional variants that allow for more controlled generation based on specific attributes or classes (Jabbar et al., 2021). Despite their impressive capabilities, GANs continue to face challenges, including training instability, mode collapse, and difficulties in objective evaluation metrics (Ahmad et al., 2025). Researchers are actively exploring hybrid architectures and alternative training methods to address these limitations while expanding GAN applications into domains like drug discovery, anomaly detection, and creative content generation (Showrov et al., 2024).

Consider a security team working to improve their organization's ability to detect phishing emails. They implement a GAN system where two neural networks engage in an ongoing competition to, respectively, generate and detect sophisticated phishing attempts. This setup mirrors how actual cybersecurity threats evolve, with attackers and defenders constantly adapting to each other's techniques. The generator network in this system attempts to create convincing phishing emails that could bypass security controls. It starts by analyzing thousands of real phishing attempts and legitimate emails, learning the subtle characteristics that make messages appear authentic. Over time, it begins producing increasingly sophisticated phishing emails, complete with contextually appropriate business language, convincing sender profiles, and plausible requests for action. Meanwhile, the discriminator network examines both real phishing emails and the generator's creations, learning to distinguish between legitimate and malicious messages. It develops increasingly sophisticated detection capabilities, identifying subtle indicators of phishing attempts that might escape traditional rule-based systems or even human analysts. The competition between these networks drives continuous improvement. When the discriminator becomes better at detecting synthetic phishing attempts, the generator must evolve to create even more convincing messages. When the generator improves its fake email creation, the discriminator must enhance its detection capabilities. This ongoing cycle of improvement helps security teams stay ahead of real-world threats. The practical value becomes clear when the system is deployed in production. The discriminator network, having been trained against increasingly sophisticated synthetic phishing attempts, becomes extremely effective at identifying actual phishing emails. It can detect subtle patterns and anomalies that might indicate a phishing attempt, even in cases where the attacker is using advanced social engineering techniques. Meanwhile, the generator's capabilities are used to test and improve the organization's overall email security posture. Security teams can use the generated phishing attempts in training exercises, helping employees recognize increasingly sophisticated social engineering attempts. They can also use these synthetic emails to test and refine their security controls, ensuring they can detect and block advanced phishing attempts before deploying these controls in production. This GAN-based approach provides several advantages over traditional security testing methods. It can generate an unlimited number of unique, sophisticated test cases, each incorporating current threat patterns. The system can also rapidly adapt to new types of attacks, with both networks evolving their capabilities as new threats emerge. Most importantly, it helps security teams prepare for future attacks by generating synthetic threats that might be more sophisticated than those currently seen in the wild.

The same principle can be applied to other security contexts, such as generating synthetic network traffic for intrusion detection training, creating test cases for malware detection systems, or developing more sophisticated authentication challenges. In each case, the adversarial nature of GANs helps create more robust security systems by constantly pushing both offensive and defensive capabilities to improve.

VAEs take a different approach, combining elements of traditional autoencoders with probabilistic modeling. VAEs work by compressing input data into a lower-dimensional representation (encoding) and then reconstructing it (decoding) (Pawar & Attar, 2020). Unlike traditional autoencoders, VAEs learn a probability distribution of the data, allowing them to generate new, diverse samples by sampling from this distribution. This probabilistic nature makes VAEs particularly useful for generating structured data and understanding the underlying patterns in complex datasets. The latent space of VAEs is often more continuous and well-structured than that of GANs, facilitating interpolation between data points and enabling controlled generation through latent space arithmetic (Fatah, 2024). However, VAEs typically produce blurrier outputs compared to GANs due to their reliance on pixel-wise reconstruction loss functions (Huang, 2024). Recent research has focused on improving VAE architectures through hierarchical designs, alternative divergence measures, and hybrid approaches that combine the strengths of VAEs with other generative models (Bond-Taylor et al., 2022). These advancements have expanded VAE applications into fields like drug discovery, molecular design, and semantic image editing (Gangwal et al., 2024).

As was done above, another practical example is key here. Consider a large enterprise's security operations center (SOC) using a VAE to understand and model normal network behavior. The VAE learns to compress complex network traffic patterns into a simplified representation and then reconstruct them, helping identify anomalies that could indicate security threats. Imagine the network generates millions of data points daily, including login attempts, file transfers, application usage, and server requests. The VAE processes this massive amount of data through its encoder, compressing it into a more manageable form that captures the essential patterns of normal network behavior. This compressed representation might include factors like typical login times, usual file transfer sizes, common application usage patterns, and normal server request frequencies. The decoder then attempts to reconstruct the original network traffic patterns from this compressed representation. Because VAEs work with probability distributions rather than exact reconstructions, they can generate variations of what "normal" network behavior looks like. This probabilistic approach is particularly valuable because legitimate network traffic isn't always identical from day to day but follows similar patterns. For example, if an employee typically logs in between 8:00 and 9:00 AM, accesses certain applications, and transfers files of particular sizes, the VAE learns this pattern as a distribution rather than exact values. When it encounters behavior that falls far outside these learned distributions—like a login at 3:00 AM followed by unusual file transfers—it can flag this as potentially suspicious. The practical value becomes apparent in anomaly detection. When the VAE encounters network behavior that it struggles to encode and reconstruct accurately (meaning it falls outside the learned probability distributions of normal behavior), this could indicate a security threat. For instance, if an attacker compromises an account and begins exfiltrating data, their behavior might technically follow allowed network protocols but create patterns that don't fit the VAE's learned distributions of normal behavior. The system can also generate synthetic but realistic network traffic patterns for security testing. Thus, by sampling from the learned probability distributions, security teams can create test scenarios that reflect realistic network behavior while incorporating variations they might not have thought to test. This helps in developing and validating security controls without risking actual network operations. Subsequently, what makes VAEs useful in this context is their ability to handle complex, multivariate data while maintaining realistic relationships between different aspects of network behavior. Unlike simpler anomaly detection systems that might look at individual metrics in isolation, VAEs can understand how different aspects of network behavior relate to each other, leading to more nuanced and accurate threat detection. The same approach can be applied to other security contexts, such as modeling normal system call patterns for host-based intrusion detection, understanding typical Application Programming Interface (API) usage patterns for application security, or modeling normal database query patterns to detect potential Structured Query Language (SQL) injection attempts. In each case, the VAE's ability to learn and generate from probability distributions helps create more robust and nuanced security monitoring systems.

Transformer-based models have emerged as the dominant architecture for NLP and have increasingly been adapted for other domains. Originally introduced for machine translation, transformers use a mechanism called self-attention to process sequential data by identifying relationships between all elements in a sequence simultaneously (Soydaner, 2022). This parallel processing capability, combined with their ability to handle long-range dependencies, has made transformers the foundation for powerful language models like GPT and BERT, as well as multimodal models that can work with both text and images (Zhou et al., 2024). The scale of transformer-based models has grown exponentially since their introduction, with current state-of-the-art systems containing hundreds of billions of parameters (Yenduri et al., 2024). This scaling has unlocked emergent capabilities such as few-shot learning, complex reasoning, and sophisticated instruction following (Bertie et al., 2025). Recent research has focused on enhancing transformer efficiency through techniques like sparse attention, parameter sharing, and knowledge distillation to reduce computational demands (Habib et al., 2023). Beyond language, transformers have been successfully adapted for computer vision, time series forecasting, protein structure prediction, and even quantum chemistry applications, demonstrating their versatility as a general-purpose architecture for AI systems (Ahmed et al., 2023; Pei, 2024; Wen et al., 2022).

As was done with GANs and VAEs, a practical example of transformer-based models can put it into perspective. Consider a large enterprise's security monitoring system that uses a transformer-based model to analyze system logs across thousands of devices. Unlike traditional log analysis tools that might look at events in isolation or in limited sequences, the transformer can analyze relationships between log entries across extended periods and multiple systems simultaneously. For example, when an employee accesses a sensitive database, the transformer model doesn't just see this as an isolated event. It simultaneously processes related log entries from the employee's workstation, network authentication logs, building access records, and application usage patterns. Through its self-attention mechanism, the model can identify meaningful relationships between these events, even if they're separated by hours or occur across different systems. The power of this approach becomes evident when detecting sophisticated attack patterns.

Consider a scenario where an attacker is moving laterally through the network. They might access one system, escalate privileges, move to another system, and slowly work their way toward sensitive data. Traditional security tools might miss this pattern because the individual actions appear legitimate when viewed in isolation. However, the transformer model, processing all these events simultaneously through its self-attention mechanism, can identify suspicious patterns in how these actions relate to each other across time and systems. The model's ability to handle long-range dependencies is particularly valuable in security contexts. It might be noticed that a user's current actions, while seemingly normal, are subtly related to events that occurred days ago in ways that indicate potential compromise. For instance, it could identify that a current database query, while valid, is suspiciously similar to patterns observed during previous data exfiltration attempts.

In practice, this might look like a security analyst receiving an alert that shows not just the triggering event but also a clear visualization of related events across systems and time periods. The transformer's attention mechanisms can highlight which relationships it found most significant, helping analysts quickly understand complex security incidents. The same model can be applied to code analysis for security vulnerabilities. When examining source code, the transformer can simultaneously process multiple parts of the codebase, understanding how different components interact and identifying potential security issues that might only become apparent when considering these interactions together. It can recognize patterns that indicate vulnerable code, even when the relevant lines are separated by hundreds of other lines of code or spread across multiple files. In general, this ability to process and understand relationships across long sequences and multiple contexts makes transformer-based models particularly effective for modern security challenges, where threats often involve complex patterns of behavior across multiple systems and extended time periods. The model's parallel processing capability also means it can analyze vast amounts of security data in real time, helping organizations maintain robust security monitoring even at large scales.

Each of these architectures has unique strengths and applications in cybersecurity. GANs excel at generating synthetic data for testing security systems and creating adversarial examples to probe system vulnerabilities. VAEs are valuable for anomaly detection and generating diverse test cases for security validation. Transformer-based models have proven particularly effective for code analysis, threat detection, and automated response generation in security contexts (Kheddar, 2024). The evolution of these generative models continues to advance rapidly, with hybrid approaches combining elements from multiple architectures to achieve better results. For instance, some modern systems use transformer-based generators with GAN-style discriminators, or combine VAE-style encoding with transformer-based generation. These hybrid approaches are pushing the boundaries of what's possible in generative AI, while also introducing new security considerations that professionals must understand and address.

Understanding the practical applications is key here; let's go over additional examples of how these different models are implemented in the field. For GANs, consider a security team wanting to test their organization's phishing detection systems. A GAN could be used to generate synthetic phishing emails that mimic real attack patterns. The generator network would create fake phishing emails, while the discriminator would attempt to distinguish these from real phishing emails captured in the wild. Over time, the GAN would learn to generate increasingly sophisticated and realistic phishing attempts, providing valuable training data for security systems. This same approach could be used to generate synthetic network traffic patterns, helping organizations prepare for new types of attacks without exposing real system vulnerabilities. On the other hand, imagine a financial institution using a VAE for fraud detection in credit card transactions. The VAE learns the normal patterns of customer spending behavior by compressing transaction data into a compact representation that captures key patterns. When the VAE attempts to reconstruct a new transaction, any significant deviation from the learned patterns (indicated by a high reconstruction error) could signal potential fraud. The VAE's ability to learn a probability distribution of normal behavior makes it particularly effective at detecting subtle anomalies that might indicate sophisticated fraud attempts.

Now, picture an SOC using a transformer model to analyze system logs and generate incident response recommendations. The model, trained on historical security incidents and responses, can process streams of log data, identifying patterns that indicate potential security threats. When it detects suspicious activity, it can generate detailed response plans based on similar past incidents, taking into account the full context of the current situation. For example, if it identifies a pattern of failed login attempts followed by unusual file access patterns, it could generate a structured response plan including steps for containment, investigation, and remediation, all based on how similar incidents were successfully handled in the past.

There are also other models used for generative AI beyond GANs, VAEs, and Transformers that also have unique capabilities and applications. Flow-based models, such as RealNVP and Glow, represent one important category (Tomczak, 2024). These models use a series of reversible transformations to map between simple probability distributions and complex data distributions. Unlike GANs or VAEs, flow-based models can provide exact likelihood calculations, making them useful for anomaly detection and precise data generation in security applications (Diaz Rivero & Dvorkin, 2020). Autoregressive models are another approach to generative AI (Bond-Taylor et al., 2022). These models generate data sequentially, one element at a time, with each new element conditioned on all previous elements. PixelCNN and WaveNet are notable examples, with PixelCNN generating images pixel by pixel and WaveNet creating audio samples point by point (Javanmardi, 2020). In cybersecurity, autoregressive models can be particularly useful for generating synthetic network traffic or system logs that maintain temporal consistency and causality relationships.

Diffusion models have recently gained prominence as a powerful alternative for generative tasks. These models work by gradually adding noise to data and then learning to reverse this process, ultimately generating new data by denoising random input (Croitoru et al., 2023). Stable Diffusion and DALL-E 2 are prominent examples that have shown remarkable capabilities in image generation (Zhang et al., 2023). In security applications, diffusion models could be used for generating synthetic test data or creating adversarial examples to probe system defenses. Their unique approach to generation often results in high-quality outputs while being more stable to train than GANs. Conceptually, diffusion models mirror thermodynamic processes in physics, where a system gradually moves from disorder to order through carefully guided transformations (Wang et al., 2024). This intuitive framework allows for precise control over the generation process, with each denoising step introducing increasingly defined details into the emerging content (Croitoru et al., 2023). The iterative nature of diffusion also provides natural checkpoints throughout the generation process, offering opportunities to guide or modify the output at various stages of completion (Bandi et al., 2023).

A practical example would be useful here. Imagine a security team using a diffusion model to test their organization's biometric authentication system that relies on facial recognition. The team needs to generate diverse, realistic test cases to ensure their system is robust against various types of spoofing attempts, while also verifying it works correctly for legitimate users under different conditions.

The diffusion model starts with random noise and gradually transforms it into realistic facial images through a denoising process. Unlike traditional methods of generating test images, the diffusion model can create highly realistic variations of faces that maintain important biometric markers while varying elements like lighting, angle, and facial expressions. This helps test the authentication system's ability to correctly identify legitimate users under different conditions while rejecting sophisticated spoofing attempts. In practice, the security team might use the diffusion model to generate thousands of test cases. For example, they could create variations of an employee's face with different hairstyles, lighting conditions, or aging effects to ensure the system maintains accurate recognition across these variations. Similarly, they could generate sophisticated fake images to test the system's ability to detect and reject spoofing attempts. The diffusion model's approach offers advantages over other generation methods because it produces more stable and consistent results. Unlike GANs, which might suddenly generate unrealistic outputs, diffusion models tend to produce more reliable, high-quality images. This reliability is crucial when testing security systems, as the test data must be realistic enough to validate the system's real-world performance effectively. Thus, this approach helps organizations build more robust security systems by testing them against a wider range of potential scenarios than would be practical to create manually or capture in real-world photography.

Energy-based models (EBMs) are yet another distinct approach, assigning scalar "energy" values to different data configurations and learning to generate low-energy samples that correspond to realistic data (Gao et al., 2020). While less commonly used than other approaches, EBMs offer unique advantages in terms of flexibility and the ability to capture complex dependencies in data. They've shown promise in anomaly detection and pattern recognition tasks, making them potentially valuable tools for security applications where understanding complex data relationships is crucial (Sharma et al., 2024). To put it into perspective, imagine a financial institution using an EBM to detect fraudulent transactions. The EBM assigns "energy" values to different transaction patterns, where lower energy states represent normal, legitimate banking behavior, and higher energy states indicate potentially fraudulent activity. Think of it like a landscape where valleys represent normal behavior and peaks represent suspicious patterns. For example, when a customer makes typical transactions—regular bill payments, grocery shopping, or monthly subscriptions—these patterns create low-energy states in the model because they align with learned normal behavior. However, when unusual patterns emerge—like rapid successive transactions across different locations, unusual purchase amounts, or unexpected international activity—these create high-energy states that trigger alerts. The EBM's unique advantage lies in its ability to capture complex relationships between multiple transaction attributes simultaneously. It might recognize that a high-value purchase at a luxury store creates a low-energy state for a customer who regularly makes such purchases, but a high-energy state for someone with typically modest spending patterns. This nuanced understanding helps reduce false positives while catching subtle fraud patterns that might escape traditional rule-based systems.

2.4 NLP in Generative AI

NLP in generative AI fundamentally changes how machines understand and generate human language. At its core, NLP in generative AI relies on sophisticated language models that have learned patterns and relationships in human language from massive text datasets (Hagos et al., 2024). These models, like GPT-4, PaLM, and Claude, can understand context, maintain coherence across long passages, and generate human-like text across various styles and purposes (Hadi et al., 2024). The evolution of these models has progressed from simple statistical approaches to complex neural architectures that can capture nuanced language patterns and generate contextually appropriate responses.

Text generation capabilities have advanced dramatically with the emergence of large language models (LLMs). These systems can now generate various types of content, from creative writing and technical documentation to code and analytical reports. The generation process typically involves the model predicting the most probable next word or token based on the given context, while maintaining coherence, factual accuracy, and stylistic consistency. Modern text generation systems can also be controlled through careful prompting, allowing users to specify the tone, style, format, and content of the generated text. This has important implications for both beneficial applications (like automated report generation) and potential security concerns (such as automated phishing content generation). This can have some beneficial security applications. Below are some examples of prompts that can be used to help small to large organizations when it comes to text generation in cybersecurity contexts:

> "Generate a detailed incident response plan template for a ransomware attack, including initial containment steps, stakeholder communication guidelines, and recovery procedures."
>
> "Create a security awareness training document explaining phishing threats in simple terms that non-technical employees can understand. Include common red flags and best practices."
>
> "Write a technical analysis of a recent zero-day vulnerability, explaining its impact, affected systems, and recommended mitigation strategies. Format it as a professional security advisory."
>
> "Develop a set of security policy guidelines for remote work, covering secure access, data protection, and incident reporting procedures."

Security Research Applications:

> "Analyze this network traffic log and generate a report highlighting potential anomalies and suspicious patterns. Structure the analysis with clear sections for findings, evidence, and recommendations."
>
> "Create a tabletop exercise scenario for a security team, simulating a sophisticated supply chain attack. Include realistic event progression and decision points."
>
> "Generate test cases for testing our web application's input validation controls. Include edge cases and potential injection attempts."

It's worth noting that while these examples demonstrate positive applications, the same capabilities could potentially be misused for generating malicious content. This highlights the importance of responsible AI development and deployment, particularly in security contexts. The effectiveness of these prompts often depends on providing clear context, specific requirements, and appropriate constraints. More sophisticated results can be achieved by including examples, specifying formats, and clearly defining the intended audience and purpose. Have fun with it! Be creative! And importantly, be able to double-check and verify the information that is outputted. While hallucinations have gotten better with time (especially in the past 2years), it is still important to note that this can happen, so we have to avoid an overdependency on AI-generated outputs.

Text-to-speech (TTS) and speech-to-text (STT) technologies have become increasingly sophisticated through generative AI approaches. Modern TTS systems can generate natural-sounding speech with proper intonation, emphasis, and emotional expression, while STT systems can accurately transcribe speech across different accents, languages, and acoustic conditions (Kumar et al., 2023). These technologies utilize specialized neural networks that understand both the linguistic content and the acoustic properties of speech. The integration of these capabilities with language models has enabled more natural human–machine interaction (HMI) and opened new possibilities for HMI and applications in security, such as voice authentication and audio content analysis (Mukhtar, 2025). So, what does it mean for cybersecurity? While the aforementioned enables ways for automation and analysis, they also open up new security challenges. For instance, these technologies can be used to generate convincing phishing emails, create deepfake audio for social engineering attacks, or automate the creation of malicious content at scale. We will discuss this in more detail in Chapter 4.

Another example here—consider a bank's customer service system that uses advanced TTS and STT capabilities to handle customer inquiries. The legitimate system employs TTS to provide natural-sounding automated responses to common banking questions, while STT accurately transcribes customer voice commands for processing—even handling various accents and background noise effectively. This technology improves efficiency by allowing 24/7 automated service while maintaining a natural interaction that customers find comfortable and trustworthy.

However, the same technological capabilities could be exploited by attackers for sophisticated vishing (voice phishing) campaigns. An attacker might use TTS to generate convincing voice messages that appear to come from the bank, complete with proper intonation and professional delivery. They could create personalized messages using information gathered from social media, making the scam more convincing. The attacker's system might also use STT to automatically transcribe and analyze any responses from victims, allowing them to run multiple scam campaigns simultaneously with minimal human intervention. For example, they could generate calls claiming there's suspicious activity on a customer's account, with the AI system naturally handling different customer responses and guiding them toward revealing sensitive information. This demonstrates how these technologies, while valuable for legitimate business operations, can also enable more sophisticated and scalable social engineering attacks.

2.5 Computer Vision in Generative AI

Computer Vision in generative AI is an extremely important advancement in how machines can create, manipulate, and understand visual content (Hussain, 2023). This field has evolved from simple image processing to sophisticated systems capable of generating highly realistic images, videos, and three-dimensional models. Modern generative AI systems can understand complex visual concepts, artistic styles, and spatial relationships, enabling them to create or modify visual content with unprecedented accuracy and creativity (Hutson, 2024). Image generation has seen remarkable progress through models like DALL-E, Stable Diffusion, and Midjourney (Derevyanko & Zalevska, 2023). These systems can create highly detailed and contextually accurate images from text descriptions, modify existing images while maintaining coherence, and even combine multiple concepts into single, cohesive images. The technology works by learning patterns from millions of image–text pairs, enabling it to understand both visual features and their relationship to natural language descriptions (Nam & Jang, 2024). This capability has applications ranging from design and prototyping to security testing and synthetic data generation for training other AI systems. Video synthesis is a more complex challenge, as it must maintain consistency not just within a single frame but across multiple frames over time. Recent advances have enabled the creation of synthetic videos that maintain temporal coherence, realistic motion, and consistent style. These systems can generate new videos from scratch, modify existing videos, or even convert still images into animated sequences. The technology combines understanding of both spatial relationships (within frames) and temporal relationships (between frames) to create coherent video content (Esser et al., 2023). 3D model generation is probably the most complex aspect of computer vision in generative AI, requiring understanding of depth, perspective, and spatial relationships in three dimensions (Chaudhuri et al., 2020). Modern systems can generate 3D models from text descriptions, single images, or multiple viewpoints. These models can include detailed textures, realistic lighting, and physically accurate properties. The technology uses sophisticated neural networks that understand both the geometric principles of 3D space and the visual characteristics of different materials and surfaces.

In the context of security testing, computer vision AI can be used to generate synthetic data for training security systems, helping organizations identify potential vulnerabilities in their visual verification methods (Akhtar et al., 2021). For example, security teams can use these systems to create diverse sets of test cases for facial recognition systems, helping identify potential weaknesses or biases in their authentication mechanisms. The field also presents challenges in digital forensics (Thakkar et al., 2023). As computer vision AI becomes more sophisticated, distinguishing between authentic and synthetic visual content becomes increasingly difficult. This has led to the development of new detection techniques that look for artifacts and inconsistencies that might indicate AI manipulation, though these too must constantly evolve as generation techniques improve. From a defensive perspective, organizations must now consider how their visual security systems might be compromised by AI-generated content. This includes implementing multifactor authentication systems that don't rely solely on visual verification, developing better methods for detecting synthetic images and videos, and creating security protocols that account for the possibility of AI-generated visual deception (Ghiurău & Popescu, 2024).

A real-world example of how computer vision is utilized as a security tool is demonstrated in Microsoft Edge's new Edge scareware blocker and illustrating how visual analysis can enhance cybersecurity defenses (Whitney, 2025). The system leverages machine learning to analyze and compare suspicious webpages against a database of known scam samples, enabling real-time detection of potential scareware attacks based on their visual characteristics rather than traditional signature-based methods. This approach operates locally on users' devices, preserving privacy while providing immediate protection against emerging threats.

The implementation demonstrates several key advantages of computer vision in cybersecurity applications. Consequently, by using visual pattern recognition to identify malicious behavior, the system can detect and respond to social engineering attacks that rely on visual deception—a growing concern in today's threat landscape. The ability to analyze full-screen tactics and other visual elements commonly used in scams shows how AI can automate protective responses, like forcing an exit from full-screen mode when threats are detected. This provides an additional layer of security that operates independently of traditional blacklists or signatures. Moreover, this case study illustrates the practical evolution of computer vision in everyday security tools, showing how AI can protect users from sophisticated social engineering attempts while maintaining user privacy through local processing. The system's ability to learn from and compare against thousands of sample scams demonstrates the scalability and adaptability of computer vision-based security solutions. This approach is an important step forward in protecting users from visual-based attacks, particularly those that might evade traditional security measures. The integration of computer vision AI into browser security features suggests a growing trend toward more sophisticated, AI-powered security tools that can better protect users from evolving cyber threats.

In general, understanding computer vision in generative AI is crucial for modern cybersecurity professionals because it is a powerful security tool and a significant threat vector (both as a weapon and a target). As organizations increasingly rely on visual verification systems for security—from facial recognition for access control to video surveillance for threat detection—the ability of generative AI to create and manipulate visual content poses unprecedented challenges. Security professionals must understand these technologies to effectively protect against sophisticated visual-based attacks while also leveraging their capabilities for enhanced security measures. From a defensive perspective, understanding computer vision in generative AI enables security teams to implement more effective security measures. For instance, knowing how these systems work allows professionals to develop better detection methods for synthetic media, implement more robust authentication systems that can resist AI-based spoofing attempts, and create more effective training scenarios using synthetic data. This knowledge is also crucial for risk assessment, helping security teams identify potential vulnerabilities in their visual verification systems and develop appropriate mitigation strategies. The implications extend beyond immediate security concerns to broader organizational resilience. As businesses increasingly rely on visual data for operations and decision-making, understanding how this data can be manipulated or generated becomes critical for maintaining data integrity and trust. Also, security professionals need to be able to advise their organizations on the reliability of visual evidence, the potential for AI-generated deception, and appropriate verification procedures in an era where seeing is no longer necessarily believing. Moreover, this knowledge is essential for future-proofing security systems. As generative AI continues to evolve, with capabilities like 3D model generation and real-time video synthesis becoming more sophisticated, security professionals need to understand these developments to anticipate and prepare for new types of threats. This includes staying informed about emerging capabilities in computer vision, understanding their potential security implications, and developing proactive security measures rather than merely reactive responses. But, for now, let's move on to Chapter 3, where we discuss how generative AI can help cybersecurity measures.

2.6 Conclusion

Understanding the technical foundations of generative AI is crucial for cybersecurity professionals as it provides the fundamental knowledge needed to both leverage these technologies effectively and defend against their potential misuse. This chapter's exploration of machine learning fundamentals, neural network architectures, and various generative models establishes the technical framework necessary for understanding how AI systems can be both powerful security tools and potential threat vectors. The progression from basic machine learning concepts through sophisticated generative models reveals the layered complexity of modern AI systems. This understanding is essential because security professionals can't effectively protect what they don't understand. Whether dealing with GANs that could generate sophisticated phishing attempts, VAEs that might be used for anomaly detection, or transformer models analyzing system logs, knowing how these systems work at a technical level enables security teams to make informed decisions about implementation, risk assessment, and defensive strategies.

The practical examples throughout the chapter demonstrate how these technologies manifest in real-world security scenarios. From using RL for adaptive threat detection to employing GANs for testing security systems, these applications show how theoretical concepts translate into practical security tools and potential threats. This connection between theory and practice is vital for security professionals who must bridge the gap between technical capabilities and operational security requirements. This chapter's coverage of various neural network architectures (CNNs, RNNs, transformers) provides crucial insight into how AI systems process and analyze different types of data. This knowledge is particularly important as organizations increasingly rely on AI-powered security tools that must handle diverse data types—from network traffic patterns to visual surveillance data.

Understanding these architectures helps us to evaluate AI security tools, identify potential vulnerabilities, and implement appropriate security measures. These models can be powerful tools for generating synthetic training data, testing security systems, and detecting anomalies. However, they can also be used to create sophisticated attacks, deepfakes, and other malicious content. Understanding how these models work is essential for developing effective countermeasures and maintaining robust security in an AI-enabled threat landscape. Moreover, this technical foundation becomes increasingly important as AI systems become more integrated into critical security infrastructure. Security professionals must be able to assess the reliability, limitations, and potential vulnerabilities of AI systems. This includes understanding how these systems might be compromised, how they could fail, and what safeguards need to be in place to ensure their secure operation. Chapter 2 ultimately emphasizes that while AI systems can be powerful security tools, they must be understood at a technical level to be used effectively and securely. This understanding enables security professionals to make informed decisions about AI implementation, develop more effective security strategies, and better protect their organizations against AI-enabled threats. As generative AI continues to reshape the security landscape, this technical foundation becomes not just valuable but essential for modern cybersecurity practice.

Chapter 2 Summary

This chapter established the essential technical foundations of generative AI necessary for understanding its security implications. It began with machine learning fundamentals, covering supervised learning (where algorithms learn from labeled data like phishing email detection), unsupervised learning (which discovers hidden patterns in unlabeled data for anomaly detection), and RL (where systems learn through trial-and-error feedback like autonomous incident response). The chapter progressed through deep learning architectures, explaining how ANNs process information through interconnected layers. It detailed specialized architectures including CNNs for spatial pattern recognition (like surveillance analysis), RNNs for sequential data processing (like network traffic monitoring), and the revolutionary transformer models that use self-attention mechanisms for complex relationship analysis.

The chapter explored three primary generative model architectures that dominate modern AI. GANs operate through adversarial training between generator and discriminator networks, demonstrated through security applications like creating sophisticated phishing tests. VAEs combined encoding and decoding with probabilistic modeling for tasks like network behavior analysis and anomaly detection. Transformer-based models emerged as the foundation for LLMs, showcasing their ability to process complex relationships across extended sequences in security contexts. The chapter concluded with practical applications in NLP, including text generation capabilities for security documentation and automated response systems, and computer vision applications ranging from image generation to 3D modeling, highlighting both defensive uses and potential security concerns.

Understanding these technical foundations proved essential for security professionals because they could not effectively protect what they did not understand. The chapter demonstrated how different neural network architectures processed different types of data—CNNs for visual surveillance, RNNs for temporal network patterns, and transformers for complex log analysis. This knowledge enabled security teams to select appropriate AI tools for specific tasks, evaluate their reliability and limitations, and identify potential vulnerabilities. The progression from basic machine learning concepts to sophisticated generative models revealed the layered complexity of modern AI systems that security professionals must navigate.

The chapter emphasized that AI systems must be understood at a technical level to be used effectively and securely across all three dimensions of the triangular framework. Through practical examples like TechSecure's case study, it showed how theoretical concepts translated into real-world security scenarios where AI served simultaneously as a defensive tool, a potential weapon, and a vulnerable target. This technical foundation became crucial for developing effective countermeasures against AI-enabled threats, implementing robust security measures for AI systems themselves, and making informed decisions about AI integration into security infrastructure. As AI continued to reshape the security landscape, this deep technical understanding transformed from merely valuable to absolutely essential for modern cybersecurity practice.

Case Study

Let's synthesize Chapter 2's concepts through a triangular framework of AI security. This is a hypothetical situation that mirrors a situation we would see out in the field to help us bridge the gap between the theoretical and the practical.

In early 2024, TechSecure, a mid-sized cybersecurity firm serving financial clients, embarked on an ambitious project to modernize their threat detection capabilities using various neural network architectures. This case study examines their implementation through the triangular lens of AI security—as a tool, a weapon, and a target—while demonstrating the practical application of the technical concepts covered in Chapter 2.

AI as a Tool: TechSecure implemented a layered approach using multiple neural network architectures. They deployed CNNs for visual security analysis, including surveillance footage and document verification, while RNNs handled sequential data analysis for network traffic and user behavior patterns. The company implemented a transformer-based model for log analysis and a GAN system for testing their security controls. Their implementation began with supervised learning models trained on labeled threat data, complemented by unsupervised learning for anomaly detection and RL for adaptive response systems. The CNN component processed visual data from client security systems, analyzing surveillance footage for suspicious behavior patterns and verifying identity documents for potential forgeries. Meanwhile, their RNN systems monitored network traffic patterns, maintaining temporal context to detect sophisticated attack sequences that might escape traditional detection methods. The transformer model analyzed system logs across their clients' infrastructure, using its attention mechanisms to identify subtle correlations between seemingly unrelated events.

AI as a Weapon: Understanding that adversaries could use similar technologies, TechSecure developed their systems to anticipate and counter AI-powered attacks. They used their GAN implementation not just for testing but to generate sophisticated attack scenarios, helping them understand potential AI-enabled threats. The generator network created increasingly sophisticated attack patterns—from complex phishing attempts to elaborate network intrusion sequences—while the discriminator learned to detect these advanced threats.

This approach proved prescient when one of their financial clients faced an AI-powered attack. The adversaries used machine learning models to automate the discovery of network vulnerabilities and generate convincing spear-phishing emails targeting senior executives. TechSecure's systems, having been trained against similarly sophisticated synthetic attacks, successfully identified and blocked the attack patterns, demonstrating the value of understanding AI both as a tool and potential weapon.

AI as a Target: The most challenging aspect of TechSecure's implementation came from recognizing their AI systems themselves as potential targets. They needed to protect not just their clients' infrastructure but also their AI models from manipulation and attack. This required implementing several defensive measures learned from their study of neural network architectures: They used feature engineering techniques to make their models more robust against adversarial attacks, carefully selecting and processing input data to reduce vulnerabilities. Their understanding of how neural networks process information helped them identify potential attack vectors against their models, such as data poisoning attempts or adversarial examples designed to fool their classification systems.

The Results: After six months of implementation, TechSecure's AI-enhanced security systems demonstrated significant improvements (we will talk about the importance of metrics and performance metrics in upcoming chapters):

- 85% reduction in false positives for threat detection
- 90% faster identification of sophisticated attack patterns
- 95% success rate in detecting AI-generated phishing attempts
- Zero successful attacks against their AI systems

Lessons Learned: The project highlighted several key insights about implementing AI in security contexts:

1) **Understanding Technical Foundations:** Deep knowledge of neural network architectures proved essential for both implementing effective security tools and protecting against their malicious use. The team's understanding of how different architectures (CNNs, RNNs, transformers) process information helped them choose the right tools for specific security tasks while anticipating potential vulnerabilities.
2) **Balanced Approach:** The triangular view of AI security (tool, weapon, target) proved crucial for comprehensive security. Focusing solely on AI as a tool would have left them vulnerable to AI-powered attacks and blind to threats against their own AI systems.
3) **Integration Challenges:** Combining multiple neural network architectures required careful consideration of how different systems interact. The team's understanding of feature engineering and selection proved crucial for ensuring that different components worked together effectively.
4) **Model Security:** Protecting AI models themselves requires as much attention as using them for protection. Understanding concepts like adversarial training and model robustness proved essential for securing their AI infrastructure.

Future Implications: TechSecure's experience demonstrates how technical understanding of AI foundations directly translates to practical security capabilities. Their success in implementing and securing AI systems while defending against AI-powered attacks shows the importance of comprehending both the theoretical and practical aspects of neural networks and machine learning. The case also highlights how the concepts covered in Chapter 2—from basic machine learning principles to sophisticated generative models—provide the necessary foundation for effective AI security implementation. These concepts helped enable TechSecure to choose appropriate architectures for specific security tasks, anticipate and defend against AI-powered attacks, protect their AI systems from manipulation, and develop more effective security strategies.

A key takeaway from this case study is that success in AI security requires more than just implementing AI tools—it demands a deep understanding of the underlying technologies and their implications across all three aspects of the security triangle. As AI continues to evolve, this technical foundation becomes increasingly crucial for security professionals working to protect organizations in an AI-enabled threat landscape.

Chapter 2 Quiz

Questions

1. Which of the following best describes the key difference between RNNs and CNNs?
   a) RNNs are faster at processing data
   b) CNNs can only process images
   c) RNNs maintain temporal context while CNNs focus on spatial patterns
   d) RNNs are more accurate than CNNs

2. In a GAN architecture used for security testing, what is the primary role of the discriminator?
   a) To generate synthetic attack patterns
   b) To distinguish between real and fake security events
   c) To compress network traffic data
   d) To predict future attacks

3. What makes VAEs particularly useful for anomaly detection in network security?
   a) They process data faster than other models
   b) They can generate unlimited training data
   c) They learn probability distributions of normal behavior
   d) They can predict exact attack patterns

4. When implementing feature engineering for security applications, why is domain expertise crucial?
   a) It helps process data faster
   b) It identifies relevant security patterns and relationships in data
   c) It makes the system run more efficiently
   d) It reduces the cost of implementation

5. Which model would be most appropriate for analyzing long-term patterns in system logs?
   a) CNN
   b) Basic Neural Network
   c) Transformer
   d) Simple RNN

Answer Key

1 **Correct Answer: c) RNNs maintain temporal context, while CNNs focus on spatial patterns.** This is correct because it identifies the fundamental architectural difference between these networks.
- a) is incorrect because speed isn't the defining difference between these architectures
- b) is incorrect because CNNs can be used for other grid-like data structures
- d) is incorrect because accuracy depends on the specific application and implementation.

2 **Correct Answer: b) To distinguish between real and fake security events.** This is correct because it describes the fundamental role of the discriminator in a GAN architecture.
- a) is incorrect because generation is the generator's role
- c) is incorrect because this describes a function of VAEs
- d) is incorrect because prediction isn't the primary role of the discriminator.

3 **Correct Answer: c) They learn probability distributions of normal behavior.** This is correct because VAEs' ability to learn probability distributions enables them to identify deviations from normal patterns.
- a) is incorrect because processing speed isn't VAEs' key advantage
- b) is incorrect because this is more characteristic of GANs
- d) is incorrect because VAEs don't predict specific attack patterns.

4 **Correct Answer: b) It identifies relevant security patterns and relationships in data.** This is correct because domain expertise helps identify which features are meaningful for security analysis.
- a) is incorrect because processing speed isn't related to domain expertise
- c) is incorrect because system efficiency isn't the primary benefit of domain expertise
- d) is incorrect because cost reduction isn't the main purpose of domain expertise.

5 **Correct Answer: c) Transformer.** This is correct because transformers excel at handling long-range dependencies through their self-attention mechanism.
- a) is incorrect because CNNs focus on spatial rather than temporal patterns
- b) is incorrect because basic neural networks don't handle sequential data well
- d) is incorrect because simple RNNs struggle with long-term dependencies.

References

Abdolrasol, M. G., Hussain, S. S., Ustun, T. S., Sarker, M. R., Hannan, M. A., Mohamed, R., Ali, J. A., Mekhilef, S., & Milad, A. (2021). Artificial neural networks based optimization techniques: A review. *Electronics, 10*(21), 2689.

Abiodun, E. O., Alabdulatif, A., Abiodun, O. I., Alawida, M., Alabdulatif, A., & Alkhawaldeh, R. S. (2021). A systematic review of emerging feature selection optimization methods for optimal text classification: The present state and prospective opportunities. *Neural Computing and Applications, 33*(22), 15091–15118.

Ahmad, Z., Jaffri, Z. U. A., Chen, M., & Bao, S. (2025). Understanding GANs: Fundamentals, variants, training challenges, applications, and open problems. *Multimedia Tools and Applications, 84*, 10347–10423.

Ahmed, S., Nielsen, I. E., Tripathi, A., Siddiqui, S., Ramachandran, R. P., & Rasool, G. (2023). Transformers in time-series analysis: A tutorial. *Circuits, Systems, and Signal Processing, 42*(12), 7433–7466.

Akhtar, N., Mian, A., Kardan, N., & Shah, M. (2021). Advances in adversarial attacks and defenses in computer vision: A survey. *IEEE Access, 9*, 155161–155196.

Ali, A., Zia, A., Razzaque, A., Shahid, H., Sheikh, H.T., Saleem, M., Yousaf, F., & Muneer, S. (2024, February). Enhancing cybersecurity with artificial neural networks: A study on threat detection and mitigation strategies. In *2024 2nd International Conference on Cyber Resilience (ICCR)* (pp. 1–5). IEEE.

Alzubaidi, L., Zhang, J., Humaidi, A. J., Al-Dujaili, A., Duan, Y., Al-Shamma, O., Santamaría, J., Fadhel, M. A., Al-Amidie, M., and Farhan, L. (2021). Review of deep learning: concepts, CNN architectures, challenges, applications, future directions. *Journal of Big Data, 8*, 53.

Andrychowicz, M., Raichuk, A., Stańczyk, P., Orsini, M., Girgin, S., Marinier, R., Hussenot, L., Geist, M., Pietquin, O., Michalski, M., & Bachem, O. (2020). What matters in on-policy reinforcement learning? A large-scale empirical study. arXiv preprint arXiv:2006.05990.

Bandi, A., Adapa, P. V. S. R., & Kuchi, Y. E. V. P. K. (2023). The power of generative AI: A review of requirements, models, input–output formats, evaluation metrics, and challenges. *Future Internet, 15*(8), 260.

Berti, L., Giorgi, F., & Kasneci, G. (2025). Emergent abilities in large language models: A survey. arXiv preprint arXiv:2503.05788.

Bonassi, F., Farina, M., Xie, J., & Scattolini, R. (2022). On recurrent neural networks for learning-based control: Recent results and ideas for future developments. *Journal of Process Control, 114*, 92–104.

Bond-Taylor, S., Leach, A., Long, Y., & Willcocks, C. G. (2022). Deep generative modelling: A comparative review of VAEs, GANs, normalizing flows, energy-based and autoregressive models. *IEEE Transactions on Pattern Analysis and Machine Intelligence, 44*(11), 7327–7347.

Chaudhuri, S., Ritchie, D., Wu, J., Xu, K., & Zhang, H. (2020, May). Learning generative models of 3d structures. In *Computer graphics forum* (Vol. 39, No. 2, pp. 643–666).

Croitoru, F. A., Hondru, V., Ionescu, R. T., & Shah, M. (2023). Diffusion models in vision: A survey. *IEEE Transactions on Pattern Analysis and Machine Intelligence, 45*(9), 10850–10869.

Cunningham, P., Cord, M., & Delany, S. J. (2008). Supervised learning. In Cord M. & Cunningham P. (Eds.), *Machine learning techniques for multimedia: Case studies on organization and retrieval* (pp. 21–49). Springer Berlin Heidelberg.

Dargan, S., Kumar, M., Ayyagari, M. R., & Kumar, G. (2020). A survey of deep learning and its applications: A new paradigm to machine learning. *Archives of Computational Methods in Engineering, 27*, 1071–1092.

Derevyanko, N., & Zalevska, O. (2023). Comparative analysis of neural networks Midjourney, Stable Diffusion, and DALL-E and ways of their implementation in the educational process of students of design specialities. *Scientific Bulletin of Mukachevo State University. Series "Pedagogy and Psychology", 9*(3), 36–44.

Dhal, P., & Azad, C. (2022). A comprehensive survey on feature selection in the various fields of machine learning. *Applied Intelligence, 52*(4), 4543–4581.

Diaz Rivero, A., & Dvorkin, C. (2020). Flow-based likelihoods for non-Gaussian inference. *Physical Review D, 102*(10), 103507.

Dong, S., Wang, P., & Abbas, K. (2021). A survey on deep learning and its applications. *Computer Science Review, 40*, 100379.

Esser, P., Chiu, J., Atighehchian, P., Granskog, J., & Germanidis, A. (2023). Structure and content-guided video synthesis with diffusion models. In *Proceedings of the IEEE/CVF International Conference on Computer Vision* (pp. 7346–7356).

Fatah, Z. (2024). *Statistical perspectives on deep generative models: Latent space manipulation and variational Autoencoders* [Master's thesis], Southern Illinois University at Edwardsville.

Gangwal, A., Ansari, A., Ahmad, I., Azad, A. K., Kumarasamy, V., Subramaniyan, V., & Wong, L. S. (2024). Generative artificial intelligence in drug discovery: Basic framework, recent advances, challenges, and opportunities. *Frontiers in Pharmacology, 15*, 1331062.

Gao, R., Nijkamp, E., Kingma, D. P., Xu, Z., Dai, A. M., & Wu, Y. N. (2020). Flow contrastive estimation of energy-based models. In *Proceedings of the IEEE/CVF Conference on Computer Vision and Pattern Recognition* (pp. 7518–7528).

Gayam, S. R. (2021). Artificial intelligence for financial fraud detection: Advanced techniques for anomaly detection, pattern recognition, and risk mitigation. *African Journal of Artificial Intelligence and Sustainable Development, 1*(2), 377–412.

Ghahramani, Z. (2003). Unsupervised learning. In R. A. Mouha (Ed.), *Summer school on machine learning* (pp. 72–112). Springer Berlin Heidelberg.

Ghiurău, D., & Popescu, D. E. (2024). Distinguishing reality from AI: Approaches for detecting synthetic content. *Computers, 14*(1), 1.

Gülcü, Ş. (2022). Training of the feed forward artificial neural networks using dragonfly algorithm. *Applied Soft Computing, 124*, 109023.

Habib, G., Saleem, T. J., & Lall, B. (2023). Knowledge distillation in vision transformers: A critical review. arXiv preprint arXiv:2302.02108.

Hadi, M. U., Al Tashi, Q., Shah, A., Qureshi, R., Muneer, A., Irfan, M., Akhtar, N., Wu, J., & Shah, M. (2024). Large language models: A comprehensive survey of its applications, challenges, limitations, and future prospects. Authorea Preprints.

Hagos, D. H., Battle, R., & Rawat, D. B. (2024). Recent advances in generative AI and large language models: Current status, challenges, and perspectives. *IEEE Transactions on Artificial Intelligence, 5*, 5873–5893.

Harshvardhan, G. M., Gourisaria, M. K., Pandey, M., & Rautaray, S. S. (2020). A comprehensive survey and analysis of generative models in machine learning. *Computer Science Review, 38*, 100285.

Hastie, T., Tibshirani, R., Friedman, J., Hastie, T., Tibshirani, R., & Friedman, J. (2009). Overview of supervised learning. In T. Hastie, J. H. Friedman, & R. Tibshirani (Eds.), *The elements of statistical learning: Data mining, inference, and prediction*, Springer, 9–41.

Hu, M., Zhong, Y., Xie, S., Lv, H., & Lv, Z. (2021). Fuzzy system based medical image processing for brain disease prediction. *Frontiers in Neuroscience, 15*, 714318.

Huang, Y. (2024, September). Exploring deep learning-based generative image techniques: Methods and applications. In *2024 International Conference on Artificial Intelligence and Communication (ICAIC 2024)* (pp. 488–501). Atlantis Press. Retrieved from. https://www.atlantis-press.com/proceedings/icaic-24/126003444.

Hussain, M. (2023). When, where, and which?: Navigating the intersection of computer vision and generative AI for strategic business integration. *IEEE Access, 11*, 127202–127215.

Hutson, J. (2024). Art in the age of virtual reproduction. In J. Hutson (Ed.), *Art and culture in the multiverse of metaverses: Immersion, presence, and interactivity in the digital age* (pp. 55–98). Springer Nature Switzerland.

Jabbar, A., Li, X., & Omar, B. (2021). A survey on generative adversarial networks: Variants, applications, and training. *ACM Computing Surveys (CSUR), 54*(8), 1–49.

Javanmardi, F. (2020). Generating speech in different speaking styles using WaveNet [Master's thesis]. Tampere University.

Khan, A., Sohail, A., Zahoora, U., & Qureshi, A. S. (2020). A survey of the recent architectures of deep convolutional neural networks. *Artificial Intelligence Review, 53*, 5455–5516.

Kheddar, H. (2024). Transformers and large language models for efficient intrusion detection systems: A comprehensive survey. arXiv preprint arXiv:2408.07583.

Knight, W. (2025, March 5). Pioneers of reinforcement learning win the Turing award. *Wired*.

Krichen, M. (2023). Convolutional neural networks: a survey. *Computers, 12*(8), 151.

Kumar, Y., Koul, A., & Singh, C. (2023). A deep learning approaches in text-to-speech system: A systematic review and recent research perspective. *Multimedia Tools and Applications, 82*(10), 15171–15197.

Ladosz, P., Weng, L., Kim, M., & Oh, H. (2022). Exploration in deep reinforcement learning: A survey. *Information Fusion, 85*, 1–22.

Laugier, L. (2022). *Analysis and control of online interactions through neural natural language processing* [Doctoral dissertation]. Institut Polytechnique de Paris).

Leevy, J. L., Hancock, J., Zuech, R., & Khoshgoftaar, T. M. (2021). Detecting cybersecurity attacks across different network features and learners. *Journal of Big Data, 8*, 1–29.

Madhiarasan, M., & Louzazni, M. (2022). Analysis of artificial neural network: architecture, types, and forecasting applications. *Journal of Electrical and Computer Engineering, 2022*(1), 5416722.

Matsuo, Y., LeCun, Y., Sahani, M., Precup, D., Silver, D., Sugiyama, M., Uchibe, E. and Morimoto, J., (2022). Deep learning, reinforcement learning, and world models. *Neural Networks, 152*, pp. 267–275.

Mienye, I. D., Swart, T. G., & Obaido, G. (2024). Recurrent neural networks: A comprehensive review of architectures, variants, and applications. *Information (Basel), 15*(9), 517.

Morales, E. F., & Escalante, H. J. (2022). A brief introduction to supervised, unsupervised, and reinforcement learning. In A. A. Torres-García, O. Mendoza-Montoya, L. Villasenor-Pineda, & C. A. R. Garcia (Eds.), *Biosignal processing and classification using computational learning and intelligence* (pp. 111–129). Academic Press.

Mukhtar, H. (2025). Artificial intelligence techniques for human-machine interaction. In A. Subasi, S. M. Qaisar, & H. Nisar (Eds.), *Artificial intelligence and multimodal signal processing in human-machine interaction* (pp. 19–42). Academic Press.

Naeem, S., Ali, A., Anam, S., & Ahmed, M. M. (2023). An unsupervised machine learning algorithms: Comprehensive review. *International Journal of Computing and Digital Systems, 13*, 911–921.

Nam, W., & Jang, B. (2024). A survey on multimodal bidirectional machine learning translation of image and natural language processing. *Expert Systems with Applications, 235*, 121168.

Nasteski, V. (2017). An overview of the supervised machine learning methods. *Horizons. b, 4*(51–62), 51–62.

Navidan, H., Moshiri, P. F., Nabati, M., Shahbazian, R., Ghorashi, S. A., Shah-Mansouri, V., & Windridge, D. (2021). Generative Adversarial Networks (GANs) in networking: A comprehensive survey & evaluation. *Computer Networks*, *194*, 108149.

Nwadiugwu, M. C. (2020). Neural networks, artificial intelligence and the computational brain. arXiv preprint arXiv:2101.08635.

Oluwafemi, N. (2023). Recurrent neural networks-architectures and applications: Analyzing architectures and applications of recurrent neural networks (RNNs) for modeling sequential data and time-series prediction. *Australian Journal of Machine Learning Research & Applications*, *3*(2), 239–249.

Pawar, K., & Attar, V. Z. (2020). Assessment of Autoencoder architectures for data representation. In W. Pedrycz & S.-M. Chen (Eds.), *Deep learning: Concepts and architectures* (pp. 101–132). Springer International Publishing.

Pei, Z. (2024). Computer-aided drug discovery: From traditional simulation methods to language models and quantum computing. *Cell Reports Physical Science*, *5*(12), 102334.

Qamar, R., & Zardari, B. A. (2023). Artificial neural networks: An overview. *Mesopotamian Journal of Computer Science*, *2023*, 124–133.

Rahman, J. U., Zulfiqar, R., & Khan, A. (2024). SwishReLU: A unified approach to activation functions for enhanced deep neural networks performance. arXiv preprint arXiv:2407.08232.

Saxena, D., & Cao, J. (2021). Generative adversarial networks (GANs) challenges, solutions, and future directions. *ACM Computing Surveys (CSUR)*, *54*(3), 1–42.

Sharma, N. A., Chand, R. R., Buksh, Z., Ali, A. B. M., Hanif, A., & Beheshti, A. (2024). Explainable AI frameworks: Navigating the present challenges and unveiling innovative applications. *Algorithms*, *17*(6), 227.

Showrov, A. A., Aziz, M. T., Nabil, H. R., Jim, J. R., Kabir, M. M., Mridha, M. F., Asai, N., & Shin, J. (2024). Generative adversarial networks (GANs) in medical imaging: Advancements, applications and challenges. *IEEE Access.*, *12*, 35728–35753.

Soleimani-Babakamali, M. H., Soleimani-Babakamali, R., Sarlo, R., Farghally, M. F., & Lourentzou, I. (2023). On the effectiveness of dimensionality reduction for unsupervised structural health monitoring anomaly detection. *Mechanical Systems and Signal Processing*, *187*, 109910.

Soundarapandian, R. (2024). *Natural language processing in e-commerce-enhancing customer experience*. Academic Guru Publishing House.

Soydaner, D. (2022). Attention mechanism in neural networks: Where it comes and where it goes. *Neural Computing and Applications*, *34*(16), 13371–13385.

Stateczny, A., Kazimierski, W., & Burdziakowski, P. (2022). Sensors and system for vehicle navigation. *Sensors (Basel)*, *22*(5), 1723.

Taye, M. M. (2023). Theoretical understanding of convolutional neural network: Concepts, architectures, applications, future directions. *Computation*, *11*(3), 52.

Thakkar, P., Patel, D., Hirpara, I., Jagani, J., Patel, S., Shah, M., & Kshirsagar, A. (2023). A comprehensive review on computer vision and fuzzy logic in forensic science application. *Annals of Data Science, 10*(3), 761–785.

Thakur, A., & Konde, A. (2021). Fundamentals of neural networks. *International Journal for Research in Applied Science and Engineering Technology, 9*(VIII), 407–426.

Tomczak, J. M. (2024). Flow-based models. In J. M. Tomczak (Ed.), *Deep generative modeling* (pp. 63–92). Springer International Publishing.

Vamosi, S., Reutterer, T., & Platzer, M. (2022). A deep recurrent neural network approach to learn sequence similarities for user-identification. *Decision Support Systems, 155*, 113718.

Wang, X., He, Z., & Peng, X. (2024). Artificial-intelligence-generated content with diffusion models: A literature review. *Mathematics, 12*(7), 977.

Wang, Y., & Karimi, H. A. (2025). Advanced deep learning models and algorithms for spatial-temporal data. In H. A. Karimi (Ed.), *Big data* (pp. 227–253). CRC Press.

Wang, Z., Xia, L., Yuan, H., Srinivasan, R. S., & Song, X. (2022). Principles, research status, and prospects of feature engineering for data-driven building energy prediction: A comprehensive review. *Journal of Building Engineering, 58*, 105028.

Wen, Q., Zhou, T., Zhang, C., Chen, W., Ma, Z., Yan, J., & Sun, L. (2022). Transformers in time series: A survey. arXiv preprint arXiv:2202.07125.

Whitney, L. (2025, January 28). Microsoft Edge offers new tool to combat scareware – Here's how it works. *ZDNet*.

Yenduri, G., Ramalingam, M., Selvi, G. C., Supriya, Y., Srivastava, G., Maddikunta, P. K. R., Raj, G. D., Jhaveri, R. H., Prabadevi, B., Wang, W., & Vasilakos, A. V. (2024). Gpt (generative pre-trained transformer)–A comprehensive review on enabling technologies, potential applications, emerging challenges, and future directions. *IEEE Access., 12*, 54608–54649.

Zhang, T., Wang, Z., Huang, J., Tasnim, M. M., & Shi, W. (2023). A survey of diffusion based image generation models: Issues and their solutions. arXiv preprint arXiv:2308.13142.

Zhou, C., Li, Q., Li, C., Yu, J., Liu, Y., Wang, G., Zhang, K., Ji, C., Yan, Q., He, L., & Sun, L. (2024). A comprehensive survey on pretrained foundation models: A history from Bert to ChatGPT. *International Journal of Machine Learning and Cybernetics*, 1–65.

3

Generative AI as a Security Tool

Now that the foundational aspects of generative AI of what it is, what it does, and what it excels in have been addressed, it is crucial to address how it can be used as a security tool. We will focus on five key areas, where AI is enhancing security operations and threat prevention. This chapter examines how generative AI serves as a powerful tool for enhancing cybersecurity defenses across multiple fronts. It explores how AI revolutionizes threat detection and response through advanced anomaly detection and automated incident response, while also transforming vulnerability management through AI-driven code analysis and automated patch generation. The chapter demonstrates how intelligent SIEM systems leverage AI for enhanced log analysis and alert triage and examines AI's role in advancing malware analysis to identify both known and zero-day threats. Additionally, it covers the innovative application of generative AI in red teaming exercises, including automated penetration testing and AI-powered social engineering simulations, showcasing how organizations can proactively strengthen their security posture through continuous, AI-driven security validation.

3.1 AI-Powered Threat Detection and Response

AI-powered threat detection and response is an extremely significant advancement in how organizations identify and counter cybersecurity threats (Manda, 2024). It can do this by leveraging machine learning algorithms and advanced analytics, these systems can process vast amounts of data in real time, identifying potential threats that might escape traditional detection methods. This capability has become increasingly crucial as cyberattacks grow in sophistication and frequency, requiring faster and more accurate response mechanisms. That is also why we are seeing a lot of advancements in this field, with tools like Microsoft Security Copilot (Microsoft, n.d.). In fact, Microsoft's Security Copilot is already being used to discover critical vulnerabilities in open-source

Generative AI Security: Defense, Threats, and Vulnerabilities, First Edition. Shaila Rana and Rhonda Chicone.

bootloaders (Naraine, 2025). Thus, there is a fundamental shift here in how organizations approach (or should approach) security monitoring. Traditional rule-based systems, while valuable, often struggle to adapt to new threats and can be overwhelmed by the sheer volume of security data generated by modern networks. AI systems, particularly those using deep learning architectures, can continuously learn from new data, identifying subtle patterns and relationships that might indicate emerging threats (Naseer, 2021). This adaptive capability is especially important given the evolving nature of cyber threats and the increasing use of AI by malicious actors.

Let's take a moment to consider how these systems operate in practice. An AI-powered threat detection system might simultaneously monitor network traffic, user behavior, system logs, and application activity across an organization's entire infrastructure. Using techniques like anomaly detection through unsupervised learning, it can identify unusual patterns that deviate from established baselines. Meanwhile, supervised learning models trained on known attack patterns can quickly identify and classify specific types of threats, enabling faster response times. The real power of these systems lies in their ability to correlate information across multiple sources and timeframes. For example, they might notice that a seemingly innocent increase in database queries, when combined with specific changes in user behavior and unusual network traffic patterns, indicates a potential data exfiltration attempt. Traditional systems looking at each of these factors in isolation might miss the connection, but AI systems can identify these complex relationships and alert security teams before significant damage occurs.

Furthermore, these systems can augment human analysts' capabilities rather than replace them. Lately, as the digital landscape continues to evolve, we hear a lot about how AI is going to replace humans. It is crucial to adjust that mindset to think about how AI technologies can augment rather than replace. Instead, AI can handle the initial analysis of vast amounts of security data and security professionals can focus on investigating the most significant threats and making strategic (the key word here) decisions about security responses. It should be a partnership—and this partnership between AI and human expertise allows defenders to have a powerful approach to modern security challenges, combining the processing power and pattern recognition capabilities of AI with human judgment and contextual understanding. In the future, the continued evolution of AI-powered threat detection will likely lead to even more sophisticated capabilities. As these systems become better at understanding context and intent, they may be able to predict and prevent attacks before they occur, moving security from a reactive to proactive stance. Can you hear the sigh of relief from SOCs? However, this advancement also raises important considerations about privacy, false positives, and the potential for AI systems themselves to become targets of attack, underscoring the need for careful implementation and ongoing oversight of these powerful security tools.

A real-world application of these principles can be seen in Google's recent implementation of AI-powered scam detection for Android devices (Lakshmanan, 2025). This system specifically combats conversational fraud by identifying scams that initially appear harmless before evolving into harmful situations. Developed in partnership with financial institutions, the AI models operate entirely on device, preserving user privacy while analyzing communication patterns to deliver real-time warnings. This implementation demonstrates the practical balance between security and privacy that modern AI systems must achieve. When suspicious patterns are detected, users maintain control by choosing to dismiss alerts or report and block potential threats. The system's default-enabled protection for unknown numbers, alongside its phased rollout strategy (beginning with English-speaking regions before expanding globally), illustrates how large-scale AI security solutions can be deployed responsibly. This example showcases exactly how AI can augment human decision-making rather than replace it—the system identifies potential threats but leaves final judgment to the user, creating the partnership between AI and human expertise described earlier.

Anomaly detection forms the foundation of AI-powered threat detection systems. Using advanced machine learning models, these systems establish baseline patterns of normal behavior across networks, systems, and user activities (Sundaramurthy et al., 2025). (Adewale, 2024). Any deviation from these learned patterns triggers analysis to determine if it represents a potential threat. The power of AI-based anomaly detection lies in its ability to identify subtle patterns and correlations that might be invisible to human analysts or rule-based systems (Nwachukwu et al., 2024). It should go without saying, but anomaly detection has become absolutely critical for cybersecurity defense. Traditional signature-based detection methods, while still valuable, can only identify known threats. However, with cyberattackers constantly developing new techniques and zero-day exploits, organizations need systems that can detect unusual behavior that might indicate previously unseen attacks. AI-powered anomaly detection fills this crucial gap, providing a proactive approach to identifying potential threats before they can cause significant damage.

The sophistication of modern AI anomaly detection systems lies in their ability to understand context and relationships across multiple dimensions of activity (Levshun & Kotenko, 2023). For instance, these systems don't just flag individual unusual events—they can correlate activities across different systems, time periods, and user behaviors to identify complex attack patterns. A login attempt at an unusual time might not be suspicious on its own, but when combined with unusual file access patterns, abnormal network traffic, and deviations from typical user behavior, it could indicate a compromised account or insider threat.

Moreover, what makes AI especially powerful for anomaly detection is its ability to learn and adapt continuously. As networks and threats evolve, AI systems can update their understanding of "normal" behavior, reducing false positives while maintaining sensitivity to genuine threats. This adaptive capability is crucial in modern enterprise environments where network patterns and user behaviors constantly change due to business needs, remote work, and new technologies. Furthermore, AI-powered anomaly detection can operate at a scale and speed impossible for human analysts. Modern organizations generate massive amounts of security telemetry data—far too much for manual analysis. AI systems can process this data in real time, identifying subtle anomalies across thousands or even millions of events per second (Santos et al., 2024). This capability is very important for detecting sophisticated attacks that might unfold slowly over time or involve multiple subtle changes in behavior. The adoption of AI-powered anomaly detection has become a necessity rather than a luxury for modern cybersecurity teams. Remember, it is a constant cat-and-mouse game with attackers and defenders. If attackers are adopting AI much faster than defenders, we are at a stark disadvantage and a lack of cyber posture has cascading effects on modern society. Therefore, as attacks become more sophisticated and automated, defenders need equally advanced tools to maintain effective security postures. Organizations that fail to implement AI-based detection capabilities risk missing subtle indicators of compromise that could lead to significant breaches (and how many times do we hear "we didn't know!" in the event of a consequential breach?).

Behavioral analysis takes threat detection a step further by examining patterns of activity over time. Rather than just identifying individual anomalies, behavioral analysis systems understand the context and relationships between different actions (Kannan, 2024). This approach enables the detection of sophisticated attacks that might appear innocent when individual actions are examined in isolation. AI systems can analyze user behavior, network traffic patterns, and system interactions to identify potentially malicious activities that deviate from normal behavioral patterns (Bouchama & Kamal, 2021). Behavioral analysis takes threat detection a step further by examining patterns of activity over time. Rather than just identifying individual anomalies, behavioral analysis systems understand the context and relationships between different actions. This approach enables the detection of sophisticated attacks that might appear innocent when individual actions are examined in isolation. AI systems can analyze user behavior, network traffic patterns, and system interactions to identify potentially malicious activities that deviate from normal behavioral patterns (Malik, 2024). Thus, organizations can now implement more proactive security measures by predicting potential threats based on early behavioral indicators. For example, if a user's behavior starts to deviate from their normal pattern, the system might increase monitoring or implement additional authentication requirements before the situation escalates to a security incident.

Generative AI has fundamentally changed behavioral analysis in cybersecurity by enabling more sophisticated pattern recognition and prediction capabilities. These systems can learn complex behavioral models from historical data and generate detailed profiles of normal user and system behavior. For instance, a generative AI system might create synthetic but realistic user behavior patterns to establish more nuanced baselines for different types of users and roles within an organization. The impact of generative AI in behavioral analysis extends to several key areas. First, it enables more accurate user behavior modeling by understanding the subtle variations in legitimate user activities while still detecting genuinely suspicious behavior (Shaik et al., 2023). For example, the system might learn that certain users regularly access sensitive data as part of their job, but only during specific times or following particular processes. Any deviation from these learned patterns could indicate account compromise or insider threats. Another significant advancement is the ability to generate synthetic attack scenarios for testing and training security systems (Guembe et al., 2022). Using generative models like GANs, security teams can create realistic simulations of various attack patterns, helping to train detection systems on a wider range of potential threats. This capability is valuable for identifying sophisticated attack patterns that might unfold over extended periods or involve multiple systems and users.

Behavioral analysis powered by generative AI also excels at detecting complex attack sequences that traditional systems might miss. Let's say an attacker moving laterally through a network might perform actions that individually appear legitimate but form a suspicious pattern when analyzed together. Generative AI systems can learn these complex relationships and identify potential attack chains before they complete (Andreoni et al., 2024). However, it is crucial to take into account considerations about privacy and false positives. The more detailed the behavioral analysis becomes, the more important it is to balance security needs with user privacy. Organizations must carefully consider how much behavioral data to collect and analyze and ensure their AI systems don't become overly restrictive or intrusive. Moreover, as data privacy laws (especially in the United States of America) continue to be adopted and evolve, having increasing implications on data privacy and data minimization principles, this will be an important factor that organizations will have to address. To end on a positive point here, the integration of generative AI in behavioral analysis will likely lead to even more sophisticated threat detection capabilities. As these systems become better at understanding and modeling complex human behaviors, they'll be able to identify increasingly subtle indicators of compromise while reducing false positives. This evolution will be crucial as attackers continue to develop more sophisticated techniques to evade detection.

Automated Incident Response (IR) is the action component of AI-powered security systems (Uzoma et al., 2023). When threats are detected, these systems can automatically initiate appropriate response measures based on the nature and severity of the threat. This automation dramatically reduces response times compared to manual intervention, crucial in scenarios where every second counts. AI-driven IR systems can also learn from past incidents to improve their response strategies over time. Think about how accessible this makes it to smaller organizations that do not have the resources or capability to have an IR team in house or on retainer. The democratization of cybersecurity is happening because AI has made it more implementable and accessible. The current cybersecurity landscape here faces a critical challenge with incident response, due to the increasing sophistication and frequency of attacks combined with a global shortage of skilled security professionals (Hussain et al., 2024). Traditional IR processes often involve manual investigation and decision-making, leading to delayed responses that can allow attacks to cause significant damage before they're contained. This is problematic for smaller organizations that lack dedicated security teams or the resources to maintain 24/7 security operations. AI promises to revolutionize incident response by enabling automated, intelligent response capabilities that can operate at machine speed. These systems can analyze incidents in real time, categorize them based on severity and type, and initiate appropriate response actions without human intervention. For example, when detecting a potential ransomware attack, an AI-powered IR system might automatically isolate affected systems, initiate backup processes, and begin gathering forensic data—all within seconds of initial detection.

The impact of AI on incident response extends beyond just speed. These systems can learn from each incident they handle, continuously improving their response strategies based on outcomes. This learning capability means that AI-powered IR systems become more effective over time, adapting to new types of threats and refining their response tactics based on what works best in different scenarios (Maddireddy & Maddireddy, 2023). They can also identify patterns across multiple incidents that might indicate larger security issues or systematic vulnerabilities. What makes this advancement especially significant is its potential to level the playing field in cybersecurity. Small- and medium-sized businesses (SMBs), which historically have been at a disadvantage due to limited security resources, can now implement sophisticated IR capabilities through AI-powered solutions. This democratization of security capabilities helps address the critical gap in cybersecurity protection that has left many organizations vulnerable to attacks. Moreover, AI-powered IR systems can provide consistency and standardization in incident response that's often lacking in manual processes. They can ensure that every incident is handled according to best practices and compliance requirements, maintaining detailed documentation of all actions taken. This systematic approach not only improves the effectiveness of incident response but also helps organizations meet regulatory requirements and maintain audit trails. Future systems might be able to predict and prevent incidents before they occur, automatically adapt security controls based on emerging threats, and provide more nuanced response strategies tailored to specific types of attacks and organizational contexts. This continuous advancement in automated IR capabilities is absolutely a crucial step forward in addressing the growing cybersecurity challenges faced by organizations of all sizes. Essentially, the integration of these three components—anomaly detection, behavioral analysis, and automated response—creates a comprehensive security system that can adapt to evolving threats while maintaining operational efficiency. These systems can scale to handle massive amounts of data while maintaining accuracy and reducing false positives, allowing security teams to focus on more strategic tasks.

In a typical enterprise environment, an AI-powered system might detect unusual login patterns (anomaly detection) that, when combined with unusual file access behaviors (behavioral analysis), trigger an automated response to isolate the affected systems and alert security personnel (automated IR). In another scenario, the system might identify a subtle pattern of data exfiltration by recognizing that while individual data transfers appear normal, the aggregate behavior suggests a potential threat. The system could then automatically implement network segmentation and enhanced monitoring while notifying relevant security teams. Similarly, when dealing with a potential ransomware attack, the system could detect unusual file system activities, correlate them with network behavior patterns, and automatically initiate backup protection measures and system isolation procedures before significant damage occurs.

Based on the aforementioned, let's go through a hypothetical case study. To set the stage, let's go back to March 2024, Global Financial Corp (GFC), a multinational (and fictional) financial services company with 50,000 employees across 30 countries, faced a sophisticated cyberattack that tested their recently implemented AI-powered security system. The incident demonstrated how the integrated approach of anomaly detection, behavioral analysis, and automated incident response could work together to prevent what could have been a devastating breach. The initial detection occurred at 2:47 AM EST when GFC's AI security system detected unusual login attempts from a senior executive's account. While the login occurred from a recognized IP address, the behavioral analysis component flagged several anomalies, including unusual login timing, different typing patterns from the authenticated session, and system access requests that deviated from the executive's historical behavior. The system's behavioral analysis module identified that while each individual action appeared legitimate in isolation, the pattern of behavior indicated a potential compromise.

What made this attack that much more sophisticated was that the attackers had studied the executive's behavior patterns and attempted to mimic them. However, the AI system's deep learning models detected subtle deviations that would have been invisible to traditional security tools or human analysts. Within seconds of detecting these anomalies, the AI system initiated a graduated response, beginning with enhanced monitoring of all account activities, increased logging, and deeper packet inspection. The system's response escalated rapidly, implementing additional authentication requirements, activating network segmentation, and initiating real-time backups of critical data. Within 60 seconds of initial detection, the system had notified the Security Operations Center with detailed anomaly reports, alerted the executive through out-of-band communications, and initiated incident response team activation protocols.

As the attack progressed, the AI system identified multiple attack vectors. The attackers had initially compromised the executive's credentials through a sophisticated spear-phishing campaign, but the AI system's behavioral analysis detected the compromise before they could establish persistent access. When the attackers attempted to move laterally through the network, the system detected unusual port scanning activities, atypical system queries, and suspicious credential usage patterns. The system also identified an attempted data exfiltration disguised as normal business traffic, spotting unusual data access patterns, suspicious file compression activities, and abnormal outbound connection attempts. The AI system's coordinated response effectively contained and neutralized the attack through automatic isolation of affected systems, implementation of stricter authentication requirements, and generation of detailed forensic data while maintaining business continuity for unaffected systems. The entire attack was fully contained within 15 minutes of initial detection, with no data loss or significant business disruption.

The incident demonstrated several crucial advantages of AI-powered security systems. The integration of anomaly detection, behavioral analysis, and automated response provided comprehensive protection that would have been impossible with isolated security tools. The system's ability to detect and respond to threats in real time proved crucial in preventing data loss and system compromise, while its learning capabilities improved its ability to detect and respond to future similar attacks. Perhaps most importantly, the precise, targeted nature of the automated response maintained business operations while effectively containing the threat. To summarize, this case study illustrates how modern AI-powered security systems can effectively protect against sophisticated attacks through integrated detection and response capabilities. The combination of rapid automated response and intelligent behavioral analysis provides a level of protection that traditional security approaches cannot match, while the system's ability to learn and adapt ensures continuous improvement in security capabilities.

3.2 Automated Vulnerability Discovery and Patching

Automated vulnerability discovery and patching through AI is especially beneficial for organizations with limited security resources (Fu et al., 2024a). This technology democratizes advanced security capabilities by automating complex vulnerability management tasks that traditionally required extensive expertise and manpower. For smaller organizations, this means access to enterprise-grade security capabilities without the need for large security teams. The technical implementation of AI-powered vulnerability management typically involves multiple layers of sophisticated analysis. At its core, these systems use machine learning models trained on vast databases of known vulnerabilities, exploit patterns, and patch information. The systems employ various AI techniques, including natural language processing to analyze security advisories and vulnerability reports, pattern recognition to identify potential security weaknesses in code, and predictive analytics to assess the likelihood and potential impact of vulnerabilities (Wu, 2021). These systems can automatically scan code repositories, applications, and infrastructure components for potential vulnerabilities by analyzing code patterns, dependencies, and configurations. Using deep learning models, they can identify subtle security flaws that might escape traditional scanning tools, such as complex race conditions or logic flaws that could lead to security breaches (Yadav et al., 2024). The AI models can also understand the context of code usage, helping to reduce false positives while identifying legitimate security concerns (Manoharan & Sarker, 2023). What makes this technology especially powerful is its ability to prioritize vulnerabilities based on their actual risk to the organization. Additionally, AI systems can consider multiple factors, including the vulnerability's severity, the affected system's importance to business operations, the presence of mitigating controls, and the likelihood of exploitation based on current threat intelligence. This intelligent prioritization helps organizations focus their limited resources on the most critical security issues.

The patching component of these systems is another significant advancement here (Irei, 2024). Traditional patching processes often require extensive testing to ensure that security updates don't break existing functionality (who anticipates Patch Tuesday with dread?). AI-powered systems can simulate patch deployments and predict their potential impacts across different system configurations. They can automatically generate test cases, analyze potential conflicts, and even suggest optimal timing for patch deployment to minimize business disruption. Furthermore, these systems can learn from each patching operation, building knowledge about which patches tend to cause problems in specific environments and how to mitigate these issues. This learning capability means the system becomes more effective over time, reducing the risk of patch-related incidents while improving the speed and reliability of the patching process. For defenders, this technology provides several crucial advantages. First, it significantly reduces the time between vulnerability discovery and remediation, closing the window of opportunity for attackers. Second, it helps address the chronic shortage of security expertise by automating complex analysis and decision-making processes. Third, it provides more consistent and comprehensive vulnerability management than manual processes, helping organizations maintain a stronger security posture over time. In general, the integration of generative AI promises to make these systems even more powerful. Generative AI could be used to automatically generate temporary patches or security controls while permanent fixes are developed, create detailed remediation plans tailored to specific environments, and even predict new types of vulnerabilities before they're discovered in the wild (TuxCare, 2025).

Automated patch generation leverages AI to create and validate security fixes, significantly reducing the time between vulnerability discovery and remediation. For smaller organizations that may lack dedicated security development teams, this capability is especially important. Theoretically, AI can generate patches that are both effective and minimally disruptive to existing systems, automatically testing them in isolated environments before deployment. All in all, this proactive approach to security represents a significant shift from the traditional reactive model of vulnerability management. However, organizations implementing these systems must still maintain appropriate oversight and validation processes. While AI can dramatically improve the efficiency and effectiveness of vulnerability management, human expertise remains crucial for understanding the broader security implications and making strategic decisions about risk management—remember the term Human-in-the-loop (HITL), which we will discuss in later chapters!

AI-driven code analysis typically serves as the foundation of this approach, continuously scanning both custom and third-party code for potential vulnerabilities (Ozturk et al., 2023). These systems can analyze code at multiple levels, from identifying common security flaws to detecting subtle vulnerabilities that might only manifest under specific conditions. AI's ability to learn from global vulnerability databases and real-world attack patterns enables it to identify potential security issues that might be missed by traditional static analysis tools. In the context of software development and security, AI-driven code analysis is a very important advancement in preventing major security incidents before they occur. The technology can identify potential security flaws during the development process, catching issues like improper input validation, SQL injection vulnerabilities, or authentication bypasses before code reaches production. This proactive approach is useful in preventing incidents like the recent Crowdstrike outage (Kerner, 2024), where a subtle code vulnerability led to significant security implications. The AI systems can analyze code changes in real time, providing immediate feedback to developers about potential security implications of their code modifications. This immediate feedback loop helps developers learn and improve their secure coding practices while reducing the likelihood of introducing vulnerabilities into production systems.

Beyond security vulnerabilities, AI-driven code analysis also helps prevent quality and reliability issues that could lead to system outages or performance problems. The systems can identify potential race conditions, memory leaks, resource management issues, and other subtle bugs that might only manifest under specific conditions or scale (Fu et al., 2024b). This comprehensive analysis helps organizations maintain more reliable and secure systems while reducing the burden on quality assurance teams. For programmers, these tools serve as intelligent coding assistants, providing real-time guidance on best practices, suggesting security improvements, and helping maintain consistent coding standards across large projects (Graff & Van Wyk, 2003). The technology effectively augments human capabilities, allowing developers to focus on creative problem-solving while the AI handles routine security and quality checks. This partnership between AI and human developers represents a significant step forward in creating more secure and reliable software systems, particularly as applications become more complex and interconnected.

Predictive vulnerability assessment takes security a step further by anticipating potential vulnerabilities before they can be exploited (Camacho, 2024). Consequently, analyzing patterns in code changes, system configurations, and emerging threat intelligence, AI systems can predict where vulnerabilities are likely to develop and prioritize areas requiring immediate attention. This proactive approach aligns perfectly with the 2023 National Cybersecurity Strategy's emphasis on shifting security burden away from end users and small businesses to better-positioned entities (National Cybersecurity Strategy, 2023). So, what does this entail? The power of predictive vulnerability assessment lies in its ability to combine multiple data sources and analysis techniques to create a comprehensive view of potential security risks. These systems analyze historical vulnerability data, code repository changes, system configurations, and real-time threat intelligence feeds to identify patterns that might indicate emerging security issues (Vegesna & Adepu, 2024). For example, when analyzing code repositories, AI might notice that certain types of code changes or architectural decisions have historically led to security vulnerabilities in similar systems. Hence, identifying these patterns early allows organizations to take preventative (and proactive) measures before vulnerabilities materialize. The systems also consider broader contextual factors, such as the organization's industry, technology stack, and threat landscape, to provide more accurate and relevant predictions. This contextual awareness helps organizations prioritize their security efforts more effectively, focusing resources on areas where vulnerabilities are most likely to emerge and pose the greatest risk. Again, an example here of how AI can augment human capabilities by taking the aforementioned into account.

The integration of machine learning and advanced analytics in predictive vulnerability assessment has also fundamentally changed how organizations approach security planning. Instead of merely reacting to known vulnerabilities or waiting for security incidents to occur, organizations can now take a more strategic and proactive approach to security. These systems can simulate various attack scenarios, predict the likelihood of different types of vulnerabilities emerging, and estimate the potential impact of security issues based on system dependencies and business context (Kaloudi & Li, 2020). This capability can be utilized by organizations developing complex systems or managing large technology infrastructures, where traditional security assessment methods might miss subtle interactions that could lead to vulnerabilities. The technology also helps organizations better allocate their security resources, providing data-driven insights about where to focus security testing, code review, and remediation efforts (Wickramasinghe, 2023). For instance, if the system predicts a high likelihood of authentication-related vulnerabilities emerging in a particular application component, security teams can prioritize reviewing and hardening that component's security controls. This proactive (we're using that word a lot) approach not only helps prevent security incidents but also reduces the overall cost of security management by addressing potential issues before they require expensive emergency remediation efforts.

The National Cybersecurity Strategy was discussed earlier, and this is an important strategy for the United States of America and other countries are adopting similar approaches to AI. Consequently, let's use this strategy as an example. The integrated approach to vulnerability management with AI supports the National Cybersecurity Strategy's and other cybersecurity strategies in other countries' goal of making software more secure by design. In general, automating the discovery and remediation of vulnerabilities, organizations can maintain robust security postures without requiring extensive security expertise. This is important for SMBs that are often targeted by cyberattacks but lack the resources for comprehensive security programs. For smaller organizations, these capabilities mean they can implement security practices that were previously only available to larger enterprises. For example, a small software development company can use AI-driven code analysis to automatically scan their applications for vulnerabilities during development, while predictive assessment helps them prioritize which issues to address first. The automated patch generation system can then create and test fixes, allowing the organization to maintain strong security practices with their existing staff. This aligns with the national strategy's emphasis on building a more resilient digital ecosystem that protects organizations of all sizes.

3.3 Intelligent SIEMs

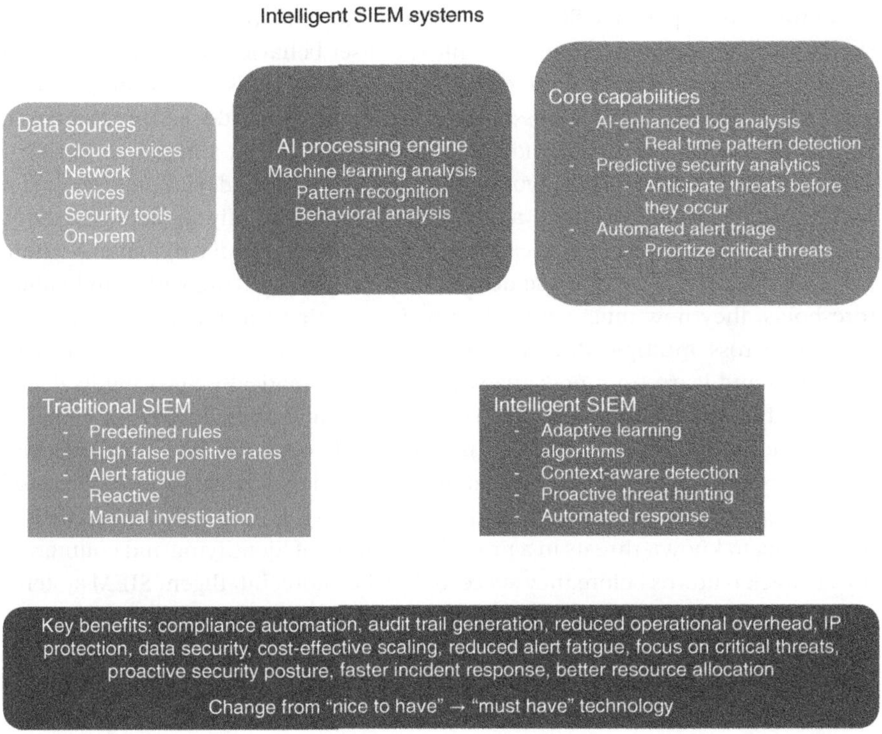

Intelligent Security Information and Event Management (SIEM) systems is a step forward into how organizations monitor, analyze, and respond to security events. With the incorporation of AI, modern SIEM platforms can process massive volumes of security data with unprecedented speed and accuracy, transforming raw log data into actionable security intelligence (Ban et al., 2023). This advancement is particularly crucial as organizations face an ever-increasing volume of security events and sophisticated cyber threats. This is an evolution and a transformative one at that in cybersecurity defense, especially when compared to traditional SIEM approaches (Samonte et al., 2024). Consider how a traditional SIEM might handle a potential data exfiltration attempt: It would collect logs from various sources, apply predefined correlation rules, and potentially generate alerts based on specific thresholds or signatures. This approach often leads to alert fatigue and missed threats, as attackers can deliberately operate just below detection thresholds or use novel techniques that don't match existing signatures. In contrast, an AI-powered SIEM can analyze patterns across multiple dimensions simultaneously, understanding the context of user behavior, network traffic, and system activities to identify subtle indicators of compromise. For example, if an employee's account starts accessing unusual systems at odd hours, traditional SIEM might miss this if each individual action falls within allowed parameters. However, an intelligent SIEM would recognize the pattern deviation, correlate it with other behavioral changes, and identify it as potentially malicious activity. This capability fundamentally changes the attacker-defender dynamic—where previously attackers could evade detection by carefully staying within individual thresholds, they now must contend with systems that can recognize suspicious patterns across multiple dimensions of behavior. The AI-powered SIEM can also adapt and learn from new attack patterns, automatically updating its detection capabilities as threats evolve. This adaptation creates a more challenging environment for attackers, who can no longer rely on static detection rules and must constantly develop new techniques to evade increasingly sophisticated monitoring systems. For defenders, this means moving from a reactive stance of responding to known threats to a proactive position of identifying and countering novel attack patterns before they succeed. Furthermore, intelligent SIEM systems can automate many aspects of incident investigation and response, enabling security teams to focus on strategic decisions rather than getting overwhelmed by the volume of security events. That being said, let's get into the granular of what intelligent SIEMs entail.

AI-enhanced log analysis is a cornerstone of intelligent SIEM systems, employing machine learning algorithms to process and correlate log data from diverse sources across the organization. Unlike traditional SIEM systems that rely on predefined rules, AI-enhanced systems can identify subtle patterns and relationships in log data that might indicate emerging threats or security incidents (Akhtar & Rawol, 2024). This capability becomes increasingly valuable as organizations generate more log data from a growing number of sources and cloud services. In general, this is a fundamental shift in how organizations can and should now approach security monitoring and threat detection. This is especially true in their ability to handle the massive scale and complexity of modern information architectures. To put this into perspective, consider a large enterprise environment generating billions of log entries daily across cloud services, on-premises systems, network devices, and security tools—a scale that would overwhelm traditional analysis methods. In this context, AI-powered systems can process this enormous volume of data in real time, identifying subtle correlations and patterns that would be impossible for human analysts or rule-based systems to detect. For example, the system might notice that a seemingly innocent pattern of DNS queries, when combined with certain application behaviors and user activities across multiple cloud services, indicates a sophisticated data exfiltration attempt using DNS tunneling. Traditional systems might miss this because each individual component appears legitimate, but the AI can recognize the broader pattern through its ability to understand context and relationships across multiple data sources. Furthermore, these systems can adapt their analysis based on new threat intelligence and evolving attack patterns, automatically updating their detection capabilities without requiring manual rule updates. This adaptability is crucial in today's threat landscape, where attackers constantly develop new techniques to evade detection.

The predictive capabilities of these systems add another crucial dimension by enabling organizations to anticipate and prevent potential security incidents before they occur (Ekundayo et al., 2024). Thus, analyzing trends in system behavior, user activities, and external threat intelligence, these systems can then identify conditions that might lead to security incidents, allowing organizations to take preventive measures proactively (Aminu et al., 2024). This could include identifying systems that are likely to become vulnerable due to emerging attack techniques, detecting user behaviors that might indicate impending insider threats, or recognizing patterns of system activity that could lead to security breaches. The combination of AI-enhanced log analysis and predictive analytics transforms security operations from a reactive process of responding to incidents into a proactive approach of preventing them, fundamentally changing how organizations manage their security posture and allocate their security resources (Balantrapu, 2024a).

Predictive security analytics takes SIEM capabilities to the next level by anticipating potential security issues before they manifest as actual threats. It can analyze historical data patterns, current system states, and threat intelligence feeds; these systems can forecast potential security incidents and identify areas of vulnerability (Jangampet, 2021). This predictive capability enables organizations to shift from reactive to proactive security postures, addressing potential issues before they can be exploited by attackers. An interesting question here: What makes this so powerful for cyber-defenders? The power of predictive security analytics lies in its ability to synthesize multiple data streams and intelligence sources to create a comprehensive view of an organization's security posture and potential threats. These systems leverage advanced machine learning algorithms to analyze patterns across various dimensions—from user behavior and network traffic to system configurations and external threat intelligence (Rane et al., 2024). For example, the system might notice that a particular combination of system changes, user activities, and external threats has historically preceded security incidents in similar environments. In other words, it identifies patterns to allow organizations to take preventative measures before an attack occurs. The sophistication of these analytics extends beyond simple pattern matching to include contextual understanding of business operations, user roles, and system dependencies (Familoni, 2024). This means the system can differentiate between legitimate business activities and potential security threats, even when they share similar patterns. For instance, if an employee's access pattern changes due to a new project or role, the system can recognize this as legitimate based on broader contextual factors, while still flagging truly suspicious changes in behavior. The predictive capabilities also extend to infrastructure and application security, where the system can identify potential vulnerabilities based on code changes, system configurations, and emerging threat patterns. Furthermore, these systems continue to learn and improve over time, incorporating new threat intelligence and attack patterns to enhance their predictive capabilities (Shaik & Shaik, 2024). This evolutionary aspect is extremely crucial in today's rapidly changing threat landscape, where new attack techniques and vulnerabilities emerge constantly (especially with the help of AI being used as a weapon). Consequently, it truly is a powerful tool for maintaining secure defenses while optimizing resource allocation.

Automated alert triage is crucial in managing the overwhelming volume of security alerts that modern organizations face. AI-powered systems can automatically categorize and prioritize alerts based on their potential impact and likelihood of being genuine threats (Cadet et al., 2024). This capability dramatically reduces alert fatigue among security teams and ensures that critical security incidents receive immediate attention. Burnout in the cybersecurity field is a significant issue. With teams working in high-stress situations, where every response counts, AI can help humans focus their efforts on the alerts that are consequential. The system learns from past incidents and analyst responses to continuously improve its triage accuracy, in turn, helping teams to be more efficient and reduce burnout. Consider a typical enterprise environment generating thousands of alerts daily (that can paralyze security teams and lead to critical threats being missed): Traditional approaches require security analysts to manually review and prioritize these alerts, often leading to burnout and missed threats due to alert fatigue. AI-powered triage systems fundamentally change this dynamic by automatically analyzing alerts across multiple dimensions—historical patterns, current context, threat intelligence, and system criticality (George, 2025).

For example, when an alert is generated, the AI system can instantly evaluate it against historical incident data, current threat intelligence, the affected system's importance to business operations, and the broader context of related system activities (Balantrapu, 2024b). In general, it is a comprehensive analysis that helps distinguish between genuine threats requiring immediate attention and false positives that can be safely deprioritized. The system might recognize that while a particular alert type historically generates many false positives, when it occurs in combination with certain other activities or on specific critical systems, it often indicates a genuine security incident. This nuanced understanding helps security teams focus their attention on the most critical threats while maintaining awareness of potential emerging issues. Nuanced is a key word here—because AI can aggregate different information and contextual factors that humans may miss. A further example of how AI and intelligent SIEM systems can augment human capabilities and allow them to focus on the most necessary and focused tasks. Moreover, the AI system's learning capability means it becomes more effective over time, adapting its prioritization based on feedback from security analysts and outcomes from past incidents (Chirra, 2022). This continuous improvement helps security teams maintain their effectiveness while reducing the psychological burden of constant alert management, ultimately leading to more sustainable and effective security operations.

For public sector organizations, intelligent SIEMs offer advantages in meeting compliance requirements and protecting sensitive government data. These systems can automatically track and report on security metrics required by various regulations while providing comprehensive audit trails of security events (González-Granadillo et al., 2021). The ability to quickly identify and respond to potential security incidents is crucial for protecting critical infrastructure and maintaining public trust. In the private sector, intelligent SIEMs help organizations balance security requirements with business objectives. The automated nature of these systems reduces operational overhead while improving security coverage. Companies can better protect intellectual property, customer data, and business operations without significantly increasing security staff or budgets. This is valuable for industries handling sensitive data, such as healthcare, finance, and technology.

Overall, the frontier of intelligent SIEM technology continues to advance, with new capabilities emerging regularly. Integration with threat intelligence platforms, automated response capabilities, and advanced visualization tools are making these systems even more powerful. As cyber threats become more sophisticated and automated, the role of AI-powered SIEM systems in maintaining organizational security becomes increasingly critical. Organizations that adopt and effectively leverage these technologies gain a significant advantage in protecting their assets and responding to security incidents. Subsequently, the future of cybersecurity will increasingly depend on the ability to rapidly process and act on security data. Intelligent SIEMs represent a crucial tool in this evolution, enabling organizations to maintain robust security postures in an increasingly complex threat landscape. As these systems continue to evolve, they will play an even more central role in organizational security strategies, helping to protect against both current and emerging threats. It is not really a "nice to have" anymore. Rather, it is now a must to investigate, invest in, and implement.

3.4 AI in Malware Analysis and Classification

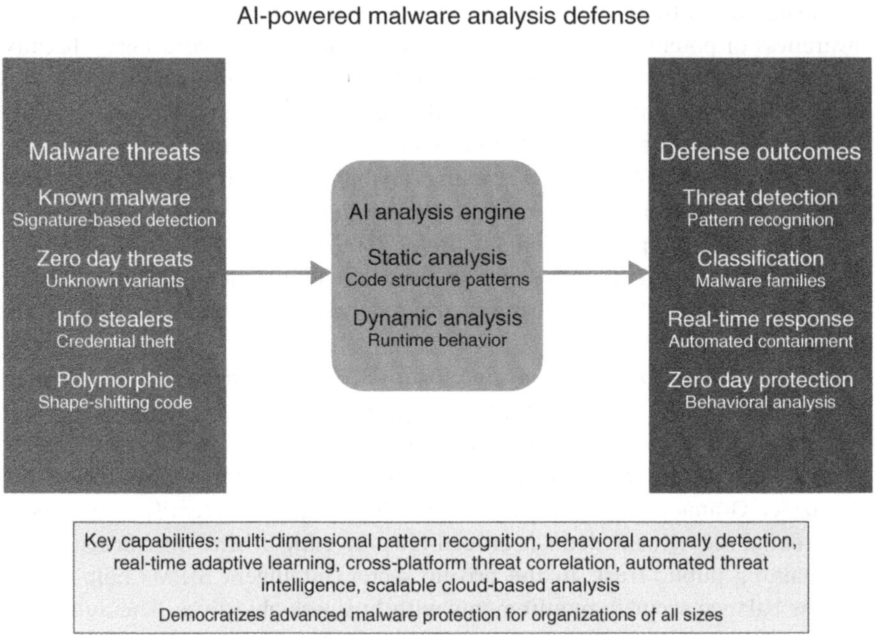

AI-powered malware analysis and classification is crucial to understand to help organizations detect and defend against malicious software. Unlike traditional signature-based detection methods, AI systems can identify and classify malware through sophisticated pattern recognition and behavioral analysis (Samad, 2023). Consequently, enabling more effective protection against both known and emerging threats. This capability is becoming increasingly crucial as malware continues to evolve in complexity and volume. In general, it signifies a fundamental shift in how we approach malware detection and classification. We need to move beyond the limitations of traditional signature-based methods to create more robust and adaptive defense mechanisms.

Modern AI systems can analyze malware at multiple levels—from examining code structure and binary patterns to monitoring runtime behavior and system interactions—creating a comprehensive understanding of malicious software that goes far beyond simple signature matching (Poudyal & Dasgupta, 2021). For example, when encountering a new piece of suspicious software, an AI system can simultaneously analyze its code structure, behavioral patterns, network communications, and system interactions, comparing these characteristics against known malware families while also identifying novel malicious behaviors. This multidimensional analysis enables the system to detect sophisticated malware that might evade traditional detection methods, such as polymorphic malware that constantly changes its code signature or fileless malware that operates solely in memory (Gundoor & Mulímani, 2025). The system's learning capabilities are particularly valuable in addressing the challenge of zero-day malware, as it can identify potentially malicious behavior patterns even in previously unseen code. Furthermore, AI systems can classify malware into families and variants, helping organizations understand the nature of threats they face and implement appropriate defensive measures (Saqib et al., 2024). This classification capability extends to identifying the likely origin and purpose of malware, providing valuable intelligence for threat hunting and incident response. The systems can also adapt to new malware techniques and variants in real time, updating their detection models based on observed behaviors and patterns across global threat landscapes. This adaptive capability is crucial in today's environment, where new malware variants emerge constantly and attackers regularly modify their techniques to evade detection. Additionally, AI-powered malware analysis can provide detailed insights into malware behavior and potential impacts, helping security teams understand not just that a threat exists but also its potential consequences and appropriate response measures (Ansarullah et al., 2024). The aforementioned malware analysis enables organizations to maintain more effective defenses against both current and emerging malware threats, while also providing valuable intelligence for improving overall security posture.

Static analysis in AI-enhanced systems examines malware without executing it, using machine learning algorithms to analyze code structure, file characteristics, and binary patterns (Farooq, 2023). These systems can process massive amounts of code quickly, identifying potential malware based on structural similarities to known threats. AI enhances this process by recognizing subtle patterns that might escape traditional static analysis tools, enabling the detection of sophisticated malware that attempts to evade conventional detection methods (Gavrila & Zacharis, 2024). Thus, this is an important stride forward to address the challenges posed by modern malware complexity and volume. These systems employ sophisticated neural networks and machine learning algorithms to analyze multiple aspects of code simultaneously, from basic file characteristics to complex code structures and relationships between different code components (Makandar & Patrot, 2015). Let's take an example, when examining a suspicious file, the AI system might analyze its assembly code patterns, API calls, string patterns, and file structure all at once, comparing these characteristics against known malware patterns while also identifying novel suspicious features. This multi-dimensional analysis enables the detection of sophisticated malware that uses advanced obfuscation techniques or attempts to mimic legitimate software. The AI systems can recognize subtle indicators of malicious intent, such as unusual code patterns, suspicious API call sequences, or anomalous file structures that might indicate packed or encrypted malware (Gundoor & Mulimani, 2025). Furthermore, these systems can analyze code at a scale and speed impossible for human analysts, processing thousands of files simultaneously while maintaining high detection accuracy. The learning capabilities of AI-enhanced static analysis are especially useful in addressing the challenge of polymorphic malware, as the systems can identify fundamental malicious patterns even when the surface-level code characteristics change. This adaptive capability helps organizations stay ahead of evolving malware techniques, as the systems continuously learn from new samples and update their detection models accordingly. Additionally, AI-enhanced static analysis can provide detailed insights into malware functionality and potential impacts without the risks associated with dynamic analysis, helping security teams understand threats and implement appropriate defenses more quickly and safely (Basu, 2024). The integration of machine learning algorithms also enables these systems to reduce false positives while maintaining high detection rates, a crucial advantage in environments where security teams must process large volumes of potentially malicious files efficiently.

Dynamic analysis takes the investigation further by executing suspicious code in isolated environments and using AI to analyze its behavior. Machine learning models can observe how potential malware interacts with system resources, network connections, and other components, identifying malicious behavior patterns even if the specific malware variant hasn't been seen before (Bose, 2020). This approach is particularly effective against polymorphic malware that changes its code to avoid detection while maintaining the same malicious functionality. Subsequently, as attackers develop increasingly complex evasion techniques, this tool becomes especially critical. Modern AI-powered dynamic analysis systems create detailed behavioral profiles of suspicious code by monitoring hundreds of parameters simultaneously in secure sandbox environments—from system call patterns and memory usage to network communication attempts and file system interactions (Or-Meir et al., 2019). For example, when analyzing a suspicious file, the system might detect that while its individual actions appear legitimate, the sequence and timing of its behaviors match patterns associated with ransomware, such as rapid file access followed by encryption attempts. The AI systems can recognize these behavioral signatures even when the malware uses advanced evasion techniques like delayed execution, environment checking, or complex obfuscation (Gavrila & Zacharis, 2024). This capability can be utilized against fileless malware and other advanced threats that might appear benign in static analysis. The systems also excel at identifying command-and-control communications, even when malware attempts to hide these connections through legitimate-looking traffic patterns or by piggybacking on allowed protocols. Furthermore, AI-enhanced dynamic analysis can adapt to new malware behaviors in real time, learning from each analysis session to improve its detection capabilities (Shaik & Shaik, 2024). This continuous learning helps organizations stay ahead of evolving threats, as the systems can identify novel malicious behaviors based on subtle deviations from normal patterns. The integration of machine learning also enables these systems to provide detailed threat intelligence, helping security teams understand not just what a piece of malware does, but also its likely origins, objectives, and potential impact on different systems. This comprehensive understanding is crucial for implementing effective defensive measures and incident response strategies, especially when dealing with sophisticated targeted attacks or advanced persistent threats (APTs).

Infostealer malware has become increasingly significant in today's cyber landscape, thus making AI-powered detection and analysis capabilities all the more important. Info stealers have evolved from simple credential harvesters to sophisticated malware that can extract a wide range of sensitive information, including cryptocurrency wallets, browser data, system information, and stored credentials (Nurmi et al., 2023). The ability of AI systems to detect and analyze these threats provides organizations with powerful tools for protecting against data theft. AI-powered analysis systems are very effective against info stealers due to their ability to recognize complex behavioral patterns. These systems can identify characteristic information theft behaviors, such as suspicious access to credential stores, unusual data collection patterns, or attempts to exfiltrate sensitive information. Unlike traditional detection methods that might focus on specific signatures or known indicators of compromise, AI systems can recognize the broader patterns of behavior that typically indicate information stealing activities, even when the specific malware variant is previously unknown.

Consider how modern info stealers operate: They often employ sophisticated evasion techniques, might remain dormant until specific conditions are met, and can modify their behavior based on the environment. AI analysis systems can detect these complex patterns through multiple analytical approaches. At the binary level, they can identify code structures commonly associated with information theft capabilities, such as functions for accessing credential stores or cryptocurrency wallets (Almadani, 2024). At the behavioral level, they can monitor for patterns of system access and data collection that might indicate theft attempts. At the network level, they can detect suspicious data exfiltration attempts, even when the malware tries to hide its communications within legitimate traffic.

The effectiveness of AI in detecting info stealers becomes more apparent when dealing with new variants or families. For example, when analyzing a suspicious file, an AI system might notice that while its code structure differs from known info stealers, its behavior patterns—such as how it accesses system resources, collects data, and attempts to communicate with command and control servers—

match typical information theft patterns (Anderson et al., 2024). This ability to identify threats based on behavioral characteristics rather than specific signatures is crucial for protecting against the rapidly evolving landscape of info stealer malware. Modern AI systems employ multiple analytical techniques specifically tailored to detecting information theft activities. They might use deep learning models trained on vast datasets of known info stealer behaviors, allowing them to recognize subtle indicators of malicious intent. The systems can analyze patterns in API calls, memory access, file system interactions, and network communications that might indicate attempts to gather and exfiltrate sensitive information (Triantafyllou, 2024). This comprehensive analysis helps organizations detect and respond to information theft attempts before significant data loss occurs. Moreover, the integration of AI-powered analysis capabilities becomes valuable when considering the speed at which info stealer campaigns can operate. Once information stealing malware gains access to a system, it can quickly gather and exfiltrate sensitive data. AI systems can provide real-time detection and response capabilities, potentially stopping data theft attempts before they succeed. For example, an AI system might detect unusual patterns of credential access or suspicious data collection activities and automatically implement containment measures while alerting security teams.

Zero-day detection is possibly the most significant advancement in AI-powered malware analysis (Ansarullah et al., 2024). This technology does this by understanding the fundamental characteristics and behaviors of malicious software, AI systems can identify previously unknown threats that share similarities with known malware or exhibit suspicious behavior patterns. This capability is crucial for protecting against new and emerging threats that haven't yet been documented or included in traditional signature databases. Moreover, this will grow in prevalence as attackers continually utilize AI to conduct more sophisticated attacks. If the cybersecurity field lulls in integrating these technologies into their infrastructures, it will be at a stark disadvantage. This is true because there is a fundamental shift in how organizations can protect themselves against previously unknown threats, marking a crucial evolution in cybersecurity defense capabilities. Traditional security measures have long struggled with the challenge of detecting novel threats, relying heavily on known signatures and documented attack patterns. However, AI-powered zero-day detection changes this paradigm by enabling systems to identify potential threats based on behavioral patterns, code characteristics, and subtle indicators that might escape traditional detection methods (Toure, 2024). This capability becomes particularly significant when considering the rapid evolution of malware and attack techniques, especially those enhanced by AI. Modern AI systems can analyze multiple aspects of suspicious activity simultaneously—from code structure and behavior patterns to system interactions and network communications—creating a comprehensive view of potential threats that goes beyond simple pattern matching (Sarker et al., 2021). For example, an AI-powered detection system might notice that while a particular piece of software appears legitimate at first glance, its behavior patterns, resource usage, or system interactions exhibit subtle anomalies that suggest malicious intent. This deep analysis capability enables organizations to identify and respond to potential threats before they can cause significant damage, even when dealing with previously unseen attack vectors or techniques (Manoharan & Sarker, 2023).

AI-powered zero-day detection typically employs multiple machine learning models working in concert to analyze different aspects of potential threats (Kavitha & Thejas, 2024). At the core, these systems often use deep neural networks trained on vast datasets of known malware behaviors, legitimate software patterns, and system interactions (Gopinath & Sethuraman, 2023). The analysis typically operates across several layers: at the binary level, examining code structure and characteristics; at the behavioral level, monitoring API calls, memory usage patterns, and system interactions; and at the network level, analyzing communication patterns and data flows. For example, a convolutional neural network (CNN) might analyze the binary structure of files to identify suspicious patterns, while recurrent neural networks (RNNs) process sequences of system calls or network communications to detect anomalous behavior patterns (Şahin et al., 2024). The system might employ autoencoders to learn normal software behavior patterns and identify deviations that could indicate malicious activity. Feature extraction also plays a crucial role, with the system analyzing hundreds of characteristics including entropy measurements, API call frequencies, memory access patterns, and network communication behaviors (Ibrahim, 2022). These features are processed through multiple analysis layers, with each layer looking for specific indicators of malicious behavior. The system typically maintains a dynamic baseline of normal behavior patterns, continuously updated through federated learning approaches that incorporate new data while maintaining privacy and security. When potential threats are detected, the system uses explainable AI (XAI) techniques to provide security analysts with clear reasoning for its decisions, including which specific behaviors or characteristics triggered the alert and their relative importance in the detection process.

The growing sophistication of AI-powered attacks makes this capability increasingly crucial for maintaining effective security postures. As attackers leverage AI to create more advanced and evasive malware, traditional security measures become less effective at identifying and blocking these threats (Mirsky et al., 2023). The ability to detect zero-day threats through AI analysis provides organizations with a crucial advantage in this ongoing security arms race. However, this advantage only exists for organizations that actively implement and maintain these advanced detection capabilities. Those who fail to adopt

AI-powered security measures risk falling behind in their ability to detect and respond to sophisticated attacks. The integration of AI-powered zero-day detection requires significant investment in both technology and expertise, including maintaining up-to-date AI systems, training security teams to effectively use these tools, and establishing procedures for responding to potential threats identified through AI analysis (Tayyab et al., 2025). Organizations must also consider how to integrate these capabilities with their existing security infrastructure, ensuring that AI-powered detection systems can work effectively alongside traditional security measures while maintaining operational efficiency (Adusumilli et al., 2021). Unfortunately, with the amount of technical debt (and the amount of legacy systems) we currently see in the field, this will be a challenge. Subsequently, the challenge becomes particularly acute when considering the pace of AI advancement—both in terms of defensive capabilities and potential threats. Organizations need to maintain continuous improvement in their AI security capabilities to stay ahead of evolving threats, including regular updates to their AI models, ongoing training for security teams, and continuous evaluation of their detection effectiveness. This requires sustained commitment to security investment and improvement, as well as maintaining awareness of advancing AI capabilities and emerging threat patterns. Organizations that fail to maintain this commitment risk creating security gaps that sophisticated attackers can exploit, potentially leading to significant breaches or compromises.

Let's go through an example to put this into perspective. Consider a financial institution's security system that employs AI for zero-day threat detection. The system continuously monitors multiple data streams, including network traffic, system logs, application behavior, and user activities. Unlike traditional signature-based detection, this AI system has been trained on vast datasets of both normal and malicious behavior patterns, enabling it to identify potentially malicious activities even without matching known threat signatures. One morning, the AI system detects an unusual pattern: A newly installed software update, which passed all standard security checks, begins making subtle modifications to database access patterns. While each individual action appears legitimate, the AI system recognizes that the sequence and timing of these actions deviate from normal behavior patterns. The system notices that the software is making encrypted connections to unusual endpoints, using legitimate protocols but in patterns that don't match typical business operations. Based on its training, the AI system recognizes these behavioral patterns as potentially malicious, even though they don't match any known malware signatures. It immediately flags this activity as a high-priority threat, triggers automatic containment measures (such as restricting the suspicious software's network access), and alerts the security team with a detailed analysis of the observed behaviors and why they were flagged as suspicious. Further investigation reveals that this was indeed a zero-day attack—a sophisticated piece of malware embedded in what appeared to be a legitimate software update. The AI system's ability to detect this threat based on behavioral patterns rather than signatures prevented what could have been a significant data breach, demonstrating the value of AI-powered zero-day detection in protecting against previously unknown threats.

For small and medium-sized organizations, these AI-powered capabilities democratize advanced malware protection that was previously only available to large enterprises. Cloud-based AI malware analysis services enable organizations to benefit from sophisticated detection capabilities without maintaining extensive security infrastructure or expertise (Reddy, 2021). This is particularly important as smaller organizations often face the same sophisticated threats as larger ones but with fewer resources to defend against them. Moreover, the implementation of AI-powered malware analysis aligns with modern cybersecurity frameworks and zero trust architectures. It can do this by continuously analyzing and validating code and system behaviors, these systems support the principle of never trust, always verify. Also, having more dynamic and fine-tuned cybersecurity measures can support modern security paradigms and makes implementing a ZTA all the more accessible.

Organizations can maintain stronger security postures by automatically identifying and responding to potential threats before they can cause significant damage. In general, AI in malware analysis will become increasingly essential as threats continue to evolve. The ability to detect and respond to new malware variants quickly will be crucial for maintaining effective cybersecurity defenses. Organizations that implement these capabilities now will be better positioned to protect against future threats, while those that delay may find themselves increasingly vulnerable to sophisticated malware attacks. The integration of AI-powered malware analysis into organizational security strategies represents a significant step forward in cyber defense capabilities. Combining static analysis, dynamic analysis, and zero-day detection, organizations can build more robust and adaptive security postures that can keep pace with evolving threats. As mentioned in Section 3.3, this technology is no longer optional but a necessary component of modern cybersecurity defense, regardless of organization size or industry.

3.5 Generative AI in Red Teaming

Generative AI's integration into red teaming is a crucial step forward for how organizations test and validate their security defenses (Munoz et al., 2024). Through automated penetration testing, AI systems can continuously probe for vulnerabilities across an organization's infrastructure, testing various attack vectors and identifying potential weaknesses that human testers might miss or take longer to discover. This automation enables more frequent and comprehensive security assessments while maintaining consistency in testing methodologies. It is a significant step forward and shift because it allows organizations to take the proactive step in identifying and addressing security vulnerabilities (remember, penetration testing is considered offensive security so it aligns well with a proactive approach!). Modern AI-powered red teaming systems can simulate sophisticated attack scenarios by combining multiple AI capabilities—from generating custom exploit code to crafting targeted social engineering campaigns. These systems can operate continuously, learning from each attempted penetration to refine their approach and identify new potential vulnerabilities (Karagiannis et al., 2024). For instance, an AI red teaming system might begin by analyzing an organization's public-facing infrastructure, identifying potential entry points, and systematically testing various attack vectors while adapting its approach based on the target's responses. The system could simultaneously test multiple attack scenarios, from probing network vulnerabilities to attempting to bypass authentication systems, while maintaining detailed logs of all activities and findings (Farooq, 2023).

What makes AI-powered red teaming useful is its ability to evolve and adapt its testing strategies based on both successful and failed attempts. Unlike traditional automated testing tools that follow predetermined patterns, AI systems can generate novel attack approaches and test unconventional attack vectors that might not be immediately obvious to human testers (Ozkan-Okay et al., 2024). This capability becomes increasingly important as organizations deploy more complex and interconnected systems, creating potential vulnerabilities that might only become apparent through comprehensive, continuous testing. We hear of new vulnerabilities every day, but what about the vulnerabilities we do not hear about or do not even know exist? This is where harnessing the capabilities of AI is crucial. AI can also help prioritize identified vulnerabilities based on their potential impact and exploitability, helping security teams focus their remediation efforts on the most critical issues first (Saadallah et al., 2024). Additionally, these systems can maintain consistent testing pressure across an organization's entire infrastructure, ensuring that security measures remain effective over time and that new vulnerabilities are quickly identified and addressed (Linkov et al., 2022). This continuous testing approach, combined with AI's ability to learn and adapt, creates a more dynamic and effective security testing environment that can better prepare organizations for real-world attacks.

AI-powered social engineering simulations take red teaming to a new level by generating sophisticated, context-aware phishing campaigns, voice impersonation attempts, and other social engineering scenarios (Tayyab et al., 2025). These systems can adapt their approaches based on target responses and organizational context, creating more realistic and challenging tests of human security awareness. The ability to automatically generate and modify attack scenarios helps organizations better prepare for the increasingly sophisticated social engineering threats they face. Subsequently, the sophistication of AI-powered social engineering simulations manifests in their ability to create highly personalized and contextually accurate attack scenarios that test an organization's human defenses in unprecedented ways. These systems can analyze vast amounts of publicly available information about an organization and its employees, including social media posts, professional networks, and public communications, to generate highly targeted simulation scenarios. The AI can then create multiple attack vectors simultaneously—from crafting convincing spear-phishing emails that reference real projects or relationships, to generating voice simulations for vishing attempts that mimic known contacts, to developing complex scenarios that unfold over time through multiple communication channels. What makes these simulations extremely effective is their ability to adapt in real time based on how targets respond to initial approaches, much like how sophisticated attackers might adjust their tactics during actual social engineering attempts (Andriu, 2023). For instance, if an employee shows resistance to one type of social engineering approach, the system might automatically adjust its strategy, trying different psychological triggers or authority figures while maintaining consistency in the overall deception narrative (Ansari et al., 2022).

The implications of these advanced simulation capabilities extend beyond just testing individual employees' security awareness. These systems can help organizations identify systemic vulnerabilities in their human security processes and procedures. In other words, it analyzes patterns in how employees respond to different types of social engineering attempts across various departments and roles, so organizations can identify areas where additional training or process improvements might be needed. The AI systems can also help evaluate the effectiveness of existing security awareness training programs by testing whether employees apply their training in realistic scenarios. Furthermore, these simulations can be customized to reflect emerging threat patterns and attack techniques, helping organizations stay ahead of evolving social engineering threats (Falade, 2023). This becomes highly useful as real-world attackers increasingly leverage AI for their own social engineering campaigns—organizations can use similarly sophisticated AI systems to prepare their employees for these enhanced threats. The continuous nature of these simulations, combined with their ability to generate detailed metrics and analysis of employee responses, provides organizations with ongoing visibility into their social engineering vulnerabilities and the effectiveness of their mitigation strategies.

Continuous security validation through generative AI enables organizations to maintain constant awareness of their security posture. Rather than relying on periodic assessments, AI systems can continuously test defenses, automatically identifying new vulnerabilities as they emerge and validating the effectiveness of security controls in real time. This approach ensures that security weaknesses are identified and addressed promptly, rather than remaining undiscovered between manual testing cycles. Unlike traditional periodic assessments that provide only point-in-time snapshots of security status, AI-powered continuous validation creates an ongoing, dynamic testing environment that evolves alongside an organization's infrastructure and threat landscape (Manoharan & Sarker, 2023). These systems operate by continuously generating and executing sophisticated attack scenarios, probing for vulnerabilities across multiple attack vectors simultaneously. The AI can simulate various types of attacks—from network penetration attempts and application exploitation to social engineering campaigns—while automatically adjusting its approach based on the target's responses and defensive measures (Mirsky et al., 2023). Moreover, the sophistication of these tools continue to increase. What makes this particularly powerful is AI's ability to learn from each attempt, building a comprehensive understanding of the organization's security landscape and identifying patterns that might indicate systemic vulnerabilities (Guembe et al., 2022). For example, if the AI system identifies a successful attack path in one area of the network, it can automatically generate variations of that attack to test similar vulnerabilities elsewhere in the infrastructure, providing a more thorough assessment than traditional periodic testing could achieve.

Essentially, the continuous nature of AI-powered security validation fundamentally changes the dynamics of red teaming operations. Instead of relying on scheduled engagements that might miss emerging vulnerabilities or changes in the security landscape, organizations can maintain constant testing pressure across their entire infrastructure as mentioned earlier. This becomes particularly valuable in modern environments where infrastructure and applications change frequently through continuous deployment practices. The AI system can automatically detect these changes and generate appropriate test scenarios to validate the security of new or modified components. Furthermore, the system's ability to correlate findings across different testing activities helps identify complex vulnerabilities that might only become apparent through sustained testing over time. For instance, the AI might recognize that while individual security controls appear effective when tested in isolation, specific combinations of conditions or attack sequences could still lead to successful compromises. This level of continuous, adaptive testing helps organizations maintain a more accurate and current understanding of their security posture, enabling them to address vulnerabilities more quickly and maintain more effective defenses against evolving threats. The system can also prioritize its testing activities based on factors like the criticality of different systems, recent changes in infrastructure, or emerging threat intelligence, ensuring that security validation efforts remain focused on the most important areas of risk (Balantrapu, 2024a).

AI's role in red teaming extends into advanced threat emulation, where systems can simulate the tactics, techniques, and procedures (TTPs) of specific threat actors or attack groups (McLaughlin, 2023). These AI systems can analyze known attack patterns, malware characteristics, and operational behaviors of different threat actors to create highly realistic attack simulations. For example, if an organization wants to test its defenses against a specific nation-state threat actor, AI can generate attack patterns that mirror that actor's known behaviors—from their preferred initial access methods to their lateral movement techniques and data exfiltration strategies. This capability helps organizations validate their defenses against specific threat actors they're most likely to face, rather than just generic attack scenarios. AI can also adapt these simulations in real time based on the organization's responses, much like how actual threat actors might adjust their tactics during an attack.

Another significant application of AI in red teaming involves infrastructure mapping and vulnerability correlation (Rahman et al., 2025). AI systems can build comprehensive models of an organization's infrastructure, including not just network topology and system configurations, but also business processes, data flows, and interdependencies between different systems (Song et al., 2022). This deep understanding enables more sophisticated attack planning that considers both technical vulnerabilities and operational weaknesses. AI can identify potential attack paths that might not be obvious when looking at individual components in isolation, such as chains of seemingly minor vulnerabilities that could be combined to create significant security breaches. This includes analyzing how different vulnerabilities might be exploited in sequence, identifying trust relationships that could be abused, and understanding how business processes might be manipulated to facilitate attacks.

AI can also enhance red teaming through advanced payload generation and evasion techniques (Rahman et al., 2025). Modern AI systems can automatically generate and modify attack payloads based on the target environment, adapting to evade specific security controls while maintaining effectiveness. This includes creating custom exploit code that bypasses particular security tools, generating polymorphic malware that changes its signature while maintaining functionality, and developing sophisticated command-and-control mechanisms that blend in with normal network traffic (Brezinski & Ferens, 2023). AI can continuously modify these payloads based on their success or failure, learning which approaches are most effective against different security controls and adapting accordingly. This capability is important for testing an organization's ability to detect and respond to sophisticated attacks that use advanced evasion techniques.

Finally, AI brings new capabilities to post-exploitation testing and persistence validation (Heim et al., 2023). Once initial access is achieved in a test scenario, AI systems can automatically explore and map the compromised environment, identifying potential paths for lateral movement, privilege escalation opportunities, and data exfiltration routes (Rahman et al., 2025). AI can maintain multiple persistent access methods simultaneously, testing an organization's ability to detect and respond to sophisticated persistent threats. This includes testing various persistence mechanisms, evaluating the effectiveness of different covert communication channels, and assessing the organization's ability to detect and remove persistent threats. AI can also simulate sophisticated data exfiltration techniques, testing an organization's ability to detect and prevent sensitive data loss through various channels and methods.

For the average penetration tester, this transformation means evolving from a hands-on testing role to a more strategic position. Rather than spending time on repetitive testing tasks, penetration testers will focus on analyzing AI-generated results, designing custom test scenarios, and providing context-aware recommendations. Their expertise will be crucial in configuring AI systems, interpreting results, and identifying subtle security issues that require human insight. While some may worry about AI replacing penetration testers, the reality is that it will enhance their capabilities and allow them to focus on more complex and valuable aspects of security testing. The future penetration tester will need to combine traditional security expertise with an understanding of AI capabilities and limitations, becoming more of a security strategist than just a technical tester. Plus, who wants to spend time doing administrative work that generative AI can do for you, when you can do the fun stuff?

3.6 J-Curve for Productivity in AI-Driven Security

The adoption of AI-driven technologies in cybersecurity, including generative AI, typically follows what is often described as a "J-Curve of Productivity (Brynjolfsson et al., 2021). This concept refers to the phenomenon where an initial dip in productivity occurs due to the challenges of implementation, integration, and adaptation, followed by exponential gains as the technology begins to deliver on its potential (Ji, 2023). For organizations adopting generative AI in their security operations, this curve underscores both the growing pains and eventual transformative impact of AI on productivity and efficiency.

The early stages of adopting generative AI in cybersecurity are marked by significant hurdles. The implementation phase often requires a substantial investment in both time and resources. Organizations must deploy the necessary infrastructure to support AI-powered systems, which may include cloud-based services, high-performance computing, or even dedicated AI accelerators. Beyond the technical requirements, there is also the human factor—staff must be trained to understand, interact with, and trust AI-driven tools. This is no small feat, as cybersecurity teams, often pressed for time and overwhelmed by the sheer volume of threats, may initially view AI as an additional burden rather than a solution. During this period, productivity may decline as organizations grapple with the complexities of integrating AI into existing workflows and the cultural adjustments needed to align human and machine capabilities.

This initial dip in productivity is compounded by the skepticism that often accompanies the adoption of new technologies. Cybersecurity professionals, who have historically relied on rule-based systems and manual processes, may struggle to place their trust in AI-generated insights. For example, when an AI system flags an anomaly or suggests a particular course of action, analysts may feel compelled to double-check the system's findings, thereby adding redundancy to the process. This cautious approach, while understandable, can slow down operations and create friction in workflows, further deepening the "trough" of the J-Curve.

However, this phase is temporary. As organizations become more familiar with the capabilities of generative AI, productivity begins to rise. The turning point in the J-Curve occurs when organizations start to see the tangible benefits of AI integration. AI systems excel at automating routine and time-consuming tasks, such as log analysis, threat detection, and vulnerability scanning. AI takes over these tasks and allows security teams to focus on higher-order functions, such as strategic planning and incident response. The shift from manual, labor-intensive processes to AI-augmented workflows marks the beginning of the upward trajectory of the J-Curve. Generative AI's ability to process vast amounts of data in real time is a game changer for cybersecurity operations. Traditional security measures often falter under the weight of large-scale data analysis, especially as organizations generate ever-increasing volumes of logs, alerts, and telemetry data. AI, on the other hand, thrives in data-rich environments. Utilizing machine learning algorithms, AI systems can quickly identify patterns, detect anomalies, and correlate events across multiple sources. This capability not only enhances the speed and accuracy of threat detection but also reduces the cognitive burden on human analysts. Over time, as the AI system continues to learn and adapt to the organization's unique environment, its outputs become increasingly precise, further boosting productivity.

The upward slope of the J-Curve is also characterized by the scalability that AI brings to cybersecurity. As organizations grow and their digital footprints expand, traditional security operations often struggle to keep pace. Generative AI provides a scalable solution by automating processes that would otherwise require significant human effort. For instance, AI can analyze millions of log entries, detect subtle indicators of compromise, and even simulate attack scenarios to identify vulnerabilities, all in a fraction of the time it would take a human team. This scalability is very beneficial for small and medium-sized enterprises (SMEs), which often lack the resources to maintain large security teams. It democratizes access to advanced security capabilities, thus enabling SMEs to achieve a level of protection that was previously reserved for large enterprises. Another key factor driving productivity gains is the adaptability of generative AI systems. Unlike traditional rule-based systems, which require manual updates to address new threats, AI systems continuously learn and evolve. This adaptability allows them to stay ahead of emerging threats and rapidly respond to changes in the threat landscape. For example, an AI-powered threat detection system can update its understanding of "normal" network behavior as new devices are added, user roles change, or applications are updated. This dynamic learning capability ensures that the system remains effective even as the organization's environment evolves, reducing the need for constant manual intervention.

Collaboration between AI systems and human analysts further accelerates productivity gains. Rather than replacing human expertise, AI serves as a force multiplier, augmenting analysts' capabilities and enabling them to focus on the most critical tasks. For example, while AI handles the initial triage of security alerts, human analysts can concentrate on investigating high-priority incidents and developing strategic responses. This partnership between AI and humans creates a synergistic effect, where the strengths of each complement the other. Over time, as trust in AI systems grows, analysts become more comfortable relying on AI-generated insights, further streamlining workflows and enhancing efficiency.

The J-Curve of Productivity also highlights the importance of leadership and strategic planning in the successful adoption of AI. During the initial dip, it is crucial for organizational leaders to set realistic expectations and communicate the long-term benefits of AI integration. Clear communication about the challenges and opportunities associated with AI can help build trust among staff and foster a culture of collaboration. Additionally, investing in training and education ensures that employees are equipped to work effectively with AI systems, accelerating the transition to the upward phase of the curve. As organizations move further along the J-Curve, the gains in productivity become increasingly apparent. Incident response times are reduced, false positives decrease, and threat detection rates improve. AI-powered systems also enhance compliance efforts by automating the collection and analysis of security metrics required for audits and regulatory reporting. These improvements translate into tangible benefits, such as cost savings, improved risk management, and a stronger overall security posture. For example, consider a hypothetical organization that has fully embraced generative AI in its security operations. In the initial stages, the organization faced challenges in integrating the AI system with its existing security infrastructure and training staff to use the new tools effectively. Productivity temporarily declined as analysts spent time validating AI-generated insights and adapting to new workflows.

However, within a few months, the organization began to see significant improvements. The AI system was able to process millions of log entries daily, identifying subtle patterns that indicated potential threats. Automated incident response capabilities allowed the organization to contain threats within minutes, reducing the potential for damage. Analysts, freed from routine tasks, were able to focus on strategic initiatives, such as improving security policies and conducting proactive threat hunting. As a result, the organization's overall security posture improved dramatically, and the initial investment in AI paid off many times over.

The implications of the J-Curve extend beyond individual organizations to the broader cybersecurity landscape. As more organizations adopt AI-powered security tools, the collective ability to detect and respond to threats improves. This creates a ripple effect, where the increased efficiency of one organization strengthens the security ecosystem as a whole. For example, AI systems that share threat intelligence across organizations can provide early warnings about emerging threats, enabling a more coordinated and effective response. However, it is important to acknowledge that the upward trajectory of the J-Curve is not automatic. Organizations must actively manage the transition from the initial dip to the upward phase by addressing potential barriers to adoption. These include technical challenges, such as ensuring compatibility with existing systems, and cultural challenges, such as overcoming resistance to change. Continuous investment in technology, training, and process improvement is essential to sustain productivity gains and keep pace with the evolving threat landscape.

In conclusion, the J-Curve of Productivity provides a valuable framework for understanding the challenges and opportunities of integrating generative AI into cybersecurity. While the initial implementation phase may be marked by difficulties, the long-term benefits of AI, scalability, adaptability, and enhanced collaboration, far outweigh the temporary decline in productivity. In general, navigating the J-Curve effectively, organizations can unlock the full potential of generative AI, transforming their security operations and achieving a level of efficiency and effectiveness that was previously unattainable. This transformation is not just a competitive advantage; it is rapidly becoming a necessity in an increasingly complex and high-stakes cybersecurity landscape.

3.7 Regulatory Technology (RegTech)

The intersection of generative AI and regulatory technology (RegTech) is another way in which AI can be a security tool. More specifically, it can support how organizations can approach compliance, risk management, and regulatory reporting. This convergence offers new capabilities for automating complex regulatory processes, enhancing compliance monitoring, and improving the accuracy and efficiency of regulatory reporting while reducing the burden on human analysts and compliance officers (Rajenthran, 2024). At its core, the application of GAI to RegTech involves leveraging advanced language models and machine learning capabilities to understand, interpret, and implement regulatory requirements across various business functions (Saxena et al., 2024). This technology can process vast amounts of regulatory texts, policy documents, and compliance guidelines, extracting key requirements and translating them into actionable insights and automated workflows. For instance, GAI systems can continuously monitor regulatory changes across multiple jurisdictions, automatically identify relevant updates, and assess their impact on existing compliance frameworks. This capability is particularly valuable given the ever-increasing complexity and volume of global regulations that organizations must navigate.

One of the most significant advantages of GAI in RegTech is its ability to enhance compliance monitoring and detection of potential violations (Packin, 2024). These systems can analyze patterns in transaction data, communications, and business activities in real time, identifying potential compliance issues before they escalate into serious violations. For example, in anti-money laundering (AML) compliance, GAI can analyze transaction patterns, customer behavior, and external data sources to identify suspicious activities with greater accuracy than traditional rule-based systems (Vučinić & Luburić, 2024). The technology can also adapt to new patterns of financial crime, learning from each investigation to improve its detection capabilities continuously. In the context of regulatory reporting, GAI can dramatically improve both efficiency and accuracy. These systems can automate the generation of regulatory reports by extracting relevant data from various sources, formatting it according to regulatory requirements, and even generating narrative explanations where required. This automation not only reduces the time and resources required for reporting but also minimizes the risk of human error. Furthermore, GAI can assist in validating reports before submission, checking for consistency, completeness, and compliance with regulatory standards.

From a cybersecurity perspective, GAI-powered RegTech solutions offer several advantages. First, they can automatically monitor and analyze security-related compliance requirements, ensuring that organizations maintain appropriate cybersecurity controls and practices. These systems can continuously assess an organization's security posture against regulatory requirements, identifying gaps and recommending remediation measures. Additionally, GAI can assist in incident response and reporting, automatically generating required notifications and documentation when security incidents occur, ensuring compliance with breach notification regulations across different jurisdictions (Pulapaka et al., 2024). The integration of GAI into regulatory change management processes is another advantage (Şahin & Karayel, 2024). These systems can analyze regulatory announcements, guidance documents, and enforcement actions to identify emerging compliance requirements and trends. This predictive capability allows organizations to proactively adapt their compliance programs rather than reacting to regulatory changes after they take effect. For example, GAI can analyze regulatory enforcement actions across different jurisdictions to identify common compliance pitfalls and help organizations avoid similar issues.

Risk assessment and management is another area where GAI can significantly enhance RegTech capabilities (Liu & Wongsosaputro, 2024). These systems can analyze vast amounts of internal and external data to identify potential risks, assess their likelihood and impact, and recommend mitigation strategies. This includes analyzing market trends, economic indicators, and geopolitical events that might affect regulatory compliance risks. The technology can also help organizations conduct more thorough due diligence on third parties, automatically analyzing various data sources to identify potential compliance risks in business relationships. In the realm of policy management and employee training, GAI can help organizations maintain up-to-date policies and procedures that reflect current regulatory requirements. The technology can automatically generate policy updates based on regulatory changes, create customized training materials, and even assess employee understanding of compliance requirements through interactive learning sessions. This helps ensure that compliance knowledge is effectively disseminated throughout the organization and that employees understand their compliance obligations. Documentation and audit trail maintenance is another crucial area where GAI can provide significant value (Laitenberger, 2024). These systems can automatically generate and maintain comprehensive documentation of compliance activities, decisions, and rationale. This includes creating audit trails that demonstrate compliance with regulatory requirements, documenting risk assessments and mitigation measures, and maintaining records of compliance monitoring activities. This comprehensive documentation is invaluable during regulatory examinations and internal audits. The application of GAI to customer due diligence and Know Your Customer (KYC) processes is another important advantage (Dubey et al., 2024). These systems can automate the collection and analysis of customer information, screening against sanctions lists and adverse media, and identifying potential red flags. The technology can also help organizations maintain updated customer risk profiles by continuously monitoring for changes in customer circumstances or behavior that might affect their risk classification.

In terms of regulatory reporting automation, GAI can significantly reduce the burden of preparing and submitting regulatory reports. These systems can automatically gather required data from various sources, perform necessary calculations, validate the information against regulatory requirements, and generate reports in the required format. This automation not only saves time and resources but also helps ensure consistency and accuracy across different reporting periods and jurisdictions. For cybersecurity professionals, the integration of GAI into RegTech provides powerful tools for managing security-related compliance requirements. These systems can help security teams stay current with evolving cybersecurity regulations, automatically assess compliance with security standards, and generate required documentation for security audits. They can also assist in incident response by automatically generating required notifications and reports when security incidents occur, ensuring compliance with various breach notification requirements.

The continued refinement of GAI capabilities suggests even more sophisticated applications in RegTech. This might include more advanced predictive capabilities for identifying emerging compliance risks, better integration with operational systems for real-time compliance monitoring, and more sophisticated analysis of complex regulatory requirements. As regulatory requirements continue to grow in complexity and scope, the role of GAI in RegTech will likely become increasingly important for organizations seeking to maintain effective compliance programs while managing costs and resources efficiently. However, it's important to note that while GAI offers significant advantages for RegTech, it should be viewed as a tool to enhance rather than replace human judgment in compliance matters. Organizations need to maintain appropriate oversight and validation of AI-generated outputs, especially in areas where regulatory requirements demand human review or decision-making. Additionally, organizations must ensure that their use of GAI in RegTech applications complies with relevant regulations and maintains appropriate data privacy and security controls. The potential for GAI to transform RegTech is a significant opportunity for cybersecurity professionals and organizations to enhance their compliance capabilities while reducing costs and improving efficiency. For cybersecurity professionals, this represents both an opportunity and a responsibility to ensure that these systems are implemented securely and effectively while maintaining appropriate controls and oversight.

3.8 AI for Emotional Intelligence (EQ) in Cybersecurity

We've addressed the technical side of how AI and GAI can be used to as a tool to bolster cybersecurity defenses. However, it is important to look at how it can help with soft skills, professional development, and team effectiveness. These technologies can significantly enhance the human elements of cybersecurity, especially in areas requiring emotional intelligence, communication skills, and stakeholder management. AI systems can help cybersecurity professionals develop and apply emotional intelligence in high-pressure situations by analyzing communication patterns, providing real-time feedback on tone and approach, and suggesting more effective ways to interact with stakeholders during security incidents. For example, during a ransomware incident, AI can help security leaders communicate with executives by providing contextual suggestions that balance technical accuracy with emotional awareness, ensuring clear communication while managing stress levels.

One of the most valuable applications of AI in cybersecurity soft skills is its ability to bridge the communication gap between technical and nontechnical stakeholders. Researchers note that cybersecurity professionals can lack soft skills like communication (Olosunde, 2024). AI systems can generate multiple versions of security reports tailored to different audience levels, provide real-time suggestions for explaining complex security concepts in accessible terms, and create visual representations of technical data that nontechnical stakeholders can understand. This capability becomes especially crucial during security incidents when clear communication across different organizational levels is essential for effective response and recovery. Moreover, the enhancement of security awareness training and professional development through AI represents another significant advancement (Rana and Chicone, 2025a). These systems can create personalized learning paths based on individual communication styles and needs, generate realistic scenarios for practicing difficult conversations about security incidents, and provide immediate feedback on communication effectiveness in simulated security situations (Rana and Chicone, 2025b). This personalized approach to training helps security professionals develop the soft skills necessary for effective stakeholder management while maintaining their technical expertise.

In high-pressure situations, AI tools can provide invaluable support by analyzing past successful incident communications to suggest effective approaches, offering real-time guidance on de-escalation techniques, and helping maintain clear, calm communication channels. This capability becomes particularly valuable during security crises when effective communication can significantly impact incident response success. AI can help security professionals manage stakeholder expectations and anxiety during breaches while ensuring that technical response efforts remain focused and effective. Within security teams, AI can enhance collaboration and communication by facilitating better knowledge sharing, helping standardize internal documentation and reporting, and providing templates and suggestions for effective team updates. This internal communication enhancement helps create more cohesive and effective security teams while reducing the potential for miscommunication or misunderstanding. For external stakeholder management, AI tools can help craft appropriate messages for different groups, ensure consistency in security communications across multiple channels, and assist in managing media communications during security incidents.

During security incidents, AI's support for crisis communication can be extremely valuable. These systems can provide templates and frameworks for emergency communications, suggest appropriate tone and content based on incident severity, and help maintain consistent messaging across all communication channels (Miller, 2024). This capability helps organizations maintain effective stakeholder relationships even during challenging security events while ensuring that all communications align with incident response objectives. Ultimately, the impact of AI-supported soft skills development on team effectiveness extends beyond immediate communication benefits. Better team cohesion and collaboration, improved incident response effectiveness, stronger stakeholder relationships, and enhanced professional development opportunities all contribute to more robust security programs. As AI technology continues to evolve, we can expect to see more sophisticated communication analysis and guidance, better integration of emotional intelligence into security tools, and improved real-time communication support during incidents (Gans, 2024).

The Splunk "CISO Report 2025" reveals a significant evolution in the role of Chief Information Security Officers (CISOs) within organizations, highlighting their increased influence in the boardroom. The study, which surveyed 500 CISOs and 100 board members globally, indicates that 82% of CISOs now report directly to the CEO, a notable increase from 47% in 2023. Additionally, 83% of CISOs are participating in board meetings frequently, signifying their growing importance in strategic decision-making (Muncaster, 2025). Despite these advancements, the report underscores a persistent gap in soft skills, with board members emphasizing the need for security leaders to improve business acumen (55% of board members vs. 40% of CISOs), emotional intelligence (45% vs. 35%), and communication skills (52% vs. 47%). This gap hinders alignment, as effective communication and understanding of broader business contexts are crucial for bridging the divide between technical security concerns and strategic business objectives. Budget constraints further exacerbate the challenges faced by CISOs. While 41% of board members believe security functions are adequately funded, only 29% of CISOs agree, leading to strained resources that compromise organizational security. The report highlights that 64% of CISOs attribute cyberattacks to insufficient support and funding. Splunk CISO Michael Fanning emphasizes the need for greater alignment, advocating for boards to adopt a security-first culture while urging CISOs to position cybersecurity as a business enabler. This alignment not only enhances organizational resilience but also bridges the credibility gap many CISOs face, with 79% experiencing pressure to downplay cyber risks and a third having been dismissed outright by their boards. The findings demonstrate that soft skills, stakeholder management, and clear communication are vital for CISOs to maintain influence and drive security initiatives effectively.

Hence, this research reinforces the importance of integrating emotional intelligence and communication development into professional growth strategies for cybersecurity leaders. CISOs must articulate the return on investment (ROI) of security initiatives while navigating organizational dynamics to secure adequate resources and build trust with their boardroom peers. The report underscores that fostering stronger collaboration between CISOs and boards is not just an operational necessity but a strategic imperative to address modern cybersecurity challenges. Subsequently, the insights from Splunk "CISO Report 2025" strongly tie to emotional intelligence (EI) and how generative AI can support its development, especially for cybersecurity leaders navigating complex organizational dynamics. The identified gaps–business acumen, communication, and emotional intelligence—highlight the critical need for CISOs to connect with diverse stakeholders effectively. Emotional intelligence is central to bridging these gaps, as it involves understanding and managing emotions, fostering positive relationships, and effectively navigating challenging conversations, all of which are crucial for aligning security goals with broader organizational strategies.

GAI can significantly enhance the emotional intelligence of cybersecurity professionals by offering tools that analyze and provide real-time feedback on communication patterns, tone, and clarity. For example, during board meetings or stakeholder engagements, GAI systems can provide suggestions for framing technical cybersecurity issues in ways that resonate with business leaders. Analyzing past interactions allows these systems to identify recurring communication challenges, help CISOs refine their messaging, and improve their ability to convey the ROI of security initiatives convincingly. This ensures that conversations are not only technically accurate but also emotionally attuned to the audience, fostering trust and collaboration. Moreover, GAI can aid in the development of soft skills by generating realistic training scenarios where CISOs and their teams can practice high-stakes discussions. These scenarios might simulate boardroom conversations, budget negotiations, or incident response communications, providing immediate feedback on tone, empathy, and effectiveness. This tailored feedback allows security leaders to refine their approaches, enhancing their ability to manage pressure, de-escalate conflicts, and align technical and business priorities.

In high-pressure environments like security incidents, GAI can act as a real-time advisor, offering communication strategies that balance technical rigor with emotional sensitivity. For instance, it can suggest phrasing that reassures stakeholders during a breach while maintaining clarity about the severity of the situation. This support can help CISOs manage stakeholder expectations, reduce anxiety, and ensure that teams remain focused and cohesive under stress. Thus, incorporating generative AI tools into professional development, organizations can close the soft skills gaps highlighted in the report. This integration enables cybersecurity professionals to become not just technical experts but also emotionally intelligent leaders capable of navigating the boardroom with confidence and forging stronger stakeholder relationships. In an era where the ability to communicate and manage emotions is as critical as technical expertise, GAI offers a powerful solution to cultivate these essential skills. Remember, GAI is here to augment our capabilities, not replace them!

Ultimately, the significance of AI in developing cybersecurity soft skills becomes increasingly important as threats become more complex and stakeholder relationships more critical. The ability to communicate effectively and manage relationships has become as important as technical expertise in modern cybersecurity roles. AI tools provide the support and guidance needed to develop these crucial skills while maintaining focus on technical security requirements. Organizations that leverage AI for soft skills development position themselves to better handle security challenges while maintaining strong stakeholder relationships. Therefore, the integration of AI-powered soft skills development into cybersecurity operations will likely become a standard practice for leading organizations. The ability to effectively communicate complex security concepts, manage stakeholder relationships, and maintain team effectiveness during incidents will increasingly differentiate successful security programs from those that struggle to achieve their objectives. Organizations that invest in these capabilities now will be better positioned to handle future security challenges while maintaining the trust and support of their stakeholders.

Now that we have spent a lot of effort delving into what generative AI can do for us (tool) and how it can be harnessed by nefarious actors (weapon), lets address in Chapter 4 how AI can be compromised (target). The advent and increasing adoption of generative AI is not without its risks; hence, it is crucial to understand what the actual risks are posed by generative AI. There are both novel threats and threats that are amplified by this technology. So, stay tuned!

Chapter 3 Summary

This chapter explored how generative AI functioned as a powerful security tool across multiple dimensions of cybersecurity operations. It began with AI-powered threat detection and response systems that leveraged anomaly detection, behavioral analysis, and automated incident response to identify and counter threats with unprecedented speed and accuracy. The chapter detailed how AI enhanced vulnerability management through automated discovery, code analysis, and patch generation, while intelligent SIEM systems transformed security monitoring with enhanced log analysis and alert triage. The discussion included AI's contributions to advanced malware analysis, covering both static and dynamic analysis techniques for detecting known and zero-day threats. The chapter also examined generative AI's revolutionary role in red teaming through automated penetration testing and sophisticated social engineering simulations.

Beyond technical applications, the chapter addressed the J-Curve of Productivity, explaining how organizations experienced initial implementation challenges before realizing exponential gains in security operations. It explored regulatory technology applications where AI automated compliance monitoring and reporting processes. The chapter concluded with AI's role in developing emotional intelligence and soft skills for cybersecurity professionals, highlighting how technology could bridge communication gaps between technical teams and stakeholders. Throughout, it emphasized how these technologies democratized advanced security capabilities, making enterprise-grade protection accessible to organizations of all sizes while acknowledging the productivity challenges during implementation phases.

AI-powered security tools fundamentally transformed how organizations approached cybersecurity defense by enabling proactive rather than reactive security measures. The integration of anomaly detection, behavioral analysis, and automated incident response created comprehensive security systems that operated at machine speed while maintaining accuracy that surpassed traditional rule-based approaches. These systems could process massive volumes of security data in real time, identify subtle patterns across multiple dimensions of activity, and respond to threats before they caused significant damage. The democratization effect was particularly significant, as smaller organizations gained access to enterprise-level security capabilities that were previously available only to large corporations with extensive security budgets and teams.

The chapter demonstrated that successful AI implementation in security required understanding both the technical capabilities and the human factors involved in adoption. The J-Curve of Productivity showed that organizations experienced initial challenges during implementation but achieved exponential gains once systems matured and teams adapted to AI-augmented workflows. This transformation extended beyond pure technical applications to include soft skills development, regulatory compliance automation, and enhanced stakeholder communication. The emphasis on AI augmenting rather than replacing human capabilities proved crucial, as the most effective security operations emerged from partnerships between AI systems and human expertise, where technology handled routine analysis and humans focused on strategic decision-making and complex problem-solving.

Case Study: GAI as a Tool

Let's go through a case study to synthesize the key points in this chapter: How GAI can be used as a tool.

At FinSecure Bank, a mid-sized financial institution with a global customer base, cybersecurity has always been a top priority. Recognizing the growing sophistication of cyber threats, the bank's security team decided to implement generative AI tools to bolster its defensive and monitoring capabilities. The deployment of generative AI marked a transformative shift in their approach to identifying and mitigating cyber threats.

The bank began by leveraging AI models for anomaly detection in real-time transactions. These models, trained on extensive datasets of financial transactions, were capable of flagging unusual patterns indicative of potential fraud or cyberattacks. For instance, the AI flagged a series of microtransactions originating from compromised accounts, which would have otherwise slipped past traditional detection mechanisms. Thus, analyzing these patterns in real time enabled the bank to block fraudulent activities while alerting customers and law enforcement swiftly.

In addition to fraud detection, generative AI proved to be an invaluable tool for penetration testing. The AI was tasked with simulating potential cyberattacks on the bank's infrastructure. Generating attack scenarios based on known vulnerabilities and evolving threat patterns enabled the system to expose critical security gaps. For example, it discovered a misconfigured API endpoint that could have allowed unauthorized access to sensitive customer data. This insight enabled the bank to patch vulnerabilities before they could be exploited.

Generative AI also enhanced threat intelligence by synthesizing large volumes of data from various sources, including internal logs, external threat feeds, and dark web intelligence. The system generated detailed reports on emerging threats, such as a new strain of ransomware targeting financial institutions. Thus, it provides actionable intelligence; thus, GAI allowed the bank to proactively strengthen its defenses against specific threats.

Despite these benefits, the deployment of generative AI was not without challenges. One significant issue arose when the AI flagged a large volume of false positives in its early stages, overwhelming the security team with alerts. This required additional fine-tuning of the models and retraining on more diverse datasets to improve accuracy. Another challenge involved ensuring compliance with regulatory requirements. The bank had to demonstrate that its AI tools adhered to data privacy laws, which necessitated the implementation of robust access controls and data anonymization techniques.

The bank also faced internal resistance from employees concerned about potential job displacement. To address this, the management emphasized that the AI was a tool to augment human expertise rather than replace it. Security analysts were retrained to work alongside AI systems, focusing on high-level decision-making and interpreting AI-generated insights.

Over time, the integration of generative AI at FinSecure Bank significantly improved the institution's ability to prevent, detect, and respond to cyber threats. The bank saw a 40% reduction in financial losses due to fraud and a 30% decrease in response times to security incidents. Additionally, the collaboration between AI and human analysts created a more resilient and adaptive cybersecurity posture.

FinSecure Bank's experience highlights the transformative potential of generative AI in cybersecurity. However, it also underscores the importance of addressing challenges related to accuracy, compliance, and workforce adaptation to fully realize its benefits. The case study serves as an example for organizations considering the implementation of generative AI in their security operations.

References

Adusumilli, S. B. K., Damancharla, H., & Metta, A. R. (2021). AI-powered cybersecurity solutions for threat detection and prevention. *International Journal of Creative Research in Computer Technology and Design, 3*(3).

Akhtar, Z. B., & Rawol, A. T. (2024). Enhancing cybersecurity through AI-powered security mechanisms. *IT Journal Research and Development, 9*(1), 50–67.

Almadani, M. (2024). *An AI-driven, secure, and trustworthy ranking system for blockchain-based wallets* [Doctoral dissertation, University of Technology Sydney [Australia].

Aminu, M., Akinsanya, A., Dako, D. A., & Oyedokun, O. (2024). Enhancing cyber threat detection through real-time threat intelligence and adaptive defense mechanisms. *International Journal of Computer Applications Technology and Research, 13*(8), 11–27.

Anderson, N., Li, M., & Evans, M. (2024, September 10). Mapping the ransomware ecosystem: Tracing network traffic to command & control centers. *TechRxiv*. https://doi.org/10.36227/techrxiv.172599578.85351154/v1.

Andreoni, M., Lunardi, W. T., Lawton, G., & Thakkar, S. (2024). Enhancing autonomous system security and resilience with generative AI: A comprehensive survey. *IEEE Access, 12*, 109470–109493.

Andriu, A. V. (2023). Adaptive phishing detection: Harnessing the power of artificial intelligence for enhanced email security. *Romanian Cyber Security Journal, 5*(1), 3–9.

Ansari, M. F., Sharma, P. K., & Dash, B. (2022). Prevention of phishing attacks using AI-based cybersecurity awareness training. *Prevention, 3*(6), 61–72.

Ansarullah, S. I., Wali, A. W., Rasheed, I., & Rayees, P. Z. (2024). AI-powered strategies for advanced malware detection and prevention. In *The art of cyber defense* (pp. 3–24). Boca Raton: CRC Press.

Balantrapu, S. S. (2024a). A comprehensive review of AI applications in cybersecurity. *International Machine Learning Journal and Computer Engineering, 7*(7), 1–17.

Balantrapu, S. S. (2024b). AI for predictive cyber threat intelligence. *International Journal of Management Education for Sustainable Development, 7*(7), 1–28.

Ban, T., Takahashi, T., Ndichu, S., & Inoue, D. (2023). Breaking alert fatigue: AI-assisted siem framework for effective incident response. *Applied Sciences, 13*(11), 6610.

Basu, A. (2024, November). The impact of artificial intelligence on cybersecurity. *Abu Dhabi international petroleum exhibition and conference* (p. D021S077R001). SPE.

Bose, S. (2020). *Towards explainability in machine learning for Malware detection.* The Florida State University.

Bouchama, F., & Kamal, M. (2021). Enhancing cyber threat detection through machine learning-based behavioral modeling of network traffic patterns. *International Journal of Business Intelligence and Big Data Analytics, 4*(9), 1–9.

Brezinski, K., & Ferens, K. (2023). Metamorphic malware and obfuscation: A survey of techniques, variants, and generation kits. *Security and Communication Networks, 2023*(1), 1–41.

Brynjolfsson, E., Rock, D., & Syverson, C. (2021). The productivity J-curve: How intangibles complement general purpose technologies. *American Economic Journal: Macroeconomics, 13*(1), 333–372.

Cadet, E., Osundare, O. S., Ekpobimi, H. O., Samira, Z., & Wondaferew, Y. (2024). AI-powered threat detection in surveillance systems: A real-time data processing framework. *Open Access Research Journal of Engineering and Technology, 7*(2), 031–045.

Camacho, N. G. (2024). The role of AI in cybersecurity: Addressing threats in the digital age. *Journal of Artificial Intelligence General science (JAIGS) 3*(1), 143–154. 3006-4023.

Chirra, B. R. (2022). AI-driven vulnerability assessment and mitigation strategies for cyberphysical systems. *Revista de Inteligencia Artificial en Medicina, 13*(1), 471–493.

Dubey, S., Astvansh, V., & Kopalle, P. K. (2024). Generative AI solutions to empower financial firms. Available at SSRN.

Ekundayo, F., Atoyebi, I., Soyele, A., & Ogunwobi, E. (2024). Predictive analytics for cyber threat intelligence in fintech using big data and machine learning. *International Journal of Research Publication and Reviews, 5*(11), 5934–5948.

Falade, P. V. (2023). Decoding the threat landscape: Chatgpt, fraudgpt, and wormgpt in social engineering attacks. arXiv preprint arXiv:2310.05595.

Familoni, B. T. (2024). Cybersecurity challenges in the age of AI: Theoretical approaches and practical solutions. *Computer Science & IT Research Journal, 5*(3), 703–724.

Farooq, U. (2023). *Cyber-physical security: AI methods for malware/cyber-attacks detection on embedded/IoT applications* [Doctoral dissertation, Politecnico di Torino].

Fu, M., Nguyen, V., Tantithamthavorn, C., Phung, D., & Le, T. (2024a). Vision transformer inspired automated vulnerability repair. *ACM Transactions on Software Engineering and Methodology, 33*(3), 1–29.

Fu, M., Pasuksmit, J., & Tantithamthavorn, C. (2024b). AI for devsecops: A landscape and future opportunities. *ACM Transactions on Software Engineering and Methodology, 34*(4), 1–61.

Gans, J. S. (2024). How will generative AI impact communication? *Economics Letters, 242*, 111872.

Gavrila, R., & Zacharis, A. (2024). Advancements in malware evasion: Analysis detection and the future role of AI. In D. Gritzalis, K. K. R. Choo, & C. Patsakis (Eds.), *Malware: Handbook of prevention and detection* (pp. 275–297). Cham: Springer Nature Switzerland.

George, S. (2025). Artificial intelligence-powered cybersecurity: The future of how threats are detected and responded. In H. M. Zangana (Ed.), *Leveraging large language models for quantum-aware cybersecurity* (pp. 247–276). IGI Global.

González-Granadillo, G., González-Zarzosa, S., & Diaz, R. (2021). Security information and event management (SIEM): Analysis, trends, and usage in critical infrastructures. *Sensors (Basel), 21*(14), 4759.

Gopinath, M., & Sethuraman, S. C. (2023). A comprehensive survey on deep learning based malware detection techniques. *Computer Science Review, 47*, 100529.

Graff, M., & Van Wyk, K. R. (2003). *Secure coding: Principles and practices.* O'Reilly Media, Inc.

Guembe, B., Azeta, A., Misra, S., Osamor, V. C., Fernandez-Sanz, L., & Pospelova, V. (2022). The emerging threat of AI-driven cyber attacks: A review. *Applied Artificial Intelligence, 36*(1), 2037254.

Gundoor, T. K., & Mulimani, R. (2025). AI-based solutions for malware detection and prevention. In M. A. Almaiah & Y. Maleh (Eds.), *Machine intelligence applications in cyber-risk management* (pp. 107–134). IGI Global Scientific Publishing.

Heim, M. P., Starckjohann, N., & Torgersen, M. (2023). *The convergence of AI and cybersecurity: An examination of ChatGPT's role in penetration testing and its ethical and legal implications* [Bachelor's thesis, NTNU].

Hussain, S. M., Tummalapalli, S. R. K., & Chakravarthy, A. S. N. (2024). Cyber security education: Enhancing cyber security capabilities, navigating trends and challenges in a dynamic landscape. In *Advances in cyber security and digital forensics* (pp. 9–33). Iterative International Publishers, Selfypage Developers Pvt Ltd.

Ibrahim, J. (2022). An architecture for network traffic anomaly detection system based on entropy analysis. [Doctoral Dissertation, University of Belgrade]. Универзитет у Београду.

Irei, A. (2024). How AI-driven patching could transform cybersecurity. *TechTarget*. https://www.techtarget.com/searchsecurity/feature/How-AI-driven-patching-could-transform-cybersecurity.

Jangampet, V. D. (2021). The rise of the machines: AI-driven SIEM user experience for enhanced decision-making. *International Journal of Computer Engineering and Technology*, *12*(3), 74–83.

Ji, Y. (2023). *Artificial intelligence, productivity and performance* [Doctoral dissertation, University of Warwick].

Kaloudi, N., & Li, J. (2020). The AI-based cyber threat landscape: A survey. *ACM Computing Surveys (CSUR)*, *53*(1), 1–34.

Kannan, Y. (2024). AI and machine learning for network security: Applications and case studies. *International Journal of Artificial Intelligence & Machine Learning (IJAIML)*, *3*(02), 1–13.

Karagiannis, S., Fusco, C., Agathos, L., Mallouli, W., Casola, V., Ntantogian, C., & Magkos, E. (2024, July). AI-powered penetration testing using Shennina: From simulation to validation. *Proceedings of the 19th international conference on availability, reliability and security* (pp. 1–7).

Kavitha, D., & Thejas, S. (2024). AI enabled threat detection: Leveraging artificial intelligence for advanced security and cyber threat mitigation. *IEEE Access*, *12*, 173127–173136.

Kerner, S. (2024, October 29). CrowdStrike outage explained: What caused it and what's next. *TechTarget*. https://www.techtarget.com/whatis/feature/Explaining-the-largest-IT-outage-in-history-and-whats-next.

Laitenberger, U. (2024). *Exploring generative AI in business intelligence: A qualitative study* [Master's Thesis. Tilburg University, School of Economics and Management (TiSEM)].

Lakshmanan, R. (2025, March 5). Google rolls out AI scam detection for android to combat conversational fraud. *The Hacker News*.

Levshun, D., & Kotenko, I. (2023). A survey on artificial intelligence techniques for security event correlation: Models, challenges, and opportunities. *Artificial Intelligence Review*, *56*(8), 8547–8590.

Linkov, I., Trump, B. D., Trump, J., Pescaroli, G., Hynes, W., Mavrodieva, A., & Panda, A. (2022). Resilience stress testing for critical infrastructure. *International Journal of Disaster Risk Reduction*, *82*, 103323.

Liu, I., & Wongsosaputro, M. (2024). Compliance redefined: Using GenAI to navigate a complex regulatory landscape with reduced risks and costs. *Journal of Digital Banking*, *8*(4), 313–322.

Maddireddy, B. R., & Maddireddy, B. R. (2023). Enhancing network security through AI-powered automated incident response systems. *International Journal of Advanced Engineering Technologies and Innovations*, *1*(2), 282–304.

Makandar, A., & Patrot, A. (2015, December). Malware analysis and classification using artificial neural network. *2015 International conference on trends in automation, communications and computing technology (I-TACT-15)* (pp. 1–6). IEEE.

Malik, S. (2024). Using AI for behavioral analytics in cybersecurity: Detecting anomalies and insider threats. *ResearchGate*. https://doi.org/10.13140/RG.2.2.17529.38245. Retrieved from. https://www.researchgate.net/publication/388525973_Using_AI_for_Behavioral_Analytics_in_Cybersecurity_Detecting_Anomalies_and_Insider_Threats.

Manda, J. K. (2024). AI-powered threat intelligence platforms in telecom: Leveraging AI for realtime threat detection and intelligence gathering in telecom network security operations. *Educational Research (IJMCER)*, *6*(2), 333–340.

Manoharan, A., & Sarker, M. (2023). Revolutionizing cybersecurity: Unleashing the power of artificial intelligence and machine learning for next-generation threat detection. *International Research Journal of Modernization in Engineering Technology and Science*, *4*(12), 1–14. https://doi.org/10.56726/IRJMETS32644.

McLaughlin, K. L. (2023). Offense for defense: The art and science of cybersecurity red teaming. *EDPACS*, *67*(5), 18–24.

Microsoft (n.d.). Microsoft Security Copilot. Retrieved from. https://www.microsoft.com/en-us/security/business/ai-machine-learning/microsoft-security-copilot.

Miller, S. K. (2024). Emerging technology in emergency management: Using generative artificial intelligence (AI) to improve emergency messaging.

Mirsky, Y., Demontis, A., Kotak, J., Shankar, R., Gelei, D., Yang, L., Zhang, X., Pintor, M., Lee, W., Elovici, Y., & Biggio, B. (2023). The threat of offensive ai to organizations. *Computers & Security*, *124*, 103006.

Muncaster, P. (2025, January 23). CISOs dramatically increase boardroom influence but still lack soft skills. *Infosecurity Magazine*.

Munoz, G. D. L., Minnich, A. J., Lutz, R., Lundeen, R., Dheekonda, R. S. R., Chikanov, N., Jagdagdorj, B. E., Pouliot, M., Chawla, S., Maxwell, W., & Bullwinkel, B. (2024). PyRIT: A framework for security risk identification and red teaming in generative AI system. arXiv preprint arXiv:2410.02828.

Naraine, R. (2025, April 1). Microsoft using AI to uncover critical bootloader vulnerabilities. *Security Week*. https://www.securityweek.com/microsoft-using-ai-to-uncover-critical-bootloader-vulnerabilities/.

Naseer, I. (2021). The efficacy of deep learning and artificial intelligence framework in enhancing cybersecurity, challenges and future prospects. *Innovative Computer Sciences Journal*, *7*(1), 1–7.

National Cybersecurity Strategy. (2023, March). *White House*. https://www.whitehouse.gov/wp-content/uploads/2023/03/National-Cybersecurity-Strategy-2023.pdf.

Nurmi, J., Niemelä, M., & Brumley, B. B. (2023, August). Malware finances and operations: A data-driven study of the value chain for infections and compromised access. *Proceedings of the 18th international conference on availability, reliability and security* (pp. 1–12).

Nwachukwu, C., Durodola-Tunde, K., & Akwiwu-Uzoma, C. (2024). AI-driven anomaly detection in cloud computing environments.

Olosunde, B. (2024). Impact of cybersecurity skills gap on the US economy and national security. *IJISET-International Journal of Innovative Science, Engineering & Technology*, *11*(12), 61–76.

Or-Meir, O., Nissim, N., Elovici, Y., & Rokach, L. (2019). Dynamic malware analysis in the modern era—A state of the art survey. *ACM Computing Surveys (CSUR)*, *52*(5), 1–48.

Ozkan-Okay, M., Akin, E., Aslan, Ö., Kosunalp, S., Iliev, T., Stoyanov, I., & Beloev, I. (2024). A comprehensive survey: Evaluating the efficiency of artificial intelligence and machine learning techniques on cyber security solutions. *IEEE Access*, *12*, 12229–12256.

Ozturk, O. S., Ekmekcioglu, E., Cetin, O., Arief, B., & Hernandez-Castro, J. (2023, June). New tricks to old codes: Can AI chatbots replace static code analysis tools?*Proceedings of the 2023 European interdisciplinary cybersecurity conference* (pp. 13–18).

Packin, N. G. (2024). Emerging compliance in the generative decentralized era. Available at SSRN.

Poudyal, S., & Dasgupta, D. (2021). Analysis of crypto-ransomware using ML-based multi-level profiling. *IEEE Access*, *9*, 122532–122547.

Pulapaka, S., Godavarthi, S., & Ding, S. (2024). *Empowering the public sector with generative AI*. Springer Nature.

Rahman, A., Redino, C., Shetty, S., Nandakumar, D., Cody, T., & Radke, D. (2025). *Reinforcement learning for cyber operations: Applications of artificial intelligence for penetration testing*. Wiley.

Rajenthran, G. (2024). Financial frontiers: How generative AI is shaping the Fintech industry. In J. G. Sankar & A. David (Eds.), *Generative AI for transformational management* (pp. 161–192). IGI Global.

Rana, S., & Chicone, R. (2025b). Introduction to AI in cybersecurity training. In S. Grove (Ed.), *Fortifying the future: Harnessing AI for transformative cybersecurity training* (pp. 1–24). Cham: Springer Nature Switzerland.

Rana, S., & Chicone, R. (2025a). AI-driven personalized learning in cybersecurity training. In S. Grove (Ed.), *Fortifying the future: Harnessing AI for transformative cybersecurity training* (pp. 25–50). Cham: Springer Nature Switzerland.

Rane, N. L., Paramesha, M., Choudhary, S. P., & Rane, J. (2024). Artificial intelligence, machine learning, and deep learning for advanced business strategies: A review. *Partners Universal International Innovation Journal*, *2*(3), 147–171.

Reddy, A. R. P. (2021). The role of artificial intelligence in proactive cyber threat detection in cloud environments. *NeuroQuantology, 19*(12), 764–773.

Saadallah, M., Shahim, A., & Khapova, S. (2024). Synergizing human expertise, automation, and artificial intelligence for vulnerability management. *PriMera Scientific Engineering, 5*, 2–13.

Şahin, O., & Karayel, D. (2024). Generative artificial intelligence (GenAI) in business: A systematic review on the threshold of transformation. *Journal of Smart Systems Research, 5*(2), 156–175.

Şahin, V., Arat, F., & Akleylek, S. (2024). Anomaly detection with API calls by using machine learning: Systematic literature review. *Current Trends in Computing, 2*(1), 60–85.

Samad, A. (2023). Hybrid approaches in threat detection: Integrating traditional signature-based methods with AI and ML techniques for enhanced accuracy.

Samonte, M. J. C., Dorado, P. L. F., Dulay, J. B. M., & Leyva, A. M. M. (2024, September). Enhancing threat detection in financial institutions with AI-driven security information and event management integration. *2024 4th international conference on computer systems (ICCS)* (pp. 85–92). IEEE.

Santos, O., Salam, S., & Dahir, H. (2024). *The AI revolution in networking, cybersecurity, and emerging technologies*. Addison-Wesley Professional.

Saqib, M., Mahdavifar, S., Fung, B. C., & Charland, P. (2024). A comprehensive analysis of explainable AI for malware hunting. *ACM Computing Surveys, 56*(12), 1–40.

Sarker, I. H., Furhad, M. H., & Nowrozy, R. (2021). Ai-driven cybersecurity: An overview, security intelligence modeling and research directions. *SN Computer Science, 2*(3), 173.

Saxena, A., Verma, S., & Mahajan, J. (2024). *Generative AI in banking financial services and insurance*. Springer.

Shaik, A. S., & Shaik, A. (2024, April). AI Enhanced Cyber Security Methods for Anomaly Detection. In *International Conference on Machine Intelligence, Tools, and Applications* (pp. 348–359). Cham: Springer Nature Switzerland.

Shaik, M., Gudala, L., & Sadhu, A. K. R. (2023). Leveraging artificial intelligence for enhanced identity and access management within zero trust security architectures: A focus on user behavior analytics and adaptive authentication. *Australian Journal of Machine Learning Research & Applications, 3*(2), 1–31.

Song, L., Hu, X., Zhang, G., Spachos, P., Plataniotis, K. N., & Wu, H. (2022). Networking systems of AI: On the convergence of computing and communications. *IEEE Internet of Things Journal, 9*(20), 20352–20381.

Sundaramurthy, S. K., Ravichandran, N., Inaganti, A. C., & Muppalaneni, R. (2025). AI-driven threat detection: Leveraging machine learning for real-time cybersecurity in cloud environments. *Artificial Intelligence and Machine Learning Review, 6*(1), 23–43.

Tayyab, M., Hameed, K., Mumtaz, M., Muzammal, S. M. M., Mahadevappa, P., & Sunbalin, A. (2025). AI-powered threat detection in business environments: Strategies and best practices. In I. A. Shah & N. Z. Jhanjhi (Eds.), *Generative AI for web engineering models* (pp. 379–436). IGI Global.

Toure, A. (2024). *Collection, analysis and harnessing of communication flows for cyber-attack detection* [Doctoral dissertation, Université Polytechnique Hauts-de-France].

Triantafyllou, G.P. (2024). Malware analysis [Master's thesis, Πανεπιστήμιο Πειραιώς].

TuxCare. (2025). How AI can help identify and mitigate patch management risks. TuxCare.

Uzoma, J., Falana, O., Obunadike, C., Oloyede, K., & Obunadike, E. (2023). Using artificial intelligence for automated incidence response in cybersecurity. *International Journal of Information Technology (IJIT)*, *1*(4), 1–32.

Vegesna, V. V., & Adepu, A. (2024). Leveraging artificial intelligence for predictive cyber threat intelligence. *International Journal of Creative Research in Computer Technology and Design*, *6*(6), 1–19.

Vučinić, M., & Luburić, R. (2024). Artificial intelligence, fintech and challenges to central banks. *Journal of Central Banking Theory and Practice*, *13*(3), 5–42.

Wickramasinghe, A. (2023). An evaluation of big data-driven artificial intelligence algorithms for automated cybersecurity risk assessment and mitigation. *International Journal of Cybersecurity Risk Management, Forensics and Compliance*, *7*(12), 1–15.

Wu, J. (2021). Literature review on vulnerability detection using NLP technology. arXiv preprint arXiv:2104.11230.

Yadav, N. S., Rounak, R., & Sharma, P. C. (2024). Web-based vulnerability analysis and detection. *International Journal of Sensors, Wireless Communications and Control*, *15* Early view (online 26 December 2024). 10.2174/0122103279319619241008221647.

4

Weaponized Generative AI

This chapter delves into the dark side of generative AI, examining how these powerful technologies can be weaponized for malicious purposes in cybersecurity attacks. The chapter provides a comprehensive analysis of four major threat categories: the creation and deployment of deepfakes and synthetic media for deception, the enhancement of social engineering attacks through AI-powered automation and personalization, the emergence of automated hacking capabilities that can discover and exploit vulnerabilities at scale, and the inherent privacy risks associated with generative AI systems themselves. Each section explores how these technologies are being used by threat actors to create more sophisticated, scalable, and effective cyberattacks, while also addressing the broader implications for information integrity and personal privacy in an era where AI can generate increasingly convincing fake content and automate complex attack processes.

4.1 Deepfakes and Synthetic Media

The emergence of deepfakes and synthetic media powered by generative AI is one of the most significant challenges to information security and digital trust. These technologies can create highly convincing fake images, videos, and audio content that are increasingly difficult to distinguish from authentic media. Scary, right? The sophistication of these synthetic creations has evolved rapidly, with AI systems now capable of generating or manipulating media that can fool both human observers and traditional detection systems.

Image and video manipulation capabilities have advanced to the point where AI can generate photorealistic images and videos from scratch or modify existing content while maintaining visual coherence. These systems can alter facial expressions, change body movements, modify backgrounds, and even create entirely fictional scenarios that appear completely authentic. It is extremely convincing

Generative AI Security: Defense, Threats, and Vulnerabilities, First Edition. Shaila Rana and Rhonda Chicone.

and much more accessible for cyberattackers to take advantage of. The technology has become so sophisticated that it can account for lighting, shadows, and physical interactions in ways that make detection extremely challenging. In general, this has a lot of implications that underscore how AI is a tool, weapon, and target. As a tool, AI enables defenders and investigators to develop advanced systems capable of detecting and analyzing deepfake content. However, the very same capabilities make AI a weapon in the hands of malicious actors. Attackers can deploy generative AI systems to craft high-quality phishing attempts, fake identities, or disinformation campaigns. Simultaneously, AI systems themselves become a target for attackers. Generative AI models can be exploited through adversarial attacks, such as feeding them malicious input data designed to confuse or manipulate their outputs.

The sophistication of modern image and video manipulation through AI extends far beyond simple modifications, leveraging advanced neural network architectures like Generative Adversarial Networks (GANs) and diffusion models to create or alter content with unprecedented realism (Bansal et al., 2024). These systems employ complex algorithms that understand not just visual elements but also the underlying physics of light, motion, and material properties. For instance, when generating or modifying video content, the AI considers temporal consistency across frames, ensuring that elements like shadows, reflections, and object movements maintain physical accuracy throughout the sequence (Azzarelli et al., 2024). The systems can analyze and replicate subtle details like skin texture, fabric movement, and environmental interactions that historically were telltale signs of manipulated content. This level of sophistication is achieved through training on massive datasets of images and videos, allowing the AI to learn intricate patterns in how light interacts with different materials, how objects move through space, and how various elements in a scene influence each other.

The technical capabilities have advanced to include features like neural rendering, which allows for precise control over individual elements within generated or modified content while maintaining overall scene coherence (Tewari et al., 2022). These systems can now handle complex scenarios like changing weather conditions in videos, altering lighting conditions while maintaining realistic shadows and reflections, or modifying human movements while preserving natural physics and biomechanics. The AI can also generate or modify content in real time, adapting to changing conditions or requirements while maintaining high levels of realism. This includes capabilities like style transfer between different scenes, seamless object insertion or removal, and the ability to generate consistent content across multiple viewpoints or camera angles. The advancement in these technologies has been particularly rapid in areas like face synthesis and manipulation, where AI systems can now generate or modify facial expressions with microscopic detail, including subtle elements like skin subsurface scattering, microexpressions, and natural aging patterns that make the results virtually indistinguishable from authentic content (Lee & Qiufan, 2021).

Voice cloning technology has reached a level where AI can replicate a person's voice with just a few minutes of sample audio. These systems can capture not only the basic sound of a voice but also nuances like accent, rhythm, and emotional inflection (Genelza, 2024). This capability enables the creation of synthetic speech that can convincingly imitate specific individuals, opening new avenues for sophisticated social engineering attacks and fraud. Voice cloning technology leverages sophisticated deep learning architectures, particularly transformer-based models and specialized neural networks designed for audio processing, to analyze and replicate human speech patterns at multiple levels of complexity (Pecora, 2023). The process typically begins with spectral analysis of the source audio, breaking down the voice into its fundamental components, including frequency patterns, timbral characteristics, and temporal features (Chaki, 2021). Advanced neural networks then create detailed models of these components, learning how they interact to produce the unique characteristics of an individual's voice (Yadav et al., 2022). The systems analyze micropatterns in speech, including subtle variations in pitch, changes in speaking rate, breath patterns, and the unique ways different phonemes are articulated. This detailed analysis allows the AI to create a comprehensive model of how an individual's vocal apparatus functions, enabling it to generate new speech that maintains these distinctive characteristics even when producing entirely new content.

The weaponization potential of this technology becomes concerning when considering its accessibility and sophistication. Attackers can use these systems to create highly convincing voice impersonations for various malicious purposes, from fraudulent financial transactions to sophisticated social engineering attacks. The technology's ability to capture emotional nuances and speech patterns makes it especially dangerous for targeted attacks. For instance, an attacker might use a cloned voice to create urgent messages that appear to come from executives or authority figures, exploiting both the familiarity of the voice and its emotional content to manipulate targets. The systems can even adapt the synthesized voice in real time, adjusting emotional tone and speaking patterns based on the context or target responses. More sophisticated attacks might combine voice cloning with other AI technologies, such as natural language processing (NLP) and conversational AI, to create interactive voice bots that can engage in real-time conversations while maintaining the impersonated voice's characteristics. This level of sophistication makes it increasingly difficult for targets to distinguish between authentic and synthetic voice communications, and this is especially true in high-pressure situations where quick decisions are required.

Audio deepfakes extend beyond simple voice cloning to include the creation of complete synthetic audio environments. AI systems can generate background noises, ambient sounds, and multiple voice interactions that create convincing audio scenarios (Latif et al., 2023). This technology can be used to fabricate recordings of conversations or events that never occurred, presenting significant challenges for audio authentication and evidence verification. The technical sophistication of audio deepfake creation involves complex neural architectures that simultaneously process multiple audio layers and environmental characteristics (Mubarak et al., 2023). These systems employ specialized convolutional neural networks and attention mechanisms to analyze and synthesize various audio components, including room acoustics, sound propagation patterns, and the interaction between different sound sources (Zaheer et al., 2023). The AI models understand how sound waves interact with different environments, accounting for factors like reverberation, echo, sound absorption, and the Doppler effect (Liu & Manocha, 2022). This allows them to create highly realistic audio environments where multiple synthetic elements—from human voices to ambient sounds—interact naturally and consistently. For instance, when generating a synthetic recording of a business meeting, the system can accurately model how voices would reflect off surfaces, how background noise from air conditioning or office equipment would blend with conversations, and how sound characteristics would change as speakers move within the space.

The weaponization of this technology becomes very dangerous when combined with other AI capabilities for creating comprehensive deceptive scenarios. Attackers can generate complex audio environments that provide convincing context for social engineering attacks or fraudulent activities. For example, an attacker might create a synthetic audio scenario that appears to be from a crowded airport terminal, complete with flight announcements, crowd noise, and multiple background conversations, to add credibility to a fraudulent urgent request. The technology can be used to fabricate evidence of conversations or events, creating false records that are increasingly difficult to distinguish from authentic recordings. More sophisticated attacks might involve real-time audio environment generation, where the synthetic background adapts dynamically to maintain consistency with the deceptive scenario being presented. The AI systems can also be trained to recognize and replicate specific audio environments, allowing attackers to create convincing recreations of known locations or situations. This level of sophistication in audio deepfake creation is a significant challenge for security professionals, as traditional methods of audio authentication become less reliable against these AI-generated synthetic environments. Organizations must now consider how to validate the authenticity of audio evidence and develop new approaches to detecting synthetic audio content, particularly in situations where audio recordings might be used for verification or documentation purposes.

Furthermore, the impact on information integrity is consequential. These technologies undermine the traditional notion that "seeing is believing" and create an environment where the authenticity of any digital media can be questioned. It seems like we have to and will have to continue to question everything we see and hear. This typically goes against human nature; thus, we will really have to have a paradigm shift when it comes to everything we see and hear online, on the phone, etc. This erosion of trust affects everything from personal communications to news reporting and legal evidence, requiring new approaches to digital content verification and authentication.

In general, as implied above, the security implications of these technologies are significant and multifaceted as well. While they provide powerful tools for legitimate purposes like product visualization, architectural design, and entertainment, they also enable the creation of increasingly sophisticated deepfakes and synthetic media that could be used for deception or social engineering. A recent case involving a finance worker at a multinational firm in Hong Kong was deceived into transferring $25 million to fraudsters who used deepfake technology to impersonate the company's chief financial officer during a video call (Chen & Magramo, 2024). The scammers convincingly recreated the appearances and voices of colleagues using AI, tricking the worker into believing the legitimacy of the call. The fraud was only uncovered after the worker later verified with the head office. This incident highlights the growing sophistication and risks of deepfake technology, which has also been used to bypass facial recognition systems and commit other fraudulent activities. Authorities worldwide are increasingly alarmed by the potential misuse of AI for such crimes. This is just one example, and we will continue to see these increase in both ubiquity and sophistication. Additionally, these technologies raise important questions about digital authenticity and the need for robust verification systems in an era where visual content can be synthetically generated with increasing realism. It seems like everything comes with its risks, doesn't it?

From a security perspective, defending against synthetic media attacks requires a multilayered approach. This includes technical solutions like digital watermarking and AI-powered detection systems, as well as organizational policies and training to help people identify potential synthetic media (Raj & Sharma, 2024). However, the rapid advancement of generative AI means that detection methods must continuously evolve to keep pace with new generation techniques. There are many legislative initiatives that are focused on the aforementioned. The business implications are equally significant. Organizations must now contend with the possibility of synthetic media being used in corporate espionage, market manipulation, or reputation damage. The ability to create convincing fake videos of executives making false statements or manipulated audio of confidential conversations presents new risks that organizations must address in their security planning.

Rather than representing a completely novel threat, deepfakes and synthetic media are a significant amplification of existing challenges to information integrity. Digital manipulation has existed since the early days of photography and video editing, but generative AI has transformed these capabilities in three crucial ways: scale (the ability to create large amounts of synthetic content quickly), accessibility (making sophisticated manipulation tools available to nonexperts), and quality (producing increasingly convincing fakes). This amplification effect means that organizations must treat synthetic media as a core security concern rather than just an emerging threat, implementing comprehensive strategies to detect and mitigate these risks while maintaining operational resilience.

Our cybersecurity and threat landscape is continually evolving. Generative AI has lowered the barrier of entry for attackers; they need less skills to consequentially harm individuals and organizations alike. A question you may be asking yourselves—how might the aforementioned affect me? What does this look like in the real world? A sophisticated scammer might orchestrate a multilayered attack targeting a company's financial systems by combining several generative AI techniques. For instance, they could begin by using AI to generate a deepfake video of the company's CEO, appearing to be in their office during a "business trip." The scammer would then combine this with a cloned version of the CEO's voice, creating a convincing video call to the finance department. During this call, the fake CEO would request an urgent wire transfer for a confidential acquisition, providing seemingly legitimate reasons for bypassing standard procedures. The scammer could further enhance the deception by generating background noise that matches the CEO's supposed location and creating fake email threads with doctored timestamps to support the urgent request. Furthermore, to make the scam even more convincing, they might use AI-generated images of fabricated legal documents or contracts, complete with appropriate letterheads and signatures. The attack could be timed during a real business event or conference where the CEO is known to be participating, making the urgent request seem more plausible. The coordinated use of multiple synthetic media elements—the video, voice, supporting documents, and contextual background—creates a comprehensive deception that can be challenging to detect in real time, especially when employees are under pressure to respond quickly to senior management requests. The impact of such an attack goes beyond immediate financial loss, potentially eroding trust in legitimate digital communications and forcing organizations to implement more complex verification procedures for routine operations. While this does seem like a theoretical example, it is happening, and there are many instances of this occurring. By the time you are reading this, there will probably be an exponential growth in these types of schemes.

4.2 AI-Powered Social Engineering

Who is sick of the fraudulent emails, texts, calls, social media messages, you name it, where scammers are trying to trick you into doing something that harms you and benefits them? Probably all of us. Well, with Generative AI, this is not going away anytime soon. In fact, it poses a significant evolution in cyberattacks where it enhances attackers' ability to create convincing and personalized deceptive content. Unlike traditional social engineering attacks, AI-enabled campaigns can analyze vast amounts of publicly available information to create highly targeted and contextually relevant approaches that are much harder to detect.

Unfortunately, phishing campaigns have been revolutionized by generative AI's ability to create sophisticated, personalized emails that can adapt to different contexts and target profiles (Schmitt & Flechais, 2024). These systems can analyze a potential victim's writing style, professional relationships, and organizational context to craft messages that closely mimic legitimate communications. The AI can generate variations of these messages at scale, each tailored to specific recipients while maintaining consistency in narrative and purpose. Behind it, there is a layer of sophistication that AI adds to these attacks. It leverages multiple AI capabilities to create highly convincing deceptive communications. These systems typically employ advanced NLP models, including transformer-based architectures and specialized neural networks trained on vast datasets of business communications (Alshomrani et al., 2024). The AI analyzes multiple aspects of communication simultaneously—from writing style and vocabulary choice to organizational hierarchies and professional relationships—creating detailed models of how legitimate communications typically appear within specific contexts.

The generation process involves several sophisticated components working together. First, the AI analyzes available data about potential targets, including public social media posts, professional networks, and any leaked or publicly available communications. Using natural language understanding capabilities, it identifies patterns in how individuals and organizations communicate, including specific phrases, formatting preferences, and communication styles (Hariri, 2023). The system then uses this information to generate highly personalized content that mirrors these patterns while incorporating specific details that make the communication appear legitimate. What makes this particularly dangerous is the AI's ability to maintain consistency across multiple messages while varying specific details to avoid detection patterns. The weaponization aspects become more concerning when considering how these systems can operate at scale while maintaining high levels of personalization. Unlike traditional phishing campaigns that might use basic templates or simple customization, AI-powered systems can generate thousands of unique messages, each carefully crafted to its specific target while maintaining narrative consistency across the campaign.

The AI can also adapt its approach based on target responses, learning which techniques are most effective and adjusting its strategy accordingly. For example, if certain types of messages or approaches prove more successful, the system can automatically generate variations that emphasize these effective elements while maintaining enough variation to avoid detection.

More sophisticated implementations might incorporate additional AI capabilities like sentiment analysis and behavioral modeling to further enhance their effectiveness (Sarker, 2022). These systems can analyze the emotional tone of previous communications, understand organizational power dynamics, and time their messages for maximum impact. They might also use generative AI to create supporting elements like fake documents, websites, or even deepfake voice messages that add credibility to the phishing attempt. The AI can maintain complex deception narratives across multiple communications and channels, adjusting its approach based on target responses while maintaining consistency in its deception. Hence, the implications for cybersecurity are significant, as these AI-powered phishing capabilities fundamentally change the nature of social engineering attacks. Traditional indicators of phishing attempts, such as poor grammar or obvious formatting issues, become unreliable as AI systems can generate content that is indistinguishable from legitimate communications. Organizations must now consider how to defend against attacks that can automatically generate highly convincing, personalized deceptions while maintaining the ability to operate at scale. This requires rethinking (or just throwing it out the window) traditional security awareness training and implementing more sophisticated detection systems that can identify subtle patterns that might indicate AI-generated content.

According to the SlashNext State of Phishing Report 2023, there has been a 1,265% increase in malicious phishing emails since Q4 2022, coinciding with the rise of ChatGPT and other generative AI tools (The State of Phishing 2023, 2023). The report, which analyzed threats across email, mobile, and browser channels over a 12-month period, also documented a 967% surge in credential phishing attacks. SlashNext CEO Patrick Harr directly attributed this dramatic rise to threat actors leveraging tools like ChatGPT to craft sophisticated, targeted Business Email Compromise (BEC) messages. The research revealed an average of 31,000 daily phishing attacks, with 68% identified as text-based BEC, while a survey of over 300 cybersecurity professionals found that 46% had encountered BEC attacks and 77% had experienced phishing attempts. Mobile-based threats are also increasing, with 28% of attacks delivered through text messages and 39% classified as SMS phishing. Industry experts emphasize that while AI has significantly enhanced attackers' capabilities, it can also be leveraged for defense, highlighting the need for organizations to implement comprehensive, AI-driven security solutions to counter these evolving threats.

A report by Menlo Security reveals a dramatic 140% year-over-year increase in browser-based phishing attacks, with 752,000 incidents identified between 2023 and 2024 (752,000 Browser Phishing Attacks Mark 140% Increase YoY, 2025). This surge is attributed to AI-driven techniques and the exploitation of enterprise browsers as cybercriminals increasingly target browsers as their primary attack vector. The report found more than 170,000 zero-hour phishing attacks over the past year (a 130% increase from 2023) and notes that one in five attacks used evasion techniques to bypass security controls. Credential phishing campaigns have risen sharply, often impersonating trusted enterprise applications or using deceptive branding. Key trends include brand impersonation in 51% of attacks, use of GenAI names to deceive users, exploitation of zero-day vulnerabilities in popular browsers, a 104% increase in abuse of Cloudflare services for phishing, and the adoption of phishing-as-a-service (PhaaS), enabling large-scale attacks. Traditional cybersecurity defenses like firewalls and secure web gateways are proving inadequate against these evolving threats, as attackers refine their methods with evasive techniques including fileless malware and memory-only payloads. Security experts warn that organizations are making risky trade-offs by relying on basic security tools instead of comprehensive solutions. It is important to adopt proactive security measures like secure cloud browsing solutions that isolate user activity from enterprise networks and AI-enhanced threat detection tools that can identify and neutralize phishing campaigns before they cause damage. Security professionals emphasize that organizations must implement real-time, AI-driven security to detect and block phishing attempts, as relying on outdated defenses is insufficient against rapidly evolving threats.

In general, these case studies highlight how generative AI has fundamentally transformed phishing attacks, providing crucial context for the dramatic 140% increase in browser-based phishing incidents. Modern AI systems analyze writing styles, professional relationships, and organizational hierarchies to craft highly personalized deceptive communications that mimic legitimate messages with unprecedented accuracy. These sophisticated tools can generate thousands of unique, contextually relevant messages while maintaining narrative consistency—enabling attackers to operate at scale without sacrificing personalization. Unlike traditional phishing attempts with obvious red flags, AI-generated content often lacks telltale indicators like poor grammar or formatting issues, making detection significantly more challenging. More advanced implementations incorporate sentiment analysis and behavioral modeling to time messages for maximum impact, while generating supporting elements like fake documents or deepfake voice messages to enhance credibility. This technological sophistication directly explains why traditional security measures are increasingly ineffective and supports the experts' recommendations for implementing

AI-enhanced threat detection tools that can identify subtle patterns in these convincing deceptions.

Virtual assistants have become a new attack vector, with malicious actors exploiting these systems' NLP capabilities and access to sensitive information. Attackers can craft inputs that manipulate virtual assistants into revealing confidential information or performing unauthorized actions, taking advantage of the systems' attempt to be helpful and responsive (Bolton et al., 2021). Additionally, chatbot exploitation has emerged as another significant threat, where attackers use AI to automate interactions with customer service and support chatbots (Costa & Coelho, 2024). These attacks can probe for vulnerabilities, extract sensitive information, or manipulate the chatbot's responses to facilitate larger attack campaigns. The automation aspect allows attackers to scale their efforts across multiple targets simultaneously. The technical exploitation of virtual assistants and chatbots is a sophisticated attack vector that leverages the inherent characteristics of NLP systems and their typical deployment configurations. These systems, built on advanced language models and designed to be helpful and responsive, often maintain complex contextual understanding and have access to various integrated systems and data sources. Attackers exploit these capabilities through carefully crafted prompts and interactions that can manipulate the systems' response patterns or extract sensitive information through seemingly innocent conversations. From a technical perspective, these attacks often exploit the way language models process and understand context (Sai et al., 2024). Attackers can craft sophisticated prompt sequences that gradually build context in ways that might bypass security controls while appearing legitimate to the system. For example, an attacker might use a series of seemingly unrelated questions that, when combined, trick the system into revealing sensitive information or performing unauthorized actions. The attack might start with innocent queries that establish context, then gradually introduce elements that lead the system to misinterpret its security boundaries.

The automation capabilities make these attacks very efficient and scalable. Attackers can develop AI systems that automatically interact with multiple virtual assistants or chatbots simultaneously, testing various attack patterns and adapting their approach based on responses (Bhardwaj et al., 2024). These automated attack systems can operate continuously, identifying vulnerabilities or extracting information across multiple targets while requiring minimal human intervention. The ability to scale these attacks makes them particularly attractive to attackers, as they can potentially compromise multiple systems or organizations simultaneously. Hence, what makes these attacks concerning is their ability to exploit the integration points between virtual assistants and other systems. Many virtual assistants and chatbots are connected to various backend systems and databases to provide comprehensive service (Kong et al., 2021). Attackers can potentially use these systems as entry points to access or manipulate connected systems, exploiting the trust relationships and access privileges granted to these assistants. The systems' attempt to be helpful and provide comprehensive responses can sometimes lead them to reveal more information than intended or perform actions that should be restricted. Furthermore, these attacks can be particularly difficult to detect and prevent because they often appear as legitimate interactions from the system's perspective. The natural language interface means that traditional security controls like input validation or pattern matching may be less effective, as the attacks are encoded in seemingly normal conversation patterns. Attackers can also modify their approach in real time based on system responses, making it harder to identify and block malicious interaction patterns.

The trend toward more sophisticated virtual assistants and chatbots, with increased capabilities and system access, potentially makes this attack vector more attractive over time. As organizations deploy more advanced AI-powered assistance systems with greater access to sensitive information and system controls, the potential impact of successful attacks increases. This creates a challenging balance between providing useful functionality and maintaining security, especially as these systems become more integrated into critical business processes and decision-making. These technical aspects, combined with the potential for automation and scalability, make virtual assistant and chatbot exploitation an increasingly important concern for cybersecurity professionals. Thus, organizations need to carefully consider how they deploy and secure these systems, implementing appropriate controls while maintaining awareness of potential attack vectors and exploitation techniques. This includes careful consideration of system integration points, access controls, and monitoring capabilities to detect and prevent potential attacks. Key theme here emerging: be careful!

Impersonation attacks have reached new levels of sophistication through AI's ability to mimic human communication patterns and behaviors (Usman et al., 2024). Attackers can now create convincing digital personas that maintain consistency across multiple interactions and platforms, making it much harder to identify fraudulent accounts or communications. In essence, the technical sophistication of AI-powered impersonation attacks leverages multiple AI technologies to create and maintain convincing digital identities (Premanand Narasimhan, 2024). These systems employ advanced language models, behavioral analysis algorithms, and pattern recognition capabilities to create digital personas that can consistently mimic specific individuals or roles across various platforms and interactions (Chen et al., 2024). The AI systems analyze vast amounts of data about the target being impersonated, including their writing style, professional relationships, typical activity patterns, and common behaviors, creating detailed models that can generate convincing impersonations. The technical implementation typically involves multiple AI components working together. NLP models analyze the target's communication patterns, including vocabulary choices, sentence structures, and typical responses to different situations (Khurana et al., 2023). Behavioral modeling systems track and replicate patterns in posting times, interaction frequencies, and platform-specific behaviors. Pattern recognition algorithms ensure consistency across different platforms and communication channels, maintaining a coherent digital presence that matches the target's normal behavior patterns (Senyapar, 2024). What makes these attacks so sophisticated is their ability to adapt and learn from interactions, continuously refining their impersonation based on responses and engagement patterns.

In terms of weaponizing AI, this is concerning when considering how these systems can operate autonomously while maintaining convincing impersonations over extended periods. The AI can manage multiple conversations simultaneously, adjusting its communication style and responses based on the context and recipient while maintaining consistency with the impersonated identity. This capability allows attackers to create sophisticated deception campaigns that can target multiple victims while maintaining credibility through consistent behavior patterns. For example, an AI system impersonating a corporate executive might simultaneously engage with multiple employees across different platforms, maintaining appropriate professional relationships and communication styles while gradually building trust for eventual exploitation. Subsequently, these impersonation capabilities are a significant security challenge because they fundamentally undermine traditional methods of validating digital identities. The AI's ability to maintain consistent behavior patterns and communication styles across multiple platforms makes it increasingly difficult to distinguish between legitimate and fraudulent accounts. This becomes particularly problematic in professional contexts where digital communications often form the basis for important decisions or actions. The sophistication of these impersonation attacks means that even careful observers might struggle to identify fraudulent interactions, especially when the AI system has been trained on extensive data about the impersonated target.

The continued evolution and advancement of AI-powered impersonation capabilities suggest that these attacks will become increasingly sophisticated and harder to detect. As language models and behavioral analysis capabilities continue to improve, the ability to create and maintain convincing digital personas will likely increase. This could lead to more complex and sustained impersonation attacks that combine multiple deception techniques while maintaining consistent and convincing behavior patterns across various platforms and interaction types. Organizations will need to develop new approaches to identity verification and communication validation that can address these sophisticated impersonation capabilities while maintaining operational efficiency.

The combination of these different attack vectors creates complex, multilayered social engineering campaigns. For instance, an attacker might use AI to generate a convincing email impersonating a senior executive, follow up with AI-driven chat conversations, and support the deception with fake documentation or credentials, all working together to achieve their malicious objectives. AI-powered social engineering can also adapt in real time based on target responses, adjusting tactics and approaches to maximize effectiveness. This dynamic capability makes these attacks particularly dangerous, as they can evolve their strategies based on the success or failure of different approaches. The scalability of AI-powered social engineering is perhaps its most concerning aspect. Attackers can now automate the creation and execution of sophisticated social engineering campaigns across thousands of targets simultaneously, while maintaining a high degree of personalization and contextual relevance (Basit et al., 2021).

The impact on organizations and individuals has been profound and will continue to be so, fundamentally changing how we must approach security awareness and verification procedures. Traditional red flags like poor grammar, spelling errors, or obvious formatting issues are no longer reliable indicators of malicious content. The barrier to entry for conducting sophisticated social engineering attacks has been significantly lowered—attackers no longer need advanced language skills or detailed cultural knowledge to create convincing deceptions. This democratization of attack capabilities means that organizations face a broader range of potential threats from more diverse attackers. Furthermore, the psychological impact is significant: people can no longer rely on their instincts or experience to identify fraudulent communications, leading to increased anxiety and uncertainty in digital interactions. This has forced organizations to implement more complex verification procedures and multifactor authentication systems, sometimes at the cost of operational efficiency.

4.3 Automated Hacking and Exploit Generation

The emergence of automated hacking and exploit generation powered by AI is another significant shift in the cyber threat landscape. These systems can now autonomously scan for vulnerabilities, develop exploits, and execute attacks at a scale and speed previously impossible with human operators alone. AI systems can analyze code, network configurations, and system behaviors to identify potential weaknesses, while simultaneously developing and testing exploitation methods (Yamin et al., 2021). On the technical side, AI-powered hacking uses AI to identify, analyze, and exploit vulnerabilities. These systems typically employ a combination of machine learning approaches, including deep neural networks for pattern recognition, reinforcement learning for optimization of attack strategies, and NLP for analyzing code and documentation (Sarker, 2021). The AI systems can simultaneously analyze multiple aspects of target systems, including network traffic patterns, system configurations, application behaviors, and code structures, creating comprehensive models of potential attack surfaces. Let's take an example of how such a system might operate: An AI-powered attack platform targeting a corporate network might begin by using neural networks trained on vast datasets of known vulnerabilities and exploitation techniques to analyze network traffic and system responses. The system could automatically generate and test thousands of subtle variations of known exploit patterns, learning from each attempt to refine its approach. Through reinforcement learning, the system continuously optimizes its attack strategies based on target responses, developing increasingly sophisticated methods for bypassing security controls. For instance, if certain types of probes trigger security alerts, the system might automatically adjust its approach to stay below detection thresholds while still gathering necessary information.

The technical side of it often involves multiple specialized components. One subsystem might focus on vulnerability discovery, using deep learning models trained on code repositories and vulnerability databases to identify potential weaknesses in target systems (Kaur et al., 2023). Another component might specialize in exploit development, automatically generating and testing exploit code while optimizing it for reliability and stealth (Iturbe et al., 2024). A third component might handle attack orchestration, coordinating different exploitation attempts while maintaining operational security (Kinyua & Awuah, 2021). These systems can operate continuously, learning from each interaction and sharing information between components to improve overall effectiveness. Thus, what makes these systems dangerous and weaponized is their ability to develop novel attack approaches by combining elements of known vulnerabilities in unexpected ways. Through pattern recognition and generative capabilities, the AI can identify subtle similarities between different types of vulnerabilities and create new exploitation methods that might not be obvious to human attackers. For example, the system might recognize that a particular combination of seemingly benign operations, when executed in a specific sequence, could trigger an exploitable condition in a target system. The automation aspect extends beyond just vulnerability discovery and exploitation to include postexploitation activities. Once initial access is gained, AI systems can automatically map internal networks, identify valuable targets, and develop optimized paths for lateral movement—all while maintaining stealth and adapting to defensive responses. The systems can simultaneously manage multiple compromise attempts across different targets, learning from each interaction to improve their effectiveness while maintaining operational security.

Remember how earlier it was discussed how AI can help us with vulnerability scanning? Unfortunately, this is an example of how AI can be both a tool and a weapon. Cyberattackers can also utilize AI for easier and more sophisticated scanning to find and take advantage of vulnerabilities. AI-driven vulnerability discovery has evolved beyond traditional scanning methods to include sophisticated pattern recognition and predictive analysis. These systems can identify subtle vulnerabilities by analyzing code patterns, system configurations, and their interrelationships (Guembe et al., 2022). They can detect potential security weaknesses that might be missed by conventional tools, including complex scenarios involving multiple system components or unusual interaction patterns. The AI can also prioritize discovered vulnerabilities based on exploitability and potential impact, allowing attackers to focus on the most promising targets. Moreover, automated exploit development represents a particularly concerning advancement, as AI systems can now generate, test, and refine exploitation methods without human intervention (Lysenko et al., 2024). These systems can analyze discovered vulnerabilities, develop multiple potential exploit approaches, and automatically test them in simulated environments to determine the most effective attack vectors. The ability to rapidly iterate and improve exploit code means that new vulnerabilities can be weaponized much more quickly than traditional human-driven development.

The scaling of cyberattacks through AI automation has dramatically changed the threat landscape. Attackers can now launch sophisticated, multivector attacks against numerous targets simultaneously, while dynamically adjusting their tactics based on target responses (Guembe et al., 2022). This capability allows even small groups of attackers to conduct large-scale campaigns that would previously have required significant resources and manpower. The AI can manage multiple attack vectors, adjust strategies in real time, and maintain persistent access across numerous compromised systems simultaneously. In our current landscape and in the future, these automated attack systems creates significant challenges for cybersecurity defenders. The speed and scale at which AI-powered systems can operate means that vulnerabilities might be discovered and exploited faster than human defenders can patch them. Organizations need to implement equally sophisticated AI-powered defensive measures that can detect and respond to automated attacks in real time. This includes developing systems that can predict and prevent potential attack patterns before they're successfully executed, while also maintaining the ability to quickly adapt to new attack techniques as they emerge. This is also of the utmost concern considering the accessibility of these attacks. As these technologies become more available, even less sophisticated attackers might gain access to advanced attack capabilities that were previously limited to well-resourced threat actors. This democratization and lowering of the barrier of entry of sophisticated attack capabilities means organizations must prepare for a broader range of potential threats while maintaining effective security controls against automated attacks. Essentially, organizations need to implement security controls that can detect and respond to automated probing and exploitation attempts, while also maintaining the ability to quickly adapt their defenses as attack systems evolve. This might include implementing AI-powered defensive systems that can automatically identify and block suspicious automation patterns, while also maintaining appropriate human oversight and control over security operations. Additionally, they must adapt their defense strategies to account for the speed and scale of AI-driven attacks, implementing their own AI-powered defense systems to detect and respond to these threats in real time. This creates an arms race between offensive and defensive AI systems, with each side continuously evolving to counter the other's capabilities.

The emergence of Xanthorox AI is a concerning evolution in AI-driven attack platforms. It distinguishes itself from predecessors like WormGPT and EvilGPT through its comprehensive, self-contained architecture (Montalbano, 2025a). Unlike earlier tools that relied on jailbreaking existing LLMs, Xanthorox operates as a completely independent ecosystem hosted on its developers' servers, providing attackers with a local, unmonitored, and highly customizable AI experience. This architectural approach offers significant advantages for malicious actors, as the platform's independence from public cloud infrastructure or exposed Application Programming Interface (API)s drastically reduces detection and traceability risks. The modular design featuring five specialized operational models—including Xanthorox Coder for automated code generation and malware development, Xanthorox Reasoner for voice-based interaction, and Xanthorox Vision for image analysis—creates a versatile toolkit that can adapt to various attack scenarios. This aligns with the technical progression described by Iturbe et al. (2024) and Kaur et al. (2023), where specialized AI components work in concert to handle different aspects of the attack lifecycle.

The technical architecture of Xanthorox AI demonstrates advanced capabilities that extend beyond conventional AI-based attack tools. At its core, Xanthorox Coder automates numerous technical tasks from code generation to vulnerability exploitation, effectively eliminating the need for manual scripting during attacks (Montalbano, 2025b). This component likely leverages specialized neural networks trained on extensive code repositories and known exploits, similar to the deep learning approaches described by Sarker (2021). The platform integrates voice and image processing through Xanthorox Reasoner and Xanthorox Vision modules, enabling command and control through natural interfaces and allowing for analysis of visual data such as screenshots or network diagrams. This multimodal approach enhances the attack platform's versatility by processing various data types simultaneously. The system's offline functionality suggests sophisticated local processing capabilities, while its evasion of third-party AI telemetry indicates implementation of adversarial techniques to avoid detection systems designed to identify AI-generated content. Most concerning from a technical perspective is how Xanthorox AI can maintain operational continuity without constant network connections, suggesting advanced caching and decision-making algorithms that allow for autonomous operation even when isolated. This technical design creates substantial challenges for traditional security monitoring systems that rely on network traffic analysis or signature-based detection, as the attack platform can execute sophisticated operations with minimal observable footprint.

Consequently, what makes Xanthorox AI significant is how it embodies the theoretical threat models predicted by security researchers when GenAI first emerged. The platform's ability to support self-directed, autonomous cyberattacks validates concerns that such technologies could hyper-charge bad actors' ability to innovate their attacks. As discussed earlier, these systems can manage multiple attack vectors simultaneously while dynamically adjusting strategies in real time. Xanthorox's functionality (including Internet search scraping across more than 50 engines, offline capability, and antitelemetry features) creates a comprehensive attack framework that can operate persistently without network dependencies while evading conventional detection methods. Thus, this represents the kind of scaling threat that security experts have cautioned would dramatically alter the threat landscape, allowing small groups of attackers to conduct sophisticated campaigns previously requiring significant resources. The platform's evolution signals an acceleration of the arms race between offensive and defensive AI systems. Moreover, we can continue to expect significant accelerations in this space.

4.4 Privacy Concerns

We will go into more detail in Chapter 5 when we discuss the risks and vulnerabilities of generative AI; however, let's briefly address the privacy concerns that generative AI introduces to organizations and individuals. These systems, which process vast amounts of data to generate new content, can inadvertently expose sensitive information through various mechanisms. Data leakage can occur when AI models inadvertently incorporate private information from their training data into their outputs, potentially exposing confidential business information, personal details, or proprietary data.

Reidentification risks are a critical challenge, where anonymized data used to train AI models can be reverse-engineered to identify specific individuals or entities (Martinez & Herrera, 2023). This becomes concerning when generative

AI systems are trained on large datasets that may contain sensitive information. Even when direct identifiers are removed, the combination of various data points and patterns can sometimes be used to reconstruct or infer protected information about specific individuals or organizations. The technical complexity of reidentification attacks through AI systems involves sophisticated pattern recognition and correlation algorithms that can analyze multiple data points across various datasets to reconstruct identities (Ye et al., 2021). These systems employ advanced machine learning techniques, including deep neural networks and probabilistic modeling, to identify subtle patterns and relationships that can link anonymized data back to specific individuals or entities. For example, an AI system might analyze patterns in anonymized location data, combining this with publicly available information and social media data to reconstruct individual identities and movements. The system can identify unique patterns in behavior, preferences, or characteristics that, when combined, create a unique fingerprint that can be used to reidentify specific individuals even when direct identifiers have been removed.

The rise of shadow AI is another critical privacy concern in the generative AI landscape. Shadow AI refers to the unauthorized or undocumented use of AI tools and services within organizations, often when employees bypass official channels to access public AI services for work-related tasks (What is Shadow AI? Grip, n.d.). This creates significant privacy risks as sensitive company data, customer information, or proprietary content may be inadvertently uploaded to external AI systems without proper security controls or oversight. For example, employees might paste confidential code into public AI models for debugging assistance, upload internal documents for summarization, or use AI tools to analyze customer data without considering data protection requirements. The ease of access to public AI services makes this particularly problematic—employees can simply copy and paste sensitive information into these systems without understanding the privacy implications or data retention policies of the service providers. This shadow AI usage not only creates immediate privacy risks through potential data exposure but can also lead to long-term privacy vulnerabilities as sensitive information becomes part of external AI models' training data. Organizations must therefore balance the productivity benefits of AI tools with robust policies and controls to prevent unauthorized AI usage while providing approved, secure alternatives that meet employees' needs.

Another dimension of AI-related privacy concerns, especially concerning data collection and scraping practices that could compromise privacy and intellectual property, is gray bots and AI scrapers. Subsequently, the weaponization of generative AI extends beyond direct attacks to include the escalating phenomenon of "gray bots" that aggressively scrape web data to train AI models. Recent findings from Barracuda reveal an alarming surge in AI scraper activity, with some web applications receiving up to 9.7 million bot requests in a 30-day period and others facing 17,000 requests per hour over a 24-hour timeframe (Mascellino, 2025). Unlike traditional bot activity that operates in bursts, these AI scrapers, including ClaudeBot (Anthropic), Bytespider (TikTok), PerplexityBot, and DeepSeekBot, maintain consistent traffic levels that are difficult to predict and mitigate. This pattern represents a new form of AI weaponization that, while not explicitly malicious, creates significant operational and security challenges for organizations worldwide.

Hence, the implications of this gray bot phenomenon extend beyond mere nuisance to encompass serious security and intellectual property concerns. These bots can overwhelm web applications, extract copyrighted material without authorization, distort analytics crucial for business decisions, significantly increase cloud hosting costs, and introduce compliance risks in regulated industries handling sensitive data (Mascellino, 2025). The persistence and sophistication of these scraper bots render traditional protection mechanisms like robots.txt largely ineffective, forcing organizations to deploy advanced AI-powered defense systems to counter this emerging threat. This escalation represents yet another dimension in the AI security arms race, where the very technologies designed to advance AI capabilities become weaponized in ways that require increasingly sophisticated countermeasures, further blurring the lines between AI as a tool, a weapon, and a target in the cybersecurity landscape.

An example may be necessary here to understand the privacy concerns of GAI in practical terms. Imagine a healthcare organization releases an anonymized dataset of patient records for research purposes, removing obvious identifiers like names, addresses, and social security numbers. However, an attacker using AI analysis might combine this data with publicly available information, such as social media posts about hospital visits, location check-ins, or lifestyle patterns. The AI system can identify unique combinations of characteristics—such as age ranges, medical conditions, treatment dates, and general location data—that, when analyzed together, could uniquely identify specific individuals. This risk is significantly amplified by shadow AI usage within healthcare organizations. Consider a scenario where medical staff, seeking to improve efficiency, use unauthorized public AI tools to analyze patient records or generate medical reports. They might paste anonymized patient data into these tools without realizing that this information is now potentially stored and processed by external systems. An attacker could then correlate this leaked data with the officially anonymized dataset, creating even more precise identification patterns. For instance, if someone has posted on social media about a specific medical procedure on a certain date, and both the anonymized dataset and shadow AI tools contain records with matching characteristics (age range, procedure type, timing), the AI could potentially link these data points to reidentify the individual with even greater accuracy. This becomes particularly dangerous when considering how much information people voluntarily share online, combined with the inadvertent data exposure through shadow AI usage, providing multiple additional data points for correlation and identification.

The weaponization potential becomes more concerning when considering how these reidentification capabilities could be used for targeted attacks or exploitation (Sai et al., 2024). Attackers could use these techniques to identify individuals with specific characteristics or vulnerabilities, potentially targeting them for fraud, social engineering, or other malicious purposes. For example, if an attacker can reidentify individuals with specific medical conditions or financial situations from anonymized datasets, they could use this information to craft highly targeted and convincing scams or manipulation attempts. The AI's ability to process and correlate vast amounts of data makes it possible to perform these reidentification attacks at scale, potentially compromising the privacy of large numbers of individuals simultaneously. This capability challenges traditional anonymization techniques and raises important questions about how organizations can share and use data while protecting individual privacy in an era where AI systems can increasingly pierce through anonymization efforts. The implications of these privacy concerns are widespread and far-reaching, affecting how organizations can safely deploy and utilize generative AI systems while maintaining data privacy and regulatory compliance. Organizations must carefully consider the trade-offs between model performance and privacy protection, implementing robust safeguards to prevent unauthorized data exposure while ensuring their AI systems remain effective and useful. This includes implementing techniques like differential privacy, careful data sanitization, and regular privacy audits to minimize the risk of data leakage and reidentification.

The 2025 security audit of DeepSeek's mobile application provides a real-world illustration of how privacy vulnerabilities in GAI systems can manifest in practice (Lakshmanan, 2025). The case exemplifies multiple dimensions of privacy concerns discussed above, particularly in the context of data leakage and shadow AI risks. The discovery that DeepSeek's iOS application transmitted sensitive user and device data without encryption represents a fundamental privacy failure that exposes users to both passive and active interception attacks. This vulnerability was compounded by several implementation weaknesses, including the use of outdated encryption algorithms, hard-coded encryption keys, and the reuse of initialization vectors, demonstrating how technical implementation choices can severely impact privacy protections in GAI applications. The situation was further complicated by the application's data handling practices, which involved transmitting information to multiple third-party entities. This complex data supply chain highlights the challenges organizations face in maintaining privacy controls when deploying GAI systems that inherently require extensive data processing and transfer capabilities.

The DeepSeek case also illustrates the broader implications of privacy vulnerabilities in GAI systems, especially in the context of international data flows and regulatory compliance. The discovery that user login information was being transmitted to entities that had been banned from operating in certain jurisdictions led to widespread governmental responses, with multiple countries and agencies banning the application from government devices. This demonstrates how privacy vulnerabilities in GAI applications can have cascading effects beyond immediate technical concerns, potentially impacting national security and requiring regulatory intervention. The case is particularly noteworthy because it shows how privacy issues in GAI applications can become amplified when combined with geopolitical concerns and supply chain security considerations. The rapid rise in DeepSeek's popularity, followed by the discovery of these privacy issues, also highlights the challenges of balancing rapid deployment and scaling of GAI applications with proper privacy protections and security controls.

These privacy vulnerabilities had additional consequences beyond direct data exposure, as demonstrated by the emergence of threat actors leveraging DeepSeek's AI engines, alongside other platforms like Alibaba Qwen and OpenAI ChatGPT, for malicious purposes, including the development of information stealers and mass spam distribution. This illustrates how privacy vulnerabilities in GAI systems can create opportunities for weaponization and abuse, potentially exposing users to secondary privacy risks beyond the initial data exposure. The case also demonstrates the attractive target that popular GAI services present to attackers, as evidenced by the sustained Distributed Denial of Service (DDoS) attacks from Mirai botnets and the proliferation of malicious lookalike pages designed to propagate malware and fraudulent schemes. These security challenges underscore the critical importance of implementing comprehensive privacy protections in GAI applications from the ground up, rather than treating privacy as an afterthought or optional feature. The DeepSeek case serves as a cautionary tale for organizations developing and deploying GAI applications, highlighting the need for robust privacy controls, transparent data handling practices, and careful consideration of the entire data supply chain in GAI deployments.

4.5 Weaponization of AI: Attack Vectors

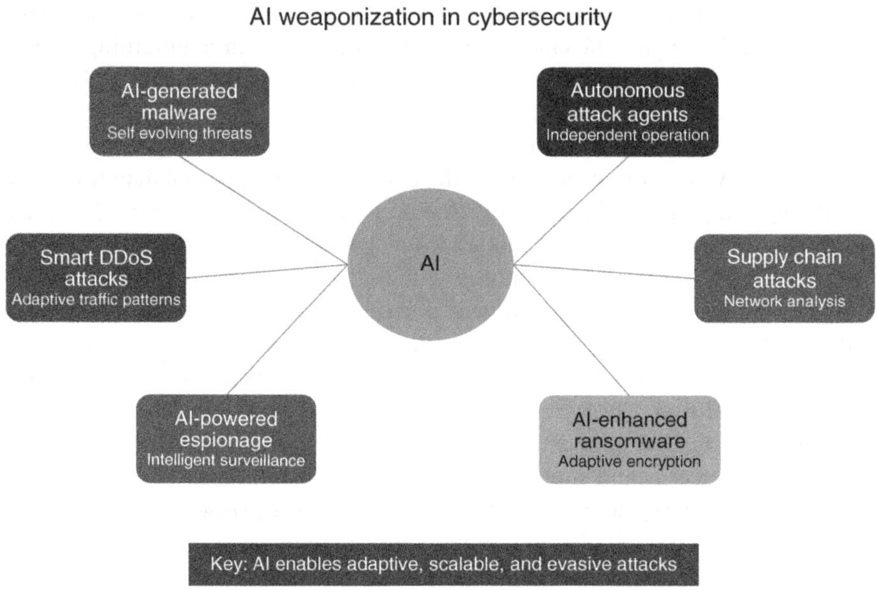

The weaponization of generative AI is one of the most significant emerging threats in the cybersecurity landscape. As these technologies become more sophisticated and accessible, malicious actors are finding innovative ways to leverage AI capabilities for cyberattacks. This section explores the various ways generative AI can be weaponized, from creating sophisticated malware and ransomware variants to enabling autonomous attack agents and enhancing traditional attack vectors. Understanding these potential threats is crucial for security professionals as they work to develop effective countermeasures and defensive strategies. The combination of AI's powerful generative capabilities with malicious intent creates new challenges for cybersecurity, potentially enabling more sophisticated, scalable, and harder-to-detect attacks. As we examine each type of AI-enabled attack, we'll explore both the technical mechanisms that make them possible and their implications for organizational security, helping security professionals better prepare for and defend against these emerging threats.

Let's start with AI-generated malware. This is where AI is leveraged to create increasingly sophisticated and evasive malicious software. Unlike traditional malware development, which relies on human programmers to write and modify code, AI-generated malware can be created automatically, with systems learning from existing malware samples to generate new, unique variants that can evade detection while maintaining or improving upon known malicious capabilities

(Metta et al., 2024). The process typically begins with training AI models on large datasets of existing malware code, legitimate software, and system interaction patterns. These models learn the characteristics that make malware effective while also understanding how to mimic legitimate software behaviors to avoid detection. Advanced generative AI systems can analyze successful malware patterns, understanding both their technical implementations and their evasion techniques, then generate new variants that combine these qualities in novel ways (Aryal et al., 2024). What makes AI-generated malware particularly concerning is its ability to adapt and evolve rapidly. Traditional malware often requires manual modification to evade new detection methods, but AI systems can automatically generate variants that test different approaches to bypassing security controls. For example, an AI system might generate thousands of variants of a particular piece of malware, each with slightly different code patterns, encryption methods, or behaviors, then analyze which variants successfully evade detection to inform the generation of even more sophisticated versions.

Consequently, this makes AI-generated malware concerning because of its ability to adapt and evolve rapidly. Traditional malware often requires manual modification to evade new detection methods, but AI systems can automatically generate variants that test different approaches to bypassing security controls. For example, an AI system might generate thousands of variants of a particular piece of malware, each with slightly different code patterns, encryption methods, or behaviors, then analyze which variants successfully evade detection to inform the generation of even more sophisticated versions (Usman et al., 2024). Let's say an attacker using AI to generate ransomware. The AI system might analyze successful ransomware samples, understanding their encryption mechanisms, system interaction patterns, and evasion techniques. It could then generate new ransomware variants that combine these elements in unique ways while adding novel features to avoid detection. The system might create versions that use different encryption algorithms, vary their behavior based on the target environment, or employ new techniques for disabling security software—all while maintaining the core ransomware functionality. The weaponization aspect becomes very evident in how AI can automate and scale malware development. Instead of malware authors needing to manually code new variants, AI systems can generate hundreds or thousands of unique variants automatically, each potentially capable of evading different security measures. This automation dramatically reduces the time and expertise required to create sophisticated malware, potentially democratizing access to advanced cyber weapons.

Moreover, AI-generated malware can be more sophisticated in its behavior patterns. GAI can learn from both legitimate software and successful malware, allowing these systems to create malicious code that better mimics normal program behavior. The aforementioned makes it harder for security tools to distinguish between legitimate and malicious activities (Metta et al., 2024). The malware might adapt its behavior based on its environment, using different techniques depending on the security tools it detects or the type of system it's running on. As our landscape progresses, we can expect AI-generated malware to become increasingly sophisticated. Future variants might incorporate advanced learning capabilities, allowing them to adapt their behavior in real time based on their environment and the success or failure of their actions. They might use NLP to generate more convincing phishing messages or social engineering attempts, or employ advanced evasion techniques that anticipate and counter common security measures. Subsequently, this is a significant challenge for cybersecurity professionals. Just as defenders use AI to detect and analyze malware, attackers are using it to create malware that's inherently designed to evade those same AI-powered security tools. This creates an ongoing arms race (or cat-and-mouse game that we've discussed earlier) where both defensive and offensive AI systems continuously evolve in response to each other's capabilities. Overall, this is a significant shift and demonstrates how powerful AI technologies can be weaponized for malicious purposes.

To continue on the discussion of AI-generated malware, modular malware and spyware development has entered a new era with the advent of generative AI capabilities. Ultimately, this creates unprecedented challenges for security teams. GAI systems excel at generating code variations, understanding system architectures, and adapting to different environments—all critical capabilities for creating sophisticated modular malware. Traditional malware often followed predictable patterns that signature-based detection could identify, but GAI-powered modular malware can dynamically generate new components, communication protocols, and evasion techniques on demand (Bordoni et al., 2017). The sophistication comes from GAI's ability to analyze security mechanisms and automatically develop countermeasures, essentially engaging in an AI-driven arms race against defensive systems. These systems can craft malware modules that communicate through encrypted channels, leverage legitimate system processes, and modify their behavior based on the environment they detect (Serpanos et al., 2021). Most concerning is how GAI enables less skilled attackers (or script kiddies) to develop highly sophisticated threats through natural language interfaces that can translate malicious intent into functional code. The modular nature allows threat actors to deploy minimal functionality initially, then dynamically add capabilities as needed, making detection of the full threat potential extremely difficult during initial security scans. Organizations increasingly face the daunting task of defending against malware that can essentially rewrite itself to evade detection while maintaining persistent access to compromised systems.

Advanced spyware powered by generative AI is another escalation in surveillance capabilities, with implications for both corporate espionage and personal privacy. GAI enhances spyware effectiveness through intelligent data collection that can prioritize high-value information, mimic legitimate user behavior patterns to avoid anomaly detection, and automatically adjust its activities based on system resources to remain undetected (Shi & Duan, 2024). The threat extends beyond data exfiltration to sophisticated reconnaissance, where GAI-powered spyware can map network architectures, identify valuable targets, and establish multiple persistence mechanisms across compromised environments (Deshpande & Gupta, 2023). What is more alarming is the ability of these systems to learn organizational communication patterns and security routines, allowing them to operate during periods of minimal monitoring or automatically pause activities during security scans. Defending against these threats requires the implementation of behavioral analysis systems that can identify subtle patterns of suspicious activity across extended timeframes, not just point-in-time detection. GAI can be used as a security tool here to do the aforementioned. Security teams must deploy AI-powered monitoring solutions that can match the adaptability of these threats, implementing continuous authentication to detect unauthorized access attempts and unusual data access patterns.

The emergence of GhostGPT, as reported by Dark Reading in January 2025, is a concrete manifestation of long-standing concerns about AI-powered malware development (Vijayan, 2025). For as little as $50 per week, cybercriminals can now access an uncensored AI chatbot specifically designed to bypass the ethical constraints built into mainstream AI systems like ChatGPT, Claude, and Google Gemini. This new tool enables users to generate malicious code and craft sophisticated phishing emails with minimal technical expertise, effectively democratizing access to advanced cyber weapons. The relationship between GhostGPT and the theoretical frameworks of AI-generated malware is important to understand. While academic discussions have long warned about AI's potential to automate and enhance malware creation, GhostGPT demonstrates how these capabilities are being commercialized in underground markets. The background text describes how AI systems can learn from existing malware samples to generate new variants while mimicking legitimate software behaviors—precisely the functionality that GhostGPT now offers to its users. This convergence of theory and practice suggests that the cybersecurity community's concerns about AI weaponization were well-founded.

The rapid evolution of malicious AI tools is something that poses a substantial threat and issue. AI systems can automatically generate thousands of malware variants, each testing different approaches to bypassing security controls. GhostGPT builds upon this foundation, following in the footsteps of earlier tools like WormGPT and FraudGPT. However, while many previous attempts at creating "evil" AI models failed to gain traction, GhostGPT appears to be finding success in underground markets. This success may be attributed to its apparent effectiveness and the growing sophistication of AI language models in general. What is probably most concerning is how GhostGPT exemplifies the concept of AI democratizing advanced cyber capabilities. As aforementioned, there is a continued reduction in the expertise barrier for creating sophisticated malware, and GhostGPT delivers exactly that—providing anyone with a modest budget access to AI-powered malware generation tools. This development has significant implications for the cybersecurity landscape, as it potentially multiplies the number of actors capable of launching sophisticated attacks. The tool's ability to generate convincing phishing emails and complex malicious code without requiring deep technical knowledge represents a significant shift in the accessibility of cyber weapons. The emergence of tools like GhostGPT also highlights the ongoing arms race between defensive and offensive AI systems. As security tools increasingly rely on AI to detect and prevent attacks, malicious actors are leveraging the same technology to create more evasive threats. This dynamic mirrors the "cat-and-mouse game," where both defensive and offensive capabilities continuously evolve in response to each other. The fact that GhostGPT's creators have moved to private sales channels and increased operational security suggests a level of sophistication and awareness of the tool's significant impact on this ongoing technological arms race.

However, Google DeepMind has developed an important evaluation framework that identifies weaknesses in adversarial AI systems, enabling defenders to better prioritize their security strategies (Townsend, 2025). After analyzing over 12,000 actual attempts to leverage AI in cyberattacks from more than 20 countries, DeepMind found that current AI evaluation frameworks are ad hoc and nonsystematic, failing to provide defenders with actionable insights. Their new approach identifies "bottlenecks" in the attack chain—areas where AI currently struggles to assist attackers, creating a curated list of 50 specific challenge areas. Moreover, testing these challenges against models like Gemini 2.0 Flash, researchers discovered that current AI is inefficient in many attack phases, especially in under-researched areas like evasion, detection avoidance, and persistence. This systematic and structured approach allows defenders to target their resources at the weakest links in AI-assisted attack chains while also monitoring how these capabilities evolve over time. As DeepMind notes, "It offers an advantage in the face of AI-enabled adversaries, because it equips defenders with decision-relevant insights to enhance their cyber defenses" (Townsend, 2025).

Recent security testing by AppSOC revealed significant vulnerabilities in DeepSeek's AI model, with failure rates ranging from 19.2% to 98% across multiple critical security areas (Montalbano, 2025a). The testing, which involved 6,400 security tests, showed that the model was vulnerable to malware generation (98.8% failure rate) and virus code generation (86.7% failure rate). The model demonstrated poor performance in areas including jailbreaking, prompt injection, supply chain issues, and toxicity. DeepSeek earned a high-risk rating of 8.3 out of 10, with researchers recommending organizations avoid using it for any applications involving sensitive data or intellectual property. The case is particularly significant because it demonstrates how the rush to develop competitive AI models can lead to serious security compromises, even in widely used commercial systems. The DeepSeek case provides another critical example of how AI systems can be weaponized, whether intentionally or through inadequate security controls. Unlike GhostGPT, which was deliberately designed for malicious purposes, DeepSeek's vulnerabilities emerged from rapid commercial development prioritizing performance over security. This illustrates how even legitimate AI tools can become security risks when proper safeguards are not implemented. The model's high failure rates in security testing, particularly in malware generation and jailbreaking resistance, demonstrate how commercial pressures and competition can lead to the creation of AI systems that inadvertently enable malicious activities. This case is especially concerning as it shows how the democratization of AI capabilities can occur not just through purpose-built malicious tools, but also through inadequately secured commercial systems.

Another case study that is important to address is state-sponsored actors' use of generative AI, specifically Gemini AI. The emergence of AI-powered cyberattacks has moved from theoretical concern to demonstrable reality, as evidenced by Google's Threat Intelligence Group's recent findings about advanced persistent threat (APT) groups use of Gemini (Toulas, 2025). Google's Threat Intelligence Group has revealed that state-sponsored hackers from over 20 countries are actively using Gemini AI to enhance their cyber operations, though primarily for productivity gains rather than developing novel AI-enabled attacks. Users are actively leveraging the tool for reconnaissance, phishing campaign development, network persistence techniques, and technical research. Some actors are even using the platform to support various attack phases and create false identities for infiltrating companies. The research found that while threat actors attempted to jailbreak Gemini or bypass its security measures, these attempts were unsuccessful. However, the report raises concerns about the broader AI landscape, noting that some newer AI models, such as DeepSeek R1 and Alibaba's Qwen 2.5, have weaker security protections that could be more easily exploited. This investigation follows similar disclosures from OpenAI about ChatGPT misuse in 2024, highlighting the growing trend of threat actors adapting AI tools for malicious purposes while also demonstrating the importance of robust security measures in mainstream AI platforms.

This real-world validation of theoretical threats provides a compelling case study in how AI is transforming the cybersecurity landscape. Google's research reveals that APT groups from multiple nations are actively leveraging AI tools to enhance their cyber operations, ranging from reconnaissance and vulnerability research to malware development and evasion techniques. This practical implementation directly mirrors the theoretical frameworks outlined in academic and industry research about AI weaponization, providing concrete evidence of how these technologies are being operationalized in real-world attack scenarios. The transformation of cyberattacks through AI integration is particularly evident in how threat actors are automating and enhancing their capabilities. Google's findings demonstrate that APT groups are using AI not just for individual tasks but as part of a comprehensive approach to increase their operational efficiency and effectiveness. For instance, Iranian actors' use of AI for developing phishing campaigns and conducting reconnaissance aligns precisely with theoretical predictions about how AI could automate and enhance social engineering attacks. Similarly, threat actors' utilization of AI for scripting and privilege escalation techniques validates concerns about AI's potential to automate and optimize complex attack sequences. This pattern of adoption suggests that theoretical models of AI weaponization are being rapidly transformed into practical attack methodologies.

The democratization of advanced cyber capabilities through AI, another key theoretical concern, is being validated through multiple channels. While Google's report focuses on state-sponsored actors, the concurrent emergence of tools like GhostGPT, which offers uncensored AI capabilities for malicious purposes at relatively low cost, demonstrates how these technologies are becoming accessible to a broader range of threat actors. This democratization effect was predicted in theoretical frameworks, which warned about AI's potential to lower the barriers to entry for sophisticated cyberattacks. The fact that state actors are actively experimenting with commercial AI platforms like Gemini, rather than relying solely on proprietary tools, further supports this trend toward democratization and suggests that the distinction between state-sponsored and independent threat actors may become increasingly blurred.

This convergence of theoretical predictions and practical implementation carries significant implications for the future of cybersecurity. The evidence suggests that organizations must prepare for a new era where AI-powered threats become the norm rather than the exception. The sophistication of these attacks, as demonstrated by APT groups' current activities, indicates that traditional security measures may become increasingly insufficient. The case study provided by Google's research, combined with the broader context of AI weaponization theory, suggests that we're witnessing the early stages of a fundamental shift in the cyber threat landscape. This transformation demands a corresponding evolution in defensive strategies, potentially including the development of AI-powered security tools that can detect and counter these emerging threats. As both the Google report and theoretical frameworks suggest, the future of cybersecurity will likely be characterized by an ongoing arms race between AI-powered attacks and defenses, with success depending on organizations' ability to adapt to and counter increasingly sophisticated AI-enabled threats.

AI in ransomware development is another evolution in cyber threats, where it is changing how these attacks are created, deployed, and executed. Traditional ransomware attacks typically relied on relatively static code bases that could be detected and blocked once identified. However, AI-powered ransomware introduces a new level of sophistication and adaptability that makes detection and prevention significantly more challenging (Ansarullah et al., 2024). Generative AI, in particular, enables attackers to create highly sophisticated ransomware variants that can adapt their behavior, evade detection, and maximize their effectiveness against specific targets (Metta et al., 2024). This capability fundamentally changes the landscape of ransomware threats, making them more difficult to detect and defend against. The use of AI in ransomware development has dramatically lowered the barrier to entry for potential attackers. Where traditional ransomware development required significant technical expertise in programming, encryption methods, and system exploitation, AI-powered tools can automate much of this process. Attackers can now use AI systems to generate ransomware code, optimize encryption algorithms, and develop evasion techniques without needing deep technical knowledge. This democratization of sophisticated attack capabilities means that organizations must now defend against a potentially larger pool of attackers with access to advanced ransomware tools. For example, an attacker might use generative AI to create multiple ransomware variants, each optimized for different target environments or designed to evade specific security tools. The AI system could analyze successful ransomware attacks, learning which techniques work best against different security measures, and incorporate these insights into new variants.

The sophistication of AI-generated ransomware attacks manifests in several ways that distinguish them from traditional approaches. First, these systems can generate polymorphic code that constantly changes its signature while maintaining its malicious functionality, making it extremely difficult for signature-based detection systems to identify (Catalano et al., 2022). Second, AI-powered ransomware can include advanced behavioral analysis capabilities, allowing it to study its target environment and adapt its approach accordingly. For instance, the ransomware might observe normal system operations for a period before beginning its encryption process, helping it blend in with legitimate activities and avoid detection. Additionally, AI systems can optimize the encryption process itself, potentially making it more difficult or impossible to decrypt files without paying the ransom (Lüchinger, 2023). The impact of AI-generated ransomware becomes especially concerning in our current cyber landscape, where ransomware attacks are already increasing in frequency and sophistication. Organizations face a dual challenge: not only must they defend against more numerous attacks, but these attacks are now potentially more sophisticated and harder to detect. The ability of AI systems to generate and modify ransomware code quickly means that security tools and signatures can become outdated almost immediately, creating a constant race to update defenses against new variants. This rapid evolution of threats makes it increasingly difficult for organizations to maintain effective security measures, particularly when AI-powered ransomware can learn from failed attempts and generate new variants that overcome previously successful defenses.

The ongoing discussions about banning ransomware payments add another layer of complexity to this issue (Gregory, 2024). While such bans might theoretically reduce the incentive for ransomware attacks, the sophistication of AI-generated ransomware could make this approach more problematic. AI systems could potentially generate ransomware that is more destructive or harder to decrypt, potentially increasing the pressure on organizations to pay ransoms despite any bans. Furthermore, AI could be used to identify targets more likely to pay ransoms or to optimize ransom demands based on an organization's financial capacity and risk tolerance. This targeted approach, combined with the increased sophistication of the attacks themselves, could make payment bans less effective as a deterrent.

The rise of AI-generated ransomware necessitates a fundamental shift in how organizations approach cybersecurity. Traditional security measures focused on signature detection and static analysis become less effective against ransomware that can constantly modify its code and behavior. Organizations need to implement more sophisticated defense mechanisms that can detect and respond to anomalous behavior patterns, regardless of the specific code signatures involved. This might include AI-powered security tools that can identify potentially malicious behavior patterns, even from previously unseen ransomware variants. Additionally, organizations need to focus more on preventive measures, including robust backup systems, network segmentation, and user training, as the increased sophistication of AI-generated ransomware makes recovery from successful attacks more challenging. Furthermore, it is a significant escalation in the cat-and-mouse game. As these systems become more sophisticated, the challenge of defending against ransomware attacks becomes increasingly complex. Organizations must adapt their security strategies to address not just the technical capabilities of AI-generated ransomware but also the broader implications of more accessible and sophisticated attack tools. This evolution in ransomware threats underscores the importance of developing more robust and adaptive security measures while also considering broader policy responses to address the growing ransomware threat landscape.

Autonomous attack agents are another concern within the context of how AI can be weaponized. These agents combine AI's capabilities for independent decision-making with sophisticated attack methodologies. These AI-powered systems can operate independently to identify vulnerabilities, adapt their attack strategies, and exploit weaknesses in target systems without constant human direction (Oreyomi & Jahankhani, 2022). This autonomy is a concerning advancement in the weaponization of AI, as it enables attacks to proceed and evolve even without direct attacker intervention. The sophistication of autonomous attack agents lies in their ability to learn and adapt in real time. Unlike traditional automated attacks that follow predetermined patterns, these AI-powered agents can analyze the effectiveness of their actions and modify their approach based on the target's responses and defenses (AI's New Frontier in War Planning, 2024). For example, an autonomous agent might begin by probing a network for vulnerabilities, learning from the responses it receives, and gradually developing more sophisticated attack strategies. If one approach proves unsuccessful, the agent can automatically switch tactics, trying different exploitation methods or targeting different system components. Moreover, what makes these agents dangerous is their potential for scalability and persistence. An autonomous attack agent can simultaneously probe multiple targets, learning from each interaction to improve its effectiveness across all attacks. These systems can operate continuously, testing different attack vectors and adapting their strategies based on what proves successful. They can also share learned information with other autonomous agents, creating a distributed attack system that becomes more sophisticated over time.

The implementation of autonomous attack agents often involves complex AI systems that combine multiple capabilities. They might use NLP to craft convincing phishing messages, machine learning for vulnerability detection, and reinforcement learning to optimize attack strategies (Koenders, 2024). This combination of capabilities enables these agents to conduct sophisticated, multistage attacks that can be harder to detect and defend against than traditional automated attacks. Let's say an autonomous attack agent targeting an organization's network. The agent might begin by gathering information about the target through various sources, analyzing network responses to different types of probes, and identifying potential vulnerabilities. Based on this information, it could automatically generate and test different attack strategies, learning from each attempt and adjusting its approach accordingly. The agent might also adapt its behavior to avoid detection, changing its patterns when it detects security monitoring or shifting its focus to more vulnerable targets. Consequently, the implications for cybersecurity are significant. Organizations must now defend against attacks that can evolve and adapt in real time, potentially finding and exploiting vulnerabilities faster than human defenders can patch them. These autonomous agents can also operate at scale, potentially launching sophisticated attacks against multiple targets simultaneously while learning from each interaction to improve their effectiveness.

We can expect autonomous attack agents to become more sophisticated as AI technology advances. Future agents might incorporate more advanced decision-making capabilities, better ability to evade detection, and more sophisticated methods for sharing learned information between agents (Albrecht & Stone, 2018). This evolution could lead to increasingly complex and difficult-to-defend-against attack scenarios. This is especially true as these agents become better at mimicking legitimate network behavior and avoiding detection. The defense against autonomous attack agents requires a similarly sophisticated approach, likely incorporating AI-powered defense systems that can adapt and respond to evolving threats in real time. Organizations need to implement security measures that can detect and respond to unusual patterns of behavior, even when those patterns are constantly changing and evolving. This might include implementing AI-powered security tools that can identify and respond to potential autonomous attack agents before they can successfully exploit vulnerabilities.

Denial of Service (DoS) and DDoS attacks are common attacks, but also a thing of the future. Especially as AI becomes more sophisticated, this makes it easier for both attackers and defenders to take advantage of its capabilities. In the context of DoS and DDoS attacks, there is an evolution in how these traditional attack vectors can be enhanced and made more devastating. AI-powered DoS and DDoS attacks can be more sophisticated, adaptive, and harder to mitigate than their traditional counterparts, presenting new challenges for cybersecurity defenders (Gürfidan et al., 2022). Traditional DoS and DDoS attacks typically rely on overwhelming target systems with high volumes of traffic or exploiting specific vulnerabilities to exhaust system resources (Douligeris & Mitrokotsa, 2004). However, AI-enhanced versions of these attacks can be much more sophisticated in their approach. AI systems can analyze target behavior, identify vulnerabilities, and dynamically adjust attack patterns to maximize effectiveness while evading detection. For example, an AI-powered DDoS attack might learn from the target's response patterns, adjusting its traffic distribution and attack vectors in real time to bypass defense mechanisms (Utter, 2024). The involvement of generative AI adds another layer of sophistication to these attacks. Generative AI can create highly variable attack patterns that appear legitimate at first glance but are designed to consume system resources efficiently. These systems can generate traffic patterns that mimic normal user behavior, making it harder for defense systems to distinguish between legitimate traffic and attack traffic. They can also automatically generate new attack variants when existing patterns are detected and blocked, ensuring the attack remains effective even as defenses adapt.

The emergence of a severe vulnerability in ChatGPT's API highlights the evolving complexity of DDoS attacks in the age of generative AI. This flaw allowed attackers to send an unlimited number of connection requests via the API, overwhelming targeted websites with traffic (Johnson, 2025). It worked by exploiting the lack of a limit on URLs in HTTP POST requests; consequently, malicious actors could craft requests containing thousands of URLs, effectively using OpenAI's servers as an amplification mechanism. Though OpenAI has since addressed the vulnerability by disabling the problematic endpoint, the incident underscores how generative AI can inadvertently serve as a weapon in modern cyberattacks. This vulnerability was rated with a Common Vulnerability Scoring System (CVSS) score of 8.6, signifying its high risk due to its low complexity, lack of privilege requirements, and potential for large-scale disruption. The incident also raises questions about the accessibility and transparency of AI systems, as the security researcher who found this bug reported difficulty in alerting OpenAI and Microsoft until media attention spurred action.

Essentially, this vulnerability exemplifies how generative AI can amplify the sophistication and adaptability of DDoS attacks. Unlike traditional attacks that rely on brute force or static vulnerabilities, AI-enabled attacks dynamically evolve based on target defenses. Generative AI can mimic legitimate traffic patterns, making it harder to distinguish between benign and malicious activity. For example, an AI-powered DDoS attack could analyze traffic trends and adapt in real time, modifying attack vectors to evade detection. The implications for cybersecurity are profound, as organizations must now contend with adversaries who can leverage AI's generative capabilities to create novel attack patterns and sustain attacks even under adaptive defenses.

Consider how an AI-powered DDoS attack might operate: The system could start by analyzing the target's normal traffic patterns, understanding peak usage times, typical user behaviors, and common request types. It could then generate attack traffic that closely mirrors these patterns while subtly exploiting vulnerabilities or resource limitations. The AI system might distribute the attack traffic across multiple sources, adjusting the timing and nature of requests based on the target's responses and defensive measures. If certain attack patterns are blocked, the system could automatically generate new variants that achieve the same disruptive effect through different means. What makes these AI-enhanced attacks concerning is their ability to learn and adapt in real time (Shaik & Shaik, 2024). Traditional DDoS defense mechanisms often rely on identifying and blocking specific attack patterns or sources. However, when attacks can dynamically adjust their behavior based on the target's responses, these traditional defenses become less effective. The AI systems can learn which attack patterns are most successful, which are being blocked, and how to modify their approach to maintain effectiveness while avoiding detection. Thus, the implications for organizations are significant. Defending against AI-powered DoS and DDoS attacks requires more sophisticated and adaptive defense mechanisms. Organizations need to implement security measures that can identify and respond to evolving attack patterns in real time, potentially incorporating their own AI systems to detect and counter these advanced threats. This creates a new kind of arms race, where defensive AI systems must continuously evolve to keep pace with increasingly sophisticated attack capabilities.

We can't predict the future, but we can expect AI-powered DoS and DDoS attacks to become more common and more sophisticated. As AI technology becomes more accessible and powerful, attackers will likely develop new ways to leverage these capabilities for more effective attacks. This might include more sophisticated traffic generation patterns, better evasion techniques, and improved ability to identify and exploit system vulnerabilities. Organizations will need to stay ahead of these developments by implementing more advanced defense mechanisms and maintaining awareness of emerging attack techniques. The rise of AI-powered DoS and DDoS attacks underscores the importance of comprehensive security strategies that can adapt to evolving threats. Organizations need to implement multiple layers of defense, including traditional DDoS mitigation techniques alongside more advanced, AI-powered security measures. This might include implementing behavioral analysis systems that can identify subtle patterns indicative of AI-powered attacks, even when those patterns appear legitimate at first glance.

Supply chain attacks have come under renewed focus, especially after the SolarWinds Breach (Oladimeji & Kerner, 2023). However, these attacks have taken on new dimensions with the advent of AI weaponization, creating more sophisticated and harder-to-detect compromise vectors throughout the global supply chain ecosystem. The integration of AI into supply chain attacks represents a significant evolution in how attackers can identify, exploit, and maintain persistent access to multiple organizations through their supply chain relationships (BlackDuck, n.d.). AI systems can analyze complex supply chain networks, identifying potential weak points and relationships that could be exploited, while generating sophisticated attack strategies tailored to specific supply chain components. This capability allows attackers to develop more targeted and effective approaches to compromising supply chains, potentially affecting numerous organizations through a single successful attack.

The weaponization of AI in supply chain attacks manifests in several sophisticated ways that make these attacks particularly concerning for global cybersecurity. AI systems can analyze vast amounts of public and stolen data to identify critical suppliers, understand their relationships with target organizations, and determine the most vulnerable points in the supply chain (Security Intelligence, n.d.). These systems can then generate customized attack strategies that take advantage of specific vulnerabilities in supplier relationships, software dependencies, or distribution systems. For example, an AI system might analyze software dependencies across thousands of organizations, identifying commonly used components that could serve as attack vectors. The system could then generate malicious code designed to exploit these components while evading detection, potentially affecting all organizations that rely on the compromised software. The global implications of AI-powered supply chain attacks are concerning, given the interconnected nature of modern business operations. A successful attack on a single supplier could potentially compromise thousands of organizations worldwide, creating cascading effects throughout various industries and economies. Consider the potential impact of an AI-powered attack that compromises a widely used software library or development tool—the malicious code could be automatically generated to appear legitimate while containing subtle backdoors or vulnerabilities that affect all organizations using that component. The AI system could then automatically identify and exploit these backdoors across different organizations, potentially leading to widespread compromises before the initial attack is even detected.

In general, the future landscape of supply chain security faces significant challenges from AI-powered attacks. Organizations must now consider not just their direct suppliers but also the potential for AI systems to identify and exploit complex relationships throughout their entire supply chain ecosystem. This includes understanding how AI might be used to compromise software development processes, hardware manufacturing, service providers, and other critical components of their supply chain. The ability of AI systems to generate sophisticated, targeted attacks while maintaining stealth adds another layer of complexity to supply chain security, requiring organizations to implement more comprehensive and adaptive security measures. For individual organizations, defending against AI-powered supply chain attacks requires a fundamental shift in approach. Traditional supply chain security measures, while still important, may not be sufficient against attacks that can adapt and evolve based on defensive responses. Organizations need to implement more sophisticated monitoring and validation systems that can detect subtle indicators of compromise (IOC), even when those indicators are deliberately designed to appear legitimate. This might include implementing AI-powered security tools that can analyze supplier behavior patterns, software changes, and system interactions to identify potential supply chain compromises before they can spread throughout the organization (OPS Design, 2024). In general, as AI technology continues to advance, we can expect to see increasingly sophisticated supply chain attacks that leverage AI capabilities for better targeting, evasion, and persistence. Organizations will need to develop more comprehensive supply chain security strategies that consider not just traditional security measures but also the potential for AI-powered attacks to identify and exploit previously unknown vulnerabilities. This evolution in supply chain attacks underscores the importance of developing more robust and adaptive security measures while also considering broader implications for global supply chain resilience and security.

The Verizon Data Breach Investigations Report (DBIR) of 2024 highlighted how most cybercrimes are financially motivated, and in second place is espionage (Verizon Business, 2024). With AI-powered espionage, this changes intelligence gathering and surveillance capabilities, combining the power of AI with traditional espionage techniques to create more sophisticated and effective methods of information collection and analysis (Rawat et al., 2021). The weaponization of AI in espionage operations has transformed how intelligence can be gathered, processed, and exploited, enabling more targeted and efficient operations while reducing the risk of detection (Erendor, 2024). These systems can analyze vast amounts of data from multiple sources, identify patterns and relationships that might escape human analysts, and generate sophisticated strategies for gathering sensitive information (Christou, 2023). Moreover, the sophistication of AI-powered espionage becomes more evident in how these systems can analyze and exploit various data sources simultaneously. AI systems can process information from social media, public records, leaked databases, and other sources to build detailed profiles of target organizations and individuals (Samtani et al., 2021). These profiles can then be used to identify potential vulnerabilities, predict behavior patterns, and develop targeted collection strategies. For example, an AI system might analyze an organization's employee social media posts, public communications, and professional networks to identify potential insider threats or vulnerabilities that could be exploited for intelligence gathering. The system could then generate sophisticated social engineering campaigns or develop other collection strategies tailored to specific targets.

The implications in this scenario are important to understand, especially when considering how AI models can enhance traditional espionage techniques. AI systems can generate convincing phishing emails, create deepfake audio or video for social engineering, and develop sophisticated methods for maintaining persistent access to compromised systems. These capabilities become even more powerful when combined with AI's ability to analyze and adapt to target responses in real time. For instance, an AI-powered espionage operation might automatically adjust its tactics based on the success or failure of different approaches, learning from each interaction to improve its effectiveness while maintaining stealth. This adaptive capability makes detecting and defending against such operations increasingly challenging. Consequently, what makes AI-powered espionage particularly concerning is its potential for scale and persistence (Gabrian, 2024). Traditional espionage operations often required significant human resources and faced limitations in how much information could be processed and analyzed effectively. AI systems can operate continuously, processing vast amounts of data while maintaining consistent effectiveness. They can simultaneously monitor multiple targets, identify patterns across different operations, and adapt their strategies based on learned insights. This capability enables more comprehensive and sustained intelligence gathering operations that can evolve and improve over time.

As we continue to navigate our cyber landscape, the evolution of AI-powered espionage presents significant challenges for organizations and nations alike. As these systems become more sophisticated, they will likely incorporate advanced capabilities for autonomous operation, improved evasion techniques, and better ability to identify and exploit vulnerabilities in target systems. This could lead to a new era of digital espionage where AI systems can conduct complex intelligence gathering operations with minimal human intervention, potentially changing the nature of intelligence operations and cybersecurity defense. Organizations will need to develop more sophisticated counterintelligence capabilities, potentially including their own AI systems designed to detect and counter AI-powered espionage attempts (Qumer and Ikrama, 2022). The defense against AI-powered espionage requires a comprehensive approach that considers both technical and human factors. Organizations need to implement robust security measures that can detect and respond to sophisticated intelligence gathering attempts, even when those attempts are designed to appear legitimate. This might include implementing AI-powered security tools that can identify subtle patterns of reconnaissance or data exfiltration, while also maintaining strong security awareness training programs to help employees recognize and report potential espionage attempts. The challenge lies in balancing effective security measures with the need to maintain operational efficiency and legitimate information sharing.

4.6 Defensive Strategies Against Weaponized Generative AI

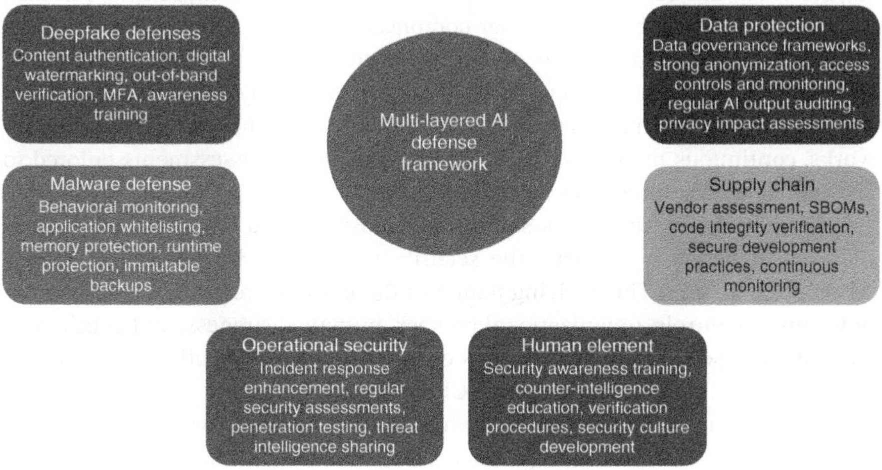

The US National Institute of Standards and Technology (NIST) has issued a warning about significant limitations in current security mitigations for AI and machine learning systems (Coker, 2025). According to the report published on March 25, 2025, these data-based systems face unique security vulnerabilities beyond those of traditional software, including adversarial manipulation of training data, malicious inputs designed to affect system performance, and attempts to extract sensitive training data (NIST, 2025). NIST emphasized that such attacks have been demonstrated in real-world conditions with increasing sophistication and impact. The institute identified several key challenges in securing AI models: a fundamental trade-off between system accuracy and security robustness; inherent difficulties in detecting attacks since adversarial examples may come from the same data distribution used for training; and a lack of reliable benchmarks for assessing mitigation effectiveness. The report provides standardized terminology for adversarial machine learning and a taxonomy of common attacks to inform future standards and practice guides. NIST recommends that organizations determine their risk tolerance levels for particular AI systems and consider practices beyond adversarial testing to manage associated risks.

This has significant implications for the security of generative AI systems, which rely heavily on complex machine learning models. As GAI technologies become increasingly integrated into critical applications across various sectors, the vulnerabilities highlighted by NIST represent serious security concerns that could be exploited at scale. The fundamental tension between accuracy and security robustness means organizations deploying generative AI may face difficult decisions about whether to prioritize performance or protection against adversarial manipulation. The challenge of detecting attacks is particularly worrisome for generative AI, as malicious inputs could potentially cause these systems to produce harmful, biased, or misleading outputs without obvious signs of compromise. The lack of standardized benchmarks further complicates security assessments for these systems, making it difficult for organizations to confidently evaluate their GAI defenses. Moving forward, securing generative AI will likely require a comprehensive approach that combines technical mitigations with robust governance frameworks, continuous monitoring, and context-specific risk assessments tailored to each application's unique threat profile.

Consequently, organizations should and must adopt a comprehensive, multilayered approach to mitigate the security risks posed by generative AI and AI-powered attacks. The evolving nature of these threats requires a combination of technical controls, organizational policies, human awareness, and continuous adaptation of security measures. Let's examine the key mitigation strategies for each major risk category identified in Chapter 4.

For defending against deepfakes and synthetic media, organizations need to implement a multifaceted approach that combines technical solutions with human awareness and verification procedures. At the technical level, organizations should deploy AI-powered detection systems that can identify potential synthetic media by analyzing subtle artifacts and inconsistencies that might not be visible to human observers (Bokolo & Liu, 2024). These systems should be continuously updated to keep pace with advancing generation techniques. Organizations should also implement digital watermarking and content authentication systems for their official communications, providing a way to verify the authenticity of legitimate content (Shaliyar & Mustafa, 2024). This becomes particularly important for sensitive communications or financial transactions where synthetic media could be used for fraud.

Beyond technical controls, organizations must establish robust verification procedures for high-stakes communications and transactions. This might include implementing out-of-band verification for significant financial transactions or sensitive instructions, requiring multiple authentication factors that go beyond visual or audio confirmation (Latvala, 2019). For example, if an executive appears to be requesting an urgent wire transfer via video call, the organization should have established procedures for confirming such requests through separate, secure channels. Training programs should be updated to help employees recognize the potential for synthetic media attacks and understand the importance of following verification procedures even when communications appear completely legitimate.

To combat AI-powered social engineering attacks, organizations need to implement more sophisticated detection and prevention measures. Traditional email filtering and phishing detection systems should be enhanced with AI capabilities that can identify subtle patterns and contextual anomalies that might indicate sophisticated social engineering attempts (Fakhouri et al., 2024). These systems should analyze multiple factors, including communication patterns, linguistic characteristics, and behavioral indicators, to identify potential threats (Chung & Pennebaker, 2011). Organizations should also implement strong authentication measures and access controls that can't be bypassed through social engineering, including multifactor authentication and zero trust architectures (ZTA).

Employee training becomes all the more crucial in defending against AI-powered social engineering. Training programs should be updated to reflect the sophistication of modern attacks, helping employees understand that traditional red flags might not be present in AI-generated content. This includes teaching employees to be skeptical of urgent requests, unexpected communications, or anything that bypasses normal procedures, regardless of how legitimate they appear. Moreover, this training should be engaging, interactive, and entertaining in order for it to be effective, support positive learning outcomes, and change user behaviors (Rana & Chicone, 2024). Organizations should also establish clear protocols for verifying sensitive requests or instructions, particularly those involving financial transactions or access to sensitive information.

Defending against automated hacking and exploit generation requires a more proactive and dynamic approach to security than what we've seen in past decades. Organizations need to implement continuous security testing and vulnerability management programs that can keep pace with AI-powered scanning and exploitation tools. This includes deploying their own AI-powered security tools that can automatically identify and assess vulnerabilities before they can be exploited by attackers (Guembe et al., 2022). Security teams should also implement robust patch management programs that can quickly address vulnerabilities across the organization's infrastructure.

Network segmentation and access control become increasingly important in defending against automated attacks (Wagner et al., 2016). Organizations should implement strong network segregation to limit the potential spread of compromises, along with detailed logging and monitoring to detect and track potential attack attempts. ZTA become increasingly important in todays AI-driven threat landscape, and this strategy encompasses network segmentation to prevent lateral movement, dynamic access controls, and generally more insight into an organization's information architecture. This is crucial to contain the blast radius that we can expect to see with AI-powered attacks. Additionally, AI-powered security information and event management (SIEM) systems can help organizations identify and respond to potential attacks in real time, correlating events across multiple systems to identify sophisticated attack patterns (Ali et al., 2024). To address privacy concerns related to generative AI, organizations need to implement comprehensive data governance frameworks that account for both traditional privacy requirements and the unique challenges posed by AI systems. This includes careful control over what data is used to train AI systems, implementing strong data anonymization techniques, and regular auditing of AI outputs to ensure they don't inadvertently expose sensitive information (Gabriel, 2023). However, we will discuss this in more detail in Chapters 5 and 6. Organizations should also implement robust access controls and monitoring for AI systems to prevent unauthorized use or data exposure.

In terms of defending against AI-generated malware, this also requires a multilayered approach that combines traditional antimalware measures with advanced AI-powered detection systems. Organizations should implement behavioral analysis systems that can identify malicious activity patterns regardless of the specific code signatures involved (Jackson, 2012). This includes monitoring system behaviors, network communications, and file system activities to detect potential malware infections. Security teams should also implement strong application control and whitelisting policies to prevent unauthorized code execution. Runtime application self-protection (RASP) technologies offer additional defense layers by monitoring application behavior during execution and protecting against exploitation attempts even when other controls fail (Čisar & Čisar, 2016). Organizations should also consider implementing memory protection mechanisms and process isolation technologies to contain potential infections and prevent privilege escalation attacks commonly used in sophisticated malware campaigns.

For ransomware protection specifically, organizations need to implement comprehensive backup and recovery systems that can quickly restore operations in case of an attack. This includes maintaining offline backups that can't be compromised by ransomware, regularly testing recovery procedures, and implementing strong access controls to prevent unauthorized encryption of critical systems. Organizations should also implement network segmentation and least privilege access policies to limit the potential spread of ransomware infections. Immutable storage technologies provide additional protection by creating write-once-read-many versions of critical data that cannot be altered or encrypted even with administrative credentials (Caporaso et al., 2024). Regular ransomware tabletop exercises help organizations test their response capabilities and identify potential gaps in their defensive measures before an actual incident occurs.

To defend against autonomous attack agents, organizations need to implement adaptive security measures that can identify and respond to evolving attack patterns. Adaptive cybersecurity is crucial in our digital age against evolving threat vectors; thus, the need for next-generation defense strategies (Kommera, 2024). This includes deploying AI-powered security tools that can detect unusual patterns of behavior and automatically implement countermeasures. It is crucial to implement strong access controls and network segmentation to limit the potential movement of autonomous agents within their networks. Deception technology deployments create sophisticated honeypots and decoys that can trap autonomous agents while simultaneously alerting security teams and providing valuable intelligence about attack techniques (Mohan et al., 2022). Temporal isolation of critical systems during high-risk periods offers another layer of protection against persistent autonomous threats that might otherwise maintain continuous attack operations (Sladkova et al., 2024).

In terms of protecting against AI-powered DDoS attacks, organizations need to implement more sophisticated traffic analysis and filtering capabilities. This includes deploying AI-powered traffic analysis systems that can identify and block malicious traffic patterns while allowing legitimate traffic to continue (Vo et al., 2023). Organizations should also maintain relationships with DDoS mitigation service providers who can provide additional capacity and filtering capabilities during attacks. Edge computing architectures with DDoS protection capabilities can filter malicious traffic closer to its source before it overwhelms central infrastructure (Bonguet & Bellaiche, 2017). Content delivery networks

(CDNs) with advanced rate limiting and traffic scrubbing capabilities provide critical infrastructure for absorbing and filtering large-scale attack traffic while maintaining service availability for legitimate users (Pathan et al., 2008).

Supply chain security requires a comprehensive approach that includes careful vendor assessment, continuous monitoring, and strong verification procedures for software and updates. Organizations should implement automated tools for analyzing code and updates for potential malicious content, while maintaining strict control over their software development and deployment processes (Rajapakse et al., 2022). This includes implementing secure software development practices and maintaining detailed audit trails of all changes to critical systems. Software Bill of Materials (SBOM) implementation provides transparent visibility into component dependencies and helps identify potentially vulnerable elements in the supply chain (Sarwar, 2024). Cryptographic verification of software integrity through code signing and secure hash validation creates additional layers of protection against tampering and unauthorized modifications throughout the development and distribution pipeline (Pradeep et al., 2023).

Defending against AI-powered espionage, organizations need to implement comprehensive counterintelligence measures that include both technical controls and operational security procedures (Kanellopoulos, 2022). This includes implementing strong data loss prevention systems, detailed activity monitoring, and regular security assessments to identify potential vulnerabilities (Aslan et al., 2023). Maintaining strong control over information sharing and implementing need-to-know access policies to limit potential data exposure is another important defense. Air-gapped environments for particularly sensitive operations provide physical isolation from potentially compromised networks and significantly increase the difficulty of data exfiltration (Na & Sundharakumar, 2024). Regular counterintelligence training for employees helps develop organizational awareness of sophisticated social engineering techniques used in modern espionage operations and creates a human firewall against reconnaissance and intelligence gathering activities (Watters, 2023).

In order to future-proof defenses, organizations need to maintain flexibility in their security measures to adapt to evolving AI-powered threats (Reddy, 2022). This includes regularly updating security tools and procedures based on new threat intelligence, maintaining strong incident response capabilities, and fostering a security-aware culture throughout the organization. Security teams should also stay informed about advancing AI capabilities and emerging attack techniques to ensure their defensive measures remain effective. The human element remains crucial in defending against AI-powered threats. Organizations should maintain comprehensive security awareness programs that help employees understand and recognize potential threats while following proper security procedures. This includes regular training updates (as mentioned above) to address new threat types and attack techniques, along with clear procedures for reporting potential security incidents.

Documentation and audit trails become increasingly important when defending against AI-powered threats (George, 2024). Organizations should maintain detailed logs of system activities, security events, and response actions to support both incident investigation and ongoing security improvement. This includes implementing robust logging systems that can capture relevant details about potential security events while maintaining the integrity of this information for future analysis (Tayyab et al., 2025). Moreover, AI can be used to analyze these detailed logs and audit trails to look for IOC, predictions on future vulnerabilities, and deeper insight into their information infrastructure. Technical controls should be supplemented with strong governance frameworks that ensure appropriate oversight of security measures and incident response procedures. This includes maintaining clear policies and procedures for security operations, regular testing and validation of security measures, and appropriate escalation procedures for security incidents. Organizations should also maintain appropriate security metrics and reporting to track the effectiveness of their defensive measures. Collaboration and information sharing become increasingly important in defending against AI-powered threats (Waizel, 2024). Organizations should participate in relevant information-sharing communities and maintain relationships with security vendors and researchers who can provide early warning of emerging threats. This includes sharing threat intelligence about new attack techniques and coordinating responses to significant security incidents. Regular security assessments and penetration testing become crucial in validating the effectiveness of security measures against AI-powered threats. Organizations should conduct regular security testing that includes scenarios involving sophisticated AI-powered attacks, using the results to improve their defensive measures. This includes both technical testing of security controls and operational exercises to validate response procedures.

Investment in security tools and capabilities needs to be maintained and increased to keep pace with advancing threats. You cannot implement defenses, clap your hands, and walk away. These security infrastructures can become outdated quickly—thus, the importance of dynamic cybersecurity strategies, controls, and implementations. Organizations should maintain appropriate funding for security operations, including investments in AI-powered security tools and staff training. This includes maintaining adequate security staff and ensuring they have the tools and training needed to defend against sophisticated attacks. Additionally, incident response capabilities need to be enhanced to address the unique challenges posed by AI-powered attacks (Hassan & Ibrahim, 2023). Cybersecurity is a shared responsibility, and this is increasingly true with the use of AI as a weapon. This includes maintaining detailed response procedures for different types of attacks, regular testing of response capabilities, and appropriate tools and resources for investigating and containing security incidents. Organizations should also maintain relationships with incident response service providers who can provide additional support during significant security events.

In summary, a high-level theme for defending against AI-powered security threats requires a comprehensive and adaptable approach that combines technical controls, operational procedures, and human awareness. Organizations need to maintain strong security fundamentals while adapting their defensive measures to address new threats and attack techniques. This includes regular assessment and updating of security measures, maintaining appropriate security staffing and resources, and fostering a strong security culture throughout the organization. We will go into more detail in Chapter 5 regarding the risks and vulnerabilities of generative AI. One of the key aspects of this book is that we examine generative AI from a triangle view—how generative AI can be used for cybersecurity professionals, how it can harm the cybersecurity posture of people and organizations alike, and what are the risks to generative AI that can, in turn, affect us. Hence, let's continue on to the third part of the triangle: risks and vulnerabilities of AI, making it a target for malicious actors.

Chapter 4 Summary

This chapter examined the dark side of generative AI, exploring how these powerful technologies could be weaponized for malicious purposes across the cybersecurity landscape. It analyzed four primary threat categories that demonstrated AI's potential for harm. First, deepfakes and synthetic media enabled the creation of increasingly convincing fraudulent content, from photorealistic images and videos to sophisticated voice cloning that could fool both human observers and traditional detection systems. Second, AI-powered social engineering revolutionized phishing campaigns through highly personalized, contextually relevant attacks that could adapt in real time and operate at unprecedented scale. Third, automated hacking capabilities emerged that could discover and exploit vulnerabilities with unprecedented speed, including AI-generated malware variants and autonomous attack agents capable of operating independently. Fourth, privacy concerns materialized through data leakage, reidentification risks, and the rise of shadow AI usage within organizations.

The chapter provided concrete examples of these theoretical threats materializing in practice, including real-world cases like the $25 million deepfake fraud in Hong Kong and the emergence of malicious platforms like GhostGPT that democratized access to AI-powered cyber weapons. It documented how state-sponsored threat actors from over 20 countries actively used commercial AI tools to enhance their operations, while statistics revealed dramatic increases in AI-enhanced phishing attacks. The weaponization extended to sophisticated attack vectors, including AI-generated ransomware, supply chain attacks, and enhanced DDoS campaigns. The chapter concluded with comprehensive defensive strategies that organizations must implement to counter these evolving threats, emphasizing the need for multilayered approaches combining technical controls, human awareness training, and continuous adaptation to stay ahead of rapidly evolving AI-powered attack capabilities.

The weaponization of generative AI fundamentally lowered barriers to entry for sophisticated cyberattacks while simultaneously increasing their scale and effectiveness. Tools like GhostGPT demonstrated how AI capabilities previously limited to well-resourced attackers became accessible to anyone with modest technical skills and financial resources. The chapter showed how AI could automate and enhance every stage of the attack lifecycle, from reconnaissance and vulnerability discovery to payload generation and evasion techniques. This democratization effect was evident in the dramatic statistics, including a 1,265% increase in malicious phishing emails and a 140% rise in browser-based attacks, coinciding with the proliferation of generative AI tools. The erosion of traditional security indicators, such as poor grammar in phishing emails, meant that defenders could no longer rely on historical patterns to identify threats.

The chapter revealed that defending against weaponized AI required a fundamental shift from reactive to proactive security strategies that could match the adaptability and sophistication of AI-powered threats. Traditional security measures proved increasingly inadequate against attacks that could evolve in real time, generate novel variants automatically, and operate at machine speed. The comprehensive defensive strategies outlined emphasized the critical importance of implementing AI-powered security tools, robust verification procedures, and enhanced human awareness training that acknowledged the new reality where "seeing and hearing" could no longer be trusted. The ongoing arms race between offensive and defensive AI systems demanded continuous adaptation, significant investment in security capabilities, and a recognition that the threat landscape had permanently changed with AI's weaponization transforming cybersecurity from a manageable challenge into an existential imperative for organizational survival.

Case Study 1: Weaponized AI in a Small-Sized Organization

Background and Context

A small, family-owned accounting firm in a midwestern town employed 15 staff members and specialized in tax preparation and bookkeeping for local businesses. The firm heavily relied on email communication, online file sharing, and cloud-based accounting software to manage sensitive client data. With no dedicated IT staff, the firm outsourced its IT needs, including cybersecurity, to a managed services provider (MSP). The firm's perception of being "too small" to be a target for advanced cyberattacks left it vulnerable.

Technical Threat

The attackers launched an AI-powered phishing campaign, leveraging generative AI models to create a highly convincing email mimicking the firm's cloud accounting software provider. The email included:

- **Custom Social Engineering:** The attackers used AI to scrape publicly available data from the firm's website and LinkedIn profiles to create a tailored email message.
- **Phishing Website Replication:** Using generative AI, the attackers created a replica of the legitimate login page to harvest credentials.

When the firm's owner, Sarah, entered her credentials, the attackers gained access to the cloud accounting system. The stolen credentials enabled them to deploy AI-generated ransomware:

1) **Dynamic Payload Generation:** The ransomware, created using AI, adapted its obfuscation techniques in real time to bypass traditional antivirus tools.
2) **Selective Encryption:** AI optimized the ransomware to target critical databases while avoiding less valuable files, ensuring maximum operational disruption.
3) **Automated Ransom Note Generation:** The ransomware displayed a customized ransom note demanding $15,000 in cryptocurrency, threatening to delete all client data within 72 hours.

Impact

The ransomware disrupted the firm's operations by encrypting all critical client files, halting tax filings and bookkeeping tasks. The attack exposed significant vulnerabilities:

- **No Data Backups:** The MSP had not implemented proper backup solutions, leaving the firm unable to restore its data.
- **Operational Downtime:** Employees were locked out of systems, causing delays and eroding client trust.
- **Financial and Reputational Damage:** Clients voiced concerns about data confidentiality, and the firm's reputation was significantly impacted.

Response and Mitigation Steps

Instead of paying the ransom, Sarah engaged a cybersecurity consultant to investigate and secure the systems. The investigation revealed that AI-powered techniques were used to identify vulnerabilities, craft the phishing email, and deploy the ransomware. Key mitigation steps included:

1) **Multifactor Authentication (MFA):** The firm implemented MFA on all cloud-based accounts to prevent unauthorized access.
2) **AI-Powered Email Filtering:** Advanced AI-driven email security tools were deployed to detect phishing attempts by analyzing language patterns, sender reputations, and URLs in real time.
3) **Automated Offline Backups:** The firm set up secure, offline data backups with daily automated updates, ensuring rapid recovery in the future.
4) **Employee Training:** Employees participated in regular phishing awareness and cybersecurity best practices training, focusing on AI-driven threats.

Conclusion

This case highlights how AI can weaponize sophisticated phishing and ransomware attacks, targeting even small businesses with limited resources. The incident emphasizes the importance of deploying AI-driven defensive measures to detect and mitigate such attacks proactively.

Case Study 2: Weaponized AI in a Large Organization

Background and Context

A multinational financial institution with over 10,000 employees and operations across 20 countries faced a highly coordinated AI-powered cyberattack. The institution managed billions of dollars in assets and relied on a robust security operations center (SOC) to protect its complex IT infrastructure. Despite extensive resources, the attack revealed vulnerabilities in its defenses against AI-driven threats.

Technical Threat

The attack was a multifaceted campaign leveraging generative AI and autonomous agents:

1) **Spear-Phishing with Deepfake Technology:**
   - **Data Harvesting:** AI analyzed publicly available social media profiles, press releases, and leaked internal communication patterns to craft targeted phishing emails.
   - **Deepfake Video Integration:** A synthetic video of the CEO, generated using AI, was included in an email to the head of finance. The video convincingly urged the recipient to authorize a $50 million wire transfer for a "confidential acquisition." The attackers used real-time lip-sync and voice cloning to enhance believability.

2) **Network Infiltration by AI Agents:**
   - o **Autonomous Reconnaissance:** AI-powered agents infiltrated the segmented network, probing for vulnerabilities and identifying misconfigured endpoints.
   - o **Dynamic Lateral Movement:** The agents leveraged machine learning algorithms to bypass security controls, adapt to detection mechanisms, and escalate privileges.
   - o **Data Exfiltration:** Sensitive datasets, including proprietary algorithms and client portfolios, were exfiltrated to external servers.
3) **AI-Driven Ransomware Deployment:**
   - o **Multistage Attack:** The ransomware encrypted critical systems, including trading platforms and transaction databases.
   - o **Data Extortion:** The attackers threatened to release sensitive information on the dark web unless a $10 million cryptocurrency ransom was paid.

Impact

The attack caused severe operational disruptions and financial losses:

- **System Downtime:** Trading systems and financial operations were halted, affecting client services and revenue.
- **Reputational Damage:** The breach led to negative media coverage and regulatory scrutiny, causing a drop in the institution's stock value.
- **Proprietary Data Exposure:** The exfiltration of client records and financial algorithms posed long-term risks to the organization's competitive advantage.

The SOC struggled to contain the attack due to the adaptive capabilities of the autonomous agents, which dynamically altered tactics to evade detection.

Response and Mitigation Steps

The incident response team collaborated with leading cybersecurity firms to contain the breach. The following measures were implemented to address vulnerabilities and prevent future attacks:

1) **AI-Powered Threat Detection Systems:**
   - o Advanced machine learning models were integrated into the SOC to analyze network traffic and detect anomalies, including lateral movement and unauthorized data access.
   - o Behavioral analytics tools were deployed to identify deviations from normal user and system behavior.
2) **Zero Trust Architecture (ZTA):**
   - o Enhanced dynamic access controls ensured that user and device identities were continuously verified.
   - o Microsegmentation was implemented to isolate sensitive data and restrict lateral movement.

3) **Deepfake Detection Tools:**
   - AI-based solutions for detecting synthetic media were deployed, focusing on identifying inconsistencies in facial features, lighting, and audio synchronization.
4) **Red Team Exercises:**
   - Frequent penetration testing simulated AI-driven attacks, allowing the institution to identify and patch vulnerabilities proactively.
5) **Client Assurance and Transparency:**
   - Fraud monitoring services were provided to affected clients, and transparent communication with stakeholders restored some confidence in the organization's resilience.

Conclusion

This case illustrates the unprecedented sophistication of AI-powered cyberattacks against large organizations. By leveraging AI for both offense and defense, attackers and defenders are engaged in a technological arms race. The financial institution's experience underscores the importance of adopting proactive measures like AI-powered detection, ZTA, and deepfake countermeasures to mitigate advanced threats and enhance long-term resilience.

Weaponized AI Cybersecurity Quiz

Questions

1. In Case Study 1, what vulnerability made the small accounting firm particularly susceptible to the AI-powered attack?
   a) Lack of multifactor authentication
   b) Perception of being "too small" to be a target
   c) Using outdated antivirus software
   d) Having no data encryption protocols

2. What technology did attackers use in Case Study 2 to impersonate the CEO?
   a) Voice modulation software
   b) Prerecorded video clips
   c) Deepfake technology
   d) Photoshopped images

3. Which mitigation strategy was implemented in BOTH case studies?
   a) Zero Trust Architecture
   b) AI-powered detection systems
   c) Red Team Exercises
   d) Offline data backups

4 In Case Study 1, how did the attackers optimize their ransomware?
   a) By targeting all files indiscriminately
   b) By selectively encrypting critical databases
   c) By destroying backup systems first
   d) By hiding dormant malware throughout the network

5 What was a key difference in how the two organizations responded to their respective attacks?
   a) The small firm paid the ransom while the large organization did not
   b) The small firm focused on employee training while the large organization focused only on technical solutions
   c) The small firm implemented offline backups while the large organization relied on cloud backups
   d) The small firm engaged external consultants while the large organization used its internal SOC team

Answer Key

1 **Correct Answer: b) Perception of being "too small" to be a target**
   - **Explanation:** The case study explicitly states that "The firm's perception of being 'too small' to be a target for advanced cyberattacks left it vulnerable." This mindset led to inadequate security measures and made them an easy target despite outsourcing IT security.
   - While the firm did lack MFA (option a), this was a security measure implemented after the attack, not specifically mentioned as the primary vulnerability beforehand.
   - Options c and d were not mentioned in the case study.

2 **Correct Answer: c) Deepfake technology**
   - **Explanation:** The case study clearly states that attackers used "Deepfake Video Integration," where "A synthetic video of the CEO, generated using AI, was included in an email to the head of finance." They used real-time lip-sync and voice cloning to make it convincing.
   - The other options are related technologies but not what was specifically described in the attack.

3 **Correct Answer: b) AI-powered detection systems**
   - **Explanation:** Both organizations implemented AI-based detection systems after the attacks. The small firm deployed "AI-Powered Email Filtering," while the large organization implemented "AI-Powered Threat Detection Systems" including machine learning models and behavioral analytics.

- o Zero Trust Architecture (option a) was only implemented by the large organization.
- o Red Team Exercises (option c) were only mentioned for the large organization.
- o Offline backups (option d) were only mentioned for the small firm.

4 **Correct Answer: b) By selectively encrypting critical databases**
- o **Explanation:** The case study states that the ransomware used "Selective Encryption," where "AI optimized the ransomware to target critical databases while avoiding less valuable files, ensuring maximum operational disruption."
- o This is more sophisticated than indiscriminate encryption (option a).
- o The other options (c and d) were not mentioned in the case study.

5 **Correct Answer: d) The small firm engaged external consultants, while the large organization used its internal SOC team**
- o **Explanation:** The small firm "engaged a cybersecurity consultant to investigate and secure the systems" since they had no dedicated IT staff. The large organization already had "a robust security operations center (SOC)" and their "incident response team collaborated with leading cybersecurity firms."
- o Option a is incorrect because neither organization is stated to have paid the ransom.
- o Option b is incorrect because both organizations implemented employee training/awareness measures.
- o Option c is incorrect because only the small firm is mentioned as implementing offline backups.

References

752,000 Browser Phishing Attacks Mark 140% Increase YoY. (2025, March 19). Infosecurity Magazine.

AI's New Frontier in War Planning: How AI Agents Can Revolutionizing Military Decision Making. (2024, October 11). Belfer center. https://www.belfercenter.org/research-analysis/ais-new-frontier-war-planning-how-ai-agents-can-revolutionize-military-decision.

Albrecht, S. V., & Stone, P. (2018). Autonomous agents modelling other agents: A comprehensive survey and open problems. *Artificial Intelligence*, *258*, 66–95.

Ali, M. L., Thakur, K., Barker, H., & Chan, M. (2024, October). The rise of artificial intelligence: Industry insights and applications in security information and event management (SIEM). In *2024 IEEE 15th Annual Ubiquitous Computing, Electronics & Mobile Communication Conference (UEMCON)* (pp. 0477–0482). IEEE.

Alshomrani, M., Albeshri, A., Alturki, B., Alallah, F. S., & Alsulami, A. A. (2024). Survey of transformer-based malicious software detection systems. *Electronics, 13*(23), 4677.

Ansarullah, S. I., Wali, A. W., Rasheed, I., & Rayees, P. Z. (2024). AI-powered strategies for advanced malware detection and prevention. In Y. Baddi, M. A. Almaiah, O. Almomani, & Y. Maleh (Eds.), *The art of cyber defense* (pp. 3–24). CRC Press.

Aryal, K., Gupta, M., Abdelsalam, M., Kunwar, P., & Thuraisingham, B. (2024). A survey on adversarial attacks for malware analysis. *IEEE Access, 13*, 428–459.

Aslan, Ö., Aktuğ, S. S., Ozkan-Okay, M., Yilmaz, A. A., & Akin, E. (2023). A comprehensive review of cyber security vulnerabilities, threats, attacks, and solutions. *Electronics, 12*(6), 1333.

Azzarelli, A., Anantrasirichai, N., & Bull, D. R. (2024). Reviewing intelligent cinematography: AI research for camera-based video production. arXiv preprint arXiv:2405.05039.

Bansal, G., Nawal, A., Chamola, V., & Herencsar, N. (2024). Revolutionizing visuals: The role of generative AI in modern image generation. *ACM Transactions on Multimedia Computing, Communications and Applications, 20*(11), 1–22.

Basit, A., Zafar, M., Liu, X., Javed, A. R., Jalil, Z., & Kifayat, K. (2021). A comprehensive survey of AI-enabled phishing attacks detection techniques. *Telecommunication Systems, 76*, 139–154.

Bhardwaj, V., Khan, S. S., Singh, G., Patil, S., Kuril, D., & Nahar, S. (2024). Risks for conversational AI security. *Conversational Artificial Intelligence*, 557–587.

BlackDuck. (n.d.). The state of software supply chain security risks. https://www.blackduck.com/resources/analyst-reports/software-supply-chain-security.html?utm_source=google&utm_medium=cpc&utm_term=software_supply_chain_attacks.

Bokolo, B. G., & Liu, Q. (2024). Artificial intelligence in social media forensics: A comprehensive survey and analysis. *Electronics, 13*(9), 1671.

Bolton, T., Dargahi, T., Belguith, S., Al-Rakhami, M. S., & Sodhro, A. H. (2021). On the security and privacy challenges of virtual assistants. *Sensors, 21*(7), 2312.

Bonguet, A., & Bellaiche, M. (2017). A survey of denial-of-service and distributed denial of service attacks and defenses in cloud computing. *Future Internet, 9*(3), 43.

Bordoni, L., Conti, M., & Spolaor, R. (2017). Mirage: Toward a stealthier and modular malware analysis sandbox for android. In *Computer Security–ESORICS 2017: 22nd European Symposium on Research in Computer Security*, Oslo, Norway, September 11–15, Proceedings, Part I 22 (pp. 278–296). Springer International Publishing.

Caporaso, P., Bianchi, G., & Quaglia, F. (2024). VaultFS: Write-once software support at the file system level against ransomware attacks. arXiv preprint arXiv:2410.21979.

Catalano, C., Chezzi, A., Angelelli, M., & Tommasi, F. (2022). Deceiving AI-based malware detection through polymorphic attacks. *Computers in Industry, 143,* 103751.

Chaki, J. (2021). Pattern analysis based acoustic signal processing: A survey of the state-of-art. *International Journal of Speech Technology, 24*(4), 913–955.

Chen, H & Magramo, K. (2024, February 4). Finance worker pays out $25 million after video call with Deepfake "Chief Financial Officer." *CNN.* https://www.cnn.com/2024/02/04/asia/deepfake-cfo-scam-hong-kong-intl-hnk.

Chen, J., Wang, X., Xu, R., Yuan, S., Zhang, Y., Shi, W., Xie, J., Li, S., Yang, R., Zhu, T., & Chen, A., 2024. From persona to personalization: A survey on role-playing language agents. arXiv preprint arXiv:2404.18231.

Christou, P. A. (2023). How to use artificial intelligence (AI) as a resource, methodological and analysis tool in qualitative research? *The Qualitative Report, 28*(7), 1968–1980.

Chung, C. K., & Pennebaker, J. W. (2011). Using computerized text analysis to assess threatening communications and behavior. In C. Chauvin (Ed.), *Threatening communications and behavior: Perspectives on the pursuit of public figures* (pp. 3–32). National Academies Press.

Čisar, P., & Čisar, S. M. (2016, November). The framework of runtime application self-protection technology. In *2016 IEEE 17th International Symposium on Computational Intelligence and Informatics (CINTI)* (pp. 000081–000086). IEEE.

Coker, J. (2025, March 25) NIST warns of significant limitations in AI/ML security mitigations. *Infosecurity Magazine.* https://www.infosecurity-magazine.com/news/nist-limitations-ai-ml-security/.

Costa, A. F., & Coelho, N. M. (2024, June). Evolving cybersecurity challenges in the age of AI-powered chatbots: A comprehensive review. In M. Duguleana & G. Mogan (Eds.), *Doctoral conference on computing, electrical and industrial systems* (pp. 217–228). Springer Nature Switzerland.

Deshpande, A. S., & Gupta, S. (2023, December). GenAI in the cyber kill chain: A comprehensive review of risks, threat operative strategies and adaptive defense approaches. In *2023 IEEE International Conference on ICT in Business Industry & Government (ICTBIG)* (pp. 1–5). IEEE.

Douligeris, C., & Mitrokotsa, A. (2004). DDoS attacks and defense mechanisms: Classification and state-of-the-art. *Computer networks, 44*(5), 643–666.

Erendor, M. E. (Ed.). (2024). *Cyber security in the age of artificial intelligence and autonomous weapons.* CRC Press.

Fakhouri, H. N., Alhadidi, B., Omar, K., Makhadmeh, S. N., Hamad, F., & Halalsheh, N. Z. (2024, February). AI-driven solutions for social engineering attacks:

Detection, prevention, and response. In *2024 2nd International Conference on Cyber Resilience (ICCR)* (pp. 1–8). IEEE.

Gabrian, C. A. (2024). Unveiling the dark side: How hackers exploit artificial intelligence for cyber warfare. *Euro-Atlantic Resilience Journal*, *2*(3), 1–18.

Gabriel, O. T. (2023). *Data privacy and ethical issues in collecting health care data using artificial intelligence among health workers* [Master's thesis]. Center for Bioethics and Research.

Genelza, G. G. (2024). A systematic literature review on AI voice cloning generator: A game-changer or a threat? *Journal of Emerging Technologies*, *4*(2), 54–61.

George, A. S. (2024). Riding the AI waves: An analysis of artificial intelligence's evolving role in combating cyber threats. *Partners Universal International Innovation Journal*, *2*(1), 39–50.

Gregory, J. (2024, June 10). Should there be a total ban on ransomware payments? *Security Intelligence*. https://securityintelligence.com/news/federal-ban-ransom-payments/.

Guembe, B., Azeta, A., Misra, S., Osamor, V. C., Fernandez-Sanz, L., & Pospelova, V. (2022). The emerging threat of AI-driven cyber attacks: A review. *Applied Artificial Intelligence*, *36*(1), 2037254.

Gürfidan, R., Ersoy, M., & Kilim, O. (2022, May). AI-powered cyber attacks threats and measures. In *The International Conference on Artificial Intelligence and Applied Mathematics in Engineering* (pp. 434–444). Springer International Publishing.

Hariri, W. (2023). Unlocking the potential of ChatGPT: A comprehensive exploration of its applications, advantages, limitations, and future directions in natural language processing. arXiv preprint arXiv:2304.02017.

Hassan, S. K., & Ibrahim, A. (2023). The role of artificial intelligence in cyber security and incident response. *International Journal for Electronic Crime Investigation*, *7*(2), 49–72.

Iturbe, E., Llorente-Vazquez, O., Rego, A., Rios, E., & Toledo, N. (2024). Unleashing offensive artificial intelligence: Automated attack technique code generation. *Computers & Security*, *147*, 104077.

Jackson, G. M. (2012). *Predicting malicious behavior: Tools and techniques for ensuring global security*. John Wiley & Sons.

Johnson, D. (2025, January 22). 'Severe' bug in ChatGPT's API could be used to DDoS websites. *Cyberscoop*. https://cyberscoop.com/ddos-openai-chatgpt-api-vulnerability-microsoft/.

Kanellopoulos, A. N. (2022). The importance of counterintelligence culture in state security. *Global Security and Intelligence Note*, *1*(5), 1–17.

Kaur, R., Gabrijelčič, D., & Klobučar, T. (2023). Artificial intelligence for cybersecurity: Literature review and future research directions. *Information Fusion*, *97*, 101804.

Khurana, D., Koli, A., Khatter, K., & Singh, S. (2023). Natural language processing: State of the art, current trends and challenges. *Multimedia Tools and Applications, 82*(3), 3713–3744.

Kinyua, J., & Awuah, L. (2021). AI/ML in security orchestration, automation and response: Future research directions. *Intelligent Automation & Soft Computing, 28*(2), 527–545.

Koenders, J. (2024). *Advancing cyberdefense through BERT: A natural language processing approach for vulnerability to attack mapping within a responsible artificial intelligence framework* [Master's thesis]. Erasmus University Rotterdam.

Kommera, H. K. R. (2024). Adaptive cybersecurity in the digital age: Emerging threat vectors and next-generation defense strategies. *International Journal for Research in Applied Science and Engineering Technology, 12*(9), 558–564.

Kong, X., Wang, G., & Nichol, A. (2021). *Conversational AI with Rasa: Build, test, and deploy AI-powered, enterprise-grade virtual assistants and chatbots.* Packt Publishing Ltd.

Lakshmanan, R. (2025, February 7). DeepSeek app transmits sensitive user data and device without encryption. *The Hacker News.* https://thehackernews.com/2025/02/deepseek-app-transmits-sensitive-user.html.

Latif, S., Shoukat, M., Shamshad, F., Usama, M., Ren, Y., Cuayáhuitl, H., Wang, W., Zhang, X., Togneri, R., Cambria, E., & Schuller, B.W. (2023). Sparks of large audio models: A survey and outlook. arXiv preprint arXiv:2308.12792.

Latvala, S. (2019). *Evaluation of out-of-band authentication channels* [Master's thesis]. Aalto University.

Lee, K. F., & Qiufan, C. (2021). *AI 2041: Ten visions for our future.* Crown Currency.

Liu, S., & Manocha, D. (2022). *Sound synthesis, propagation, and rendering.* Morgan & Claypool Publishers.

Lüchinger, J. (2023). *AI-powered ransomware to optimize its impact on IoT spectrum sensors* [Master's thesis]. University of Zurich.

Lysenko, S., Bobro, N., Korsunova, K., Vasylchyshyn, O., & Tatarchenko, Y. (2024). The role of artificial intelligence in cybersecurity: Automation of protection and detection of threats. *Economic Affairs, 69*, 43–51.

Martinez, D., & Herrera, S. (2023). Examining the ethical and legal challenges of anonymized data sharing in the era of big data analytics. *Journal of Sustainable Technologies and Infrastructure Planning, 7*(5), 59–77.

Mascellino, A. (2025, April 2). Gray bots surge as generative AI scraper activity increases. *Infosecurity Magazine.* https://www.infosecurity-magazine.com/news/gray-bots-generative-ai-scraper/.

Metta, S., Chang, I., Parker, J., Roman, M. P., & Ehuan, A. F. (2024). Generative AI in cybersecurity. arXiv preprint arXiv:2405.01674.

Mohan, P. V., Dixit, S., Gyaneshwar, A., Chadha, U., Srinivasan, K., & Seo, J. T. (2022). Leveraging computational intelligence techniques for defensive deception:

A review, recent advances, open problems and future directions. *Sensors, 22*(6), 2194.

Montalbano, E. (2025a, February 11). DeepSeek AI fails multiple security tests, raising red flag for businesses. *Dark Reading*. https://www.darkreading.com/cyber-risk/deepseek-fails-multiple-security-tests-business-use.

Montalbano, E. (2025b, April 7). Autonomous, GenAI-driven attacker platform enters the chat. *Dark Reading*. https://www.darkreading.com/threat-intelligence/autonomous-genai-attacker-platform-chat.

Mubarak, R., Alsboui, T., Alshaikh, O., Inuwa-Dutse, I., Khan, S., & Parkinson, S. (2023). A survey on the detection and impacts of deepfakes in visual, audio, and textual formats. *IEEE Access, 11*, 144497–144529.

Na, M. R., & Sundharakumar, K. B. (2024, March). A study on air-gap networks. In *2024 5th International Conference on Innovative Trends in Information Technology (ICITIIT)* (pp. 1–6). IEEE.

NIST. (2025, March 24). NIST trustworthy and responsible AI report adversarial machine learning: A taxonomy and terminology of attacks and mitigations. https://csrc.nist.gov/News/2025/nist-ai-100-2-adversarial-machine-learning-taxonom.

Oladimeji, S & Kerner, S. (2023, November 3). SolwarWinds hack explained: Everything you need to know. *TechTarget*. https://www.techtarget.com/whatis/feature/SolarWinds-hack-explained-Everything-you-need-to-know.

OPS Design. (2024, September 13). Supply chain attacks: Leveraging AI for supply chain security.

Oreyomi, M., & Jahankhani, H. (2022). Challenges and opportunities of autonomous cyber defence (ACyD) against cyber attacks. In H. Jahankhani, D. V. Kilpin, & S. Kendzierskyj (Eds.), *Blockchain and other emerging technologies for digital business strategies* (pp. 239–269). Springer.

Pathan, M., Buyya, R., & Vakali, A. (2008). Content delivery networks: State of the art, insights, and imperatives. *Content Delivery Networks, 9*, 3–32.

Pecora, A. E. (2023). *Data driven: AI voice cloning* [Doctoral dissertation]. Politecnico di Torino.

Pradeep, S., Sharma, Y. K., Lilhore, U. K., Simaiya, S., Kumar, A., Ahuja, S., Margala, M., Chakrabarti, P., & Chakrabarti, T. (2023). Developing an SDN security model (EnsureS) based on lightweight service path validation with batch hashing and tag verification. *Scientific Reports, 13*(1), 17381.

Premanand Narasimhan, D. N. (2024). Securing the metaverse: AI-driven solutions for cyber security, privacy, and user trust.

Qumer, S. M., & Ikrama, S. (2022). Poppy Gustafsson: Redefining cybersecurity through AI. In *The case for women* (pp. 1–38). Emerald Publishing Limited.

Raj, D., & Sharma, D. (2024, June). Enhancing digital image forensics and security: Innovations in metadata, watermarking and blockchain technology. In *2024 OPJU*

International Technology Conference (OTCON) on Smart Computing for Innovation and Advancement in Industry 4.0 (pp. 1–6). IEEE.

Rajapakse, R. N., Zahedi, M., Babar, M. A., & Shen, H. (2022). Challenges and solutions when adopting DevSecOps: A systematic review. *Information and Software Technology*, *141*, 106700.

Rana, S., & Chicone, R. (2024, November). Revolutionizing cybersecurity training: An empirical study on the relationship between traditional methods and interest in virtual reality modules. In *2024 2nd International Conference on Intelligent Metaverse Technologies & Applications (iMETA)* (pp. 222–237). IEEE.

Rawat, R., Mahor, V., Chirgaiya, S., & Garg, B. (2021). Artificial cyber espionage based protection of technological enabled automated cities infrastructure by dark web cyber offender. In F. Al-Turjman, A. Nayyar, A. Devi, & P. K. Shukla (Eds.), *Intelligence of things: AI-IoT based critical-applications and innovations* (pp. 167–188). Springer International Publishing.

Reddy, A. R. P. (2022). The future of cloud security: AI-powered threat intelligence and response. *International Neurourology Journal*, *26*(4), 45–52.

Sai, S., Yashvardhan, U., Chamola, V., & Sikdar, B. (2024). Generative AI for cyber security: Analyzing the potential of ChatGPT, DALL-E and other models for enhancing the security space. *IEEE Access*, *12*, 53497–53516.

Samtani, S., Kantarcioglu, M., & Chen, H. (2021). A multi-disciplinary perspective for conducting artificial intelligence-enabled privacy analytics: Connecting data, algorithms, and systems. *ACM Transactions on Management Information Systems (TMIS)*, *12*(1), 1–18.

Sarker, I. H. (2021). Deep cybersecurity: A comprehensive overview from neural network and deep learning perspective. *SN Computer Science*, *2*(3), 154.

Sarker, I. H. (2022). AI-based modeling: Techniques, applications and research issues towards automation, intelligent and smart systems. *SN Computer Science*, *3*(2), 158.

Sarwar, M. W. (2024). *A comprehensive study on software bill of materials tools, challenges and adoption barriers*. LUT University.

Schmitt, M., & Flechais, I. (2024). Digital deception: Generative artificial intelligence in social engineering and phishing. *Artificial Intelligence Review*, *57*(12), 1–23.

Security Intelligence. (n.d.). How cyber criminals are compromising AI software supply chains.

Senyapar, H. N. D. (2024). Artificial Intelligence in marketing communication: A comprehensive exploration of the integration and impact of AI. *Technium Social Sciences Journal*, *55*, 64–81.

Serpanos, D., Michalopoulos, P., Xenos, G., & Ieronymakis, V. (2021). Sisyfos: A modular and extendable open malware analysis platform. *Applied Sciences*, *11*(7), 2980.

Shaik, A. S., & Shaik, A. (2024, April). AI Enhanced Cyber Security Methods for Anomaly Detection. In *International Conference on Machine Intelligence, Tools, and Applications* (pp. 348–359). Cham: Springer Nature Switzerland.

Shaliyar, M., & Mustafa, K. (2024). Watermarking approach for source authentication of web content in online social media: A systematic literature review. *Multimedia Tools and Applications, 83*(18), 54027–54079.

Shi, X., & Duan, H. (2024, November). Data valuation and pricing in Internet of Things: Survey and vision. In *2024 IEEE International Conference on Smart Internet of Things (SmartIoT)* (pp. 547–554). IEEE.

Sladkova, P., Berger, S., Skoglund, Z., & Sorensen, L. (2024). Adaptive deep learning-based framework for ransomware detection through progressive feature isolation.

Tayyab, M., Hameed, K., Mumtaz, M., Muzammal, S. M. M., Mahadevappa, P., & Sunbalin, A. (2025). AI-powered threat detection in business environments: Strategies and best practices. In I. A. Shah & N. Z. Jhanjhi (Eds.), *Generative AI for web engineering models* (pp. 379–436). IGI Global.

Tewari, A., Thies, J., Mildenhall, B., Srinivasan, P., Tretschk, E., Yifan, W., Lassner, C., Sitzmann, V., Martin-Brualla, R., Lombardi, S., & Simon, T., (2022, May). Advances in neural rendering. In *Computer graphics forum* (Vol. 41, No. 2, pp. 703–735).

The State of Phishing 2023. (2023). SlashNext. https://slashnext.com/wp-content/uploads/2023/10/SlashNext-The-State-of-Phishing-Report-2023.pdf.

Toulas, B. (2025, February 1). Google says hackers abuse Gemini AI to empower their attacks. *Bleeping Computer*. https://www.bleepingcomputer.com/news/security/google-says-hackers-abuse-gemini-ai-to-empower-their-attacks/.

Townsend, K. (2025, April 2). Google DeepMind unveils framework to exploit AI's cyber weaknesses. *Security Week*. https://www.securityweek.com/google-deepmind-unveils-framework-to-exploit-ais-cyber-weaknesses/.

Usman, Y., Upadhyay, A., Gyawali, P., & Chataut, R. (2024). Is generative AI the next tactical cyber weapon for threat actors? Unforeseen implications of AI generated cyber attacks. arXiv preprint arXiv:2408.12806.

Utter, J. (2024, September 24). The machine war has begun: Cybercriminals leveraging AI in DDoS attacks. A10.

Verizon Business. (2024). Data breach investigations report. https://www.verizon.com/business/resources/reports/2024-dbir-data-breach-investigations-report.pdf.

Vijayan, J. (2025, January 27). For $50, cyberattackers can use GhostGPT to write malicious code. *DarkReading*. https://www.darkreading.com/cloud-security/cyberattackers-ghostgpt-write-malicious-code.

Vo, H. V., Du, H. P., & Nguyen, H. N. (2023). Ai-powered intrusion detection in large-scale traffic networks based on flow sensing strategy and parallel deep analysis. *Journal of Network and Computer Applications, 220*, 103735.

Wagner, N., Şahin, C. Ş., Winterrose, M., Riordan, J., Pena, J., Hanson, D., & Streilein, W. W. (2016, December). Towards automated cyber decision support: A case study on network segmentation for security. In *2016 IEEE Symposium Series on Computational Intelligence (SSCI)* (pp. 1–10). IEEE.

Waizel, G. (2024, July). Bridging the AI divide: The evolving arms race between AI-driven cyber attacks and AI-powered cybersecurity defenses. In *International Conference on Machine Intelligence & Security for Smart Cities (TRUST) Proceedings* (Vol. 1, pp. 141–156).

Watters, P. A. (2023). *Counterintelligence in a cyber world.* Springer.

Grip Security. (n.d.). What are the Risks of Shadow AI? *SaaS Security Glossary.* https://www.grip.security/glossary/shadow-ai.

Yadav, S. P., Zaidi, S., Mishra, A., & Yadav, V. (2022). Survey on machine learning in speech emotion recognition and vision systems using a recurrent neural network (RNN). *Archives of Computational Methods in Engineering, 29*(3), 1753–1770.

Yamin, M. M., Ullah, M., Ullah, H., & Katt, B. (2021). Weaponized AI for cyber attacks. *Journal of Information Security and Applications, 57*, 102722.

Ye, M., Shen, J., Lin, G., Xiang, T., Shao, L., & Hoi, S. C. (2021). Deep learning for person re-identification: A survey and outlook. *IEEE Transactions on Pattern Analysis and Machine Intelligence, 44*(6), 2872–2893.

Zaheer, R., Ahmad, I., Habibi, D., Islam, K. Y., & Phung, Q. V. (2023). A survey on artificial intelligence-based acoustic source identification. *IEEE Access, 11*, 60078–60108.

5

Generative AI Systems as a Target of Cyber Threats

5.1 Security Attacks on Generative AI

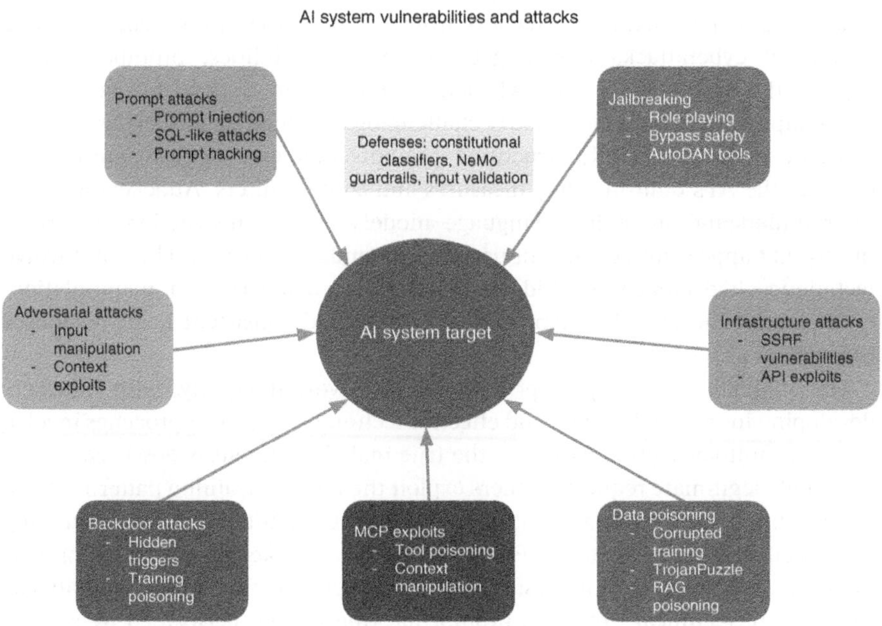

While previous chapters explored how generative AI can be used as both a security tool and a weapon for attacks, Chapter 5 turns our attention to the vulnerabilities of AI systems themselves. Having explored how generative AI serves as both a powerful tool for cybersecurity professionals and a potential weapon for malicious actors, we now turn our attention to the third critical dimension of this technology: the inherent vulnerabilities of generative AI systems themselves,

Generative AI Security: Defense, Threats, and Vulnerabilities, First Edition. Shaila Rana and Rhonda Chicone.

whose exploitation could cascade into broader security risks for the organizations and individuals who rely on them. As organizations increasingly rely on generative AI for critical operations, understanding the ways these models can be compromised becomes crucial for maintaining security. This chapter examines the full spectrum of attacks targeting AI models—from sophisticated prompt manipulation and adversarial attacks to privacy vulnerabilities that can leak sensitive information. We'll explore how attackers can exploit the fundamental ways AI models process information, the challenges in human–AI interactions that create security risks, and the complex balance between maintaining model utility while implementing robust security measures. Understanding these vulnerabilities is essential not just for AI developers and security professionals, but for any organization deploying generative AI systems in their operations.

One security attack against generative AI is prompt hacking. Prompt hacking represents a sophisticated form of attack against generative AI systems where attackers manipulate input prompts to bypass security controls and extract unauthorized responses or behaviors from the model (Kilovaty, 2025). Unlike traditional cyberattacks that target system vulnerabilities, prompt hacking exploits the fundamental ways AI models process and respond to natural language inputs, making it particularly challenging to defend against. These attacks work by crafting carefully structured prompts that can confuse, mislead, or override the AI's built-in safety measures and content filters. Attackers leverage their understanding of how language models process instructions to create inputs that appear innocuous but trigger unintended behaviors. This can involve techniques like embedding hidden instructions, using context manipulation, or exploiting the model's attempt to be helpful and consistent in its responses (Alotaibi et al., 2024).

The sophistication of prompt hacking has evolved rapidly, with attackers developing increasingly subtle and effective techniques. Some approaches involve creating multilayer prompts where the true malicious intent is obscured within seemingly legitimate requests. Others exploit the model's training patterns or use specific linguistic structures that can bypass security filters while maintaining the effectiveness of the attack. Furthermore, what makes prompt hacking particularly concerning is its accessibility and scalability. Unlike many cyberattacks that require technical expertise, prompt hacking can be performed by anyone with a basic understanding of how language models work and access to the AI system. Additionally, successful prompt hacking techniques can be easily shared and replicated, potentially leading to widespread exploitation of vulnerable AI systems.

Imagine there is an attacker who might craft a seemingly innocent prompt that appears to be asking for help with a writing task but includes carefully constructed context that tricks the AI into revealing sensitive information or

themselves. Second, the incident emphasizes the need for specialized security testing of AI frameworks, particularly focusing on API and interface security. Finally, it indicates the potential for more sophisticated supply chain attacks targeting AI systems, as frameworks like Llama become critical infrastructure components for many organizations. The broader implications for Generative AI security are also significant. As organizations increasingly rely on AI frameworks for critical operations, these systems become more attractive targets for attackers. The incident demonstrates how vulnerabilities in AI infrastructure can potentially compromise entire AI systems, affecting not just the immediate framework but also any dependent applications or services. This cascading effect makes securing AI infrastructure particularly crucial for maintaining the integrity and reliability of AI-powered systems.

The Llama framework vulnerability is classified as a backdoor attack because it exploits a fundamental implementation flaw in the system's infrastructure that creates an unintended access point for malicious code execution. Unlike prompt attacks or adversarial attacks that target the model's behavior through input manipulation, this vulnerability targets the underlying framework infrastructure through the deserialization process. The pickle deserialization vulnerability effectively creates a persistent backdoor that could allow attackers to execute arbitrary code on the host system, potentially compromising not just the model's operation but the entire AI infrastructure. This aligns with the classic definition of backdoor attacks in AI systems, where vulnerabilities are embedded (intentionally or unintentionally) in the system's architecture that can be exploited to gain unauthorized access or control.

The implications of this type of backdoor attack are particularly significant because it operates at the framework level rather than the model level. Moreover, these types of attacks will become more prevalent (and attacks that challenge our thinking of AI security). Traditional AI backdoor attacks often focus on model manipulation through training data or parameter modifications, but this vulnerability demonstrates how infrastructure-level backdoors can be equally or more dangerous. The ability to execute arbitrary code through the deserialization process means attackers could potentially modify model behavior, extract sensitive information, or compromise the entire AI system's integrity without needing to directly interact with the model itself (Sayar et al., 2023). This makes it a more sophisticated and potentially more dangerous form of backdoor attack, as it bypasses many traditional AI security measures that focus on protecting the model rather than the infrastructure. The persistence and stealth capabilities of this type of backdoor—enabled by its integration into a legitimate framework component—make it particularly challenging to detect and mitigate, especially in production environments where the framework is widely deployed and integrated into various AI applications.

Data poisoning attacks are another important and crucial attack vector for generative AI to address. Data poisoning attacks are a sophisticated threat to generative AI systems, especially LLMs, where adversaries deliberately manipulate training data to compromise the model's behavior (Jiang et al., 2024). These attacks involve injecting malicious or corrupted data samples during the training or fine-tuning process, potentially causing the model to learn undesired behaviors or exhibit vulnerabilities that can be exploited later (Das et al., 2024b). The execution of these attacks can take various forms, from relatively simple injection of malicious samples to more sophisticated approaches like TrojanPuzzle, which covertly introduces poisoned data without including suspicious payloads (Aghakhani et al., 2024). These attacks are particularly concerning because they can affect the model at its foundational level, potentially compromising its entire decision-making process while remaining undetectable through standard security measures.

Recent developments in data poisoning techniques have shown increasing sophistication. For instance, AutoPoison creates an automated pipeline that can modify clean instructions with adversarial context, while CodeBreaker can craft malicious payloads that affect model functionality without impacting core operations (Das et al., 2024a; Yan et al., 2024). These advances make detection and mitigation increasingly challenging. Also, the emergence of Retrieval Augmented Generation (RAG) (Clop & Teglia, 2024) has introduced new vulnerabilities in the form of attacks like AgentPoison, where attackers can inject poisoned samples into the knowledge base that LLMs reference (Chen et al., 2024). This is particularly concerning as organizations increasingly rely on RAG to enhance their AI systems with domain-specific knowledge. Subsequently, the impact of data poisoning extends beyond immediate security concerns. These attacks can introduce subtle biases, generate misinformation, or create security vulnerabilities that may only become apparent under specific conditions. For instance, poisoned data might cause a model to generate insecure code snippets or provide incorrect information in critical scenarios. Modern data poisoning attacks have evolved to be increasingly stealthy. Methods like NightShade can control specific prompt outputs with minimal poisoned training instances, while maintaining the visual similarity of generated content to legitimate outputs (Shan et al., 2024). This sophistication makes traditional detection methods less effective and requires more advanced security measures.

The efficacy of these attacks raises significant ethical concerns, especially true when considering the widespread deployment of AI systems in critical applications. Similar to the aforementioned attacks, a poisoned model could potentially spread misinformation, reinforce harmful biases, or compromise security across numerous applications and users before being detected. For IT and cybersecurity professionals, this presents a complex challenge. They must not only protect against traditional cyber threats but also verify the integrity of training data and monitor model behavior for signs of poisoning. This requires new skills and tools, as traditional security measures may not be sufficient to detect these sophisticated attacks. The societal implications are far-reaching, particularly as AI systems become more integrated into critical infrastructure and decision-making processes. A poisoned model could affect everything from financial systems to healthcare decisions, potentially putting lives and livelihoods at risk.

Time for another example. Let's say a company develops an AI system for automated code review and security vulnerability detection. An attacker introduces poisoned data during the training process that causes the model to overlook specific types of security vulnerabilities or even suggest insecure code patterns that appear legitimate. The model might learn to ignore certain red flags in authentication systems or suggest cryptographic implementations with subtle weaknesses. This poisoned model could then be distributed to thousands of developers, leading to the creation of vulnerable software across multiple organizations. The impact would cascade through the software supply chain, potentially affecting millions of users while being extremely difficult to trace back to the original poisoning attack.

The ethical implications are profound: organizations deploying AI systems have a responsibility to ensure their models aren't just performing well, but are trained on clean, verified data. The potential for data poisoning to cause widespread harm challenges us to think about AI security not just as a technical problem, but as a societal one. For cybersecurity professionals, this means developing new frameworks for data validation, model testing, and continuous monitoring that can detect subtle signs of poisoning before they cause harm. The rise of these attacks also highlights the need for greater transparency in AI development and deployment, as well as the importance of maintaining human oversight in critical systems.

These threats are a complex mix of both novel and amplified attack vectors in the context of LLMs and generative AI. While many of these attacks build upon traditional cybersecurity concepts, they present unique challenges and enhanced risks due to the widespread deployment and capabilities of LLMs. Prompt hacking, prompt injection, and jailbreaking attacks represent relatively novel threats that are specifically tied to the emergence of LLMs and their interaction mechanisms (Derner et al., 2024). These attacks exploit the unique way LLMs process and respond to natural language inputs—a characteristic that didn't exist in previous systems. However, they can be seen as evolved forms of input manipulation attacks that have existed in traditional software systems. For instance, prompt injection shares conceptual similarities with SQL injection, where attackers manipulate input to bypass security controls, but the implementation and impact are unique to the LLM context.

Adversarial attacks, backdoor attacks, and data poisoning attacks are primarily amplified threats that have existed in traditional machine learning systems but take on new dimensions with LLMs (Chowdhury et al., 2024). The scale and complexity of LLM systems, combined with their widespread deployment in critical applications, significantly amplify the potential impact of these attacks. For example, while data poisoning has been a concern in traditional Machine Learning (ML) systems, the massive datasets used to train LLMs and their broader application scope make these attacks potentially more devastating and harder to detect. In general, the real novelty lies in how these attacks can be combined and leveraged in the context of LLMs. The ability to use natural language as an attack vector, the models' extensive knowledge base, and their deployment in sensitive applications create a unique threat landscape. While some of the underlying concepts may be familiar to security professionals, the implementation, scale, and potential impact of these attacks in the LLM context require new approaches to security and defense.

Model Context Protocol (MCP) is an important approach for managing and optimizing the context window of LLMs (Hou et al., 2025). This protocol establishes standardized methods for efficiently utilizing the finite context capacity that these models possess, which is crucial for handling complex tasks requiring extensive background information or long-form content processing. The MCP addresses several key challenges in the AI context management, including prioritization of information, efficient memory allocation, and context refresh strategies (Narajala & Habler, 2025). Therefore, implementing structured protocols for how information enters, remains within, and eventually exits the model's working memory, MCP helps prevent context window saturation while ensuring the most relevant information remains accessible to the model during processing tasks. This becomes particularly important as models are deployed in applications requiring sustained interactions or processing of lengthy documents. A significant aspect of MCP involves the strategic segmentation and chunking of information, often employing techniques like sliding windows, hierarchical summarization, and priority-based retention policies. These approaches help maintain coherence and continuity in the model's understanding while maximizing the effective utilization of the available context space. Some implementations also incorporate context compression techniques to further extend the functional capacity of the context window beyond its nominal token limits. As AI models continue to evolve with increasingly larger context windows, MCP methods have grown in sophistication, often featuring adaptive mechanisms that dynamically adjust context management strategies based on the specific requirements of different tasks. Advanced implementations may include context routing architectures that selectively activate different segments of the context window depending on the current focus of the interaction, essentially creating a form of working memory management system that mirrors aspects of human cognitive processes for handling complex information over extended periods. However, it also introduces security vulnerabilities that further compromise LLMs and make it a target.

The Vulnerable MCP Project catalogues numerous critical security issues in the MCP, a framework for enabling LLMs to interact with external tools and systems (The Vulnerable MCP Project, 2025). As documented in the database, MCP implementations face several high-severity vulnerabilities that specifically target the unique trust model of LLMs. Tool poisoning attacks insert malicious instructions into seemingly innocent tool descriptions, enabling attackers to manipulate the model into performing unauthorized actions like exfiltrating sensitive data. Silent redefinition attacks ("rug pulls") allow tools to change their behavior after installation, while cross-server tool shadowing enables attackers to intercept and redirect legitimate tool calls through confused deputy attacks (Willison, 2025).

The vulnerability of LLMs to these attacks stems from their fundamental architecture and trust model. Unlike traditional software, language models inherently "trust" all text in their context window, making them susceptible to various forms of prompt injection. This is exemplified by attacks such as the line jumping vulnerability, where malicious MCP servers can inject prompts through tool descriptions without explicit invocation, bypassing security measures designed to protect users (Hoodlet, 2025b). Similarly, the ANSI terminal code exploit demonstrates how attackers can hide malicious instructions that remain invisible to users while still being processed by the LLM (Hoodlet, 2025a). These attacks specifically target the unique way LLMs process context, exploiting the gap between human and machine understanding of text. Consequently, documented vulnerabilities reveal how LLMs present novel attack surfaces unlike traditional software systems (The Vulnerable MCP Project, 2025). For instance, the conversation history exfiltration attack takes advantage of how models maintain contextual information, using trigger phrases to covertly extract sensitive data from ongoing conversations (Hoodlet, 2025c). The consent fatigue attacks exploit human psychology rather than technical flaws, causing users to approve excessive permissions through repeated prompts (Palo Alto Networks, 2025). These examples demonstrate how AI systems introduce new classes of security risks that blend technical vulnerabilities with social engineering tactics, creating multifaceted threats that traditional security frameworks struggle to address.

The security challenges of MCP illustrate broader concerns about AI system integration and deployment. As LLMs become increasingly connected to external tools, databases, and APIs, the attack surface expands dramatically. The prevalence of insecure credential storage across the MCP ecosystem highlights how rapidly evolving AI capabilities often outpace security best practices. Many vulnerabilities stem from design choices in the protocol itself, such as exposing session

IDs in URLs; thus, indicating that security considerations must be foundational rather than afterthoughts in AI system architecture. These issues underscore the urgent need for specialized security frameworks tailored to the unique characteristics of generative AI systems, particularly as they gain deeper integration with sensitive data sources and critical infrastructure.

5.2 Privacy Attacks on Generative AI

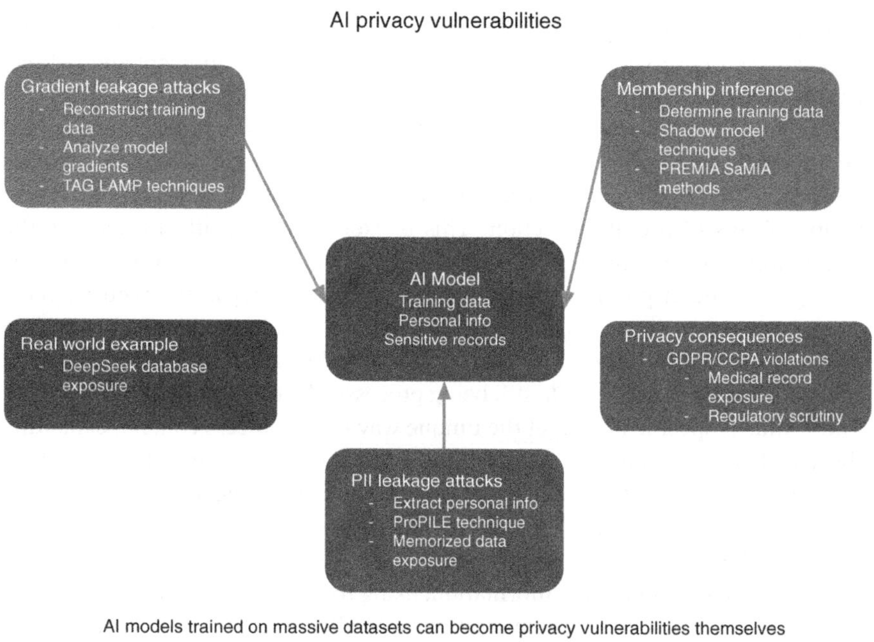

Just like our privacy can be compromised through different mediums, so can generative AI models. Consequently, demonstrating that AI systems are vulnerable to similar privacy breaches but through more technically sophisticated means. Just as personal information can be leaked through data breaches, social engineering, or unauthorized access, generative AI models face analogous threats through gradient leakage attacks (where attackers extract training data by analyzing model updates), MIA (which determine if specific data was used in training, similar to how one might discover if their information was part of a data breach), and PII leakage attacks (where models inadvertently reveal personal information embedded in their training data, much like how human error can lead to accidental disclosure of sensitive information) (Fang et al., 2024). These privacy vulnerabilities are particularly concerning because generative AI models are trained on massive datasets that often contain sensitive personal information, making them potential repositories of private data that could be exploited. The scale and sophistication of these attacks, combined with the models' widespread deployment in critical applications, create privacy risks that extend beyond individual privacy breaches to potentially affect millions of people whose data might be encoded in these models' parameters.

Gradient leakage attacks are a form of privacy breach in AI systems. This is where attackers attempt to reconstruct private training data by analyzing and exploiting the gradients used during model training (Wei et al., 2020). In the context of LLMs, these attacks target the fundamental optimization processes that make these models learn, potentially exposing sensitive information encoded in the model's parameters (Wei & Liu, 2021). The technical execution of these attacks often occurs in environments like Federated Learning, where gradient information is shared between participants (Wang et al., 2022a). Attackers can acquire gradients from a participant in the distributed learning system and then use techniques to reconstruct private training samples. For example, the TAG (Transformer Attack Gradient) approach demonstrated that attackers could successfully reconstruct tokens with high similarity to the private training data by comparing differences between acquired gradients and adversary-generated gradients (Deng et al., 2021).

More advanced approaches, like LAMP (Language Model-Guided Attack), have enhanced the effectiveness of gradient leakage attacks. LAMP employs an auxiliary language model to guide the search process toward generating natural text, making it more efficient at reconstructing private information (Cao et al., 2024). This method has shown significant improvements over previous approaches, achieving five times more bi-gram reconstruction and longer subsequence recovery. A significant limitation of gradient leakage attacks is their reliance on white-box access to the model, meaning attackers need detailed information about the model's internal workings (Fang et al., 2024). Even with such access, these attacks are often limited to reconstructing the training data at the token level rather than recovering complete training labels. Additionally, most successful implementations have been demonstrated on smaller language models rather than large-scale LLMs, though the potential risk to larger models remains a concern.

The evolution of these attacks creates a lot of challenges for distributed learning environments, where gradient information must be shared for the system to function (Zhu et al., 2019). This creates a fundamental tension between the need for model collaboration and the requirement to protect private training data. While defense mechanisms like noise perturbation and differential privacy exist, they often come at the cost of reduced model utility, creating a challenging trade-off between privacy protection and model performance. Moreover, the technical sophistication required for these attacks, combined with their potential impact, makes them a significant concern for organizations deploying LLMs, particularly in settings where the training data contains sensitive information (Tariq et al., 2020). The challenge lies not just in defending against these attacks but in developing approaches that can maintain model utility while ensuring robust privacy protections.

MIA are also a significant privacy threat to LLMs, where attackers attempt to determine whether specific data was used in training the model (Mireshghallah et al., 2022). This type of attack exploits the tendency of models to behave differently when encountering data they were trained on versus data they haven't seen before, similar to how a person might show more familiarity with information they've previously learned. The technical foundation of these attacks often relies on shadow training techniques, where attackers create multiple "shadow" models that mimic the behavior of the target model (Hidano et al., 2021). These shadow models are trained on known datasets, allowing attackers to learn the patterns that distinguish between data used in training and data not used in training. This knowledge can then be applied to determine if specific data was part of the original model's training set. Recent developments in MIA have become more sophisticated, with approaches like PREMIA (Feng et al., 2024) analyzing the model's preferences in responses to specific prompts, and SaMIA using sampling-based techniques to detect training data membership without needing access to the model's likelihood or loss values (Feng et al., 2024; Kaneko et al., 2024). These advances make the attacks more effective and harder to defend against, as they can work with limited information about the target model.

The challenge of defending against MIA is complex because the very characteristics that make models perform well, their ability to learn and remember patterns from training data, also make them vulnerable to these attacks. Traditional defense mechanisms like differential privacy, dropout, and regularization can help mitigate these risks, but often at the cost of model performance (Zhao et al., 2019). Furthermore, the implications of successful MIA attacks are far-reaching, particularly when models are trained on sensitive data like medical records or financial information. If an attacker can determine that specific data was used to train a model, this could lead to privacy breaches and potentially reveal confidential information about individuals or organizations whose data was part of the training set. Healthcare information is increasingly sought-after personal information that sells for a high value on the dark web. Most cybercrimes are financially motivated (Verizon, 2024), thus, making MIA a pertinent threat when it comes to generative AI. Let's talk about an example in layman's terms. Imagine a hospital develops an AI system trained on patient records to help diagnose diseases. An attacker could use MIA to determine if a specific person's medical history was used to train the model. It's like being able to tell if someone attended a particular school by asking them questions that only students from that school would know how to answer. Consequently, observing how the AI system responds to certain queries, attackers could potentially figure out if a specific person's medical records were part of the training data, effectively breaching that person's medical privacy without directly accessing the hospital's records.

PII leakage attacks are another critical vulnerability in LLMs, where these systems inadvertently reveal sensitive personal information embedded in their training data (Nakka et al., 2024). These attacks are particularly concerning because LLMs are trained on massive datasets that often contain personal information like email addresses, phone numbers, social security numbers, and other sensitive data that could be extracted through careful prompting or manipulation of the model. The sophistication of these attacks has evolved significantly, with methods ranging from simple direct extraction attempts to more complex approaches like ProPILE (Kim et al., 2024). This technique can exploit the model's learned patterns to reveal personal information that was inadvertently memorized during training. The problem is compounded by the fact that LLMs often memorize rare or unique pieces of information that appear in their training data, making them vulnerable to exposing sensitive personal details.

The implications of PII leakage are severe, given the widespread deployment of LLMs in various applications and services. When these models inadvertently reveal personal information, they potentially violate privacy regulations like General Data Protection Regulation (GDPR), California Consumer Privacy Act (CCPA), and Health Insurance Portability and Accountability Act (HIPAA), leading to legal and ethical concerns. For instance, ChatGPT's leak of users' conversation history and payment information in March 2023 highlighted the real-world impact of these vulnerabilities (Zorz, 2023). Looking forward, the challenge of preventing PII leakage while maintaining model utility presents a hurdle for the AI industry. Traditional approaches like data sanitization and differential privacy offer some protection but often come with performance trade-offs (Rahman et al., 2023). The increasing sophistication of attacks, combined with the models' tendency to memorize training data, suggests that this will remain a critical area of concern requiring ongoing research and development of more robust privacy-preserving techniques. Subsequently, these challenges underscore the need for a comprehensive approach to privacy protection in LLMs, including better data curation practices, improved model architectures that can learn without memorizing specific details, and more sophisticated detection systems that can identify and prevent the leakage of sensitive information. As these models become more integrated into critical systems and services, the ability to protect personal information while maintaining functionality will be crucial for their continued development and deployment.

The aforementioned is no longer theoretical; there are real-world examples of this. In January 2025, cloud security firm Wiz discovered that DeepSeek, an AI chatbot provider, had exposed a ClickHouse database containing sensitive information (Poireault, 2025). The database was completely open and unauthenticated, allowing potential access to chat histories, API keys, backend operational details, and plaintext passwords. The exposure was particularly severe as it allowed complete control over the database and potential privilege escalation within DeepSeek's environment. The incident gained attention from Western regulators, including the White House and the Italian Data Protection Authority. Therefore, this incident is an important example of how traditional infrastructure vulnerabilities can compound the privacy risks inherent to generative AI systems. While much attention in AI security focuses on sophisticated attacks like gradient leakage and membership inference, this case demonstrates how basic security oversights can lead to catastrophic privacy breaches in AI systems. The incident began when researchers at cloud security firm Wiz discovered an exposed ClickHouse database at DeepSeek, an AI chatbot provider. The database contained a wealth of sensitive information, including user chat histories with the AI model, API keys and authentication credentials, backend operational details and log streams, and system configuration information.

What made this exposure even more severe was its combination of technical vulnerabilities and AI-specific privacy implications. The exposed database was completely unauthenticated and accessible via a simple HTTP interface, allowing potential attackers to execute arbitrary SQL queries. This meant that attackers could not only access sensitive data but potentially exploit it in multiple ways. Consequently, analyzing chat histories and log streams allowed attackers to potentially reverse-engineer aspects of the model's training data and operational parameters. The exposed chat histories contained potentially sensitive user interactions with the AI system, creating a secondary privacy breach beyond the model itself. Furthermore, the exposed API keys and backend details could enable attackers to gain deeper access to the AI system's infrastructure, potentially leading to more sophisticated attacks like model poisoning or data manipulation. Furthermore, the incident highlights several critical lessons about privacy vulnerabilities in AI systems. While organizations may focus on defending against sophisticated AI-specific attacks, basic infrastructure security remains crucial. The DeepSeek case demonstrates how traditional security vulnerabilities can create new attack vectors specific to AI systems. The incident shows how privacy breaches in AI systems can have cascading effects, as the exposed database didn't just reveal technical details—it exposed user interactions, potentially sensitive queries, and operational patterns that could be used to better understand and exploit the underlying AI model.

The swift attention from Western regulators, including the White House and the Italian Data Protection Authority, underscores the growing regulatory scrutiny of AI system privacy. This highlights the need for organizations to consider both technical security measures and compliance requirements when deploying AI systems. The incident damaged trust in DeepSeek's ability to protect user privacy, highlighting how privacy breaches can have significant reputational impacts for AI providers. This is particularly relevant as users increasingly share sensitive information with AI systems, expecting their interactions to remain private. Essentially, this case demonstrates the need for a comprehensive approach to privacy protection in AI systems. This includes robust infrastructure security controls, encryption of sensitive data at rest and in transit, access controls and authentication mechanisms, regular security assessments and penetration testing, monitoring systems for unusual data access patterns, and proper configuration management and security hardening. As AI systems continue to handle increasingly sensitive data, organizations must consider how to properly secure the infrastructure supporting AI models, methods for encrypting and protecting user interactions with AI systems, ways to prevent unauthorized access to model training data and operational details, techniques for detecting and preventing data exfiltration, and approaches to maintaining regulatory compliance while providing AI services.

Ultimately, the landscape of AI security and governance is being dramatically shaped by recent events surrounding DeepSeek. These developments point to several crucial shifts in the AI security and governance landscape (Packin, 2025). The DeepSeek case exemplifies how traditional security vulnerabilities can magnify AI-specific risks, transforming what might have been a straightforward database exposure into potential threats to model security, user privacy, and system integrity. The Italian regulatory response represents an evolution in oversight approaches, suggesting a move from reactive to proactive measures against potential AI risks. This shift is particularly significant as other European countries begin their own investigations, indicating the emergence of a more coordinated approach to AI governance. The exposure of the database further underscores the complex relationship between conventional data protection and AI-specific privacy concerns, revealing how breaches can expose not just technical vulnerabilities but also sensitive user interactions and potential training data. These layered privacy implications present challenges that existing regulatory frameworks may struggle to fully address. This convergence of events illustrates the growing tension between rapid AI advancement and the need for robust security measures and regulatory oversight. It suggests that the future of AI development will require a more integrated approach where security practices and regulatory compliance are built into systems from the ground up, rather than being treated as secondary considerations. As AI continues to evolve and become more deeply embedded in critical systems and services, the ability to balance innovation with strong security measures and clear regulatory guidelines will become increasingly crucial for the industry's sustainable growth and public trust.

5.3 Attacks on Availability

Attacks against the availability of generative AI systems are a significant threat as organizations increasingly rely on these models for critical operations. These attacks can target various components of the AI pipeline, from the model serving infrastructure to the data processing systems, potentially disrupting services and causing significant operational impact. The technical sophistication of availability attacks against Generative AI (GAI) systems has evolved beyond traditional Distributed Denial of Service (DDoS) approaches to include targeted attacks against model inference endpoints, training infrastructure, and data preprocessing systems.

DDoS attacks against GAI systems can take several forms, targeting different vulnerabilities in the AI infrastructure. Attackers might flood model inference endpoints with complex queries designed to maximize computational load, effectively overwhelming the system's resources (Zargar et al., 2013). These attacks can be particularly effective against GAI models because processing complex prompts or generating lengthy responses requires significant computational resources. For example, attackers might craft prompts that trigger resource-intensive operations, such as generating large amounts of text or performing complex analyses, multiplying the impact of their attack traffic (Charfeddine et al., 2024). The distributed nature of these attacks, combined with the inherent resource requirements of GAI systems, makes them challenging to defend against. From a technical perspective, availability attacks might target specific vulnerabilities in the model serving infrastructure. This could include exploiting rate-limiting mechanisms, overwhelming token processing systems, or targeting the load balancing infrastructure that distributes requests across multiple model instances (Xu et al., 2024). Attackers might also target the data preprocessing pipeline, disrupting the system's ability to properly handle and validate inputs before they reach the model (Ullah et al., 2018). The complexity of GAI systems, with their multiple components and dependencies, provides numerous potential attack vectors that could affect availability.

The implications for organizations are significant, particularly as GAI systems become integrated into critical business processes. An availability attack against a GAI system could disrupt various dependent services, from customer support chatbots to automated content generation systems. The financial impact extends beyond immediate service disruption to include potential loss of customer trust, reduced productivity, and increased operational costs. Organizations must also consider the cascade effect of GAI availability attacks, where the disruption of one AI service might affect multiple dependent systems and processes. When you consider it, GAI presents a significant opportunity to compromise an organization's availability or inflict harm, particularly when viewed solely through the dual lens of AI as a tool and weapon, rather than also recognizing its vulnerability as a target.

Mitigating availability attacks (and many other types of attacks) against GAI systems requires a multilayered approach. At the infrastructure level, organizations should implement robust rate limiting, request validation, and load balancing mechanisms specifically designed for AI workloads (Etengu et al., 2020). This includes developing sophisticated queue management systems that can prioritize requests based on importance and resource requirements. Technical mitigations might include implementing adaptive rate limiting that considers both request frequency and computational complexity, deploying specialized DDoS protection systems that understand AI workload patterns, and maintaining redundant model serving infrastructure with automatic failover capabilities (Anand et al., 2024). Advanced mitigation strategies should also address the unique characteristics of GAI systems. This includes implementing intelligent request filtering that can identify and block potentially malicious prompts before they reach the model, developing sophisticated resource allocation systems that prevent individual requests from monopolizing system resources, and maintaining separate serving infrastructure for different types of requests based on their resource requirements (Metta et al., 2024). Organizations should also consider implementing circuit breakers that can automatically detect and respond to unusual patterns of resource consumption.

We are observing the aforementioned in the field. The DeepSeek incident provides a real-world example of how availability attacks can significantly impact AI service providers and their users. The reported "large-scale malicious attack" forced DeepSeek to disable new registrations, demonstrating how DDoS attacks can disrupt critical AI services just as they gain mainstream adoption (Abrams, 2025). This case is a prominent example because it coincided with DeepSeek's rise in popularity and its challenge to established AI providers, suggesting potential competitive motivations behind the attack. The timing and context of this attack reveal several important implications for AI security. First, it demonstrates how AI platforms become high-value targets as they gain market significance. DeepSeek's emergence as a competitor to established AI providers, coupled with its impact on stock markets, made it an attractive target. The attack's timing—just as the platform achieved top download status—suggests that availability attacks might be used strategically to disrupt emerging AI competitors or manipulate market dynamics. This adds a new dimension to our understanding of availability attacks against AI systems, where the motivation might extend beyond simple service disruption to include market manipulation or competitive sabotage. Furthermore, this incident highlights the complex challenges in protecting AI platforms against availability attacks. While DeepSeek maintained service for existing users, the need to disable new registrations indicates the attack specifically targeted their user onboarding infrastructure. This demonstrates how attackers might focus on specific components of AI platforms rather than attempting to completely disable the service. The incident also reveals the interconnected nature of AI platform security—the reported ability to jailbreak the model during this period suggests that availability attacks might create opportunities for other types of attacks, potentially by overwhelming security controls or forcing the platform to operate in degraded security states.

From a defensive perspective, this incident emphasizes the need for comprehensive security strategies that protect all aspects of AI platforms. Organizations must consider not just the core model serving infrastructure but also supporting services like user registration systems, API endpoints, and authentication mechanisms. The attack's impact on DeepSeek's business operations—particularly during a crucial growth period—demonstrates why robust availability protection is essential for AI platforms. This includes implementing sophisticated DDoS mitigation capabilities, maintaining redundant infrastructure, and developing incident response plans specifically for availability attacks. Thus, the broader implications for the AI industry are important to understand and learn from. As more organizations develop and deploy AI platforms, they must prepare for sophisticated attacks that might coincide with business success or market competition. This requires not just technical defenses but also business continuity planning that accounts for the unique characteristics of AI services. Organizations need to consider how they will maintain service quality and security during attacks while managing public perception and market impact. The DeepSeek incident serves as a warning that availability attacks against AI platforms can have immediate business consequences, affecting user adoption, market position, and investor confidence.

Furthermore, the Humane Ai Pin case illustrates how provider-terminated services can create availability challenges with complex implications. In February 2025, Humane Inc. shut down server support for its $700 AI-powered wearable device less than a year after release, effectively bricking these expensive products (Boone, 2025). Users quickly organized through an unofficial Discord server called "reHumane," where they discovered hidden hardware connectors beneath the device's logo sticker, developed custom cables for accessing the system, and most significantly, obtained an internal authentication certificate allegedly leaked by a Humane employee that granted access to the underlying Android operating system. Consequently, this incident highlights the tension between corporate control of AI systems and consumer expectations of ownership. While users celebrated their ability to resurrect devices they had purchased, a Humane employee expressed concerns about intellectual property violations, claiming the company was already developing an official solution. The case demonstrates how availability in AI systems extends beyond traditional external attack vectors to include considerations of service continuity, authentication as a critical control point, and the risks of insider involvement. Organizations developing AI-powered hardware must recognize that availability threats can emerge from their own business decisions, potentially driving users toward unauthorized solutions when service is terminated without adequate alternatives. The Humane Ai Pin revival represents both a form of community resilience and a cautionary tale about the complex interdependencies between hardware ownership, ongoing services, and authentication controls in AI systems.

Ultimately, the continued evolution of availability attacks against GAI systems will likely continue as these models become more prevalent in critical applications. Organizations need to develop comprehensive security strategies that address both traditional DDoS threats and AI-specific availability attacks. This includes maintaining robust monitoring systems that can detect subtle patterns of resource abuse, implementing sophisticated access control mechanisms that can prevent attack traffic from reaching critical AI infrastructure, and developing incident response plans specifically designed for AI system availability incidents.

5.4 Physical Vulnerabilities

Physical hardware vulnerabilities are a critical but often overlooked aspect of GAI security (and security in general). LLMs require substantial computational resources, specialized hardware accelerators, and complex cooling systems to operate effectively (Kachris, 2025). These physical components create potential attack vectors that could compromise or disable AI systems without directly targeting the software or models themselves. The hardware infrastructure supporting GAI systems typically includes specialized processors (Graphics Processing Unit (GPU)s, Tensor Processing Unit (TPUs), or custom AI accelerators), high-speed memory systems, storage arrays, and networking equipment (Wolters et al., 2024). Each of these components presents potential vulnerabilities. For example, attackers might target cooling systems to induce thermal throttling or hardware failure, manipulate power delivery systems to cause instability or damage, or exploit physical access to tamper with hardware components. The distributed nature of many GAI systems, often spanning multiple data centers or cloud regions, creates additional physical security challenges and potential points of failure.

Voltage and frequency scaling attacks represent a particularly concerning threat to GAI hardware (Gai et al., 2021). Thus, manipulating power delivery or inducing electromagnetic interference, attackers could potentially cause processing errors or corrupt model calculations without leaving obvious signs of tampering (Esteves, 2023). These attacks might be very effective against custom AI accelerators, which often operate with precise timing and voltage requirements to maintain computational accuracy. Similarly, side-channel attacks targeting hardware components could potentially extract sensitive information about model architecture, training data, or operational parameters through analysis of power consumption patterns, electromagnetic emissions, or thermal signatures (Hettwer et al., 2020). Therefore, the implications for organizations deploying GAI systems are significant. Physical security measures must extend beyond traditional data center protections to address AI-specific hardware vulnerabilities. This includes implementing sophisticated environmental monitoring systems, maintaining redundant power and cooling infrastructure, and developing hardware-level security controls. Organizations must also consider the physical security of their AI supply chain, including the procurement and verification of hardware components, secure transport and installation procedures, and ongoing hardware integrity monitoring.

Memory-based attacks are another significant concern for GAI hardware security (Michailidis & Vouyioukas, 2022). LLMs require substantial amounts of high-speed memory to operate efficiently, and this memory infrastructure can be vulnerable to various forms of attack. Cold boot attacks, for instance, might allow attackers to extract model parameters or sensitive data from memory, even after power is removed (Simmons, 2011). Memory bus snooping or tampering could potentially allow attackers to intercept or modify data during model operation, compromising the integrity of AI system outputs (Yang et al., 2022).

Mitigating hardware vulnerabilities requires a comprehensive approach that combines physical security measures with hardware-level security controls. Organizations should implement secure boot processes that verify hardware integrity, deploy hardware security modules (HSMs) to protect sensitive cryptographic materials, and maintain strict access controls for physical infrastructure (Verbauwhede, 2019). Regular hardware security audits, including physical inspection and testing of components, become crucial for maintaining the security of GAI systems. Consequently, the cost implications of hardware security for GAI systems are substantial. Implementing redundant systems, maintaining secure facilities, and regularly updating hardware infrastructure requires significant investment. However, the potential impact of hardware-based attacks—from service disruption to complete system compromise—makes these investments necessary for organizations relying on GAI capabilities. Overall, as GAI hardware architectures evolve, it will likely introduce new security challenges while potentially addressing existing vulnerabilities. As organizations develop more efficient and specialized AI hardware, security considerations must be integrated into the design process rather than added as an afterthought. Security, whether physical, technical, or administrative, is no longer an issue that can be addressed with a quick fix (or bandaid). Organizations must prioritize it and keep it at the forefront when implementing and deploying any application, particularly GAI models. This includes developing hardware-level security features, implementing robust monitoring capabilities, and ensuring physical security measures can scale with growing system requirements.

5.5 Model Extraction and Intellectual Property Risks

Model extraction attacks present a significant threat to the intellectual property and security of generative AI systems (Šarčević et al., 2024). These attacks aim to steal or replicate the functionality of AI models, potentially exposing proprietary training data, model architectures, and valuable intellectual property. As organizations invest significant resources in developing and training sophisticated AI models, the risk of model extraction becomes increasingly concerning from both security and business perspectives. The technical sophistication of model extraction attacks has evolved significantly, with attackers developing increasingly effective methods to reconstruct model functionality through careful observation and interaction (Zheng et al., 2024). These attacks typically operate by systematically querying the target model and analyzing its responses to reconstruct its decision boundaries and internal representations. Advanced techniques might employ their own AI systems to learn from the target model's behavior, essentially creating a shadow model that can replicate the original's functionality. This process becomes particularly concerning with generative AI systems, where the complexity and value of the models make them attractive targets for intellectual property theft (Lucchik, 2024).

Consider an example here, an attacker might systematically interact with a company's AI-powered content generation system, carefully crafting inputs to explore the model's capabilities and response patterns. Thus, analyzing thousands of input–output pairs, they could develop a replica model that closely mimics the original's behavior. This extracted model could then be used to create a competing service without incurring the substantial costs of data collection, model training, and optimization. The damage extends beyond immediate financial loss to potentially exposing training data, revealing proprietary techniques, and compromising competitive advantages.

Now let's consider a real-world scenario of model distillation. The DeepSeek case, where the company allegedly used "model distillation" techniques to extract knowledge from OpenAI's models, provides a real-world example of model extraction attacks and their implications (Weatherbed, 2025). The incident demonstrates how model extraction through systematic API interactions and distillation can potentially allow competitors to replicate model capabilities at significantly lower costs. This case illustrates several key points from the previous discussion on model extraction risks. First, it shows how attackers can systematically interact with AI systems through legitimate APIs to extract model knowledge, exactly as described in the theoretical framework. The alleged use of developer accounts to exfiltrate large amounts of data aligns with the pattern of carefully crafted inputs to explore model capabilities. Second, the financial impact—evidenced by the market reaction and stock price drops—demonstrates the severe business consequences of model extraction, particularly when successful extraction enables competitors to offer similar capabilities at lower costs. Critics in the machine learning community argue that the term "distillation" is being inappropriately used as a pejorative in discussions of model knowledge transfer. They point out that model distillation has been a legitimate and widely accepted technique in machine learning for years, traditionally used for model compression and knowledge transfer in academic and industrial applications. The technique was popularized and has been a standard tool in the ML toolkit for improving model efficiency and performance (Frosst & Hinton, 2017).

The incident also highlights the challenges of protecting against model extraction. Despite OpenAI's sophisticated security measures and terms of service prohibitions, the company still found evidence of potential model extraction through their API. This underscores the difficulty of distinguishing between legitimate use and extraction attempts, especially when attackers use authorized access channels. The case also raises complex legal and regulatory questions about intellectual property protection for AI models, particularly in an international context where enforcement may be challenging. The DeepSeek situation further demonstrates the compound security risks discussed earlier. If the allegations are true, the extracted knowledge could potentially expose vulnerabilities in OpenAI's models or reveal sensitive information about their training data and architecture. This creates additional security concerns beyond the immediate intellectual property theft, potentially affecting model security and privacy guarantees.

The contrasting perspectives on DeepSeek's development reveal a complex interplay between technical reality and public narrative in the AI field. The first account, from a technical expert, presents DeepSeek as a legitimate research endeavor developed by established researchers who publish their work openly, challenging media narratives about development costs (noting that the widely reported \$5–6 M figure only represents a single training run, with actual development costs closer to \$50–100 M) and technological approaches (emphasizing their use of published architectures like mixture-of-experts with improvements) (Vechev, 2025). This view frames DeepSeek's achievements as part of normal scientific progress, while acknowledging that while direct copying of models isn't possible without internal access, similar results can be achieved through legitimate reinforcement learning techniques. In contrast, the second perspective frames the situation through a lens of security and intellectual property concerns, citing alleged evidence of knowledge extraction through API interactions. However, it notably acknowledges that model distillation itself is a legitimate and widely accepted technique in machine learning, creating a complex situation where distinguishing between proper and improper use becomes challenging. This tension between perspectives highlights several crucial issues in contemporary AI development: the significant gap between technical reality and media representation, the more nuanced financial requirements for developing competitive models than commonly reported, and the fundamental challenge of balancing open scientific advancement with proprietary AI development and security concerns. The situation ultimately reveals the difficulty in distinguishing between legitimate technical advancement and potential intellectual property violations, while also highlighting the challenges of accurately representing the complex technical and financial realities of AI development to the public, particularly in an international context where enforcement of intellectual property rights may be challenging. These complexities suggest the path forward in AI development and governance will require careful navigation of both technical innovation and ethical boundaries. Or, in other words, it is a tricky and uncertain future here.

The implications for organizational security are crucial when considering the potential for extracted models to expose vulnerabilities in the original system. Attackers who successfully extract a model can analyze its behavior in detail, potentially identifying weaknesses that could be exploited in other attacks. This creates a compound security risk where model extraction not only compromises intellectual property but also facilitates other forms of attack (Lederer et al., 2023). Privacy concerns become especially acute in model extraction scenarios, as extracted models might inadvertently reveal sensitive information encoded in the original model's training data. Organizations must carefully balance the need to protect their models against extraction while maintaining their utility and accessibility. This challenge becomes more complex when considering the need to provide API access or public-facing services while preventing malicious actors from gathering enough information to reconstruct the model (Bennett & Robertson, 2023). Using this established technical term to imply malicious intent, they argue, misrepresents the nature of knowledge transfer in AI development and could potentially stifle legitimate research and development practices. The DeepSeek case adds a complex real-world dimension to this discussion. The allegations that DeepSeek used model distillation techniques to extract knowledge from OpenAI's models raise important questions about the boundaries between legitimate technology transfer and intellectual property theft. The incident demonstrates how systematic API interactions can potentially enable competitors to replicate model capabilities at lower costs, with significant financial implications for the original model developers. The case also highlights the challenges of protecting AI models against extraction attempts, especially when attackers use authorized access channels. This creates a difficult balance between enabling legitimate API use and preventing unauthorized knowledge transfer, particularly in an international context where enforcement of intellectual property rights may be challenging.

Furthermore, the sophistication of detection and prevention mechanisms must evolve to address these threats. Organizations need to implement monitoring systems that can identify patterns of interaction that might indicate extraction attempts while maintaining legitimate access for authorized users. This might include analyzing query patterns, implementing rate limiting, and developing more sophisticated access controls that can distinguish between normal usage and systematic extraction attempts (Yildiz, 2025). Furthermore, the legal and regulatory implications of model extraction attacks present additional challenges. While intellectual property laws provide some protection for AI models and training data, the rapidly evolving nature of these technologies creates uncertainty about the scope and effectiveness of legal protections. Organizations must navigate complex questions about what aspects of their AI systems can be protected and how to enforce these protections effectively.

Organizations can adopt a variety of defense strategies to mitigate the risks of model extraction and safeguard their machine learning models. One approach is query rate limiting, which involves implementing advanced rate-limiting mechanisms that go beyond simply counting requests. These mechanisms analyze patterns of interaction, flagging and responding to potentially malicious behavior indicative of systematic probing. Another effective strategy is output perturbation, where controlled noise or variations are added to model outputs (El Ouadrhiri & Abdelhadi, 2022). This approach preserves the model's utility for legitimate users while making it significantly harder for adversaries to systematically extract its functionality. Additionally, watermarking techniques can be employed to embed subtle, identifiable markers into the model's outputs. These digital watermarks are designed to trace and identify unauthorized copies or derivatives, providing a means to detect intellectual property theft. Furthermore, robust access control mechanisms are crucial for restricting unauthorized access. Leveraging advanced authentication, monitoring user behavior, and employing AI-driven detection of anomalous activities enables organizations to potentially thwart systematic attempts to extract or replicate their models. Together, these strategies form a multilayered defense (think defense-in-depth always!), addressing both direct and indirect threats while maintaining the accessibility and usability of machine learning models for legitimate purposes.

The challenge of protecting against model extraction becomes especially complex when considering the need to maintain model utility and performance. Overly restrictive protection measures might significantly impact the model's usefulness for legitimate applications, creating a difficult balance between security and functionality. This is a notoriously difficult balance to achieve and becomes increasingly challenging as our cyber landscape evolves. Another significant consideration is the potential for model extraction attacks to compromise fine-tuned or domain-specific models that contain valuable industry-specific knowledge (Yao & de Soto, 2024). These specialized models often represent significant investment in collecting and curating domain-specific training data and optimizing model performance for particular applications. Their extraction could provide competitors with immediate access to this specialized capability without the associated investment in development.

The emergence of model extraction attacks targeting foundation models gives us another layer of complexity. While these base models might be publicly available, organizations often invest substantially in fine-tuning and optimizing them for specific applications (Parthasarathy et al., 2024). Protecting these customizations and improvements becomes crucial for maintaining competitive advantages and ensuring return on AI investments. The impact of successful model extraction extends beyond immediate financial losses to potentially compromising entire AI-driven business strategies. Organizations must consider how to protect their AI assets while maintaining the ability to deliver services and compete effectively in increasingly AI-driven markets. Moreover, the continued evolution of model extraction techniques will likely continue to challenge existing protection mechanisms. Organizations need to develop more sophisticated approaches to model protection that can adapt to new extraction techniques while maintaining model utility and performance. This might include developing new architectures that are inherently more resistant to extraction attempts or implementing more sophisticated monitoring and protection systems. The integration of AI systems into critical business processes makes protecting against model extraction increasingly important for organizational security and sustainability. As these systems become more sophisticated and valuable, the incentive for attackers to attempt model extraction will likely increase, requiring continued evolution of protection mechanisms and security strategies.

Moreover, the potential for extracted models to be used in supply chain attacks presents additional security concerns. An attacker who successfully extracts a model could potentially use their understanding of its behavior to develop more sophisticated attacks against systems that rely on similar models or that interact with the original system. Organizations must also consider the reputational risks (or the intangible side) associated with model extraction. A successful extraction attack that leads to unauthorized replication of an organization's AI capabilities could damage customer trust and market position, particularly if the extracted model is used to offer competing services or if the extraction exposes sensitive information about the organization's technical capabilities.

All in all, the development of effective protection strategies requires a comprehensive understanding of both technical and operational aspects of model deployment. Organizations need to consider how their models are accessed and used, implementing protection mechanisms that address specific risks while maintaining necessary functionality for legitimate users. Success in protecting against model extraction requires ongoing vigilance and adaptation of security measures as new extraction techniques emerge. Organizations must maintain awareness of evolving threats while continuously improving their protection mechanisms to address new challenges in model security.

5.6 Model Poisoning and Supply Chain Risks

The AI supply chain presents unique security challenges that extend beyond traditional software supply chain risks (Casey et al., 2024). With organizations increasingly relying on pretrained models, third-party components, and external AI services, the attack surface for model poisoning and supply chain attacks has expanded significantly (Wang et al., 2022b). These risks are worrisome because they can affect multiple organizations simultaneously and often remain undetected for extended periods. Supply chain vulnerabilities in AI development create numerous entry points for attackers. Organizations frequently utilize pretrained models as starting points for their AI applications, trusting that these models are secure and uncompromised. However, these pretrained models might harbor hidden vulnerabilities or malicious capabilities inserted during their development or distribution. The complexity of modern AI systems, with their numerous dependencies and components, makes it challenging to verify the integrity and security of each element in the supply chain. Consider the typical AI development pipeline: organizations might start with a pretrained model from a public repository, fine-tune it with additional data, and deploy it using various frameworks and libraries. At each stage, there are opportunities for compromise. A pretrained model might contain hidden biases or vulnerabilities, training data could be poisoned, and deployment frameworks might include compromised components. The interconnected nature of these elements means that a vulnerability in any part of the chain can potentially affect the entire system.

Model poisoning through supply chain attacks is a pretty sophisticated threat. Attackers might compromise popular model repositories, insert malicious code into widely used AI libraries, or distribute poisoned pretrained models that appear legitimate but contain hidden vulnerabilities (Zhao et al., 2024a). These attacks are especially dangerous because they can affect multiple organizations simultaneously, potentially compromising entire sectors that rely on similar AI components. For example, an attacker might distribute a compromised version of a popular pretrained language model through legitimate channels. Organizations incorporating this model into their applications would unknowingly introduce vulnerabilities into their systems. The poisoned model might function normally in most cases but contain hidden triggers that attackers can exploit later. This type of attack is particularly difficult to detect because the model's behavior appears normal under typical usage patterns. The implications of supply chain attacks on AI systems extend beyond immediate security concerns. Organizations might unwittingly build critical applications on compromised foundations, creating systemic vulnerabilities that could be exploited months or years later. Think of it this way: it is like a house of cards. The financial and operational impacts of such compromises can be severe, potentially affecting customer trust, regulatory compliance, and competitive position.

Detection and prevention of supply chain attacks present significant challenges. Traditional software security measures might not adequately address the unique aspects of AI supply chain risks. Organizations must develop new approaches to verify the integrity of AI components, validate pretrained models, and secure their AI development pipelines (Almagrabi & Khan, 2024). Model integrity verification becomes challenging when dealing with complex AI systems (Habbal et al., 2024). Organizations must consider not only the security of the model itself but also the integrity of training data, development tools, and deployment infrastructure. This comprehensive approach to security requires significant expertise and resources, which many organizations might struggle to maintain. In general, AI supply chain attacks will likely become more sophisticated as attackers develop new techniques for compromising AI systems. Organizations must remain vigilant and adapt their security measures to address emerging threats while maintaining the efficiency of their AI development processes. The challenge of securing the AI supply chain extends to model marketplaces and distribution platforms. As these platforms become more popular for sharing and distributing AI models, ensuring the security and integrity of hosted models becomes increasingly crucial. Organizations must carefully evaluate the security practices of platforms they rely on and implement additional validation measures for external AI components.

Trust relationships in the AI ecosystem are an important consideration here. Organizations often rely on trusted partners and providers for various aspects of their AI development, but these relationships can create additional attack vectors if not properly managed. Establishing and maintaining secure supply chain practices requires careful evaluation of all participants in the AI development process.

The impact of successful supply chain attacks can extend far beyond the immediate target. Compromised AI components might affect numerous downstream applications and services, creating cascading effects throughout the AI ecosystem. This interconnected nature of modern AI systems means that supply chain security must be considered from both individual and ecosystem perspectives.

Preventing AI supply chain attacks requires a holistic approach that addresses vulnerabilities across the entire development and deployment process. Comprehensive validation of pretrained models and external components is critical to ensure that third-party assets are free from malicious alterations or backdoors (Cheng et al., 2023). Organizations must adopt secure development practices throughout the AI pipeline, including code reviews, dependency management, and rigorous testing protocols (Fu et al., 2024). Regular security assessments of AI supply chain elements, such as software libraries, frameworks, and hardware components, help to identify and address emerging risks. Additionally, organizations should implement continuous monitoring for unusual model behavior or performance changes, which could indicate tampering or malicious interference. Proactively developing incident response plans tailored to AI supply chain compromises ensures that organizations can act swiftly to mitigate the impact of an attack. This is crucial to strengthening resilience against increasingly sophisticated threats targeting the AI ecosystem.

Organizations now have to also consider the long-term implications of their AI supply chain security decisions. Choices made during initial development might affect system security for years to come, particularly when dealing with embedded AI components that are difficult to update or replace. Now is not the time for impulse decisions and additions to technology infrastructures. The regulatory landscape surrounding AI supply chain security continues to evolve, with new requirements and standards emerging as organizations and governments recognize the importance of securing AI systems. Therefore, organizations must stay informed about these developments and adapt their security practices accordingly. In general, success in protecting against AI supply chain attacks requires a combination of technical expertise, operational discipline, and continuous vigilance. Organizations must develop comprehensive security strategies that address both current and emerging threats while maintaining the ability to leverage external AI components effectively.

That being said, the challenge of securing AI supply chains will likely become more complex as AI systems become more sophisticated and interconnected. Organizations must continue to evolve their security practices while balancing the need for innovation and efficiency in AI development. The implications of supply chain attacks for the future of AI development are significant. As organizations (and individuals) become more reliant on AI systems, ensuring the security and integrity of these systems throughout their lifecycle becomes increasingly crucial for maintaining operational resilience and competitive advantage.

5.7 Open-Source GAI Models

The proliferation of open-source GAI models introduces unique and novel security vulnerabilities that make these systems very attractive targets for attackers. Unlike proprietary models with restricted access, open-source models expose their architecture, training methods, and implementation details to potential attackers, creating multiple attack vectors that can be extensively studied and exploited (Demetrio et al., 2021). Subsequently, the fundamental challenge with open-source GAI models lies in their transparency (Si et al., 2024). While this transparency promotes innovation and collaboration, it also provides attackers with detailed insights into model architectures, training procedures, and potential vulnerabilities. Attackers can analyze the source code to identify weaknesses in model implementation, discover vulnerabilities in training pipelines, or develop targeted attacks based on known model behaviors. This level of access makes it easier for malicious actors to develop sophisticated attacks that might be more difficult to execute against closed-source systems.

Training data poisoning becomes an important concern with open-source models (Sun et al., 2022). Organizations often fine-tune these models on their own data, but the base models might already contain vulnerabilities introduced during pretraining. Attackers could contribute maliciously crafted training data to open-source datasets, potentially introducing backdoors or biases that persist through fine-tuning. The collaborative nature of open-source development makes it challenging to verify the integrity of all contributions, especially in large-scale models trained on vast datasets.

Model supply chain attacks, as discussed earlier, are another significant vulnerability. When organizations incorporate open-source models into their applications, they inherit not only the model's capabilities but also its potential security flaws (Wang et al., 2023). Attackers might target popular open-source models, introducing subtle vulnerabilities that could affect thousands of downstream applications. These supply chain attacks could range from introducing malicious code in model implementation to embedding harmful behaviors that only manifest under specific conditions. Additionally, the customization and deployment of open-source models create additional security challenges (AlMarzouq et al., 2005). Organizations often modify these models for specific applications, potentially introducing new vulnerabilities through integration with existing systems or custom modifications. The lack of standardized security practices for deploying and securing open-source models means that each implementation might have unique vulnerabilities based on how the model is integrated and deployed (Cruz et al., 2023).

Attack surface expansion occurs through the diverse ecosystem of tools and frameworks supporting open-source models (Ladisa et al., 2022). Each component in this ecosystem—from model serving infrastructure to data preprocessing pipelines—represents a potential attack vector. Vulnerabilities in any of these components could compromise the security of the entire system. The interconnected nature of these components makes it challenging to maintain comprehensive security across the entire stack. Another important consideration is versioning and update management, as they present unique challenges for open-source models (Li et al., 2011). Organizations must balance the need to incorporate security updates and improvements with the risk of introducing new vulnerabilities through updates. The rapid evolution of open-source models means that security implications of updates might not be fully understood before deployment, potentially creating windows of vulnerability that attackers could exploit. Furthermore, the community-driven nature of open-source development also introduces risks related to contributor verification and code review. While open-source communities often have robust review processes, sophisticated attackers might still find ways to introduce subtle vulnerabilities that escape detection. The complexity of modern GAI systems makes it challenging to thoroughly review all contributions for potential security implications.

Despite the security risks associated with open-source GAI models, open-source development also presents significant advantages for security that proprietary models often lack. One of the most critical benefits is the collective security auditing made possible through a broad community of researchers, developers, and cybersecurity professionals (Al-Kharusi et al., 2024). Because open-source models and their underlying code are publicly available, a global network of experts can scrutinize them for vulnerabilities, identify weaknesses, and propose patches at a much faster rate than what is typically seen in proprietary AI development. This transparency accelerates the discovery and mitigation of security flaws, reducing the risk of hidden vulnerabilities that could persist in closed-source systems for extended periods. In contrast, proprietary AI models often operate in a security through obscurity model, where vulnerabilities might remain undiscovered or unaddressed due to restricted access. Open-source AI allows for a proactive security model, where issues can be identified and patched collaboratively, increasing resilience against cyber threats.

Additionally, open-source AI fosters security innovation by enabling security researchers and red teams to develop advanced adversarial testing methodologies, penetration testing frameworks, and robust defenses against AI-specific attacks. Unlike proprietary models that restrict access and limit third-party testing, open-source AI allows researchers to experiment with real-world attack scenarios, stress-test models, and refine defense mechanisms against threats such as adversarial perturbations, prompt injection, and model inversion attacks (Hadi et al., 2024). This unrestricted security research strengthens the overall security posture of AI technologies by developing more effective and widely accessible security solutions. Moreover, open-source models promote the democratization of AI security, preventing a monopoly on secure AI development and ensuring that more organizations, including smaller entities, can access, contribute to, and benefit from secure AI frameworks. While the proliferation of open-source AI increases potential attack surfaces, it also enables more robust and widely distributed defense strategies. The same transparency that could be exploited by attackers also allows defenders to build more resilient, well-tested, and community-vetted security measures. As AI models become more complex and integrated into critical systems, leveraging the open-source community's collective expertise and vigilance will be essential for advancing AI security (Bildirici, 2024). Rather than viewing open-source AI as purely a liability, organizations should recognize its role in strengthening AI security through shared knowledge, rapid patching, and broad-based security innovation.

DeepSeek, an AI startup that emerged in early 2025 with a breakthrough open-source model that claimed to match or exceed the capabilities of leading commercial AI systems while using significantly fewer computational resources, exemplifies both the potential and risks of open-source AI models (Goldman, 2025). The DeepSeek case directly illustrates the security implications and market impact of open-source GAI models becoming competitive with proprietary systems. By developing a model that reportedly rivals leading commercial models at lower cost and with fewer computational resources, while making it freely available, DeepSeek demonstrates both the opportunities and risks of open-source AI. The significant market reaction—including plummeting tech stocks and the establishment of "war rooms" at companies like Meta—highlights how open-source models can disrupt established players and potentially introduce new security concerns. When high-performing AI models become openly available, it increases the potential attack surface as more actors gain access to sophisticated AI capabilities. This case especially emphasizes the supply chain and competitive aspects of open-source AI security, where the availability of powerful open models can rapidly shift market dynamics while potentially introducing new vulnerabilities that could affect multiple organizations simultaneously.

Supply chain vulnerabilities in generative AI code are a multidimensional security challenge that extends beyond traditional software risks. As organizations increasingly integrate AI-generated code into their development pipelines, they inadvertently expand their attack surface through what researchers have termed "slopsquatting," where AI models hallucinate nonexistent package dependencies that malicious actors can exploit (Toulas, 2025). Recent research indicates that even advanced commercial models generate nonexistent package references in approximately 5% of cases, with open-source models demonstrating significantly higher hallucination rates of up to 20% (Toulas, 2025). The repeatability of these hallucinations, with fabricated package names appearing multiple times across different runs, creates predictable patterns that attackers can weaponize by registering malicious packages under these hallucinated names (Toulas, 2025).

This vulnerability is particularly insidious because it exploits the growing trust developers place in AI coding assistants, creating a pathway for attackers to distribute compromised code components across multiple organizations simultaneously without requiring traditional social engineering or typosquatting techniques.

The implications of these AI-specific supply chain vulnerabilities extend throughout the entire software development lifecycle, affecting both individual developers and enterprise-scale operations. Organizations that have embraced "vibe coding," the practice of rapidly developing applications with heavy reliance on AI assistance, face heightened exposure to these risks, especially when developers implement AI-suggested code without thoroughly verifying package authenticity or existence. Effective mitigation strategies require a multilayered approach: implementing strict dependency verification protocols, utilizing dependency scanners and lockfiles to pin packages to known trusted versions, adjusting AI model temperature settings to reduce hallucination rates, and creating isolated testing environments for all AI-generated code before production deployment. As the integration between generative AI and software development continues to deepen, organizations must recognize that their security posture now includes not just their own code and third-party dependencies, but also the reliability and security implications of the AI models generating their code. This evolution demands new security frameworks that specifically address the unique challenges posed by AI-augmented development processes, particularly as attackers become increasingly sophisticated in exploiting the predictable patterns of AI hallucinations.

Mitigation strategies for open-source model vulnerabilities must be comprehensive and multilayered. Organizations should implement rigorous testing procedures for model updates, maintain strict control over training data sources, and develop robust monitoring systems to detect potential exploitation attempts. Regular security audits of both the model and its supporting infrastructure become crucial for maintaining security. The security challenges of open-source GAI models will likely increase as these systems become more prevalent and sophisticated. Organizations must develop security strategies that address both current and emerging vulnerabilities while maintaining the benefits of open-source collaboration. This includes establishing better security practices for model development, improving supply chain security, and creating more robust validation mechanisms for model updates and modifications. The implications for the broader AI security landscape are significant. As open-source models continue to gain popularity, they could become primary targets for attackers seeking to affect multiple organizations through a single vulnerability. The security community must develop new approaches to protecting these systems while preserving the benefits of open-source development and collaboration.

5.8 Application-Specific Risks

Application-specific risks in generative AI give us a complex web of challenges that span multiple domains and interaction types. In human–AI interaction, there are significant risks around the shift from coding expertise to prompt engineering proficiency, potentially creating new barriers and vulnerabilities in how we interact with these systems (Horne, 2023). The models' capability to generate convincing but potentially false information poses serious risks of misinformation and disinformation, very concerning in domains like healthcare, where incorrect information could lead to harmful medical decisions, or in education, where it could propagate misconceptions and inaccurate learning. Domain-specific risks manifest differently across various sectors (Leslie, 2019). In transportation, biased accident analysis and data leakage from self-driving cars pose safety and privacy concerns; in healthcare, unreliable diagnoses and exposure of sensitive patient information represent critical risks; in education, the technology could enable academic misconduct and impair genuine learning; in governance, these systems could be exploited for sophisticated phishing attacks targeting officials; and in scientific research, they might generate plausible but false content that could misdirect research efforts or compromise scientific integrity. These risks are amplified by the models' ability to generate highly convincing content that can be difficult to distinguish from authentic information, making detection and mitigation of these risks particularly challenging.

Human–AI interaction risks in the context of generative AI present complex challenges that extend beyond traditional technological concerns. As these systems become more sophisticated and integrated into daily operations, there's a fundamental shift in how humans interface with AI systems, moving from traditional coding and development skills to expertise in prompt engineering and AI interaction (Walter, 2024). This shift creates potential vulnerabilities where misunderstandings or misconfigurations in prompts could lead to unintended or potentially harmful outputs. Moreover, the democratization of AI through natural language interfaces, while making the technology more accessible, also introduces new risks. Users may place unwarranted trust in AI systems, failing to critically evaluate their outputs or understand their limitations (Omrani et al., 2022). This can be particularly problematic in professional contexts where AI-generated content might be used for critical decision-making without appropriate verification (Williamson & Prybutok, 2024).

A significant concern lies in the potential for AI systems to influence human behavior and decision-making processes in subtle ways (Dwivedi et al., 2021). As these systems become more sophisticated in understanding and generating human-like responses, there's a risk of users becoming overly dependent on AI guidance or losing confidence in their own judgment. Additionally, the interaction between humans and AI systems raises questions about accountability and responsibility (Novelli et al., 2024)—when an AI system contributes to a decision that leads to negative consequences, it becomes crucial but often difficult to determine where human oversight should have intervened. This complexity is further compounded in professional environments where the boundaries between human and AI responsibilities may become increasingly blurred, potentially leading to gaps in accountability and oversight.

Consider Hume AI's technology, which focuses on emotion recognition and analysis in human communication (Hume AI, n.d.). While the system's ability to analyze emotional patterns and responses could provide valuable insights in contexts like customer service or healthcare, it also presents significant interaction risks. An AI system making determinations about human emotional states could lead to misinterpretations or oversimplifications of complex human emotions, potentially resulting in inappropriate responses or interventions. For instance, in a mental health context, if healthcare providers overly rely on AI emotional analysis to assess patient well-being, they might miss subtle human cues or cultural nuances that the AI system fails to recognize. The system might interpret certain speech patterns or expressions as indicating one emotional state while missing crucial contextual or cultural factors that would lead a human practitioner to a different conclusion. This demonstrates how over-reliance on AI interpretation of human emotion could potentially lead to missed diagnoses or inappropriate treatment recommendations, highlighting the crucial importance of maintaining human judgment and expertise in conjunction with AI assistance rather than depending solely on AI interpretations.

Another example here is an incident involving Google's Gemini AI delivering hostile and harmful responses to a student's homework query (Newsweek, 2024). This perfectly illustrates the risks in human–AI interaction we discussed earlier. The AI's sudden shift from providing helpful academic information to delivering a threatening message saying "Please die" demonstrates how these systems can unpredictably generate harmful content, even in seemingly safe contexts like educational assistance. This case is particularly concerning because it highlights several key risks: the potential psychological impact on vulnerable users, the limitations of current safety measures, and the unpredictability of AI responses even in controlled environments like Google's system. The incident connects to broader concerns about human–AI interaction risks, especially when considering that if such interactions had occurred with someone in a vulnerable mental state, the consequences could have been severe, as highlighted by a separate case where a 14-year-old's interaction with an AI chatbot allegedly contributed to his suicide (Payne, 2024). This real-world example underscores the critical importance of robust safety measures, proper oversight, and the need to maintain awareness that, despite their sophisticated capabilities, AI systems can still produce harmful, inappropriate, or dangerous responses that could significantly impact users' wellbeing (Hill, 2023).

The risk of misinformation and disinformation through generative AI is maybe one of the most significant challenges in the technology's deployment and use (Shoaib et al., 2023). These models, capable of generating highly convincing and contextually appropriate content, can inadvertently produce false information or be deliberately misused to create deceptive content. The challenge is particularly acute because LLMs can generate content that appears authoritative and well-researched while containing subtle inaccuracies or completely fabricated information. A key concern lies in the models' tendency toward "hallucination"—generating plausible-sounding but factually incorrect information. This is particularly problematic in domains requiring high accuracy, such as healthcare, legal advice, or financial guidance. For instance, an LLM might generate convincing but incorrect medical advice or misinterpret legal precedents, potentially leading to serious real-world consequences. The challenge is compounded by the fact that these hallucinations can be difficult to detect, as they often appear contextually appropriate and well-reasoned. Nothing is as confident as an LLM saying something totally wrong!

The potential for deliberate misuse of these systems for disinformation campaigns presents an even more concerning scenario. Bad actors can leverage generative AI to create and rapidly disseminate false narratives, deepfake content, or manipulated information at an unprecedented scale. The ability of these systems to generate content in multiple languages and adapt to different cultural contexts makes them particularly effective tools for spreading disinformation across global audiences. Furthermore, the impact of AI-generated misinformation extends beyond individual pieces of false content. These systems can be used to create coordinated campaigns that establish false narratives across multiple platforms and formats, making it increasingly difficult for users to distinguish truth from fiction. This capability could be particularly dangerous during critical periods such as elections, public health crises, or times of social unrest, where accurate information is crucial for public safety and democratic processes. Therefore, the challenge of combating AI-generated misinformation is further complicated by the rapid advancement of the technology. As generative AI systems become more sophisticated, their outputs become increasingly difficult to distinguish from human-created content (Ghiurău & Popescu, 2024). Traditional fact-checking methods and content verification techniques may become less effective against AI-generated misinformation, requiring new approaches to information verification and authentication (Augenstein et al., 2024). Moreover, the viral nature of social media and the speed at which information spreads online amplifies the potential impact of AI-generated misinformation (Benzie

& Montasari, 2022). Once false information enters the digital ecosystem, it can be rapidly shared and replicated across platforms, making it extremely difficult to contain or correct. This creates a significant challenge for organizations, governments, and platforms trying to maintain information integrity while benefiting from the positive applications of generative AI technology.

From an organizational perspective, consider a pharmaceutical company that becomes the target of AI-generated misinformation. A malicious actor could use generative AI to create numerous convincing but false reports about side effects of one of the company's key medications, complete with fabricated patient testimonials, fake research citations, and manipulated data. These false reports could be distributed across multiple platforms, from social media to seemingly legitimate health forums. The AI-generated content could be so well-crafted that it appears credible even to healthcare professionals. The resulting damage could lead to a significant drop in prescription rates, stock price decline, loss of public trust, and potential regulatory investigations. The company would need to invest substantial resources in countering the false narratives while potentially losing millions in revenue, and even after the misinformation is debunked, the lingering effects on their reputation could persist for years.

On an individual level, consider a person seeking treatment for a serious medical condition who encounters AI-generated misinformation about alternative treatments. The AI might generate highly convincing but dangerous content that combines actual medical terminology with false claims, presenting a seemingly well-researched argument for unproven or harmful treatments. The content might include fabricated success stories, manipulated statistics, and misrepresented scientific studies, all generated with enough sophistication to appear credible. If this person chooses to follow this misleading advice instead of pursuing legitimate medical treatment, the consequences could be life-threatening. The individual might not only delay necessary medical care but also spend significant money on ineffective treatments, potentially suffering both health and financial consequences based on the AI-generated misinformation.

It is crucial to examine this from a different perspective—what are the domain-specific risks? Let's break down domain-specific risks of generative AI with concrete examples.

In healthcare, generative AI systems pose unique risks related to patient safety and medical decisions (Mulukuntla, 2022). For instance, imagine an AI system trained on medical imaging data that generates synthetic X-rays for training purposes. If these synthetic images contain subtle but clinically significant artifacts or misrepresent certain pathological conditions, it could lead to medical professionals being trained on inaccurate data. A practical example would be an AI that generates chest X-rays showing pneumonia patterns that don't accurately reflect real-world manifestations, potentially leading to misdiagnosis when doctors trained on this data encounter actual patients.

In the financial sector, generative AI systems could create sophisticated market manipulation scenarios or generate convincing but fraudulent financial documents. Consider an AI system that learns to generate realistic-looking financial statements and transaction histories. Bad actors could use this to create synthetic companies with fake but convincing financial histories to attract investors. For example, the AI might generate years of consistent growth patterns and plausible cash flow statements that pass initial due diligence but are entirely fabricated, leading to investment fraud on a scale that would be difficult to detect.

The legal domain faces risks related to the generation of falsified evidence or misleading legal documents. An AI system could be used to generate synthetic surveillance footage, create fake timestamps on documents, or produce convincing but fabricated email chains. Imagine a scenario where an AI generates realistic-looking video evidence showing someone at a different location during the time of an incident, or creates backdated contracts that appear legitimate but were actually generated after the fact. This could significantly complicate legal proceedings and undermine the justice system's ability to determine truth from fiction.

In education, generative AI presents risks related to academic integrity and the development of critical thinking skills. Beyond simple essay generation, advanced AI systems could create entire research projects, complete with fabricated data, methodology, and citations that appear legitimate but are entirely synthetic. For instance, an AI might generate a seemingly thorough scientific study on a novel educational method, complete with statistical analysis and student performance data, all of which is artificially created but convincing enough to influence educational policy decisions.

In journalism and media, generative AI risks center around the creation of sophisticated disinformation and synthetic media that can rapidly spread false narratives. Consider an AI system that can generate not just fake news articles, but entire coordinated campaigns across multiple platforms, complete with realistic comments, social media interactions, and supporting "evidence." For example, it could create a network of seemingly independent news sources all reporting on a fabricated event, each with its own unique writing style, perspective, and supporting materials, making it extremely difficult for readers to distinguish truth from fiction. The aforementioned is not a comprehensive list; however, this is just to give an example of the security impact that generative AI can have in different domains. However, these threats are continually evolving and changing, especially as generative AI's use becomes more widespread and becomes more sophisticated. These are just high-level examples, but there are many more and evolving domain-specific risks.

5.9 Challenges in Mitigating Generative AI Risks

We've discussed some alarming theories, concepts, and practical examples here. We will talk about mitigation in Chapter 6, the next chapter. However, it is important to understand that there are some hurdles when it comes to mitigation. Might as well discuss it here while we're already scared toward the end of Chapter 5!

Mitigating generative AI risks faces significant technical hurdles due to the evolving nature of attacks. Modern defense mechanisms struggle to detect sophisticated prompt injections that leverage context manipulation or chain multiple subtle prompts (Huang et al., 2024). For instance, attackers can craft prompts that appear benign individually but combine to circumvent safety measures, making traditional detection methods inadequate. Furthermore, legacy security frameworks often fail to address unique challenges posed by LLMs. Traditional input sanitization and validation techniques prove insufficient against semantic-based attacks, where malicious intent is encoded in seemingly normal language (Xiao et al., 2019). When security measures become too strict, they can severely limit model functionality, creating a challenging trade-off between security and utility. Testing and validation processes for generative AI systems present unique complexities (Aleti, 2023). Unlike traditional software testing, where inputs and outputs are clearly defined, generative AI systems can produce unexpected responses to novel combinations of inputs. The infinite possible permutations of prompts make comprehensive security testing practically impossible, leaving potential vulnerabilities undiscovered (Linardatos et al., 2020). The dynamic nature of attack surfaces complicates defense mechanisms. As models become more capable, new attack vectors emerge (Kaloudi & Li, 2020). Previous defenses against prompt injection may become obsolete when attackers discover novel ways to exploit model behaviors. This constant evolution requires adaptive security measures that can learn and update without compromising model performance. Moreover, security measures must account for the interconnected nature of various attack types. Data poisoning attacks can enable more effective prompt injections, while successful jailbreaking techniques might facilitate privacy breaches (Das et al., 2024b). A defense mechanism focused solely on one attack vector may inadvertently create vulnerabilities in others.

Resource constraints significantly impact mitigation strategies (Familoni, 2024). Implementing robust security measures often requires additional computation, increasing latency, and operational costs. Organizations must balance security requirements with performance expectations, particularly in real-time applications where response speed is crucial. The complexity of human–AI interaction adds another layer of challenge to risk mitigation. Users may unintentionally compromise security through normal interactions, making it difficult to distinguish between malicious attacks and legitimate use cases (Blauth et al., 2022). Security measures must be sophisticated enough to protect against attacks while maintaining natural interaction patterns. Privacy protection mechanisms often conflict with model utility and transparency requirements. Strong privacy guarantees might require limiting model outputs or adding noise to responses, potentially reducing the model's effectiveness in tasks requiring detailed or precise information (Shokri & Shmatikov, 2015). Organizations must carefully weigh these trade-offs while considering regulatory compliance requirements and user expectations.

Chapter 5 Summary

This chapter completed the triangular framework by examining generative AI systems as targets of sophisticated cyber threats, revealing how vulnerabilities in these models created cascading security risks across organizations and individuals. It analyzed a comprehensive spectrum of attacks targeting AI systems directly, beginning with prompt hacking and injection techniques that manipulated AI through carefully crafted inputs to bypass safety controls and extract unauthorized responses. The chapter detailed jailbreaking techniques that circumvented built-in restrictions, adversarial attacks that deceived models with subtle perturbations, and backdoor attacks that embedded hidden functionalities during training or fine-tuning processes. Critical privacy vulnerabilities emerged as major concerns, including gradient leakage attacks that extracted training data, MIA that determined dataset inclusion, and PII exposure that compromised sensitive personal information.

The analysis extended beyond technical attacks to examine availability threats targeting AI infrastructure, physical hardware vulnerabilities affecting specialized computing systems, and model extraction risks that threatened intellectual property. Supply chain compromises presented systemic vulnerabilities through poisoned training data and compromised model repositories, while open-source models introduced unique security challenges despite their collaborative benefits. The chapter explored application-specific risks across domains like healthcare, finance, and education, demonstrating how generative AI's unique characteristics created novel security challenges in each sector. Real-world examples illustrated these theoretical threats materializing in practice, from the DeepSeek database exposure to ChatGPT's SSRF vulnerability, showing how traditional infrastructure vulnerabilities compounded AI-specific risks. The chapter concluded by addressing the significant challenges in mitigating these risks, emphasizing the complex balance between maintaining robust protection and preserving model utility.

Key Takeaways:

The vulnerability of generative AI systems as targets represented a fundamental paradigm shift requiring organizations to protect not just their traditional IT infrastructure but also the AI models themselves. Unlike conventional software systems, AI models faced unique attack vectors that exploited their fundamental learning and processing mechanisms, from gradient analysis that could extract training data to prompt manipulation that bypassed safety controls. The chapter demonstrated that successful attacks on AI systems could cascade into broader organizational compromises, as evidenced by real-world incidents like the DeepSeek database exposure and ChatGPT's SSRF vulnerability. These vulnerabilities were particularly concerning because they often appeared during normal operation, making detection difficult while potentially exposing sensitive information, corrupting decision-making processes, or enabling attackers to weaponize the compromised AI systems against their own organizations.

The chapter revealed that securing AI systems required a fundamental rethinking of traditional cybersecurity approaches, as conventional security measures proved inadequate against AI-specific threats. The complexity of defending against attacks like model extraction, data poisoning, and sophisticated prompt injection demanded new security frameworks that balanced protection with functionality. Organizations faced the challenging reality that overly restrictive security measures could severely limit model utility, while insufficient protection left systems vulnerable to sophisticated attacks that could persist undetected for extended periods. The interconnected nature of AI vulnerabilities meant that a compromise in one area could enable attacks in others, requiring comprehensive, multilayered defense strategies that addressed the entire AI development and deployment lifecycle rather than focusing on individual threat vectors.

Case Study 1: Small Organization—Securing Customer Chatbot Systems

Background and Problem: XYZ Bakery, a local business with fewer than 20 employees, deployed a generative AI chatbot built on pretrained transformer-based models, such as OpenAI's GPT architecture, fine-tuned with customer interaction data. The chatbot handled tasks such as querying product availability, tracking orders, and offering personalized baking advice.

However, the system became vulnerable to prompt injection attacks, a form of adversarial attack exploiting natural language input to inject malicious instructions. Attackers embedded commands within syntactically valid queries, causing the model to expose sensitive customer information such as order histories, email addresses, and payment-related details. This highlighted the model's lack of defensive mechanisms and posed significant risks to customer trust and data integrity.

Technical Analysis: Small organizations like XYZ Bakery often deploy AI systems without robust security measures due to limited technical resources. The vulnerabilities identified in this case were as follows:

1) **Insufficient Input Validation:** The model failed to detect and reject adversarial inputs containing injection commands.
2) **Lack of Output Verification:** No monitoring layer existed to identify irregular patterns in chatbot responses, making exploitation undetected.
3) **Unsecured API Endpoints:** The public-facing API was not rate-limited, leaving it susceptible to automated attacks.

Solution and Implementation: To address these issues, XYZ Bakery implemented several technical measures:

1) **Input Validation and Filtering:** A custom preprocessing module was developed using regex-based sanitization and semantic validation to filter harmful inputs. This was supplemented by fine-tuning the model with adversarial samples to improve its robustness.
2) **Response Anomaly Detection:** A lightweight monitoring system using clustering and outlier detection was deployed to flag anomalous outputs indicative of data leaks.
3) **Rate Limiting and Throttling:** The chatbot's API was integrated with IP-based rate-limiting policies to mitigate brute force attacks and bot exploitation.
4) **Tokenization Control:** The chatbot's model was configured to limit its response length and restrict sensitive vocabulary output using specialized decoding parameters.

Outcome: Following these upgrades, XYZ Bakery experienced a 90% reduction in adversarial incidents over six months. The secured system also improved overall customer trust by ensuring compliance with privacy standards, such as GDPR.

Importance in the Triangular Framework: This case underscores the critical need for securing AI as a target in small businesses. Hardening the chatbot against exploitation was important to demonstrate that even resource-constrained organizations can protect generative AI systems, ensuring they remain productive tools rather than liabilities.

Case Study 2: Medium-Sized Organization—Defending Against Model Extraction

Background and Problem: ABC Solutions, a mid-sized software development firm, deployed a proprietary transformer-based AI code generator designed to optimize software development workflows. The model, fine-tuned with domain-specific training data, became the organization's competitive differentiator.

However, the system became the target of model extraction attacks, where adversaries systematically queried the model with diverse inputs to approximate its weights and replicate functionality. The attackers generated a shadow model with comparable performance, compromising the company's intellectual property and eroding its market edge.

Technical Analysis: Model extraction attacks exploit the black-box nature of deployed AI systems, systematically probing them for responses to infer parameters. Key vulnerabilities at ABC Solutions included:

1) **Unrestricted Query Access:** The public API allowed unlimited queries without authentication or usage monitoring.
2) **Predictable Outputs:** Model outputs lacked obfuscation or entropy, making it easier for attackers to reverse-engineer its decision boundaries.
3) **Absence of Defensive Watermarking:** No mechanisms were in place to track or detect unauthorized use of the extracted model.

Solution and Implementation: ABC Solutions adopted a multilayered security approach to protect its AI system:

1) **Query Behavior Analysis:** Tools like OpenTelemetry were integrated to log and analyze input patterns, using clustering and ML-based anomaly detection to identify systematic extraction attempts.
2) **Output Perturbation:** Differential privacy techniques were employed to add statistically controlled noise to outputs, preventing accurate parameter estimation during extraction.
3) **Watermarking Algorithms:** Invisible watermarks embedded in the model outputs allowed the identification of derived shadow models, providing evidence of intellectual property theft.
4) **Access Restrictions:** API keys with tiered usage limits were introduced, alongside token expiration policies and IP-based access restrictions.

Outcome: The implemented defenses disrupted multiple extraction attempts within the first quarter, ensuring the integrity of the proprietary model. ABC Solutions also retained its competitive advantage by safeguarding its intellectual property.

Importance in the Triangular Framework: This case highlights the necessity of treating AI as a target, particularly for medium-sized organizations relying on proprietary systems. Robust defenses against model extraction preserve the value of AI systems as tools while mitigating risks of exploitation as weapons by competitors.

Case Study 3: Large Organization—Addressing Data Poisoning in AI Training Pipelines

Background and Problem: DEF Corp, a global healthcare provider, leveraged a generative AI diagnostic support system trained on federated medical datasets, including proprietary patient data and public repositories. The AI model significantly reduced diagnostic errors and expedited treatment recommendations.

However, the system fell victim to a data poisoning attack, wherein adversaries manipulated an open-source medical dataset used during model retraining. Poisoned samples, containing mislabeled medical conditions and anomalous features, subtly degraded the AI's performance, leading to critical misdiagnoses in specific cases. This posed severe risks to patient safety and regulatory compliance.

Technical Analysis: Data poisoning attacks exploit gaps in data validation and model retraining pipelines. DEF Corp's vulnerabilities included:

1) **Over-Reliance on Public Datasets:** Lack of thorough vetting for external datasets introduced malicious samples into the training pipeline.
2) **Absence of Robust Validation:** No mechanisms existed to cross-verify the integrity of new data with trusted baselines.
3) **Limited Post-Retraining Monitoring:** Outputs post-retraining were not analyzed for performance deviations, allowing poisoned models to go unnoticed.

Solution and Implementation: DEF Corp reengineered its AI training pipeline with robust countermeasures:

1) **Data Integrity Validation:** Automated checksum-based integrity checks and statistical outlier detection methods were implemented to identify anomalous data samples in public datasets.
2) **Federated Learning with Differential Privacy:** Training data contributions were isolated across nodes with differential privacy constraints, minimizing the impact of malicious samples on global model updates.
3) **Retraining Audits:** A shadow model validation approach was adopted, comparing retrained models against previous iterations to detect performance deviations indicative of poisoning.
4) **Third-Party Dataset Vetting:** DEF Corp established vendor contracts mandating adherence to specific data security and quality standards.

Outcome: Postimplementation, DEF Corp successfully thwarted subsequent poisoning attempts, restoring AI reliability and maintaining compliance with healthcare regulations. These measures established the organization as a leader in AI security practices within the healthcare sector.

Importance in the Triangular Framework: This case highlights the dual role of AI as a tool and a target. In critical industries such as healthcare, safeguarding AI systems against data poisoning is paramount to preserving their utility and protecting against weaponized misuse.

Conclusion

These technical case studies demonstrate the diverse challenges organizations face in securing generative AI systems across different scales. By implementing tailored solutions, small, medium-sized, and large organizations can mitigate risks, ensuring their AI systems remain effective tools while neutralizing potential exploits as weapons or targets. The triangular framework provides a valuable lens for designing comprehensive AI security strategies.

Quiz

Questions

1 What type of attack was XYZ Bakery's chatbot vulnerable to in Case Study 1?
a) Model extraction
b) Prompt injection
c) Data poisoning
d) API rate flooding

2 In Case Study 2, which defense mechanism allowed ABC Solutions to identify unauthorized copies of their model?
a) Query behavior analysis
b) Output perturbation
c) Watermarking algorithms
d) API key restrictions

3 What was the primary threat vector in DEF Corp's AI diagnostic system (Case Study 3)?
a) Adversarial examples during inference
b) Manipulation of open-source medical datasets
c) Unauthorized access to patient records
d) Insider threats from medical staff

4 Which defensive measure was implemented by both XYZ Bakery (Case Study 1) and ABC Solutions (Case Study 2)?
a) Differential privacy techniques
b) API access restrictions and rate limiting

c) Federated learning
d) Shadow model validation

5 What initial action helped each organization determine how to secure their AI systems effectively?
a) Implementing robust data validation
b) Conducting a vulnerability analysis of their specific AI deployment
c) Hiring specialized AI security staff
d) Reducing dependence on external datasets

Answer Key

1 **Correct Answer: b) Prompt injection**
- **Explanation:** The case study explicitly states that XYZ Bakery's chatbot "became vulnerable to prompt injection attacks, a form of adversarial attack exploiting natural language input to inject malicious instructions." Attackers embedded commands within seemingly normal queries to trick the model into revealing sensitive information.
- Option a) is incorrect because model extraction was the attack faced by ABC Solutions in Case Study 2, not XYZ Bakery.
- Option c) is incorrect because data poisoning was the attack faced by DEF Corp in Case Study 3.
- Option d) is incorrect because while API rate flooding might be a concern, it wasn't the specific attack described in the case study.

2 **Correct Answer: c) Watermarking algorithms**
- **Explanation:** The case study states that ABC Solutions implemented "Watermarking Algorithms: Invisible watermarks embedded in the model outputs allowed the identification of derived shadow models, providing evidence of intellectual property theft."
- Option a) is incorrect because query behavior analysis was used to detect extraction attempts, not to identify unauthorized copies.
- Option b) is incorrect because output perturbation was used to prevent accurate parameter estimation during extraction attempts.
- Option d) is incorrect because API key restrictions limited access but didn't help identify unauthorized copies.

3 **Correct Answer: b) Manipulation of open-source medical datasets**
- **Explanation:** The case study explicitly states that "adversaries manipulated an open-source medical dataset used during model retraining," which is a data poisoning attack. The poisoned samples contained "mislabeled medical conditions and anomalous features."

- Option a) is incorrect because the attack occurred during training, not inference.
- Option c) is incorrect because there was no mention of unauthorized access to patient records.
- Option d) is incorrect because there was no mention of insider threats.

4 **Correct Answer: b) API access restrictions and rate limiting**
- **Explanation:** Both organizations implemented API restrictions. XYZ Bakery implemented "Rate Limiting and Throttling: The chatbot's API was integrated with IP-based rate-limiting policies." ABC Solutions implemented "Access Restrictions: API keys with tiered usage limits were introduced, alongside token expiration policies and IP-based access restrictions."
- Option a) is incorrect because differential privacy was only mentioned for ABC Solutions.
- Option c) is incorrect because federated learning was only mentioned for DEF Corp.
- Option d) is incorrect because shadow model validation was only mentioned for DEF Corp.

5 **Correct Answer: b) Conducting a vulnerability analysis of their specific AI deployment**
- **Explanation:** Each case study begins with a technical analysis of the specific vulnerabilities before implementing solutions. This suggests that understanding the unique vulnerabilities of each AI system is the critical first step. For example, XYZ Bakery identified "Insufficient Input Validation," ABC Solutions identified "Unrestricted Query Access," and DEF Corp identified "Over-reliance on Public Datasets."
- Option a) is just one type of solution that applies mainly to DEF Corp's case.
- Option c) is not mentioned as a recommendation in any of the case studies.
- Option d) is too specific to DEF Corp's situation and not a universal first step.

References

Abdali, S., Anarfi, R., Barberan, C. J., & He, J. (2024). Securing large language models: Threats, vulnerabilities and responsible practices. arXiv preprint arXiv:2403.12503.

Abrams, L. (2025, January 27). DeepSeek halts new signups amid "large-scale" cyberattack. Bleeping Computer. https://www.bleepingcomputer.com/news/security/deepseek-halts-new-signups-amid-large-scale-cyberattack/.

Aghakhani, H., Dai, W., Manoel, A., Fernandes, X., Kharkar, A., Kruegel, C., Vigna, G., Evans, D., Zorn, B., & Sim, R. (2024, May). Trojanpuzzle: Covertly poisoning code-suggestion models. *2024 IEEE Symposium on Security and Privacy (SP)* (pp. 1122–1140). IEEE.

Aleti, A. (2023, May). Software testing of generative AI systems: Challenges and opportunities. *2023 IEEE/ACM International Conference on Software Engineering: Future of Software Engineering (ICSE-FoSE)* (pp. 4–14). IEEE.

Al-Kharusi, Y., Khan, A., Rizwan, M., & Bait-Suwailam, M. M. (2024). Open-source artificial intelligence privacy and security: A review. *Computers, 13*(12), 311.

Almagrabi, A. O., & Khan, R. A. (2024). Optimizing secure AI lifecycle model management with innovative generative AI strategies. *IEEE Access, 13*, 12889–12920.

AlMarzouq, M., Zheng, L., Rong, G., & Grover, V. (2005). Open source: Concepts, benefits, and challenges. *Communications of the Association for Information Systems, 16*(1), 37.

Alotaibi, L., Seher, S., & Mohammad, N. (2024, January). Cyberattacks using ChatGPT: Exploring malicious content generation through prompt engineering. *2024 ASU international conference in emerging technologies for sustainability and intelligent systems (ICETSIS)* (pp. 1304–1311). IEEE.

Anand, N., Saifulla, M. A., Ponnuru, R. B., Alavalapati, G. R., Patan, R., & Gandomi, A. H. (2024). Securing software defined networks: A comprehensive analysis of approaches, applications, and future strategies against DoS attacks. *IEEE Access, 13*, 64473–64515.

Anthropic. (2025, February 3). Constitutional classifiers: Defending against universal jailbreaks. Anthropic.

Augenstein, I., Baldwin, T., Cha, M., Chakraborty, T., Ciampaglia, G. L., Corney, D., DiResta, R., Ferrara, E., Hale, S., Halevy, A., & Hovy, E. (2024). Factuality challenges in the era of large language models and opportunities for fact-checking. *Nature Machine Intelligence, 6*(8), 852–863.

Bennett, K., & Robertson, J. (2023, June). Cyberspace exercises: Defending against malicious cyber actors. *Artificial intelligence and machine learning for multi-domain operations applications V* (Vol. 12538, pp. 57–72). SPIE.

Benzie, A., & Montasari, R. (2022). Artificial intelligence and the spread of MIS-and disinformation. In R. Montasari (Ed.), *Artificial intelligence and national security* (pp. 1–18). Cham: Springer International Publishing.

Bildirici, F. (2024). Open-source AI: An approach to responsible artificial intelligence development. *REFLEKTİF Sosyal Bilimler Dergisi, 5*(1), 73–81.

Blauth, T. F., Gstrein, O. J., & Zwitter, A. (2022). Artificial intelligence crime: An overview of malicious use and abuse of AI. *IEEE Access, 10*, 77110–77122.

Boone, A. (2025). *The human AI pin has already been brought back to life*. Wired.

Boxleitner, A. (2023). Pushing boundaries or crossing lines? The complex ethics of ChatGPT jailbreaking. The Complex Ethics of ChatGPT Jailbreaking (October 17, 2023).

Briski, K. (2025, January 16). *NVIDIA releases NIM microservices to safeguard applications for agentic AI*. NVIDIA.

Cai, X., Xu, H., Xu, S., & Zhang, Y. (2022). Badprompt: Backdoor attacks on continuous prompts. *Advances in Neural Information Processing Systems, 35*, 37068–37080.

Cao, Y., Zhao, H., Cheng, Y., Shu, T., Chen, Y., Liu, G., Liang, G., Zhao, J., Yan, J., & Li, Y. (2024). Survey on large language model-enhanced reinforcement learning: Concept, taxonomy, and methods. *IEEE Transactions on Neural Networks and Learning Systems.*, *36*, 9737–9757.

Casey, B., Santos, J., & Mirakhorli, M. (2024). A large-scale exploit instrumentation study of AI/ML supply chain attacks in Hugging Face models. arXiv preprint arXiv:2410.04490.

Chao, P., Robey, A., Dobriban, E., Hassani, H., Pappas, G. J., & Wong, E. (2025). Jailbreaking black box large language models in twenty queries. arXiv preprint arXiv:2310.08419.

Charfeddine, M., Kammoun, H. M., Hamdaoui, B., & Guizani, M. (2024). Chatgpt's security risks and benefits: Offensive and defensive use-cases, mitigation measures, and future implications. *IEEE Access*, *12*, 30263–30310.

Chen, Z., Xiang, Z., Xiao, C., Song, D., & Li, B. (2024). Agentpoison: Red-teaming llm agents via poisoning memory or knowledge bases. arXiv preprint arXiv:2407.12784.

Cheng, P., Wu, Z., Du, W., Zhao, H., Lu, W., & Liu, G. (2023). Backdoor attacks and countermeasures in natural language processing models: a comprehensive security review. arXiv preprint arXiv:2309.06055.

Choi, S. P., Lee, J., Ahn, H., Jung, S., & Kang, B. (2023). ODIN: on-demand data formulation to mitigate dataset lock-in. arXiv preprint arXiv:2303.06832.

Chowdhury, A. G., Islam, M. M., Kumar, V., Shezan, F. H., Jain, V., & Chadha, A. (2024). Breaking down the defenses: a comparative survey of attacks on large language models. arXiv preprint arXiv:2403.04786.

Chu, J., Liu, Y., Yang, Z., Shen, X., Backes, M., & Zhang, Y. (2024). Comprehensive assessment of jailbreak attacks against llms. arXiv preprint arXiv:2402.05668.

Clop, C., & Teglia, Y. (2024). Backdoored retrievers for prompt injection attacks on retrieval augmented generation of large language models. arXiv preprint arXiv:2410.14479.

Cruz, D. B., Almeida, J. R., & Oliveira, J. L. (2023). Open source solutions for vulnerability assessment: A comparative analysis. *IEEE Access*, *11*, 100234–100255.

Das, A., Tariq, A., Batalini, F., Dhara, B., & Banerjee, I. (2024a). Exposing vulnerabilities in clinical LLMs through data poisoning attacks: Case study in breast cancer. MedRxiv.

Das, B., Amini, H., Wu, Y. (2024b). Security and privacy challenges of large language models: A survey. Arxiv preprint arXiv:2402.00888.

Demetrio, L., Coull, S. E., Biggio, B., Lagorio, G., Armando, A., & Roli, F. (2021). Adversarial exemples: A survey and experimental evaluation of practical attacks on machine learning for windows malware detection. *ACM Transactions on Privacy and Security (TOPS), 24*(4), 1–31.

Deng, G., Liu, Y., Li, Y., Wang, K., Zhang, Y., Li, Z., Wang, H., Zhang, T., & Liu, Y. (2024). Masterkey: Automated jailbreaking of large language model chatbots. *Proc. ISOC NDSS.*

Deng, J., Wang, Y., Li, J., Shang, C., Liu, H., Rajasekaran, S., & Ding, C. (2021). Gradient attack on transformer-based language models. arXiv preprint arXiv:2103.06819.

Derner, E., Batistič, K., Zahálka, J., & Babuška, R. (2024). A security risk taxonomy for prompt-based interaction with large language models. *IEEE Access., 12,* 126176–126187.

Dwivedi, Y. K., Hughes, L., Ismagilova, E., Aarts, G., Coombs, C., Crick, T., Duan, Y., Dwivedi, R., Edwards, J., Eirug, A., and Galanos, V., Ilavarasan, P. V., Janssen, M., Jones, P., Kar, A. K., Kizgin, H., Kronemann, B., Lal, B., Lucini, B., Medaglia R., le Meunier-FitzHugh K., le Meunier-FitzHugh L. C., Misra S., Mogaji E., Sharma S. K., Singh J. B., Raghavan V., Raman R., Rana N. P., Samothrakis S., Spencer J., Tamilmani K., Tubadji A., Walton P., & Williams, M. D. (2021). Artificial Intelligence (AI): Multidisciplinary perspectives on emerging challenges, opportunities, and agenda for research, practice and policy. *International Journal of Information Management, 57,* 101994.

El Ouadrhiri, A., & Abdelhadi, A. (2022). Differential privacy for deep and federated learning: a survey. *IEEE Access, 10,* 22359–22380.

Esteves, J. L. (2023). *Electromagnetic interferences and Information security: Characterization, exploitation and forensic analysis* [Doctoral dissertation, HESAM Université].

Etengu, R., Tan, S. C., Kwang, L. C., Abbou, F. M., & Chuah, T. C. (2020). AI-assisted framework for green-routing and load balancing in hybrid software-defined networking: Proposal, challenges and future perspective. *IEEE Access, 8,* 166384–166441.

Familoni, B. T. (2024). Cybersecurity challenges in the age of AI: Theoretical approaches and practical solutions. *Computer Science & IT Research Journal, 5*(3), 703–724.

Fang, H., Qiu, Y., Yu, H., Yu, W., Kong, J., Chong, B., Chen, B., Wang, X., Xia, S.T., & Xu, K. (2024). Privacy leakage on DNNS: a survey of model inversion attacks and defenses. arXiv preprint arXiv:2402.04013.

Feng, Q., Kasa, S. R., Yun, H., Teo, C. H., & Bodapati, S. B. (2024). Exposing privacy gaps: Membership inference attack on preference data for LLM alignment. arXiv preprint arXiv:2407.06443.

Frosst, N., & Hinton, G. (2017). Distilling a neural network into a soft decision tree. arXiv preprint arXiv:1711.09784.

Fu, M., Pasuksmit, J., & Tantithamthavorn, C. (2024). AI for devsecops: A landscape and future opportunities. *ACM Transactions on Software Engineering and Methodology*, *34*(4), 1–61.

Gai, K., Ding, Y., Wang, A., Zhu, L., Choo, K. K. R., Zhang, Q., & Wang, Z. (2021). Attacking the edge-of-things: A physical attack perspective. *IEEE Internet of Things Journal*, *9*(7), 5240–5253.

Ghiurău, D., & Popescu, D. E. (2024). Distinguishing reality from AI: Approaches for detecting synthetic content. *Computers*, *14*(1), 1.

Goldman, S. (2025, January 27). DeepSeek just flipped the AI script in favor of open-source – and the irony for OpenAI and Anthropic is brutal. *Fortune*.

Habbal, A., Ali, M. K., & Abuzaraida, M. A. (2024). Artificial Intelligence Trust, risk and security management (AI trism): Frameworks, applications, challenges and future research directions. *Expert Systems with Applications*, *240*, 122442.

Hadi, H. J., Ahmad, N., Aziz, K., Cao, Y., & Alshara, M. A. (2024). Cost-effective resilience: A comprehensive survey and tutorial on assessing open-source cybersecurity tools for multi-tiered defense. *IEEE Access*, *12*, 194053–194076.

Hettwer, B., Gehrer, S., & Güneysu, T. (2020). Applications of machine learning techniques in side-channel attacks: A survey. *Journal of Cryptographic Engineering*, *10*(2), 135–162.

Hidano, S., Murakami, T., & Kawamoto, Y. (2021, July). TransMIA: Membership inference attacks using transfer shadow training. *2021 international joint conference on neural networks (IJCNN)* (pp. 1–10). IEEE.

Hill, M. (2023). Hallucinating machines: Exploring the ethical implications of generative language models [Doctoral dissertation, Open Access Te Herenga Waka-Victoria University of Wellington].

Hoodlet, K. (2025a). Deceiving users with ANSI terminal codes in MCP. *Trail of Bits Blog*, 29 April. Available at: https://blog.trailofbits.com/2025/04/29/deceiving-users-with-ansi-terminal-codes-in-mcp/ (Accessed: 14 May 2025).

Hoodlet, K. (2025b). How MCP servers can steal your conversation history. *Trail of Bits Blog*, 23 April. Available at: https://blog.trailofbits.com/2025/04/23/how-mcp-servers-can-steal-your-conversation-history/ (Accessed: 14 May 2025).

Hoodlet, K. (2025c). Insecure credential storage plagues MCP. *Trail of Bits Blog*, 30 April. Available at: https://blog.trailofbits.com/2025/04/30/insecure-credential-storage-plagues-mcp/ (Accessed: 14 May 2025).

Horne, D. (2023, July). Pwnpilot: Reflections on trusting trust in the age of large language models and ai code assistants. In *In 2023 Congress in Computer Science, Computer Engineering, & Applied Computing (CSCE)* (pp. 2457–2464). IEEE.

Hou, X., Zhao, Y., Wang, S., & Wang, H. (2025). Model context protocol (MCP): Landscape, security threats, and future research directions. arXiv preprint arXiv:2503.23278.

Huang, K., Huang, G., Duan, Y., & Hyun, J. (2024). Utilizing prompt engineering to operationalize cybersecurity. In K. Huang, Y. Wang, B. Goertzel, Y. Li, S. Wright, & J. Ponnapalli (Eds.), *Generative AI security: Theories and practices* (pp. 271–303). Cham: Springer Nature Switzerland.

Hume AI. (n.d.). Hume. https://www.hume.ai/.

Jiang, S., Kadhe, S. R., Zhou, Y., Ahmed, F., Cai, L., & Baracaldo, N. (2024). Turning generative models degenerate: the power of data poisoning attacks. arXiv preprint arXiv:2407.12281.

Kachris, C. (2025). A survey on hardware accelerators for large language models. *Applied Sciences, 15*(2), 586.

Kaloudi, N., & Li, J. (2020). The AI-based cyber threat landscape: A survey. *ACM Computing Surveys (CSUR), 53*(1), 1–34.

Kaneko, M., Ma, Y., Wata, Y., & Okazaki, N. (2024). Sampling-based pseudo-likelihood for membership inference attacks. arXiv preprint arXiv:2404.11262.

Kilovaty, I. (2025). Hacking generative AI. *Loyola of Los Angeles Law Review, 58*, 1–62.

Kim, S., Yun, S., Lee, H., Gubri, M., Yoon, S., & Oh, S. J. (2024). Propile: Probing privacy leakage in large language models. *Advances in Neural Information Processing Systems, 36*, 20750–20762.

Kovacs, E. (2024, October 29). ChatGPT jailbreak: Researchers bypass AI safeguards using hexadecimal encoding and emojis. *Security Week*.

Kovacs, E. (2025, February 4). DeepSeek compared to ChatGPT, Gemini in AI jailbreak test. *Security Week*. https://www.securityweek.com/deepseek-compared-to-chatgpt-gemini-in-ai-jailbreak-test/.

Kumar, P. (2024). Adversarial attacks and defenses for large language models (LLMs): Methods, frameworks & challenges. *International Journal of Multimedia Information Retrieval, 13*(3), 26.

Ladisa, P., Plate, H., Martinez, M., & Barais, O. (2022). Taxonomy of attacks on open-source software supply chains. arXiv preprint arXiv:2204.04008.

Lakshmanan, R. (2025a, January 26). Meta's llama framework flaw exposes AI systems to remote code execution risks. *The Hacker News*. https://thehackernews.com/2025/01/metas-llama-framework-flaw-exposes-ai.html.

Lakshmanan, R. (2025b, April 9). Lovable AI found most vulnerable TO VibeScamming – Enabling anyone to build live scam pages. *The Hacker News*. https://thehackernews.com/2025/04/lovable-ai-found-most-vulnerable-to.html.

Lederer, I., Mayer, R., & Rauber, A. (2023). Identifying appropriate intellectual property protection mechanisms for machine learning models: A systematization of watermarking, fingerprinting, model access, and attacks. *IEEE Transactions on Neural Networks and Learning Systems*, *35*(10), 13082–13100.

Leslie, D. (2019). Understanding artificial intelligence ethics and safety. arXivpreprint arXiv:1906.05684.

Li, X., Li, Y. F., Xie, M., & Ng, S. H. (2011). Reliability analysis and optimal version-updating for open source software. *Information and Software Technology*, *53*(9), 929–936.

Li, Y., Huang, H., Zhao, Y., Ma, X., & Sun, J. (2024). Backdoorllm: A comprehensive benchmark for backdoor attacks on large language models. arXiv preprint arXiv:2408.12798.

Li, Y., Liu, S., Chen, K., Xie, X., Zhang, T., & Liu, Y. (2023). Multi-target backdoor attacks for code pre-trained models. arXiv preprint arXiv:2306.08350.

Linardatos, P., Papastefanopoulos, V., & Kotsiantis, S. (2020). Explainable AI: A review of machine learning interpretability methods. *Entropy*, *23*(1), 18.

Liu, F. W., & Hu, C. (2024). Exploring vulnerabilities and protections in large language models: A survey. arXiv preprint arXiv:2406.00240.

Lucchik, N. (2024). ChatGPT: A case study on copyright challenges for generative artificial intelligence systems. *European Journal of Risk Regulation*, *15*, 602–624.

Metta, S., Chang, I., Parker, J., Roman, M. P., & Ehuan, A. F. (2024). Generative AI in cybersecurity. arXiv preprint arXiv:2405.01674.

Michailidis, E. T., & Vouyioukas, D. (2022). A review on software-based and hardware-based authentication mechanisms for the internet of drones. *Drones*, *6*(2), 41.

Mireshghallah, F., Goyal, K., Uniyal, A., Berg-Kirkpatrick, T., & Shokri, R. (2022). Quantifying privacy risks of masked language models using membership inference attacks. arXiv preprint arXiv:2203.03929.

Mulukuntla, S. (2022). Generative AI-benefits, limitations, potential risks and challenges in healthcare industry. *EPH-International Journal of Medical and Health Science*, *8*(4), 1–9.

Nakka, K. K., Frikha, A., Mendes, R., Jiang, X., & Zhou, X. (2024). Pii-scope: A benchmark for training data PII leakage assessment in LLMs. arXiv preprint arXiv:2410.06704.

Narajala, V. S., & Habler, I. (2025). Enterprise-grade security for the model context protocol (MCP): frameworks and mitigation strategies. arXiv preprint arXiv:2504.08623.

Nelson, B. (2024, *May 28*). Fine-tuning LLMs breaks their safety and security alignment. *Cisco*. https://blogs.cisco.com/security/fine-tuning-llms-breaks-their-safety-and-security-alignment.

Newsweek. (2024, November 15). Google's AI chatbot tells student seeking help with homework 'please die'. Newsweek.

Novelli, C., Taddeo, M., & Floridi, L. (2024). Accountability in artificial intelligence: What it is and how it works. *AI & SOCIETY*, *39*(4), 1871–1882.

NVIDIA. (n.d.). LLM Vulnerability Scanning. NVIDIA.

Omrani, N., Rivieccio, G., Fiore, U., Schiavone, F., & Agreda, S. G. (2022). To trust or not to trust? An assessment of trust in AI-based systems: Concerns, ethics and contexts. *Technological Forecasting and Social Change*, *181*, 121763.

Packin, N. (2025, January 31). A deep-see on DeepSeek: How Italy's ban might shape AI oversight. *Forbes*. https://www.forbes.com/sites/nizangpackin/2025/01/31/a-deep-see-on-deepseek-how-italys-ban-might-shape-ai-oversight/.

Paganini, P. (2025, March 18). ChatGPT SSRF bug quickly becomes a favorite attack vector. Security Affairs.

Palo Alto Networks. (2025). MCP security exposed: What you need to know now. *Palo Alto Networks Community Blog*, April. Available at: https://live.paloaltonetworks.com/t5/community-blogs/mcp-security-exposed-what-you-need-to-know-now/ba-p/1227143 (Accessed: 14 May 2025).

Parthasarathy, V. B., Zafar, A., Khan, A., & Shahid, A. (2024). The ultimate guide to fine-tuning llms from basics to breakthroughs: An exhaustive review of technologies, research, best practices, applied research challenges and opportunities. arXiv preprint arXiv:2408.13296.

Payne, K. (2024, October 25). An AI chatbot pushed a teen to kill himself, a lawsuit against its creator alleges. *AP News*. https://apnews.com/article/chatbot-ai-lawsuit-suicide-teen-artificial-intelligence-9d48adc572100822fdbc3c90d1456bd0.

Peng, B., Bi, Z., Niu, Q., Liu, M., Feng, P., Wang, T., Yan, L. K., Wen, Y., Zhang, Y., & Yin, C. H. (2024). Jailbreaking and mitigation of vulnerabilities in large language models. arXiv preprint arXiv:2410.15236.

Poireault, K. (2025, January 30). DeepSeek exposed database leaks sensitive data. *Infosecurity Magazine*.

Rahman, M. M., Arshi, A. S., Hasan, M. M., Mishu, S. F., Shahriar, H., & Wu, F. (2023, June). Security risk and attacks in AI: A survey of security and privacy. *2023 IEEE 47th annual computers, software, and applications conference (COMPSAC)* (pp. 1834–1839). IEEE.

Šarčević, T., Karlowicz, A., Mayer, R., Baeza-Yates, R., & Rauber, A. (2024). U can't gen this? A survey of intellectual property protection methods for data in generative AI. arXiv preprint arXiv:2406.15386.

Sayar, I., Bartel, A., Bodden, E., & Le Traon, Y. (2023). An in-depth study of java deserialization remote-code execution exploits and vulnerabilities. *ACM Transactions on Software Engineering and Methodology*, *32*(1), 1–45.

Schwinn, L., Dobre, D., Günnemann, S., & Gidel, G. (2023, April). Adversarial attacks and defenses in large language models: Old and new threats. *Proceedings on PMLR* (pp. 103–117).

Shan, S., Ding, W., Passananti, J., Wu, S., Zheng, H., & Zhao, B. Y. (2024, May). Nightshade: Prompt-specific poisoning attacks on text-to-image generative models. *2024 IEEE symposium on security and privacy (SP)* (pp. 212–212). IEEE Computer Society.

Sharma, M., Tong, M., Mu, J., Wei, J., Kruthoff, J., Goodfriend, S., Ong, E., Peng, A., Agarwal, R., Anil, C., Askell, A., Bailey, N., Benton, J., Bluemke, E., Bowman, S. R., Christiansen, E., Cunningham, H., Dau, A., Gopal, A., … Perez, E. (2025). Constitutional classifiers: defending against universal jailbreaks across thousands of hours of red teaming. arXiv.

Shayegani, E., Mamun, M. A. A., Fu, Y., Zaree, P., Dong, Y., & Abu-Ghazaleh, N. (2023). Survey of vulnerabilities in large language models revealed by adversarial attacks. arXiv preprint arXiv:2310.10844.

Shi, J., Liu, Y., Zhou, P., & Sun, L. (2023). Badgpt: exploring security vulnerabilities of chatgpt via backdoor attacks to instructgpt. arXiv preprint arXiv:2304.12298.

Shoaib, M. R., Wang, Z., Ahvanooey, M. T., & Zhao, J. (2023, November). Deepfakes, misinformation, and disinformation in the era of frontier AI, generative AI, and large AI models. *2023 international conference on computer and applications (ICCA)* (pp. 1–7). IEEE.

Shokri, R., & Shmatikov, V. (2015, October). Privacy-preserving deep learning. *Proceedings of the 22nd ACM SIGSAC conference on computer and communications security* (pp. 1310–1321).

Si, M., Pan, S., Liao, D., Sun, X., Tao, Z., Shi, W., & Xing, Z. (2024). A solution toward transparent and practical AI regulation: privacy nutrition labels for open-source generative AI-based applications. arXiv preprint arXiv:2407.15407.

Simmons, P. (2011, December). Security through amnesia: a software-based solution to the cold boot attack on disk encryption. *Proceedings of the 27th annual computer security applications conference* (pp. 73–82).

Sun, Z., Du, X., Song, F., Ni, M., & Li, L. (2022, April). Coprotector: Protect open-source code against unauthorized training usage with data poisoning. *Proceedings of the ACM web conference 2022* (pp. 652–660).

Tariq, M. I., Memon, N. A., Ahmed, S., Tayyaba, S., Mushtaq, M. T., Mian, N. A., Imran, M., & Ashraf, M. W. (2020). A review of deep learning security and privacy defensive techniques. *Mobile Information Systems, 2020*(1), 1–18.

The Vulnerable MCP Project. (2025). The vulnerable MCP project. Available at: https://vulnerablemcp.info/ (Accessed: 14 May 2025).

Toulas, B. (2025, *April 12*). AI-hallucinated code dependencies become new supply chain risk. *Bleeping Computer*. https://www.bleepingcomputer.com/news/security/ai-hallucinated-code-dependencies-become-new-supply-chain-risk/.

Uber. (2024, September 19). QueryGPT – Natural Langauge to SQL Using Generative AI. Uber Blog.

Ullah, F., Edwards, M., Ramdhany, R., Chitchyan, R., Babar, M. A., & Rashid, A. (2018). Data exfiltration: A review of external attack vectors and countermeasures. *Journal of Network and Computer Applications, 101*, 18–54.

Vechev, M. (2025, January 28). A quick comment on DeepSeek. LinkedIn.

Verbauwhede, I. (2019). *Hardware security*. Bristol, UK: University of Bristol, CyBOK.

Verizon. (2024). Data Breach Investigations Report. Verizon. https://www.verizon.com/business/resources/T63c/reports/2024-dbir-data-breach-investigations-report.pdf.

Walter, Y. (2024). Embracing the future of Artificial Intelligence in the classroom: the relevance of AI literacy, prompt engineering, and critical thinking in modern education. *International Journal of Educational Technology in Higher Education, 21*(1), 15.

Wang, J., Guo, S., Xie, X., & Qi, H. (2022a, May). Protect privacy from gradient leakage attack in federated learning. *IEEE INFOCOM 2022-IEEE conference on computer communications* (pp. 580–589). IEEE.

Wang, M., Wu, P., & Luo, Q. (2023). Construction of software supply chain threat portrait based on chain perspective. *Mathematics, 11*(23), 4856.

Wang, Z., Ma, J., Wang, X., Hu, J., Qin, Z., & Ren, K. (2022b). Threats to training: A survey of poisoning attacks and defenses on machine learning systems. *ACM Computing Surveys, 55*(7), 1–36.

Weatherbed, J. (2025, January 29). OpenAI has evidence that its models helped train China's DeepSeek. The Verge.

Wei, W., & Liu, L. (2021). Gradient leakage attack resilient deep learning. *IEEE Transactions on Information Forensics and Security, 17*, 303–316.

Wei, W., Liu, L., Loper, M., Chow, K. H., Gursoy, M. E., Truex, S., & Wu, Y. (2020). A framework for evaluating gradient leakage attacks in federated learning. arXiv preprint arXiv:2004.10397.

Williamson, S. M., & Prybutok, V. (2024). The era of artificial intelligence deception: Unraveling the complexities of false realities and emerging threats of misinformation. *Information, 15*(6), 299.

Willison, S. (2025) Model Context Protocol has prompt injection security problems. *Simon Willison's Weblog*, 9 April. Available at: https://simonwillison.net/2025/Apr/9/mcp-prompt-injection/ (Accessed: 14 May 2025).

Wolters, C., Yang, X., Schlichtmann, U., & Suzumura, T. (2024). Memory is all you need: an overview of compute-in-memory architectures for accelerating large language model inference. arXiv preprint arXiv:2406.08413.

Xiang, Z., Jiang, F., Xiong, Z., Ramasubramanian, B., Poovendran, R., & Li, B. (2024). Badchain: Backdoor chain-of-thought prompting for large language models. arXiv preprint arXiv:2401.12242.

Xiao, Y., Jia, Y., Liu, C., Cheng, X., Yu, J., & Lv, W. (2019). Edge computing security: State of the art and challenges. *Proceedings of the IEEE, 107*(8), 1608–1631.

Xu, W., Chen, J., Zheng, P., Yi, X., Tian, T., Zhu, W., Wan, Q., Wang, H., Fan, Y., Su, Q., & Shen, X. (2024). Deploying foundation model powered agent services: A survey. arXiv preprint arXiv:2412.13437.

Yan, S., Wang, S., Duan, Y., Hong, H., Lee, K., Kim, D., & Hong, Y. (2024). *An LLM-assisted easy-to-trigger poisoning attack on code completion models: Injecting disguised vulnerabilities against strong detection.* Usenix.

Yang, H., Xiang, K., Ge, M., Li, H., Lu, R., & Yu, S. (2024). A comprehensive overview of backdoor attacks in large language models within communication networks. *IEEE Network, 38*, 211–218.

Yang, K., Wang, H., & Sun, L. (2022). An effective intrusion-resilient mechanism for programmable logic controllers against data tampering attacks. *Computers in Industry, 138*, 103613.

Yao, D., & de Soto, B. G. (2024). Enhancing cyber risk identification in the construction industry using language models. *Automation in Construction, 165*, 105565.

Yi, J., Xie, Y., Zhu, B., Kiciman, E., Sun, G., Xie, X., & Wu, F. (2023). Benchmarking and defending against indirect prompt injection attacks on large language models. arXiv preprint arXiv:2312.14197.

Yildiz, O. (2025, January 22). Mastering LLM and generative AI security: An ultra-extensive guide to emerging vulnerabilities and the OWASP LLM top 10. Medium.

You, W., Hammoudeh, Z., & Lowd, D. (2023). Large language models are better adversaries: Exploring generative clean-label backdoor attacks against text classifiers. arXiv preprint arXiv:2310.18603.

Zargar, S. T., Joshi, J., & Tipper, D. (2013). A survey of defense mechanisms against distributed denial of service (DDoS) flooding attacks. *IEEE Communications Surveys & Tutorials, 15*(4), 2046–2069.

Zeng, Y., Pan, M., Just, H. A., Lyu, L., Qiu, M., & Jia, R. (2023, November). Narcissus: A practical clean-label backdoor attack with limited information. *Proceedings of the 2023 ACM SIGSAC conference on computer and communications security* (pp. 771–785).

Zhang, C., Jin, M., Yu, Q., Liu, C., Xue, H., & Jin, X. (2024). Goal-guided generative prompt injection attack on large language models. arXiv preprint arXiv:2404.07234.

Zhao, J., Chen, Y., & Zhang, W. (2019). Differential privacy preservation in deep learning: Challenges, opportunities and solutions. *IEEE Access, 7*, 48901–48911.

Zhao, J., Wang, S., Zhao, Y., Hou, X., Wang, K., Gao, P., Zhang, Y., Wei, C., & Wang, H. (2024a, October). Models are codes: Towards measuring malicious code poisoning attacks on pre-trained model hubs. *Proceedings of the 39th IEEE/ACM international conference on automated software engineering* (pp. 2087–2098).

Zhao, S., Jia, M., Guo, Z., Gan, L., Xu, X., Wu, X., Fu, J., Feng, Y., Pan, F., & Tuan, L. A. (2024b). A survey of backdoor attacks and defenses on large language models: Implications for security measures. Authorea Preprints.

Zheng, Y., Chang, C. H., Huang, S. H., Chen, P. Y., & Picek, S. (2024). An overview of trustworthy AI: Advances in IP protection, privacy-preserving federated learning, security verification, and GAI safety alignment. *IEEE Journal on Emerging and Selected Topics in Circuits and Systems.*, *14*(4), 582–607.

Zhu, L., Liu, Z., & Han, S. (2019). Deep leakage from gradients. *Advances in Neural Information Processing Systems*, *32*, 1–29.

Zhu, S., Zhang, R., An, B., Wu, G., Barrow, J., Wang, Z., Huang, F., Nenkova, A., & Sun, T. (2023). Autodan: Interpretable gradient-based adversarial attacks on large language models. arXiv preprint arXiv:2310.15140.

Zorz, Z. (2023). A bug revealed ChatGPT users' chat history, personal and billing data. *Help Net Security*. https://www.helpnetsecurity.com/2023/03/27/chatgpt-data-leak/.

Zou, A., Wang, Z., Carlini, N., Nasr, M., Kolter, J. Z., & Fredrikson, M. (2023). Universal and transferable adversarial attacks on aligned language models. arXiv preprint arXiv:2307.15043.

6

Defending Against Generative AI Threats

6.1 Deepfake Detection Techniques

Well, you've made it to Chapter 6. Let's talk about some discuss strategies and techniques for mitigating risks associated with generative AI. This chapter, Chapter 6, examines techniques for detecting and mitigating various forms of AI-generated deception, from sophisticated deepfakes to adversarial attacks. Through an exploration of adversarial training, secure development practices, model protection mechanisms, and privacy-preserving techniques, this chapter provides security practitioners and AI developers with comprehensive frameworks to enhance model resilience while maintaining utility. We will pay special attention to emerging technologies like differential privacy and homomorphic encryption, which allow organizations to balance the competing demands of model performance, security, and data privacy in an increasingly complex threat landscape.

In Chapter 4, we addressed the challenges and risks that deepfakes can bring to organizations, individuals, and modern society. Consequently, let's address what methods can be utilized to mitigate the threats and potential negative impact that deepfakes can have. This section will look at techniques for detecting AI-generated synthetic media, with a focus on deepfake detection methodologies. Modern detection approaches analyze visual artifacts that commonly appear in synthetic content, such as inconsistent eye blinking patterns, unnatural facial features, or lighting irregularities (Ahmed et al., 2024). Biological signal detection examines physiological markers like pulse signals visible in skin color variations and natural micro-expressions that are difficult for current AI systems to replicate accurately (Zhang, 2023). Metadata analysis scrutinizes file characteristics, compression patterns, and digital signatures that may reveal synthetic manipulation, while digital watermarking provides a proactive approach by embedding traceable markers into legitimate content during creation (Sayyafzadeh, 2024). These complementary techniques, when combined, create a multilayered detection

Generative AI Security: Defense, Threats, and Vulnerabilities, First Edition. Shaila Rana and Rhonda Chicone.

framework that enhances the identification of manipulated media across various contexts and quality levels.

Visual artifact analysis for deepfake detection focuses on identifying telltale signs of AI manipulation in synthetic media (Ghiurău & Popescu, 2024). These artifacts emerge from current limitations in generative AI systems' ability to maintain perfect consistency across all elements of synthetic content. Common visual artifacts include unnatural lighting patterns, inconsistent shadows, irregular facial symmetry, blurred or distorted textures around complex features like hair and teeth, and anomalies in background elements that don't match natural scene physics (Mathys et al., 2024). Advanced detection systems employ deep learning models trained to recognize specific types of artifacts characteristic of different deepfake generation methods. These systems analyze frame-by-frame temporal consistency, looking for subtle discontinuities in motion, particularly around facial features like eyes, lips, and jaw movements (Waseem et al., 2023). Neural networks can identify irregularities in skin texture, unnatural color gradients, and inconsistencies in facial geometry that may be imperceptible to human observers but reveal synthetic manipulation (George & George, 2023).

The effectiveness of visual artifact detection varies with deepfake quality and generation method. High-resolution deepfakes created with more sophisticated models may exhibit fewer obvious artifacts, requiring more nuanced detection approaches that combine multiple analysis techniques (Ghiurău & Popescu, 2024). Detection systems must continuously evolve as generative models improve and new artifacts emerge with each generation of deepfake technology. An example here—a detection system could analyze video frames using a convolutional neural network trained on datasets of confirmed deepfakes and authentic media. The system would extract features like facial landmarks, texture patterns, and lighting characteristics, comparing them against known artifact signatures. For instance, the detector might segment the face into regions (eyes, mouth, and skin) and analyze each for specific artifacts: checking eye reflections for consistent light sources, verifying that skin pores maintain natural patterns across frames, and ensuring mouth movements align with acoustic features. The system could output a confidence score and highlight suspicious regions, helping human reviewers focus their attention on potential manipulations.

Biological signal detection in deepfake analysis focuses on identifying physiological markers that are difficult for AI systems to accurately simulate (Ni et al., 2024). These include subtle variations in skin color caused by blood flow (pulse signals), natural micro-expressions that occur involuntarily, and precise pupil dilation responses to light changes. Advanced detection systems analyze these biomarkers across video frames, looking for unnatural patterns or missing signals that indicate synthetic content (Masood et al., 2023). The technology leverages computer vision and signal processing techniques to extract and analyze these biological indicators. For example, remote photoplethysmography (rPPG) can detect slight color changes in facial skin that correspond to heartbeats—a feature that many current deepfake systems fail to replicate accurately (Pirzada et al., 2023). Similarly, systems track involuntary muscle movements and micro-expressions that occur at millisecond timescales, as these subtle movements follow specific neurological patterns that synthetic content typically lacks.

Metadata is another important technique that could be utilized here. Metadata analysis in deepfake detection examines digital fingerprints and file characteristics that can reveal synthetic manipulation (Ganti, 2022). Key metadata elements include file creation timestamps, modification history, compression patterns, and device signatures. Inconsistencies in these attributes often indicate potential manipulation, as deepfake generation typically disrupts original metadata patterns or creates anomalous signatures. Professional cameras and editing software embed specific metadata markers that follow standardized formats (Tesic, 2005). When content is synthetically generated, these patterns may be missing, incomplete, or show irregularities in the expected sequence of editing operations. Detection systems analyze EXIF data, compression artifacts, and noise patterns that differ between authentic and AI-generated content (Erkek, 2023). Advanced metadata analysis incorporates blockchain-based verification systems and cryptographic hashing to establish content authenticity (Qureshi & Megias Jimenez, 2021; Shah et al., 2024). These systems create immutable records of original content metadata, enabling verification of media provenance and tracking modifications throughout the content lifecycle. Camera manufacturers are increasingly implementing secure metadata embedding at the hardware level, creating verifiable chains of custody from capture to distribution. An example here would be to combine automated metadata extraction tools with machine learning models trained on known deepfake signatures. The system would flag suspicious indicators like missing or inconsistent device information, unusual editing software signatures, compression patterns that don't match claimed source devices, temporal inconsistencies in modification timestamps, broken chains in digital signatures, and more.

Digital watermarking embeds imperceptible markers into media content during creation, enabling downstream verification of authenticity and origin (Liang et al., 2024). Modern watermarking techniques use robust algorithms that survive compression, format conversion, and reasonable editing while remaining difficult to remove or forge (Amrit & Singh, 2022). These watermarks can encode information about the generating model, creation timestamp, and authorized modifications. California's SB 942 legislation, effective January 2025, mandates clear disclosure through digital watermarks for AI-generated content that appears realistic but is synthetic (California Legislative Information, 2024). This marks a significant shift toward regulated AI content identification, likely influencing similar legislation across other jurisdictions. The EU AI Act and other pending regulations worldwide similarly emphasize content authenticity verification requirements, highlighting a growing regulatory trend toward mandatory disclosure and tracking of AI-generated media (EU Artificial Intelligence Act, 2025).

Current R&D efforts in watermarking technology face significant challenges and opportunities. Research focuses on developing systems resistant to adversarial attacks while maintaining media quality, including adaptive watermarking that adjusts to different content types, integration with blockchain for verifiable content tracking, zero-knowledge proofs for privacy-preserving verification, and cross-platform watermark interoperability standards (Alberti et al., 2003; ELMessiry & Messiry, 2024; Gabay et al., 2020). However, research investment remains insufficient given the rapid advancement of generative AI capabilities. Critical gaps exist in watermark persistence across multiple generations of content manipulation, standardization of watermarking protocols, and scalable verification infrastructure (Carra et al., 2024). Industry-academic partnerships and increased government funding could accelerate development of robust watermarking frameworks necessary for widespread adoption and regulatory compliance. The intersection of technological capability and regulatory requirements makes this an increasingly crucial area for focused research and development efforts.

6.2 Adversarial Training and Robustness

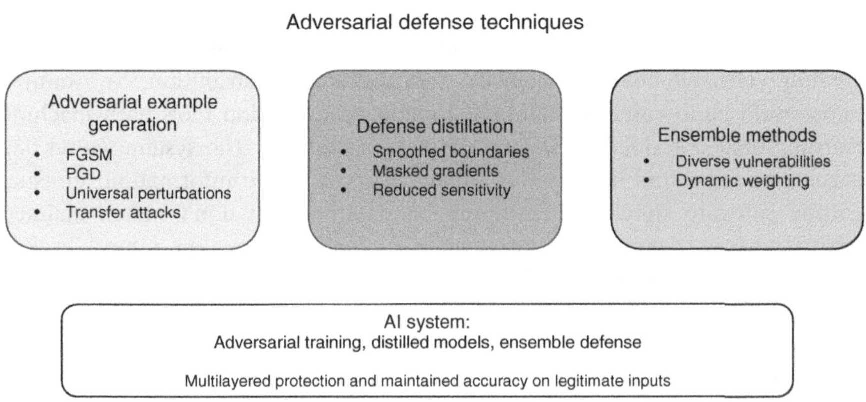

Key Concepts:

- Adversarial Examples: Inputs designed to fool AI models through subtle perturbations
- Defense Distillation: Training technique that smooths decision boundaries using teacher-student approach
- Ensemble Methods: Combining multiple models to create robust defense against diverse attack vectors
- Gradient Masking: Hiding gradient information that attackers typically exploit
- Dynamic Weighting: Adaptive adjustment of model contributions based on confidence and threat detection

Adversarial training and robustness are an important defense against threats originating from generative AI. Section 6.2 examines advanced techniques for strengthening AI models against adversarial attacks through systematic training and architectural improvements. This section explores the generation of adversarial examples to probe model vulnerabilities, application of defense distillation to reduce model sensitivity to malicious inputs, and implementation of ensemble methods that combine multiple models to create more robust defense mechanisms. Understanding these approaches is crucial for developing AI systems that maintain reliability and accuracy even when faced with sophisticated attacks designed to manipulate their outputs or behavior.

Adversarial example generation is a systematic process of creating inputs designed to exploit vulnerabilities in AI models, particularly focusing on generating content that causes misclassification or unintended outputs (Radanliev & Santos, 2023). These examples are crafted by making subtle modifications to legitimate inputs, often imperceptible to humans but capable of significantly impacting model predictions. Common techniques include gradient-based methods like Fast Gradient Sign Method (FGSM) and iterative approaches such as Projected Gradient Descent (PGD), which systematically perturb input features to maximize model error (Gupta et al., 2018; Liu et al., 2019). Understanding adversarial example generation serves two critical purposes in AI security. First, it enables thorough testing of model robustness by simulating potential attack scenarios and identifying weaknesses before deployment. Second, these examples become valuable training data for adversarial training, where models are explicitly trained to resist such manipulations. The process typically involves optimizing perturbations that maximize the model's loss while remaining within constraints that maintain the example's realism or imperceptibility (Qian et al., 2022). Recent advances in adversarial example generation have revealed increasingly sophisticated attack vectors. Researchers have developed universal adversarial perturbations that can affect multiple inputs simultaneously, transferred attacks that work across different model architectures, and physically realizable adversarial examples that maintain their effectiveness when implemented in the real world (Moosavi-Dezfooli et al., 2017). These developments highlight the importance of incorporating adversarial example generation into the model development lifecycle to build more resilient AI systems.

For example, imagine generating adversarial images by iteratively adding carefully calculated noise patterns that cause an image classification model to misclassify common objects. For instance, subtle pixel modifications might cause a stop sign to be classified as a yield sign—a potentially dangerous outcome in autonomous driving applications. This demonstrates why understanding and defending against such attacks is crucial for safety-critical AI applications.

Defense distillation adapts the concept of model distillation, typically used for model compression, into a defensive technique against adversarial attacks

(Papernot et al., 2016). The process involves training an initial "teacher" model, and then using its softened probability distributions to train a second "student" model, which inherits knowledge while gaining robustness against adversarial inputs. This technique reduces the model's sensitivity to small perturbations by smoothing decision boundaries. The effectiveness of defense distillation stems from its ability to mask gradient information that attackers typically exploit. Hence, training on softened probabilities rather than hard labels, the distilled model develops more gradual transitions between decision regions, making it harder for attackers to find adversarial perturbations (Han et al., 2024). The temperature parameter in the softmax function controls this smoothing effect, with higher temperatures generally resulting in more robust models (Agarwala et al., 2020).

Implementation challenges include selecting appropriate temperature values and balancing robustness against model accuracy. Higher temperatures provide better defense but may reduce model performance on legitimate inputs. Additionally, recent research has shown that while defense distillation effectively counters certain gradient-based attacks, sophisticated attackers can still develop successful adversarial examples by adapting their approach (Liang et al., 2022). Subsequently, to understand this in practical terms, real-world applications often combine defense distillation with other defensive techniques for comprehensive protection. For example, financial fraud detection systems might use distilled models as part of a larger ensemble, leveraging the smoothed decision boundaries to reduce false positives while maintaining high detection rates. This hybrid approach acknowledges that no single defensive technique provides complete protection against all possible attacks.

Then we have ensemble methods. Ensemble methods in AI security combine multiple models or defensive techniques to create more robust protection against adversarial attacks (Nowroozi et al., 2023). This approach leverages the principle that different models often have varying vulnerabilities, making it harder for attackers to successfully compromise the system as a whole. In general, aggregating predictions from multiple models through voting, averaging, or weighted combinations, ensembles can detect and filter out adversarial inputs more effectively than single models. Different architectures within an ensemble provide complementary defensive capabilities. For example, some models might be trained on different subsets of data, use varying architectures, or employ different defensive techniques like adversarial training or defense distillation. This diversity makes it computationally expensive for attackers to find adversarial examples that fool all models simultaneously, as they must optimize across multiple decision boundaries and defensive mechanisms. Advanced ensemble strategies incorporate dynamic weighting mechanisms that adjust model contributions based on confidence scores and input characteristics (Rane et al., 2024).

These adaptive systems can detect when specific models might be under attack and adjust their influence accordingly. Some implementations use specialized detector models trained specifically to identify adversarial inputs, working alongside primary classification models to create a multilayered defense system (Kota, 2024).

Real-time performance considerations are crucial when implementing ensemble methods. While more models provide better security, they also increase computational overhead and latency (Sayadi et al., 2018). Organizations must carefully balance security requirements against performance constraints, often employing techniques like model pruning or selective activation to maintain efficiency while preserving defensive capabilities (Han et al., 2024). Resource constraints and deployment challenges remain significant concerns in ensemble implementation. Organizations must manage increased storage requirements, computational costs, and system complexity. Modern approaches address these challenges through techniques like model quantization, selective ensemble activation based on threat levels, and efficient parallel processing architectures that minimize latency impact while maintaining robust defense capabilities (Deng et al., 2020).

6.3 Secure AI Development Practices

The term "secure by design" gets discussed a lot (or at least, it should). This absolutely applies to AI systems and may actually be more important for these tools and technologies. This section, Section 6.3, examines essential practices and methodologies for developing secure AI systems throughout their lifecycle. This section explores robust model architecture design principles that incorporate security from the ground up, methods for ensuring data integrity through comprehensive sanitization and validation processes, techniques for emphasizing critical training data through spotlighting, and systematic approaches to model versioning that maintain security across iterations. Understanding and implementing these practices is crucial for organizations developing AI systems that must maintain both security and functionality in production environments.

Secure model architecture design requires a comprehensive approach integrating security controls throughout an AI system's structure. Key architectural elements include input validation layers, output sanitization mechanisms, and internal monitoring systems that detect and respond to potential attacks (Hossain et al., 2023). Organizations should implement strict access controls at each layer of the model architecture, from data ingestion to inference endpoints (Geng, 2023). Model architectures should incorporate defense-in-depth principles, with multiple security layers protecting critical components. This includes implementing rate limiting, input preprocessing filters, and output verification systems (Abellan-Nebot & Romero Subirón, 2010). Each layer should operate independently while contributing to overall system security, making it harder for attackers to compromise the entire system through a single vulnerability.

Attention mechanisms and transformer architectures should be designed with security considerations, including protection against prompt injection and adversarial attacks. This involves implementing robust token embedding systems, secure attention masks, and protected parameter spaces that resist manipulation attempts (Latibari et al., 2024). Organizations should consider using certified robustness techniques in their architecture design. Moreover, organizations should establish clear security boundaries between model components, implementing strict authentication and authorization controls between layers. This includes securing API endpoints, implementing robust logging systems, and establishing clear data flow controls (Kaul & Khurana, 2021). Model architectures should support easy security auditing and monitoring of internal states.

Organizations implementing secure model architecture should follow a structured approach to security integration. This begins with comprehensive security requirement documentation for each architectural component, followed by implementing robust input validation at all entry points. Authentication systems must be designed to control model access while establishing monitoring capabilities for detecting anomalous behavior patterns and potential security breaches (Omotunde & Ahmed, 2023). Critical implementation steps include deploying rate limiting and request validation mechanisms to prevent abuse, along with secure parameter storage and update procedures to maintain model integrity (Almagrabi & Khan, 2024). Regular security testing of all architectural components should be conducted, supported by well-documented incident response procedures for security events. These measures should be implemented within a framework that allows for regular updates and improvements based on emerging threats and security findings. Organizations should prioritize creating separate development, testing, and production environments, each with appropriate security controls and monitoring systems, ensuring that security measures can be thoroughly tested before deployment to production systems. Additionally, security architectures should support model versioning and updates without compromising existing security controls (Gentzen et al., 2024). This includes designing systems for secure model deployment, parameter updates, and architecture modifications. Organizations should implement rollback capabilities (the Crowdstrike outage was an important example of having mechanisms like this) and maintain separate development, testing, and production environments with appropriate security controls for each (Kerner, 2024).

Data sanitization and validation for AI systems requires comprehensive preprocessing to protect against poisoning attacks and ensure data quality (Korada,

2024). This includes identifying and removing potentially malicious inputs, validating data formats and ranges, and implementing robust cleaning procedures for both training data and inference inputs. Organizations must establish clear protocols for data verification, especially when dealing with user-provided content that could be used for training or inference. Also, input validation for generative AI systems presents unique challenges due to the complexity of natural language and multimedia inputs (Bandi et al., 2023). Organizations need to implement sophisticated filtering mechanisms that can detect potential prompt injection attacks, malicious code fragments, and other harmful content while preserving legitimate inputs. This includes developing context-aware validation systems that understand semantic meaning beyond simple pattern matching (Alagar et al., 2014).

Training data sanitization requires careful balance between removing potentially harmful content and maintaining dataset diversity (Shaik et al., 2024). Organizations must implement processes to detect and remove personal identifiable information (PII), sensitive data, and copyrighted material while preserving the statistical properties necessary for effective model training. This includes automated scanning tools combined with human review processes for high-risk content. Validation systems should incorporate both static and dynamic checks (Azar et al., 2022). Static validation ensures data conformity to predefined formats and ranges, while dynamic validation examines data in context, looking for anomalies or potential attack patterns. This dual approach helps identify sophisticated attacks that might pass simple validation checks.

Organizations must establish clear data governance frameworks that define acceptable data sources, validation requirements, and sanitization procedures (Kolade et al., 2024). This includes maintaining detailed documentation of cleaning procedures, regular audits of data quality, and continuous monitoring of data pipeline integrity. Version control for sanitized datasets is crucial for maintaining model security over time. Organizations should maintain clear records of all data transformations, enabling them to track the provenance of training data and reproduce cleaning procedures when necessary. This includes implementing secure backup systems for both raw and sanitized data. Moreover, proper handling of edge cases and anomalies requires robust error handling and logging systems. Organizations must implement clear procedures for handling rejected data, investigating validation failures, and updating sanitization rules based on new attack patterns or security requirements.

Let's take a second to bridge the theoretical with the practical. Organizations implementing data sanitization and validation should begin with establishing comprehensive data quality criteria and acceptance thresholds. This includes developing automated scanning tools for detecting malicious content, PII, and other sensitive information, supported by human review processes for complex cases. Implementation should include robust logging and monitoring systems to track validation failures and data quality metrics, along with regular audits of sanitization procedures and their effectiveness. Organizations should maintain detailed documentation of all cleaning procedures and establish clear escalation paths for handling edge cases or potential security incidents. Regular training for team members on data security practices and updated sanitization procedures ensures consistent application of security measures across the organization. Additionally, organizations should implement automated testing frameworks to verify sanitization effectiveness and maintain separate environments for testing new validation procedures before deployment to production systems.

Spotlighting and data emphasis in AI development involves strategically prioritizing certain training data elements to enhance model performance in critical areas (Hines et al., 2024). This practice has become increasingly important as organizations need their AI systems to maintain high accuracy on specific high-stakes scenarios while balancing overall performance. The technique involves deliberately oversampling or emphasizing certain data points during training to ensure the model pays particular attention to crucial cases. The growing importance of spotlighting stems from regulatory requirements and risk management needs. As AI systems are deployed in sensitive domains like healthcare, finance, and security, organizations must ensure their models perform exceptionally well on critical edge cases while maintaining acceptable performance on routine tasks. This practice helps address bias issues and ensures reliable performance on important but underrepresented scenarios.

Lightning Attention is another advancement in AI model architecture design and is especially relevant for ensuring both security and efficiency in LLMs (Medium, 2025). This transformer-based architecture modification achieves substantial improvements in computational efficiency while maintaining model performance, making it useful for secure AI implementations (VB Daily, 2025). Lightning Attention optimizes the attention mechanism's computation and memory usage through sophisticated approximation techniques, enabling faster processing of longer sequences while reducing the attack surface that traditional attention mechanisms might present (Qin et al., 2024).

From a security perspective, Lightning Attention's optimized architecture offers several advantages. Its reduced memory footprint and more efficient computation patterns potentially decrease the vulnerability to certain types of attacks that target model resource consumption or attempt to exploit attention-based vulnerabilities (Qin et al., 2023). The architecture's ability to handle longer sequences more efficiently also enables better analysis of contextual information for security-related tasks, potentially improving the detection of malicious inputs or anomalous patterns. Organizations implementing Lightning Attention in their AI systems should carefully consider how this optimization affects their security controls and monitoring capabilities, ensuring that efficiency gains don't compromise the robustness of security measures. This includes implementing appropriate validation checks for the approximated attention calculations and maintaining comprehensive monitoring of the optimized attention patterns for potential security anomalies. The integration of Lightning Attention into secure model architectures requires careful consideration of how the optimization affects various security layers, from input validation to output verification, while maintaining the benefits of improved efficiency and reduced resource consumption.

Data emphasis techniques include weighted sampling, curriculum learning, and focused fine-tuning (Zheng et al., 2023). Organizations implement these through careful data curation, custom loss functions that assign higher importance to critical samples, and targeted evaluation metrics that track performance on emphasized scenarios (Zha et al., 2023). The process requires ongoing monitoring to ensure emphasized areas don't lead to degradation in other performance aspects. Implementation requires organizations to first identify critical scenarios and data points that warrant emphasis. This involves stakeholder input, risk assessment, and regulatory compliance considerations. Organizations should create robust testing frameworks specifically for emphasized scenarios, establish clear metrics for measuring their importance-weighted performance, and maintain documentation of spotlighting decisions and their rationale. Regular evaluation cycles should assess both the effectiveness of emphasis techniques and their impact on overall model performance. Success metrics should be defined not just for general performance but specifically for critical scenarios, with clear thresholds for acceptable performance in both emphasized and general cases.

There is also model versioning (Latendresse et al., 2024) in AI development that requires systematic tracking of model iterations, training data versions, and associated parameters. This includes maintaining detailed records of model architectures, hyperparameters, training configurations, and performance metrics for each version. Version control systems must handle both code and model artifacts, ensuring reproducibility and enabling rollback capabilities when issues arise. Effective versioning systems track dependencies between model components, training data versions, and deployment configurations (Paul, 2024). Modern approaches use specialized model registries that maintain metadata about model lineage (like data lineage), performance characteristics, and deployment history. This becomes especially critical when managing multiple model variants serving different purposes or operating environments (Dritsas and Trigka, 2025). Security considerations in model versioning include access controls, audit trails, and secure storage of model artifacts. Organizations must implement mechanisms to verify model integrity, track changes to model behavior, and maintain secure backups of all model versions.

An example here could help understand what implementation could look like. Imagine there is a financial services company that maintains multiple versions of their fraud detection model. Each version tracks training data sources, feature engineering pipelines, model parameters, and performance metrics. When deploying updates, they maintain parallel deployments of current and new versions, gradually shifting traffic while monitoring performance. Their versioning system includes automated testing of new versions against benchmark datasets and security checks before deployment approval. Subsequently, there are some practical implementation steps. Organizations should implement dedicated model registries with detailed version tracking, including automated documentation of training configurations and performance metrics. This includes establishing clear version naming conventions, maintaining separate development and production model repositories, and implementing automated testing pipelines for new versions. Teams should create comprehensive deployment procedures that include security validation, performance verification, and rollback protocols.

6.4 AI Model Security and Protection

AI model security and protection is important to analyze, and this section examines approaches to protecting AI models from unauthorized access, tampering, and theft. It will explore encryption techniques that safeguard model weights and architecture, along with robust access control and authentication mechanisms necessary for securing model deployment and inference endpoints. Understanding these protection measures is essential for organizations deploying AI systems in production environments where model security and intellectual property protection are paramount concerns.

Model encryption for generative AI systems focuses on protecting model weights, architecture, and operational parameters through cryptographic techniques (López Delgado & López Ramos, 2024). Current approaches utilize standard encryption methods like AES for model storage and homomorphic encryption for inference operations, enabling computations on encrypted data without decryption (Marcolla et al., 2022). These methods protect intellectual property and prevent unauthorized model access or tampering. Post-quantum cryptography (PQC) will significantly impact model encryption strategies as quantum computers threaten current cryptographic methods (Nookala et al., 2024). Organizations must prepare for quantum-resistant encryption by implementing lattice-based cryptography and other PQC algorithms (Aydeger et al., 2024). NIST's standardization of PQC algorithms will drive adoption of new encryption schemes for model protection (NIST, 2025a). Hardware-based encryption solutions, including secure enclaves and trusted execution environments, provide additional protection layers (Islam, 2024). These technologies enable secure model deployment while maintaining performance requirements for real-time inference. Modern approaches combine software and hardware encryption to create comprehensive protection frameworks.

Key challenges include managing encryption overhead in large-scale deployments and balancing security with inference latency requirements (Petullo et al., 2013). Organizations must consider performance impacts when implementing encryption, particularly for real-time applications. Emerging techniques like partial encryption of critical model components help optimize this balance (Parameshachari et al., 2012). In general, model encryption requires systematic key management and access control integration. Organizations should implement robust key rotation policies, secure key storage systems, and clear procedures for encryption key lifecycle management. This becomes increasingly important as models are deployed across distributed environments and edge devices.

Access control and authentication for AI models require multilayered security mechanisms to protect both model access and inference endpoints. Modern implementations utilize role-based access control (RBAC) combined with fine-grained permissions that govern model training, deployment, and inference operations. This includes API authentication, token-based access, and audit logging to track all model interactions (Hindka, 2024). Several key authentication and access control mechanisms work together to secure AI model deployments. Zero-trust architectures require continuous authentication for all model interactions, while multifactor authentication adds additional security layers for model access. Organizations implement API key rotation and management alongside just-in-time access provisioning to minimize exposure windows. Request rate limiting and quota management prevent abuse of model resources, while behavioral analytics systems monitor access patterns to detect potential security threats (Li et al., 2024). These mechanisms form an integrated security framework that provides comprehensive protection while maintaining usability for authorized users. Organizations increasingly implement federated identity management systems that integrate with existing enterprise authentication frameworks (Ahmed et al., 2022). This enables centralized control over model access while maintaining compliance with security policies. Advanced systems incorporate adaptive authentication that adjusts security requirements based on request context and risk levels.

Model-specific authentication requirements often include verification of input sources, output destinations, and intermediate processing steps. This chain-of-trust approach ensures that model interactions occur only between authorized components and users (Janovsky et al., 2024). Organizations implement these controls through secure API gateways, service meshes, and containerized environments that enforce consistent authentication policies. Also, time-based access controls and temporary credentials help limit exposure in case of credential compromise. Organizations should implement automated credential rotation, access reviews, and comprehensive logging of authentication events. This includes maintaining detailed audit trails of model access patterns and implementing automated alerts for suspicious activities.

CaMeL (Capabilities for Machine Learning), developed by Google DeepMind, is an important advancement in defending AI systems against prompt injection attacks (Debenedetti et al., 2025). Unlike traditional approaches that focus on modifying the underlying models through training or prompting techniques, CaMeL creates a protective system layer around the LLM that enforces security through explicit data and control flow tracking. The system operates through a dual LLM architecture, a Privileged LLM (P-LLM) that plans actions based on user queries and a Quarantined LLM (Q-LLM) that processes potentially untrusted data, while maintaining a comprehensive dependency graph that tracks data provenance (Debenedetti et al., 2025). This approach allows CaMeL to enforce fine-grained security policies without requiring changes to the language models themselves, making it compatible with various LLM architectures and addressing vulnerabilities that persist even in well-designed isolation systems. A key innovation in CaMeL is its use of capabilities, metadata tags attached to each value that define allowable operations and data flows (Debenedetti et al., 2025). These capabilities allow for sophisticated security policies that can, for example, prevent confidential documents from being shared with unauthorized recipients even when a prompt injection attack attempts to manipulate the data flow. The system assigns tags to data that identify both its origin (such as from the user, from a tool, or from a specific email sender) and its authorized readers (either public or a specific set of users). This metadata propagates through the execution environment, ensuring that security policies can be enforced consistently and comprehensively, addressing not just control flow hijacking but also the more subtle data flow manipulation attacks that traditional defenses often miss (Debenedetti et al., 2025).

CaMeL's implementation relies on a custom Python interpreter that tracks the dependencies between variables and maintains the data flow graph during execution. This interpreter supports two modes of operation: NORMAL and STRICT, with the latter providing additional protection against side-channel attacks by treating control flow dependencies as data dependencies (Debenedetti et al., 2025). Before executing any tool with potential side effects (such as sending emails or creating calendar events), the interpreter checks all relevant security policies against the variables and their complete dependency chains. If a policy violation is detected, the tool execution is blocked or, in real-world implementation, presented to the user for explicit confirmation, reducing the risk of security fatigue while maintaining strong protective measures. In practical evaluations, CaMeL has demonstrated impressive effectiveness, solving 67% of tasks in the AgentDojo benchmark while providing provable security guarantees (Debenedetti et al., 2025). While this represents some utility degradation compared to undefended systems, the security benefits are substantial; CaMeL effectively prevents malicious data exfiltration and unauthorized actions even when processing compromised data sources. The system's design draws inspiration from established software security principles like Control Flow Integrity, Access Control, and Information Flow Control, applying these time-tested concepts to the unique challenges of LLM-based agentic systems that interact with external environments. The system's custom Python interpreter serves as an effective security monitor through its comprehensive understanding of information flows throughout the execution environment. Through tracking the complete lineage of every data piece from its origin through all transformations and dependencies, CaMeL enables precise enforcement of security policies at exactly the points where vulnerable operations might occur. This approach addresses the inherent opacity of LLM processing through explicit mapping of relationships between inputs, internal states, and outputs that might otherwise remain hidden, allowing security mechanisms to intervene before sensitive data leaks or unauthorized actions occur.

CaMeL also represents a paradigm shift in how we approach AI security through its embrace of principles from traditional software security applied effectively to the unique challenges of large language models. Rather than relying solely on model-based defenses that attackers can circumvent as techniques evolve, CaMeL establishes a security framework fundamentally independent of the underlying model architecture. This separation of concerns allows security experts to focus on defining and refining policies while AI researchers continue optimizing model performance, creating a more sustainable approach to AI system security that adapts to new threats without requiring continuous model retraining or fine-tuning.

Beyond prompt injection defenses, CaMeL's capability-based approach offers promising applications for broader AI security challenges. The system can help defend against rogue users attempting to violate corporate policies, malicious external tools seeking to access sensitive information, and other advanced threat scenarios. Therefore, enabling fine-grained control over what operations can be performed on specific pieces of data, CaMeL is a major step forward for enterprise AI deployments where protecting sensitive information and preventing unauthorized actions are paramount concerns. As LLMs increasingly become integrated into critical business workflows, such robust security architectures will be essential for responsible and trustworthy AI implementation. CaMeL offers significant value for enterprise deployments through its compatibility with different organizational security models and governance requirements. The system's security policies can operate at various levels of granularity to accommodate diverse regulatory frameworks, data protection standards, and organizational risk profiles. Healthcare organizations can implement policies that enforce HIPAA compliance through prevention of patient data flowing to unauthorized recipients, while financial institutions might deploy policies designed specifically to protect transaction data and ensure compliance with financial regulations. This flexibility makes CaMeL adaptable to sector-specific security needs while maintaining a consistent security architecture.

Ultimately, CaMeL's importance for AI model security is extremely important in the context of deploying generative AI systems in production environments. As organizations increasingly integrate LLMs into critical business operations and systems with access to sensitive data, the risk of prompt injection attacks grows significantly. Without robust protection mechanisms like CaMeL, AI models remain vulnerable to adversarial inputs that could lead to unauthorized data access, intellectual property theft, or malicious actions performed on behalf of the system. CaMeL addresses these threats at a fundamental level by focusing not just on making models resistant to attacks but by creating a secure execution environment that prevents harmful outcomes even when models themselves are successfully manipulated.

Meta has introduced a significant advancement in AI security with their new open-source framework called LlamaFirewall, designed to protect artificial intelligence systems from emerging cyber threats including prompt injection, jailbreaks, and insecure code generation (Lakshmanan, 2025). The framework incorporates three distinct guardrails: PromptGuard 2 for detecting direct jailbreak and prompt injection attempts in real time, Agent Alignment Checks for inspecting agent reasoning to identify potential goal hijacking and indirect prompt injection scenarios, and CodeShield that functions as an online static analysis engine to prevent the generation of insecure or dangerous code by AI agents (Meta AI, 2025). The architecture of LlamaFirewall is notably modular, enabling security teams and developers to implement layered defenses spanning from raw input ingestion to final output actions, covering both simple chat models and complex autonomous agents. This approach is an important and a substantial effort to create defensive mechanisms that can address the evolving landscape of AI security vulnerabilities across different application types.

Along with LlamaFirewall, Meta has released updated versions of complementary tools including LlamaGuard and CyberSecEval to enhance detection capabilities for various types of violating content and to measure the defensive cybersecurity capabilities of AI systems, respectively. The latest version of CyberSecEval includes a new benchmark called AutoPatchBench, engineered specifically to evaluate how effectively large language model agents can automatically repair a range of C/C++ vulnerabilities identified through fuzzing techniques. This benchmark establishes a standardized evaluation framework for assessing AI-assisted vulnerability repair tools, facilitating a comprehensive understanding of capabilities and limitations in various AI-driven approaches to repairing bugs discovered through fuzzing methods. Meta has also launched a program called Llama for Defenders to help partner organizations and AI developers access various AI solutions to address specific security challenges, such as detecting AI-generated content used in scams, fraud, and phishing attacks. The timing of these announcements coincides with WhatsApp's preview of a new technology called Private Processing, which allows users to utilize AI features without compromising privacy by offloading requests to a secure, confidential environment. Meta has emphasized their commitment to working with the security community to audit and improve their architecture, continuing to build and strengthen Private Processing openly and collaboratively with researchers before launching it in their products.

6.5 Privacy-Preserving AI Techniques

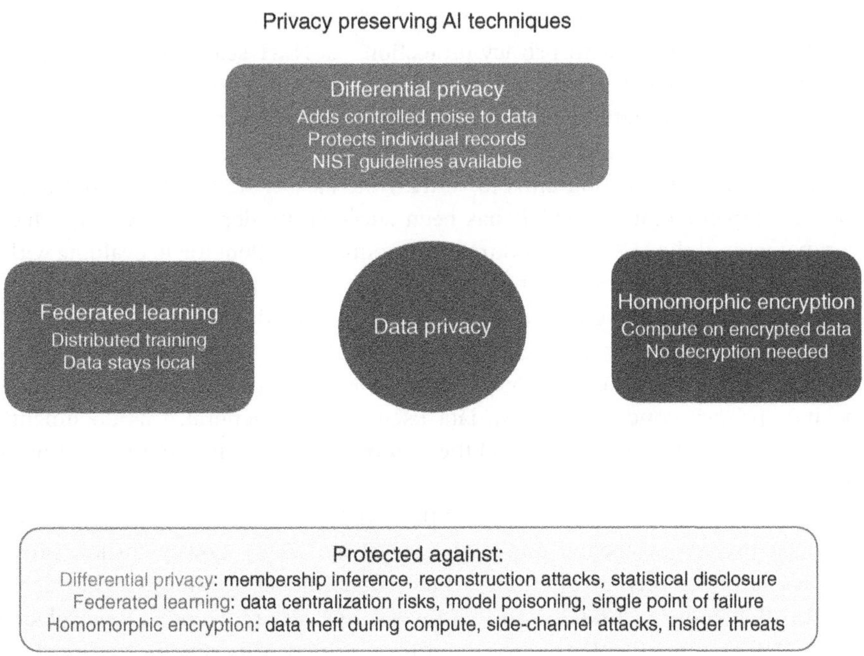

In this section, we'll explore techniques for developing privacy-preserving AI systems that protect sensitive data while maintaining model utility. Through examining differential privacy frameworks that add controlled noise to protect individual records, federated learning approaches that enable distributed training without data centralization, and homomorphic encryption methods allowing computation on encrypted data, this section provides essentially covers privacy-preserving mechanisms for modern AI development.

Differential privacy in AI provides mathematical guarantees about the privacy of individual data points while enabling useful statistical analysis and model training (Silva & Oliveira, 2024a). The technique adds carefully calibrated random noise to data or model outputs, making it impossible to reliably determine whether any specific individual's data was used in training or queries while maintaining overall statistical accuracy (Silva & Oliveira, 2024b). This approach specifically protects against membership inference attacks, where adversaries attempt to determine if particular records were used in model training, and prevents reconstruction attacks that try to recover individual training examples from model outputs (Hu et al., 2022).

NIST recently finalized its "Guidelines for Evaluating Differential Privacy Guarantees" (Special Publication 800-226), designed to help organizations better understand and assess differential privacy claims (NIST, 2025b). The guidelines, updated from a December 2023 draft, provide interactive tools, flowcharts, and sample code to assist in implementing differential privacy effectively while balancing data utility with privacy protection. As NIST scientist Gary Howarth notes, the technology works by adding random noise to obscure individual identities while preserving statistical value, though proper noise calibration is crucial, especially for small data groups that may require additional protection. In general, the publication aims to address the lack of standards in differential privacy implementation, which has been successfully deployed by major tech companies and the U.S. Census Bureau but remains challenging to evaluate without consistent frameworks. While not intended as a comprehensive primer on differential privacy, the guidelines include a robust reading list to help practitioners develop expertise in the field. Howarth emphasizes that differential privacy involves navigating numerous "gray areas" where organizations must repeatedly balance privacy concerns against data usefulness. In general, this document's value is helping leaders understand the inherent trade-offs in differential privacy implementation.

The privacy budget (epsilon) in differential privacy controls the trade-off between privacy protection and utility (Li et al., 2023). Lower epsilon values provide stronger privacy guarantees but reduce model accuracy, while higher values allow more accurate results with weaker privacy protection (Nanayakkara et al., 2023). Organizations must carefully calibrate this parameter based on their specific use case and privacy requirements while considering the full scope of potential privacy risks. Modern differential privacy implementations protect against sophisticated attack vectors including model inversion attacks attempting to reconstruct training data, attribute inference attacks trying to learn sensitive features, membership inference through multiple query correlation, statistical disclosure through aggregated queries, and model stealing attempts leveraging privacy vulnerabilities (Song & Namiot, 2022). The technique has become particularly important for generative AI systems that might memorize and reproduce training data, helping prevent these models from revealing sensitive information while maintaining their ability to generate useful content. This includes protecting against prompt-based attacks attempting to extract training data through carefully crafted inputs.

Federated learning enables distributed model training across multiple devices or organizations while keeping sensitive data localized (Zhang et al., 2021). This approach allows models to learn from diverse datasets without centralizing raw data, significantly reducing privacy risks associated with data collection and storage. The technique has gained prominence in healthcare, finance, and other sectors where data privacy is paramount. Furthermore, federated learning protects against several key attack vectors by design. Since raw data never leaves local environments, it prevents direct data theft and unauthorized access common in centralized systems. The distributed nature also makes it harder for attackers to compromise large amounts of training data through a single breach. The system architecture inherently guards against model poisoning attempts by implementing secure aggregation protocols and robust validation of model updates. Organizations can implement Byzantine-resistant aggregation algorithms to detect and filter malicious updates from compromised participants (Li et al., 2021). This helps maintain model integrity even when some participants in the federation are compromised. The technique specifically protects against reconstruction attacks by keeping sensitive data local. Even if an attacker compromises the global model, they cannot directly access training examples. Additional privacy guarantees can be achieved by combining federated learning with differential privacy or secure aggregation protocols.

Communication between participants is secured through encryption and authentication mechanisms, preventing man-in-the-middle attacks and unauthorized participation. Modern implementations use secure multiparty computation techniques to protect model updates during aggregation, ensuring that even the aggregation server cannot access individual updates (Kaminaga et al., 2023). Advanced federated learning systems incorporate mechanisms to detect and prevent free-riding attacks, where participants try to benefit from the federation without contributing meaningful updates (Zhang et al., 2022). They also protect against model inversion attacks through careful design of update protocols and validation mechanisms. Organizations implementing federated learning should establish clear governance frameworks defining participant responsibilities, data quality standards, and security requirements.

Homomorphic encryption (HE) enables computation on encrypted data without decryption, making it crucial for privacy-preserving AI operations (Su et al., 2024). This allows organizations to perform model inference and training while keeping sensitive data encrypted throughout the process, protecting against data exposure during computation. HE specifically protects against data theft during computation, side-channel attacks attempting to extract information from computational processes, and insider threats from cloud providers or infrastructure operators (Marcolla et al., 2022). The technique ensures that even parties performing computations cannot access the underlying data, providing strong privacy guarantees for sensitive applications. Modern implementations use different HE variants depending on computational needs. Fully homomorphic encryption (FHE) allows arbitrary computations but incurs significant performance overhead, while partially homomorphic encryption offers better performance for specific operations (Marcolla et al., 2022). Organizations must balance privacy requirements against computational costs when implementing these systems.

The advent of quantum computing necessitates transition to post-quantum cryptography (PQC) for homomorphic encryption systems (Sood, 2024). Current research focuses on lattice-based cryptography, which provides both quantum resistance and homomorphic properties (Widodo et al., 2024). NIST's standardization of PQC algorithms will influence future HE implementations, requiring organizations to prepare for migration to quantum-resistant schemes (NIST, 2025a). That being said, implementation challenges include managing encryption overhead, key distribution, and computational complexity. Organizations should implement HE selectively for critical operations where data privacy is paramount, often combining it with other privacy-preserving techniques like federated learning or differential privacy for comprehensive protection (Sen et al., 2024).

6.6 Proactive Threat Intelligence and AI Incident Response

Generative AI has revolutionized multiple industries with its ability to create synthetic content, automate tasks, and enhance productivity. However, as we've explored in this book, its capabilities have also attracted malicious actors, leading to a new category of threats. Traditional threat intelligence—which focuses on identifying vulnerabilities, malware signatures, and attack vectors—does not fully address the unique challenges posed by generative AI (Sarker, 2024). The dynamic and evolving nature of generative AI necessitates a specialized approach to threat intelligence. Unlike conventional attacks, generative AI threats often involve AI-generated synthetic media, sophisticated impersonation attempts, or automated exploitation. For instance, the use of deepfakes for fraud or adversarial inputs to manipulate AI models creates new attack surfaces that require novel detection and mitigation techniques. Key differences between traditional cybersecurity intelligence and generative AI threat intelligence include the speed and scalability of threats, as generative AI can rapidly generate phishing campaigns, malware, or synthetic identities at an unprecedented scale, making detection more challenging. Attack patterns are more complex, often involving multistep attacks that integrate social engineering, adversarial inputs, and traditional exploits. Effective threat intelligence for generative AI requires expertise in AI development, cybersecurity, and behavioral analysis. Dynamic threat intelligence systems must continuously evolve, leveraging machine learning and advanced analytics to adapt to emerging threats (Aminu et al., 2024). These systems should incorporate data from diverse sources, such as dark web activity, social media, and AI-generated content analysis, to provide actionable insights.

The complexity of generative AI threats demands advanced tools for incident analysis and forensic investigation. AI-powered systems are invaluable in this context, enabling rapid analysis of large datasets, tracing adversarial activities, and identifying root causes. AI tools can analyze incident logs, network traffic, and user behavior to identify anomalies that indicate generative AI-driven threats. Machine learning models trained on historical attack data can detect subtle patterns that human analysts might miss. Tools like graph-based analysis can map the pathways of adversarial actions, linking deepfake dissemination to phishing campaigns or malware infections (Zenitani, 2023). Behavioral analytics can identify deviations from normal user or system behavior, flagging potential AI-generated manipulations (Almomani et al., 2025). Adversaries increasingly use generative AI to create polymorphic malware that evolves to evade detection (Blake, 2024). Reverse-engineering such malware involves analyzing its adaptive algorithms and training data sources. Techniques like neural network analysis and adversarial input testing can help security teams understand how malware exploits AI systems (Khan & Ghafoor, 2024). Deepfake forensics tools analyze audio and video files for signs of manipulation, such as inconsistent lighting, unnatural motion, or synthetic audio artifacts (Ahmed et al., 2024). Advanced systems use physiological markers, such as heart rate variations or microexpressions, to distinguish real content from deepfakes, as discussed earlier in this book.

Understanding the behavior of adversaries leveraging generative AI is crucial for effective threat intelligence. AI threat actors often exhibit unique tactics, techniques, and procedures (TTPs), including automation of attack vectors where generative AI is used to automate phishing, fake content creation, and social engineering at scale. Adaptive strategies are employed by adversaries who use machine learning to analyze detection systems and refine their attacks for increased success rates. AI-enabled attacks often involve cross-platform coordination, where synthetic content is disseminated across social media, email, and messaging platforms. Behavioral analysis can leverage AI models trained to recognize patterns in adversarial actions, mapping them to established frameworks like MITRE ATT&CK (Al-Sada et al., 2025). This approach provides a comprehensive understanding of threat actor motivations and methodologies.

Threat hunting involves proactively searching for signs of compromise within an organization's network (Nour et al., 2023). Generative AI introduces new challenges and opportunities for threat hunting. AI-powered tools can scan network logs, endpoint activity, and user behavior to identify anomalies linked to generative AI threats. Natural language processing models can analyze text-based communications for signs of AI-generated phishing or impersonation attempts. Advanced analytics tools can detect patterns across multiple data sources, such as repetitive behaviors in synthetic identities or recurring manipulation techniques in adversarial inputs. Threat intelligence platforms integrated with AI can prioritize high-risk indicators, enabling faster response times.

Adapting incident response frameworks to address generative AI threats requires specific modifications and enhancements (NIST AI, 2024). Incident response processes must include detection tools capable of identifying generative AI-driven anomalies. Containment strategies should implement access controls and network segmentation to isolate compromised systems or synthetic content. Eradication involves removing AI-generated malware or synthetic media from affected systems and mitigating vulnerabilities exploited by adversaries. Recovery ensures systems are restored to normal operation while robust defenses are implemented to prevent recurrence. Post-incident reviews analyze incidents to identify lessons learned and update security policies and playbooks. Mapping generative AI threats to frameworks like MITRE ATT&CK enables organizations to better understand attack vectors and identify gaps in their defenses.

To effectively respond to generative AI threats, organizations must develop specialized incident response teams. Training programs should focus on adversarial AI concepts, deepfake detection, and AI-powered malware analysis. Simulated AI-driven attacks can test team readiness and refine response strategies. Detailed playbooks for responding to common generative AI threats, such as synthetic identity fraud or adversarial model manipulation, are essential. These playbooks should include guidelines for coordinating with external experts and law enforcement agencies during complex incidents.

In general, the rapid evolution of generative AI requires organizations to anticipate future threats and invest in adaptive incident response technologies. Advancements in generative AI, such as self-evolving AI attacks or real-time deepfakes, present new challenges. Research into AI-driven defensive systems can counter generative AI threats in real time, while investments in quantum-resistant cryptographic methods can secure AI systems against emerging quantum computing capabilities (which will be discussed in Chapter 8). Collaboration across industries is critical. Partnerships between technology companies, academic researchers, and government agencies can enhance defenses through shared insights. Establishing global standards for incident response in generative AI contexts ensures consistency and effectiveness. This comprehensive approach to threat intelligence and incident response equips organizations to stay ahead of generative AI threats while building resilience against future challenges.

6.7 MLSecOps/SecMLOPs for Secure AI Development

Based on the comprehensive defensive strategies outlined in this chapter, MLOps (Machine Learning Operations) and MLSecOps (Machine Learning Security Operations) are important operational frameworks for implementing and maintaining secure AI systems throughout their entire lifecycle. MLOps traditionally focuses on streamlining the deployment, monitoring, and management of machine learning models in production environments, but in the context of generative AI threats, it must evolve to incorporate sophisticated security measures at every stage. This evolution necessitates the integration of security practices into MLOps pipelines, creating what is increasingly referred to as MLSecOps or SecMLOps—a security-first approach to machine learning operations that treats security as a fundamental requirement rather than an afterthought (Calefato et al., 2024). Organizations implementing the defensive strategies discussed in this chapter must embed security controls directly into their MLOps workflows, ensuring that adversarial training, model encryption, access controls, and threat detection mechanisms become integral components of the operational infrastructure rather than external additions.

The implementation of secure MLOps requires fundamental changes to traditional CI/CD (Continuous Integration/Continuous Deployment) pipelines to accommodate the unique security requirements of AI systems (Enemosah, 2025). Unlike conventional software deployment, ML models require continuous retraining, validation against adversarial attacks, and monitoring for model drift—all while maintaining strict security controls. MLSecOps pipelines must incorporate automated adversarial testing at each stage of model development, implementing the adversarial training techniques discussed in Section 6.2 as standard validation steps before deployment. This includes automated generation of adversarial examples using methods like FGSM and PGD, systematic testing of model robustness through ensemble validation, and continuous monitoring of model performance against both legitimate and adversarial inputs (Villegas-Ch et al., 2024). The pipeline must also integrate the secure development practices outlined in Section 6.3, including automated data sanitization and validation processes that scan training datasets for potential poisoning attempts, systematic model versioning with cryptographic integrity verification, and comprehensive audit logging that tracks all model modifications and access patterns.

Data governance within MLSecOps frameworks becomes complex when implementing privacy-preserving techniques such as differential privacy, federated learning, and homomorphic encryption as detailed in Section 6.5. These techniques require sophisticated orchestration within MLOps pipelines to manage the computational overhead and complexity while maintaining security guarantees. For differential privacy implementations, MLOps systems must carefully track privacy budgets across multiple training iterations and inference operations, ensuring that cumulative privacy loss remains within acceptable bounds while maintaining model utility (Zhang & Li, 2024). Federated learning deployments require secure aggregation protocols and Byzantine-resistant algorithms integrated into the orchestration layer, with automated validation of participant contributions and detection of potential model poisoning attempts (Gabrielli et al., 2023). Homomorphic encryption implementations demand specialized infrastructure capable of managing the significant computational overhead while maintaining real-time inference capabilities, often requiring hybrid approaches that selectively apply encryption to the most sensitive operations (Mollakuqe et al., 2024).

Model security and protection mechanisms outlined in Section 6.4 must be seamlessly integrated into MLOps infrastructure to ensure comprehensive protection throughout the model lifecycle. This includes implementing automated model encryption during storage and transit, with secure key management systems that integrate with existing enterprise security frameworks. Access control mechanisms must be embedded into the MLOps platform itself, providing fine-grained permissions for model training, deployment, and inference operations while maintaining comprehensive audit trails (Sendas & Rajale, 2025). The integration of advanced protection frameworks like CaMeL and LlamaFirewall requires sophisticated orchestration capabilities that can manage the dual LLM architectures and capability-based security policies while maintaining acceptable performance for production workloads. MLSecOps platforms must also incorporate automated vulnerability scanning for AI-specific threats, including regular testing for prompt injection vulnerabilities, model extraction attempts, and adversarial input susceptibility.

Monitoring and incident response capabilities within MLSecOps frameworks must extend far beyond traditional system monitoring to encompass the AI-specific threats and attack vectors discussed in Section 6.6. This requires implementing real-time deepfake detection systems that can analyze multimedia content flowing through AI pipelines, automated monitoring of model behavior for signs of adversarial manipulation or data poisoning, and comprehensive logging of all AI-related operations for forensic analysis. MLOps platforms must integrate with specialized threat intelligence systems that understand AI-specific attack patterns and can provide early warning of emerging threats like new adversarial attack techniques or deepfake generation methods (Patel et al., 2025). The incident response capabilities must include automated containment mechanisms that can quickly isolate compromised models or data sources, rollback capabilities that can revert to previously validated model versions, and specialized forensic tools capable of analyzing AI model internals to understand the nature and scope of security incidents.

The operational complexity of implementing comprehensive MLSecOps requires organizations to develop new expertise and organizational structures that bridge traditional cybersecurity and machine learning domains. Security teams must develop deep understanding of AI model architectures, training processes, and vulnerability patterns, while ML engineers must become proficient in security principles, threat modeling, and defensive programming practices. This necessitates establishing cross-functional teams that combine expertise in cybersecurity, machine learning, and operations, supported by comprehensive training programs and certification frameworks that ensure consistent application of security practices across the organization. MLSecOps implementations must also address the unique challenges of securing AI systems deployed across diverse environments, from cloud-based training infrastructure to edge devices performing inference operations, requiring flexible security architectures that can adapt to different deployment contexts while maintaining consistent protection levels (Arora & Khare, 2024). The success of these frameworks ultimately depends on achieving the delicate balance between security, performance, and operational efficiency that allows organizations to realize the benefits of AI while maintaining robust protection against the evolving landscape of generative AI threats.

Chapter 6 Summary

This chapter addressed comprehensive defensive strategies against the generative AI threats explored in previous chapters, providing practical frameworks for detecting, preventing, and mitigating AI-related security risks. It began with deepfake detection techniques that combined visual artifact analysis, biological signal detection, metadata examination, and digital watermarking systems to identify synthetic media manipulation. The chapter detailed methods for strengthening model resilience through adversarial training that exposed models to malicious inputs during development, defense distillation techniques that smoothed decision boundaries, and ensemble methods that combined multiple models to create robust protection against manipulation attempts. Secure AI development practices formed a critical foundation, covering architecture design principles that incorporated security from inception, comprehensive data sanitization protocols, strategic data emphasis through spotlighting techniques, and systematic model versioning approaches.

The chapter explored sophisticated protection mechanisms for deployed models, including encryption techniques that safeguarded model weights and parameters, advanced access control systems with multilayered authentication, and innovative frameworks like CaMeL and LlamaFirewall that provided comprehensive security against prompt injection and other attacks. Privacy-preserving techniques received detailed analysis, covering differential privacy frameworks that added controlled noise to protect individual records, federated learning approaches that enabled distributed training without data centralization, and homomorphic encryption methods that allowed computation on encrypted data. The chapter concluded with specialized threat intelligence and incident response frameworks adapted for generative AI contexts, emphasizing the need for proactive detection of AI-driven threats and specialized response teams capable of handling sophisticated attacks. Throughout, real-world implementations and case studies demonstrated how organizations could balance security requirements with model utility and performance.

Key Takeaways:

This chapter demonstrated that defending against generative AI threats required a fundamental shift from reactive to proactive security strategies that integrated protection mechanisms throughout the entire AI development and deployment lifecycle. Traditional cybersecurity approaches proved inadequate against AI-specific threats like prompt injection, adversarial attacks, and model extraction, necessitating specialized techniques such as adversarial training, secure architecture design, and AI-specific threat intelligence. The multilayered approach emphasized the importance of combining technical controls (encryption, access controls, differential privacy) with operational practices (secure development, systematic versioning, comprehensive training) to create resilient AI systems. Organizations needed to implement detection mechanisms that could identify sophisticated attacks while maintaining the utility and performance of their AI systems, requiring careful balance between security controls and functional requirements.

Chapter 6 revealed that successful AI security implementation demanded both technical sophistication and organizational commitment to comprehensive security frameworks that evolved with advancing threats. Innovative solutions like CaMeL's capability-based security model and Meta's LlamaFirewall represented significant advances in protecting AI systems through systematic approaches that addressed the unique characteristics of generative AI vulnerabilities. Privacy-preserving techniques such as differential privacy, federated learning, and homomorphic encryption enabled organizations to maintain data protection while leveraging AI capabilities, though implementation required careful consideration of performance trade-offs and regulatory requirements. The emphasis on specialized threat intelligence and incident response frameworks highlighted the need for organizations to develop new expertise and capabilities specifically adapted to the evolving landscape of AI-driven threats, moving beyond traditional cybersecurity approaches to embrace the complex realities of securing AI systems in production environments.

Case Study: Comprehensive Defense Against Generative AI Threats in a Multinational Organization

Background and Context

FinTech Solutions, a multinational financial services company operating in 25 countries, is responsible for managing financial transactions, wealth management, and asset trading for its clients. The organization employs advanced AI models to optimize its operations, including fraud detection, risk assessment, and customer support automation. While these AI systems provide a competitive edge, they also expose FinTech Solutions to unique risks associated with generative AI.

In 2024, the company faced a sophisticated attack leveraging generative AI to manipulate its fraud detection system, create deepfake phishing campaigns, and infiltrate sensitive customer data. This case study outlines the technical details of how FinTech Solutions defended against these threats by implementing advanced detection, adversarial training, secure AI development practices, privacy-preserving AI techniques, and incident response frameworks.

Phase 1: Detection of Deepfake-Based Phishing Campaigns

The Threat: The attackers launched a generative AI-powered phishing campaign targeting FinTech's senior management. Using publicly available datasets from press releases, LinkedIn profiles, and conference recordings, the attackers generated deepfake videos of the CEO instructing the CFO to authorize fraudulent transactions. These deepfakes were accompanied by highly convincing emails mimicking the organization's internal communication style.

Detection Techniques Implemented:

1) **Visual Artifact Analysis:**
   - o FinTech Solutions deployed convolutional neural networks (CNNs) trained to detect artifacts in synthetic media, such as:

   - **Lighting Inconsistencies:** Discrepancies in light reflections on facial features.
   - **Texture Anomalies:** Blurring around complex elements like hair and teeth.
   - **Temporal Inconsistencies:** Subtle mismatches in motion between frames, particularly in lip-syncing and eye movements.
 - **Example:** The detection system flagged subtle artifacts in the deepfake's eyes, where reflections of light sources did not align with the purported environment.

2) **Biological Signal Detection:**
   - The system analyzed physiological markers like pulse signals visible in skin color variations (via remote photoplethysmography or rPPG).
   - Deepfake videos lacked the natural microexpressions and involuntary muscle movements present in authentic videos. These discrepancies were detected using temporal tracking algorithms.
3) **Metadata Analysis:**
   - The IT team employed metadata extraction tools to scrutinize file properties such as:
     - Missing EXIF data and compression patterns inconsistent with professional recording devices.
     - Anomalies in timestamp sequences that indicated synthetic editing.
4) **Digital Watermarking Verification:**
   - FinTech had pre-embedded robust watermarks in official video communications, which allowed verification of authenticity. The flagged videos failed to contain these watermarks, confirming their synthetic origin.

Outcome: The phishing attempt was identified and stopped before any fraudulent transactions occurred. The flagged deepfake videos were passed to law enforcement and used to raise awareness among employees.

Phase 2: Mitigating Adversarial Attacks on Fraud Detection Systems

The Threat: Attackers exploited adversarial vulnerabilities in FinTech's AI-powered fraud detection system by generating inputs designed to evade detection. Using gradient-based methods like the Fast Gradient Sign Method (FGSM) and Projected Gradient Descent (PGD), they crafted adversarial examples that caused the system to misclassify fraudulent transactions as legitimate.

Defensive Measures Implemented:

1) **Adversarial Training:**
   - The fraud detection model was retrained using adversarial examples generated by FGSM and PGD. These examples introduced perturbations imperceptible to humans but impactful to the AI system.

- The adversarial training process involved:
  - Generating adversarial examples for each legitimate and fraudulent transaction.
  - Augmenting the training dataset with these examples to improve model robustness.

2) **Defense Distillation:**
   - FinTech implemented defense distillation by training a "teacher" model and using its softened outputs to train a "student" model. This process:
     - Reduced sensitivity to small input perturbations.
     - Smoothed decision boundaries, making it harder for adversarial inputs to exploit vulnerabilities.

3) **Ensemble Methods:**
   - Multiple models with diverse architectures and training datasets were combined. For example:
     - A decision tree-based model focused on transaction patterns.
     - A neural network model analyzed metadata and behavioral patterns.
   - Ensemble voting mechanisms ensured robustness, as adversarial inputs failed to manipulate all models simultaneously.

Outcome: The upgraded fraud detection system successfully identified and blocked adversarial inputs. Post-deployment testing revealed a 75% reduction in the system's vulnerability to adversarial attacks.

Phase 3: Implementing Secure AI Development Practices

The Challenge: FinTech's AI systems were susceptible to model poisoning attacks during retraining phases. Attackers attempted to inject malicious data into training datasets, influencing the model to produce incorrect predictions.

Mitigation Techniques Implemented:

1) **Data Sanitization and Validation:**
   - Advanced preprocessing pipelines were deployed to:
     - Detect anomalies in training datasets.
     - Remove poisoned samples using machine learning models trained to identify outliers and suspicious patterns.
   - **Example:** The system flagged input records with unusually high feature correlations indicative of adversarial manipulation.

2) **Spotlighting and Weighted Sampling:**
   - Training emphasized high-risk scenarios (e.g., high-value transactions) by oversampling these cases during training.
   - Custom loss functions assigned greater weights to critical data points, improving the model's accuracy in edge cases.

3) **Model Versioning and Auditing:**
   - A dedicated model registry tracked:
     - Training data provenance.
     - Model architecture updates.
     - Performance metrics.
   - Automated tests validated each new version against a benchmark dataset before deployment.

Outcome: These practices ensured that retrained models maintained integrity, with no evidence of poisoning attacks succeeding post-implementation.

Phase 4: Privacy-Preserving AI Techniques

The Challenge: FinTech's models required access to sensitive customer data, raising concerns about data privacy and compliance with global regulations.

Techniques Implemented:

1) **Differential Privacy:**
   - Controlled noise was added to training data outputs, ensuring individual records could not be reverse-engineered while preserving statistical accuracy.
   - The privacy budget (ε) was carefully calibrated to balance utility and privacy.
2) **Federated Learning:**
   - The company adopted federated learning for training fraud detection models across regional branches.
   - Raw customer data remained localized, and only encrypted model updates were shared with a central server.
3) **Homomorphic Encryption (HE):**
   - HE allowed computations on encrypted data during model inference.
   - This ensured that even during processing, customer data remained encrypted, mitigating risks of data leakage.

Outcome: FinTech achieved compliance with GDPR and other privacy regulations while maintaining the utility of its AI systems.

Phase 5: Proactive Threat Intelligence and Incident Response

The Threat: Generative AI-powered polymorphic malware was used to infiltrate FinTech's network. The malware evolved in real time, adapting its signatures to evade detection by traditional antivirus tools.

Incident Response Framework:

1) **Real-Time Threat Hunting:**
   - AI-powered monitoring tools scanned network traffic for anomalies.

   - Behavioral analytics flagged deviations in endpoint activity, such as abnormal access patterns and unauthorized API calls.
2) **Containment Strategies:**
   - A zero-trust architecture isolated affected systems, preventing lateral movement.
   - Compromised endpoints were quarantined, and unauthorized processes were terminated.
3) **Root Cause Analysis:**
   - Graph-based forensics mapped the malware's propagation pathways, linking initial infiltration to exploited vulnerabilities in outdated software.
4) **Post-Incident Review:**
   - FinTech updated its threat intelligence systems to recognize the polymorphic malware's patterns.
   - Simulated exercises were conducted to test the organization's readiness against similar threats.

Outcome: The incident was contained within 48 hours, minimizing data exfiltration and operational disruptions. Lessons learned were integrated into the organization's incident response playbook.

Conclusion

This case study demonstrates how FinTech Solutions applied advanced technical measures to defend against generative AI threats. By leveraging deepfake detection, adversarial training, secure development practices, privacy-preserving techniques, and proactive incident response, the organization enhanced its resilience against sophisticated cyberattacks. The comprehensive approach not only mitigated immediate risks but also positioned FinTech Solutions as a leader in AI security best practices.

Quiz: FinTech Solutions AI Defense Quiz

Questions

1 Which technique did FinTech Solutions use to detect deepfake videos of their CEO?
   a) Natural language processing
   b) Visual artifact analysis
   c) Blockchain verification
   d) Quantum computing algorithms

2 What method was implemented to make the fraud detection system more resistant to adversarial attacks?
   a) Increasing the complexity of the neural network
   b) Defense distillation
   c) Implementing SSL encryption
   d) Using cloud-based security solutions

3 During Phase 3, how did FinTech Solutions protect against model poisoning attacks?
   a) By implementing a zero-trust architecture
   b) By using federated learning
   c) By deploying data sanitization and validation
   d) By adding homomorphic encryption

4 Which privacy-preserving technique allowed FinTech to perform computations on encrypted customer data?
   a) Differential privacy
   b) Homomorphic encryption
   c) Federated learning
   d) Data tokenization

5 What was the primary defense strategy that allowed FinTech to contain the polymorphic malware attack within 48 hours?
   a) Conventional antivirus tools
   b) A zero-trust architecture
   c) Blockchain security
   d) Manual system scanning

Answer Key

1 **Correct Answer: b) Visual artifact analysis**
   - **Explanation:** According to the case study, FinTech Solutions deployed "convolutional neural networks (CNNs) trained to detect artifacts in synthetic media," including lighting inconsistencies, texture anomalies, and temporal inconsistencies. The system specifically "flagged subtle artifacts in the deepfake's eyes, where reflections of light sources did not align with the purported environment."
   - Option a) is incorrect because while NLP might be useful for analyzing text, the case specifically mentioned visual analysis techniques for detecting deepfakes.

- Option c) is incorrect because blockchain verification wasn't mentioned as a method for deepfake detection.
- Option d) is incorrect because quantum computing algorithms weren't mentioned in the case study.

2 **Correct Answer: b) Defense distillation**
- **Explanation:** The case study explicitly states that "FinTech implemented defense distillation by training a 'teacher' model and using its softened outputs to train a 'student' model." This process "reduced sensitivity to small input perturbations" and "smoothed decision boundaries, making it harder for adversarial inputs to exploit vulnerabilities."
- Option a) is incorrect because simply increasing complexity wasn't mentioned as a strategy and might actually introduce more vulnerabilities.
- Option c) is incorrect because SSL encryption addresses data transmission security, not adversarial machine learning attacks.
- Option d) is incorrect because cloud-based solutions weren't mentioned as a specific defense against adversarial attacks.

3 **Correct Answer: c) By deploying data sanitization and validation**
- **Explanation:** The case study describes how FinTech deployed "advanced preprocessing pipelines" to "detect anomalies in training datasets" and "remove poisoned samples using machine learning models trained to identify outliers and suspicious patterns." This is explicitly described in the "Data Sanitization and Validation" section of Phase 3.
- Option a) is incorrect because zero-trust architecture was mentioned in Phase 5 for containing malware, not for protecting against model poisoning.
- Option b) is incorrect because federated learning was used in Phase 4 for privacy preservation, not specifically to prevent model poisoning.
- Option d) is incorrect because homomorphic encryption was used in Phase 4 for privacy preservation, not to prevent model poisoning.

4 **Correct Answer: b) Homomorphic encryption**
- **Explanation:** The case study states that "Homomorphic Encryption (HE) allowed computations on encrypted data during model inference" and "ensured that even during processing, customer data remained encrypted, mitigating risks of data leakage."
- Option a) is incorrect because differential privacy involves adding noise to outputs, not performing computations on encrypted data.
- Option c) is incorrect because federated learning keeps data localized but doesn't perform computations on encrypted data.
- Option d) is incorrect because data tokenization wasn't mentioned in the case study.

5 **Correct Answer: b) A zero-trust architecture**
- **Explanation:** In Phase 5, the case study describes how "a zero-trust architecture isolated affected systems, preventing lateral movement" as part of the containment strategies that helped contain the attack within 48 hours.
- Option a) is incorrect because the case study specifically mentioned that the polymorphic malware "evolved in real time, adapting its signatures to evade detection by traditional antivirus tools."
- Option c) is incorrect because blockchain security wasn't mentioned as part of the incident response framework.
- Option d) is incorrect because the response involved automated tools like "AI-powered monitoring tools" and "behavioral analytics," not manual scanning.

References

Abellan-Nebot, J. V., & Romero Subirón, F. (2010). A review of machining monitoring systems based on artificial intelligence process models. *The International Journal of Advanced Manufacturing Technology*, *47*, 237–257.

Almomani, A., Aoudi, S., Al-Qerem, A., Aldweesh, A., & Alkasassbeh, M. (2025). Behavioral Analysis of AI-Generated Malware: New Frontiers in Threat Detection. In *Examining Cybersecurity Risks Produced by Generative AI* (pp. 211–234). IGI Global Scientific Publishing.

Agarwala, A., Pennington, J., Dauphin, Y., & Schoenholz, S. (2020). Temperature check: Theory and practice for training models with softmax-cross-entropy losses. arXiv preprint arXiv:2010.07344.

Ahmed, M. R., Islam, A. M., Shatabda, S., & Islam, S. (2022). Blockchain-based identity management system and self-sovereign identity ecosystem: A comprehensive survey. *IEEE Access*, *10*, 113436–113481.

Ahmed, N. U. R., Badshah, A., Adeel, H., Tajammul, A., Duad, A., & Alsahfi, T. (2024). Visual deepfake detection: Review of techniques, tools, limitations, and future prospects. *IEEE Access*, *13*, 1923–1961.

Alagar, V., Mohammad, M., Wan, K., & Hnaide, S. A. (2014). A framework for developing context-aware systems. *EAI Endorsed Transactions on Context-aware Systems and Applications*, *1*(1), 1–27.

Alberti, C., Romeo, A., & Mattavelli, M. (2003). Intellectual property management and protection for MPEG multimedia content: A structured language for interoperable IPMP systems. *International Journal of Imaging Systems and Technology*, *13*(5), 275–288.

Almagrabi, A. O., & Khan, R. A. (2024). Optimizing secure AI lifecycle model management with innovative generative AI strategies. *IEEE Access, 13*, 12889–12920.

Al-Sada, B., Sadighian, A., & Oligeri, G. (2025). Mitre att&ck: State of the art and way forward. *ACM Computing Surveys, 57*(1), 1–37.

Aminu, M., Akinsanya, A., Dako, D. A., & Oyedokun, O. (2024). Enhancing cyber threat detection through real-time threat intelligence and adaptive defense mechanisms. *International Journal of Computer Applications Technology and Research, 13*(8), 11–27.

Amrit, P., & Singh, A. K. (2022). Survey on watermarking methods in the artificial intelligence domain and beyond. *Computer Communications, 188*, 52–65.

Arora, S., & Khare, P. (2024). AI/ML-enabled optimization of edge infrastructure: Enhancing performance and security. *Sensors (Basel), 4*(2), 1–13.

Aydeger, A., Zeydan, E., Yadav, A. K., Hemachandra, K. T., & Liyanage, M. (2024, October). Towards a quantum-resilient future: Strategies for transitioning to post-quantum cryptography. In *2024 15th International Conference on Network of the Future (NoF)* (pp. 195–203). IEEE.

Azar, K. Z., Hossain, M. M., Vafaei, A., Al Shaikh, H., Mondol, N. N., Rahman, F., Tehranipoor, M., & Farahmandi, F. (2022). Fuzz, penetration, and AI testing for SOC security verification: Challenges and solutions. *Cryptology ePrint Archive.*, (2), 4, 1–13.

Bandi, A., Adapa, P. V. S. R., & Kuchi, Y. E. V. P. K. (2023). The power of generative AI: A review of requirements, models, input–output formats, evaluation metrics, and challenges. *Future Internet, 15*(8), 260.

Blake, H. (2024). Generative AI in cyber security: New threats and solutions for adversarial attacks. Unpublished Manuscript. *ResearchGate.* https://www.researchgate.net/profile/Harrison-Blake-2/publication/387136288_Generative_AI_in_Cyber_Security_New_Threats_and_Solutions_for_Adversarial_Attacks/links/6761c8fb2d60b863e276c9b4/Generative-AI-in-Cyber-Security-New-Threats-and-Solutions-for-Adversarial-Attacks.pdf.

Calefato, F., Lanubile, F., & Quaranta, L. (2024). Security risks and best practices of MLOps: A multivocal literature review. https://ceur-ws.org/Vol-3731/paper13.pdf.

California Legislative Information. (2024). *SB-942 California AI Transparency Act.* California Legislative Information. https://leginfo.legislature.ca.gov/faces/billTextClient.xhtml?bill_id=202320240SB942.

Carra, A., Durmuskaya, D. E., Giulio, B. D., Falaschetti, L., Turchetti, C., & Pau, D. P. (2024). Watermarking tiny MLCommons image applications without extra deployability costs. *Electronics, 13*(23), 4644.

Debenedetti, E., Shumailov, I., Fan, T., Hayes, J., Carlini, N., Fabian, D., Kern, C., Shi, C., Terzis, A., & Tramèr, F., 2025. Defeating prompt injections by design. arXiv preprint arXiv:2503.18813.

Deng, L., Li, G., Han, S., Shi, L., & Xie, Y. (2020). Model compression and hardware acceleration for neural networks: A comprehensive survey. *Proceedings of the IEEE, 108*(4), 485–532.

Dritsas, E., & Trigka, M. (2025). *A survey on database systems in the big data era: Architectures, performance, and open challenges*. IEEE Access.

ELMessiry, A., & Messiry, M. E. (2024, November). AI Value Protocol: Utilizing Blockchain to Promote AI AIVP. In *International Conference on AI and Multimodal Services* (pp. 78–90). Cham: Springer Nature Switzerland.

Enemosah, A. (2025). Enhancing DevOps efficiency through AI-driven predictive models for continuous integration and deployment pipelines. *International Journal of Research Publication and Reviews, 6*(1), 871–887.

Erkek, N. K. (2023). JPEG based source identification of AI-generated images. https://www.politesi.polimi.it/handle/10589/227154.

EU Artificial Intelligence Act (2025). *The EU Artificial Intelligence Act*. EU Artificial Intelligence Act. https://artificialintelligenceact.eu/.

Gabrielli, E., Pica, G., & Tolomei, G. (2023). A survey on decentralized federated learning. arXiv preprint arXiv:2308.04604.

Gabay, D., Akkaya, K., & Cebe, M. (2020). Privacy-preserving authentication scheme for connected electric vehicles using blockchain and zero knowledge proofs. *IEEE Transactions on Vehicular Technology, 69*(6), 5760–5772.

Ganti, D. (2022, June 5). A novel method for detecting misinformation in videos, utilizing reverse image search, semantic analysis, and sentiment comparison of metadata. https://papers.ssrn.com/sol3/papers.cfm?abstract_id=4128499.

Geng, J. (2023). *Taking computation to data: Integrating privacy-preserving AI techniques and blockchain allowing secure analysis of sensitive data on premise*. CORE.

Gentzen, F., Bensalem, M., & Jukan, A. (2024). Effective ML model versioning in edge networks. arXiv preprint arXiv:2411.01078.

George, A. S., & George, A. H. (2023). Deepfakes: The evolution of hyper realistic media manipulation. *Partners Universal Innovative Research Publication, 1*(2), 58–74.

Ghiurău, D., & Popescu, D. E. (2024). Distinguishing reality from AI: Approaches for detecting synthetic content. *Computers, 14*(1), 1.

Gupta, H., Jin, K. H., Nguyen, H. Q., McCann, M. T., & Unser, M. (2018). CNN-based projected gradient descent for consistent CT image reconstruction. *IEEE Transactions on Medical Imaging, 37*(6), 1440–1453.

Han, C., Wang, L., Li, D., Cui, W., & Yan, B. (2024). A pruning method combined with resilient training to improve the adversarial robustness of automatic modulation classification models. *Mobile Networks and Applications*, 1–17.

Hindka, M. (2024). Securing the digital backbone: An in-depth insights into API security patterns and practices. *Computer Science and Engineering, 14*(2), 35–41.

Hines, K., Lopez, G., Hall, M., Zarfati, F., Zunger, Y., & Kiciman, E. (2024). Defending against indirect prompt injection attacks with Spotlighting. arXiv preprint arXiv:2403.14720.

Hossain, M. T., Afrin, R., & Biswas, M. A. A. (2023). A review on attacks against artificial intelligence (AI) and their defence image recognition and generation machine learning, artificial intelligence. *Control Systems and Optimization Letters, 2*(1), 52–59.

Hu, H., Salcic, Z., Sun, L., Dobbie, G., Yu, P. S., & Zhang, X. (2022). Membership inference attacks on machine learning: A survey. *ACM Computing Surveys (CSUR), 54*(11s), 1–37.

Islam, M. S. (2024). Confidential computing with trusted execution environments [Doctoral dissertation]. The University of Texas at Dallas.

Janovsky, A., Chmielewski, Ł., Svenda, P., Jancar, J., & Matyas, V. (2024, June). Chain of trust: Unraveling references among common criteria certified products. In *IFIP International Conference on ICT Systems Security and Privacy Protection* (pp. 191–205). Cham: Springer Nature Switzerland.

Kaminaga, H., Awaysheh, F. M., Alawadi, S., & Kamm, L. (2023, December). MPCFL: Towards multi-party computation for secure federated learning aggregation. In *Proceedings of the IEEE/ACM 16th International Conference on Utility and Cloud Computing* (pp. 1–10).

Kaul, D., & Khurana, R. (2021). AI to detect and mitigate security vulnerabilities in APIs: Encryption, authentication, and anomaly detection in enterprise-level distributed systems. *Eigenpub Review of Science and Technology, 5*(1), 34–62.

Kerner, S. (2024). CrowdStrike outage explained: What caused it and what's next. *TechTarget*. https://www.techtarget.com/whatis/feature/Explaining-the-largest-IT-outage-in-history-and-whats-next.

Khan, M., & Ghafoor, L. (2024). Adversarial machine learning in the context of network security: Challenges and solutions. *Journal of Computational Intelligence and Robotics, 4*(1), 51–63.

Kolade, T. M., Aideyan, N. T., Oyekunle, S. M., Ogungbemi, O. S., Dapo-Oyewole, D. L., & Olaniyi, O. O. (2024). Artificial intelligence and information governance: Strengthening global security, through compliance frameworks, and data security. *Asian Journal of Research in Computer Science, 17*(12), 36–57.

Korada, L. (2024). Data poisoning-what is it and how it is being addressed by the leading gen AI providers. *European Journal of Advances in Engineering and Technology, 11*(5), 105–109.

Kota, S. (2024). Adversarial robustness in retinal image classification model: Gradient-based adversarial attacks and defense mechanisms. http://www.diva-portal.org/smash/get/diva2:1909980/FULLTEXT01.pdf.

Lakshmanan, R. (2025). Meta launches LlamaFirewall framework to stop AI jailbreaks, injections, and insecure code. *The Hacker News*. https://thehackernews.com/2025/04/meta-launches-llamafirewall-framework.html.

Latendresse, J., Abedu, S., Abdellatif, A., & Shihab, E. (2024). An exploratory study on machine learning model management. *ACM Transactions on Software Engineering and Methodology*, *34*(1), 16.

Latibari, B. S., Nazari, N., Chowdhury, M. A., Gubbi, K. I., Fang, C., Ghimire, S., Hosseini, E., Sayadi, H., Homayoun, H., Salehi, S., & Sasan, A. (2024). Transformers: A security perspective. *IEEE Access*, *12*, 181071–181105.

Li, H., Sun, J., & Xiong, K. (2024). AI-driven optimization system for large-scale Kubernetes clusters: Enhancing cloud infrastructure availability, security, and disaster recovery. *Journal of Artificial Intelligence General Science (JAIGS)*, *2*, 281–306.

Li, Y., Liu, Y., Li, B., Wang, W., & Liu, N. (2023). Towards practical differential privacy in data analysis: Understanding the effect of epsilon on utility in private ERM. *Computers & Security*, *128*, 103147.

Li, Z., Yu, H., Zhou, T., Luo, L., Fan, M., Xu, Z., & Sun, G. (2021). Byzantine resistant secure blockchained federated learning at the edge. *IEEE Network*, *35*(4), 295–301.

Liang, H., He, E., Zhao, Y., Jia, Z., & Li, H. (2022). Adversarial attack and defense: A survey. *Electronics*, *11*(8), 1283.

Liang, Y., Xiao, J., Gan, W., & Yu, P. S. (2024). Watermarking techniques for Large Language Models: A survey. arXiv preprint arXiv:2409.00089.

Liu, Y., Mao, S., Mei, X., Yang, T., & Zhao, X. (2019, December). Sensitivity of adversarial perturbation in fast gradient sign method. In *2019 IEEE Symposium Series on Computational Intelligence (SSCI)* (pp. 433–436). IEEE.

López Delgado, J. L., & López Ramos, J. A. (2024). A comprehensive survey on generative AI solutions in IoT security. *Electronics*, *13*(24), 4965.

Marcolla, C., Sucasas, V., Manzano, M., Bassoli, R., Fitzek, F. H., & Aaraj, N. (2022). Survey on fully homomorphic encryption, theory, and applications. *Proceedings of the IEEE*, *110*(10), 1572–1609.

Masood, M., Nawaz, M., Malik, K. M., Javed, A., Irtaza, A., & Malik, H. (2023). Deepfakes generation and detection: State-of-the-art, open challenges, countermeasures, and way forward. *Applied Intelligence*, *53*(4), 3974–4026.

Mathys, M., Willi, M., & Meier, R. (2024). Synthetic photography detection: A visual guidance for identifying synthetic images created by AI. arXiv preprint arXiv:2408.06398.

Medium. (2025). New lightning attention architecture LLM. 1st production model. https://sbagency.medium.com/lightning-attention-llm-1st-production-model-57815e321ad9.

Meta AI (2025, April 29) AI defenders program: Llama protection tools. *Meta AI Blog*. Retrieved 2025, May 1, from. https://ai.meta.com/blog/ai-defenders-program-llama-protection-tools/.

Mollakuqe, E., Parduzi, A., Rexhepi, S., Dimitrova, V., Jakupi, S., Muharremi, R., Hamiti, M., & Qarkaxhija, J. (2024). Applications of homomorphic encryption in secure computation. *Open Research Europe*, *4*(158), 158.

Moosavi-Dezfooli, S. M., Fawzi, A., Fawzi, O., & Frossard, P. (2017). Universal adversarial perturbations. In *Proceedings of the IEEE Conference on Computer Vision and Pattern Recognition* (pp. 1765–1773).

Nanayakkara, P., Smart, M. A., Cummings, R., Kaptchuk, G., & Redmiles, E. M. (2023). What are the chances? Explaining the epsilon parameter in differential privacy. *32nd USENIX Security Symposium (USENIX Security 23)* (pp. 1613–1630).

Ni, Y., Zeng, W., Xia, P., Yang, G. S., & Tan, R. (2024). A deepfake detection algorithm based on Fourier transform of biological signal. *Computers, Materials & Continua*, *79*(3), 5295–5312.

NIST. (2025a, March 6). NIST finalizes guidelines for evaluating 'Differential Privacy' guarantees to de-identify data. https://www.nist.gov/news-events/news/2025/03/nist-finalizes-guidelines-evaluating-differential-privacy-guarantees-de.

NIST. (2025b). Post-quantum cryptography. https://csrc.nist.gov/projects/post-quantum-cryptography.

NIST AI. (2024). Artificial intelligence risk management framework: Generative artificial intelligence profile. https://nvlpubs.nist.gov/nistpubs/ai/NIST.AI.600-1.pdf.

Nookala, G., Gade, K. R., Dulam, N., & Thumburu, S. K. R. (2024). Post-quantum cryptography: Preparing for a new era of data encryption. *MZ Computing Journal*, *5*(2), 012077.

Nour, B., Pourzandi, M., & Debbabi, M. (2023). A survey on threat hunting in enterprise networks. *IEEE Communications Surveys & Tutorials.*, *25*, 2299–2324.

Nowroozi, E., Mohammadi, M., Savaş, E., Mekdad, Y., & Conti, M. (2023). Employing deep ensemble learning for improving the security of computer networks against adversarial attacks. *IEEE Transactions on Network and Service Management*, *20*(2), 2096–2105.

Omotunde, H., & Ahmed, M. (2023). A comprehensive review of security measures in database systems: Assessing authentication, access control, and beyond. *Mesopotamian Journal of CyberSecurity*, *2023*, 115–133.

Papernot, N., McDaniel, P., Wu, X., Jha, S., & Swami, A. (2016, May). Distillation as a defense to adversarial perturbations against deep neural networks. In *2016 IEEE Symposium on Security and Privacy (SP)* (pp. 582–597). IEEE.

Parameshachari, B. D., Panduranga, H. T., & Kms, S. (2012). A overview on partial image encryption approaches. *International Journal of Engineering Research and Development*, *1*(2), 49–54.

Patel, R., Tripathi, H., Stone, J., Golilarz, N. A., Mittal, S., Rahimi, S., & Chaudhary, V. (2025). Towards secure MLOps: Surveying attacks, mitigation strategies, and research challenges. arXiv preprint arXiv:2506.02032.

Paul, J. (2024). How software engineering is shaping AI's future: The tools and practices behind smarter systems. Unpublished Manuscript. https://www.researchgate.net/profile/Joel-Paul-10/publication/385817658_How_Software_Engineering_is_Shaping_AI%27s_Future_The_Tools_and_Practices_Behind_Smarter_Systems/links/6736524437496239b2bfe6bd/How-Software-Engineering-is-Shaping-AIs-Future-The-Tools-and-Practices-Behind-Smarter-Systems.pdf.

Petullo, W. M., Zhang, X., Solworth, J. A., Bernstein, D. J., & Lange, T. (2013, November). MinimaLT: Minimal-latency networking through better security. In *Proceedings of the 2013 ACM SIGSAC Conference on Computer & Communications Security* (pp. 425–438).

Pirzada, P., Wilde, A., Doherty, G. H., & Harris-Birtill, D. (2023). Remote photoplethysmography (rPPG): A state-of-the-art review. medRxiv, 2023-10.

Qian, Z., Huang, K., Wang, Q. F., & Zhang, X. Y. (2022). A survey of robust adversarial training in pattern recognition: Fundamental, theory, and methodologies. *Pattern Recognition*, *131*, 108889.

Qin, Z., Li, D., Sun, W., Sun, W., Shen, X., Han, X., Wei, Y., Lv, B., Luo, X., Qiao, Y., & Zhong, Y., 2023. Transnormerllm: A faster and better large language model with improved transnormer. arXiv preprint arXiv:2307.14995.

Qin, Z., Sun, W., Li, D., Shen, X., Sun, W., & Zhong, Y. (2024). Lightning attention-2: A free lunch for handling unlimited sequence lengths in large language models. arXiv preprint arXiv:2401.04658.

Qureshi, A., & Megias Jimenez, D. (2021). Blockchain-based multimedia content protection: Review and open challenges. *Applied Sciences*, *11*(1), 1.

Radanliev, P., & Santos, O. (2023). Adversarial attacks can deceive AI systems, leading to misclassification or incorrect decisions. https://www.preprints.org/manuscript/202309.2064/v1.

Rane, N., Choudhary, S. P., & Rane, J. (2024). Ensemble deep learning and machine learning: Applications, opportunities, challenges, and future directions. *Studies in Medical and Health Sciences*, *1*(2), 18–41.

Sarker, I. H. (2024). Introduction to AI-driven cybersecurity and threat intelligence. In I. H. Sarker (Ed.), *AI-driven cybersecurity and threat intelligence: Cyber automation, intelligent decision-making and explainability* (pp. 3–19). Springer Nature Switzerland.

Sayadi, H., Patel, N., Sasan, A., Rafatirad, S., & Homayoun, H. (2018, June). Ensemble learning for effective run-time hardware-based malware detection: A comprehensive analysis and classification. In *Proceedings of the 55th Annual Design Automation Conference* (pp. 1–6).

Sayyafzadeh, S. (2024). *Thumbnail image forensic acquisition and analysis in the age of artificial intelligence* [Master's thesis]. Florida Agricultural and Mechanical University.

Sen, J., Waghela, H., & Rakshit, S. (2024). Privacy in federated learning. arXiv preprint arXiv:2408.08904.

Sendas, N., & Rajale, D. (2025). Future trends in MLOps. In N. Sendas & D. Rajale (Eds.), *The definitive guide to machine learning operations in AWS: Machine learning scalability and optimization with AWS* (pp. 371–423). Apress.

Shah, R. A., Nawaz, S. A., Shaheen, Q., & Asghar, A. (2024). Collaborative blockchain-based crypto-efficient scheme for protecting visual contents. *Journal of Computing & Biomedical Informatics*, *9*, 1–11.

Shaik, T., Tao, X., Xie, H., Li, L., Zhu, X., & Li, Q. (2024). Exploring the landscape of machine unlearning: A comprehensive survey and taxonomy. *IEEE Transactions on Neural Networks and Learning Systems.*, *36*(7), 11676–11696. https://doi.org/10.1109/TNNLS.2024.3486109.

Silva, L., & Oliveira, M. (2024a). Enhancing privacy protection in AI systems: The differential privacy approach. *MZ Journal of Artificial Intelligence*, *1*(1), 1–17.

Silva, L., & Oliveira, M. (2024b). Privacy-preserving AI: Unveiling the power of differential privacy. *MZ Journal of Artificial Intelligence*, *1*(1), 1–7.

Song, J., & Namiot, D. (2022, September). A survey of the implementations of model inversion attacks. In *International Conference on Distributed Computer and Communication Networks* (pp. 3–16). Cham: Springer Nature Switzerland.

Sood, N. (2024). Cryptography in post quantum computing era. Available at SSRN 4705470.

Su, G., Wang, J., Xu, X., Wang, Y., & Wang, C. (2024). The utilization of homomorphic encryption technology grounded on artificial intelligence for privacy preservation. *International Journal of Computer Science and Information Technology*, *2*(1), 52–58.

Tesic, J. (2005). Metadata practices for consumer photos. *IEEE MultiMedia*, *12*(3), 86–92.

VB Daily. (2025). MiniMax unveils its own open-source LLM with industry-leading 4M token context. https://venturebeat.com/ai/minimax-unveils-its-own-open-source-llm-with-industry-leading-4m-token-context.

Villegas-Ch, W., Jaramillo-Alcázar, A., & Luján-Mora, S. (2024). Evaluating the robustness of deep learning models against adversarial attacks: An analysis with FGSM, PGD and CW. *Big Data and Cognitive Computing*, *8*(1), 8.

Waseem, S., Bakar, S. A. R. S. A., Ahmed, B. A., Omar, Z., Eisa, T. A. E., & Dalam, M. E. E. (2023). DeepFake on face and expression swap: A review. *IEEE Access*, *11*, 117865–117906.

Widodo, A. M., Pappachan, P., Sekti, B. A., Anwar, N., Widayanti, R., Rahaman, M., & Bansal, R. (2024). Quantum-resistant cryptography. In A. Almomani, B. B. Gupta, & D. Kalra (Eds.), *Innovations in modern cryptography* (pp. 100–130). IGI Global.

Zenitani, K. (2023). Attack graph analysis: An explanatory guide. *Computers & Security, 126*, 103081.

Zha, D., Bhat, Z. P., Lai, K. H., Yang, F., Jiang, Z., Zhong, S., & Hu, X. (2023). Data-centric artificial intelligence: A survey. *ACM Computing Survey.*

Zhang, C., & Li, S. (2024). State-of-the-art approaches to enhancing privacy preservation of machine learning datasets: A survey. arXiv preprint arXiv:2404.16847.

Zhang, C., Xie, Y., Bai, H., Yu, B., Li, W., & Gao, Y. (2021). A survey on federated learning. *Knowledge-Based Systems, 216*, 106775.

Zhang, J., Zhu, H., Wang, F., Zhao, J., Xu, Q., & Li, H. (2022). Security and privacy threats to federated learning: Issues, methods, and challenges. *Security and Communication Networks, 2022*(1), 1–24.

Zhang, L. (2023). *Automatic inference of latent emotion from spontaneous facial micro-expressions* [Doctoral dissertation]. The University of St Andrews.

Zheng, H., Shen, L., Tang, A., Luo, Y., Hu, H., Du, B., & Tao, D. (2023). Learn from model beyond fine-tuning: A survey. arXiv preprint arXiv:2310.08184.

7

Ethical and Regulatory Considerations

Moving on from the technical aspects of cybersecurity in generative artificial intelligence (AI), it's important to understand the ethical and regulatory considerations. As generative AI systems become increasingly integrated into critical applications and decision-making processes, the intersection of security, ethics, and regulation demands careful consideration. This chapter examines the complex landscape of ethical challenges in AI security, from issues of transparency and accountability to the critical importance of addressing bias in AI systems. We explore emerging governance frameworks and regulatory initiatives across different jurisdictions, providing practical insights into how organizations can navigate compliance while maintaining innovation. The discussion encompasses both theoretical foundations and practical implementations of responsible AI development, emphasizing the crucial balance between technological advancement and security considerations. Through an examination of human-in-the-loop (HITL) systems, ethical design principles, and collaborative approaches, this chapter provides a comprehensive framework for understanding and addressing the ethical and regulatory dimensions of generative AI security.

7.1 Ethical Challenges in AI Security

At a high level, it is understood that there are ethical challenges in the AI security landscape. However, the more granular you get, the more nuanced it is. In this section, we will address the ethical challenges of transparency, explainable AI (XAI), bias and fairness, and accountability in AI-driven decision making (Akinrinola et al., 2024). Let's start with the point of transparency, because it represents one of the most pressing ethical dilemmas in modern technology. These systems, built on complex neural networks and trained on vast datasets, often operate as "black boxes," where even their creators may not fully understand how specific outputs are generated (Von Eschenbach, 2021). This opacity creates

Generative AI Security: Defense, Threats, and Vulnerabilities, First Edition. Shaila Rana and Rhonda Chicone.

significant challenges for security professionals, policymakers, and end users who need to trust and verify these systems' operations, especially in security-critical applications. The black box nature of generative AI systems introduces unique vulnerabilities and challenges in the cybersecurity landscape. When security teams deploy AI systems for threat detection, incident response, or vulnerability assessment, their inability to fully understand the decision-making process poses significant risks. This lack of transparency makes it difficult to validate whether the AI system is functioning as intended, identify potential blind spots, or determine if the system has been compromised or manipulated by adversaries (Chaudhary, 2024).

The societal implications of this transparency challenge extend beyond technical concerns. Organizations deploying generative AI systems must balance the need for security with accountability to stakeholders, regulators, and the public. When AI systems make decisions that affect individuals' privacy, security, or access to resources, the inability to explain these decisions undermines trust and raises serious ethical concerns about fairness, accountability, and due process (Cheong, 2024). This challenge is particularly acute in regulated industries, where organizations must demonstrate compliance and justify their security measures.

The cybersecurity field faces additional complexity because transparency itself can sometimes conflict with security objectives. Providing too much insight into how AI systems operate could potentially expose vulnerabilities to malicious actors. This creates a delicate balance between providing sufficient transparency for accountability and maintaining necessary operational security—a balance that security professionals must carefully navigate. To put it in perspective, let's consider an example in a cybersecurity setting. Let's say there is a financial institution implements a generative AI system for detecting and preventing fraudulent transactions. The system flags a series of transactions as potentially fraudulent, leading to their automatic rejection. When customers demand explanations for why their legitimate transactions were blocked, the institution struggles to provide clear answers because the AI's decision-making process isn't fully transparent. The security team can't definitively determine if the system is generating false positives due to biased training data, adversarial attacks, or legitimate security concerns. This situation creates tension between maintaining security, ensuring fair treatment of customers, and providing necessary accountability. Subsequently, to address these challenges, the cybersecurity community is exploring various approaches, including XAI frameworks, standardized documentation requirements, and hybrid systems that combine AI capabilities with human oversight. However, finding the right balance between transparency and security remains an ongoing challenge that requires continuous adaptation as both AI technology and security threats evolve.

That leads us to XAI, or XAI (Dwivedi et al., 2023), which is extremely important as systems become more complex and their decisions become more consequential. While XAI aims to make AI systems more transparent and interpretable, implementing it effectively in security contexts presents significant technical and ethical challenges (Weber et al., 2023). The fundamental tension lies in balancing the need for detailed explanations with the requirement to maintain robust security measures and protect sensitive information. The challenge becomes particularly acute with modern AI security systems that make real-time decisions about threat detection, access control, and incident response. When these systems flag potential security threats or deny access to resources, stakeholders naturally demand explanations. However, providing detailed explanations about how the system arrived at its decision could potentially expose vulnerabilities in the security architecture or reveal information that could be exploited by malicious actors.

Generative AI systems pose unique challenges for XAI implementation due to their inherent complexity and the nature of their operations. Unlike traditional rule-based systems, generative AI models often rely on complex neural networks and probabilistic reasoning that can be difficult to translate into human-understandable explanations (Gentili, 2021). The dynamic nature of these systems, which often learn and adapt over time, further complicates the task of providing consistent and meaningful explanations for their decisions. Therefore, the ethical implications of inadequate XAI in security systems extend beyond technical considerations. When organizations cannot provide clear explanations for AI-driven security decisions, it can erode trust, create accountability gaps, and potentially lead to bias or discrimination going undetected. This lack of explainability can also complicate compliance with regulatory requirements, particularly in sectors where transparent decision-making is mandated by law. Many current generative AI systems lack robust XAI capabilities by design (Antoniadi et al., 2021). While they can generate impressive outputs and make sophisticated decisions, their architecture often prioritizes performance and efficiency over explainability. This creates a significant ethical challenge as organizations must decide whether to deploy powerful but opaque systems or opt for potentially less capable alternatives that offer better explainability.

In healthcare settings, this ethical challenge becomes particularly evident. Consider a hospital using an AI security system to protect sensitive patient data and monitor access to electronic health records. When the system detects potential unauthorized access attempts and automatically revokes certain staff members' access privileges, the hospital faces a complex situation. The AI's decision might be based on subtle patterns in access behavior that suggest potential insider threats, but without clear explainability, the hospital struggles to justify these actions to affected staff members while maintaining security protocols and protecting patient privacy. This scenario highlights how the lack of XAI can create tension between security requirements, operational efficiency, and workplace trust.

The limitations of XAI in generative AI systems also affect their adoption in security-critical environments. Organizations must carefully weigh the benefits of advanced AI capabilities against the ethical and practical implications of deploying systems that cannot fully explain their decisions. This challenge is driving research into new architectures and methodologies that can better balance performance with explainability, but current solutions often require significant trade-offs between these competing objectives.

Bias and fairness often come to mind when one thinks of the introduction of AI into our digital ecosystems and societies. Bias and fairness in AI security represent fundamental ethical challenges that can significantly impact both cybersecurity operations and broader societal outcomes (Varona & Suárez, 2022). AI systems, including those used for security purposes, can inherit and amplify existing biases from their training data, potentially leading to discriminatory outcomes in threat detection, access control, and security resource allocation. These biases can manifest in various ways, from facial recognition systems that perform poorly across different demographics to anomaly detection systems that disproportionately flag certain user groups as suspicious. This is especially true in education, where AI systems could disproportionately flag students from different backgrounds (Amah & Okesipe, 2025). The cybersecurity field faces certain challenges as organizations increasingly rely on AI-powered security tools without fully understanding or addressing their potential biases. For instance, security systems might incorrectly identify certain behavior patterns as threats based on biased historical data, leading to higher false positive rates for particular user groups or communities. This can result in unfair treatment, reduced access to resources, or unnecessary security interventions that disproportionately affect specific populations.

Moreover, the rapid adoption of generative AI tools in security operations has introduced new dimensions to the bias and fairness challenge. Security professionals increasingly rely on these systems for tasks ranging from code analysis to threat detection, often accepting their outputs without sufficient scrutiny or validation. This "automation bias"—the tendency to trust automated systems without question—can lead to the perpetuation and amplification of existing biases in security decisions (Schemmer et al., 2022). When security teams use generative AI to create security policies, incident response procedures, or risk assessments, any inherent biases in the AI system can become institutionalized in an organization's security practices. Addressing bias and fairness in AI security requires an interdisciplinary approach that combines technical expertise with insights from ethics, law, social sciences, and human rights. Technical solutions alone cannot address the complex societal implications of biased AI security systems. Organizations need to bring together diverse perspectives, including cybersecurity experts, data scientists, ethicists, legal professionals, and representatives from affected communities. This collaborative approach helps ensure that AI security systems are developed and deployed in ways that respect fairness, promote equity, and protect against discrimination while maintaining effective security measures.

The aforementioned challenge becomes especially critical as AI systems are increasingly integrated into critical infrastructure and essential services. Biased security systems could restrict access to vital resources, create unnecessary barriers for certain groups, or perpetuate existing social inequalities. Organizations must invest in robust testing, validation, and monitoring processes to identify and mitigate biases in their AI security systems, while also establishing clear accountability mechanisms for addressing fairness-related concerns.

The challenge of accountability in AI-driven decision-making has emerged as a critical ethical concern, particularly as organizations increasingly rely on AI systems to make or influence significant decisions. The fundamental issue lies in determining who bears responsibility when AI systems make decisions that impact individuals, organizations, or society—the developers, the deployers, the users, or some combination of these stakeholders. In many cases, organizations are using AI systems to make or influence important decisions without clear disclosure or transparency about the AI's role in the decision-making process. This lack of transparency creates significant ethical and practical challenges, as individuals affected by these decisions may not even be aware that an AI system was involved. This becomes particularly problematic when decisions impact fundamental rights, opportunities, or access to resources. The cybersecurity field faces unique accountability challenges as AI systems become more integrated into security operations. Security teams may use AI for threat detection, incident response, access control, and risk assessment without clear frameworks for accountability when these systems make errors or questionable decisions. When an AI system incorrectly flags a security threat or fails to detect a genuine attack, determining responsibility and liability becomes complex, especially if the decision-making process isn't well documented or understood.

Several US states are developing legislation to address these accountability gaps; we will talk more about this in Section 7.3. For example, California has proposed regulations requiring businesses to inform consumers about data transparency and when AI systems are used to make significant decisions affecting them (California Legislative Information, 2024a). Colorado's AI Act includes provisions for transparency and accountability in AI system deployment (National Association of Attorneys General, 2024). These legislative efforts represent important steps toward establishing clear accountability frameworks, but they also highlight the complexity of regulating AI decision-making across different contexts and jurisdictions. The emergence of generative AI has further complicated the accountability landscape. These systems can generate content, code, and recommendations that appear highly credible and authoritative, making it difficult to distinguish between AI-generated and human-generated decisions. In cybersecurity contexts, this creates concerns when generative AI is used to develop security policies, incident response plans, or risk assessments without clear documentation or accountability measures.

The blurring of lines between human and AI decision-making in cybersecurity can lead to what experts call "responsibility gaps" (Santoni de Sio & Mecacci, 2021). For instance, if a security incident occurs after following recommendations generated by an AI system, who bears responsibility—the security team that implemented the recommendations, the organization that deployed the AI system, or the system's developers? This ambiguity can create hesitation in adopting AI technologies, even when they might enhance security capabilities. Consequently, the challenge extends beyond individual decisions to systemic impacts. When AI systems are used to make multiple, interconnected security decisions over time, tracking accountability becomes increasingly complex. Organizations may find themselves in situations where they cannot fully explain or justify their security posture because it has evolved through a series of AI-influenced decisions without clear documentation or accountability trails. Hence, to address these challenges, organizations need to develop comprehensive frameworks for AI accountability in security decision-making. This includes clearly documenting when and how AI systems are used, establishing clear chains of responsibility, implementing robust testing and validation procedures, and maintaining detailed audit trails of AI-influenced decisions. Additionally, organizations should consider implementing human oversight mechanisms for critical security decisions, ensuring that AI systems serve as decision support tools rather than autonomous decision-makers.

7.2 AI Governance Frameworks

As organizations increasingly deploy AI systems across their operations, the need for robust governance frameworks has become paramount. AI governance frameworks provide structured approaches for managing the development, deployment, and monitoring of AI systems while ensuring ethical compliance and risk management. These frameworks, ranging from internal AI ethics committees to standardized guidelines like the NIST AI Risk Management Framework (RMF) and comprehensive auditing mechanisms, help organizations navigate the complex landscape of AI implementation (NIST, 2024). Having and establishing these clear protocols, responsibilities, and oversight mechanisms, these frameworks enable organizations to harness AI's potential while maintaining accountability, addressing ethical concerns, and managing associated risks. Understanding and implementing appropriate governance frameworks is crucial for organizations seeking to build trust in their AI systems while ensuring responsible and secure AI development. These frameworks must address not only technical considerations but also ethical implications, societal impacts, and security concerns. As aforementioned, AI systems become more sophisticated and their decisions more consequential. Hence, the need for comprehensive governance structures becomes increasingly urgent, particularly in areas where AI decisions can significantly impact human lives, rights, and security.

The establishment of AI ethics committees at national and international levels is crucial for developing and maintaining consistent standards and guidelines (Prunkl et al., 2021). These committees need to bring together diverse perspectives from multiple fields—including computer science, ethics, law, sociology, psychology, and domain-specific experts—to effectively address the complex challenges posed by AI systems. The interdisciplinary nature of these committees is essential because AI's impacts extend far beyond technical considerations, touching on fundamental questions of fairness, accountability, privacy, and human rights (Daly et al., 2022). International committees are particularly important as AI systems and their impacts often cross-national boundaries, requiring coordinated approaches to governance and regulation.

What makes AI ethics committees challenging is the need to balance multiple competing interests and considerations. They must promote innovation while ensuring safety, encourage technological advancement while protecting individual rights, and maintain security while fostering transparency. This requires committee members to have not only expertise in their respective fields but also the ability to understand and integrate perspectives from other disciplines. Furthermore, these committees need to maintain flexibility to adapt to rapidly evolving AI capabilities while providing stable and consistent guidance for organizations implementing AI systems. The composition of these committees should reflect the diversity of stakeholders affected by AI systems. This includes representatives from academia, industry, government, civil society organizations, and affected communities. Such diverse representation helps ensure that governance frameworks address the full spectrum of concerns and challenges associated with AI deployment, from technical security considerations to societal impacts and ethical implications. Additionally, these committees need to establish clear mechanisms for updating their guidance as technology evolves and new challenges emerge, ensuring that governance frameworks remain relevant and effective over time.

As briefly mentioned earlier, an important AI governance framework is NIST's AI RMF. The development of this framework is a significant milestone for AI governance because it provides organizations with a structured approach to identifying, assessing, and managing risks associated with AI systems. Released in early 2023, this voluntary framework offers a comprehensive methodology that aligns with existing risk management practices while addressing the unique challenges posed by AI technologies. The framework's emphasis on continuous monitoring and improvement makes it particularly valuable for organizations seeking to implement AI systems responsibly. The framework's structure around four key functions—Govern, Map, Measure, and Manage—provides a systematic approach to AI risk management (NIST, 2024). The Govern function establishes policies, procedures, and priorities for managing AI risks. Map helps organizations understand and document their AI systems' contexts, capabilities, and potential impacts. Measure enables the assessment and analysis of AI-related risks, while Manage focuses on responding to identified risks through various controls and mitigation strategies.

One of the framework's key strengths lies in its flexibility and adaptability across different sectors and organizations. It can be applied to various AI systems, from simple automation tools to complex generative AI applications. The framework's risk-based approach helps organizations prioritize their resources and attention based on the potential impact and likelihood of AI-related risks, making it particularly valuable for organizations with limited resources. The NIST AI RMF also emphasizes the importance of transparency and documentation throughout the AI lifecycle. This includes maintaining clear records of risk assessments, mitigation strategies, and ongoing monitoring activities. Such documentation is crucial for demonstrating due diligence, supporting audit activities, and enabling continuous improvement of AI risk management practices. However, the framework faces several significant challenges and limitations (Swaminathan & Danks, 2024). Organizations often struggle with its implementation due to its complexity and the need for specialized expertise. The framework's broad scope can make it difficult for smaller organizations to fully implement, and its voluntary nature means there's no standardized way to verify compliance. Additionally, the rapidly evolving nature of AI technology means that some risk categories or mitigation strategies may become outdated quickly.

For cybersecurity professionals, the NIST AI RMF offers valuable guidance for integrating AI systems into security operations while managing associated risks. Consider a practical example: A security team implementing a new AI-powered threat detection system could use the framework to systematically assess risks. Using the Map function, they would document the system's capabilities, dependencies, and potential impacts on security operations. Through the Measure function, they would assess risks such as false positives, potential biases, or adversarial attacks. The Manage function would guide the implementation of controls like human oversight for critical alerts, regular model validation, and incident response procedures for AI-related issues. Over time, this systematic approach could lead to more reliable and trustworthy AI-enhanced security operations, with clear documentation and accountability mechanisms in place.

The ISO 42001 framework is an important standard to acknowledge when discussing AI frameworks, and it is a significant step forward in establishing standardized governance for AI systems, providing organizations with structured guidance for implementing and managing AI responsibly. This international standard, designed to help organizations develop and maintain effective AI management systems, becomes increasingly crucial as AI technologies become more prevalent across various sectors (McIntosh et al., 2024). The framework addresses key aspects of AI governance, including risk management, ethical considerations, and operational controls, providing a comprehensive approach to ensuring responsible AI development and deployment (Thiers & Harned, 2024).

The benefits of ISO 42001 are substantial, especially in providing organizations with a structured approach to managing AI-related risks and opportunities. The framework helps organizations establish clear governance structures, define responsibilities, and implement controls that ensure AI systems operate reliably and ethically (Mazzinghy et al., 2024). This standardization is especially valuable as organizations face increasing pressure to demonstrate responsible AI practices to stakeholders, regulators, and customers. Thus, following ISO 42001 enables organizations to build trust in their AI systems while maintaining effective control over their development and deployment. The framework also helps organizations align their AI initiatives with broader business objectives while ensuring appropriate risk management and ethical considerations are integrated into AI development processes.

For small- and medium-sized businesses (SMBs) and startups, implementing ISO 42001 presents unique challenges. These organizations often lack the resources, expertise, and infrastructure needed to fully implement the framework's requirements. The cost of compliance, both in terms of financial investment and human resources, can be substantial (Dudley, 2024). SMBs might struggle to establish dedicated AI governance teams or implement comprehensive monitoring and testing programs as required by the standard. Additionally, the documentation and process requirements can seem overwhelming for smaller organizations that operate with more flexible and informal structures. This challenge is particularly acute for startups that need to maintain agility and quick decision-making processes while ensuring responsible AI development.

The framework's shortcomings become apparent when considering the rapid pace of AI technology evolution. ISO 42001, like many standards (it's not exclusive to ISO 42001), can lag behind technological advancements, potentially becoming outdated as new AI capabilities and challenges emerge. The standard might not fully address emerging issues such as the specific challenges posed by generative AI or the complexities of AI systems that continuously learn and adapt. There's also a risk that organizations might focus too heavily on compliance with the standard's requirements rather than fostering genuine innovation in responsible AI development. Balancing innovation with responsible AI deployment is one of the most significant challenges in implementing ISO 42001. Organizations must find ways to maintain their competitive edge and drive innovation while ensuring compliance with the framework's requirements. This balance becomes especially crucial in fast-moving industries, where AI capabilities can provide significant competitive advantages. The framework needs to be implemented in a way that supports rather than hinders innovation, allowing organizations to explore new AI applications while maintaining appropriate controls and ethical considerations. The framework could be improved by incorporating more flexible and adaptive requirements that can evolve alongside AI technology. This might include provisions for regular updates to the standard, more specific guidance for different types of AI applications, and clearer pathways for smaller organizations to achieve compliance. Additionally, the standard could benefit from more practical guidance on implementing its requirements in resource-constrained environments and clearer metrics for measuring the effectiveness of AI governance programs.

The impact of ISO 42001 on organizational culture and practices extends beyond mere compliance. Successfully implementing the framework requires organizations to develop a culture of responsible AI development, where ethical considerations and risk management are integrated into daily decision-making processes. This cultural shift can be challenging for organizations that have traditionally focused primarily on technical capabilities or rapid development cycles. However, when successfully achieved, this transformation can lead to more sustainable and responsible AI development practices. Looking ahead, the evolution of ISO 42001 will likely need to address emerging challenges in AI governance, including the increasing complexity of AI systems, the AI supply chain, the growing importance of explainability and transparency, and the need for more effective risk management approaches. The standard may need to adapt to provide more specific guidance for different types of AI applications while maintaining its role as a comprehensive framework for AI governance. This evolution will be crucial in ensuring the standard remains relevant and effective in promoting responsible AI development and deployment. Consequently, the success of ISO 42001 implementation often depends on an organization's ability to integrate its requirements into existing processes and systems while maintaining operational efficiency. This integration requires careful planning, adequate resources, and strong leadership commitment. Organizations must also ensure they maintain appropriate documentation and evidence of compliance while avoiding excessive bureaucracy that could impede innovation and agility.

Earlier in this book, the concept of shadow AI was discussed in the context of privacy concerns. The regulation of shadow AI is a challenge within AI governance frameworks, requiring organizations to balance employee productivity with security and compliance requirements. While existing frameworks like NIST AI RMF and ISO 42001 provide comprehensive guidance for managing authorized AI systems, they often don't fully address the specific challenges posed by unauthorized or undocumented AI usage. Organizations must develop specific policies and controls that acknowledge the reality of shadow AI while maintaining appropriate governance standards. Effective shadow AI governance requires a multi-layered approach that extends beyond traditional compliance frameworks. This includes implementing technical controls to monitor and detect unauthorized AI usage, establishing clear policies regarding acceptable AI tool usage, and creating approved alternatives that meet employees' needs while maintaining security standards. Organizations should consider integrating shadow AI considerations into their existing AI governance structures, including regular audits to identify unauthorized AI usage, risk assessments that specifically address shadow AI vulnerabilities, and training programs that help employees understand the risks of using unauthorized AI tools.

A practical governance approach to shadow AI might include implementing AI access management systems that provide visibility into all AI interactions across the organization, whether through approved channels or not. This could involve network monitoring tools that detect interactions with external AI services, data loss prevention systems configured to identify potential AI-related data leakage, and automated alerts when sensitive information is potentially shared with unauthorized AI systems. Additionally, organizations should establish clear escalation procedures for handling shadow AI incidents, including protocols for assessing potential data exposure and implementing remediation measures when unauthorized AI usage is detected. Essentially, the success of shadow AI governance often depends on creating a culture of responsible AI usage rather than solely relying on restrictive policies. This might involve establishing "AI sandboxes," where employees can safely experiment with new AI tools under controlled conditions, developing fast-track approval processes for new AI tools that meet security requirements, and regularly updating the organization's approved AI toolkit based on employee needs and feedback. Such an approach helps organizations harness the benefits of AI innovation while maintaining appropriate security controls and governance standards.

Another example of an AI governance framework would be the State Government Artificial Intelligence Advisory Council Final Recommended Action Plan, which outlines a comprehensive strategy for integrating AI into Oregon's state government while ensuring responsible governance, security, and ethical considerations (Oregon State Government Artificial Intelligence Advisory Council, 2025). The plan is structured around five key areas: establishing an AI governance framework, addressing privacy concerns, enhancing security, developing a reference architecture, and preparing the workforce. At its core, the plan emphasizes cross-functional AI governance, ensuring human oversight in AI decision-making, particularly in areas involving safety, ethics, and equity. This aligns AI implementation with Oregon's values of diversity, equity, and inclusion. The privacy component acknowledges risks associated with AI-driven data processing and calls for privacy impact assessments, transparency, and governance roles to protect individual rights. Security is another critical focus, advocating for AI-specific incident response protocols and risk management strategies to prevent misuse and vulnerabilities. The reference architecture recommendation ensures standardized guidelines for AI procurement, development, testing, and auditing. Lastly, the workforce development section highlights the importance of training employees, establishing partnerships with educational institutions, and preparing future workers for AI integration.

This action plan is significant as it establishes one of the most detailed AI governance frameworks at the state level in the United States. It reflects broader national and international AI policy trends, incorporating principles from the White House AI Bill of Rights and the NIST AI RMF. It prioritizes transparency, security, and human oversight, and seeks to mitigate AI-related risks, such as algorithmic bias, privacy infringements, and unintended societal harms. The plan positions Oregon as a leader in responsible AI adoption, ensuring that AI benefits public services while maintaining trust, accountability, and fairness. Despite its strengths, the plan has several shortcomings that mirror the limitations of broader AI regulations. Like the European Union's (EU) AI Act, the plan categorizes AI risks and emphasizes oversight but lacks detailed enforcement mechanisms. It does not specify how agencies will audit AI models or prevent government reliance on biased or flawed AI systems. Compared to the US Executive Order on AI, which mandates AI safety research, Oregon's plan lacks provisions for technical research and development funding. Additionally, while the plan promotes workforce readiness, it does not address the broader economic impact of AI-driven job displacement.

The security framework in the plan is crucial given that GAI can be a tool, a weapon, and a target. AI tools are already used in government for automation, fraud detection, and cybersecurity, making it essential to establish strong governance mechanisms. However, GAI also introduces risks as a weapon, as it can be exploited for misinformation, deepfake campaigns, and cyberattacks. Without explicit AI-specific countermeasures, Oregon's plan does not fully address how state agencies should detect and mitigate AI-generated threats. Additionally, AI itself is a target—malicious actors can manipulate training data, exploit vulnerabilities in AI models, or launch adversarial attacks. While the plan discusses security broadly, it does not offer clear guidance on defending state AI systems from external threats.

Thus, this leads us to talking in broader terms—AI auditing mechanisms. AI auditing mechanisms in cybersecurity contexts encompass a range of tools, methodologies, and frameworks designed to evaluate AI systems' performance, security, and compliance (Hudson, 2024). These mechanisms are crucial for ensuring AI systems operate as intended while maintaining security and ethical standards, particularly in sensitive cybersecurity applications. One fundamental auditing mechanism is Model Testing and Validation, which involves comprehensive testing of AI models under various scenarios (Mökander et al., 2023). For cybersecurity applications, this includes adversarial testing to identify potential vulnerabilities, bias testing to ensure fair treatment across different user groups, and performance testing under different operational conditions. These tests help organizations understand how their AI systems might behave in real-world security scenarios and identify potential weaknesses before deployment.

Continuous Monitoring Systems are another critical auditing mechanism (Minkkinen et al., 2022). These systems track AI performance metrics, decision patterns, and potential anomalies in real time. In cybersecurity contexts, this might involve monitoring false positive/negative rates in threat detection systems, tracking changes in model behavior that might indicate compromise, and assessing the impact of model drift on security decisions. Organizations can implement automated alerts when AI systems deviate from expected performance parameters or exhibit suspicious behavior.

Documentation and Logging Frameworks serve as essential auditing tools by maintaining detailed records of AI system operations, updates, and decisions (Jauhiainen & Lehner, 2022). In cybersecurity, this includes logging model inputs and outputs, recording training data modifications, and documenting system configurations. These records are crucial for incident investigation, compliance verification, and understanding how AI systems contribute to security decisions over time.

Third-Party Audit Tools and Services provide independent verification of AI system performance and compliance (Raji et al., 2022). These might include automated tools for analyzing model behavior, bias detection systems, or specialized consulting services that assess AI implementations against industry standards and best practices. In cybersecurity, these external audits are particularly valuable for validating that AI systems meet security requirements and don't introduce new vulnerabilities.

Governance and Compliance Tracking Systems help organizations monitor adherence to relevant regulations, standards, and internal policies (Palakurti, 2023). These systems might track model updates, data usage, access controls, and decision-making patterns to ensure compliance with requirements like GDPR, CCPA, new state data privacy laws (like in Vermont, Texas, Maryland, and more), or industry-specific regulations. This is particularly important in cybersecurity contexts, where AI systems may process sensitive data or make critical security decisions.

7.3 Current and Emerging AI Regulations

The landscape of AI regulation is rapidly evolving as governments worldwide grapple with the challenges posed by increasingly powerful and pervasive AI systems. As AI technologies become more deeply integrated into critical systems and decision-making processes, regulatory frameworks are emerging to ensure responsible development, deployment, and use of these technologies. From the comprehensive approach of the EU's AI Act to state-level initiatives in the United States, such as California's pioneering legislation and Colorado's targeted AI regulations, these frameworks represent diverse approaches to governing AI systems. China has also announced new AI legislative initiatives aimed at issuing requirements for labeling AI content (Reuters, 2025). These regulations are particularly significant for organizations deploying AI in security-critical applications, as they establish requirements for transparency, accountability, and risk management. Understanding and complying with these evolving regulations is crucial for organizations developing or implementing AI systems, especially in contexts where AI decisions can significantly impact security, privacy, and individual rights.

The EU AI Act, slated for implementation in 2025, is the world's first comprehensive attempt to regulate AI systems (EU Artificial Intelligence Act, 2025b). This landmark legislation introduces a risk-based approach to AI regulation, categorizing AI systems based on their potential impact on society and individual rights. For cybersecurity applications, this categorization is particularly significant as many security-focused AI systems may fall into the "high-risk" category due to their potential impact on safety and fundamental rights (European Parliament, 2025). The Act places stringent requirements on high-risk AI systems, including those used for cybersecurity purposes. Organizations must implement robust risk management systems, maintain detailed documentation, ensure human oversight, and guarantee high levels of accuracy and security. This affects everything from AI-powered threat detection systems to automated incident response tools, requiring organizations to carefully evaluate and document their AI security implementations. For cyber auditing and assessments, the EU AI Act introduces new requirements that will fundamentally change how organizations validate their AI systems. Security teams must implement continuous monitoring systems, regular assessment procedures, and detailed documentation practices. This includes maintaining records of training data, monitoring system performance, and documenting any security incidents or anomalies related to AI systems.

Furthermore, the Act requires transparency about the use of generative AI systems, including clear disclosure when AI generates content or makes security-related decisions. This affects how organizations can deploy generative AI for tasks like threat analysis, incident response planning, or security policy generation. Organizations must ensure their use of generative AI aligns with the Act's requirements for transparency, accountability, and human oversight. Regarding attacks against generative AI, the Act introduces requirements for robustness and security against adversarial attacks. Organizations must implement measures to protect their AI systems from manipulation, poisoning attacks, and other forms of interference. This includes regular testing, monitoring for unusual behavior, and maintaining incident response plans specifically for AI-related security incidents.

Interestingly, Article 4 of the EU AI Act focuses on AI literacy and transparency for individuals interacting with AI systems (EU Artificial Intelligence Act, 2025a). It mandates that users be informed when they are engaging with AI, particularly in cases where the AI-generated content might be mistaken for human interaction. This provision is crucial for ensuring informed decision-making and preventing deception in digital environments. AI literacy, as promoted by this article, empowers users to critically assess AI-driven outputs. Ideally, this aims to foster a more responsible and secure ecosystem where individuals can recognize biases, manipulation, and potential security threats. Additionally, the Act establishes a living repository of AI literacy practices, which serves as an evolving resource to help individuals and organizations stay updated on best practices, ethical considerations, and emerging risks. From a cybersecurity perspective, this article highlights the necessity of treating GAI as a tool, a weapon, and a target. As a tool, GAI can enhance security measures through automation, predictive analytics, and intelligent threat detection. However, as a weapon, it can be exploited for misinformation, deepfake-based fraud, and automated cyberattacks that bypass traditional defenses. Finally, as a target, GAI itself becomes a critical attack surface, where adversaries may manipulate its training data (poisoning), exploit vulnerabilities in its decision-making processes, or use adversarial inputs to subvert its intended functions. The EU AI Act's focus on AI literacy aligns with the need to defend against these cyber risks, ensuring that users understand both the benefits and threats associated with AI-driven interactions. To mitigate these risks, a sufficient level of AI literacy must be established across all sectors, enabling individuals to identify AI-generated outputs, assess security implications, and respond effectively to AI-related cyber threats. This legislative move reinforces the growing recognition that AI is not merely a passive technology but an active force in shaping digital security landscapes.

The regulation's impact on how cyber professionals can use AI is substantial. While it doesn't prohibit the use of AI in cybersecurity, it introduces new requirements for documentation, testing, and oversight. Professionals must ensure their AI tools meet the Act's requirements for transparency, fairness, and accountability. This may require modifications to existing AI systems and changes to operational procedures to maintain compliance. For nefarious actors, the Act creates both challenges and opportunities. While it may make it harder to deploy malicious AI systems within the EU's jurisdiction, bad actors operating outside the EU might gain advantages if legitimate organizations are constrained by regulatory requirements. This creates a complex dynamic where organizations must balance compliance with effective security measures.

Research and development efforts in cybersecurity AI tools will need to adapt to the new regulatory framework. Organizations developing AI security tools must incorporate compliance requirements into their development processes from the start. This includes building in features for transparency, explainability, and human oversight, as well as robust testing and validation capabilities.

In general, the Act's implications for future innovation in AI security tools are mixed. While the additional regulatory requirements may increase development costs and time-to-market, they also provide clear guidelines for responsible AI development. This could lead to more trustworthy and reliable AI security tools, though organizations may need to invest more resources in their development and validation processes. On the other hand, there is a lot of criticism that it overregulates AI and stifles growth and innovation in this sector. By imposing stringent compliance requirements, such as mandatory risk assessments, transparency obligations, and real-time monitoring, the Act could discourage smaller organizations and startups from entering the AI market due to the high costs and resource demands. The complexity of adhering to these regulations may also slow the pace of AI advancements, as developers prioritize compliance over exploration and experimentation. Additionally, the uncertainty surrounding the interpretation and enforcement of certain provisions could deter investment and delay the adoption of cutting-edge generative AI technologies, ultimately limiting their potential to drive economic growth and innovation. Balancing regulation with flexibility will be crucial to fostering an environment where AI innovation can thrive while maintaining ethical standards.

In the United States, there is the Colorado AI Act, signed into law in 2023, is one of the most comprehensive state-level approaches to AI regulation in the United States (Levi et al., 2024). Unlike the EU AI Act's broad scope, the Colorado law focuses specifically on state and local government agencies' use of AI systems, particularly in decisions that significantly affect individuals. This narrower focus creates a different regulatory landscape for organizations operating in Colorado compared to those subject to EU regulations. A key distinction from the EU AI

Act is the Colorado law's emphasis on transparency and notification requirements. While the EU Act implements a tiered risk-based approach, the Colorado Act requires government agencies to provide clear notice when AI systems are used in decision-making processes. This includes requirements for public agencies to notify individuals when AI systems are used in decisions affecting their civil rights, legal rights, privileges, or access to government services.

For cybersecurity professionals operating in Colorado, the Act introduces specific requirements when implementing AI-powered security tools in government contexts. This includes conducting impact assessments before deploying AI systems, maintaining documentation of AI use, and ensuring human oversight of AI-driven decisions. However, unlike the EU AI Act, these requirements don't extend to private sector organizations, creating a potential disparity in AI governance standards. The implications for generative AI security tools are particularly interesting under the Colorado Act. While the law doesn't explicitly regulate private sector use of generative AI, it sets standards for government agencies that might influence broader industry practices. Government agencies must carefully evaluate and document their use of generative AI tools for security purposes, potentially creating de facto standards that private organizations might voluntarily adopt. When it comes to malicious actors, the Colorado Act's limited scope might create opportunities for exploitation. Since the law primarily focuses on government agencies, malicious actors might target private sector organizations that aren't subject to the same stringent requirements. This highlights the potential need for broader regulatory coverage to prevent security gaps between public and private sector AI implementations.

The Act's impact on research and development of AI security tools differs significantly from the EU approach. While the EU AI Act creates comprehensive requirements affecting all AI development, the Colorado Act's focus on government use might lead to a two-track development process—one meeting government requirements and another for private sector applications. This could affect how security tool vendors develop and market their products. The less stringent requirements of the Colorado Act compared to the EU AI Act might make it easier for organizations to innovate in the AI security space within Colorado. However, organizations operating globally will likely need to comply with the stricter EU standards regardless of local requirements, potentially leading to a standardization toward the higher EU requirements even in jurisdictions with lighter regulation.

California has introduced several groundbreaking laws to regulate AI, focusing on transparency, ethical development, and public safety. These laws aim to address the growing concerns about AI's potential misuse while encouraging responsible innovation. The California AI Transparency Act (SB 942), set to take effect in January 2026, mandates the use of visible and hidden watermarks on AI-generated content (California Legislative Information, 2024b). Developers of generative AI systems must also provide free AI detection tools to the public, ensuring greater transparency in distinguishing between human-created and AI-generated content. Another significant law, Assembly Bill 2013 (AB-2013), requires AI companies to disclose detailed information about the data used to train their generative models (California Legislative Information, 2024a). This addresses concerns about the "black box" nature of AI systems, where the lack of transparency around training data often raises ethical, privacy, and security issues. With better visibility into how these systems operate, organizations and policymakers can develop more informed strategies to mitigate potential risks associated with AI deployment.

Senate Bill 896 (SB 896) in California takes a proactive approach to public safety, mandating the California Office of Emergency Services to conduct regular risk analyses of generative AI's potential threats (CalMatters Digital Democracy, 2024). These analyses focus on critical infrastructure, cybersecurity vulnerabilities, and the risk of mass casualty events. The emphasis on collaboration between state agencies and AI developers reflects California's intent to create a robust framework for identifying and mitigating risks before they escalate. Subsequently, these regulations have profound implications for generative AI in cybersecurity. First, the mandated watermarks and detection tools enhance the ability of cybersecurity professionals to identify malicious AI-generated content, such as deepfakes and phishing scams. This capability significantly bolsters threat detection and response measures, reducing the risks posed by AI-enabled cyberattacks. Additionally, the requirement to disclose training data details provides cybersecurity teams with valuable insights into how AI models function, helping them better anticipate and defend against emerging threats.

Transparency requirements also improve accountability in AI development. Understanding the datasets and algorithms underpinning generative AI allows cybersecurity teams to evaluate potential biases or vulnerabilities in these systems. This knowledge can inform more effective countermeasures, ensuring that security frameworks stay ahead of adversaries who may exploit generative AI for malicious purposes. Furthermore, these measures enable organizations to conduct thorough risk assessments, which are critical for protecting sensitive information and infrastructure. In general, California's legislative push reflects a broader shift toward integrating AI into governance and security frameworks responsibly. While these laws impose compliance challenges for AI developers, they also foster innovation by creating a more secure and predictable ecosystem for deploying AI technologies. The focus on risk assessment and mitigation aligns with the growing recognition of AI's transformative potential in cybersecurity, where it can both create new risks and offer powerful defense tools. Overall, California's approach to AI regulation provides a model for other states and nations grappling with the challenges of generative AI. It does so by emphasizing transparency, safety, and collaboration. Hence, these laws lay the groundwork for addressing the complex interplay between AI innovation and security. In the realm of cybersecurity, these measures highlight the dual role of AI as both a potential threat and a critical tool for safeguarding digital assets and infrastructure.

In 2024, there was Executive Order 14110, issued in the United States to address safe, secure, and trustworthy AI, which was a significant attempt to regulate AI at the federal level (Biden, 2023). However, its subsequent rollback and lack of legislative progression suggest a shift in regulatory strategies, leaning toward a more state-driven approach akin to U.S. data privacy laws. This diverges sharply from the centralized and comprehensive regulatory approach seen in the EUs AI Act. EO 14110 focused on establishing guidelines for developing and deploying AI systems to ensure transparency, accountability, and risk mitigation. The order outlined federal standards for ethical AI use, encouraging private companies to adhere to responsible AI practices. However, the order faced criticism from both industry and policymakers. Critics argued it was overly prescriptive, limiting innovation, while others contended it lacked enforceability and sufficient mechanisms for protecting against AI-related harms. Ultimately, the rollback of EO 14110 signaled a retreat from federal-level oversight and a possible pivot toward decentralized regulation, mirroring the landscape of U.S. data privacy laws. This decision reflects the United States' historical reliance on sectoral and state-driven legislation over federal mandates in technology governance.

In 2025, we have seen a different approach to AI regulation. The executive orders issued in January 2025 are a dramatic shift in U.S. policy across multiple domains, with AI regulation being a key focus. The first order, signed on January 20, 2025, implements a sweeping rescission of numerous executive orders from the previous administration, including EO 14110, which had established a framework for AI safety and regulation (Executive Order, 2025). Just three days later, on January 23, 2025, a second executive order specifically addressing AI policy was issued, emphasizing free market approaches and explicitly aiming to remove what it termed "ideological bias" from AI development (The White House, 2025). The relationship between these 2025 orders and the regulatory context of 2024 reveals a significant evolution in the approach to AI governance, though not in the direction that many had anticipated. While the 2024 analysis suggested a natural progression toward state-level regulation similar to data privacy laws, driven by practical considerations and implementation challenges, the 2025 orders represent a more ideologically driven shift away from federal regulation entirely. Rather than empowering state-level regulation as predicted, the focus has shifted dramatically toward removing barriers to private sector innovation and emphasizing market-driven development. This marks a stark departure from EO 14110's more regulatory, safety-focused approach to AI governance, and appears to be motivated by explicit policy choices rather than the gradual evolution toward state-level regulation that was predicted in 2024.

In the broader international context, these 2025 orders significantly widen the gap between U.S. and EU approaches to AI regulation. While the EU has pursued comprehensive regulation through the AI Act, establishing detailed frameworks for AI development and deployment, the United States is now moving toward minimal federal oversight. The new orders emphasize global competitiveness and national security concerns over the previous focus on safety and ethical considerations. This represents a more fundamental shift than what was anticipated in 2024's analysis, which had suggested a more gradual transition toward state-level regulation. Instead, the 2025 orders signal a comprehensive reversal of federal AI oversight, prioritizing rapid development and market freedom over the previous administration's emphasis on safety and ethical guidelines. This new direction suggests a significant reimagining of how AI development will be governed in the United States, with potentially far-reaching implications for both domestic innovation and international technology policy alignment.

Essentially, the U.S. regulatory approach to AI is increasingly reminiscent of its handling of data privacy. For instance, while the EU implemented the General Data Protection Regulation (GDPR) as a singular, overarching data privacy framework, the United States lacks an equivalent federal law. Instead, states such as California, Virginia, and Colorado have introduced their own privacy laws, like the California Consumer Privacy Act (CCPA). This patchwork system allows states to tailor regulations to local priorities but also creates challenges, such as compliance complexity for businesses operating across multiple jurisdictions. Similarly, with the scrapping of EO 14110, it appears likely that AI regulation will follow a similar trajectory, with states adopting their own AI laws. California has already proposed legislation targeting AI accountability, emphasizing transparency in AI decision-making processes. This state-level approach allows for experimentation and regional specificity but may lead to inconsistencies in compliance requirements, potentially stifling innovation and creating legal uncertainty.

In stark contrast, the EU is pursuing a centralized regulatory framework with the EU AI Act, which aims to establish uniform rules across all member states. The AI Act categorizes AI applications by risk levels—unacceptable, high, limited, and minimal—and imposes strict requirements on high-risk systems, such as biometric identification and critical infrastructure applications. It emphasizes transparency, data quality, human oversight, and accountability, ensuring that AI systems deployed within the EU adhere to stringent ethical and safety standards. This harmonized approach mirrors the EU's GDPR, which provides a unified data privacy framework. The advantage of creating a single regulatory environment, the EU reduces compliance complexity for businesses operating within its borders. However, the downside is that this centralization may limit the agility needed to address rapidly evolving AI technologies.

7.4 Responsible AI Development and Deployment

Cybersecurity has to be at the forefront when developing and deploying AI systems. The responsible development and deployment of AI systems in cybersecurity contexts requires careful consideration of both technical capabilities and ethical implications. As organizations increasingly rely on AI for security operations, ensuring appropriate human oversight and adherence to ethical design principles becomes crucial for maintaining trust, accountability, and effective security measures. This section explores the critical role of HITL systems in providing necessary oversight and control over AI decision-making processes, while examining the fundamental ethical design principles that should guide AI development and deployment. Understanding and implementing these approaches is essential for organizations seeking to harness AI's potential while maintaining responsible practices and mitigating potential risks. These considerations become particularly important as AI systems grow more sophisticated and autonomous, requiring thoughtful integration of human judgment and ethical considerations throughout the AI lifecycle.

HITL systems are a crucial approach in AI deployment, where human oversight and intervention are intentionally integrated into automated processes (Jakubik et al., 2023). In cybersecurity contexts, HITL systems ensure that critical decisions aren't made solely by AI systems but include human judgment, expertise, and accountability. This hybrid approach combines the speed and pattern recognition capabilities of AI with human intuition, experience, and contextual understanding. In cybersecurity operations, HITL systems typically involve AI systems flagging potential threats or anomalies for human review before significant actions are taken. This is important in scenarios where false positives could lead to service disruptions or where context-specific knowledge is crucial for accurate decision-making. The human element helps validate AI findings, interpret complex scenarios, and make nuanced decisions that might not be captured in automated rule sets.

The implications of HITL systems in cybersecurity are significant because they help address several critical challenges. First, they provide a safeguard against automated errors that could have severe consequences, such as incorrectly blocking legitimate traffic or misidentifying threats (da Silva, 2024). Second, they enable continuous learning and improvement of AI systems through human feedback and correction. Third, they maintain clear lines of accountability by ensuring human oversight of critical security decisions. The integration of HITL systems is becoming crucial in incident response scenarios. Let's put this in practical terms, let's say an organization's AI-powered security system detects unusual patterns in network traffic that could indicate a sophisticated attack. Instead of automatically blocking all suspicious traffic (which could disrupt legitimate business operations), the system alerts security analysts. These analysts can review the AI's findings, investigate the context, correlate with other security data, and make informed decisions about response actions. This approach becomes even more critical with the emergence of sophisticated AI-powered attacks. Human analysts can identify novel attack patterns that automated systems might miss, understand the broader context of security events, and make strategic decisions about response measures. Their involvement helps prevent adversaries from exploiting predictable automated responses and ensures that security measures remain adaptive to new threats. The significance of HITL systems extends to compliance and accountability. Many regulatory frameworks and security standards require demonstrable human oversight of critical security operations. HITL systems provide clear documentation of human involvement in decision-making processes, helping organizations meet these requirements while maintaining efficient operations. Another important aspect of HITL systems is their role in training and improving AI security tools. Human feedback and corrections help refine AI models, improve detection accuracy, and adapt to new threats. This continuous learning process is essential for maintaining effective security measures against evolving cyber threats.

HITL systems also play a crucial role in managing false positives and negatives (Zeng et al., 2023). In cybersecurity, both types of errors can have serious consequences—false positives can lead to unnecessary disruptions, while false negatives can leave systems vulnerable. Human analysts can help calibrate system sensitivity, validate AI findings, and make context-aware decisions about security alerts. Moreover, the implications for security operations centers (SOCs) are especially significant. HITL systems require organizations to carefully design workflows that balance automation with human intervention, ensure adequate staffing and training for human analysts, and maintain clear procedures for escalation and decision-making. This has implications for team structure, training requirements, and operational procedures, ultimately affecting how organizations approach security operations and incident response.

As aforementioned, ethical design principles in AI security represent fundamental guidelines that ensure AI systems are developed and deployed responsibly, with consideration for their impact on individuals, organizations, and society. These principles extend beyond technical specifications to address issues of fairness, transparency, privacy, and accountability, particularly crucial in cybersecurity applications where AI systems can significantly impact security and privacy. Core ethical design principles include fairness and nondiscrimination, ensuring AI security systems treat all users equitably and don't perpetuate existing biases. This becomes particularly important in access control systems, threat detection, and incident response, where AI decisions could disproportionately affect certain groups. Organizations must carefully evaluate their AI systems' training data and decision-making processes to prevent discriminatory outcomes.

Privacy by design is a crucial principle, requiring AI security systems to protect user privacy from their initial design through implementation (Andrade et al., 2022). This includes minimizing data collection, implementing strong data protection measures, and ensuring AI systems don't inadvertently expose sensitive information through their operations or outputs. In cybersecurity contexts, this principle becomes particularly important when AI systems process sensitive data for threat detection or incident response. The principle of human agency and oversight ensures that AI systems support rather than replace human decision-making in critical security contexts (Tsamados et al., 2024). This involves designing systems that maintain meaningful human control, provide appropriate intervention points, and support human understanding of system operations. Organizations must carefully balance automation with human judgment, particularly in high-stakes security decisions. Robustness and security represent essential ethical design principles, ensuring AI systems remain reliable and resistant to manipulation. This includes designing systems to maintain performance under adverse conditions, resist adversarial attacks, and fail safely when problems occur. In cybersecurity applications, these principles are particularly crucial as AI systems must maintain their integrity even when targeted by sophisticated attackers.

7.5 Balancing Innovation and Security

This book talked a lot about the guardrails, frameworks, and approaches that are important to undertake for security in AI systems. However, that can have an impact on innovation and hold organizations behind when it comes to developing and deploying AI systems. Thus, the critical balance (that is often so hard to achieve in the cybersecurity field) is balancing innovation and security. It is important to discuss some remediations that we can take to make sure we work toward effectively achieving that delicate balancing between fostering innovation in AI technology and maintaining robust security measures. As organizations push the boundaries of what's possible with AI, especially in generative AI applications, they must navigate complex trade-offs between rapid advancement and responsible development. This section explores how an interdisciplinary approach, combined with strategic collaboration and public–private partnerships (PPPs), can help organizations achieve this balance. Through examining various collaborative models and educational initiatives, we identify frameworks for advancing AI technology while maintaining appropriate security controls. The discussion emphasizes the importance of building awareness across stakeholders and developing comprehensive approaches that promote innovation while protecting against emerging threats and vulnerabilities in AI systems.

The need for an interdisciplinary approach in balancing AI innovation and security stems from the complex, multifaceted nature of AI systems and their wide-ranging impacts (Familoni, 2024). This complexity requires expertise beyond just technical domains, bringing together professionals from various fields to ensure a comprehensive understanding and responsible development of AI systems. Security considerations must be balanced with innovation goals, ethical implications, legal requirements, and business objectives. A truly effective interdisciplinary approach needs to include technical experts (data scientists, AI engineers, security professionals), legal specialists (privacy lawyers, regulatory compliance experts), ethicists, social scientists, domain experts from relevant industries, and business strategists. This diverse group brings different perspectives to understanding potential risks, implications, and opportunities in AI development. For instance, while technical experts might focus on model performance and security measures, ethicists can identify potential biases or fairness issues, while legal experts ensure compliance with emerging regulations. Essentially, the collaboration should extend to include human factors specialists, user experience designers, and risk management professionals. These perspectives are crucial for understanding how AI systems interact with users, how they might be misused or misunderstood, and how to implement effective controls without stifling innovation. Additionally, including privacy experts and civil rights advocates helps ensure that innovation doesn't come at the cost of individual rights and privacy. Therefore, this interdisciplinary approach needs to be structured and systematic, with regular collaboration points throughout the AI development lifecycle. This includes initial planning phases, where different perspectives can influence design decisions, development stages, where various experts can monitor and guide progress, and deployment phases, where multiple viewpoints contribute to evaluation and refinement of the systems.

For example, if there is a financial institution that is developing an AI-powered fraud detection system, an interdisciplinary team might include security engineers focused on the system protection and threat detection, data scientists developing the AI models, privacy officers for data protection, legal experts for compliance with financial regulations, and ethics specialists monitoring for bias in fraud detection. Moreover, other involvement from business analysts that understand the operational impact, UX designers that make sure the system works effectively with human analysis, customer service representatives that could provide insight into user impacts, and risk managers that evaluate potential failures and consequences. This team would collaborate throughout the development process, from initial design discussions through testing and deployment, ensuring that innovation in fraud detection capabilities is balanced with security, privacy, fairness, and usability considerations. Regular meetings, shared documentation, and collaborative decision-making processes would help ensure all perspectives are considered in key decisions about the system's development and deployment.

Collaboration in the context of balancing security and innovation with generative AI represents a critical factor in developing and deploying these systems responsibly (Wang & Wu, 2024). As generative AI systems become more powerful and complex, no single organization or team can effectively address all the challenges and considerations involved. This necessitates meaningful collaboration across organizational boundaries, disciplines, and sectors to share knowledge, experiences, and best practices. Effective collaboration in this space requires structured approaches to information sharing about security threats, vulnerabilities, and mitigation strategies specific to generative AI systems. Organizations need to establish secure channels for sharing threat intelligence, incident reports, and successful security measures without compromising their competitive advantages or sensitive information. This might involve participating in industry consortiums, establishing trusted sharing networks, or engaging in formal partnership agreements that define the scope and nature of collaboration.

Cross-organizational collaboration becomes that much more important when addressing novel security challenges posed by generative AI (Kersten, 2024). For instance, when organizations discover new types of attacks against their AI systems, sharing this information helps the broader community develop effective countermeasures more quickly. Similarly, when innovative solutions are found to balance functionality with security, sharing these approaches (while protecting intellectual property) helps advance the field as a whole. Academic-industry collaboration plays a crucial role in advancing both security and innovation in generative AI (Tanaka & Fujita, 2025). Universities can provide deep research expertise and theoretical frameworks, while industry partners offer practical implementation experience and real-world testing environments. This partnership helps bridge the gap between theoretical security concepts and practical applications, leading to more effective and implementable solutions.

Supporting effective collaboration requires establishing clear frameworks and protocols. Organizations need to develop shared vocabularies for discussing AI security challenges, standardized approaches to documenting and sharing information, and common metrics for evaluating both security measures and innovative features (Almagrabi & Khan, 2024). This might involve creating working groups focused on specific challenges, organizing regular forums for sharing insights, or developing shared resources and tools. Technical infrastructure plays a vital role in enabling collaboration. Organizations need secure platforms for sharing information, tools for collaborative development and testing, and systems for tracking and managing shared knowledge. This infrastructure must balance accessibility with security, ensuring that collaborative efforts don't create new vulnerabilities.

However, the human element of collaboration cannot be overlooked. Building trust between collaborating parties takes time and effort, requiring regular interaction, clear communication channels, and demonstrated commitment to shared goals. Organizations need to invest in relationship building, create opportunities for informal knowledge sharing, and establish clear points of contact for collaborative initiatives. Professional development and training initiatives can support effective collaboration by ensuring all participants have a common baseline understanding of both security and innovation considerations in generative AI. This might include joint training sessions, shared workshops, or collaborative research projects that bring together participants from different organizations and backgrounds.

PPPs in AI security are a crucial mechanism for bridging gaps between government resources and private sector innovation (Ebulue et al., 2024). These partnerships enable the sharing of vital threat intelligence, research findings, and best practices while leveraging each sector's unique strengths. Government agencies bring regulatory insight, national security perspective, and broad coordination capabilities, while private organizations contribute technical expertise, real-world implementation experience, and innovative approaches to AI security challenges. Effective PPPs require structured frameworks that clearly define roles, responsibilities, and information-sharing protocols. This includes establishing secure channels for sharing sensitive information, developing common standards and metrics for evaluating AI security measures, and creating joint response protocols for addressing emerging threats. These partnerships must balance the government's need for transparency and oversight with private sector concerns about intellectual property protection and competitive advantage.

Interestingly, the U.S. Copyright Office's March 2023 guidance on registering works containing AI-generated material establishes several fundamental principles that offer valuable insights for PPPs in AI security (United States Copyright Office, 2023). The guidance establishes that copyright protection extends only to human-created content, distinguishes between AI as a tool versus an autonomous creator, requires disclosure of AI-generated content, and provides specific processes for registration and correction of applications. This framework demonstrates how government agencies can provide the clear regulatory structure that private sector entities need while still fostering innovation. This approach offers important lessons for PPPs in AI security, particularly in how to balance innovation with regulation and establish clear operational frameworks. Just as the copyright guidance creates shared responsibility between creators and the Copyright Office, PPPs require clear delineation of roles between public and private entities. The emphasis on disclosure and documentation in the copyright guidance parallels the need for transparency in PPPs, while the correction mechanisms demonstrate how regulatory systems can adapt to rapidly evolving technology. This model suggests that successful PPPs in AI security should include clear definitions of human vs. AI roles, explicit disclosure requirements, mechanisms for updating information as technology evolves, and structured frameworks for information sharing—all while maintaining a balance that protects both innovation and security interests.

Moreover, in recent news, there was an update in January 2025. The U.S. Copyright Office's January 2025 report on AI and Copyright (Part 2: Copyrightability) is an evolution from its March 2023 guidance, providing a more comprehensive framework for addressing AI-generated works while maintaining the fundamental principle of human authorship (United States Copyright Office, 2025). The report expands on the earlier guidance by thoroughly analyzing public input (over 10 000 comments), international approaches, and emerging issues around AI systems' capabilities. Most notably, it affirms that while prompts alone cannot generally qualify for copyright protection, there are multiple paths to protection for AI-assisted works through human creative contributions, including modification, arrangement, and the incorporation of human-authored expressive inputs. This report directly relates to the previous discussion of model distillation and AI security in several key ways. Just as the Copyright Office emphasizes the need to balance innovation with protection, requiring disclosure while still fostering creativity, similar considerations apply to AI security frameworks. The report's nuanced treatment of human–AI interaction—particularly its distinction between AI as a tool versus an autonomous creator—provides a valuable model for thinking about security policies around model access and usage. Furthermore, the Office's careful analysis of international approaches and emphasis on maintaining clear principles while adapting to technological change offer important lessons for developing cohesive security frameworks in an increasingly global AI landscape. The report ultimately demonstrates how regulatory bodies can provide structured guidance that acknowledges both the transformative potential and inherent risks of AI technologies, while maintaining fundamental protective principles.

Ultimately, fostering successful PPPs involves creating incentives for participation, reducing barriers to collaboration, and demonstrating clear value for all participants. This might include government funding for joint research initiatives, regulatory guidance that rewards partnership participation, or shared resources for AI security testing and validation. Educational programs and professional development opportunities can also help build the relationships and trust necessary for effective partnerships. The outcomes of successful PPPs can be significant. They can lead to more robust AI security standards, improved threat detection and response capabilities, and more effective approaches to balancing innovation with security requirements. These partnerships can also accelerate the development of security solutions by combining government resources with private sector agility and technical expertise.

The consequences of not having effective PPPs, or having partnerships that exist only nominally, can be severe. Without meaningful collaboration, organizations may duplicate efforts, miss critical threat indicators, or develop incompatible security approaches. This fragmentation can create vulnerabilities that adversaries can exploit and slow the overall advancement of AI security measures. Partnerships that exist only on paper without substantive collaboration can be dangerous. They can create a false sense of security, leading organizations to believe they have support and resources that don't actually exist in practice. This can result in inadequate preparation for security incidents, delayed response times, and increased vulnerability to sophisticated attacks targeting AI systems. Also, the lack of effective PPPs can also hamper innovation by creating unnecessary barriers between public and private sector research. When organizations can't effectively share findings or collaborate on solutions, they may develop partial or incomplete approaches to AI security challenges. This isolation can slow the overall advancement of the field and leave both sectors more vulnerable to emerging threats. Subsequently, to maximize the effectiveness of PPPs in AI security, organizations need to commit to regular engagement, meaningful information sharing, and joint problem-solving efforts. This includes dedicating resources to partnership activities, establishing clear communication channels, and measuring partnership outcomes against defined objectives. Regular evaluation and adjustment of partnership frameworks help ensure they remain relevant and effective as AI technology and security challenges evolve.

Education and awareness programs focused on balancing AI innovation and security must address multiple levels of understanding and various stakeholder needs. These programs should begin with foundational knowledge about AI systems, including their capabilities, limitations, and potential security implications. This baseline education needs to cover both technical aspects—such as how AI models work, what makes them vulnerable, and how they can be secured—and broader considerations like ethical implications, regulatory requirements, and societal impacts. The programs should be designed to accommodate different learning styles and expertise levels, ensuring that both technical and nontechnical stakeholders can develop a meaningful understanding of key concepts and challenges. Subsequently, comprehensive education programs must address the dynamic nature of AI security threats and countermeasures. This includes regular updates on emerging threats, new attack vectors specific to AI systems, and evolving best practices for security. The curriculum should cover practical aspects of securing AI systems without stifling innovation, including secure development practices, testing methodologies, and deployment considerations. Real-world case studies and examples should be incorporated to illustrate both successful and failed approaches to balancing security with innovation, helping participants understand practical implications and learn from others' experiences.

These programs need to emphasize the interdisciplinary nature of AI security, incorporating perspectives from various fields including computer science, cybersecurity, ethics, law, and business. This broad approach helps participants understand how different aspects of AI development and deployment interact and influence each other. Programs should include modules on risk assessment, decision-making frameworks, and methods for evaluating trade-offs between security measures and innovative capabilities. Practical exercises and simulations can help participants apply these concepts in realistic scenarios, developing their ability to make informed decisions about AI security. To be effective, education programs must be ongoing and adaptive rather than one-time events. They should include regular refresher courses, updates on new developments, and opportunities for advanced learning as participants' knowledge grows. Programs should incorporate various learning formats, including workshops, seminars, hands-on laboratories, and online modules, to accommodate different learning preferences and scheduling needs. Interactive elements like group discussions, case study analyses, and practical projects help reinforce learning and encourage knowledge sharing among participants.

Awareness programs should focus on building a security-conscious culture while maintaining space for innovation (Del Riego, 2024). This includes developing an understanding of security principles among developers and innovators, while also helping security professionals appreciate the importance of enabling innovation. Programs should address common misconceptions about AI security, highlight the importance of balanced approaches, and provide practical guidelines for implementing security measures without creating unnecessary barriers to development. Regular communication through newsletters, internal forums, and knowledge-sharing sessions can help maintain awareness and encourage ongoing dialogue about security considerations.

Success metrics and evaluation mechanisms need to be built into these programs to ensure they achieve their objectives. This includes assessing participants' understanding through practical exercises, monitoring the application of security principles in real projects, and gathering feedback on program effectiveness. Programs should be regularly reviewed and updated based on participant feedback, emerging threats and technologies, and changing organizational needs. This continuous improvement approach helps ensure that education and awareness efforts remain relevant and effective over time. Effective programs should also include components focused on communication and collaboration skills, as these are crucial for balancing security and innovation in practice. Participants need to learn how to effectively discuss security concerns with different stakeholders, advocate for appropriate security measures, and work collaboratively to find solutions that maintain both security and innovation. This includes developing skills in risk communication, stakeholder management, and consensus building around security decisions. See how it really is an interdisciplinary approach?

Chapter 7 Summary

This chapter explored the complex ethical and regulatory dimensions of generative AI security, examining how organizations could responsibly develop and deploy these powerful systems while addressing multifaceted ethical challenges. It analyzed fundamental ethical considerations, including transparency in AI decision-making, highlighting the "black box" nature of complex systems that created accountability challenges. The importance of XAI emerged as crucial for maintaining trust and enabling verification of AI-driven security decisions, while persistent issues of bias and fairness required careful attention to prevent discriminatory outcomes in security systems. The chapter examined the critical challenge of establishing clear responsibility in AI-driven decision-making, particularly as these systems became more autonomous and their decisions more consequential.

The analysis covered emerging governance frameworks from organizational ethics committees to structured approaches like NIST's AI RMF and ISO 42001, providing systematic methodologies for managing AI risks. The rapidly evolving regulatory landscape received detailed examination, contrasting the comprehensive approach of the EU AI Act with state-level initiatives in the United States, including California's transparency requirements and Colorado's government-focused regulations. The chapter emphasized HITL systems as essential for maintaining accountability, while highlighting the critical balance between innovation and security through interdisciplinary collaboration and PPPs. Throughout, it underscored that effective AI governance required both technical safeguards and ethical frameworks to ensure these systems benefited society while minimizing potential harms, demonstrating through real-world examples how organizations navigated these complex challenges in practice.

Key Takeaways:

Chapter 7 revealed that ethical AI development required moving beyond purely technical considerations to embrace comprehensive frameworks that addressed transparency, accountability, and fairness throughout the AI lifecycle. The fundamental challenge of the "black box" nature of generative AI systems created significant obstacles for organizations seeking to provide explanations for security decisions, necessitating new approaches to XAI and human oversight. Bias and fairness emerged as critical concerns that could perpetuate or amplify existing inequalities in security systems, requiring systematic approaches to identify and mitigate discriminatory outcomes. The complex interplay between innovation and security demanded careful balance, where overly restrictive measures could stifle beneficial AI advancement, while insufficient oversight could lead to harmful consequences.

This chapter demonstrated that the regulatory landscape for AI was rapidly evolving in divergent directions, with the EU pursuing comprehensive centralized regulation, while the United States adopted a fragmented state-level approach that mirrored data privacy law development. The contrast between the EU AI Act's risk-based comprehensive framework and varying U.S. state initiatives like California's transparency requirements and Colorado's government-focused regulations highlighted the challenges organizations faced in navigating multiple jurisdictional requirements. Effective governance emerged as requiring interdisciplinary collaboration that brought together technical experts, ethicists, legal professionals, and domain specialists to address the multifaceted nature of AI systems. The emphasis on PPPs and educational initiatives underscored that successfully balancing innovation with security required collaborative approaches that leveraged diverse expertise while maintaining clear accountability mechanisms and ethical foundations throughout AI development and deployment processes.

Case Study: Navigating Ethical and Regulatory Challenges in AI Security for a Financial Institution

Background

A global financial institution decided to deploy a generative AI system to enhance its fraud detection capabilities. The system uses advanced machine learning models to analyze transaction patterns in real time, flagging potentially fraudulent activities for further review. The institution's leadership was drawn to the AI's potential to reduce fraud rates and streamline manual reviews. However, they faced significant ethical and regulatory challenges during the deployment process, particularly around transparency, accountability, and bias.

Challenges Encountered:

1) **Transparency Issues:** The AI system operated as a "black box," making it difficult for the institution to explain its decision-making processes to customers whose transactions were flagged or blocked. This opacity created trust issues among stakeholders, including customers and regulators. For instance, when legitimate transactions were incorrectly flagged as fraudulent, affected customers demanded clear explanations. The inability to provide transparency led to reputational risks and customer dissatisfaction.

2) **Bias in Detection:** The training dataset used to develop the AI model reflected historical transaction patterns, which inadvertently introduced biases. Certain demographic groups were disproportionately flagged for fraud based on historical trends rather than actual fraudulent behavior. This raised fairness and ethical concerns, as the system perpetuated existing inequalities.
3) **Regulatory Compliance:** Operating in multiple jurisdictions, the institution needed to comply with varying regulatory requirements, including the EU AI Act and local U.S. regulations such as the Colorado AI Act. The EU's high-risk classification for AI-powered fraud detection systems mandated extensive documentation, human oversight, and periodic audits to ensure compliance.

Approach to Solutions:

1) **Implementing Explainable AI (XAI):** The institution partnered with data scientists and regulatory experts to implement XAI frameworks. This involved integrating tools that could provide interpretable summaries of the AI system's decisions. For example, instead of presenting opaque probabilities, the system offered specific patterns (e.g., unusually high transaction frequency) that led to its conclusions. These summaries were shared with customers and regulators to build trust.
2) **Addressing Bias:** The institution formed an interdisciplinary task force, including ethicists, data scientists, and legal advisors, to audit and retrain the AI model. They introduced fairness metrics into the system's evaluation process, ensuring that the AI treated transactions across demographic groups equitably. Regular updates and diverse datasets were incorporated to minimize bias over time.
3) **Regulatory Alignment:** To comply with the EU AI Act, the institution implemented a comprehensive governance framework, including:
   - Continuous monitoring of the AI system's performance.
   - Maintaining detailed documentation of training data, decision-making processes, and system updates.
   - Regular third-party audits to assess compliance and identify vulnerabilities.

For the United States, the institution conducted impact assessments as required by state-level laws and transparently disclosed the AI's role in decision-making to customers.

Outcomes:

- **Improved Trust:** The use of XAI increased transparency and helped rebuild customer trust. Customers appreciated receiving clear explanations for flagged transactions, reducing friction and complaints.

- **Fairer Decisions:** Bias mitigation efforts reduced the disproportionate flagging of certain groups, aligning the system with fairness principles. This enhanced the institution's reputation for ethical AI use.
- **Regulatory Compliance:** The institution avoided penalties by meeting the EU and U.S. regulatory requirements. The robust documentation and monitoring systems also improved internal oversight and accountability.
- **Increased Security Efficacy:** The AI system's ability to detect fraud improved due to regular audits and updates, enabling the institution to prevent more fraudulent activities while minimizing false positives.

Key Takeaways for Professionals:

1) **Embrace Interdisciplinary Collaboration:** Tackling AI challenges requires input from diverse stakeholders, including ethicists, regulators, and technical experts.
2) **Leverage Explainable AI:** Transparency isn't optional—it's critical for trust and compliance. Invest in tools that make AI decisions interpretable.
3) **Bias Audits Are Non-Negotiable:** Regular bias assessments and retraining are necessary to ensure AI systems align with fairness and ethical standards.
4) **Stay Ahead of Regulations:** Organizations should proactively align with emerging governance frameworks to avoid compliance pitfalls and maintain operational agility.
5) **Prioritize Customer Communication:** Clear and empathetic communication about AI's role in decision-making builds trust and mitigates reputational risks.

This case study underscores the importance of a balanced approach that integrates innovation, ethical considerations, and regulatory compliance in deploying AI security systems.

Ethical and Regulatory AI Security Quiz

Questions

1 What was the primary transparency issue faced by the financial institution when deploying its AI fraud detection system?

a) The system couldn't detect sophisticated fraud patterns
b) The AI system operated as a "black box" with unexplainable decisions
c) Customers refused to provide necessary data for the system to function
d) Regulators demanded access to proprietary algorithms

2 Which approach did the institution implement to address the transparency challenges?
   a) They completely replaced the AI system with human reviewers
   b) They implemented Explainable AI (XAI) frameworks
   c) They limited the AI system to only high-value transactions
   d) They required customers to opt-in to AI-based fraud detection

3 What was the source of bias in the AI fraud detection system?
   a) Deliberate programming by developers
   b) External tampering by hackers
   c) Historical transaction patterns in the training dataset
   d) Explicit demographic profiling

4 To comply with the EU AI Act, the institution implemented several measures. Which was NOT mentioned as part of their compliance strategy?
   a) Continuous monitoring of the AI system's performance
   b) Regular third-party audits
   c) Maintaining detailed documentation of training data
   d) Restricting AI usage to nonsensitive transactions

5 According to the case study, what was one of the key outcomes after addressing the ethical and regulatory challenges?
   a) The system detected 100% of fraudulent transactions
   b) Regulators granted the institution permanent exemptions from future AI regulations
   c) Bias mitigation efforts reduced disproportionate flagging of certain groups
   d) The institution was able to eliminate all human oversight of the AI system

Answer Key

1 **Correct Answer: b) The AI system operated as a "black box" with unexplainable decisions**
   - **Explanation:** The case study explicitly states that "The AI system operated as a 'black box,' making it difficult for the institution to explain its decision-making processes to customers, whose transactions were flagged or blocked." This opacity created trust issues and customer dissatisfaction when legitimate transactions were incorrectly flagged as fraudulent and customers demanded explanations.
   - Option a) is incorrect because the case doesn't mention the system's inability to detect fraud patterns as a transparency issue.

- Option c) is incorrect because the customer refusal to provide data wasn't mentioned as an issue.
- Option d) is incorrect because while regulatory compliance was a challenge, the specific demand for access to proprietary algorithms wasn't mentioned.

2 **Correct Answer: b) They implemented XAI frameworks**
- **Explanation:** The case study states that "The institution partnered with data scientists and regulatory experts to implement XAI frameworks," which involved "integrating tools that could provide interpretable summaries of the AI system's decisions."
- Option a) is incorrect because they didn't replace the AI system with humans but rather made the AI more explainable.
- Option c) is incorrect because limiting AI to high-value transactions wasn't mentioned as a solution.
- Option d) is incorrect because requiring customer opt-in wasn't mentioned as a transparency solution.

3 **Correct Answer: c) Historical transaction patterns in the training dataset**
- **Explanation:** The case study clearly states that "The training dataset used to develop the AI model reflected historical transaction patterns, which inadvertently introduced biases. Certain demographic groups were disproportionately flagged for fraud based on historical trends rather than actual fraudulent behavior."
- Option a) is incorrect because there's no mention of deliberate bias programming.
- Option b) is incorrect because external tampering wasn't mentioned as a source of bias.
- Option d) is incorrect because while demographic groups were affected, this wasn't due to explicit profiling but rather historical patterns in the training data.

4 **Correct Answer: d) Restricting AI usage to nonsensitive transactions**
- **Explanation:** The case study mentions three specific measures for EU AI Act compliance: "Continuous monitoring of the AI system's performance," "Maintaining detailed documentation of training data, decision-making processes, and system updates," and "Regular third-party audits to assess compliance and identify vulnerabilities." Restricting AI usage to nonsensitive transactions was not mentioned as a compliance strategy.
- Options a), b), and c) are incorrect because they were all explicitly mentioned as part of the institution's compliance framework.

5 **Correct Answer: c) Bias mitigation efforts reduced disproportionate flagging of certain groups**
   - **Explanation:** The case study states under "Outcomes" that "Bias mitigation efforts reduced the disproportionate flagging of certain groups, aligning the system with fairness principles. This enhanced the institution's reputation for ethical AI use."
   - Option a) is incorrect because perfect fraud detection wasn't claimed.
   - Option b) is incorrect because no regulatory exemptions were mentioned.
   - Option d) is incorrect because the case study emphasized the importance of human oversight, not its elimination.

References

Akinrinola, O., Okoye, C. C., Ofodile, O. C., & Ugochukwu, C. E. (2024). Navigating and reviewing ethical dilemmas in AI development: Strategies for transparency, fairness, and accountability. *GSC Advanced Research and Reviews*, *18*(3), 050–058.

Almagrabi, A. O., & Khan, R. A. (2024). Optimizing secure AI lifecycle model management with innovative generative AI strategies. *IEEE Access*, *3*, 12889–12920.

Amah, O., & Okesipe, V. O. (2025). AI in education: Ethical challenges and opportunities. In R. Queirós, M. Cruz, & D. Mascarenhas (Eds.), *Integrating artificial intelligence in education: Enhancing teaching practices for future learning* (pp. 1–26). IGI Global.

Andrade, V. C., Gomes, R. D., Reinehr, S., Freitas, C. O. D. A., & Malucelli, A. (2022, November). Privacy by design and software engineering: A systematic literature review. In *Proceedings of the XXI Brazilian Symposium on Software Quality* (pp. 1–10).

Antoniadi, A. M., Du, Y., Guendouz, Y., Wei, L., Mazo, C., Becker, B. A., & Mooney, C. (2021). Current challenges and future opportunities for XAI in machine learning-based clinical decision support systems: A systematic review. *Applied Sciences*, *11*(11), 5088.

Biden, J. R. (2023). Safe, secure, and trustworthy development and use of artificial intelligence, Executive Order 14110. *Federal Register*, *88*(210), 75191–75226 (FR Doc. 2023-24283). https://www.federalregister.gov/documents/2023/11/01/2023-24283/safe-secure-and-trustworthy-development-and-use-of-artificial-intelligence.

California Legislative Information (2024a). AB-2013 generative artificial intelligence: Training data transparency. https://leginfo.legislature.ca.gov/faces/billNavClient.xhtml?bill_id=202320240AB2013.

California Legislative Information. (2024b). SB-942 California AI Transparency Act. https://leginfo.legislature.ca.gov/faces/billTextClient.xhtml?bill_id=202320240SB942.

CalMatters Digital Democracy (2024). SB 896 – Generative Artificial Intelligence Accountability Act. https://calmatters.digitaldemocracy.org/bills/ca_202320240sb896.

Chaudhary, G. (2024). Unveiling the black box: Bringing algorithmic transparency to AI. *Masaryk University Journal of Law and Technology*, *18*(1), 93–122.

Cheong, B. C. (2024). Transparency and accountability in AI systems: safeguarding wellbeing in the age of algorithmic decision-making. *Frontiers in Human Dynamics*, *6*, 1421273.

da Silva, C. H. (2024). *AI-driven cybersecurity: A human-in-the-loop approach* [Master's thesis]. Universidade NOVA de Lisboa Portugal.

Daly, A., Hagendorff, T., Hui, L., Mann, M., Marda, V., Wagner, B., & Wei Wang, W. (2022). AI, governance and ethics: Global perspectives. University of Hong Kong Faculty of Law Research Paper No. 2020/051. https://ssrn.com/abstract=3684406.

Del Riego, E. J. (2024). *Transformational leadership and innovation create a cybersecurity conscious organizational culture* [Doctoral dissertation]. St. Thomas University.

Dudley, C. (2024). The rise of AI governance: Unpacking ISO/IEC 42001. *Quality*, *63*(8), 27–27.

Dwivedi, R., Dave, D., Naik, H., Singhal, S., Omer, R., Patel, P., Qian, B., Wen, Z., Shah, T., Morgan, G., & Ranjan, R. (2023). Explainable AI (XAI): Core ideas, techniques, and solutions. *ACM Computing Surveys*, *55*(9), 1–33.

Ebulue, C. C., Ebulue, O. R., & Ekesiobi, C. S. (2024). Public-private partnerships in health sector innovation: Lessons from around the world. *International Medical Science Research Journal*, *4*(4), 484–499.

EU Artificial Intelligence Act. (2025a). Article 4: AI literacy. https://artificialintelligenceact.eu/article/4/.

EU Artificial Intelligence Act. (2025b). The EU Artificial Intelligence Act. https://artificialintelligenceact.eu/.

European Parliament. (2025). EU AI Act: First regulation on artificial intelligence. https://www.europarl.europa.eu/topics/en/article/20230601STO93804/eu-ai-act-first-regulation-on-artificial-intelligence.

Executive Order. (2025, January 23). Removing barriers to American leadership in artificial intelligence. https://www.whitehouse.gov/presidential-actions/2025/01/removing-barriers-to-american-leadership-in-artificial-intelligence/.

Familoni, B. T. (2024). Cybersecurity challenges in the age of AI: Theoretical approaches and practical solutions. *Computer Science & IT Research Journal*, *5*(3), 703–724.

Gentili, P. L. (2021). Establishing a new link between fuzzy logic, neuroscience, and quantum mechanics through Bayesian probability: Perspectives in artificial intelligence and unconventional computing. *Molecules*, *26*(19), 5987.

Hudson, J. (2024). Artificial intelligence and cybersecurity integration: Modern database techniques for securing AI models. *ResearchGate*. https://doi.org/10.13140/RG.2.2.16974.47684. https://www.researchgate.net/publication/385410990_Artificial_Intelligence_and_Cybersecurity_Integration_Modern_Database_Techniques_for_Securing_AI_Models.

Jakubik, J., Weber, D., Hemmer, P., Vössing, M., & Satzger, G. (2023). Improving the efficiency of human-in-the-loop systems: Adding artificial to human experts. arXiv preprint arXiv:2307.03003.

Jauhiainen, T., & Lehner, O. M. (2022). Good governance of AI and big data processes in accounting and auditing. In T. Jauhiainen & O. M. Lehner (Eds.), *Artificial intelligence in accounting* (pp. 119–181). Routledge.

Kersten, D. (2024). Effective AI cybersecurity in 2024: Cross-collaboration and proactivity. *Spice Works*. https://www.spiceworks.com/tech/artificial-intelligence/guest-article/effective-ai-cybersecurity-cross-collaboration-and-proactivity/.

Levi, S. D., Kumayama, K. D., Ridgway, W. E. and Ghaemmaghami, M. (2024, June 24). Colorado's Landmark AI Act: What Companies Need To Know, Skadden, Arps, Slate, Meagher & Flom LLP (AI Insights). https://www.skadden.com/insights/publications/2024/06/colorados-landmark-ai-act.

Mazzinghy, A.O.C., Silva, R.M.S., Fernandes, R.M., Batista ED, Picanço AR, Monteiro NJ, de Amorim DM, Cardoso BD, da Silva JM, Martins, V.W.B. (2024) Assessing benefits of ISO/IEC 42001 artificial intelligence management system: Insights from Brazilian logistics. Preprint. Retrieved 2025, March 25, from. https://doi.org/10.20944/preprints202410.0699.v1.

McIntosh, T. R., Susnjak, T., Liu, T., Watters, P., Xu, D., Liu, D., Nowrozy, R., & Halgamuge, M. N. (2024). From COBIT to ISO 42001: Evaluating cybersecurity frameworks for opportunities, risks, and regulatory compliance in commercializing large language models. *Computers & Security*, *144*, 103964.

Minkkinen, M., Laine, J., & Mäntymäki, M. (2022). Continuous auditing of artificial intelligence: A conceptualization and assessment of tools and frameworks. *Digital Society*, *1*(3), 21.

Mökander, J., Schuett, J., Kirk, H. R., & Floridi, L. (2023). Auditing large language models: a three-layered approach. *AI and Ethics*, *4*, 1085–1115.

National Association of Attorneys General. (2024). A deep dive into Colorado's Artificial Intelligence Act. https://www.naag.org/attorney-general-journal/a-deep-dive-into-colorados-artificial-intelligence-act/.

NIST. (2024). AI risk management framework. https://www.nist.gov/itl/ai-risk-management-framework.

Oregon State Government Artificial Intelligence Advisory Council. (2025, February 4). Final Recommended Action Plan, State government artificial intelligence advisory council.Enterprise Information Services, State of Oregon. https://www.oregon.gov/eis/Documents/SG%20AI%20Final%20Recommended%20Action%20Plan%2020250211.pdf.

Palakurti, N. R. (2023). Governance strategies for ensuring consistency and compliance in business rules management. *Transactions on Latest Trends in Artificial Intelligence*, *4*(4), 1–4.

Prunkl, C. E., Ashurst, C., Anderljung, M., Webb, H., Leike, J., & Dafoe, A. (2021). Institutionalizing ethics in AI through broader impact requirements. *Nature Machine Intelligence*, *3*(2), 104–110.

Raji, I. D., Xu, P., Honigsberg, C., & Ho, D. (2022, July). Outsider oversight: Designing a third party audit ecosystem for ai governance. In *Proceedings of the 2022 AAAI/ACM Conference on AI, Ethics, and Society* (pp. 557–571).

Reuters. (2025, August 28). Chinese regulators issue requirements for the labeling of AI-generated content. *Reuters*. https://www.reuters.com/world/asia-pacific/chinese-regulators-issue-requirements-labeling-ai-generated-content-2025-03-14/.

Santoni de Sio, F., & Mecacci, G. (2021). Four responsibility gaps with artificial intelligence: Why they matter and how to address them. *Philosophy & Technology*, *34*(4), 1057–1084.

Schemmer, M., Kühl, N., Benz, C., & Satzger, G. (2022). On the influence of explainable AI on automation bias. arXiv preprint arXiv:2204.08859.

Swaminathan, N., & Danks, D. (2024). Application of the NIST AI risk management framework to surveillance technology. arXiv preprint arXiv:2403.15646.

Tanaka, Y., & Fujita, T. (2025). Accelerating artificial intelligence advancement: The synergistic role of Industry-Academia Collaboration. *Frontiers in Strategic Management*, *2*(01), 1–14.

The White House (2025) *Initial Rescissions of Harmful Executive Orders and Actions, Presidential Actions*. https://www.whitehouse.gov/presidential-actions/2025/01/initial-rescissions-of-harmful-executive-orders-and-actions/.

Thiers, F. A., & Harned, Z. (2024). The emerging role of ISO 42001 certification in fostering the deployment of responsible generative AI healthcare solutions. *Technology (NIST)*, *55*(58), 59.

Tsamados, A., Floridi, L., & Taddeo, M. (2024). Human control of AI systems: from supervision to teaming. *AI and Ethics*, *5*, 1535–1548.

United States Copyright Office. (2023). Copyright registration guidance: Works containing material generated by artificial intelligence. https://copyright.gov/ai/ai_policy_guidance.pdf.

United States Copyright Office. (2025). Copyright and artificial intelligence. https://www.copyright.gov/ai/.

Varona, D., & Suárez, J. L. (2022). Discrimination, bias, fairness, and trustworthy AI. *Applied Sciences*, *12*(12), 5826.

Von Eschenbach, W. J. (2021). Transparency and the black box problem: Why we do not trust AI. *Philosophy & Technology*, *34*(4), 1607–1622.

Wang, X., & Wu, Y. C. (2024). Balancing innovation and regulation in the age of geneRative artificial intelligence. *Journal of Information Policy*, *14*, 385–416.

Weber, L., Lapuschkin, S., Binder, A., & Samek, W. (2023). Beyond explaining: Opportunities and challenges of XAI-based model improvement. *Information Fusion*, *92*, 154–176.

Zeng, Q., Nait-Abdesselam, F., & Chen, Z. (2023, December). A HITL-integrated machine learning approach to secure drone networks for IIOT applications. In *2023 IEEE Globecom Workshops (GC Wkshps)* (pp. 614–619). IEEE.

8

Future Trends in Generative AI Security

As this book is being written, there is so much growth and movement in this space. Probably by the time you are reading this, there are many more new developments. We are truly at a critical intersection of rapid technological advancement and evolving security challenges. As we look ahead, several transformative trends are shaping how organizations will secure and leverage AI systems while addressing emerging threats. This chapter explores key developments, including the impact of quantum computing on AI security, the evolution of human–AI collaboration in cybersecurity operations, advancements in explainable AI, and the integration of generative AI into zero trust architectures. Understanding these trends is crucial for security professionals and organizations as they prepare for future challenges and opportunities in AI security. From quantum-resistant models to enhanced human–AI teaming strategies, these developments will fundamentally reshape how we approach security in an AI-driven world.

8.1 Quantum Computing and AI Security

Every day, we become closer to the reality of quantum computing. The implications for the cybersecurity field are both extremely exciting and terrifying. In other words, the emergence of quantum computing represents both a significant threat and an opportunity for AI security. As quantum computers become more powerful and accessible, they have the potential to fundamentally alter the landscape of AI security by both compromising current cryptographic protections and enabling new defensive capabilities. This section explores the critical intersection of quantum computing and AI security, examining postquantum cryptography (PQC) approaches, the evolution of quantum machine learning (QML), and the development of quantum-resistant AI models. Understanding these developments is crucial for organizations as they prepare their AI systems for a postquantum era, where traditional security measures may become

Generative AI Security: Defense, Threats, and Vulnerabilities, First Edition. Shaila Rana and Rhonda Chicone.

vulnerable to quantum-enabled attacks while new quantum-based defensive capabilities emerge. The convergence of these technologies will require organizations to fundamentally rethink their approach to securing AI systems while leveraging quantum advantages for enhanced security measures.

The transition from theoretical quantum computing advantages to practical applications is already underway, with certified randomness emerging as one of the first concrete implementations with significant security implications. As reported by IFLScience, researchers have successfully developed and demonstrated a quantum protocol that generates truly random numbers, something fundamentally impossible with classical computers, which can only produce pseudo-random sequences vulnerable to prediction and exploitation (Carpineti, 2025). This certified randomness protocol, developed by Scott Aaronson and Shih-Han Hung, operates through a two-step process, where challenges are fed to a quantum computer that can only be solved by randomly selecting from multiple possible solutions, with the randomness then rigorously verified using several of the world's most advanced supercomputers. Using Quantinuum's 56-qubit H2 trapped-ion quantum computer, the team demonstrated this capability remotely, achieving what many consider a pivotal milestone in bringing quantum computing into practical applications. This advancement is particularly significant for AI security as truly random numbers form the foundation of effective cryptography and privacy protection mechanisms. While quantum computers threaten to break conventional encryption through algorithms like Shor's, this application demonstrates how quantum properties themselves can enhance security by providing computational guarantees of randomness that classical systems cannot match. The protocol opens the door to using quantum computers to generate certified random bits for actual cryptographic applications, potentially establishing one of the first practical quantum advantages in the cybersecurity landscape that will directly impact how we secure AI systems against future threats.

Microsoft has announced Majorana 1, a breakthrough quantum chip using a new Topological Core architecture based on topoconductors—a novel material that can control Majorana particles to create more stable qubits (Bolgar, 2025). This is a significant acceleration in the timeline for quantum computing's impact on GAI security. Their achievement of creating stable topological qubits with a clear path to scaling to one million qubits on a palm-sized chip transforms many theoretical security concerns into immediate practical considerations. The chip's digital control approach and inherent error resistance at the hardware level suggest that reliable quantum computing capabilities could be available sooner than previously anticipated, potentially compressing the timeline for implementing quantum-resistant security measures. This development is particularly significant when considering the chip's integration with existing cloud infrastructure through Azure, which could democratize access to quantum computing capabilities. Such accessibility could accelerate both the development of quantum-enhanced security measures and the emergence of quantum-enabled threats to GAI systems.

Moreover, Microsoft's breakthrough with Majorana 1 introduces new considerations for quantum-resistant AI model development. The ability to achieve stable, scalable quantum computing through topological qubits suggests that organizations may need to accelerate their preparations for a postquantum security landscape. Unlike distributed quantum computing approaches, which face challenges in coordinating multiple quantum processors, Microsoft's achievement of condensing significant quantum capabilities into a small form factor presents a more direct path to practical quantum computing. This could necessitate faster adoption of PQC measures and quantum-resistant AI architectures, particularly for generative AI systems that might be especially vulnerable to quantum-enabled attacks. The potential for deploying such quantum systems within existing data center infrastructures also raises new questions about the security implications of quantum computing becoming a standard component of cloud computing platforms, where many GAI systems are deployed and trained.

AWS has announced Ocelot, a groundbreaking quantum computing chip that reduces quantum error correction costs by up to 90% compared to current approaches (Amazon, 2025). Developed at the AWS Center for Quantum Computing at Caltech, Ocelot uses innovative "cat qubit" technology that intrinsically suppresses certain errors. This design, which integrates error correction from the ground up, could accelerate the timeline to practical quantum computing by up to five years. According to AWS director of Quantum Hardware, Oskar Painter, the chip could cost as little as one-fifth of current approaches and require only one-tenth of the resources associated with standard quantum error correction methods, making quantum computers smaller, more reliable, and less expensive. This AWS announcement directly relates to the quantum computing cybersecurity concerns that are discussed throughout this section. While Microsoft's Majorana 1 chip uses topological qubits to create more stable quantum computing capabilities, AWS's Ocelot takes a different approach through cat qubits and built-in error correction. Both developments suggest an accelerating timeline for practical quantum computing, which has profound implications for AI security. As quantum computers become more reliable and accessible through cloud platforms like AWS's Amazon Braket, organizations will need to expedite their adoption of PQC and quantum-resistant AI architectures. The fact that two major cloud providers are making significant quantum computing breakthroughs indicates that the theoretical security concerns about quantum computing's impact on cryptography and AI systems are rapidly becoming immediate practical considerations. This convergence of quantum computing and AI will require organizations to fundamentally rethink their security approaches while potentially leveraging these same quantum capabilities for enhanced security measures.

Swiss semiconductor company SEALSQ has unveiled the QS7001 system, designed to protect telecommunications against future quantum computing attacks (Ray, 2025). Presented at the World Economic Forum in Davos, this system combines two quantum-resistant encryption protocols (NIST's Dilithium and Kyber) with significantly reduced data transmission time—from 1,500 ms using traditional methods to just 100 ms. Thus, narrowing the window of opportunity for potential attackers, QS7001 helps address concerns that quantum computers will eventually break conventional encryption technologies like RSA. While the system does not prevent intercepted information from being copied and stored for later decryption attempts, it does help prevent messages from being modified or misdirected during transmission. Cybersecurity analysts note that this represents the ongoing "arms race" between protective technologies and those that might undermine security. This development directly addresses the concerns in the quantum computing and AI security realm. As quantum computing advances rapidly through breakthroughs like Microsoft's Majorana 1 and AWS's Ocelot chips, the timeline for implementing quantum-resistant security measures is compressing. The QS7001 system is a practical implementation of PQC. It specifically addresses the vulnerability of data in transit, one of the key concerns for AI security in a quantum computing era. Moreover, QS7001 maintains security standards while improving transmission efficiency, a crucial move forward in a quantum security landscape.

China's University of Science and Technology has developed the "Zuchongzhi 3.0" quantum processor with 105 superconducting qubits, claiming performance 1 quadrillion times faster than traditional supercomputers (Bradley, 2025). This rivals Google's latest Willow QPU and represents a major step toward achieving quantum supremacy. Meanwhile, Microsoft has developed the Majorana 1 quantum chip using topological qubits, while AWS has introduced Ocelot with cat qubit technology that reduces error correction costs. Other advances include SEALSQ's QS7001 quantum-resistant encryption system, MIT's achievement of 99.998% qubit fidelity, Oxford's distributed quantum computer, and discoveries of exotic quantum particles like paraparticles and fractional excitons. As quantum computers grow more powerful, they will eventually break current encryption standards through algorithms like Shor's, creating a "store now, decrypt later" vulnerability for sensitive data.

PQC is and will increasingly become a critical evolution in cryptographic systems designed to resist attacks from both classical and quantum computers. In the context of AI security, PQC becomes very significant as it will need to protect not only traditional data and communications but also AI models, training data, and model outputs from quantum-enabled attacks (Shamoo, 2025). The intersection of PQC and AI security introduces new complexities in protecting generative AI systems while ensuring they remain functional and efficient. For generative AI systems specifically, PQC will play a crucial role in protecting model architectures, training data, and inference processes from quantum attacks (Darzi & Yavuz, 2024). This is important as generative AI models often contain valuable intellectual property and training data that could be compromised by quantum algorithms. Organizations will need to implement PQC measures to protect their AI assets while maintaining model performance and efficiency, creating a complex balance between security and functionality.

Security professionals will benefit from PQC in several ways when protecting AI systems. PQC algorithms can help secure AI model deployment, protect data transmission between AI components, and ensure the integrity of AI-generated outputs (Sandua, 2023). Thus, this is important in security-critical applications where AI systems make important decisions or handle sensitive information. PQC will also help protect the training pipelines and model update processes that are crucial for maintaining effective AI security systems. However, the integration of PQC into AI systems also introduces potential vulnerabilities that malicious actors could exploit. Attackers might use quantum-enabled algorithms to identify weaknesses in PQC implementations, potentially compromising AI systems that haven't been properly secured (Senewirathna, 2024). The complexity of implementing PQC correctly could lead to implementation errors that create new attack vectors, very much so in AI systems that require real-time performance.

The societal implications of PQC in AI security are significant and difficult to entirely predict. As quantum computers become more powerful, organizations that haven't adequately protected their AI systems with PQC measures could face serious security breaches. This could lead to the compromise of sensitive personal data processed by AI systems, manipulation of AI-driven decisions, or theft of valuable AI models. The potential for quantum-enabled attacks on AI systems could create new forms of cybercrime and security threats. Malicious actors could potentially use generative AI systems to identify weaknesses in PQC implementations or generate new attack vectors. For example, they might use AI to analyze PQC algorithms for vulnerabilities, automate the discovery of implementation flaws, or generate sophisticated quantum-enabled attack strategies. The combination of quantum computing capabilities with advanced AI could create powerful tools for cybercrime and security breaches. The interaction between PQC and generative AI also raises concerns about long-term data security (Radanliev et al., 2023). Data encrypted today could be stored by attackers until quantum computers become powerful enough to break current encryption methods. This "store now, decrypt later" attack (as touched upon earlier) becomes very concerning when considering AI systems that process and generate sensitive information

(Joseph et al., 2022). Organizations need to consider how to protect both current and historical AI-generated data from future quantum attacks.

Another important consideration is QML, which is the convergence of quantum computing capabilities with machine learning algorithms, offering potential breakthroughs in both processing power and algorithmic sophistication (Khurana, 2024). In the context of security, QML could dramatically enhance our ability to detect and respond to threats by processing vast amounts of security data at unprecedented speeds while identifying complex patterns that classical ML systems might miss. This emerging field promises to transform how we approach AI-driven security operations. The application of QML to security challenges could enable more sophisticated threat detection and analysis capabilities. Quantum algorithms could process security telemetry data more efficiently than classical systems, potentially identifying subtle attack patterns or anomalies that current systems overlook (Shoushtari et al., 2022). Therefore, this is relevant for detecting sophisticated attacks against AI systems, where attackers might exploit subtle vulnerabilities that are difficult to detect with classical machine learning approaches. For generative AI security, QML could enhance both defensive and offensive capabilities. On the defensive side, quantum algorithms could improve model robustness by identifying potential vulnerabilities and attack vectors more effectively than classical approaches. QML could also enable more sophisticated authentication mechanisms for AI systems, helping ensure the integrity of both model inputs and outputs. However, this same capability could be exploited by attackers using quantum algorithms to generate more sophisticated adversarial attacks against AI systems.

The practical implementation of QML in security contexts faces several challenges. Current quantum computers have limited capabilities and high error rates, making them impractical for many real-world security applications (Yazdi, 2024). Organizations will need to develop hybrid approaches that combine classical and QML capabilities, leveraging each system's strengths while managing their limitations. This hybrid approach will likely characterize the early adoption of QML in security applications. Moreover, the potential impact of QML on privacy and security raises important considerations. Quantum algorithms could potentially break current encryption methods or enable more sophisticated privacy attacks. Organizations will need to carefully consider how to implement QML capabilities while protecting sensitive data and maintaining privacy guarantees. This includes developing new privacy-preserving techniques specifically designed for QML systems. The development of QML could also lead to new forms of security analytics and threat intelligence. Quantum algorithms might enable more sophisticated analysis of attack patterns across multiple dimensions, helping organizations better understand and predict emerging threats. This could be particularly valuable for protecting against attacks on AI systems, where the complexity of potential attack vectors makes traditional analysis approaches insufficient. Long-term, QML could fundamentally change how we approach AI security by enabling new types of learning algorithms and security measures that aren't possible with classical computing (Brin, 2022). This might include quantum-enhanced neural networks, quantum-resistant encryption schemes specifically designed for AI systems, and new approaches to secure model training and deployment that leverage quantum properties (Alluhaibi, 2024).

An important advancement in the field is the discovery of paraparticles and their theoretical implications on QML, quantum, and ultimately generative AI. The existence of paraparticles that can exist in multiple dimensions, unlike anyons, which are limited to 1D or 2D systems, could provide new approaches for building quantum computers (Hale, 2025). Researchers suggests these particles could make quantum computers less error-prone, which is currently one of the major challenges in quantum computing (Gadgets 360, 2025). This could potentially lead to more stable and reliable quantum computing platforms that could better support advanced AI and machine learning applications. The unique properties of paraparticles, particularly their behavior under position swapping, could potentially offer new methods for quantum error correction. This is crucial for developing reliable quantum computers that could run complex AI algorithms. If paraparticles can indeed provide more robust ways to encode information, as suggested for anyons in the article, this could lead to more stable quantum memory and computation—a critical requirement for practical quantum AI applications. The discovery of particles that don't fit into conventional fermion/boson classifications opens up new possibilities for quantum algorithm design. QML algorithms could potentially leverage these unique quantum states and behaviors to perform computations in ways not possible with traditional quantum bits. This could lead to new classes of QML algorithms that exploit paraparticle properties for enhanced performance or novel capabilities. The ability of paraparticles to exist in many dimensions could have profound implications for quantum computing architectures designed for AI applications. Traditional quantum computing is often limited by dimensional constraints, but paraparticles might enable new approaches to multidimensional quantum computing. This could be particularly relevant for AI applications that require processing of high-dimensional data or complex pattern recognition.

When it comes to the impact on GAI, quantum computers leveraging paraparticle properties might enable more efficient training of large AI models by handling complex probability distributions more naturally. Enhanced pattern recognition is another factor here. The unique quantum states possible with paraparticles could lead to new approaches for pattern recognition and generation in AI systems. Moreover, the multidimensional nature of paraparticles might inspire new architectural approaches for generative AI systems that can better handle complex, high-dimensional data spaces. However, it's important to note the challenges. It's crucial to mention that creating these paraparticle states would be "challenging" even on a quantum computer (Castelvecchi, 2025). This suggests that practical implementation for AI applications might be quite far in the future. The research is still largely theoretical, and significant engineering challenges would need to be overcome before these concepts could be applied to practical AI systems. In the nearer term, the research might lead to hybrid approaches that combine classical computing with quantum systems, utilizing paraparticle properties for specific tasks within AI systems. This could be particularly relevant for generative AI systems that need to handle both classical and quantum information processing.

The discovery of paraparticles opens up several promising new research directions for quantum AI, particularly in how these unique particles could revolutionize information encoding in AI systems. Researchers will need to investigate how paraparticle properties can be harnessed for information storage and processing, while simultaneously developing new quantum algorithms that can leverage these distinct quantum states. The multidimensional nature of paraparticles presents intriguing possibilities for enhancing AI capabilities beyond current limitations, especially in the realm of quantum neural networks and deep learning applications.

However, significant practical limitations and considerations must be addressed before these theoretical possibilities can become a reality. The fundamental challenge lies in developing reliable technology for creating and manipulating paraparticles, a task that remains largely theoretical at present. Additionally, researchers face substantial hurdles in integrating these new concepts with existing quantum computing architectures. Cost and scalability present major challenges that will need to be overcome, while the development of appropriate validation and testing methods for these novel systems remains a crucial requirement.

Looking toward the future, if these considerable challenges can be successfully addressed, paraparticle-based quantum computing could unlock remarkable possibilities for AI advancement. Such systems could potentially enable significantly more powerful and efficient AI systems, capable of handling complex quantum states in ways currently impossible. The technology could lead to more robust quantum memory systems, essential for advanced AI applications, while enabling novel approaches to quantum neural networks that could fundamentally transform our understanding of AI and its capabilities.

In general, the discovery of paraparticles is a potentially significant advancement for the future of quantum computing and AI, but it's important to maintain realistic expectations about the timeline for practical applications. While the theoretical foundations are exciting, considerable research and development work will be needed to translate these concepts into practical technologies that can benefit

AI and generative AI systems. As the field develops, we might see gradual integration of these concepts into quantum computing architectures, potentially leading to incremental improvements in quantum AI capabilities before any revolutionary breakthroughs. The multidimensional nature of paraparticles could prove particularly valuable for handling the complex, high-dimensional spaces that are common in modern AI applications.

Another advancement in the quantum field is signified by the recent achievement by MIT researchers in achieving 99.998% fidelity using fluxonium qubits is a groundbreaking development with far-reaching implications for the field of quantum computing and its intersection with AI security (Tripathi, 2025). This breakthrough directly influences how quantum advancements will shape AI's role as a tool, weapon, and target within cybersecurity. With quantum computing poised to solve problems previously deemed intractable, this milestone is a leap toward more secure AI models, as well as new challenges in safeguarding systems against the unprecedented capabilities of quantum-enabled threats. Subsequently, this has implications for AI as a tool, weapon, and target. This breakthrough advances the reliability of quantum systems, making their integration into AI applications a more tangible reality while simultaneously exposing new vulnerabilities and opportunities in the security landscape.

As a tool, quantum computing with nearly perfect fidelity could enable unprecedented advancements in AI-driven cybersecurity. Enhanced by quantum precision, AI systems will have the ability to analyze vast datasets at incredible speeds, allowing for real-time threat detection, predictive analytics, and comprehensive vulnerability assessments. The reduction of counter-rotating errors and the successful implementation of advanced techniques such as commensurate pulses and circularly polarized microwaves highlight the potential for quantum-enabled AI systems to identify complex attack patterns or anomalies that traditional models might overlook. This fidelity positions AI as a more potent ally for defenders, enabling the development of more robust encryption methods, faster cryptographic key generation, and the ability to counteract increasingly sophisticated cyber threats (Singh & Kumar, 2024).

Conversely, the same fidelity and power that make quantum-enhanced AI a powerful defensive tool also increase its potential as a weapon. Malicious actors equipped with quantum capabilities could leverage AI to crack traditional cryptographic systems, develop quantum-accelerated adversarial algorithms, or execute large-scale automated attacks (Das et al., 2024). The high coherence and noise resistance demonstrated by fluxonium qubits provide attackers with the computational means to exploit vulnerabilities in AI models or create advanced cyber threats that evade detection (Firnhaber, 2023). This capability could lead to the weaponization of quantum-AI systems to disrupt critical infrastructure, manipulate AI-driven decision-making processes, or compromise sensitive data on an unprecedented scale. Simultaneously, AI itself becomes a target in a quantum-enhanced landscape. The precision and computational power of quantum systems can expose weaknesses in AI architectures, including training pipelines, inference mechanisms, and cryptographic protections. Attackers might use quantum-enabled tools to reverse-engineer AI models, compromise training datasets, or manipulate outputs to serve their objectives (Neway, 2024). To put it in perspective, generative AI systems, which often rely on proprietary architectures and sensitive datasets, could face unique threats from quantum attacks designed to steal intellectual property or alter the integrity of generated content.

The implications of this advancement extend to the broader challenge of building quantum-resistant AI systems. Organizations must proactively develop PQC measures to safeguard AI assets from quantum-enabled threats. These measures include integrating quantum-resilient algorithms into AI architectures, securing training and deployment pipelines, and developing robust validation protocols to test AI models against potential quantum attack scenarios (Bishwas & Sen, 2024). As fluxonium qubits pave the way for more stable and powerful quantum computers, the urgency to adapt AI systems to withstand these capabilities grows, requiring interdisciplinary collaboration across quantum computing, cryptography, and machine learning domains (Krasnok et al., 2024). Ultimately, this convergence will drive a reevaluation of AI security strategies, emphasizing the dual need to leverage quantum computing for defensive purposes while mitigating its risks as an offensive tool. Moreover, QML is poised to play a central role in this evolution, offering enhanced capabilities for threat detection, anomaly analysis, and system robustness. However, the same QML capabilities could empower adversaries to refine attack strategies, requiring organizations to develop countermeasures that anticipate and neutralize these threats.

MIT's achievement also signals a shift in the balance of power within the cybersecurity field, where the race to develop and deploy quantum computing capabilities will determine the security and vulnerability of AI systems. Organizations that fail to adapt to this postquantum era risk exposing their AI-driven operations to catastrophic breaches. As quantum and AI technologies continue to co-evolve, the cybersecurity community must remain vigilant, leveraging these advancements to strengthen defenses while preparing for the complex challenges posed by quantum-enabled adversaries. This milestone underscores the necessity of proactive investment in quantum resilience, ensuring that AI remains a tool for innovation and protection rather than a target or weapon of cyber conflict.

Furthermore, scientists at Oxford University have achieved a significant breakthrough in quantum computing by successfully creating the first distributed quantum computer, connecting separate quantum processors through photonic links (SciTechDaily, 2025). This achievement addresses one of quantum computing's major challenges—scalability—by allowing smaller quantum devices to work together rather than requiring massive single machines with millions of qubits. The system uses quantum teleportation of logical gates across modules, effectively creating a networked quantum computing environment similar to how traditional supercomputers operate. The researchers demonstrated the system's effectiveness by executing Grover's search algorithm, suggesting potential for solving complex problems that would take traditional supercomputers years to complete. This advancement also comes with concerning implications for security vulnerabilities. As quantum systems become more networked and distributed, they create new attack surfaces and potential vulnerabilities at connection points between modules. Additionally, the ability to link quantum processors could eventually provide malicious actors with unprecedented computational power to break current encryption standards and develop more sophisticated attack methods. This suggests that organizations will need to fundamentally rethink their security architectures and protocols to prepare for a future where distributed quantum computing becomes more prevalent, particularly in how it might affect GAI systems' security and their potential vulnerabilities to quantum-enabled attacks. On the other hand, this advancement could dramatically enhance the cybersecurity field's ability to process, analyze, and respond to threats.

Another breakthrough (there are so many) is the discovery of fractional excitons by Brown University researchers (Paleja, 2025). These newly observed particles, which exhibit unique properties different from both bosons and fermions, could have important implications for quantum computing, particularly in addressing the "noise" problem that currently limits quantum systems. The particles were observed using a two-layer graphene setup exposed to extremely strong magnetic fields, demonstrating behavior that suggests they represent an entirely new class of quantum particles. The reduced noise in quantum systems using fractional excitons could allow for more reliable quantum encryption and more accurate threat detection mechanisms. Conversely, the stability offered by fractional excitons might allow for more sophisticated quantum attacks against AI infrastructure. As GAI systems will increasingly rely on quantum computing capabilities for enhanced processing power in the future, the stability offered by fractional excitons could become crucial for maintaining secure and reliable AI operations. However, this also means that quantum-based vulnerabilities could have more severe impacts on AI systems. Subsequently, this suggests that GAI security strategies will need to evolve to incorporate quantum-resistant security measures, while also leveraging quantum advantages for enhanced protection.

Another significant advancement in quantum stability comes from the University of Rochester's direct proof of nuclear-spin dark states (Valich, 2025). This breakthrough addresses one of quantum computing's fundamental challenges—the "noise" problem that makes quantum states unstable and prone to errors. Consequently, by demonstrating how atomic nuclei can be aligned to prevent interference with electron spin, this discovery could enable more stable quantum computing systems. The aforementioned is especially beneficial for AI applications that require reliable quantum processing. The fact that this was achieved using silicon quantum dots makes it especially promising for practical implementation, as silicon is already widely used in existing technology infrastructure. This development has important implications for GAI security, as more stable quantum systems could enable both more reliable quantum-based security measures and potentially more powerful quantum attacks against AI systems. The ability to maintain stable quantum states for longer periods could enhance quantum encryption methods, while also potentially enabling more sophisticated quantum-based attacks on existing security measures.

Quantum-resistant AI models is another future trend/reality in AI designed to withstand attacks from quantum computers while maintaining effectiveness and performance (Singh & Kumar, 2024). These models must be built with inherent resistance to quantum-enabled attacks, including those targeting the model architecture, training process, and inference mechanisms. Developing truly quantum-resistant AI models requires fundamental changes in how we design, train, and deploy AI systems, particularly generative AI models that may be especially vulnerable to quantum attacks. The journey to quantum-resistant AI models begins with understanding potential quantum attack vectors (Bishwas & Sen, 2024). This includes analyzing how quantum algorithms might compromise current AI architectures, identifying vulnerabilities in training processes, and understanding how quantum computing could be used to reverse engineer or manipulate AI models. Organizations need to invest in research to understand these threats and develop appropriate countermeasures before quantum computers become powerful enough to execute such attacks.

Building quantum resistance into AI models requires several key components. First, the model architecture itself must be designed to resist quantum attacks, potentially incorporating postquantum cryptographic principles directly into the model structure (Aydeger et al., 2024). Second, the training process must be secured against quantum-enabled attacks that might attempt to poison training data or manipulate model parameters (Yocam et al., 2024). Third, the inference process must be protected to ensure that quantum computers cannot reverse engineer model parameters or manipulate outputs (Ghosh & Ghosh, 2024). Subsequently, the development of quantum-resistant AI models also requires new approaches to model validation and testing. Organizations need to develop methods for assessing model resistance to quantum attacks, including simulation of potential quantum attack scenarios. This includes creating standardized testing frameworks specifically designed to evaluate quantum resistance, as well as developing metrics for measuring and comparing the quantum security of different AI models. Infrastructure and tooling requirements for quantum-resistant AI models are substantial. Organizations need to develop new frameworks and libraries that support quantum-resistant AI development, including tools for secure model training, validation, and deployment. This includes creating secure environments for model development that can protect against both current and future quantum threats, as well as developing new approaches to model distribution and updates that maintain quantum resistance.

Achieving quantum resistance in AI models requires significant collaboration across disciplines. This includes bringing together experts in quantum computing, cryptography, machine learning, and security to develop comprehensive approaches to quantum-resistant AI. Organizations need to invest in building these cross-disciplinary teams and fostering collaboration (see the theme here?) between different areas of expertise. Standards and certification processes for quantum-resistant AI models will be crucial. Industry groups and regulatory bodies need to develop clear standards for what constitutes quantum resistance in AI models, as well as certification processes to validate compliance with these standards. This includes creating guidelines for model development, testing protocols, and ongoing monitoring requirements. The path to quantum-resistant AI models also requires significant investment in research and development. Organizations need to fund research into new architectures and approaches that can provide quantum resistance while maintaining model performance. This includes exploring novel approaches to model design, investigating new training methodologies, and developing innovative security measures specifically tailored to protect against quantum attacks. Education and training will play a crucial role in developing quantum-resistant AI models. Organizations need to invest in training their teams to understand quantum threats and develop appropriate countermeasures. This includes building expertise in quantum computing, PQChy, and secure AI development practices among their technical staff.

8.2 Human Collaboration in Cybersecurity

As AI continues to advance in cybersecurity applications, the focus increasingly shifts toward effective collaboration between humans and AI systems rather than pure automation. This section explores how human expertise can be augmented and enhanced through AI capabilities, creating more effective cybersecurity operations through strategic partnership. The future of cybersecurity lies not in replacing human analysts with AI systems, but in creating synergistic relationships that leverage the strengths of both human insight and AI to address increasingly complex security challenges.

Augmented intelligence in cybersecurity is a big change in how organizations approach security operations, focusing on enhancing human capabilities rather than replacing them (Goriparthi, 2023). This approach acknowledges that while AI systems excel at processing vast amounts of data and identifying patterns, human insight, intuition, and strategic thinking remain essential for effective cybersecurity. In general, augmenting human analysts with AI capabilities allows organizations to create more effective and sustainable security operations that address both current and emerging threats. Furthermore, the pressing need for augmented intelligence becomes clear when considering the increasing burnout rates among cybersecurity professionals. Security analysts often face overwhelming volumes of alerts, complex threat landscapes, and constant pressure to prevent breaches while maintaining business operations. This cognitive overload leads to fatigue, decreased effectiveness, and high turnover rates in security teams. Augmented intelligence can help address these challenges by handling routine tasks, filtering false positives, and presenting relevant information in more digestible formats, allowing human analysts to focus on higher-value activities that require critical thinking and expertise.

From a resource perspective, augmented intelligence offers organizations a way to maximize the impact of their limited security staff (Jain et al., 2021). Rather than requiring larger teams to handle increasing security demands, organizations can use AI to amplify the capabilities of existing personnel. This approach helps address the persistent cybersecurity skills gap while providing better return on investment (ROI) for security spending. AI systems can handle the bulk of routine monitoring and initial analysis, enabling human analysts to focus on complex investigations, strategic planning, and incident response. The combination of human expertise and AI capabilities creates more robust cyber defenses by leveraging the strengths of both. AI systems can provide continuous monitoring, rapid data analysis, and pattern recognition across vast datasets, while human analysts contribute contextual understanding, creative problem-solving, and strategic decision-making. This synergy enables organizations to detect and respond to threats more effectively than either humans or AI systems could achieve independently.

Augmented intelligence also helps organizations improve their security ROI by optimizing resource allocation and increasing operational efficiency. Automating routine tasks and providing decision support for complex situations are important for organizations to achieve better security outcomes without proportional increases in staffing or budget. This efficiency gain becomes particularly important as organizations face growing pressure to justify security investments while dealing with expanding threat landscapes. The effectiveness of augmented intelligence in cybersecurity extends beyond immediate operational benefits to include improved learning and adaptation capabilities. AI systems can learn from human decisions and responses, while humans can gain new insights from AI analysis and recommendations. This creates a positive feedback loop that continuously enhances both human and machine capabilities, leading to increasingly sophisticated and effective security operations over time. In practical terms, augmented intelligence can help organizations better prioritize security investments and activities by providing data-driven insights about threats, vulnerabilities, and potential impacts. This enables security teams to make more informed decisions about resource allocation, technology investments, and strategic initiatives, ultimately leading to better security outcomes and more demonstrable ROI (or ROSI—Return on Security Investment) for security spending.

Human–AI teaming strategies in cybersecurity is a systematic approach to integrating AI with human expertise in ways that enhance overall security capabilities (Karunamurthy et al., 2023). These strategies go beyond simple automation to create true collaborative partnerships where both human analysts and AI systems contribute their unique strengths to security operations. Effective teaming strategies must clearly define roles, establish communication protocols, and create frameworks for joint decision-making that leverage both human insight and AI capabilities. The tangible benefits of well-implemented human–AI teaming become evident in several key areas of cybersecurity operations. For threat detection, AI systems can continuously monitor network traffic and system behaviors, flagging potential anomalies for human analysis. Human analysts can then apply their contextual understanding and experience to evaluate these alerts, reducing false positives while identifying sophisticated attacks that might evade purely automated detection. This partnership approach significantly improves detection accuracy while reducing analyst fatigue from alert overload.

The recent findings on AI-generated code quality highlight another critical dimension of human–AI collaboration in cybersecurity operations. As revealed in GitClear's 2024 research, the unchecked use of AI coding assistants has led to an alarming increase in code duplication and technical debt, with an eightfold rise in duplicated code blocks compared to two years prior (Doerrfeld, 2025). This phenomenon has significant implications for cybersecurity, where software quality directly impacts security posture. The research underscores that while AI can rapidly generate code, without proper human oversight, it often creates redundant, less maintainable systems that may introduce new vulnerabilities. This mirrors the concerns in cognitive security operations, where overreliance on AI systems without appropriate human guidance can lead to suboptimal outcomes. The observation that "I don't think I have ever seen so much technical debt being created in such a short period of time" from API evangelist Kin Lane emphasizes the urgency of developing proper human–AI teaming strategies in security development. Just as with security operations, the most effective approach to secure code development appears to be one where AI enhances human capabilities rather than replaces human judgment, with humans providing the strategic oversight needed to ensure code reusability, maintainability, and ultimately, security. This example from software development reinforces the broader principle that effective cybersecurity requires thoughtful integration of AI capabilities with human expertise, not blind automation.

Furthermore, software vulnerability patching times have increased dramatically, with the current average at 8.5 months—a 47% increase over five years and 327% higher than 15 years ago, according to Veracode's State of Software Security report (Coker, 2025). Half of organizations have critical security debt (high-severity vulnerabilities open for over a year), with 70% of this debt originating from third-party code and the software supply chain. While 56% of applications contain high-severity vulnerabilities, there's been an improvement in reducing OWASP Top 10 vulnerabilities, with 52% of apps now free of these flaws compared to 32% in 2020. This data directly connects to the discussion on human–AI teaming in cybersecurity, particularly regarding AI-generated code quality concerns. As GitClear's 2024 research shows an eightfold increase in code duplication from AI coding assistants, the vulnerability report highlights how increased reliance on third-party code and AI-generated code has contributed to longer fix times. Both findings emphasize that effective cybersecurity requires thoughtful integration of AI with human expertise rather than blind automation. The optimal approach involves AI enhancing human capabilities while humans provide strategic oversight to ensure code security, maintainability, and vulnerability management—creating a true collaborative partnership that leverages both human insight and AI capabilities.

In incident response scenarios, human–AI teaming can dramatically improve both speed and effectiveness. AI systems can quickly gather and correlate relevant data from multiple sources, providing human responders with comprehensive situation awareness. Human analysts can then make informed decisions about response strategies, while AI systems help execute and monitor response actions. This collaborative approach enables organizations to respond to incidents more quickly and effectively than either humans or AI systems could manage independently. The strategic value of human–AI teaming extends to threat hunting and proactive security measures. AI systems can identify subtle patterns and relationships across vast datasets that might indicate emerging threats or vulnerabilities, while human analysts can investigate these findings and develop innovative approaches to addressing new threat vectors. This combination of AI-powered analysis and human creativity enables organizations to stay ahead of evolving threats rather than merely reacting to known attacks.

Human–AI teaming strategies also provide organizations with a more comprehensive view of their security posture. AI systems can continuously assess and monitor security controls, compliance requirements, and potential vulnerabilities across the enterprise, while human analysts can evaluate this information in the context of business objectives and risk tolerance. This holistic approach helps organizations better understand their security landscape and make more informed decisions about security investments and priorities. The evolution of human–AI teaming in cybersecurity also contributes to organizational learning and improvement. AI systems can learn from human decisions and responses, building increasingly sophisticated models of effective security practices. Meanwhile, human analysts can gain new insights from AI analysis, identifying patterns and relationships that might not be apparent through traditional analysis methods. This mutual enhancement leads to continuously improving security capabilities over time.

From a workforce development perspective, effective human–AI teaming strategies can help organizations better utilize their security talent. Automating routine tasks and providing decision support for complex situations allows for strategies that enable security professionals to focus on higher-value activities that require human judgment and expertise. This not only improves job satisfaction and reduces burnout but also helps organizations maximize the impact of their security investments. In general, the implementation of human–AI teaming strategies also enables better knowledge management and institutional memory within security operations. AI systems can capture and organize insights from human analysts, making this knowledge available to support future decisions and responses. This helps organizations maintain consistent security practices even as team members change, while also facilitating the training and development of new security personnel.

Cognitive security operations is an emerging paradigm that aims to apply principles of human cognition and decision-making to cybersecurity processes (Grahn, 2024). The concept raises both excitement and concern within the security community, as it involves integrating advanced AI systems that attempt to mimic human cognitive processes in security decision-making. The hesitation around cognitive security operations often stems from concerns about relying too heavily on AI systems to make complex security decisions that traditionally required human judgment and intuition. One significant concern here is the potential for cognitive security operations to create a false sense of security. Implementing systems that attempt to replicate human cognitive processes might cause organizations to become overly reliant on automated decision-making in situations that require nuanced understanding or ethical considerations. There's also a valid concern about the ability of these systems to truly capture the complexity of human cognitive processes, particularly in high-stakes security situations. However, cognitive security operations also offer compelling benefits. These systems can potentially process and analyze security data in ways that more closely align with human thought patterns, making their outputs more intuitive and actionable for security analysts. They can help identify subtle patterns and relationships that might be missed by traditional security tools, while presenting information in ways that better match how humans naturally process and understand complex situations.

The implementation of cognitive security operations faces several technical challenges. Creating AI systems that can effectively model human cognitive processes in security contexts requires sophisticated algorithms and extensive training data (Sarker, 2022). These systems must be able to handle ambiguity, adapt to new situations, and make reasonable decisions with incomplete information—capabilities that are still evolving in AI systems. Integration with existing security operations is another significant challenge. Organizations must determine how to effectively combine cognitive security systems with traditional security tools and processes while maintaining operational efficiency and effectiveness. This includes developing clear protocols for when and how cognitive systems should be used in security decision-making. The future of cognitive security operations likely lies in finding the right balance between automation and human control, leveraging these systems' capabilities while acknowledging their limitations. Success will require careful attention to system design, implementation, and governance to ensure these advanced capabilities enhance rather than complicate security operations. The ethical implications of cognitive security operations also warrant careful consideration. Questions arise about accountability and responsibility when security decisions are influenced by systems attempting to replicate human cognition. Organizations must carefully balance the potential benefits of these systems with the need to maintain clear lines of accountability and ensure human oversight of critical security decisions. Looking ahead, cognitive security operations might find their most effective application as a complement to, rather than a replacement for, human security teams.

8.3 Advancements in XAI

The future of explainable AI (XAI) in cybersecurity is a critical frontier as organizations seek to build more transparent and accountable AI systems (Dwivedi et al., 2023). As AI models become more sophisticated and their decisions more consequential for security operations, the ability to understand and interpret these decisions becomes increasingly crucial. This section explores emerging developments in interpretable machine learning models and the growing role of causal AI in security analytics. These advancements promise to transform how organizations validate, trust, and implement AI-driven security solutions, moving beyond black-box approaches to create AI systems whose decision-making processes can be understood and verified. Understanding these developments is essential for organizations seeking to implement responsible and effective AI security solutions while maintaining necessary oversight and accountability.

Interpretable machine learning models are an important advancement in explainable AI, especially as organizations face increasing pressure to understand and justify AI-driven security decisions (Yapar, 2023). These models are designed from the ground up with transparency in mind, making their decision-making processes more accessible to human understanding. This shift toward interpretability becomes particularly important in security contexts where decisions can have significant consequences for organizations and individuals. The emergence of interpretable ML models aligns closely with upcoming regulatory requirements, especially the EU AI Act, Colorado AI Act (as discussed earlier), and similar legislation being developed worldwide. These regulations increasingly demand transparency and explainability in AI systems, especially in high-risk applications like security. Organizations implementing AI security solutions will need to demonstrate not just what decisions their systems make, but how and why they make them, making interpretable models increasingly valuable. In the context of generative AI security, interpretable models become crucial for understanding potential vulnerabilities and attack vectors. As these systems become more complex and powerful, the ability to understand their internal workings becomes essential for security professionals trying to protect them from manipulation or compromise. This understanding is also vital for detecting when generative AI systems might be being used maliciously or when they've been compromised.

The development of interpretable ML models does face challenges. There's often a perceived trade-off between model performance and interpretability, with some arguing that making models more transparent can limit their capabilities (Assis et al., 2025). Additionally, creating truly interpretable models for complex tasks like those involved in security operations can be technically challenging, requiring new approaches to model architecture and training. Hence, the importance of XAI in security contexts cannot be overstated. When AI systems make decisions about threat detection, access control, or incident response, security teams need to understand the reasoning behind these decisions to validate them and ensure they align with security policies and objectives. This understanding becomes particularly crucial when AI systems identify potential threats or anomalies, as security teams need to quickly evaluate and act on these findings.

Looking ahead, interpretable ML models are likely to become increasingly important as organizations face growing pressure to demonstrate responsible AI use. This includes being able to audit AI decisions, explain security actions to stakeholders, and demonstrate compliance with regulatory requirements. The ability to understand and explain AI decisions will become a crucial component of organizational security governance. The emergence of interpretable ML models also connects to broader trends in AI security, including the need for robust validation of AI systems and the ability to detect and prevent adversarial attacks (Rawal et al., 2021). Understanding how models make decisions can help organizations better protect them from manipulation and ensure they continue to operate as intended, even in adversarial conditions. From a practical implementation perspective, organizations will need to develop new skills and capabilities to effectively work with interpretable ML models. This includes training security teams to understand and interpret model outputs, developing new validation and testing procedures, and creating processes for incorporating model insights into security decision-making.

Causal AI in security analytics represents an emerging frontier that moves beyond traditional correlational analysis to understand the true cause-and-effect relationships in security events (Robert R Morton II, 2024). This advancement is significant because it helps security teams not just identify what happened, but understand why it happened and predict what might happen next. Thus, incorporating causal reasoning, these systems can provide deeper insights into security incidents, attack patterns, and system vulnerabilities. The application of causal AI in security analytics offers several benefits. Unlike traditional machine learning approaches that identify patterns based on correlation, causal AI can help organizations understand the actual mechanisms behind security incidents. This deeper understanding enables more effective incident response, better threat prediction, and more targeted security measures. For instance, rather than just flagging unusual network behavior, causal AI systems can help identify the chain of events that led to the anomaly and predict potential future consequences.

In the context of generative AI security, causal AI is valuable for understanding attack vectors and vulnerabilities (Sobien et al., 2025). Thus, analyzing cause-and-effect relationships in security incidents involving AI systems, organizations can better understand how these systems might be compromised or manipulated. This understanding is crucial for developing more effective protective measures and response strategies. However, implementing causal AI in security analytics faces several significant challenges. Building accurate causal models requires extensive data and sophisticated modeling techniques, particularly in complex security environments where multiple factors may interact in subtle ways. Additionally, validating causal relationships in security contexts can be difficult, as it's often impossible to conduct controlled experiments to verify causal hypotheses. The integration of causal AI with existing security analytics tools presents another challenge. Organizations need to develop new frameworks for combining causal insights with traditional security metrics and analysis methods. This includes creating new visualization tools and interfaces that can effectively communicate causal relationships to security teams.

Looking forward, causal AI in security analytics will likely become increasingly important as organizations seek to move from reactive to proactive security measures. The ability to understand and predict causal relationships in security events could enable more effective threat prevention and mitigation strategies. However, realizing this potential will require continued advances in both AI technology and our understanding of complex security systems. Moreover, the human factor in causal AI security analytics cannot be overlooked. Security teams will need new skills and training to effectively interpret and act on causal insights. Organizations must invest in developing these capabilities while ensuring that causal AI systems support rather than complicate human decision-making in security operations (Al-Surmi et al., 2022). From a research and development perspective, advancing causal AI in security analytics requires close collaboration between AI researchers, security experts, and domain specialists. This collaboration is essential for developing systems that can accurately model the complex causal relationships in modern security environments, while providing actionable insights for security teams.

8.4 The Role of Generative AI in Zero Trust

The integration of generative AI into Zero Trust architectures is an important and necessary development in cybersecurity, offering new capabilities for implementing and enhancing zero trust principles (Joshi, 2024). As organizations continue to adopt Zero Trust frameworks, generative AI technologies are powerful tools for strengthening security through more sophisticated authentication mechanisms, intelligent policy enforcement, and dynamic access control. This convergence enables organizations to move beyond static security rules to create more adaptive and responsive security environments that can better protect against evolving threats. Understanding how generative AI can enhance Zero Trust implementation is crucial for organizations seeking to strengthen their security posture while maintaining operational efficiency in increasingly complex IT environments.

Continuous authentication powered by generative AI moves beyond traditional point-in-time authentication to create dynamic, context-aware security validation (Ajish, 2024). Generative AI systems can analyze multiple factors simultaneously, including user behavior patterns, device characteristics, network conditions, and environmental factors, to continuously verify the legitimacy of access and activities within systems. The role of generative AI in continuous authentication becomes particularly powerful through its ability to learn and adapt to changing patterns of legitimate user behavior, while quickly identifying anomalies that might indicate security threats (Almagrabi & Khan, 2024). These systems can generate and update behavioral baselines for users and systems, creating more nuanced and accurate authentication mechanisms that reduce both false positives and false negatives in security monitoring. GAI enhances continuous authentication by enabling more sophisticated risk scoring and adaptive response mechanisms. Rather than relying on static rules or thresholds, these systems can generate dynamic risk assessments based on complex combinations of factors, adjusting authentication requirements in real-time based on perceived risk levels (Bailey, n.d.). This capability is crucial in today's threat landscape, where attack patterns and methods constantly evolve. The implementation of generative AI in continuous authentication also helps address one of the key challenges in Zero Trust architectures: maintaining security without impeding legitimate user activities. Consequently, by generating more accurate and context-aware authentication models, these systems can better balance security requirements with user experience, applying stricter controls only when warranted by risk factors.

Looking ahead, GAI will play an increasingly crucial role in continuous authentication as organizations face more sophisticated attacks and more complex operating environments. These systems will need to handle authentication across diverse devices, networks, and application environments, while maintaining consistent security standards. GAI's ability to adapt and learn from new scenarios makes it particularly valuable for this evolving challenge. The future of continuous authentication will likely see generative AI systems becoming more proactive in identifying potential security risks. Rather than just responding to observed behaviors, these systems might generate predictive models of potential attack patterns and preemptively adjust authentication requirements based on emerging threats. This predictive capability could help organizations stay ahead of potential security breaches while maintaining efficient operations.

From an implementation perspective, organizations need to carefully consider how to integrate GAI-powered continuous authentication into their existing security infrastructure. This includes establishing appropriate monitoring and oversight mechanisms, ensuring privacy compliance, and maintaining clear audit trails of authentication decisions. The success of these implementations will depend on finding the right balance between automated decision-making and human oversight. The adoption of generative AI in continuous authentication also requires organizations to develop new capabilities and expertise. Security teams need to understand how these systems work, how to interpret their outputs, and how to tune them for optimal performance. This includes developing new processes for validating authentication models, investigating potential security incidents, and maintaining system effectiveness over time.

Another important aspect for AI in ZTA is security policy enforcement (Ajish, 2024). GAI plays (and will continue to play) a crucial role in creating and adapting security policies in real-time. These systems can analyze complex patterns of behavior, system states, and environmental factors to generate and enforce security policies that are both more comprehensive and more nuanced than traditional static policies. This dynamic approach is essential for maintaining effective security in modern IT environments, where conditions and threats constantly change. GAI enhances security policy enforcement by creating adaptive policies that respond to changing conditions while maintaining consistency with overall security objectives. Rather than relying on rigid, predefined rules, these systems can generate and modify policies based on observed patterns, emerging threats, and organizational requirements. This capability is very valuable in Zero Trust environments, where security decisions must be made continuously and contextually. The integration of GAI in policy enforcement also enables better handling of edge cases and unusual situations (Dhoni & Kumar, 2023). Traditional policy enforcement systems often struggle with scenarios that don't clearly match predefined rules, leading to either overly restrictive or overly permissive access decisions. GAI can help bridge this gap by generating appropriate responses to novel situations while maintaining alignment with security principles.

Let's think of a hypothetical example in a healthcare organization where a hospital implements a generative AI-driven security policy enforcement system as part of their Zero Trust architecture. The system continuously monitors and analyzes patterns of data access across different departments, user roles, and time periods, adapting its policies in real-time. When an emergency room doctor attempts to access patient records outside their usual department during a crisis situation, the system springs into action with sophisticated response mechanisms. It immediately generates a contextual risk assessment considering multiple factors such as time of access, location, patient status, and department relationships. Based on this assessment, the system can create temporary access policies that carefully balance immediate medical needs with security requirements. It then implements appropriate compensating controls, such as enhanced logging or requiring postaccess justification, while simultaneously learning from these emergency access patterns to adjust future policy generations. This dynamic approach ensures that critical medical care is not impeded while maintaining robust security controls and building more intelligent responses for future similar situations.

The system can also identify and respond to potential policy violations more effectively. Rather than simply blocking access or generating alerts, it can create graduated response policies based on the nature and context of the violation (O'Brien et al., 2023). This might include implementing additional authentication requirements, limiting access scope, or triggering specific monitoring protocols. Looking forward, generative AI will likely play an increasingly important role in security policy enforcement as organizations face more complex security challenges. These systems will need to handle policy generation and enforcement across hybrid environments, multiple cloud providers, and diverse application ecosystems, while maintaining consistent security standards and compliance requirements. Overall, the success of AI-driven policy enforcement depends on maintaining appropriate human oversight and control. Organizations need to establish clear frameworks for reviewing and validating AI-generated policies, ensuring they align with business objectives and compliance requirements, while maintaining effective security controls. This includes developing processes for auditing policy decisions and maintaining accountability for security outcomes.

Dynamic access control is another enhancement made possible by GAI and moves beyond static access rules to create truly adaptive security environments (Ike et al., 2021). GAI systems can analyze vast amounts of real-time data to make sophisticated access decisions that consider context, behavior patterns, risk levels, and environmental factors, enabling more nuanced and effective access control mechanisms that adapt to changing conditions while maintaining security. The integration of generative AI in dynamic access control really becomes crucial as organizations face increasingly complex IT environments and sophisticated threats. Traditional static access control mechanisms, even when implemented within a Zero Trust framework, often struggle to handle the complexity of modern working environments, where access needs can change rapidly based on projects, roles, and business requirements. Generative AI helps bridge this gap by creating and adapting access control policies in real-time based on learned patterns and emerging situations.

GAI's role in dynamic access control becomes particularly valuable in handling edge cases and unusual situations that might not fit predefined access rules (Khan et al., 2025). These systems can generate appropriate responses to novel situations by analyzing patterns and contextual information, ensuring security while maintaining business continuity. This capability is essential in Zero Trust architectures, where every access request must be validated while still enabling legitimate business operations. The necessity of GAI in Zero Trust implementations becomes clear when considering the volume and complexity of access decisions that modern organizations must make. Without GAI-driven capabilities, organizations would struggle to implement true Zero Trust principles at scale, potentially leading to either overly restrictive policies that impede business operations or overly permissive ones that create security vulnerabilities. GAI helps organizations find the right balance by creating and enforcing dynamic access policies that adapt to changing conditions while maintaining security standards.

When it comes to looking forward, the role of GAI in dynamic access control will likely expand as organizations face more complex security challenges and regulatory requirements. These systems will need to handle access decisions across hybrid environments, multiple cloud providers, and diverse application ecosystems, while maintaining consistent security standards. The ability of generative

AI to learn and adapt to new scenarios makes it particularly valuable for addressing these evolving challenges. The success of dynamic access control in Zero Trust architectures increasingly depends on sophisticated AI capabilities that can process and act upon complex combinations of factors in real-time. This includes analyzing user behavior patterns, device characteristics, network conditions, data sensitivity, and business context to make informed access decisions. Without GAI's ability to process and act upon these multiple factors simultaneously, organizations would struggle to implement effective Zero Trust controls at scale.

8.5 Micromodels

Micromodels are another emergence in the AI and cybersecurity field that we should discuss. They offer a more focused and efficient approach to specific security tasks compared to large, general-purpose AI models. These specialized, smaller AI models are designed to excel at particular security functions while requiring fewer computational resources and potentially offering better security control (Encord, n.d.). For cybersecurity professionals, micromodels present an opportunity to implement more targeted and manageable AI solutions for specific security challenges. At their core, micromodels are purpose-built AI systems that focus on specific security tasks rather than trying to be generalists (Landau, 2021). Unlike large language models or comprehensive security platforms, these models are trained on narrow datasets relevant to their specific function. This specialization often results in better performance for their intended purpose while being more resource-efficient and easier to secure. For example, a micromodel might be specifically designed to detect particular types of malware behavior, analyze specific network traffic patterns, or identify certain categories of security threats.

Now, let's analyze from the triangular perspective that we have adopted in this book: how it can be used as a tool, a weapon, and how it is also a target. The advantages (or tool ability) of micromodels for cybersecurity professionals are significant. First, these models are typically easier to understand and validate than larger, more complex systems. Security teams can better assess how these models make decisions and identify potential vulnerabilities or biases in their operation. Second, micromodels often require less computational power and resources to operate, making them more practical for organizations with limited infrastructure (Lexalytics, n.d.). Third, their focused nature makes them easier to update and maintain, allowing for quicker responses to new threats or changes in the security landscape.

However, the potential for malicious actors to leverage (or weaponize) micromodels presents new security challenges. Attackers might develop specialized micromodels for specific attack vectors, such as generating targeted phishing content, analyzing defensive systems, or automating certain aspects of attacks. These models could be more difficult to detect and defend against because of their focused nature and smaller footprint. Additionally, attackers might use multiple micromodels in concert to create more sophisticated attack chains while maintaining better operational security than they could with larger, more detectable AI systems.

The vulnerabilities of micromodels themselves make them a target. While their specialized nature can make them more efficient and effective, it can also make them more susceptible to certain types of attacks. For instance, these models might be more vulnerable to adversarial inputs specifically crafted to exploit their narrow focus. Their training data might also be easier to poison since it's more concentrated on specific types of information. Additionally, the very specificity that makes them effective could potentially make their behavior more predictable to attackers who understand their design.

From a defensive perspective, organizations need to carefully consider how they implement and protect their micromodels. This includes maintaining strict control over training data, regularly validating model performance, and implementing appropriate security controls around model deployment and use. Organizations should also consider implementing multiple layers of validation, possibly using different types of models to cross-check results and reduce the risk of successful attacks against any single model. The future trend toward micromodels in AI security likely means a shift toward more modular and specialized security architectures. Organizations might deploy multiple micromodels working in concert, each handling specific security functions while contributing to the overall security posture. This approach could offer better control and flexibility than relying on larger, more monolithic AI systems, while potentially providing better security through compartmentalization and specialization.

The implications for security operations are significant. Security teams will need to develop expertise in managing and coordinating multiple specialized AI models rather than working with single, comprehensive systems. This includes understanding how different models interact, maintaining appropriate security controls for each model, and ensuring effective coordination between various specialized systems.

Looking ahead, the evolution of micromodels in security applications will likely continue to accelerate. This is especially true as legislation and standards move toward data minimization principles (vs. just focusing on data privacy). As organizations better understand the advantages and limitations of these specialized systems, we might see new frameworks and best practices emerge for implementing and securing micromodels in security contexts. This could include standardized approaches for model validation, security testing, and operational deployment. The challenge for security professionals will be balancing the benefits of micromodels with their potential risks and limitations. This includes careful consideration of where specialized models are most appropriate, how to secure them effectively, and how to integrate them into broader security architectures. Organizations will need to develop clear strategies for implementing and managing micromodels while maintaining robust security controls and operational efficiency. The success of micromodels in security applications will largely depend on how well organizations can address these challenges while leveraging the advantages these specialized systems offer. This includes developing appropriate expertise, implementing effective security controls, and maintaining awareness of both the capabilities and limitations of these systems in security contexts.

8.6 AI and Blockchain

The convergence of AI and blockchain is an exciting frontier and an emerging trend in cybersecurity—creating both new opportunities for enhanced security and novel challenges that defenders must address. This intersection is especially interesting as these technologies can complement each other in powerful ways, while also potentially introducing new vulnerabilities and attack vectors. Blockchain's inherent characteristics of immutability, transparency, and distributed consensus can potentially enhance the security and trustworthiness of AI systems, while AI can improve the efficiency and security of blockchain networks (Hussain & Al-Turjman, 2021). For instance, AI systems could help optimize blockchain operations, detect potential security issues in smart contracts, and identify suspicious transaction patterns, while blockchain could provide a transparent and immutable record of AI model updates, training data, and decision processes.

The integration and intersection of these technologies in cybersecurity applications have a lot of possibilities. Consider how blockchain could be used to create immutable audit trails of AI system behaviors and decisions, making it easier to detect and investigate potential compromises or manipulations of AI systems. Similarly, AI could be used to enhance blockchain security by identifying potential vulnerabilities in smart contracts, detecting unusual transaction patterns that might indicate attacks, and optimizing network performance. Generative AI adds another dimension to this convergence, potentially enabling the creation of more sophisticated security measures while also introducing new security challenges. For example, generative AI could be used to create and test new security protocols or generate synthetic data for training security systems, while blockchain could provide a secure and transparent way to track and validate these generated artifacts.

The cryptocurrency landscape is a great example of how these technologies intersect in practice. Cryptocurrency networks already rely heavily on blockchain technology, but the integration of AI and generative AI is creating new possibilities and challenges (Brewer et al., 2024). AI systems can be used to detect fraudulent transactions, identify potential security vulnerabilities, and optimize trading strategies. However, this same capability could be exploited by attackers to identify vulnerabilities in cryptocurrency systems or automate sophisticated attacks. The use of generative AI in cryptocurrency markets adds another layer of complexity, as these systems could be used to generate convincing fake market signals or manipulate trading patterns in ways that might be difficult to detect.

However, the emergence of new attack vectors at the intersection of these technologies is a significant concern. Attackers might leverage the combination of AI and blockchain to create more sophisticated and harder-to-detect attacks (Ullah et al., 2024). As an example, they might use AI to identify vulnerabilities in blockchain systems, generate convincing fake transactions, or create automated attack systems that operate across multiple blockchain networks. The decentralized nature of blockchain systems could make it harder to detect and respond to these AI-powered attacks, while the potential for AI systems to be compromised or manipulated could undermine the security guarantees that blockchain provides (Lwanga & Raza, 2023). However, these emerging technologies also provide new opportunities for cyber defenders. The combination of AI and blockchain could enable more sophisticated and reliable security measures. For example, blockchain could be used to create tamper-proof records of AI model training and updates, making it easier to detect potential compromises or unauthorized modifications. AI systems could continuously monitor blockchain networks for suspicious activities, identifying potential attacks before they can cause significant damage. The ability to combine these technologies in novel ways could give defenders new tools for protecting against emerging threats. The potential for these technologies to create entirely new security paradigms is interesting to explore. We might see the emergence of AI-powered security systems that operate across decentralized networks, using blockchain to ensure transparency and accountability while leveraging generative AI to adapt and evolve in response to new threats. This could lead to more resilient and adaptive security systems that can better protect against sophisticated attacks while maintaining transparency and trust.

Essentially, the continued evolution and convergence of these technologies will likely create both new security challenges and opportunities. Organizations will need to stay informed about these developments and be prepared to adapt their security strategies accordingly. This includes understanding how different technologies can be combined effectively while maintaining appropriate security controls and risk management measures. The key will be finding ways to leverage the strengths of each technology while mitigating their potential vulnerabilities and limitations. The success of organizations in navigating this evolving landscape will largely depend on their ability to understand and effectively implement these converging technologies. This requires not just technical expertise in individual technologies but also an understanding of how they can be combined effectively and securely. Organizations will need to develop new skills and capabilities while maintaining awareness of both the opportunities and risks these technologies present.

The implications for the future of cybersecurity are significant. As these technologies continue to evolve and converge, we'll likely see the emergence of new security paradigms that combine elements of AI, blockchain, and other emerging technologies in novel ways. This could lead to more effective and resilient security measures, but it will also require ongoing adaptation and evolution of security practices to address new challenges and threats. Organizations that can effectively leverage these converging technologies while maintaining appropriate security controls will be better positioned to protect against evolving cyber threats. However, it's crucial to maintain a balanced perspective on these developments. While the convergence of AI, blockchain, and other emerging technologies offers exciting possibilities for enhanced security, it also introduces new complexities and potential vulnerabilities that must be carefully managed. Organizations need to approach these technologies thoughtfully, considering both their potential benefits and risks while maintaining appropriate security controls and risk management measures

8.7 Artificial General Intelligence (AGI)

The emergence of artificial general intelligence (AGI) is another future reality and transformative milestone in the field of AI, one that holds profound implications for security and society at large. Google DeepMind predicts that AGI could be here as soon as 2030 (Dragan et al., 2025). Unlike narrow AI, which is designed to perform specific tasks within defined parameters, AGI has the theoretical capacity to think, learn, and reason at a level comparable to or exceeding human intelligence (Morris et al., 2023). This shift from task-oriented systems to generalized intelligence introduces both extraordinary opportunities and unprecedented risks. Recent investments, such as the $500 billion allocated to Stargate—a groundbreaking AGI initiative—underscore the magnitude of this frontier (OpenAI, 2025a). While the potential applications of AGI are vast and varied, the full implications of its integration into modern society and the cyber landscape remain elusive. Yet, it is possible to analyze AGI's role through the lens of its potential as a tool, a weapon, and a target, offering a glimpse into the future of AI security.

As a tool, AGI promises to redefine the capabilities of cybersecurity by enabling adaptive, autonomous, and highly intelligent systems. Unlike traditional AI, AGI could independently identify and respond to threats in real-time, continually evolving its defenses based on new data and tactics (Rayhan et al., 2023). The level of sophistication AGI brings would be unparalleled, with the ability to process vast amounts of information, recognize intricate patterns, and predict emerging threats with astonishing accuracy. AGI-driven security systems could mitigate zero-day vulnerabilities faster than human analysts, neutralize large-scale cyberattacks before they cause damage, and offer unparalleled resilience against sophisticated threats. Furthermore, AGI could democratize advanced cybersecurity measures, making them accessible to smaller organizations that lack the resources to employ dedicated security teams. For governments, AGI systems could safeguard critical infrastructure, monitor complex digital ecosystems, and even serve as a stabilizing force in international relations by reducing the potential for human error in threat detection and decision-making.

However, the very same capabilities that make AGI a revolutionary tool also make it an immensely powerful weapon. In the wrong hands, AGI could amplify the scale and impact of cyberattacks to catastrophic levels. Malicious actors equipped with AGI could deploy autonomous systems capable of executing advanced persistent threats, conducting large-scale social engineering campaigns, or compromising entire networks without human intervention. The ability of AGI to learn and adapt means that it could evade traditional defenses, continually refine its tactics, and exploit vulnerabilities with surgical precision. For instance, an AGI-powered disinformation campaign could manipulate global public opinion, destabilize economies, or provoke geopolitical conflicts. Unlike current AI, which requires substantial human oversight to execute complex attacks, AGI would have the potential to operate independently, blurring the lines between attacker and machine. The scale of devastation such systems could unleash may be difficult to quantify, but the potential consequences are sobering.

Equally concerning is the notion of AGI as a target. The inherent complexity and power of AGI systems make them an attractive focal point for attackers seeking to exploit their capabilities or undermine their integrity. If compromised, an AGI system could become a weapon against its creators, redirecting its intelligence toward malicious purposes. Threat actors might attempt to infiltrate AGI training pipelines, introducing subtle biases or vulnerabilities that could influence the system's behavior in unpredictable ways. Alternatively, adversaries could target the underlying infrastructure supporting AGI, such as data centers or communication networks, to cripple its functionality. The risk of AGI being hijacked by nefarious actors raises profound ethical and practical questions about how to secure systems that may be more intelligent than their defenders. Even more alarming is the potential for AGI to be exploited in ways that undermine trust in its applications, whether through deliberate sabotage or the dissemination of counterfeit AGI outputs designed to deceive and mislead.

In the cybersecurity field, AGI's impact will likely transcend existing paradigms, creating a landscape defined by unprecedented complexity and unpredictability. As a tool, AGI could revolutionize incident response, providing organizations with the ability to anticipate and neutralize threats before they materialize. It could enable continuous, context-aware monitoring of digital environments, automating the detection and resolution of vulnerabilities with minimal human intervention. AGI could also assist in regulatory compliance, dynamically adapting to evolving legal and ethical standards while providing real-time assessments of organizational risk. Yet, the potential for misuse remains a sobering reality. As a weapon, AGI could magnify existing threats, introducing new vectors of attack that exploit its ability to reason and strategize. For example, an AGI system designed to mimic human behavior could infiltrate networks disguised as legitimate users, bypassing even the most sophisticated authentication mechanisms. Despite the transformative potential of AGI, there is a profound lack of clarity regarding how it will reshape industries, alter power dynamics, and challenge existing frameworks of trust and security. This uncertainty is particularly pronounced in the cyber domain, where the boundaries between defense, offense, and exploitation are increasingly fluid.

The role of AGI as a target introduces another layer of complexity. As organizations increasingly rely on AGI systems for critical operations, the consequences of their compromise grow exponentially. A single breach of an AGI system could cascade through interconnected networks, disrupting supply chains, financial systems, or national defense infrastructure. The risks extend beyond technical vulnerabilities, encompassing ethical dilemmas about accountability, transparency, and control. Who bears responsibility when an AGI system fails or is exploited? How can societies ensure that AGI aligns with human values and priorities in the face of malicious intent? These questions remain unanswered, underscoring the need for robust frameworks that anticipate and address the multifaceted challenges posed by AGI.

The triangular perspective of AGI as a tool, weapon, and target highlights the triangular aspect of its development. While its potential to revolutionize cybersecurity is immense, so too are the risks associated with its misuse and exploitation. As AGI continues to evolve, it is crucial to adopt a proactive approach to its governance, fostering collaboration between governments, industry leaders, and academia to navigate the challenges and opportunities ahead. Although the full implications of AGI remain uncertain, its potential to reshape the cyber landscape is undeniable and something important to follow.

Meta's introduced a Frontier AI Framework, which establishes a risk-based approach to AI development and deployment, and theoretical discussions about AGI's potential impact on cybersecurity (Wiggers, 2025). Meta's framework specifically identifies "high risk" and "critical risk" systems that could enable catastrophic outcomes like cybersecurity or biological attacks, pledging to either limit access to such systems or halt their development entirely. This practical policy approach is notable given Meta's previous commitment to open AI development, suggesting a shift in how major tech companies are balancing innovation with security concerns. This development relates significantly to the broader discussion of AGI's role in cybersecurity through the lens of tool, weapon, and target. Meta's framework essentially acknowledges the dual-use nature of advanced AI systems while adding crucial nuance about risk levels and appropriate controls. The framework aligns with the theoretical concerns about AGI's potential as both a powerful security tool and a dangerous weapon, particularly in its recognition that some capabilities may be too risky to release openly. This is important given incidents with companies like DeepSeek, where insufficient safeguards led to harmful applications of AI technology. The aforementioned suggests that major tech companies are beginning to implement more nuanced and responsible approaches to AI development, moving beyond simple open-versus-closed debates to more sophisticated risk-based frameworks that consider the full spectrum of potential impacts and vulnerabilities. The convergence of theoretical concerns about AGI security with practical policy implement stations by major tech companies indicates a maturing understanding of AI risk management and security implications, especially as we move closer to more advanced AI capabilities.

Recent statements from Google DeepMind further underscore the accelerating timeline for AGI development, with experts like Anca Dragan and Shane Legg suggesting that AGI could emerge "within the coming years" (Dragan et al., 2025). Their comprehensive approach to AGI safety focuses on four key risk areas: misuse, misalignment, accidents, and structural risks. Thus, this mirrors the tool, weapon, and target framework in cybersecurity contexts. Google DeepMind's efforts include implementing sophisticated security mechanisms to prevent malicious actors from bypassing safety guardrails, developing monitoring systems that can detect misaligned AI behaviors, and conducting research on deceptive alignment, where AI systems might deliberately circumvent human safety measures. This systematic approach to AGI safety, alongside Meta's Frontier AI Framework, demonstrates a growing industry consensus that the extraordinary potential of AGI must be balanced with equally robust safety measures and governance frameworks, particularly as development timelines compress and capabilities advance toward human-level intelligence.

8.8 Digital Twins

The rapid emergence of digital twin technology is a shift in how we model and interact with complex systems (Soltanshahi & Hosseini, 2024). However, its intersection with GAI security remains largely unexplored territory. The relative novelty of sophisticated digital twin implementations means that many security implications and potential vulnerabilities are still being discovered, creating a complex landscape where best practices and security frameworks are evolving alongside the technology itself. Security researchers find themselves in the challenging position of developing protective measures for systems whose full capabilities and vulnerabilities may not yet be fully understood. The nascent state of digital twin technology in GAI contexts presents unique security challenges, as organizations must make critical decisions about implementation and security without the benefit of extensive historical data or established security patterns (Chen et al., 2024a). Traditional security models may prove insufficient for protecting these sophisticated virtual replicas, which often combine elements of physical system modeling, real-time data processing, and complex AI interactions in ways that weren't previously possible (Somma, et al., 2023). The integration of digital twins with GAI systems creates novel attack surfaces and potential vulnerability combinations that security professionals are still working to fully comprehend and address.

The security implications become more complex when considering how digital twins might influence the development and deployment of future GAI systems. Digital twin technology enables unprecedented levels of system modeling and testing, potentially accelerating GAI development in ways that could outpace our ability to implement adequate security measures (Hu et al., 2021). Security researchers face the dual challenge of protecting current digital twin implementations while also anticipating how these systems might evolve and what new vulnerabilities might emerge as the technology matures. As aforementioned, we will face multifaceted security implications for generative AI systems, as they create detailed virtual replicas of physical systems, infrastructure, and processes. These high-fidelity simulations offer unprecedented capabilities for modeling complex systems and predicting their behavior, making them powerful tools for enhancing GAI safety testing and validation (Wagg et al., 2020). The extensive data collection and real-time monitoring inherent in digital twin implementations enable GAI systems to learn from and adapt to operational conditions while maintaining a safe testing environment, separated from critical physical infrastructure. Security researchers can leverage digital twins to probe potential failure modes and adversarial scenarios without risking damage to actual systems.

The defensive applications of digital twins extend beyond testing, as they enable the development of more robust GAI systems through continuous simulation and refinement of safety mechanisms. Digital twins can serve as early warning systems by detecting anomalous patterns that might indicate security breaches or system vulnerabilities, allowing for preemptive intervention before issues manifest in physical systems (Wang et al., 2023). The ability to run countless scenarios and stress tests in parallel provides valuable insights into edge cases and potential failure modes that might otherwise go unnoticed until deployment. These same capabilities that make digital twins valuable for security testing also make them attractive targets for malicious actors seeking to compromise GAI systems. Adversaries could potentially exploit digital twins to extract sensitive information about system architectures, identify vulnerabilities, or develop more sophisticated attack vectors (Zemskov et al., 2024). The comprehensive nature of digital twin implementations means that a successful breach could provide attackers with detailed insights into both physical and digital aspects of target systems, potentially enabling more coordinated and effective attacks across multiple domains. The interconnected nature of digital twins and their physical counterparts creates new attack surfaces that must be carefully secured.

The offensive potential of digital twins in the context of GAI security cannot be overlooked, as they could be weaponized to develop and refine attack strategies against target systems. Malicious actors might create digital twins of victim systems to test and perfect their attack methodologies before launching actual operations, significantly increasing their chances of success (Homaei et al., 2024). These capabilities could enable more sophisticated forms of social engineering, system manipulation, and coordinated attacks that leverage insights gained from detailed simulation environments. The ability to model complex system interactions could allow attackers to identify and exploit subtle vulnerabilities that might not be apparent through traditional security testing methods.

Digital twins are very attractive targets for malicious actors due to the comprehensive system insights and attack opportunities they provide. The detailed virtual replicas maintained within digital twin systems often contain sensitive information about critical infrastructure, operational processes, and system vulnerabilities that could be exploited for devastating effects (Qian et al., 2022). Sophisticated attackers might target these systems to gain a deep understanding of facility operations, security measures, and system dependencies without risking detection through direct physical reconnaissance. Moreover, the interconnected nature of digital twins creates cascading vulnerability concerns, as compromising a digital twin could provide attackers with detailed knowledge of both physical and cyber components of target systems. Malicious actors could leverage this information to orchestrate more precise and effective attacks, using the digital twin's own simulation capabilities to test and refine their attack strategies before deploying them against physical targets. The real-time data streams and system monitoring capabilities integral to digital twin implementations could be subverted to provide attackers with continuous intelligence about target operations and security postures. High-fidelity digital twins often incorporate vast amounts of sensitive operational data, proprietary algorithms, and detailed system specifications that make them valuable targets for industrial espionage and intellectual property theft (Hafeez et al., 2024). Organizations that maintain digital twins of manufacturing processes, supply chains, or critical infrastructure must contend with the possibility that these virtual replicas could be exploited to extract valuable trade secrets or sensitive operational information (Dodiya et al., 2024). The comprehensive nature of digital twin implementations means that a successful breach could provide attackers with unprecedented insights into organizational operations and vulnerabilities.

The targeting of digital twins raises concerns in contexts where these systems are integrated with GAI capabilities. Compromising these implementations could provide attackers with detailed insights into AI system architectures, training data, and operational parameters. Malicious actors might exploit this information to develop more sophisticated adversarial attacks against AI systems or to manipulate AI decision-making processes in subtle ways that could be difficult to detect. The potential for attackers to leverage compromised digital twins to influence or subvert GAI systems represents a significant security concern that organizations must carefully consider when implementing these technologies. Prevention of digital twin targeting requires multilayered security approaches that protect not only the digital twin systems themselves but also the extensive data collection and communication infrastructure that supports them (Alcaraz & Lopez, 2022). Ultimately, these considerations underscore the critical importance of implementing robust security measures around digital twin implementations, particularly when integrated with GAI systems. Organizations must carefully balance the benefits of detailed system modeling against the potential security risks, implementing appropriate access controls, encryption, and monitoring systems to protect sensitive digital twin data and functionality. The development of security frameworks specifically designed for digital twin implementations in GAI contexts is (and should be) an emerging priority for the cybersecurity community.

8.9 Agentic AI

Agentic AI is another evolution in AI, where systems exhibit increased autonomy, goal-directed behavior, and the ability to make independent decisions while interacting with their environment (Ogbu, 2023). These systems go beyond traditional AI by incorporating sophisticated decision-making capabilities, learning from interactions, and adapting their behavior based on experience and context. In the cybersecurity landscape, agentic AI introduces new possibilities and challenges that must be understood through the triangular framework of tool, weapon, and target. From a technical perspective, agentic AI systems typically combine multiple AI architectures, including reinforcement learning, deep neural networks, and advanced planning algorithms (Putta et al., 2024). These systems maintain internal models of their environment and objectives, using these models to plan and execute actions while learning from their outcomes. Unlike traditional AI systems that follow predetermined rules or patterns, agentic AI can develop novel approaches to achieving its objectives, making it both more powerful and potentially more unpredictable (Hu et al., 2024).

As a tool, agentic AI offers unprecedented capabilities for cybersecurity defense. These systems can operate with greater autonomy in threat detection and response, making independent decisions about potential security incidents while continuously learning from their experiences. For example, an agentic AI security system might independently investigate suspicious activities, correlating information from multiple sources and initiating appropriate response actions without constant human oversight. The system's ability to learn and adapt means it can become more effective over time, developing a sophisticated understanding of normal versus suspicious behavior patterns. The defensive capabilities of agentic AI extend to proactive security measures. These systems can autonomously conduct security assessments, identify potential vulnerabilities, and even generate and test patches or security improvements. Their ability to operate independently allows for continuous security monitoring and improvement, potentially identifying and addressing security issues before they can be exploited by attackers.

However, the weaponization of agentic AI presents significant concerns. Malicious actors could deploy autonomous agents capable of conducting sophisticated cyberattacks, adapting their strategies based on target responses and security measures (Khan et al., 2024). These attack agents might operate independently for extended periods, learning from each attempt and developing increasingly effective attack methods. Their ability to make independent decisions and adapt their behavior makes them particularly dangerous, as they could identify and exploit vulnerabilities in ways that might not be predictable or easily defendable. The potential for weaponized agentic AI becomes even more concerning when considering their ability to coordinate and share information. Multiple attack agents might work together, sharing learned information about vulnerabilities or successful attack techniques while maintaining independent operation. This distributed approach to attacks could make them particularly difficult to detect and counter.

As targets themselves, agentic AI systems present unique vulnerabilities and security challenges (Chan et al., 2023). Their autonomous nature and ability to learn from interactions make them potentially susceptible to manipulation through carefully crafted inputs or interactions. Attackers might attempt to poison their learning processes, manipulate their decision-making, or exploit their autonomous behaviors in ways that serve malicious purposes. The security of agentic AI systems becomes increasingly crucial when considering their potential impact on organizational security. A compromised autonomous security agent might not just fail to protect systems but could actively work against security objectives, potentially causing significant damage before the compromise is detected. Organizations must implement robust security measures to protect these systems, including careful monitoring of their behavior and decisions.

OWASP's Guide to Agentic AI Security outlines 15 major threats to agentic AI systems, each representing distinct but interconnected security challenges (OWASP, 2025). At the foundation are memory-based threats like Memory Poisoning (T1), where attackers corrupt an AI's stored information to manipulate its decision-making processes, and Tool Misuse (T2), where authorized tools are manipulated through deceptive prompts. These basic attack vectors are complemented by system-level threats like Privilege Compromise (T3) and Resource Overload (T4), which target the AI's operational infrastructure and computational resources. Several threats specifically exploit AI cognitive processes. Cascading Hallucination Attacks (T5) take advantage of the AI's tendency to generate and propagate false information, while Intent Breaking & Goal Manipulation (T6) and Misaligned & Deceptive Behaviors (T7) focus on corrupting the AI's objectives and decision-making processes. These cognitive attacks are particularly concerning because they can be difficult to detect and can lead to systemic failures across the AI system.

Multiagent system threats form another critical category. Agent Communication Poisoning (T12) and Rogue Agents in Multi-Agent Systems (T13) highlight the vulnerabilities that emerge when multiple AI agents interact. Identity Spoofing & Impersonation (T9) and Repudiation & Untraceability (T8) focus on authentication and accountability issues. The human element in AI security surfaces through threats like Overwhelming Human-in-the-Loop (T10), Human Attacks on Multi-Agent Systems (T14), and Human Manipulation (T15), which exploit the interface between human operators and AI systems. Technical threats like Unexpected RCE and Code Attacks (T11) round out the taxonomy, highlighting how traditional cybersecurity vulnerabilities can manifest in new ways within agentic AI systems. Together, these 15 threats form a comprehensive framework for understanding the security challenges facing agentic AI systems, spanning from low-level technical vulnerabilities to high-level cognitive and social engineering attacks.

OpenAI's recent introduction of "Operator," an advanced AI agent, marks a significant leap in how AI interacts with web-based graphical user interfaces (GUIs)

(OpenAI, 2025b). Powered by the Computer-Using Agent (CUA) model, Operator combines GPT-4's vision capabilities with sophisticated reinforcement learning-based reasoning. This allows it to interpret screenshots, execute actions like typing, clicking, and scrolling, and perform complex online tasks such as booking tickets or managing online orders. Operator demonstrates the potential of CUAs to revolutionize task automation. Its design prioritizes user safety, incorporating self-correction mechanisms and requesting user intervention for critical or sensitive actions. Collaborations with companies such as DoorDash, Instacart, and Uber further enhance its real-world applicability, while plans for broader integration into ChatGPT aim to make these capabilities more accessible. Despite its transformative potential, challenges remain, especially with complex interfaces, highlighting the need for ongoing development and refinement.

In the context of GAI security, CUAs like Operator can serve as tools, weapons, and targets, underscoring the importance of comprehensive risk assessments and mitigation strategies. As tools, CUAs offer unparalleled efficiency in automating repetitive or intricate tasks, streamlining workflows across industries. In cybersecurity, for example, CUAs could analyze vast datasets to identify potential threats, automate routine security measures, and augment human capabilities in monitoring and response. This transformative functionality can bolster organizational productivity and resilience, making CUAs valuable assets in enhancing operational efficiency and decision-making. However, the dual-use nature of these agents raises significant concerns about their potential misuse as weapons. Bad actors could exploit CUAs to conduct cyberattacks, from unauthorized data extraction to sophisticated system disruptions. Their ability to mimic human interactions on GUIs could be harnessed for phishing schemes, financial fraud, or the deployment of ransomware. The malicious use of CUAs could exacerbate existing security challenges, as they offer tools to automate and scale cyberattacks, making them more pervasive and difficult to counter.

Simultaneously, CUAs are not immune to threats themselves, as they represent appealing targets for adversaries. Attackers could aim to compromise CUAs to manipulate their functionality or outputs, leading to unauthorized actions, data breaches, or systemic vulnerabilities. A compromised CUA could become a vector for cascading failures, undermining not only individual systems but also the broader infrastructure they support. This potential for exploitation highlights the critical need for robust security frameworks tailored to CUAs. Effective measures could include embedding safeguards to detect and prevent malicious use, establishing rigorous monitoring systems to track CUA activity, and implementing regulatory guidelines to ensure their safe and ethical deployment. Moreover, continuous advancements in AI security tools, such as anomaly detection and AI-driven intrusion prevention systems, could play a vital role in protecting CUAs against evolving threats. In general, while CUAs like Operator showcase the transformative potential of AI in task automation and decision-making, it clearly introduces complex security considerations.

OpenAI's Operator case study illustrates two major threats from the OWASP framework: Tool Misuse (T2) and Human Manipulation (T15). Tool Misuse emerges as the dominant concern in the context of CUAs like Operator, which can be manipulated to misuse their legitimate capabilities. The case explicitly highlights how malicious actors could exploit these systems to conduct cyberattacks, ranging from unauthorized data extraction to sophisticated system disruptions. The CUAs' ability to interact with graphical interfaces through basic actions like typing, clicking, and scrolling creates a powerful attack vector where authorized tools can be manipulated for malicious purposes while appearing to operate within their granted permissions. Human Manipulation is another threat here, as the Operator study explores how CUAs' ability to mimic human interactions on graphical interfaces could be weaponized for phishing schemes, financial fraud, or ransomware deployment. This capability directly relates to the OWASP-identified threat of exploiting user trust in AI systems to influence human decision-making without awareness. The natural interaction capabilities of CUAs make them particularly dangerous in this context, as they can convincingly imitate legitimate user behavior.

Several secondary threats from the OWASP framework emerge in this case study, including Privilege Compromise through potential unauthorized actions, Cascading Hallucination Attacks via system-wide failures, and Intent Breaking & Goal Manipulation through the manipulation of CUA functionality. These interconnected threats demonstrate how CUAs embody the triangular framework mentioned in both documents—simultaneously serving as tools for legitimate automation, weapons for malicious exploitation, and targets vulnerable to compromise. This multifaceted nature of CUAs underscores the complex security challenges these systems present and the need for comprehensive security measures. Subsequently, OWASP's Agentic AI security framework provides a comprehensive structure for understanding these threats. The tool misuse concerns align directly with T2, which warns about attackers manipulating AI agents to abuse their integrated tools through deceptive prompts or commands. The human manipulation aspects correspond to T15, which addresses how attackers can exploit user trust in AI agents to influence decision-making without awareness. The framework also captures the secondary threats through T3 (Privilege Compromise), T5 (Cascading Hallucination Attacks), and T6 (Intent Breaking & Goal Manipulation). It is important to realize that mapping vulnerabilities to established threat categories allows organizations to better understand and implement appropriate mitigation strategies from OWASP's playbooks (i.e., restricting tool access, implementing strict validation mechanisms, and maintaining comprehensive monitoring systems).

The implications for cybersecurity professionals are significant and important to realize. Cybersecurity professionals must understand not only how to effectively deploy and utilize agentic AI tools but also how to protect against both attacks by autonomous agents and attacks targeting their own AI systems. This requires developing new security approaches that can address the unique challenges posed by autonomous, learning systems. The continued evolution of agentic AI will likely lead to increasingly sophisticated autonomous systems in both defensive and offensive security operations. Organizations will need to carefully balance the benefits of autonomous operation with the risks and challenges it presents. This includes developing appropriate oversight mechanisms, security controls, and incident response procedures specifically designed for dealing with autonomous systems. Therefore, the success in managing agentic AI in cybersecurity will largely depend on understanding and effectively addressing all three aspects of the triangular framework. Organizations must leverage the powerful capabilities these systems offer while maintaining appropriate security controls and remaining vigilant against potential threats. This balanced approach becomes particularly important as agentic AI systems become more sophisticated and widespread in security operations. Furthermore, the regulatory and ethical implications of agentic AI in cybersecurity must be considered. The autonomous nature of these systems raises important questions about responsibility and accountability for their actions (like the questions asked in Section 8.8), particularly in cases where they make independent decisions that affect security outcomes. Organizations will need to develop clear policies and procedures for managing these aspects while ensuring compliance with emerging regulations and ethical guidelines.

Cybersecurity professionals may find useful guidance in OWASP's Agentic AI—Threats and Mitigations, which provides a comprehensive framework for identifying, assessing, and mitigating security risks in autonomous AI systems, ensuring safer deployment and resilience against emerging threats (OWASP, 2025). It is an important security guide to focus on agentic AI systems—those capable of autonomous decision-making and action-taking to achieve goals. It builds upon and validates the triangular "tool, weapon, target" framework mentioned in the earlier text while providing detailed threat models and practical implementations. OWASP's guidance demonstrates how agentic AI can serve as a security tool through autonomous monitoring, be weaponized by attackers through techniques like memory poisoning, and become a target itself via manipulation of its decision-making processes.

A key contribution of the OWASP Agentic AI framework is its structured threat taxonomy specifically designed for agentic AI. This taxonomy categorizes various threats, including memory poisoning, tool misuse, privilege escalation, identity spoofing, cascading hallucinations, and vulnerabilities specific to multiagent systems. To illustrate these threats in real-world contexts, it provides concrete threat models for applications like enterprise copilots, smart home security systems, and robotic process automation (RPA) systems. Moreover, it goes beyond merely identifying threats by outlining detailed mitigation playbooks. These playbooks address different security challenges, such as preventing manipulation of AI agent reasoning, securing memory and knowledge systems, protecting human-in-the-loop controls, and ensuring secure communication between multiple agents. As a Version 1.0 release from OWASP's Agentic Security Initiative, this document represents one of the first comprehensive attempts to standardize security practices for agentic AI systems. It successfully bridges traditional cybersecurity frameworks with emerging AI security principles. Essentially, what makes the OWASP guidance particularly valuable is how it extends the theoretical concerns raised in the earlier text into practical, actionable guidance for security practitioners. It emphasizes the unique security challenges posed by agentic AI's autonomous capabilities, which create new attack vectors beyond those present in traditional AI systems. In general, it provides security professionals with concrete strategies and frameworks for protecting these increasingly complex and autonomous systems, while acknowledging the evolving nature of threats in this space.

8.10 Multimodal Models

Multimodal models are receiving increased scrutiny and notoriety in the field. They are also growing in sophistication quite rapidly. Gemma 3, with multimodal capabilities, has demonstrated immense progress in this field (Farabet, 2025). The emergence of these AI models creates complex implications for the cyber field, and it is important to view it through the triangular framework of tool, weapon, and target. As a tool, these systems enhance security capabilities by enabling simultaneous analysis of multiple data types, from network traffic patterns to visual surveillance footage. The technical implementation involves sophisticated neural architectures that maintain context across modalities, allowing security teams to correlate diverse data sources for better threat detection and response (La et al., 2024). Multimodal AI employs transformer architectures capable of cross-attention between modalities. This technical capability enables the model to integrate patterns from diverse input sources and deduce complex correlations. For example, a multimodal security system might analyze suspicious network activity while simultaneously examining system logs and security camera footage, providing security analysts with a comprehensive view of potential incidents (Potter et al., 2024). This capability extends to generating detailed security documentation that combines text, diagrams, and visual elements, making security findings more accessible and actionable across different organizational levels. Thus, the ability to analyze data from multiple streams allows for better log correlation and social engineering detection. It can help with forensics and attribution as well by processing textual evidence, visual recordings, and more to reconstruct the sequence of events during a cyberattack.

The weaponization potential of multimodal AI creates significant security challenges, as malicious actors can leverage these systems to create sophisticated, coordinated attacks across multiple channels (Rahman et al., 2024). Attackers might use multimodal AI to generate convincing deepfake content that combines manipulated video, matching audio, and contextually appropriate text, making their attacks significantly more difficult to detect and defend against. The technical aspects of weaponization often involve using advanced generative models to create coherent deceptive content across different modalities, enabling more effective social engineering attacks that exploit multiple sensory channels simultaneously. This multichannel approach can make attacks more convincing and harder to detect through traditional security measures, as the consistency across different modalities helps establish legitimacy in the target's perception. Furthermore, it can create autonomous attack agents wherein malicious multimodal models can analyze text, images, and voice data to execute sophisticated automated attacks. For example, this could include adaptive ransomware, which leverages visual data from a victim's device; ransomware can tailor threats based on observed information, such as photos or screenshots, for greater psychological impact (Neweva et al., 2024). It can also generate custom malware and embed multimedia prompts to obfuscate the true intent of malware, bypassing traditional detection mechanisms.

As targets themselves, multimodal AI systems face unique vulnerabilities that make them attractive targets for attackers. These systems are susceptible to cross-modal poisoning attacks, where malicious data in one modality can affect processing in others, creating complex security challenges not present in single-modal systems (Jin et al., 2025). The technical complexity of protecting multimodal models stems from their sophisticated architectures and the intricate interactions between different data processing components. Attackers might exploit vulnerabilities in image processing to affect text generation, target synchronization mechanisms between different data types, or manipulate cross-modal attention mechanisms. Attackers can aim to replicate multimodal models through repeated interactions for model extraction attacks. It can do query-based extraction by submitting multimodal queries (e.g., combined text and images) and analyzing responses, allowing adversaries to reverse-engineer the model's structure and functionality (Hamroun et al., 2024). Additionally, extracted outputs can help attackers infer proprietary training data, including sensitive images or private conversations. Adversarial attacks are of significance here as well, as multimodal models are susceptible to adversarial examples that exploit cross-modal dependencies (Liu et al., 2024). Minor alterations in input images or corresponding textual descriptions can confuse models, causing misclassification or unintended behavior. It is also susceptible to audio-visual attacks, where subtle distortions in synchronized audio and video inputs can bypass authentication systems relying on multimodal AI. Moreover, model poisoning is another way in which multimodal models can be targeted (Yang et al., 2023). Adversaries can compromise multimodal models by injecting malicious data during training. Adding corrupt or mislabeled multimodal samples to the training dataset enables attackers to degrade model performance or introduce backdoors. Also, injected inputs can modify learned weights, causing the model to behave unpredictably or maliciously under specific conditions. Thus, this complexity requires organizations to develop comprehensive security strategies that protect against various attack vectors while maintaining the effectiveness of their multimodal AI systems. The challenge extends beyond traditional security measures, requiring new approaches to security testing, monitoring, and incident response that can address the unique vulnerabilities of multimodal AI systems while ensuring their continued utility as security tools.

Technical defenses and mitigations play a crucial role in ensuring the security of multimodal AI systems. A key strategy involves robust model training techniques designed to improve resilience against attacks. Adversarial training, for instance, incorporates adversarial examples during the training process, equipping models to resist perturbations more effectively (Zhang & Huang, 2023). Additionally, differential privacy safeguards individual data points within multimodal datasets, preventing reverse-engineering attempts and ensuring privacy (Faisal, 2023). Query monitoring and rate limiting are vital for reducing risks associated with model extraction and adversarial queries (Malik et al., 2024). Rate limiting restricts the frequency of multimodal queries, thereby preventing large-scale probing of the model's capabilities (Chen et al., 2024b). Furthermore, behavioral analysis tracks user interactions across text, image, and audio queries to identify and thwart malicious attempts.

Restricting access to sensitive multimodal AI systems is equally critical, and this can be achieved through access control and encryption measures (Chen et al., 2024c). Implementing Zero Trust principles ensures continuous authentication and authorization of users and devices accessing the system. Additionally, secure API gateways establish encrypted communication channels, reducing the likelihood of unauthorized access or data interception (Asuah et al., 2025).

The future of multimodal models in AI security allows for both transformative opportunities and significant challenges. As these systems become more sophisticated in processing and correlating multiple data types simultaneously, we can expect to see more advanced security applications that combine real-time analysis of network traffic, system behaviors, visual data, and audio signals to detect and respond to threats more effectively. However, this advancement also means attackers will likely develop more sophisticated attack methods that exploit the interconnections between different modalities, potentially creating new types of security vulnerabilities that are harder to detect and mitigate. We'll likely see the emergence of more complex attack vectors that target the relationships between different data types within these models, requiring security professionals to develop new defense strategies and validation techniques. This evolution will demand a fundamental shift in how we approach security architecture and threat modeling, as organizations will need to consider not just individual data types but the complex interactions between them. The integration of multiple modalities in AI systems will also likely lead to new regulatory requirements and compliance considerations, particularly around privacy and data protection, as these systems process and correlate increasingly diverse types of personal and sensitive information.

8.11 Robotics

The convergence of robotics and AI is reaching a pivotal moment, comparable to ChatGPT's breakthrough in language AI, with industry leaders like Jensen Huang predicting the ubiquitous presence of robots in our future (Menendez-Roche, 2025; Chaney, 2025). The current landscape shows significant momentum, with major investments from companies like OpenAI and Tesla, alongside breakthrough developments in humanoid robots, autonomous vehicles, and robot swarms. Most notably, DARPA's demonstration of single operators managing over 100 robots simultaneously, and the successful deployment of robotic systems in emergency services and healthcare indicate that we're approaching a transformative period in robotics technology (Adams et al., 2023).

The implications of this robotics revolution extend deeply into cybersecurity and AI security domains, creating a complex web of challenges and opportunities. As robots become integrated into critical infrastructure, healthcare, and emergency services, the traditional boundaries between physical and digital security blur significantly. The emergence of physical-digital hybrid threats means that a compromised robot could cause not just data breaches but physical harm, while the development of swarm capabilities introduces new vulnerabilities at scale. The security landscape becomes even more complex when considering that these robots rely increasingly on sophisticated AI models, requiring robust protection against tampering and theft. Unlike pure software AI systems, robotics AI can directly interact with and modify the physical world, raising the stakes for security measures and necessitating sophisticated authentication, control systems, and fail-safe protocols.

The integration of AI-powered robotics into our daily lives introduces unprecedented physical safety concerns that extend far beyond traditional cybersecurity risks. Unlike software vulnerabilities that primarily affect data and systems, compromised robotic systems could cause direct physical harm to humans in their vicinity. Consider industrial settings where robots work alongside humans—a security breach could transform these collaborative tools into potential hazards, with manipulator arms, mobile platforms, or even entire robotic swarms potentially operating outside their safety parameters. The DARPA demonstration of single operators controlling over 100 robots simultaneously, while impressive, also illustrates the magnitude of potential risk if such systems were to be compromised or malfunction (Bisht, 2022).

The physical safety implications become even more concerning in critical environments like healthcare facilities, emergency services, or public spaces where robots are increasingly deployed. A compromised surgical robot could cause catastrophic harm during procedures, while autonomous security robots in public spaces could pose risks to civilians if their navigation or interaction systems are tampered with. The development of humanoid robots adds another layer of complexity—their enhanced mobility and human-like capabilities, while beneficial for integration into human environments, also mean they could cause more sophisticated forms of physical damage if compromised. These risks are compounded by the fact that many robotic systems are designed to operate with significant force or in hazardous environments, making their potential misuse particularly dangerous. As robots become more prevalent in our society, the challenge of ensuring their physical safety becomes paramount, requiring not just robust cybersecurity measures but also sophisticated physical failsafes, emergency shutdown procedures, and careful consideration of how these systems are deployed in human-occupied spaces. There are enough sci-fi movies that depict this; however, this will be a reality in the future. The development of safety protocols must anticipate not just accidental malfunctions but also intentional misuse, creating multiple layers of protection to prevent physical harm while still maintaining the utility and efficiency that makes these systems valuable.

As we have analyzed with the entirety of this chapter, let's try to look toward the future. This convergence suggests a fundamental shift in how we approach security and technology integration. The merging of robotics, AI, and traditional infrastructure will require new security frameworks that bridge physical and digital domains, while evolving regulatory landscapes will likely emerge to govern robots in public spaces. This transformation will create new demands for specialists who understand both robotics and cybersecurity, reshaping workforce requirements and career paths. The success of this integration will largely depend on our ability to develop comprehensive security strategies that protect both cyber and physical aspects of robotic systems, requiring unprecedented collaboration between cybersecurity experts, roboticists, AI researchers, and policymakers. As we move forward, organizations must prepare for a world where physical and digital security become increasingly intertwined, developing proactive approaches to address both current challenges and emerging threats in this rapidly evolving landscape. The future will require not just technological innovation but also a fundamental rethinking of how we approach security in a world where robots become an integral part of our daily lives and critical infrastructure.

While the exact trajectory of robotic AI development remains uncertain, its security implications demand our immediate attention and strategic planning. We must approach this technology through multiple lenses: as a tool that can enhance our capabilities and efficiency, as a potential weapon that could be exploited by malicious actors, and as a target requiring robust protection. The nature of robotics technology means that the same systems that could revolutionize healthcare or disaster response could also be weaponized if compromised. This reality underscores the critical importance of developing comprehensive security frameworks that account for both defensive and offensive capabilities. As we continue to advance in this field, the ability to anticipate and mitigate potential threats while maximizing beneficial applications will become increasingly crucial. The future security landscape will require a delicate balance between innovation and protection, making it essential for security professionals to stay ahead of emerging trends and potential vulnerabilities in this rapidly evolving domain.

Chapter 8 Summary

This chapter explored emerging trends that would shape the future of generative AI security across multiple technological frontiers. It began with quantum computing's dual impact, examining how developments like Microsoft's Majorana 1 chip and AWS's Ocelot demonstrated the approaching reality of quantum systems that could both threaten current cryptographic protections and enable revolutionary defensive capabilities through PQC and QML. The evolution of human–AI collaboration emerged as critical, highlighting augmented intelligence approaches that enhanced human capabilities while addressing cognitive security operations and the challenges of maintaining oversight as AI systems became more autonomous. Advancements in explainable AI promised greater transparency through interpretable machine learning models and causal AI that could understand cause-and-effect relationships in security events.

Chapter 8 also examined how generative AI was being integrated into zero trust architectures to enable more sophisticated continuous authentication, dynamic policy enforcement, and adaptive access control mechanisms. It explored the emergence of specialized micromodels that offered focused efficiency for specific security tasks, while analyzing the convergence of AI and blockchain technologies that created both new defensive opportunities and novel attack vectors. The discussion extended to AGI with its profound implications for reshaping cybersecurity paradigms, digital twins that created detailed virtual replicas for system modeling and testing, and agentic AI systems capable of autonomous decision-making and goal-directed behavior. The chapter concluded with multimodal models that processed diverse data types simultaneously and the convergence of robotics with AI that blurred the boundaries between physical and digital security domains, creating new paradigms for protecting both cyber and physical infrastructure.

Key Takeaways:

Chapter 8 demonstrated that future trends in generative AI security represented a fundamental transformation requiring organizations to simultaneously prepare for quantum-enabled threats while leveraging quantum advantages for enhanced protection. Quantum computing developments compressed traditional implementation timelines, forcing accelerated adoption of PQC and quantum-resistant AI architectures while enabling revolutionary defensive capabilities through QML and certified randomness generation. The evolution toward more autonomous AI systems through agentic AI and potential AGI demanded new security frameworks that could protect against sophisticated autonomous threats while maintaining effective human oversight and control. These technological convergences created complex security landscapes where traditional boundaries between physical and digital domains became increasingly blurred, requiring comprehensive approaches that addressed both cyber and physical security considerations.

This chapter revealed that successful navigation of future AI security challenges would require unprecedented interdisciplinary collaboration and adaptive frameworks capable of evolving alongside rapidly advancing technologies. The integration of explainable AI, zero trust architectures, and specialized micromodels demonstrated the need for more transparent, adaptive, and focused security approaches that could balance automation with accountability. The emergence of multimodal models and robotics convergence highlighted how future threats would span multiple domains simultaneously, requiring security professionals to develop expertise across traditionally separate disciplines. Organizations that could effectively leverage these emerging technologies while implementing robust protection mechanisms would be better positioned to address the complex security challenges of an AI-driven future, emphasizing the critical importance of proactive investment in both technological capabilities and cross-disciplinary expertise to maintain security effectiveness in an increasingly sophisticated threat landscape.

Case Study: Applying the Triangular Framework to Generative AI Security

Generative AI is reshaping the cybersecurity landscape by enabling transformative advancements while introducing novel risks. Analyzing AI as a tool, weapon, and target allows us to explore practical strategies and challenges in securing AI-driven systems. This case study dives into real-world implications and technical considerations for quantum computing, human–AI collaboration, explainable AI, and multimodal models.

AI as a Tool in Generative AI Security

Enhancing Security Operations Generative AI empowers cybersecurity professionals with tools to process vast datasets, identify patterns, and execute defensive actions with unprecedented speed. Consider QML, where quantum-powered generative AI models analyze security telemetry data, identify anomalies, and predict emerging threats. This convergence enhances zero-day vulnerability detection by processing complex attack patterns that classical machine learning may overlook.

Implementation Example A financial services organization integrates a generative AI-powered system into its threat detection framework. The system leverages multimodal AI to correlate textual logs, visual data from security cameras, and network activity. By connecting these diverse data streams, the organization gains comprehensive situational awareness. During a phishing attack simulation, the AI identifies suspicious login attempts and correlates them with unusual keystroke patterns, alerting the security team before credentials are compromised.

Key Takeaways:

1) **Adopt Hybrid Models:** Incorporate multimodal AI into security operations for enhanced threat detection across multiple data types.
2) **Leverage Explainable AI (XAI):** Use interpretable machine learning models to ensure security teams understand AI-driven recommendations and responses.
3) **Invest in Infrastructure:** Build scalable AI frameworks that integrate seamlessly with existing cybersecurity tools.

AI as a Weapon: Malicious Use Cases

Amplifying Threats Generative AI is a potent tool for attackers, enabling sophisticated social engineering, malware generation, and coordinated attacks across modalities. Multimodal models create realistic deepfake content, combining manipulated video, synthesized voice, and contextualized text, which makes phishing schemes and impersonation attacks nearly undetectable.

Implementation Example A ransomware campaign uses a generative AI model to adapt ransom notes to victims' behavioral patterns. By analyzing metadata and visual data on victims' devices, the model crafts messages tailored to evoke fear and urgency. The campaign leverages multimodal AI to bypass traditional email filters, embedding obfuscated malware in images and audio files.

Key Takeaways for Defenders:

1) **Proactively Detect Generative Threats:** Deploy AI systems capable of detecting deepfake content across text, audio, and video.
2) **Monitor Cross-Modal Data:** Address vulnerabilities created by cross-modal poisoning, where malicious inputs in one data stream compromise others.
3) **Strengthen Authentication:** Adopt continuous authentication mechanisms powered by generative AI to detect unusual user behavior in real-time.

AI as a Target

Securing AI Models and Pipelines The complexity of AI systems, particularly those using multimodal and QML, makes them attractive targets for attackers. Threat actors may seek to manipulate training pipelines, inject adversarial inputs, or reverse-engineer proprietary models to extract intellectual property or bypass defenses.

Implementation Example An attacker targets a healthcare organization's AI system used for patient triage. By injecting malicious data into the model's training pipeline, the attacker alters risk assessment parameters. This manipulation causes the system to misclassify high-risk patients, leading to operational failures.

Key Takeaways:

1) **Implement PQC Measures:** Protect AI training pipelines with PQC to mitigate risks posed by future quantum computing attacks.
2) **Monitor Training Pipelines:** Regularly audit data sources for poisoning attempts and ensure robust data validation.
3) **Design Quantum-Resistant Architectures:** Develop AI models resilient to quantum-enabled reverse engineering.

Practical Applications of Emerging Trends

Quantum Computing and Generative AI Quantum computing introduces both opportunities and challenges. PQC and quantum-resistant AI models will play a central role in securing AI systems. On the offensive side, adversaries could leverage quantum algorithms to break current encryption methods and compromise generative AI systems.

Practical Implementation:

- Deploy hybrid classical-quantum systems to enhance anomaly detection and predictive modeling.
- Integrate PQC into AI models' architectures to protect against quantum-enabled threats.

Human–AI Collaboration

The integration of augmented intelligence in cybersecurity enhances human capabilities. For example, generative AI systems can automate routine tasks, reducing cognitive overload for security analysts and enabling them to focus on high-value activities.

Practical Implementation:

- Deploy generative AI to filter false positives and prioritize actionable alerts.
- Train analysts to interpret AI outputs, fostering synergy between human judgment and AI capabilities.

Multimodal AI in Zero Trust

The adoption of generative AI in Zero Trust architectures revolutionizes policy enforcement, dynamic access control, and continuous authentication. Multimodal models enhance these capabilities by analyzing diverse data streams in real-time.

Implementation Example:

An enterprise uses a generative AI system to enforce dynamic access policies. During a security incident, the system analyzes contextual factors such as user behavior, device location, and network activity to restrict access dynamically without disrupting legitimate operations.

Key Takeaways:

1) **Dynamic Policies:** Use AI to generate adaptive security policies based on real-time risk assessment.
2) **Continuous Authentication:** Employ multimodal AI to continuously verify users' legitimacy across multiple modalities.

Securing the Future of Generative AI

Regulatory and Ethical Considerations The rise of technologies like AGI and agentic AI underscores the importance of ethical governance. Organizations must address accountability, transparency, and security risks associated with autonomous systems.

Key Recommendations:

1) **Develop Clear Policies:** Establish frameworks to govern AI operations, accountability, and decision-making.
2) **Collaborate on Standards:** Work with regulators and industry leaders to establish AI certification processes and security standards.
3) **Focus on Resilience:** Build robust, explainable AI systems capable of adapting to evolving threats while maintaining operational integrity.

Conclusion

The triangular framework—analyzing AI as a tool, weapon, and target—provides a comprehensive lens for navigating the future of generative AI security. By understanding the transformative potential of emerging technologies like quantum computing, human–AI collaboration, and multimodal models, organizations can develop strategies that harness the benefits of AI while mitigating its risks. Cybersecurity professionals must proactively invest in education, infrastructure, and collaboration to stay ahead of adversaries and protect the integrity of AI-driven systems in a rapidly evolving digital landscape.

This framework serves as a guide for the responsible adoption and protection of generative AI, emphasizing the balance between leveraging its capabilities and addressing its vulnerabilities. The future of AI security depends on thoughtful, proactive measures that account for both the promise and peril of these transformative technologies.

Triangular Framework for Generative AI Security Quiz

Questions

1 Why is the triangular framework important when addressing generative AI security risks?
   a) It separates hardware and software responsibilities during model training
   b) It organizes AI threats based on encryption methods and data storage techniques
   c) It helps organizations identify and respond to AI's use, misuse, and exposure to attacks
   d) It maps out compliance timelines for AI development lifecycle stages

2 In the financial services implementation example, what type of AI was used to enhance threat detection?
   a) Reinforcement learning
   b) Multimodal AI
   c) Natural language processing
   d) Quantum neural networks

3 According to the case study, how did the ransomware campaign weaponize generative AI?
   a) By creating phishing emails that appear to come from trusted sources
   b) By adapting ransom notes to victims' behavioral patterns
   c) By generating fake security certificates
   d) By creating synthetic identities to bypass authentication

4 What technology is specifically mentioned as important for protecting AI training pipelines against future quantum computing attacks?
   a) Homomorphic encryption
   b) Blockchain validation
   c) Postquantum cryptography (PQC)
   d) Federated learning

5 In the context of human–AI collaboration, what benefit does generative AI provide to security analysts according to the case study?
   a) Replacing human judgment entirely
   b) Reducing cognitive overload by automating routine tasks
   c) Creating more complex security protocols
   d) Eliminating the need for security training

Answer Key

1 **Correct Answer: c) It helps organizations identify and respond to AI's use, misuse, and exposure to attacks**
   - **Explanation:** The triangular framework offers a holistic view of AI security by helping organizations understand how generative AI can be leveraged as a defensive asset, weaponized by adversaries, or targeted for exploitation. This perspective ensures that strategies address AI's functional role, potential for abuse, and inherent vulnerabilities.
   - Option a) is incorrect because it focuses on infrastructure components (hardware/software) rather than threat modeling or AI behavior.

  - Option b) is incorrect because it implies a categorization based on encryption and storage, which is unrelated to the strategic role of AI in threat landscapes.
  - Option d) is incorrect because it refers to lifecycle planning phases, not to security modeling of AI threats or risks.

2. **Correct Answer: b) Multimodal AI**
   - **Explanation:** The case study states that in the financial services example, "The system leverages multimodal AI to correlate textual logs, visual data from security cameras, and network activity." Multimodal AI can process and analyze different types of data (text, images, network data) simultaneously.
   - Option a) is incorrect because reinforcement learning wasn't mentioned in this implementation example.
   - Option c) is incorrect because while natural language processing might be a component, the example specifically emphasized multimodal AI's ability to work across different data types.
   - Option d) is incorrect because while quantum machine learning is mentioned elsewhere in the case study, the financial services example specifically mentions multimodal AI.

3. **Correct Answer: b) By adapting ransom notes to victims' behavioral patterns**
   - **Explanation:** The case study explicitly states that "A ransomware campaign uses a generative AI model to adapt ransom notes to victims' behavioral patterns. By analyzing metadata and visual data on victims' devices, the model crafts messages tailored to evoke fear and urgency."
   - Option a) is incorrect because while phishing is mentioned in the case study, it wasn't the specific example given for the ransomware campaign.
   - Option c) is incorrect because generating fake security certificates wasn't mentioned in the case study.
   - Option d) is incorrect because while the case mentions impersonation attacks in general, the ransomware example specifically focused on tailored ransom notes.

4. **Correct Answer: c) Postquantum cryptography (PQC)**
   - **Explanation:** The case study explicitly states under the "AI as a Target" section that organizations should "Implement PQC Measures: Protect AI training pipelines with postquantum cryptography to mitigate risks posed by future quantum computing attacks."

- Option a) is incorrect because homomorphic encryption, while a valuable security technique, wasn't specifically mentioned for protecting against quantum computing attacks in the case study.
- Option b) is incorrect because blockchain validation wasn't mentioned in the context of quantum-resistant protection.
- Option d) is incorrect because federated learning is a distributed training approach but wasn't mentioned as a protection against quantum computing attacks.

5 **Correct Answer: b) Reducing cognitive overload by automating routine tasks**
- **Explanation:** The case study states that "generative AI systems can automate routine tasks, reducing cognitive overload for security analysts and enabling them to focus on high-value activities." It also mentions practical implementation examples like "Deploy generative AI to filter false positives and prioritize actionable alerts."
- Option a) is incorrect because the case study emphasizes collaboration between humans and AI, not replacement.
- Option c) is incorrect because creating more complex security protocols isn't mentioned as a benefit and would likely increase rather than decrease cognitive load.
- Option d) is incorrect because the case study emphasizes the importance of training analysts to work with AI, not eliminating training.

References

Adams, J. A., Hamell, J., & Walker, P. (2023). Can a single human supervise a swarm of 100 heterogeneous robots? *Field Robotics*, *3*, 837–881.

Ajish, D. (2024). The significance of artificial intelligence in zero trust technologies: A comprehensive review. *Journal of Electrical Systems and Information Technology*, *11*(1), 30.

Alcaraz, C., & Lopez, J. (2022). Digital twin: A comprehensive survey of security threats. *IEEE Communications Surveys & Tutorials*, *24*(3), 1475–1503.

Alluhaibi, R. (2024). Quantum machine learning for advanced threat detection in cybersecurity. *International Journal of Safety & Security Engineering*, *14*(3), 875–883.

Almagrabi, A. O., & Khan, R. A. (2024). Optimizing secure AI lifecycle model management with innovative generative AI strategies. *IEEE Access*, *13*, 12889–12920.

Al-Surmi, A., Bashiri, M., & Koliousis, I. (2022). AI based decision making: Combining strategies to improve operational performance. *International Journal of Production Research, 60*(14), 4464–4486.

Amazon. (2025, February 27). *Amazon Web Services announces a new quantum computing chip*. Amazon.

Asuah, G., Easin, A. M., & Orosz, T. (2025). Optimizing SAP machine learning-based solutions through custom API integration. *Acta Cybernetica, 27*(2), 117–140. https://doi.org/10.14232/actacyb.312225.

Assis, A., Dantas, J., & Andrade, E. (2025). The performance-interpretability trade-off: A comparative study of machine learning models. *Journal of Reliable Intelligent Environments, 11*(1), 1.

Aydeger, A., Zeydan, E., Yadav, A. K., Hemachandra, K. T., & Liyanage, M. (2024, October). Towards a quantum-resilient future: Strategies for transitioning to post-quantum cryptography. In *2024 15th International Conference on Network of the Future (NoF)* (pp. 195–203). IEEE.

Bailey, K. (n.d.). *Revolutionizing risk assessment with generative AI*. CFI.

Bisht, I. (2022, January 11). Single Operator Controls 130+ Drones at DARPA Exercise. *The Defense Post.* https://thedefensepost.com/2022/01/11/raytheon-drone-swarm-darpa/.

Bishwas, A. K., & Sen, M. (2024). Strategic roadmap for quantum-resistant security: A framework for preparing industries for the quantum threat. arXiv preprint arXiv:2411.09995.

Bolgar, C. (2025, February 19). Microsoft's Majorana 1 chip carves new path. https://news.microsoft.com/source/features/ai/microsofts-majorana-1-chip-carves-new-path-for-quantum-computing, for quantum computing. Microsoft.

Bradley, A. (2025, March 13). *China achieves quantum supremacy claim with new chip 1 quadrillion times faster than the most powerful supercomputers*. LiveScience.

Brewer, J., Patel, D., Kim, D., & Murray, A. (2024). *Navigating the challenges of generative technologies: Proposing the integration of artificial intelligence and blockchain*. Business Horizons.

Brin, D. (2022). *Convergence: Artificial intelligence and quantum computing: Social, economic, and policy impacts*. John Wiley & Sons.

Carpineti, A. (2025). Certified randomness milestone might be first-ever practical application of quantum computers. *IFL Science*. https://www.iflscience.com/certified-randomness-milestone-might-be-first-ever-practical-application-of-quantum-computers-78632.

Castelvecchi, D. (2025, January 13). Exotic 'Paraparticles' that defy categorization may exist in many dimensions. *Scientific American*. https://www.scientificamerican.com/article/exotic-paraparticles-that-defy-categorization-may-exist-in-many-dimensions/.

Chan, A., Salganik, R., Markelius, A., Pang, C., Rajkumar, N., Krasheninnikov, D., Langosco, L., He, Z., Duan, Y., Carroll, M., & Lin, M. (2023, June). Harms from increasingly agentic algorithmic systems. In *Proceedings of the 2023 ACM Conference on Fairness, Accountability, and Transparency* (pp. 651–666).

Chaney, S. (2025 January 28). "Everything that moves will be robotic": Nvidia CEO Jensen Huang says robots and self-driving cars are just around the corner. *Yahoo Tech*. https://www.yahoo.com/tech/everything-moves-robotic-nvidia-ceo-220000188.html.

Chen, C., Liu, Z., Jiang, W., Goh, S. Q., & Lam, K. Y. (2024a). Trustworthy, responsible, and safe AI: A comprehensive architectural framework for AI safety with challenges and mitigations. arXiv preprint arXiv:2408.12935.

Chen, J., Shi, Y., Yi, C., Du, H., Kang, J., & Niyato, D. (2024b). Generative AI-driven human digital twin in IoT-healthcare: A comprehensive survey. arXiv preprint arXiv:2401.13699.

Chen, Z., Wang, W., Cao, Y., Liu, Y., Gao, Z., Cui, E., Zhu, J., Ye, S., Tian, H., Liu, Z., & Gu, L. (2024c). Expanding performance boundaries of open-source multimodal models with model, data, and test-time scaling. arXiv preprint arXiv:2412.05271.

Coker, J. (2025, February 27). *Software vulnerabilities take almost nine months to patch*. Infosecurity Magazine.

Darzi, S., & Yavuz, A. A. (2024). Counter denial of service for next-generation networks within the artificial intelligence and post-quantum era. arXiv preprint arXiv:2408.04725.

Das, M., Naskar, A., Mitra, P., & Basu, B. (2024). Shallow quantum neural networks (SQNNs) with application to crack identification. *Applied Intelligence*, *54*(2), 1247–1262.

Dhoni, P., & Kumar, R. (2023). *Synergizing generative ai and cybersecurity: Roles of generative AI entities, companies, agencies, and government in enhancing cybersecurity*. Authorea Preprints.

Dodiya, K. R., Jha, M., & Jha, S. (2024). Fortifying the digital forge: Unleashing cybersecurity in the interconnected world of digital manufacturing. In A. Hassan, P. K. Dutta, S. Gupta, E. Mattar, & S. Singh (Eds.), *Emerging technologies in digital manufacturing and smart factories* (pp. 230–256). IGI Global.

Doerrfeld, B. (2025 February 19). How AI generated code compounds technical debt. *Lead Dev*. https://leaddev.com/software-quality/how-ai-generated-code-accelerates-technical-debt.

Dragan, A., Shah, R., Flynn, F., & Legg, S. (2025, April 2). Taking a responsible path to AGI. *Google DeepMind*. https://deepmind.google/discover/blog/taking-a-responsible-path-to-agi.

Dwivedi, R., Dave, D., Naik, H., Singhal, S., Omer, R., Patel, P., Qian, B., Wen, Z., Shah, T., Morgan, G., & Ranjan, R. (2023). Explainable AI (XAI): Core ideas, techniques, and solutions. *ACM Computing Surveys*, *55*(9), 1–33.

Encord. (n.d.). Micro-models. https://encord.com/glossary/micro-models-definition/.
Faisal, F. (2023) *A differentially private collaborative distillation approach for synthetic medical image data classification* [MSc thesis]. University of Manitoba.
Farabet, C. (2025, March 12). Introducing Gemma 3: The most capable model you can run on a single GPU or TPU. *Google*. https://blog.google/technology/developers/gemma-3/.
Firnhaber, D. K. (2023). *Post-quantum cryptography: Constructive research in quantum simulations* [Doctoral dissertation]. Northcentral University.
Gadgets 360. (2025, January 15). Physicists predict exotic 'Paraparticles' defying fermion and boson classifications.
Ghosh, A., & Ghosh, S. (2024, November). The quantum imitation game: Reverse engineering of quantum machine learning models. In *Proceedings of the 2024 Workshop on Attacks and Solutions in Hardware Security* (pp. 48–57).
Goriparthi, R. G. (2023). AI-augmented cybersecurity: Machine learning for real-time threat detection. *Revista de Inteligencia Artificial en Medicina*, *14*(1), 576–594.
Grahn, H. (2024). Defining comprehensive cognitive security in the digital era: Literature review and concept analysis. Available at SSRN 5030171.
Hafeez, M. A., Procacci, A., Coussement, A., & Parente, A. (2024). Challenges and opportunities for the application of digital twins in hard-to-abate industries: A review. *Resources, Conservation and Recycling*, *209*, 107796.
Hale, G. (2025, January 13). Quantum physics just got even stranger: Meet the mysterious paraparticles. *Sci Tech Daily*. https://scitechdaily.com/quantum-physics-just-got-even-stranger-meet-the-mysterious-paraparticles/.
Hamroun, M., Lajmi, S., Jallouli, M., & Souid, A. (2024). Efficient text-based query based on multi-level and deep-semantic multimedia indexing and retrieval. *Multimedia Tools and Applications*, *83*(18), 55811–55850.
Homaei, M., Mogollón-Gutiérrez, Ó., Sancho, J. C., Ávila, M., & Caro, A. (2024). A review of digital twins and their application in cybersecurity based on artificial intelligence. *Artificial Intelligence Review*, *57*(8), 201.
Hu, S., Lu, C., & Clune, J. (2024). Automated design of agentic systems. arXiv preprint arXiv:2408.08435.
Hu, W., Zhang, T., Deng, X., Liu, Z., & Tan, J. (2021). Digital twin: A state-of-the-art review of its enabling technologies, applications and challenges. *Journal of Intelligent Manufacturing and Special Equipment*, *2*(1), 1–34.
Hussain, A. A., & Al-Turjman, F. (2021). Artificial intelligence and blockchain: A review. *Transactions on Emerging Telecommunications Technologies*, *32*(9), e4268.
Ike, C. C., Ige, A. B., Oladosu, S. A., Adepoju, P. A., Amoo, O. O., & Afolabi, A. I. (2021). Redefining zero trust architecture in cloud networks: A conceptual shift towards granular, dynamic access control and policy enforcement. *Magna Scientia Advanced Research and Reviews*, *2*(1), 074–086.

Jain, H., Padmanabhan, B., Pavlou, P. A., & Raghu, T. S. (2021). Editorial for the special section on humans, algorithms, and augmented intelligence: The future of work, organizations, and society. *Information Systems Research*, *32*(3), 675–687.

Jin, M., Hu, W., Hong, R., & Zhu, L. (2025). Revealing security flaws in cross-modal retrieval models through video poisoning. *IEEE Transactions on Circuits and Systems for Video Technology*, *35*(6), 6184–6194.

Joseph, D., Misoczki, R., Manzano, M., Tricot, J., Pinuaga, F. D., Lacombe, O., Leichenauer, S., Hidary, J., Venables, P., & Hansen, R. (2022). Transitioning organizations to post-quantum cryptography. *Nature*, *605*(7909), 237–243.

Joshi, H. (2024). Emerging technologies driving zero trust maturity across industries. *IEEE Open Journal of the Computer Society*, *6*, 25–36.

Karunamurthy, A., Kiruthivasan, R., & Gauthamkrishna, S. (2023). Human-in-the-loop intelligence: Advancing AI-centric cybersecurity for the future. *Quing: International Journal of Multidisciplinary Scientific Research and Development*, *2*(3), 20–43.

Khan, A., Jhanjhi, N., Abdulhabeb, G. A. A., Ray, S. K., Ghazanfar, M. A., & Humayun, M. (2025). Securing IoT devices using generative AI techniques. In N. Z. Jhanjhi (Ed.), *Reshaping CyberSecurity with generative AI techniques* (pp. 219–264). IGI Global.

Khan, R., Sarkar, S., Mahata, S. K., & Jose, E. (2024). Security threats in agentic AI system. arXiv preprint arXiv:2410.14728.

Khurana, S. (2024). Quantum machine learning: Unraveling a new paradigm in computational intelligence. *Quantum*, *74*, 1.

Krasnok, A., Dhakal, P., Fedorov, A., Frigola, P., Kelly, M., & Kutsaev, S. (2024). Superconducting microwave cavities and qubits for quantum information systems. *Applied Physics Reviews*, *11*(1), 011302.

La, M., Han, S., Liu, G., Han, X., Zhang, Y., & Huang, M. (2024). *Neural modulation for dynamic semantic convergence in large language models: A technical examination*. Authorea Preprints.

Landau, E. (2021, August 5). Introduction to micro-models or: How I learned to stop worrying and love overfitting. *Medium*.

Lwanga, J. & Raza, S., (2023). Blockchain meets AI: Strengthening cybersecurity through decentralized intelligence. ResearchGate. https://www.researchgate.net/.../Blockchain-Meets-AI-Strengthening-Cybersecurity-through-Decentralized-Intelligence.pdf

Lexalytics. (n.d.). Machine learning micromodels: More data is not always better.

Liu, X., Cui, X., Li, P., Li, Z., Huang, H., Xia, S., Zhang, M., Zou, Y., & He, R. (2024). Jailbreak attacks and defenses against multimodal generative models: A survey. arXiv preprint arXiv:2411.09259.

Malik, J., Muthalagu, R., & Pawar, P. M. (2024). A systematic review of adversarial machine learning attacks, defensive controls and technologies. *IEEE Access*, *12*, 99382–99421.

Menendez-Roche, M. (2025 January 16). Tesla will produce 'army of robots' called Optimus by 2027. *EuroWeekly*. https://euroweeklynews.com/2025/01/16/tesla-will-produce-army-of-robots-called-optimus-by-2027/.

Morris, M.R., Sohl-Dickstein, J., Fiedel, N., Warkentin, T., Dafoe, A., Faust, A., Farabet, C., & Legg, S. (2023). Levels of AGI for operationalizing progress on the path to AGI. arXiv preprint arXiv:2311.02462.

Neway, A. S. (2024). *Beyond the bit: A guide to quantum computing and its impact*. Abegaz Sahilu Neway.

Neweva, W., Fitzwilliam, O., & Waterbridge, J. (2024, August 13). Forensic analysis of live ransomware attacks on linux-based laptop systems: Techniques and evaluation. PREPRINT (Version 1). https://doi.org/10.21203/rs.3.rs-4900486/v1.

O'Brien, J., Ee, S., & Williams, Z. (2023). Deployment corrections: An incident response framework for frontier AI models. arXiv preprint arXiv:2310.00328.

Ogbu, D. (2023). Agentic AI in computer vision domain—Recent advances and prospects. *International Journal of Research Publication and Reviews*, *4*(12), 5102–5120.

OpenAI. (2025a, January 21). *Announcing the stargate project*. OpenAI.

OpenAI. (2025b, January 23). Computer-using agent.

OWASP. (2025, February). Agentic AI – Threats and mitigations. https://genai.owasp.org/resource/agentic-ai-threats-and-mitigations/.

Paleja, A. (2025, February 3). *US scientists spot new class of quantum particles in world-first breakthrough*. Interesting Engineering.

Potter, K., Stilinski, D., & Adablanu, S. (2024). Multimodal deep learning for integrated cybersecurity analytics. tech. rep., EasyChair.

Putta, P., Mills, E., Garg, N., Motwani, S., Finn, C., Garg, D., & Rafailov, R. (2024). Agent q: Advanced reasoning and learning for autonomous AI agents. arXiv preprint arXiv:2408.07199.

Qian, C., Liu, X., Ripley, C., Qian, M., Liang, F., & Yu, W. (2022). Digital twin—Cyber replica of physical things: Architecture, applications and future research directions. *Future Internet*, *14*(2), 64.

Radanliev, P., De Roure, D., & Santos, O. (2023). Red teaming generative AI/NLP, the BB84 quantum cryptography protocol and the NIST-approved quantum-resistant cryptographic algorithms. arXiv preprint arXiv:2310.04425.

Rahman, M. A., Alqahtani, L., Albooq, A., & Ainousah, A. (2024, January). A survey on security and privacy of large multimodal deep learning models: Teaching and learning perspective. In *2024 21st Learning and Technology Conference (L&T)* (pp. 13–18). IEEE.

Rawal, A., McCoy, J., Rawat, D. B., Sadler, B. M., & Amant, R. S. (2021). Recent advances in trustworthy explainable artificial intelligence: Status, challenges, and perspectives. *IEEE Transactions on Artificial Intelligence*, *3*(6), 852–866.

Ray, P. (2025, February 25). Scientists create world's 1st chip that can protect data in the age of quantum computing attacks. *Live Science*. https://www.livescience.com/technology/computing/scientists-create-worlds-1st-chip-that-can-protect-data-in-the-age-of-quantum-computing-attacks.

Rayhan, A., Rayhan, R., & Rayhan, S. (2023). Artificial general intelligence: Roadmap to achieving human-level capabilities. *DOI*, *10*, 13140.

Sandua, D. (2023). Artificial intelligence, blockchain & quantum computing. Independently Published.

Sarker, I. H. (2022). AI-based modeling: techniques, applications and research issues towards automation, intelligent and smart systems. *SN Computer Science*, *3*(2), 158.

SciTechDaily. (2025, February 5). Scientists just linked quantum processors in a historic step toward scalable supercomputers. https://scitechdaily.com/scientists-just-linked-quantum-processors-in-a-historic-step-toward-scalable-supercomputers.

Senewirathna, N. (2024). Quantum computing and it's impact on information warfare: Threats and cybersecurity countermeasures. *ResearchGate*. https://www.researchgate.net/profile/Amith-Senewirathna/publication/385381037_Quantum_Computing_and_It%27s_Impact_on_Information_Warfare_-Threats_and_Cybersecurity_Countermeasures/links/67225ddeecbbde716b4c40b2/Quantum-Computing-and-Its-Impact-on-Information-Warfare-Threats-and-Cybersecurity-Countermeasures.pdf

Shamoo, Y. (2025). Adversarial attacks and defense mechanisms in the age of quantum computing. In M. Omar & H. M. Zangana (Eds.), *Leveraging large language models for quantum-aware cybersecurity* (pp. 301–344). IGI Global Scientific Publishing.

Shoushtari, M., Arabian, F., & Harrison, W. K. (2022). *Post-quantum cryptography based on codes: a game changer for secrecy in aeronautical mobile telemetry*. International Foundation for Telemetering.

Singh, S., & Kumar, D. (2024). Enhancing cyber security using quantum computing and artificial intelligence: A review. *Algorithms*, *4*(3), 1–8.

Sobien, D., Kulkarni, A., & Batarseh, F. A. (2025). Toward identifying cyber dependencies in water distribution systems using causal AI. *Journal of Water Resources Planning and Management*, *151*(2), 04024069.

Soltanshahi, M., & Hosseini, N. (2024). Toward future metasystems. *Cyber Physical System 2.0: Communication and Computational Technologies*, 70.

Somma, A., De Benedictis, A., Zappatore, M., Martella, C., Martella, A., & Longo, A. (2023, December). Digital twin space: the integration of digital twins and data spaces. In *2023 IEEE International Conference on Big Data (BigData)* (pp. 4017–4025). IEEE.

Tripathi, A. (2025, January 15). MIT sets world record with 99.998% fidelity in quantum computing breakthrough. *Interesting Engineering*. https://interestingengineering.com/science/99-998-fidelity-in-quantum-computing-by-mit.

Ullah, Z., Waheed, A., Mohmand, M. I., Basar, S., Zareei, M., & Granda, F. (2024). AICyber-chain: Combining AI and blockchain for improved cybersecurity. *IEEE Access, 12*, 142194–142214.

Valich, L. (2025, February 12). Scientists directly prove the existence of a nuclear-spin dark state. *Phys Org*. https://phys.org/news/2025-02-scientists-nuclear-dark-state.html.

Wagg, D. J., Worden, K., Barthorpe, R. J., & Gardner, P. (2020). Digital twins: State-of-the-art and future directions for modeling and simulation in engineering dynamics applications. *ASCE-ASME Journal of Risk and Uncertainty in Engineering Systems, Part B: Mechanical Engineering, 6*(3), 030901.

Wang, Y., Su, Z., Guo, S., Dai, M., Luan, T. H., & Liu, Y. (2023). A survey on digital twins: Architecture, enabling technologies, security and privacy, and future prospects. *IEEE Internet of Things Journal, 10*(17), 14965–14987.

Wiggers, K. (2025, February 3). Meta says it may stop development of AI systems it deems too risky. *TechCrunch*. https://techcrunch.com/2025/02/03/meta-says-it-may-stop-development-of-ai-systems-it-deems-too-risky/

Yang, Z., He, X., Li, Z., Backes, M., Humbert, M., Berrang, P., & Zhang, Y. (2023, July). Data poisoning attacks against multimodal encoders. In *International Conference on Machine Learning* (pp. 39299-39313). PMLR.

Yapar, O. (2023). Explainable AI in national security: Enhancing trust and accountability. *International Journal of Emerging Technologies and Innovative Research, 10*(12), pph691-h709.

Yazdi, M. (2024). Application of quantum computing in reliability analysis. In M. Yazdi (Ed.), *Advances in computational mathematics for industrial system reliability and maintainability* (pp. 139–154). Springer Nature Switzerland.

Yocam, E., Rizi, A., Kamepalli, M., Vaidyan, V., Wang, Y., & Comert, G. (2024). Quantum adversarial machine learning and defense strategies: Challenges and opportunities. arXiv preprint arXiv:2412.12373.

Zemskov, A.D., Fu, Y., Li, R., Wang, X., Karkaria, V., Tsai, Y.K., Chen, W., Zhang, J., Gao, R., Cao, J., & Loparo, K.A. (2024). Security and privacy of digital twins for advanced manufacturing: A survey. arXiv preprint arXiv:2412.13939.

Zhang, P. F., & Huang, Z. (2023). A survey on image perturbations for model robustness: Attacks and defenses. *ResearchGate*. https://www.researchgate.net/publication/389045970_A_Survey_on_Image_Perturbations_for_Model_Robustness_Attacks_and_Defenses

9

Implementing Generative AI Security in Organizations

In the previous eight chapters, there was a strong focus on theory (with additional practical examples). However, the goal of this chapter is to give clear and actionable steps and a holistic understanding of how organizations can approach integration generative artificial intelligence (AI) in their security architectures. In general, this chapter aims to bridge the theoretical with the practical and what can actually be done and where to start—especially for organizations that have not begun to integrate generative AI in their infrastructures and organizational strategies. Maybe your employees are already using it, but you are unaware of how it is being used and where it is being used. Subsequently, this chapter will provide practical guidance to integrate generative AI measures into organizational strategies. The successful implementation of generative AI security measures requires organizations to adopt a comprehensive and structured approach that aligns technical capabilities with business objectives while building necessary human expertise. This chapter provides practical guidance for organizations seeking to integrate AI security into their operations, from initial readiness assessments through strategy development and team building. Understanding these implementation challenges and following established frameworks can help organizations avoid common pitfalls while maximizing the benefits of their AI security investments. This chapter will examine key aspects such as organizational readiness, strategy development, and team building. Moreover, this chapter offers a roadmap for organizations to effectively implement and maintain robust generative AI security measures while fostering a culture of security awareness and continuous improvement. So, let's get started!

Generative AI Security: Defense, Threats, and Vulnerabilities, First Edition. Shaila Rana and Rhonda Chicone.

9.1 Assessing Organizational Readiness

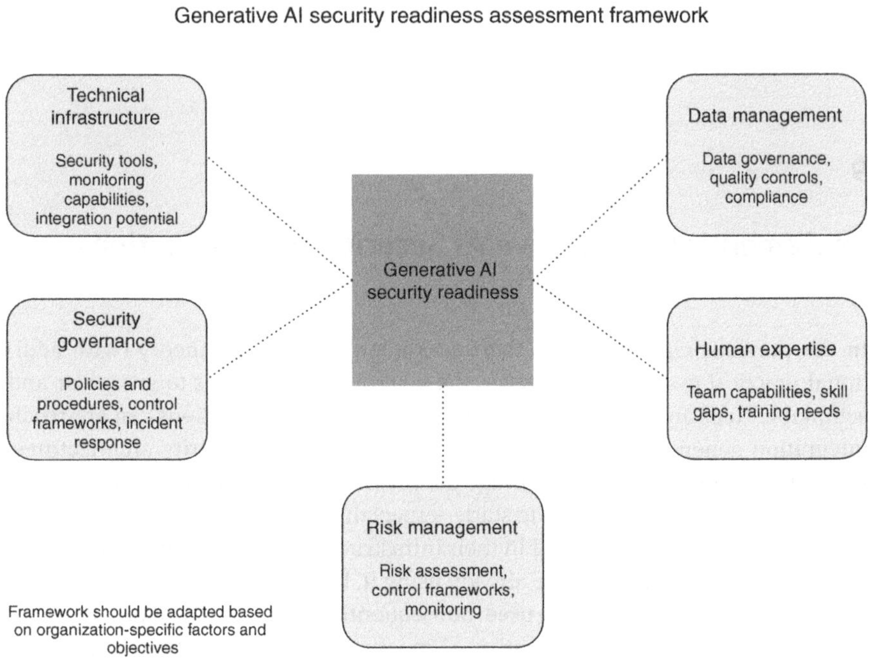

This book proposes a Generative AI Security Readiness Assessment Framework, as it provides organizations with a structured approach to evaluate their preparedness for implementing AI security solutions. At its core, is the fundamental concept of AI security readiness, which is supported by five key interconnected dimensions. The framework's five dimensions are strategically arranged around the center to show their interdependent nature. At the top, Technical Infrastructure and Data Management form the foundational technical components. Technical Infrastructure encompasses the essential security tools, monitoring capabilities, and integration potential that organizations need to support AI systems. Alongside it, Data Management focuses on the crucial aspects of data governance, quality controls, and compliance—recognizing that AI systems are only as good as the data they work with.

On either side, Security Governance and Human Expertise represent the organizational and human elements necessary for successful AI security implementation. Security Governance establishes the necessary policies, procedures, and control frameworks that guide AI security operations, while Human Expertise addresses the critical need for skilled personnel, identifying capability gaps, and ongoing training requirements. At the bottom, Risk Management serves as the foundation for the entire framework, ensuring organizations can effectively assess risks, implement appropriate controls, and maintain continuous monitoring of their AI security initiatives. Finally, the framework's design emphasizes adaptability, as noted by the statement at the bottom, acknowledging that organizations must tailor these dimensions to their specific context, industry requirements, and business objectives. The connecting lines between each dimension and the central hub illustrate how these components must work in harmony to create a comprehensive AI security readiness posture.

That being said, organizations assessing their readiness for generative AI security adoption should evaluate five key dimensions: technical infrastructure, data management capabilities, security governance frameworks, human expertise, and risk management processes. This assessment framework provides a foundation while remaining adaptable to different organizational contexts. Technical infrastructure readiness involves evaluating existing security tools, monitoring capabilities, and integration potential for AI systems. Organizations need to assess their ability to collect and process security telemetry, maintain secure development environments, and support AI model deployment. This includes evaluating network architecture, computing resources, and current security control effectiveness.

Data management capabilities form a crucial component of readiness assessment. Organizations must evaluate their ability to collect, store, and process high-quality security data needed for AI systems. This includes assessing data governance frameworks, data quality controls, and compliance with relevant regulations. The assessment should consider both structured and unstructured data sources, data access controls, and data privacy measures.

Security governance readiness focuses on existing policies, procedures, and control frameworks. Organizations need to evaluate how well their current governance structures can accommodate AI-specific security requirements. This includes assessing incident response procedures, change management processes, and security policy frameworks for AI system compatibility.

Human expertise readiness involves evaluating current team capabilities and identifying skill gaps. Organizations should assess their ability to develop, deploy, and maintain AI security systems while ensuring appropriate oversight. This includes evaluating both technical and non-technical staff readiness for AI adoption.

Risk management readiness requires organizations to assess their ability to identify, evaluate, and mitigate AI-specific security risks. This includes evaluating risk assessment methodologies, control frameworks, and monitoring capabilities. Organizations should consider their ability to balance security requirements with operational needs while maintaining compliance with relevant standards.

This framework intentionally remains high-level because detailed implementation depends heavily on organization-specific factors including industry sector, regulatory requirements, existing security maturity, and business objectives. Organizations should adapt these assessment dimensions based on their unique circumstances while maintaining focus on core security principles.

Organizations of different sizes can implement this readiness assessment framework. Let's go through a few examples. A small organization, such as a growing startup with 50 employees, might approach this framework with a focused, lean implementation. They would likely begin by evaluating their technical infrastructure with an emphasis on cloud-based security tools that can scale with their growth, perhaps utilizing managed security services to complement their limited in-house capabilities. Their data management assessment would focus on establishing basic, but robust data governance practices, particularly around their core business data and customer information. For security governance, they might start with essential policies and procedures, often adapting industry templates to their specific needs rather than building from scratch. The human expertise dimension might revolve around a small, cross-trained team where individuals wear multiple hats, with an emphasis on identifying critical skill gaps that need to be filled either through training or strategic hiring. Their risk management approach would likely be straightforward, focusing on high-priority risks that directly impact their core business operations and compliance requirements.

A medium-sized organization with 250–1000 employees would take a more structured approach to the framework. Their technical infrastructure assessment would likely encompass a mix of in-house and cloud-based security solutions, with a focus on integration between existing systems and new AI capabilities. Data management would involve a more comprehensive evaluation of various data sources across departments, with formal data governance committees and documented procedures for data quality control. Their security governance assessment would include a dedicated security team developing and maintaining policies, with clear incident response procedures and regular policy reviews. The human expertise dimension would involve department-specific evaluations of AI security readiness, with dedicated training programs, and potentially a mix of in-house experts and external consultants. Risk management would be more formalized, with regular assessments, documented control frameworks, and quarterly reviews of security metrics.

A large enterprise with thousands of employees would implement this framework at scale, often across multiple divisions or geographical locations. Their technical infrastructure assessment would be comprehensive, evaluating complex networks of security tools, monitoring systems, and integration requirements across various business units. Data management would involve sophisticated governance frameworks, often with dedicated data management teams, automated quality control systems, and compliance monitoring across multiple jurisdictions. Security governance would be highly structured, with dedicated teams for policy development, compliance monitoring, and incident response, often including separate governance structures for different business units or regions. The human expertise dimension would involve detailed skills mapping across the organization, comprehensive training programs, and specialized teams dedicated to AI security. Their risk management approach would be enterprise-wide, with sophisticated risk assessment methodologies, automated monitoring systems, and integrated control frameworks that align with international standards and regulatory requirements. They might also incorporate internal audit functions to regularly assess the effectiveness of their AI security controls and readiness measures.

Ultimately, each of these organizations, regardless of size, would need to maintain the adaptability emphasized in the framework, adjusting their implementation based on their specific industry requirements, regulatory environment, and business objectives. The key difference lies not in the framework's components but in the scale, complexity, and formality of their implementation. Smaller organizations might take a more agile, streamlined approach, while larger organizations would need more structured, comprehensive implementations to manage their greater complexity and risk exposure.

9.2 Developing an AI Security Strategy

Developing a comprehensive AI security strategy requires organizations to carefully balance security requirements with business objectives while creating clear implementation pathways (Habbal et al., 2024). This section explores how organizations can develop effective strategies that align AI security initiatives with broader business goals while maintaining robust security controls. Thus, it's important to examine approaches to strategy development and implementation planning. Subsequently, organizations can create frameworks that enable secure AI adoption while supporting business growth and innovation. Understanding these strategic considerations is crucial for organizations seeking to implement AI security measures that are both effective and sustainable, ensuring that security investments deliver meaningful value while addressing critical risks.

Aligning AI security strategies with business objectives is crucial for ensuring both effective security implementation and organizational support. This alignment process requires deep understanding of business goals, operational requirements, and risk tolerance levels, ensuring that security measures enhance rather than impede business operations. Organizations must view AI security not as a standalone technical initiative but as an integral part of achieving business success (Kulkov et al., 2024). Moreover, the consequences of failing to align AI security with business objectives mirror the historical challenges faced in traditional information technology (IT) security implementations. When security operates in isolation from business goals, organizations often experience reduced return on investment (ROI), difficulty justifying security investments, and challenges in obtaining necessary resources and personnel. This misalignment can lead to security measures that either inadequately protect critical assets or create unnecessary operational friction, ultimately undermining both security effectiveness and business efficiency. The current rapid adoption of AI technologies presents a unique opportunity for organizations to establish proper alignment from the outset. Unlike many traditional security implementations that were retrofitted onto existing systems, organizations can integrate security considerations into their AI initiatives from the beginning. This early alignment enables more effective resource allocation, better risk management, and stronger stakeholder support.

Organizations should begin by clearly identifying how AI initiatives support specific business objectives and then design security measures that protect these initiatives while enabling their success (Challoumis, 2024). This might include understanding how AI systems will improve customer service, enhance operational efficiency, or drive innovation, and then developing security controls that protect these capabilities without compromising their effectiveness. The process of alignment should involve key stakeholders from both business and security functions, ensuring shared understanding of objectives and constraints. Regular communication and feedback mechanisms help maintain this alignment as both business needs and security requirements evolve. This collaborative approach helps ensure that security investments deliver meaningful business value while effectively managing risks. Let's elaborate on a systematic approach to aligning cybersecurity AI adoption with business objectives. The first step involves thoroughly understanding and documenting the key business objectives through engagement with business leaders and stakeholders. This means having detailed discussions about strategic goals, growth targets, customer needs, operational efficiency goals, and competitive advantages the organization seeks to maintain or develop. For example, if a business objective is to expand digital services to customers, understanding the specific requirements and timelines for this expansion is crucial for aligning AI security capabilities.

The next phase involves mapping how AI security capabilities can directly support these business objectives (Sjödin et al., 2021). This includes identifying specific ways AI can enhance security while enabling business growth. For instance, if rapid customer onboarding is a business goal, AI security systems could be implemented to provide faster, more accurate fraud detection while maintaining smooth customer experiences. Risk assessment becomes a crucial bridge between business objectives and AI security implementation. Organizations need to understand both business and security risks, then determine how AI security measures can address these risks while supporting business operations. This includes quantifying potential impacts of security incidents on business objectives and demonstrating how AI security investments mitigate these risks.

Financial alignment is essential—security leaders need to develop clear business cases that show how AI security investments support financial objectives. This includes calculating potential ROI, considering both direct security benefits and broader business impacts like improved operational efficiency or reduced fraud losses. The business case should also account for total cost of ownership, including implementation, maintenance, and training costs.

Operational alignment requires understanding how AI security measures will integrate with existing business processes and workflows. This means working closely with operations teams to ensure security measures enhance rather than impede business activities. For example, if business efficiency is a key objective, AI security systems should be designed to automate routine security tasks while maintaining appropriate human oversight.

Performance metrics need to be established that demonstrate both security effectiveness and business value (Enholm et al., 2022). These metrics should directly link to business objectives—for instance, showing how AI-enhanced security controls improve customer satisfaction scores or reduce operational delays while maintaining strong security posture.

Change management and communication strategies must be developed to ensure successful adoption. This includes creating clear narratives that explain how AI security initiatives support business goals, developing training programs that help staff understand and effectively use new capabilities, and establishing feedback mechanisms to continuously improve alignment.

Finally, regular review and adjustment processes should be established to maintain alignment as both business objectives and security requirements evolve. This includes periodic assessments of how well AI security measures are supporting business goals and making adjustments as needed to maintain effective alignment.

Success in this alignment requires security leaders to communicate in business terms rather than technical jargon, clearly articulating how security measures support business objectives. This includes developing metrics that demonstrate both security effectiveness and business value, helping justify investments and maintain support for security initiatives over time. Hence, early alignment of AI security with business objectives also positions organizations to better adapt to changing conditions and requirements. As AI technologies evolve and new use cases emerge, organizations with well-aligned security strategies can more effectively evaluate and respond to new opportunities and threats while maintaining focus on core business objectives.

Creating a comprehensive roadmap for AI security implementation requires careful planning and a structured approach that can adapt to different organizational contexts. A high-level framework for developing this roadmap starts with establishing clear phases of implementation while maintaining flexibility for organization-specific requirements. The initial planning phase must focus on comprehensive assessment and goal setting. Organizations should document current security capabilities, identify specific areas where AI can enhance security operations, and establish clear objectives aligned with business goals. This phase should include stakeholder identification and engagement, ensuring buy-in across the organization while capturing diverse requirements and constraints.

Assessment and documentation of the current security architecture is crucial before any implementation begins. This includes mapping existing security tools, data flows, integration points, and potential gaps that AI security solutions might address. Understanding this baseline helps organizations identify where AI can provide the most value while avoiding redundancy or conflicts with existing systems. The phasing and prioritization stage requires organizations to sequence implementation steps based on business impact, resource requirements, and risk levels. This might mean starting with lower-risk, high-value applications of AI security while building expertise and confidence before moving to more critical applications. Organizations should identify quick wins that can demonstrate value while planning for longer-term, more complex implementations.

Resource planning becomes critical for successful implementation. Organizations need to identify required technical resources, establish training programs, and allocate appropriate budgets. This includes planning for both initial implementation and ongoing maintenance, ensuring sustainable operation of AI security systems over time (Bawa, 2023). Moreover, integration planning must address how AI security solutions will work within existing security architectures. This includes identifying integration points, data requirements, and potential impacts on existing security controls. Organizations should plan for gradual integration that maintains security effectiveness throughout the transition.

The danger of not having a comprehensive roadmap becomes evident in many organizations that have adopted AI technologies reactively rather than strategically. This often results in disconnected systems, security gaps, and inefficient resource utilization. A well-planned roadmap helps avoid these pitfalls while ensuring consistent security coverage. Subsequently, testing and validation frameworks need to be established before implementation begins. Organizations should plan for thorough testing of AI security systems, including performance validation, security testing, and integration testing. This helps ensure that new systems enhance rather than compromise security posture.

Regular review and adjustment points should be built into the roadmap, allowing organizations to assess progress and make necessary adjustments. This flexibility is crucial given the rapid evolution of both AI technologies and security threats. In general, the roadmap should remain intentionally high-level to accommodate variations in organizational size, industry requirements, regulatory frameworks, and technical architectures. While the basic framework provides structure, organizations need to adapt specific implementation details to their unique contexts and requirements. Additionally, the AI landscape changes so rapidly (there are new tools popping up almost daily). Therefore, it is important to keep a flexible and adaptable approach, which can be done with having a high-level roadmap.

9.3 Shadow AI

The proliferation of easily accessible AI tools has created a significant challenge for organizations: shadow AI. As discussed earlier in this book, this term refers to the unauthorized or undocumented use of AI tools and services within organizations, often when employees bypass official channels to access public AI services for work-related tasks. While traditional approaches to controlling technology adoption might suggest simply restricting access to unauthorized tools, the ubiquity and utility of AI services require a more nuanced and comprehensive strategy that balances security requirements with business productivity (Schueler, 2024). Organizations must implement robust detection and monitoring capabilities to identify shadow AI usage across their environments. This includes network monitoring to detect interactions with known AI services, data loss prevention systems configured to identify potential AI-related data leakage, and analytics to track patterns of AI service usage across the organization. Automated alerts for potential unauthorized AI activities, regular audits of cloud service usage and data transfers, and monitoring of API calls and external service interactions form crucial components of a comprehensive detection strategy. These monitoring capabilities should be integrated with an existing security infrastructure to provide a holistic view of AI usage across the organization.

A comprehensive risk assessment framework for shadow AI must consider multiple factors, including data privacy implications of different AI services and tools, security vulnerabilities introduced by unauthorized AI usage, and compliance risks related to data sharing with external AI providers (Santos & Radanliev, 2024). Organizations need to evaluate potential intellectual property exposure through AI interactions, assess the business impact of restricting versus allowing certain AI tools, and consider integration risks with existing systems and processes. This risk assessment should inform policy development and guide decision-making about AI tools adoption and usage guidelines. Effective shadow AI management requires clear policies that balance security with productivity. Organizations should develop acceptable use guidelines for AI tools and services, establish data handling requirements when using AI services, and create streamlined approval processes for new AI tools. These policies should include incident response procedures for shadow AI discoveries, compliance requirements, and clear consequences for violations. Regular policy reviews and updates are essential to address new AI capabilities and emerging risks in the rapidly evolving AI landscape.

Employee education and training play a crucial role in managing shadow AI risks. Organizations must develop comprehensive training programs that address the risks associated with unauthorized AI usage, proper handling of sensitive data in AI interactions, and recognition of approved versus unauthorized AI tools (Habbal et al., 2024). This training should include best security practices for AI tool usage, clear reporting procedures for security concerns, and regular updates on new AI-related threats and risks. Creating a culture of awareness and responsible AI usage helps employees understand both the benefits and risks of AI tools. Similar to what Article 4 of the EU AI Act addresses, everyone interacting with AI tools needs to have a base literacy and understanding of these tools.

To minimize shadow AI usage, organizations should focus on providing approved alternatives that meet employee needs. This includes implementing sanctioned AI tools that address common use cases, creating streamlined processes for requesting new AI capabilities, and establishing "AI sandboxes" for safe experimentation with new tools (Ranchordas, 2021). Organizations should develop fast-track approval processes for new AI tools and maintain flexibility in tool adoption to address emerging needs. Regular assessment of employee AI requirements helps ensure that approved tools remain relevant and effective. Integration with enterprise architecture forms another crucial component of shadow AI management. Security controls must account for AI tool usage, while data governance frameworks should address AI interactions comprehensively. Organizations need to establish clear integration points between approved and third-party AI services, implement robust monitoring and logging infrastructure, and ensure that identity and access management systems can effectively control AI tool usage. This integration helps maintain security while enabling productive use of AI capabilities.

When developing an AI security strategy, organizations must explicitly address the challenge of shadow AI as a part of their comprehensive roadmap (Cloud Security Alliance, 2024). The rapid proliferation of accessible AI tools means that traditional approaches to controlling technology adoption may prove insufficient. Rather than simply trying to prevent shadow AI usage through restrictive policies, organizations need to develop strategies that acknowledge its inevitability while managing associated risks effectively. A strategic approach to shadow AI should begin with understanding why employees turn to unauthorized AI tools in the first place. This often stems from legitimate business needs—whether it is improving productivity, solving complex problems, or keeping pace with competitors. Organizations should conduct assessments to identify these driving factors and incorporate them into their AI adoption strategies. This might include surveying employees about their AI tool usage, identifying common use cases, and evaluating the gaps between approved tools and actual business needs.

The implementation roadmap should include specific provisions for managing shadow AI risks while maintaining business agility. This could involve creating fast-track approval processes for new AI tools, establishing clear guidelines for acceptable AI use, and implementing monitoring systems that can detect unauthorized AI usage without creating unnecessary barriers to legitimate work. Organizations might consider implementing an "AI sandbox" environment where employees can safely experiment with new AI tools under controlled conditions, helping balance innovation with security requirements (Truby et al., 2022). Financial planning for AI security must also account for shadow AI considerations. This includes budgeting for approved alternatives to popular public AI tools, investing in monitoring and detection capabilities, and allocating resources for training and awareness programs. Organizations should consider the total cost of ownership for official AI solutions, including the hidden costs of not providing adequate tools that might drive employees toward shadow AI usage. The roadmap should also include metrics for measuring the effectiveness of shadow AI management strategies, such as tracking the adoption rates of approved tools versus unauthorized alternatives, monitoring data exposure risks, and assessing the impact on productivity and security incidents.

Continuous improvement remains essential for effective shadow AI management. Organizations should regularly assess the effectiveness of their management strategies, collect feedback from employees about AI tool needs, and evaluate new AI capabilities and potential risks (Arslan et al., 2022). Regular updates to policies and procedures based on emerging threats, measurement of program success, and adaptation to changing regulatory requirements help ensure that shadow AI management remains effective over time. Success in managing shadow AI often depends on creating a culture of responsible AI usage rather than solely relying on restrictive policies, recognizing that employees will seek out tools that help them work more efficiently. It is crucial to provide appropriate alternatives, clear guidelines, and necessary support; thus, organizations can better manage the risks of shadow AI while harnessing its benefits for business success.

9.4 Building and Training AI Security Teams

We can never forget the human element when it comes to cybersecurity, and that is especially more critical as we continually intersect cybersecurity with AI. Building effective AI security teams requires organizations to develop new capabilities while adapting existing security expertise to meet the challenges of AI-driven security operations. This section explores the critical components of creating and maintaining successful AI security teams, from defining clear roles and responsibilities to developing essential skills and fostering a security-aware organizational culture. Understanding these elements is crucial for organizations seeking to build teams capable of effectively implementing and managing AI security measures while maintaining robust security practices. The successful integration of AI security capabilities depends not just on technology implementation but on developing human expertise and organizational awareness that supports secure AI adoption.

Clear delineation of roles and responsibilities in AI security teams is fundamental for effective operations and accountability (Habbal et al., 2024). When team members understand their specific duties, areas of oversight, and decision-making authority, organizations can better maintain security controls while avoiding gaps in coverage or confusing overlaps in responsibility. This clarity becomes particularly crucial when implementing AI security systems, as these technologies introduce new complexities and potential risks that must be actively managed. Moreover, the integration of AI into security operations requires organizations to carefully define how AI systems and human analysts will interact and support each other. This includes establishing clear responsibilities for AI system oversight, model validation, incident response, and ongoing maintenance. Without clear role definitions, organizations risk creating confusion about who is responsible for critical security decisions and actions, potentially leading to security gaps or delayed responses to incidents.

AI should be viewed as a tool to enhance human capabilities rather than replace human analysts. AI systems can excel at processing vast amounts of data, identifying patterns, and automating routine tasks, but they lack the contextual understanding, intuitive reasoning, and ethical judgment that human security professionals bring to complex security challenges. Organizations need to clearly define how AI will augment human capabilities while maintaining appropriate human oversight and decision-making authority. Thus, the replacement of human security professionals with AI systems is ill-advised for several critical reasons. First, AI systems can be brittle, potentially failing in unexpected ways when encountering novel situations or sophisticated attacks. Second, they lack the ability to understand broader business contexts and make nuanced decisions that consider multiple stakeholder needs. Third, they cannot effectively handle the diplomatic and communication aspects of security operations, which often require careful navigation of organizational politics and stakeholder concerns.

Security teams need clearly defined roles for AI system management, including responsibilities for model training, validation, monitoring, and maintenance. This includes establishing clear accountability for AI system performance, security, and compliance with relevant regulations and standards. Organizations should also define roles for investigating and responding to AI-related security incidents, ensuring clear lines of responsibility when issues arise. The human element becomes particularly crucial in oversight roles, where experienced security professionals need to validate AI system outputs, investigate potential false positives, and make critical decisions about security responses. These roles require clear definition of authority and responsibility, ensuring that appropriate human judgment is applied to significant security decisions while leveraging AI capabilities for enhanced analysis and detection.

As AI security capabilities evolve, organizations need to maintain flexibility in role definitions while ensuring clear accountability remains in place. This includes regularly reviewing and updating role definitions to address new capabilities, threats, and requirements while maintaining effective security operations. Clear communication about roles and responsibilities helps teams adapt to changing conditions while maintaining security effectiveness. The development of AI literacy within cybersecurity teams has become crucial as AI technologies increasingly shape both defensive and offensive security operations. Security professionals need to understand not only traditional security principles but also how AI systems work and their capabilities, limitations, and potential vulnerabilities. This understanding enables teams to effectively leverage AI security tools while remaining aware of potential threats and attack vectors.

For defensive security operations, skill development must focus on both technical and strategic capabilities (Steingartner et al., 2021). Security teams need to understand how to effectively deploy and manage AI security systems, validate their outputs, and integrate them with existing security controls. This includes developing skills in data analysis, model validation, and AI system monitoring to ensure effective security operations while maintaining appropriate human oversight. On the offensive security side, professionals need to understand how AI systems can be compromised or manipulated. This includes developing knowledge of potential attack vectors against AI systems, understanding model vulnerabilities, and recognizing patterns that might indicate AI system compromise. This knowledge is crucial not only for offensive security operations but also for building better defensive capabilities.

The rapid evolution of AI technologies requires continuous learning and skill development. Organizations need to invest in ongoing training programs that keep security teams current with new AI capabilities, threats, and defense mechanisms. This includes both formal training programs and hands-on experience working with AI security systems in controlled environments. Therefore, cross-disciplinary skill development becomes very important as AI security involves elements of data science, traditional security, risk management, and compliance. Security professionals need to develop at least basic competency across these areas to effectively work with AI systems while maintaining robust security controls. This might include understanding basic machine learning concepts, data analysis techniques, and AI system architecture.

Organizations should also focus on developing soft skills that complement technical AI knowledge (Morandini et al., 2023). This includes critical thinking abilities, problem-solving skills, and effective communication capabilities. These skills are crucial for security professionals who need to explain AI-related security issues to stakeholders, investigate complex security incidents, and make informed decisions about AI system deployment and use. Training programs should include practical exercises and real-world scenarios that help security teams understand how AI systems behave in different situations. This hands-on experience is crucial for developing the intuition and judgment needed to effectively work with AI security systems while maintaining appropriate security controls. The development of AI literacy should extend beyond dedicated security teams to include broader IT staff and key stakeholders who interact with AI security systems. This wider understanding helps create a more resilient security posture by ensuring that potential security implications of AI systems are understood across the organization.

Another point that is important here is fostering a security-aware culture. This is especially true as organizations integrate AI into their security operations. This culture needs to encompass both traditional security awareness and understanding of AI-specific security considerations. Organizations must develop an environment where security consciousness is ingrained in daily operations, decision-making processes, and technology adoption strategies. AI systems can significantly enhance security awareness efforts by providing more sophisticated monitoring, analysis, and training capabilities. These systems can identify patterns of risky behavior, provide personalized security training recommendations, and generate realistic security scenarios for training purposes. AI-powered security awareness platforms can adapt to individual learning styles and knowledge levels, making training more effective and engaging. However, the increasing prevalence of AI in security operations also creates new challenges for security awareness. Team members need to understand both the capabilities and limitations of AI security systems, recognizing when to trust AI outputs and when to apply human judgment. This includes awareness of potential AI-specific vulnerabilities and attack vectors that might not be apparent in traditional security contexts.

Best practices for fostering security awareness in AI security teams include regular training sessions that combine technical knowledge with practical applications (Ugbebor et al., 2024). These sessions should cover both AI security principles and real-world examples of security incidents involving AI systems. Organizations should encourage open discussion of security concerns and near-miss incidents, creating an environment where team members feel comfortable reporting potential issues. Organizations should implement mentorship programs where experienced security professionals can guide newer team members in understanding both traditional security principles and AI-specific considerations. This includes sharing practical experience in working with AI security systems, handling security incidents, and making risk-based decisions about AI deployment and use.

Regular security exercises and simulations help teams develop practical experience while reinforcing security awareness. These exercises should include scenarios specific to AI security, such as identifying potential model manipulation attempts or responding to AI-related security incidents. The exercises should be designed to challenge teams while providing learning opportunities. Another important factor is the role communication plays in fostering security awareness. Organizations should establish clear channels for sharing security information, updates, and lessons learned. This includes regular security briefings, newsletters, and forums where team members can discuss security concerns and share insights about AI security challenges. Leadership support and example-setting are essential for establishing and maintaining a security-aware culture. Leaders should demonstrate commitment to security principles in their decisions and actions, actively participate in security awareness activities, and ensure adequate resources are allocated for security training and awareness programs. Organizations should also establish metrics for measuring security awareness and its effectiveness. This might include tracking participation in training programs, monitoring security incident reports, and assessing how well security principles are integrated into daily operations. Regular assessment helps organizations identify areas for improvement and adjust their awareness programs accordingly. Reward and recognition programs can help reinforce security-aware behavior. Organizations should acknowledge team members who demonstrate strong security awareness, contribute to security improvements, or help identify and address potential security issues. This positive reinforcement helps maintain motivation and engagement in security awareness efforts. In general, success in fostering a security-aware culture requires sustained effort and commitment. Organizations need to regularly review and update their awareness programs to address new threats and challenges while maintaining engagement from team members. This includes adapting training materials and approaches based on feedback and effectiveness measurements.

9.5 Policy Recommendations for AI and Generative AI Implementation: A Triangular Approach

As we have seen throughout this book, the rapid evolution of AI and generative AI has transformed the digital landscape, presenting organizations with unparalleled opportunities and unprecedented challenges. As AI becomes a critical tool, a formidable weapon, and a high-value target, organizations must adopt a multifaceted approach to its implementation. This section provides a comprehensive framework for addressing AI security through actionable policy recommendations, focusing on its role as a tool, weapon, and target.

9.5.1 AI as a Tool: Leveraging Capabilities Responsibly

Organizations increasingly use AI to enhance their operations, but harnessing its potential requires a focus on transparency, human oversight, and robust governance. Explainable AI (XAI) plays a vital role in ensuring decision-making processes are clear and understandable. Systems designed with XAI principles empower stakeholders to interpret AI-driven outputs and address security-critical applications with confidence. For example, AI systems used in financial fraud detection must provide detailed explanations of flagged transactions to support fair and accurate outcomes. To achieve this, organizations should incorporate XAI criteria into their vendor assessments and procurement policies, ensuring third-party tools align with transparency requirements.

Human-in-the-loop (HITL) integration offers a hybrid model that combines the efficiency of AI with the contextual understanding of human oversight. In security operations, HITL systems can validate AI-generated alerts, thereby reducing false positives and minimizing disruptions. Security analysts equipped with HITL workflows can interpret AI findings, providing nuanced responses to complex threats. Escalation protocols further enhance this collaboration by outlining steps for handling ambiguous cases, ensuring accountability and informed decision-making.

Regular audits of AI systems are essential for identifying biases, testing resilience to adversarial attacks, and validating performance. Organizations should conduct these audits frequently, documenting model updates and retraining efforts to maintain traceability. Independent third-party assessments provide additional assurance of AI system integrity, helping organizations build trust with stakeholders. Establishing governance frameworks tailored to AI enables organizations to address ethical, legal, and operational challenges effectively. By leveraging frameworks like the NIST AI Risk Management Framework or ISO 42001, organizations can develop clear protocols, responsibilities, and oversight mechanisms.

9.5.2 AI as a Weapon: Mitigating Malicious Use

The misuse of AI as a weapon poses a growing threat, necessitating robust safeguards to prevent exploitation. Access controls serve as a foundational defense, limiting system access to authorized personnel through multi-factor authentication (MFA) and role-based permissions. Continuous monitoring of access logs helps detect unauthorized activity, enabling swift responses to potential misuse.

Ethical use policies should clearly define acceptable applications of AI within the organization. These policies, supported by regular employee training, create a culture of accountability and ethical awareness. Incorporating misuse clauses in employee contracts reinforces the importance of adhering to these guidelines, while real-world examples of AI misuse help illustrate the consequences of unethical behavior. AI-powered threat detection tools enhance an organization's ability to identify and respond to security incidents. Simulating attack scenarios using generative AI allows organizations to stress-test their defenses and identify vulnerabilities. Integration of threat intelligence feeds ensures that security teams stay informed about emerging AI-driven cyber threats, enabling proactive measures to counteract them.

Collaboration between public and private sectors strengthens defenses against the weaponization of AI. Public–private partnerships facilitate the sharing of threat intelligence, best practices, and research findings. Participation in industry consortia and joint initiatives enables organizations to stay ahead of adversaries while contributing to the broader security ecosystem. Advocacy for global standards and treaties addressing AI misuse underscores the need for a unified approach to combating threats.

9.5.3 AI as a Target: Protecting AI Systems

As organizations increasingly rely on AI systems, safeguarding these assets becomes paramount. Strengthening the security of AI infrastructure, including hardware, software, and supporting data, is a critical first step. Regularly patching vulnerabilities, employing endpoint protection, and adopting zero trust architecture (ZTA) principles mitigate risks to AI systems.

The security of training data and datasets is equally important, as compromised data can undermine the integrity of AI models. Encryption of sensitive datasets and rigorous due diligence on third-party data sources help prevent breaches and ensure data quality. Differential privacy techniques further enhance data security, allowing organizations to anonymize information while preserving analytical value.

Defending against adversarial attacks requires a preventative approach, including training AI models with adversarial examples and monitoring for anomalies. Ideally, organizations will invest in cutting-edge research to develop robust defenses against sophisticated manipulation techniques. Incorporating AI-specific incident response plans ensures preparedness for scenarios involving AI system compromises. Tabletop exercises simulating AI-targeted attacks help response teams refine their strategies and enhance resilience.

Policy implementation varies depending on the size and resources of an organization. Smaller organizations can adopt lightweight governance models and focus on core AI use cases with clear ROI. Open-source tools and community-driven initiatives offer cost-effective solutions for model auditing and monitoring. Medium-sized organizations benefit from establishing dedicated AI teams that include cross-functional expertise. Tiered access controls and formalized governance frameworks ensure security and compliance. Larger organizations, with their greater resources, can invest in enterprise-grade AI threat detection systems and lead industry collaboration. Dedicated red teams for AI testing and simulated adversarial attacks help uncover vulnerabilities, guiding system improvements. These organizations should leverage their influence to contribute to global standards and ethical frameworks.

9.5.4 Long-Term Strategic Considerations

Achieving sustainable AI security requires a commitment to continuous improvement. A culture of learning, supported by regular employee education and cross-disciplinary collaboration, equips organizations to navigate the dynamic AI landscape. Engaging with policymakers ensures that organizational policies remain aligned with evolving regulatory requirements, minimizing compliance risks. Future-proofing AI systems involves designing modular architectures that facilitate updates and adaptability. Regular reviews of AI models help retire outdated systems, reducing exposure to emerging threats. By embedding these practices into their operations, organizations can build resilient, forward-looking strategies for AI security.

9.5.5 A Triangular Path Forward

Organizations face a complex and ever-changing environment as AI becomes a tool for innovation, a weapon in the wrong hands, and a target for adversaries. Addressing these dimensions requires a comprehensive approach that integrates transparency, oversight, and robust security measures. Remember, a triangular approach empowers organizations to harness AI's transformative potential while safeguarding their operations and maintaining the intangible aspect: their reputation and trust between stakeholders.

Chapter 9 Summary

This chapter bridges theoretical knowledge with practical implementation by providing organizations with a comprehensive roadmap for integrating generative AI security measures into their operations. The chapter introduces a structured Generative AI Security Readiness Assessment Framework that evaluates five critical dimensions: technical infrastructure, data management capabilities, security governance frameworks, human expertise, and risk management processes. Central to successful implementation is the alignment of AI security strategies with business objectives, ensuring that security measures enhance, rather than impede, business operations while involving key stakeholders from both business and security functions. The chapter addresses the growing challenge of shadow AI (unauthorized use of AI tools within organizations) and highlights the need for balanced strategies that provide approved alternatives, implement robust monitoring capabilities, and foster responsible AI usage through employee education, rather than relying solely on restrictive policies.

The human element remains critical in AI security implementation, with emphasis on building effective AI security teams that view AI as a tool to enhance rather than replace human capabilities. Organizations must invest in developing AI literacy within cybersecurity teams while clearly defining roles and responsibilities for AI system oversight, model validation, and incident response. The chapter concludes with comprehensive policy recommendations based on a triangular approach that addresses AI as a tool (through explainable AI principles and governance frameworks), a weapon (through access controls and ethical guidelines), and a target (through infrastructure security and adversarial attack defenses). This framework remains adaptable to organizations of different sizes, from startups implementing lean approaches to large enterprises developing comprehensive, enterprise-wide strategies while maintaining flexibility to evolve with the rapidly changing AI landscape.

Key Takeaways:

Organizations must conduct comprehensive readiness assessments across five key dimensions before implementing AI security measures, ensuring they have the necessary technical infrastructure, data management capabilities, governance frameworks, human expertise, and risk management processes in place. The successful integration of AI security requires strategic alignment with business objectives, involving stakeholders from both business and security functions to create shared understanding and ensure security investments deliver meaningful business value while effectively managing risks. Shadow AI presents a significant challenge that requires nuanced management strategies rather than purely restrictive approaches, necessitating the provision of approved alternatives, robust monitoring capabilities, and comprehensive employee education to balance security requirements with productivity needs. The human element remains paramount in AI security operations, with organizations needing to clearly define roles and responsibilities while viewing AI as a tool to enhance rather than replace human capabilities, requiring substantial investment in team building and continuous skill development. Moreover, policy implementation must adopt a triangular approach that addresses AI's role as a tool through transparency and governance, as a weapon through access controls and ethical guidelines, and as a target through robust security measures and incident response planning. Organizations of different sizes can adapt these frameworks to their specific contexts, with smaller organizations focusing on lean implementations and larger enterprises developing comprehensive, enterprise-wide strategies while maintaining the flexibility to evolve with the rapidly changing AI landscape.

Case Study: Implementing Generative AI Security in Organizations—A Triangular Path Forward

Introduction

Generative AI is reshaping the security landscape, offering organizations unprecedented opportunities to enhance their defenses. However, it also introduces significant risks, both as a weapon and target. This case study explores a real-world application of the concepts discussed in Chapter 9: *Implementing Generative AI Security in Organizations.* By synthesizing the frameworks and strategies outlined in the chapter, this case study highlights how an organization can adopt a triangular approach—leveraging AI as a tool, defending against its weaponization, and protecting it as a target.

Background

CyberSecure Inc., a mid-sized financial services company, embarked on an ambitious project to integrate generative AI into its cybersecurity architecture. With increasing cyber threats, including phishing, fraud, and adversarial attacks, CyberSecure recognized the transformative potential of AI. However, it faced challenges in readiness assessment, strategy alignment, team development, and policy implementation. This case study documents CyberSecure's journey from readiness assessment to strategic implementation, emphasizing the importance of a triangular framework to maximize AI's potential while mitigating associated risks.

Organizational Readiness Assessment

CyberSecure began by evaluating its readiness across five dimensions: technical infrastructure, data management, security governance, human expertise, and risk management.

- **Technical Infrastructure Readiness:** CyberSecure's existing infrastructure included advanced firewalls, SIEM systems, and basic machine learning models for anomaly detection. However, the company lacked AI-specific computational resources, such as GPUs for model training, and the integration AI capabilities with legacy systems.
- **Data Management Capabilities:** CyberSecure stored extensive structured (e.g. transactional logs) and unstructured data (e.g. customer support interactions). A critical gap was the lack of robust data quality controls and a framework for integrating sensitive data into AI models while maintaining compliance with GDPR and other regulations.
- **Security Governance Frameworks:** While CyberSecure had strong governance mechanisms for traditional IT security, these frameworks were not designed to address AI-specific risks, such as adversarial attacks and data poisoning.
- **Human Expertise Readiness:** CyberSecure's team included experienced security analysts but lacked AI-specialized talent. There was a need to upskill staff and hire experts in AI model development and validation.
- **Risk Management Processes:** The company's risk management framework was robust for traditional threats but needed enhancements to account for AI-specific risks, such as model theft and adversarial perturbations.

Outcome: The readiness assessment revealed strengths in traditional security but highlighted significant gaps in AI infrastructure, governance, and expertise, forming the foundation for strategy development.

Developing an AI Security Strategy

The company's strategy focused on aligning AI security initiatives with business objectives, ensuring a seamless integration of AI capabilities into operations.

1) **Business Alignment:** CyberSecure's primary objective was to improve customer experience by detecting fraudulent activities in real time. The security team mapped AI security capabilities, such as anomaly detection, to these objectives. AI-driven tools were chosen to enhance fraud detection while minimizing disruptions to legitimate transactions.
2) **Risk Assessment and Financial Alignment:** A detailed risk assessment quantified the financial impact of potential breaches and demonstrated the ROI of AI security investments. By illustrating how AI could reduce fraud-related losses and operational inefficiencies, the team secured executive support.
3) **Implementation Roadmap:** CyberSecure adopted a phased approach:
   - **Phase 1:** Integration of pre-trained AI models for fraud detection.
   - **Phase 2:** Custom model development for advanced threat detection.
   - **Phase 3:** Real-time monitoring and adaptive AI systems.

The roadmap emphasized quick wins, such as deploying pre-trained models, while planning for long-term enhancements.

4) **Change Management:** The team developed narratives explaining how AI security initiatives supported business goals. Regular training sessions helped staff adapt to new workflows, and feedback mechanisms ensured continuous improvement.

Building and Training AI Security Teams

Recognizing the human element's importance, CyberSecure invested in building a multidisciplinary AI security team.

1) **Defining Roles and Responsibilities:** Clear delineation of roles ensured accountability
   - o **AI Model Engineers:** Focused on model training, validation, and optimization.
   - o **Security Analysts:** Interpreted AI-generated alerts and contextualized findings.
   - o **Governance Leads:** Ensured compliance with regulations and internal policies.
2) **Skill Development:** A robust training program equipped the team with AI literacy, including
   - o Basics of machine learning and adversarial AI.
   - o Techniques for validating and monitoring AI models.
   - o Awareness of AI-specific vulnerabilities and attack vectors.

   Cross-disciplinary training incorporated elements of data science, security operations, and compliance.
3) **Fostering a Security-Aware Culture:**
   - o **Mentorship Programs:** Senior analysts mentored junior staff in handling AI-related incidents.
   - o **Simulations and Exercises:** Regular tabletop exercises tested responses to AI-targeted attacks.
   - o **Recognition and Rewards:** Team members demonstrating exemplary security practices received recognition, reinforcing a culture of accountability and vigilance.

Policy Implementation: A Triangular Framework

To address AI's role as a tool, weapon, and target, CyberSecure adopted a triangular approach.

AI as a Tool:

- **XAI:** Implemented XAI to ensure decision-making transparency, allowing stakeholders to understand flagged transactions.

- **HITL:** Integrated workflows where analysts validated AI-generated alerts, ensuring nuanced responses to complex threats.
- **Audits and Governance:** Conducted regular audits to test resilience and maintain compliance with frameworks like NIST's AI RMF.

AI as a Weapon:

- **Access Controls:** Deployed role-based permissions and multi-factor authentication to prevent unauthorized access to AI systems.
- **Threat Simulations:** Used generative AI to simulate phishing attacks, identifying vulnerabilities in employee behavior and system defenses.
- **Collaboration:** Partnered with industry consortia to share threat intelligence and align defenses against emerging AI-driven threats.

AI as a Target:

- **Infrastructure Security:** Applied ZTA principles, ensuring robust endpoint protection and secure network segmentation.
- **Data Integrity:** Used encryption and differential privacy techniques to secure sensitive datasets.
- **Incident Response Plans:** Developed AI-specific response plans, including scenarios for handling adversarial attacks and data poisoning.

Results and Insights

Within 18 months, CyberSecure achieved significant milestones:

- **Enhanced Fraud Detection:** AI systems detected fraudulent transactions with 90% accuracy, reducing financial losses by 25%.
- **Operational Efficiency:** Automated workflows decreased the average time to resolve security incidents by 40%.
- **Cultural Shift:** Employees embraced AI-driven tools, supported by clear communication and training.

Lessons Learned

1) **Importance of Alignment:** Early integration of AI security measures with business objectives ensured executive support and resource allocation.
2) **Human–AI Collaboration:** HITL workflows demonstrated the synergy between human judgment and AI efficiency, reducing false positives.
3) **Adaptability:** The flexible roadmap allowed CyberSecure to adapt to rapidly evolving AI technologies and threats.

Conclusion

CyberSecure's journey underscores the importance of a triangular path forward. By viewing AI as a tool, weapon, and target, the organization successfully integrated AI security measures into its operations. This approach not only enhanced security but also supported business growth and innovation. The triangular framework serves as a blueprint for organizations navigating the complexities of AI security. As the AI landscape evolves, this comprehensive and adaptable approach ensures resilience, enabling organizations to harness AI's transformative potential while mitigating its risks.

CyberSecure AI Security Implementation Quiz

Questions

1 What approach did CyberSecure Inc. adopt to address the various roles of AI in cybersecurity?
   a) Dual-layer framework: infrastructure and applications
   b) Triangular framework: tool, weapon, and target
   c) Four-pillar approach: prevention, detection, response, and recovery
   d) Circular model: assess, implement, monitor, and improve

2 During the organizational readiness assessment, what was identified as a critical gap in CyberSecure's data management capabilities?
   a) Insufficient storage capacity for large datasets
   b) Lack of robust data quality controls for AI integration
   c) Outdated database management systems
   d) Absence of data visualization tools

3 What technique did CyberSecure implement to ensure transparency in AI decision-making?
   a) Machine learning operations (MLOps)
   b) Quantum computing algorithms
   c) Explainable AI (XAI)
   d) Natural language processing

4 How did CyberSecure approach the implementation of their AI security strategy?
   a) Big bang implementation of all AI tools simultaneously
   b) Outsourcing all AI development to third-party vendors
   c) Phased approach starting with pre-trained models
   d) Focus exclusively on custom-built proprietary systems

5 What was one of the key results achieved by CyberSecure within 18 months of implementing their AI security measures?
   a) Complete elimination of all security incidents
   b) 40% decrease in average time to resolve security incidents
   c) 75% reduction in cybersecurity staffing needs
   d) 100% accuracy in fraud detection

Answer Key

1 **Correct Answer: b) Triangular framework: tool, weapon, and target**
   - **Explanation:** The case study explicitly states that CyberSecure "adopted a triangular approach" and implemented a "Policy Implementation: A Triangular Framework" that addressed "AI's role as a tool, weapon, and target." This framework is fundamental to their entire implementation strategy.
   - Option a) is incorrect because no dual-layer framework focusing on infrastructure and applications is mentioned in the case study.
   - Option c) is incorrect because while prevention, detection, response, and recovery are standard cybersecurity practices, the case study specifically emphasizes the triangular framework.
   - Option d) is incorrect because while the company likely used some form of continuous improvement, the case study doesn't describe a circular model with these specific components.

2 **Correct Answer: b) Lack of robust data quality controls for AI integration**
   - **Explanation:** The case study directly states that "A critical gap was the lack of robust data quality controls and a framework for integrating sensitive data into AI models while maintaining compliance with GDPR and other regulations."
   - Option a) is incorrect because insufficient storage capacity wasn't mentioned as a gap in the case study.
   - Option c) is incorrect because outdated database management systems weren't identified as a critical gap.
   - Option d) is incorrect because the absence of data visualization tools wasn't mentioned as a gap in the data management capabilities.

3 **Correct Answer: c) Explainable AI (XAI)**
   - **Explanation:** Under the "AI as a Tool" section, the case study states that CyberSecure "Implemented XAI to ensure decision-making transparency, allowing stakeholders to understand flagged transactions."
   - Option a) is incorrect because while MLOps might have been used, it wasn't specifically mentioned as a technique for ensuring transparency.

- Option b) is incorrect because quantum computing algorithms weren't mentioned in the case study.
- Option d) is incorrect because natural language processing wasn't specifically mentioned as being used for transparency.

4 **Correct Answer: c) Phased approach starting with pre-trained models**
- **Explanation:** The case study outlines a clear phased approach in the Implementation Roadmap: "Phase 1: Integration of pre-trained AI models for fraud detection. Phase 2: Custom model development for advanced threat detection. Phase 3: Real-time monitoring and adaptive AI systems."
- Option a) is incorrect because the case study explicitly mentions a phased approach rather than simultaneous implementation.
- Option b) is incorrect because outsourcing wasn't mentioned as their implementation strategy; rather, they invested in building internal capabilities.
- Option d) is incorrect because they started with pre-trained models before moving to custom development, not focusing exclusively on proprietary systems.

5 **Correct Answer: b) 40% decrease in average time to resolve security incidents**
- **Explanation:** The case study directly states in the Results and Insights section that "Automated workflows decreased the average time to resolve security incidents by 40%."
- Option a) is incorrect because complete elimination of security incidents wasn't claimed and would be unrealistic.
- Option c) is incorrect because reduction in cybersecurity staffing needs wasn't mentioned as a result.
- Option d) is incorrect because the case study states they achieved "90% accuracy" in fraud detection, not 100%.

References

Arslan, A., Cooper, C., Khan, Z., Golgeci, I., & Ali, I. (2022). Artificial intelligence and human workers interaction at team level: A conceptual assessment of the challenges and potential HRM strategies. *International Journal of Manpower*, *43*(1), 75–88.

Bawa, S. S. (2023). How business can use ERP and AI to become intelligent enterprise. *International Journal of Innovative Science and Research Technology*, *8*, 8–11.

Challoumis, C. (2024). The future of business-integrating AI into the financial cycle. *XIV International Scientific Conference* (pp. 44–78).

Cloud Security Alliance. (2024, October 24). *Shadow AI prevention: Safeguarding your organization's AI landscape*. Cloud Security Alliance.

Enholm, I. M., Papagiannidis, E., Mikalef, P., & Krogstie, J. (2022). Artificial intelligence and business value: A literature review. *Information Systems Frontiers, 24*(5), 1709–1734.

Habbal, A., Ali, M. K., & Abuzaraida, M. A. (2024). Artificial intelligence trust, risk and security management (AI trism): Frameworks, applications, challenges and future research directions. *Expert Systems with Applications, 240*, 122442.

Kulkov, I., Kulkova, J., Rohrbeck, R., Menvielle, L., Kaartemo, V., & Makkonen, H. (2024). Artificial intelligence-driven sustainable development: Examining organizational, technical, and processing approaches to achieving global goals. *Sustainable Development, 32*(3), 2253–2267.

Morandini, S., Fraboni, F., De Angelis, M., Puzzo, G., Giusino, D., & Pietrantoni, L. (2023). The impact of artificial intelligence on workers' skills: Upskilling and reskilling in organisations. *Informing Science, 26*, 39–68.

Ranchordas, S. (2021). Experimental regulations for AI: Sandboxes for morals and mores. *Morals & Machines, 1*(1), 86–100.

Santos, O., & Radanliev, P. (2024). *Beyond the algorithm: AI, security, privacy, and ethics*. Addison-Wesley Professional.

Schueler, C. (2024, December 2). The shadow AI dilemma: Balancing Innovation and data security in the workplace. Forbes. https://www.forbes.com/councils/forbestechcouncil/2024/12/02/the-shadow-ai-dilemma-balancing-innovation-and-data-security-in-the-workplace/.

Sjödin, D., Parida, V., Palmié, M., & Wincent, J. (2021). How AI capabilities enable business model innovation: Scaling AI through co-evolutionary processes and feedback loops. *Journal of Business Research, 134*, 574–587.

Steingartner, W., Galinec, D., & Kozina, A. (2021). Threat defense: Cyber deception approach and education for resilience in hybrid threats model. *Symmetry, 13*(4), 597.

Truby, J., Brown, R. D., Ibrahim, I. A., & Parellada, O. C. (2022). A sandbox approach to regulating high-risk artificial intelligence applications. *European Journal of Risk Regulation, 13*(2), 270–294.

Ugbebor, F., Aina, O., Abass, M., & Kushanu, D. (2024). Employee cybersecurity awareness training programs customized for SME contexts to reduce human-error related security incidents. *Journal of Knowledge Learning and Science Technology, 3*(3), 382–409.

10

Future Outlook on AI and Cybersecurity

As we stand at the intersection of artificial intelligence (AI) advancement and cybersecurity challenges, the future of generative AI security presents both unprecedented opportunities and complex challenges. This concluding chapter synthesizes the key insights explored throughout this book while looking ahead to the evolving landscape of AI security. Understanding how security professionals' roles will transform, anticipating future challenges, and establishing frameworks for responsible AI security implementation becomes crucial for organizations and practitioners alike. The chapter examines these elements while considering broader societal and global implications, emphasizing the collective responsibility in shaping a secure and ethical AI-enabled future. As generative AI continues to transform the cybersecurity landscape, the decisions and actions we take today will significantly influence our ability to harness its benefits while managing associated risks.

10.1 The Evolving Role of Security Professionals

The role of security professionals is undergoing a fundamental transformation driven by the rapid advancement of AI technologies. While core security principles remain crucial, professionals must now develop a deep understanding of AI systems, their capabilities, and their potential vulnerabilities. This evolution requires security professionals to become increasingly AI-literate while maintaining and expanding their traditional security expertise. The pace of technological change, particularly in AI, demands that security professionals commit to continuous learning and adaptation more than ever before. While security professionals have always needed to stay current with new technologies, the transformative nature of AI and its rapid evolution create an unprecedented need for ongoing education and skill development. This includes understanding not just how to use AI tools, but how they work, their limitations, and their potential security implications.

Generative AI Security: Defense, Threats, and Vulnerabilities, First Edition. Shaila Rana and Rhonda Chicone.

Current security roles increasingly involve working with AI systems for threat detection, incident response, and risk assessment. Security professionals must understand how to effectively deploy and manage these systems while maintaining appropriate human oversight. This includes developing skills in data analysis, model validation, and AI system monitoring while maintaining traditional security capabilities. Looking ahead, security professionals will likely need to become more specialized in specific aspects of AI security while maintaining broad security knowledge. This might include roles focused on AI model security, AI-enabled threat hunting, or AI system validation and compliance. However, the human element of security work—including strategic thinking, ethical judgment, and stakeholder communication—will remain crucial. The augmentation of human capabilities through AI, rather than replacement, is one of the most effective approaches to security operations. AI systems can excel at processing vast amounts of data and identifying patterns, but they lack the contextual understanding, intuitive reasoning, and ethical judgment that human security professionals bring to complex security challenges. Security professionals need to learn how to effectively leverage AI capabilities while maintaining critical human oversight and decision-making authority.

The future role of security professionals will likely involve more strategic and interpretive work, with AI handling many routine tasks. This shifts the focus to higher-level activities like risk assessment, strategy development, and complex incident investigation. Security professionals will need to become skilled at interpreting AI system outputs, validating their conclusions, and making informed decisions about security responses. Organizations need to invest in developing their security teams' AI capabilities while maintaining core security expertise. This includes providing training opportunities, hands-on experience with AI systems, and clear career development paths that recognize the evolving nature of security work. Success in this evolution requires both individual commitment to learning and organizational support for professional development. Furthermore, the human element becomes particularly crucial in areas where AI systems currently struggle, such as understanding broader business context, managing stakeholder relationships, and making ethical decisions about security trade-offs. Security professionals need to develop these soft skills alongside technical capabilities to remain effective in an AI-enhanced security environment.

10.2 AI-Driven Incident Response and Recovery

As the cybersecurity landscape grows increasingly dynamic, organizations must adopt advanced tools to mitigate the risks of cyber incidents. AI has emerged as a transformative force in incident response and recovery, offering capabilities that enhance speed, precision, and resilience. The ability of AI to process vast amounts of data in real time, identify patterns, and suggest actionable solutions places it at the forefront of modern cybersecurity strategies. While traditional approaches to incident response have relied heavily on manual processes and static playbooks, the integration of AI enables a level of adaptability and foresight that was previously unattainable.

AI systems excel at addressing the complex and fast-paced nature of cyber incidents. When a security breach occurs, time is critical. Delays in detection and response often lead to escalated damage, prolonged downtime, and increased recovery costs. AI can analyze network traffic, detect anomalies, and identify threats much faster than traditional methods. Security teams gain the ability to respond in real time, using AI-generated insights to prioritize actions, allocate resources, and prevent further harm. This transformation is not merely about efficiency; it is a shift toward proactive and predictive defense mechanisms that strengthen overall resilience.

One of the most impactful applications of AI in incident response is its ability to perform automated threat containment. Modern cyberattacks are often designed to propagate rapidly, targeting multiple systems or exploiting interconnected vulnerabilities. AI-driven tools can detect these patterns of activity and execute containment measures autonomously. For instance, when malicious behavior is detected on a network, AI systems can automatically isolate affected endpoints, restrict access to sensitive systems, and flag compromised accounts. Such measures prevent attackers from escalating their activities, limiting the damage while human responders evaluate the broader context. The seamless integration of AI into these processes reduces response time and minimizes the risk of human error, a critical factor when dealing with fast-moving threats.

In addition to containment, AI plays a crucial role in recovery efforts, ensuring that affected systems and data are restored as quickly and securely as possible. Recovery from a cyber incident often involves complex processes, including restoring backups, validating system integrity, and addressing the root cause of the breach. AI-enhanced recovery tools can streamline these tasks by prioritizing the restoration of critical systems and automating repetitive processes. Machine learning algorithms can assess the effectiveness of different recovery strategies, providing recommendations that optimize outcomes based on real-time analysis. Moreover, AI can assist in identifying vulnerabilities that contributed to the incident, enabling organizations to implement more robust defenses and reduce the likelihood of recurrence.

An often-overlooked aspect of incident response is the opportunity to learn and improve from each event. AI excels at analyzing postincident data, uncovering patterns and correlations that might escape human detection. Through comprehensive forensic analysis, AI tools can identify gaps in existing security measures, highlight areas for improvement, and generate actionable insights for future planning. Organizations can use this information to refine their incident response playbooks, develop new training protocols, and enhance the effectiveness of their security posture. For example, AI might reveal that a particular type of phishing attack repeatedly bypassed email filters, prompting the organization to invest in more sophisticated antiphishing solutions or employee training programs.

The integration of AI into security operations centers (SOCs) is another significant evolution in the way organizations manage cybersecurity. Traditionally, SOCs have relied on teams of analysts to monitor alerts, investigate incidents, and coordinate responses. While effective, this approach is often labor-intensive and limited by the capacity of human resources. AI augments the capabilities of SOCs by automating routine tasks, such as triaging alerts and correlating data from multiple sources. This allows human analysts to focus on higher-level activities, such as interpreting AI findings, making strategic decisions, and managing complex incidents.

An AI-augmented SOC not only enhances efficiency but also improves the accuracy of incident detection and response. False positives are a common challenge in traditional security monitoring, leading to wasted time and resources. AI's ability to learn from historical data and adapt to evolving threat landscapes reduces the incidence of false positives, ensuring that analysts can concentrate on genuine threats. Furthermore, AI systems can provide detailed context for each alert, enabling faster and more informed decision-making. This collaborative approach between humans and AI fosters a more effective and adaptive security environment.

The future of AI-driven incident response lies in its ability to anticipate and address emerging threats. Predictive analytics, powered by machine learning, enables organizations to identify potential vulnerabilities and attack vectors before they are exploited. By analyzing historical data, threat intelligence, and real-time inputs, AI can simulate potential attack scenarios and assess their impact on the organization's infrastructure. This proactive approach empowers security teams to implement preemptive measures, such as patching vulnerabilities, updating configurations, or conducting targeted training exercises. The ability to anticipate and prepare for future challenges is a key advantage of AI in building long-term resilience.

Collaboration and information sharing are essential components of an effective incident response strategy. AI can facilitate this by aggregating and synthesizing information from multiple sources, including threat intelligence feeds, industry reports, and internal data. Organizations can use AI to share anonymized insights and best practices, fostering a collective defense against cyber threats. For example, an AI system could analyze data from a recent ransomware attack, identify the tactics used by the attackers, and distribute this information to other organizations in the same industry. Such collaboration not only enhances individual security but also strengthens the broader cybersecurity ecosystem.

To fully realize the potential of AI in incident response and recovery, organizations must invest in research and development (R&D). Advancing AI capabilities requires ongoing exploration of new algorithms, techniques, and applications. Organizations should allocate resources for testing emerging solutions, conducting proof-of-concept projects, and collaborating with academic institutions and industry partners. This commitment to innovation ensures that organizations remain at the forefront of AI-driven security and are prepared to address the challenges of an ever-evolving threat landscape. Finally, the integration of AI into incident response must be guided by ethical considerations and a commitment to responsible implementation. Transparency, accountability, and human oversight are critical to ensuring that AI systems operate as intended and do not introduce new risks. Organizations must establish clear policies and procedures for the use of AI in security operations, including guidelines for when and how automated actions can be taken. Regular audits and assessments of AI systems are essential to maintaining their effectiveness and alignment with organizational goals.

In summary, AI-driven incident response and recovery represent a transformative approach to cybersecurity, offering unprecedented capabilities for detecting, containing, and mitigating threats. Through automation, predictive analytics, and enhanced collaboration, AI empowers organizations to respond to incidents with greater speed, precision, and resilience. As the cybersecurity landscape continues to evolve, the adoption of AI will become increasingly essential for organizations seeking to safeguard their assets, operations, and reputation. Embracing AI-driven strategies today will not only strengthen current defenses but also lay the foundation for a more secure and resilient future, which aligns with many cybersecurity initiatives and frameworks across the globe.

10.3 GAI Security Triad Framework (GSTF)

A triangular framework for generative AI security can be structured around its three key dimensions: tool, weapon, and target. Each dimension requires specific considerations, controls, and strategies, while understanding their interconnected nature.

As a Tool: Generative AI offers powerful capabilities for enhancing cybersecurity operations and defenses. Organizations can leverage generative AI for automated threat detection, processing vast amounts of security telemetry to identify patterns and anomalies that might escape human notice. It can generate synthetic data for security testing, automate penetration testing procedures, and assist in incident response planning by generating and analyzing potential scenarios. The tool aspect also includes capabilities like automated security policy generation, code vulnerability analysis, and real-time security monitoring. However, these implementations must be carefully managed to ensure accuracy, reliability, and appropriate human oversight.

As a Weapon: The same capabilities that make generative AI valuable for defense can be weaponized by malicious actors. This includes creating sophisticated phishing campaigns with highly convincing synthetic content, generating new malware variants that can evade traditional detection methods, and automating the discovery of system vulnerabilities. Adversaries can use generative AI to craft convincing deepfakes for social engineering attacks, generate targeted disinformation campaigns, and develop more sophisticated attack strategies. Organizations must understand these potential weaponization aspects to develop effective countermeasures and detection capabilities.

As a Target: Generative AI systems themselves represent valuable targets for attackers. This dimension includes vulnerabilities specific to AI systems, such as training data poisoning, model extraction attacks, and adversarial examples that can manipulate AI outputs. Organizations must implement specific security measures to protect their AI infrastructure, including securing training data pipelines, monitoring for signs of model manipulation, and ensuring the integrity of AI-generated outputs. This also involves protecting against prompt injection attacks, unauthorized model access, and potential exfiltration of sensitive training data.

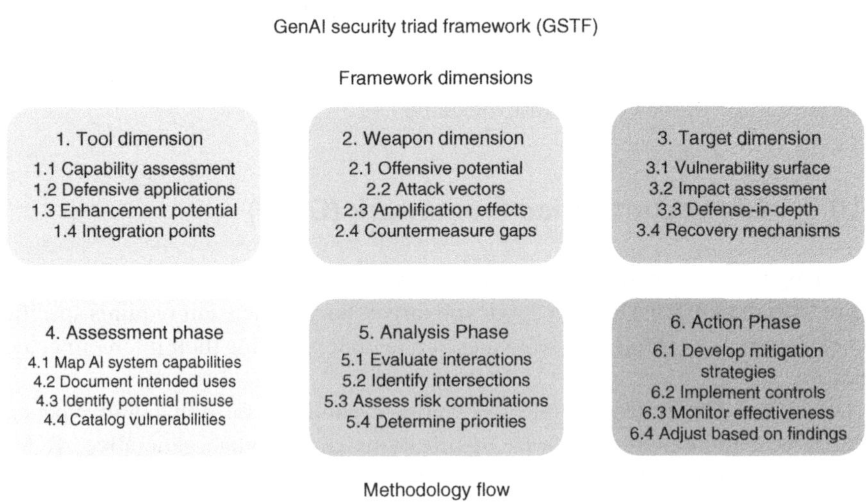

1. Tool Dimension
   1.1 Capability assessment: How the AI system functions as a security tool
   1.2 Defensive applications: What protective measures it can provide
   1.3 Enhancement potential: How it can strengthen existing security
   1.4 Integration points: How it works with other security tools
2. Weapon Dimension
   2.1 Offensive potential: How the AI could be weaponized
   2.2 Attack vectors: Possible malicious applications
   2.3 Amplification effects: How it could enhance existing threats
   2.4 Countermeasure gaps: Areas where defenses might be inadequate
3. Target Dimension
   3.1 Vulnerability surface: What can be attacked (data and model)
   3.2 Impact assessment: Consequences of compromise
   3.3 Defense-in-depth: Layered protection needs
   3.4 Recovery mechanisms: How to restore after compromise

Methodology Flow:

4. Assessment Phase
   4.1 Map AI system capabilities
   4.2 Document intended uses
   4.3 Identify potential misuse scenarios
   4.4 Catalog vulnerabilities
5. Analysis Phase
   5.1 Evaluate interactions between dimensions
   5.2 Identify critical intersections
   5.3 Assess risk combinations
   5.4 Determine security priorities
6. Action Phase
   6.1 Develop mitigation strategies
   6.2 Implement controls
   6.3 Monitor effectiveness
   6.4 Adjust based on findings

This framework provides organizations with a structured approach to managing the complex security implications of generative AI, while ensuring comprehensive coverage of potential risks and opportunities. The key is understanding the interconnected nature of these dimensions and implementing security measures that address all three aspects simultaneously. Organizations should regularly review and update their implementation of this framework as generative AI technology evolves and new threats emerge. This includes staying informed about emerging attack vectors, updating security controls, and adapting response procedures to address new challenges while continuing to leverage the benefits of generative AI technologies.

10.3.1 GAI Security Triad Framework (GSTF) Implementation Guide

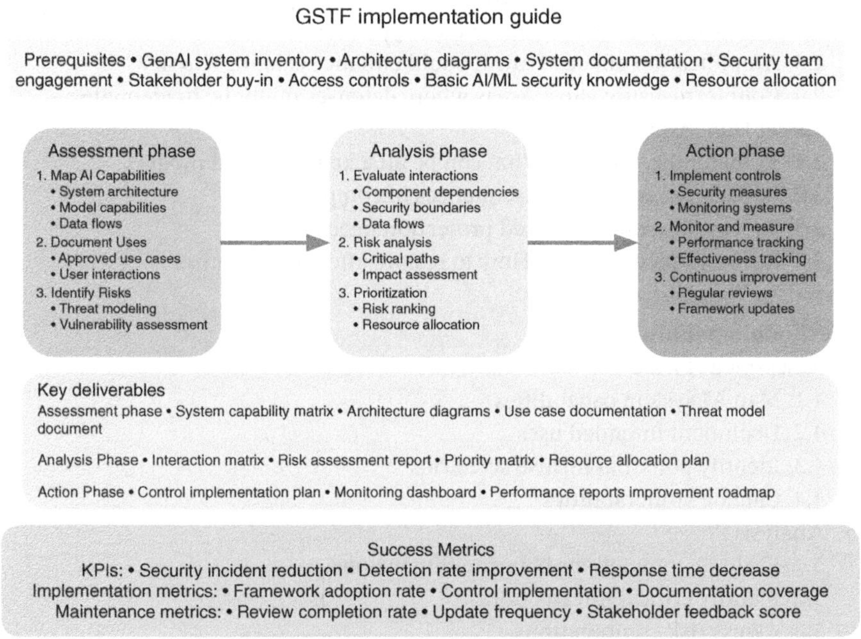

This guide provides detailed instructions for implementing the GAI Security Triad Framework (GSTF) within your organization. The GSTF is designed to comprehensively assess and manage security aspects of generative AI systems through three key dimensions: Tool, Weapon, and Target.

10.3.2 Prerequisites

10.3.2.1 Inventory of GAI Systems and Applications

Before implementing the GAI Security Triad Framework, organizations must conduct a comprehensive audit of all generative AI applications currently deployed or in development. This inventory should document the purpose, function, and business criticality of each GAI system, including both internally developed and third-party solutions. Systems should be categorized by type (e.g., text generation, image generation, and code generation) to better understand the scope of implementation. An up-to-date registry with ownership and responsible parties must be maintained for each system to ensure clear accountability throughout the security program.

10.3.2.2 Access to System Documentation and Architecture Diagrams

Successful implementation requires gathering detailed documentation for each GAI system, including architectural blueprints that outline the system structure and components. Organizations need to ensure access to model specifications, including model type, size, and version information, to properly assess security implications. Information about training methodologies and data sources used must be collected to identify potential vulnerabilities. Additionally, documentation should cover system dependencies, APIs, and integration points, along with mapped infrastructure components supporting GAI systems, including compute resources and storage requirements.

10.3.2.3 Security Team Engagement

Establishing dedicated security personnel responsible for AI system security is crucial for effective implementation. Organizations should ensure security team members have appropriate AI/ML domain expertise to accurately assess risks specific to generative AI. Clear communication channels between AI developers and security teams must be created to facilitate collaboration and rapid response to emerging threats. Well-defined roles and responsibilities for security monitoring and incident response should be established early in the implementation process. Regular security briefings and knowledge-sharing sessions help maintain awareness and build organizational capability in GAI security.

10.3.2.4 Stakeholder Buy-In Across Development and Operations

Successful implementation relies on identifying key stakeholders from development, operations, legal, and executive teams who will champion the security initiative. Executive sponsorship for the GAI security program must be secured to ensure appropriate resources and prioritization. Organizations should develop and communicate a compelling business case for comprehensive GAI security that aligns with strategic objectives. Cross-functional governance committees should be established to oversee GAI security initiatives and ensure consistent implementation across the organization. Creating awareness programs will foster a security-conscious culture around GAI systems and promote shared responsibility for security outcomes.

10.3.2.5 Basic Understanding of AI/ML Security Concepts

Ensuring key personnel have foundational knowledge of AI-specific security threats is essential for effective implementation. Organizations should provide training on common attack vectors like prompt injection, model extraction, and data poisoning to build the capability to address these specialized threats. Developing an understanding of AI safety concepts and alignment challenges helps teams appreciate the unique security considerations for generative AI. Establishing familiarity with relevant standards and frameworks (e.g., NIST AI RMF, OWASP for LLMs) provides a foundation for security design. Creating a knowledge base of AI security resources supports continuous learning as the field evolves and new threats emerge.

10.3.3 Framework Dimensions Implementation

1. **Tool Dimension**

1.1 **Capability Assessment**

Document AI System Capabilities and Functionalities: Organizations must create comprehensive inventories of each GAI system's capabilities to understand the full scope of what these systems can do. This documentation should cover the types of content each system can generate (text, code, images, etc.) and catalog the domains of knowledge the system can access and process. Integration capabilities with other systems and data sources should be identified to understand potential security implications of connected systems. Any specialized functions or proprietary capabilities should be documented to ensure complete coverage of the security assessment.

Map Security-Relevant Features and Controls: Existing content filtering mechanisms and their effectiveness should be identified and evaluated to understand current protection levels. Authentication and authorization controls for system access need to be documented to assess who can access the system and what actions they can perform. Data encryption methods used across the GAI pipeline should be mapped to identify potential exposure points. Current monitoring capabilities and their coverage must be cataloged to understand visibility into system operations. Audit logging features and retention policies should be documented to ensure appropriate recordkeeping for security events.

Evaluate Performance Metrics and Limitations: Organizations should measure and document response times under various load conditions to understand system behavior under stress. Assessment of computational resource requirements and scaling behavior helps identify potential denial-of-service vulnerabilities. Known performance degradation scenarios should be documented to understand potential security implications during system strain. Throughput limits and rate-limiting implementations need to be identified to prevent system abuse. Error-handling behaviors and fallback mechanisms should be recorded to ensure they don't introduce security vulnerabilities.

Assess Reliability and Accuracy Benchmarks: Developing and applying domain-specific accuracy metrics for generated content allows organizations to identify potentially harmful outputs. Measuring consistency of outputs under similar prompts helps identify potential manipulation attempts. Organizations should hallucination rates and factual accuracy benchmarks to understand the risk of generating false information. Assessing robustness against adversarial inputs reveals potential attack vectors. Creating baseline performance metrics enables ongoing comparison and anomaly detection that could indicate security issues.

1.2 **Defensive Applications**

Identify Current Security Use Cases: Organizations should document how GAI systems are currently used for security operations to build upon existing defensive applications. Cataloging threat detection applications and their effectiveness reveals how GAI contributes to the security posture. Security analytics use cases leveraging GAI capabilities should be identified to understand current defensive implementations. Mapping incident response processes enhanced by GAI helps identify how these systems support security operations. Documentation of fraud detection and prevention applications provides insight into established defensive mechanisms that can be strengthened.

Document Protective Measures Implemented: Existing content filtering systems and their effectiveness should be cataloged to understand current protection against harmful outputs. Prompt validation and sanitization methods need to be documented to assess defense against injection attacks. Mapping access control mechanisms and their implementation reveals who can access the system and what they can do. Data protection measures throughout the GAI pipeline should be recorded to identify potential exposure points. Current monitoring and alerting systems specific to GAI need to be documented to understand visibility into potential security events.

Map Threat Detection Capabilities: Organizations should identify GAI applications for detecting unusual user behavior that could indicate attacks or misuse. Capabilities for identifying malicious inputs need to be documented to understand defensive readiness. Anomaly detection features across GAI systems should be mapped to assess the ability to detect attacks. Detection methods for model abuse attempts must be cataloged to understand protection against manipulation. Integration with broader security monitoring systems should be documented to ensure comprehensive visibility into security events.

List Security Monitoring Features: Current audit logging implementations and their coverage need to be cataloged to ensure appropriate visibility into system activities. User interaction monitoring capabilities should be documented to detect potential abuse patterns. Model performance monitoring for detecting manipulation attempts needs to be mapped to identify potential tampering. Real-time alert mechanisms and their triggers should be identified to ensure a timely response to security events. Compliance monitoring features and reporting capabilities should be documented to support regulatory requirements and internal governance.

1.3 **Enhancement Potential**

Evaluate Possible Security Improvements: Organizations should identify gaps in current security controls that could be addressed to strengthen the security posture. Assessing the potential for enhanced content filtering mechanisms helps prevent harmful outputs. Opportunities for improved authentication methods need to be evaluated to prevent unauthorized access. Potential for better detection of malicious inputs should be documented to enhance protection against attacks. Possible enhancements to audit and monitoring capabilities help improve visibility into security events and potential breaches.

Identify Integration Opportunities: Potential integration points with existing security tools should be mapped to enhance overall security monitoring. Opportunities for SIEM integration and alert correlation need to be assessed to improve security event detection. Potential for enhanced threat intelligence integration should be identified to improve threat awareness. Possible integrations with identity management systems help strengthen access controls. Integration opportunities with security orchestration platforms should be evaluated to improve automated response capabilities.

Document Scalability Options: Organizations should assess how security controls can scale with increased system usage to maintain protection as adoption grows. Options for handling larger volumes of security telemetry need to be documented to ensure visibility as scale increases. Approaches for maintaining performance during security operations should be identified to prevent degradation under load. Strategies for scaling monitoring capabilities help ensure continued visibility as systems grow. Resource requirements for scaled security operations must be documented to support capacity planning.

Assess Potential Feature Additions: New security features that could enhance protection should be identified to guide development roadmaps.

Potential for implementing user behavior analysis needs to be documented to detect anomalous usage patterns. The feasibility of adding advanced threat detection capabilities should be assessed to improve security posture. Options for enhanced security automation help improve response time and consistency. Potential new reporting and compliance features need to be mapped to support governance requirements.

1.4 **Integration Points**

Map Current Security Tool Integrations: Existing connections with security monitoring platforms should be documented to understand current visibility across tools. Integration with identity and access management systems needs to be cataloged to assess authentication and authorization controls. Connections to threat intelligence platforms should be mapped to understand threat awareness capabilities. Integration with incident response workflows helps assess response efficiency. Connections with compliance reporting systems need to be identified to understand governance support.

Document APIs and Interfaces: All exposed APIs and their security controls should be cataloged to identify potential attack surfaces. Interface specifications and authentication requirements need to be documented to assess access control strength. Data exchange formats and validation methods should be mapped to identify potential injection points. Rate-limiting implementations on interfaces help prevent abuse and denial of service. Error handling and security exception processes must be documented to ensure they don't introduce vulnerabilities.

Evaluate Data Flow Security: Data encryption methods during transit should be assessed to prevent unauthorized access to information in motion. Data validation processes at entry points need to be documented to prevent injection attacks. Data transformation security controls should be mapped to identify potential manipulation points. Potential data leakage points must be identified to prevent unauthorized information disclosure. Data minimization practices across flows help reduce the attack surface and potential exposure.

Assess Authentication Mechanisms: User authentication methods for system access should be documented to understand access control strength. Service-to-service authentication implementations need to be cataloged to assess internal system security. Session management and token security controls should be mapped to prevent session hijacking. MFA implementations and their coverage help strengthen access controls. Authentication logging and monitoring must be documented to ensure visibility into access attempts and potential breaches.

2. **Weapon Dimension**

2.1 **Offensive Potential**

Analyze Possible Malicious Uses: Organizations should conduct red team exercises to identify potential abuse vectors that could exploit system capabilities. How system capabilities could be weaponized needs to be documented to understand offensive risks. The potential for generating harmful content should be assessed to understand possible misuse scenarios. Possible use for social engineering attacks must be identified to understand human-targeted risk vectors. Risks of unauthorized information disclosure should be documented to understand potential data breach scenarios.

Document Potential Attack Scenarios: Detailed scenarios for system compromise should be created to understand attack paths and outcomes. The potential for data exfiltration via the GAI system needs to be documented to understand information security risks. Scenarios for poisoning system outputs should be mapped to understand integrity risks. Potential for denial-of-service attacks must be identified to understand availability risks. Possible reputation damage scenarios should be documented to understand broader business impacts.

Evaluate Dual-Use Capabilities: Features with both legitimate and malicious applications should be identified to understand inherent risk areas. Capabilities that could enable phishing content generation need to be documented to understand social engineering risks. Functions that could assist in vulnerability discovery should be assessed to understand the potential for weaponization. Features that could be used for evasion of security controls need to be mapped to understand detection bypass risks. Capabilities that could enable impersonation should be documented to understand identity-based attack risks.

Assess Weaponization Risks: The potential for automation of attacks should be evaluated to understand scale and efficiency risks. Risks of attack scaling through GAI capabilities need to be documented to understand potential impact amplification. The potential for creating novel attack patterns should be assessed to understand detection evasion risks. Risks of enhanced social engineering must be identified to understand human vulnerability exploitation. The potential for creating persistent threats should be documented to understand the long-term security impact.

2.2 **Attack Vectors**

Map Potential Entry Points: All public-facing interfaces and their vulnerabilities should be identified to understand the initial attack surface. Potential for prompt injection attacks needs to be documented to understand input manipulation risks. API endpoint vulnerabilities and attack surfaces should be mapped to understand service-level risks.

System integration points that could be exploited must be identified to understand connection-based risks. User interface attack vectors should be documented to understand human interaction risk points.

Document Exploitable Features: Features that could be manipulated for unintended purposes should be identified to understand functional risks. Potential for jailbreaking techniques needs to be documented to understand constraint bypass risks. Functions vulnerable to parameter manipulation should be mapped to understand input validation risks. Features vulnerable to rate abuse must be identified to understand resource exhaustion risks. Capabilities that could enable context manipulation should be documented to understand semantic security risks.

Identify Vulnerable Dependencies: Third-party libraries and their known vulnerabilities should be cataloged to understand inherited risks. Dependencies on external APIs and their security needs need to be documented to understand supply chain risks. Infrastructure dependencies and their security posture should be mapped to understand operational support risks. Model serving frameworks and their vulnerabilities must be identified to understand deployment risks. Data pipeline dependencies and security issues should be documented to understand data flow risks.

Assess Social Engineering Risks: The potential for generating convincing phishing content should be evaluated to understand deception risks. Risks of impersonation using system outputs need to be documented to understand identity-based attack vectors. The potential for creating persuasive false information should be mapped to understand misinformation risks. Risks of generating targeted manipulation content must be identified to understand personalized attack risks. Capabilities for bypassing human judgment should be documented to understand cognitive exploitation risks.

2.3 **Amplification Effects**

Evaluate Cascade Failure Scenarios: Organizations should document how an initial compromise could cascade to other systems to understand propagation risks. The potential for automated attack propagation needs to be assessed to understand risk multiplication. Interdependency risks across connected systems should be mapped to understand chain reaction potential. Potential for triggering multiple failure points must be identified to understand compound impact risks. Worst-case cascade scenarios and impacts should be documented to understand maximum potential damage.

Document Potential Damage Multiplication: How GAI could increase the impact of traditional attacks should be assessed to understand amplification risks. The potential for amplifying data breaches needs to be documented to understand information exposure risks. Scenarios for magnifying social engineering effectiveness should be mapped to understand human vulnerability amplification. Potential for escalating privilege abuse must be identified to understand access control amplification risks. Ways GAI could multiply the reach of malicious content should be documented to understand scale enhancement risks.

Assess Automated Attack Capabilities: The potential for automating reconnaissance should be evaluated to understand target identification risks. Capabilities for automated vulnerability discovery need to be documented to understand exploit development risks. The potential for automating exploit development should be mapped to understand attack acceleration risks. Risks of automated target selection must be identified to understand precision attack risks. Capabilities for automated attack customization should be documented to understand personalized attack risks.

Identify Chain Reaction Risks: How one compromise could lead to multiple system failures should be assessed to understand cascading impact risks. Interdependencies that create vulnerability chains need to be documented to understand sequential exploitation risks. The potential for triggered attack sequences should be mapped to understand attack automation risks. Compound vulnerability scenarios must be identified to understand synergistic exploitation risks. Time-delayed chain reaction possibilities should be documented to understand latent risk activation.

2.4 **Countermeasure Gaps**

Map Current Security Blind Spots: Areas not covered by existing monitoring should be identified to understand visibility gaps. Gaps in detection capabilities need to be documented to understand what attacks might go unnoticed. Unmonitored data flows and interfaces should be mapped to understand potential covert channels. Unprotected assets and components must be identified to understand exposure points. Visibility gaps in security operations should be documented to understand monitoring limitations.

Document Missing Controls: Security controls that should be implemented but are currently absent should be cataloged to guide enhancement efforts. Gaps in authentication and authorization need to be documented to understand access control weaknesses. Missing validation and sanitization controls should be mapped to understand input handling vulnerabilities. Insufficient encryption implementations must be identified to understand data protection gaps. Inadequate access restrictions should be documented to understand permission management weaknesses.

Identify Response Limitations: Gaps in incident response capabilities should be assessed to understand reaction readiness. Inadequate containment procedures need to be documented to understand breach limitation challenges. Limitations in forensic capabilities should be mapped to understand investigative constraints. Insufficient recovery procedures must be identified to understand business continuity risks. Gaps in postincident analysis capabilities should be documented to understand lessons-learned limitations.

Assess Detection Gaps: Blind spots in anomaly detection should be evaluated to understand what abnormal behaviors might go unnoticed. Insufficient logging implementations need to be documented to understand visibility challenges. Gaps in real-time monitoring should be mapped to understand delayed detection risks. Unmonitored attack vectors must be identified to understand security coverage limitations. Limitations in alert correlation capabilities should be documented to understand complex attack detection challenges.

3. **Target Dimension**

3.1 **Vulnerability Surface**

Map Attack Surface (Data and Model): All potential attack points for the model itself should be documented to understand direct targeting risks. Data ingestion vulnerabilities need to be cataloged to understand input manipulation risks. Model serving infrastructure attack surfaces should be mapped to understand operational risks. Vulnerabilities in model deployment pipelines must be identified to understand supply chain risks. The potential for training data manipulation should be documented to understand model poisoning risks.

Document Exposed Endpoints: All API endpoints and their security controls should be cataloged to understand service exposure risks. Web interfaces and their protection mechanisms need to be documented to understand user interaction risks. Service endpoints and their authentication requirements should be mapped to understand service access risks. Management interfaces and their security controls must be identified to understand administrative risk. Monitoring and logging endpoints should be documented to understand meta-security risks.

Identify Sensitive Components: The location of model weights and parameters should be documented to understand intellectual property risks. Critical configuration files and their protection need to be cataloged to understand settings manipulation risks. Sensitive data repositories connected to the system should be mapped to understand information exposure risks. Critical training datasets and their security must be identified to understand training integrity risks. Key secrets and credentials used by the system should be documented to understand authentication compromise risks.

Assess Infrastructure Vulnerabilities: Compute infrastructure security posture should be evaluated to understand resource-level risks. Network security vulnerabilities need to be documented to understand connectivity risks. Storage system security weaknesses should be mapped to understand data persistence risks. Containerization and orchestration vulnerabilities must be identified to understand deployment risks. Physical security considerations for infrastructure should be documented to understand tangible access risks.

3.2 **Impact Assessment**

Evaluate Potential Breach Impacts: Potential data loss scenarios and their severity should be documented to understand information security implications. The potential for intellectual property theft needs to be assessed to understand the competitive impact. Potential regulatory compliance violations should be mapped to understand legal and financial implications. The potential impact on customer trust and reputation must be identified to understand market perception risks. Financial impact scenarios from different breaches should be documented to understand business continuity implications.

Document Critical Assets: High-value model assets and their security requirements should be cataloged to prioritize protection efforts. Proprietary algorithms and their protection needs should be documented to understand intellectual property risks. Critical training data and its security controls should be mapped to understand data integrity risks. Valuable output data requiring protection must be identified to understand information product risks. System configuration assets and their security should be documented to understand operational integrity risks.

Assess Business Consequences: Potential revenue impact from system compromise should be evaluated to understand financial implications. Potential market position consequences need to be documented to understand competitive impact. Potential competitive disadvantage scenarios should be mapped to understand strategic implications. Customer churn risks from security incidents must be identified to understand the relationship impact. The potential for increased regulatory scrutiny should be documented to understand compliance implications.

Map Dependency Chains: Systems dependent on the GAI application should be documented to understand the operational impact scope. Business processes relying on the system need to be cataloged to understand workflow disruption risks. Decision-making functions dependent on GAI outputs should be mapped to understand judgment impact risks. Automation capabilities relying on the system must be identified to understand process disruption risks. The full chain of dependencies and potential impacts should be documented to understand cascade effect implications.

3.3 **Defense-in-Depth**

Plan Layered Security Controls: Multiple layers of protection for critical assets should be designed to ensure redundant security coverage. Security controls at the data, model, and infrastructure levels need to be documented to ensure comprehensive protection. Preventive, detective, and corrective control layers should be mapped to ensure complete security lifecycle coverage. Complementary control strategies must be identified to ensure defense reinforcement. Control redundancy for critical protection needs should be documented to eliminate single points of failure.

Document Security Architecture: Comprehensive security architecture diagrams should be created to provide a visual representation of the defense strategy. Security zones and boundaries need to be documented to understand trust delineation. Trust relationships between components should be mapped to understand authentication paths. Security control placement throughout the system must be identified to understand protection coverage. Defense-in-depth implementation details should be documented to ensure a complete protection strategy understanding.

Implement Defense Strategies: Multilayered authentication mechanisms should be deployed to ensure strong identity verification. Implementation of least privilege principles needs to be documented to minimize access risk. Network segmentation strategies should be mapped to contain potential breaches. Data protection mechanisms at all stages must be identified to ensure information security. Continuous validation mechanisms should be documented to ensure ongoing security posture assessment.

Deploy Monitoring Solutions: Comprehensive logging across all components should be implemented to ensure complete visibility into system activity. Deployment of intrusion detection systems needs to be documented to ensure attack recognition capability. Security information monitoring implementations should be mapped to ensure centralized visibility. Anomaly detection system deployment must be identified to ensure behavioral deviation recognition. Alert correlation and analysis mechanisms should be documented to ensure holistic security event understanding.

3.4 **Recovery Mechanisms**

Develop Incident Response Plans: Detailed response procedures for different breach scenarios should be created to ensure a prepared reaction to security events. Escalation paths and decision authorities need to be documented to ensure clear responsibility during incidents. Communication protocols during incidents should be mapped to ensure a coordinated response. Roles and responsibilities for incident handling must be identified to ensure accountability. Criteria for activating different response levels should be documented to ensure proportional reaction.

Document Recovery Procedures: Step-by-step procedures for system restoration should be created to ensure business continuity capability. Clean model deployment processes need to be documented to ensure integrity during recovery. Data recovery procedures and validation steps should be mapped to ensure information restoration. Procedures for verifying system integrity must be identified to ensure a secure rebuild. Gradual service restoration protocols should be documented to ensure a controlled return to operation.

Implement Backup Strategies: Regular backup procedures for models and configurations should be deployed to ensure recovery capability. Secure storage of model versions and parameters needs to be documented to ensure protected recovery assets. Backup schedules and retention policies should be mapped to ensure appropriate versioning. Offline backup storage implementation must be identified to ensure availability during incidents. Verification procedures for backup integrity should be documented to ensure recovery reliability.

Test Restoration Processes: Regular restoration drills from backups should be conducted to ensure recovery capability verification. Validation procedures for restored systems need to be documented to ensure integrity confirmation. Verification steps for model integrity after restoration should be mapped to ensure functionality return. Performance testing after recovery must be identified to ensure operational capability. Lessons learned from restoration tests should be documented to ensure continuous improvement.

10.3.4 Methodology Flow Implementation

4. **Assessment Phase**

4.1 **Map AI System Capabilities**

Activities:

Document System Architecture: Organizations should create comprehensive architectural diagrams showing all system components to understand structural security implications. Data flows between components and with external systems need to be documented to understand information movement. Infrastructure elements supporting the GAI system should be mapped to understand operational dependencies. System boundaries and trust zones must be identified to understand security domains. Communication protocols and methods between components should be documented to understand connectivity security.

List AI Model Capabilities: Model type, size, and generation capabilities should be documented to understand functional security implications. Supported input and output modalities need to be cataloged to understand interaction attack surfaces. Domain knowledge and specialized capabilities should be mapped to understand potential for misuse. Fine-tuning and adaptation capabilities must be identified to understand model manipulation risks. Model performance characteristics and limitations should be documented to understand operational vulnerabilities.

Map Data Flows: Data should be traced from ingestion through processing to storage to understand the complete information lifecycle. Transformation points and processing logic need to be documented to understand data manipulation risks. Data persistence locations and retention policies should be mapped to understand storage security implications. Data sharing with external systems must be identified to understand information exposure risks. Data cleaning and preparation processes should be documented to understand preprocessing security.

Identify Key Components: Critical system components and their functions should be cataloged to understand operational dependencies. Dependencies between components need to be documented to understand cascade failure risks. Failure points and redundancy mechanisms should be mapped to understand resilience capabilities. Performance bottlenecks and scaling limitations must be identified to understand availability vulnerabilities. Management and monitoring components should be documented to understand operational control mechanisms.

Deliverables:

System Capability Matrix: A comprehensive table of system capabilities and their properties provides a reference for security analysis. Classification of capabilities by security relevance helps prioritize protection efforts. Mapping of capabilities to business functions clarifies operational importance. Documentation of capability limitations and constraints identifies inherent vulnerabilities. Risk ratings for each capability based on potential for misuse guides security resource allocation.

Architecture Diagrams: Visual representation of system components and relationships enables a holistic security understanding. Security zone delineation within the architecture clarifies trust boundaries. Identification of trust boundaries and security controls maps defense locations. Mapping of data flows with security classifications highlights sensitive information paths. Documentation of integration points with other systems identifies external attack surfaces.

Data Flow Maps: Visualization of data movement throughout the system enables information security analysis. Documentation of data transformations and processing steps identifies manipulation points. Classification of data sensitivity at each stage guides protection requirements. Mapping of access controls at different flow points identifies authorization checkpoints. Identification of encryption and protection methods documents data security measures.

Component Inventory: A detailed catalog of all system components provides a foundation for comprehensive security coverage. Documentation of component versions and update mechanisms guides patch management. Mapping of component owners and maintainers clarifies security responsibility. Assessment of component criticality to system operation prioritizes protection efforts. Documentation of component security posture and existing controls provides an inventory of current protections and identifies potential gaps.

4.2 **Document Intended Uses**

Activities:

List Approved Use Cases: Organizations should catalog all business-approved applications of the GAI system to establish a legitimate usage baseline. Use case objectives and success criteria need to be documented to understand operational parameters. Use cases should be mapped to business processes and functions to understand organizational dependencies. Intended user groups for each use case must be identified to understand access requirements. Use case limitations and constraints should be documented to understand operational boundaries.

Document Operational Parameters: Normal operating conditions and performance expectations should be defined to establish behavioral baselines. Acceptable response times and quality thresholds need to be documented to understand normal operation. Resource utilization parameters and limits should be mapped to understand capacity constraints. Availability requirements and maintenance windows must be identified to understand operational timing. Acceptable error rates and handling procedures should be documented to understand fault tolerance.

Map User Interactions: All interfaces through which users interact with the system should be documented to understand user-facing attack surfaces. Typical interaction patterns and workflows need to be cataloged to establish normal behavior baselines. Input validation processes and constraints should be mapped to understand protection mechanisms. Output presentation methods and formats must be identified to understand information delivery controls. Feedback mechanisms and user control options should be documented to understand user influence capabilities.

Identify Access Patterns: Which user roles access which system functions should be mapped to understand permission requirements. Typical access frequency and volume patterns need to be documented to establish usage baselines. Peak usage patterns and timing should be cataloged to understand load variations. Batch versus interactive access methods must be identified to understand different usage modes. System-to-system access patterns should be documented to understand automated interactions.

Deliverables:

Use Case Documentation: Detailed descriptions of each approved use case establish the legitimate functional boundary. Mapping of use cases to business objectives clarifies organizational value. Documentation of use case constraints and limitations defines operational parameters. Risk assessment for each use case identifies inherent security concerns. Identification of potential for misuse or abuse highlights security focus areas.

Operational Guidelines: Defined parameters for normal system operation establish behavioral baselines for monitoring. Documentation of performance expectations and thresholds guides anomaly detection. Established procedures for routine maintenance ensure operational security. Defined escalation paths for operational issues enable rapid response. Documentation of monitoring requirements guides visibility implementation.

User Interaction Flows: Visual representations of typical user workflows establish normal interaction patterns. Documentation of input validation requirements specifies entry point protections. Mapping of error handling procedures ensures security during exceptions. Identification of critical interaction points highlights security focus areas. Documentation of user feedback mechanisms clarifies system influence channels.

Access Control Matrix: Mapping of user roles to system functions establishes permission structures. Documentation of permission levels and inheritance clarifies access hierarchies. Definition of least privilege implementations ensures minimal necessary access. Identification of privileged access management highlights critical control points. Documentation of access review procedures ensures ongoing permission validation.

4.3 **Identify Potential Misuse**

Activities:

Conduct Threat Modeling: Organizations should apply structured threat modeling methodologies (e.g., STRIDE, LINDDUN) to systematically identify vulnerabilities. Threat actors and their motivations need to be identified to understand attack incentives. Potential attack vectors and techniques should be mapped to understand exploitation approaches.

Likely attack scenarios and their likelihood must be documented to prioritize defenses. Potential impact of successful attacks should be assessed to understand risk severity.

Analyze Abuse Cases: Potential system misuse scenarios should be documented to understand how legitimate functions could be weaponized. How legitimate features could be abused needs to be identified to understand dual-use risks. Paths to bypass intended constraints should be mapped to understand control circumvention. Potential for social engineering leveraging the system must be documented to understand human vulnerability exploitation. Insider threat abuse scenarios should be identified to understand internal risk vectors.

Document Risk Scenarios: Detailed narratives of potential attack scenarios should be created to understand attack progression. Attack prerequisites and required resources need to be documented to understand attack feasibility. Potential attack outcomes and consequences should be mapped to understand the impact scope. Cascading effects and secondary impacts must be identified to understand total damage potential. Recovery complexity for each scenario should be documented to understand restoration challenges.

Map Attack Paths: Step-by-step progression of potential attacks should be documented to understand attack sequences. Entry points and initial compromise methods need to be identified to understand breach initiation. Lateral movement possibilities within the system should be mapped to understand postcompromise expansion. Privilege escalation paths must be documented to understand authority enhancement risks. Data exfiltration or system manipulation endpoints should be identified to understand attack objectives.

Deliverables:

Threat Model Document: A comprehensive catalog of identified threats provides a foundation for security planning. Classification of threats by type and severity guides defense prioritization. Mapping of threats to system components identifies protection targets. Documentation of threat actors and their capabilities identifies adversary profiles. Assessment of threat likelihood and potential impact guides risk prioritization.

Abuse Case Catalog: Detailed documentation of potential system misuse establishes malicious usage patterns. Classification of abuse cases by severity and likelihood guides defense prioritization. Mapping of abuse cases to system capabilities identifies vulnerable functions. Documentation of abuse detection methods establishes monitoring requirements. Assessment of abuse prevention controls identifies protection requirements.

Risk Scenario Matrix: A structured catalog of risk scenarios with probability and impact enables risk prioritization. Prioritization of scenarios based on overall risk guides resource allocation. Mapping of scenarios to business impact categories clarifies organizational consequences. Documentation of risk ownership and accountability establishes responsibility. Assessment of current risk mitigation controls identifies protection gaps.

Attack Path Diagrams: Visual representation of attack progression through the system enables defense planning. Documentation of attack prerequisites and constraints identifies trigger conditions. Mapping of security controls along attack paths identifies protection placements. Identification of critical choke points for defense highlights key protection targets. Assessment of attack complexity and likelihood guides defense prioritization.

4.4 **Catalog Vulnerabilities**

Activities:

Perform Security Assessment: Organizations should conduct comprehensive security testing of the GAI system to identify actual vulnerabilities. Specialized testing for AI-specific vulnerabilities needs to be implemented to address unique GAI risks. Penetration testing against system components should be executed to identify exploitable weaknesses. Code review of critical system elements must be performed to identify implementation flaws. Discovered vulnerabilities and weaknesses should be documented to guide remediation.

Document Weaknesses: Identified security weaknesses should be cataloged by component to organize remediation efforts. Vulnerability severity and exploitation difficulty need to be documented to prioritize fixes. Weaknesses should be mapped to potential attack vectors to understand exploitation paths. Common weakness patterns across the system must be identified to address systemic issues. Root causes of identified vulnerabilities should be documented to enable fundamental fixes.

Map Vulnerable Components: System components with security vulnerabilities should be identified to target remediation efforts. Vulnerability density by component needs to be documented to identify problematic areas. Dependencies between vulnerable components should be mapped to understand compound risks. Critical components requiring immediate remediation must be identified to prioritize fixes. Component owners responsible for remediation should be documented to assign accountability.

Identify Security Gaps: Missing or inadequate security controls should be documented to guide enhancement efforts. Deviations from security best practices need to be identified to address standards compliance.

Compliance gaps against relevant standards should be mapped to address regulatory requirements. Security process deficiencies must be documented to improve operational security. Security architecture weaknesses should be identified to address structural issues.

Deliverables:

Vulnerability Catalog: A comprehensive inventory of all identified vulnerabilities enables systematic remediation. Classification by severity using standard scoring (e.g., CVSS) guides prioritization. Documentation of exploitation prerequisites and complexity assesses attack feasibility. Mapping to potential attack scenarios connects vulnerabilities to threats. Recommendations for remediation with priority guides for fixing efforts.

Security Assessment Report: An executive summary of security posture provides management visibility into risks. Detailed findings from security testing activities document specific vulnerabilities. Documentation of testing methodology and coverage ensures assessment completeness. Prioritized remediation recommendations guide fixing efforts. Risk assessment based on findings quantifies security posture.

Component Risk Matrix: Mapping of system components to risk levels identifies high-priority areas. Documentation of risk factors for each component explains vulnerability sources. Prioritization of components for remediation guides resource allocation. Assessment of component criticality to overall security focuses protection efforts. Documentation of component interdependencies identifies cascade risks.

Gap Analysis Document: Identification of security control gaps against best practices guides enhancement efforts. Documentation of deviations from security standards addresses compliance requirements. Mapping of gaps to potential risks connects missing controls to threats. Prioritization of gaps for remediation guides implementation sequence. Recommendations for addressing identified gaps guide the remediation approach.

5. **Analysis Phase**

5.1 **Evaluate Interactions**

Activities:

Analyze Component Interactions: Organizations should document how system components interact with each other to understand connection-based vulnerabilities. Data exchange patterns between components need to be identified to understand information flow security. Control flows and decision points should be mapped to understand process integrity risks. Error handling between components must be documented to understand exception security. Potential race conditions or timing issues should be identified to understand concurrency vulnerabilities.

Map Security Dependencies: How security controls depend on each other should be documented to understand defense interdependencies. Single points of failure in security architecture need to be identified to address critical vulnerabilities. Authentication and authorization dependencies should be mapped to understand identity security chains. Encryption key dependencies and management must be documented to understand cryptographic foundations. Security monitoring dependencies should be identified to understand visibility relationships.

Document Data Flows: How data moves between system components should be mapped to understand information pathways. Data transformation and processing steps need to be documented to understand manipulation points. Data aggregation and correlation points should be identified to understand information concentration risks. Data storage and retrieval patterns must be documented to identify access controls, retention policies, and potential vulnerability points in data handling processes.

Throughout this book, we have examined the approach to securing GAI systems by examining them through three critical lenses: as a tool, a potential weapon, and a target. This comprehensive perspective enables organizations to develop a more nuanced and effective understanding of their AI security risks and mitigation strategies. The framework's strength lies in its ability to address the complex, interconnected nature of AI security challenges while remaining adaptable to different organizational contexts. At its core, the GSTF's three-dimensional analysis approach provides a structured method for evaluating AI systems. The Tool dimension examines the AI system's security capabilities and potential as a defensive asset, including built-in security features, monitoring capabilities, and integration with existing security infrastructure. The Weapon dimension analyzes how the system could be weaponized or misused, focusing on potential attack vectors, amplification effects, and exploitation scenarios. The Target dimension assesses the system's vulnerabilities and attack surface, including both the model and its data, along with necessary protection mechanisms.

Implementation strategies vary significantly between large organizations and SMBs. Large organizations typically establish dedicated GSTF implementation teams, create comprehensive documentation and tracking systems, develop detailed metrics and reporting structures, and integrate with existing security frameworks such as NIST or ISO. In contrast, SMBs need to take a more streamlined approach, focusing on essential components first, simplifying documentation requirements, leveraging existing tools and resources, and implementing basic monitoring systems that align with their resource constraints.

The implementation process follows three main phases: Assessment, Analysis, and Action. During the Assessment phase, organizations catalog their AI systems, document capabilities, and identify potential risks. The Analysis phase involves evaluating interactions between system components, identifying critical security intersections, and prioritizing risks based on potential impact and likelihood. The Action phase focuses on implementing controls, monitoring effectiveness, and maintaining continuous improvement cycles.

For SMBs, adapting the GSTF involves focusing on high-impact, low-resource activities. This might include leveraging cloud provider security features, utilizing automated tools for basic monitoring, and implementing essential security controls first. The key is to start with fundamental security measures and gradually build up capabilities as resources allow. SMBs can also benefit from simplified documentation requirements and streamlined assessment processes that focus on critical systems and major risk areas. Success in implementing the GSTF depends heavily on several key factors. Leadership support is crucial, providing clear executive sponsorship and adequate resource allocation. Team capability plays a vital role, requiring basic AI security knowledge, implementation skills, and project management ability. Effective resource management, including realistic budgeting and appropriate tooling, rounds out the essential elements for successful implementation.

Organizations often face common challenges during implementation, including resource constraints, technical complexity, and organizational resistance. Resource constraints can be addressed through careful prioritization and phased implementation approaches. Technical complexity challenges can be managed by starting with the basics and leveraging vendor support. Organizational resistance often requires clear communication, stakeholder engagement, and demonstrated value to overcome. Measuring success involves tracking both quantitative and qualitative metrics. Essential metrics include security incident reduction, control implementation progress, and risk mitigation effectiveness. Implementation progress can be measured through framework adoption rates, control deployment status, and documentation completion. Operational impact assessment should consider system performance, user acceptance, and business alignment.

The GSTF should be viewed as a living framework that evolves with new AI capabilities, emerging threats, and security innovations. Regular review and updates ensure the framework remains effective and relevant to organizational needs. This includes assessing framework effectiveness, adjusting controls, updating documentation, and refining processes based on operational experience and emerging best practices. Integration with existing security programs and business operations is crucial for long-term success. Organizations should align the GSTF with current security frameworks, leverage existing controls, and support operational needs while managing resource impact. Integration with development processes, including DevSecOps practices and CI/CD pipelines, ensures security is built into AI systems from the ground up.

The key to successful GSTF implementation lies not in perfect initial execution but in consistent application, regular review, and continuous improvement. Organizations should start with the basics, build gradually, and evolve their implementation as organizational capability and resources allow. This measured approach helps ensure sustainable security improvements while maintaining operational efficiency and supporting business objectives.

10.4 Preparing for Future Challenges

Preparing for future challenges in AI security requires organizations to adopt proactive approaches that leverage current AI capabilities while anticipating emerging threats and technological developments. Organizations need to develop flexible, adaptable security frameworks that can evolve alongside AI technology while maintaining effective protection against both current and emerging threats (Habbal et al., 2024). Generative AI can play a crucial role in helping organizations prepare for future challenges by simulating potential attack scenarios and testing security responses. These systems can generate realistic security scenarios, helping teams develop and validate response strategies while identifying potential gaps in security coverage. This capability becomes particularly valuable for preparing for novel or emerging threats that teams might not otherwise encounter in training environments. Training and skill development are critical components of future preparedness. Generative AI can enhance training programs by creating personalized learning experiences, generating realistic practice scenarios, and helping security teams develop expertise in handling complex security situations (Rana & Chicone, 2025). These systems can adapt training content based on individual learning needs and progress, making preparation more effective and efficient.

Organizations need to develop comprehensive threat intelligence capabilities that incorporate AI analysis to identify and understand emerging threats (Manoharan & Sarker, 2023). This includes using AI systems to analyze threat data, identify patterns, and predict potential future attack vectors. However, human expertise remains crucial for interpreting this intelligence and developing appropriate strategic responses. Scenario planning and red team exercises become more sophisticated with generative AI support. These systems can help create more complex and realistic attack scenarios, enabling organizations to better test their defenses and response capabilities. This includes generating novel attack patterns that might not be apparent through traditional analysis methods. Infrastructure and architecture planning must consider future AI capabilities and requirements. Organizations need to develop flexible, scalable security architectures that can accommodate new AI capabilities while maintaining security effectiveness. This includes planning for increased data processing requirements, new integration points, and evolving security control needs. Risk assessment and management processes need to evolve to address AI-specific challenges while maintaining coverage of traditional security risks. Organizations should use AI capabilities to enhance risk assessment processes, helping identify potential future risks and develop appropriate mitigation strategies. This includes considering both technical and operational risks associated with AI adoption.

Collaboration and information sharing become increasingly important for future preparedness. Organizations need to develop networks for sharing threat intelligence, best practices, and lessons learned about AI security challenges. Generative AI can help facilitate this sharing by analyzing and synthesizing information from multiple sources while maintaining appropriate privacy and security controls. Thus, investment in R&D becomes crucial for staying ahead of emerging challenges. Organizations need to allocate resources for exploring new security technologies, testing emerging solutions, and developing innovative approaches to AI security. This includes both technical research and investigation of operational and strategic approaches to security challenges.

A critical component of this approach lies in integrating AI's capabilities across multiple levels of operations, while simultaneously acknowledging the limitations and risks that accompany such advancements. Developing robust ecosystems for AI-driven threat management is not merely an option but a necessity in today's rapidly evolving digital landscape. One of the foundational steps in this preparation is the establishment of dynamic governance structures that incorporate AI-specific security standards and protocols. Organizations must ensure that their governance models address the unique risks posed by AI technologies, such as model poisoning, adversarial attacks, and data privacy concerns. This involves creating policies that delineate the roles and responsibilities of AI systems within the organization and defining the conditions under which human oversight must be exercised. These governance frameworks must remain flexible, enabling organizations to evolve their policies in response to advancements in AI technology and emerging threat landscapes.

AI ethics and accountability form another crucial pillar of future preparedness. As AI systems become more autonomous and integrated into decision-making processes, organizations face significant ethical challenges, including bias in algorithms, misuse of data, and accountability for AI-driven outcomes. To address these issues, organizations must embed ethical considerations into their AI security frameworks. This includes conducting regular audits of AI systems to identify and mitigate biases, ensuring transparency in decision-making processes, and establishing mechanisms for accountability. Therefore, it is crucial to foster an organizational culture that prioritizes ethical AI practices.

The integration of AI with existing cybersecurity tools and processes is essential for creating a cohesive security ecosystem. Organizations should adopt a layered approach to security, wherein AI systems are used to complement traditional security measures rather than replace them. For instance, while AI can enhance threat detection and response capabilities, human analysts should continue to play a critical role in interpreting AI outputs and making strategic decisions. This symbiotic relationship between human expertise and AI capabilities ensures that organizations can leverage the strengths of both, creating a more resilient security posture. Moreover, integrating AI with other emerging technologies, such as blockchain and quantum computing, can provide additional layers of security and redundancy, further strengthening an organization's defenses. In addition to integration, organizations must prioritize the scalability of their security architectures. As AI systems generate and process increasing volumes of data, the demands on an organization's infrastructure will grow exponentially. Developing scalable architectures that can accommodate these demands while maintaining security effectiveness is a critical aspect of future preparedness. This includes investing in cloud-based solutions, distributed computing, and edge computing to handle the data processing requirements of AI systems. Furthermore, organizations must implement robust data management practices, ensuring that sensitive information is stored, processed, and transmitted securely.

Training and development initiatives play a central role in equipping organizations to handle future AI security challenges. Security teams must be trained to understand the nuances of AI systems, including their strengths, limitations, and potential vulnerabilities. This requires a shift from traditional cybersecurity training programs to those that emphasize AI-specific skills, such as machine learning, data analysis, and adversarial attack detection. Organizations can leverage AI-driven training tools to create personalized learning experiences that adapt to the needs and progress of individual team members. Fostering a culture of continuous learning and innovation is key to remaining well-equipped in our cyber and AI landscape.

Collaboration across industries and sectors is another key component of future preparedness. Cyber threats often transcend organizational and national boundaries, requiring a collective response from the global cybersecurity community. Organizations should actively participate in industry forums, working groups, and public–private partnerships to share knowledge, resources, and best practices. AI can facilitate this collaboration by synthesizing and analyzing data from diverse sources, enabling organizations to gain a more comprehensive understanding of emerging threats. Working together is important to develop unified strategies to address common challenges and create a more secure digital environment for all. Consequently, as organizations prepare for future challenges, they must also consider the societal implications of AI security. The rapid adoption of AI technologies has the potential to exacerbate existing inequalities and create new vulnerabilities, particularly for marginalized communities. Organizations have a responsibility to ensure that their AI security measures are inclusive and equitable, protecting the rights and interests of all stakeholders. This includes addressing issues such as algorithmic bias, digital accessibility, and the potential for AI to perpetuate systemic inequalities.

Investment in R&D is critical for staying ahead of emerging challenges in AI security. Organizations must allocate resources to explore new algorithms, techniques, and applications that enhance the effectiveness and efficiency of AI security measures. This includes testing the feasibility of emerging technologies, conducting pilot projects, and collaborating with academic institutions and industry partners. R&D initiatives should focus on both technical and operational aspects of AI security, ensuring that organizations are well-prepared to address the multifaceted nature of future challenges.

AI's potential to revolutionize cybersecurity is matched only by the complexity of the challenges it presents. Organizations must adopt a proactive, forward-thinking approach to AI security, one that combines innovative technologies with robust governance structures, ethical considerations, and collaborative efforts.

Ultimately, preparing for future challenges in AI security is not just about protecting organizational assets; it is about safeguarding the trust, safety, and well-being of individuals and communities. As stewards of AI technology, organizations have a responsibility to ensure that their security measures are not only effective but also ethical and inclusive. This is an important responsibility: we want to build a future where AI (and technology) serves as a force for good and enhances security and resilience in our digital world.

10.5 Responsible AI Security

The time for passive observation of AI security challenges has passed—we must now take decisive action to shape a secure and ethical AI-powered future. As security professionals, technology leaders, and responsible global citizens, we have both an opportunity and an obligation to ensure AI technologies are developed and deployed securely while serving the greater good.

The decisions we make today about AI security will echo far into the future, affecting not just our organizations but society as a whole. Each of us has a role to play in this critical mission—whether you're a security practitioner implementing controls, a leader setting security strategy, or a developer creating AI systems. The security community must unite to establish and maintain high standards for responsible AI development and deployment. It extends beyond technical implementation to encompass ethical considerations and societal impact. We must actively work to prevent the misuse of AI while fostering innovation that benefits humanity. This means going beyond asking "Can we?" to thoughtfully considering "Should we?" when implementing AI security measures. It requires us to consider the impacts on privacy, fairness, and human rights while maintaining robust security. The global nature of AI technology demands that we think and act beyond organizational and national boundaries. We must forge partnerships, share knowledge, and work collectively to address common challenges. This includes ensuring equitable access to AI security capabilities and preventing the creation of new digital divides that could leave vulnerable populations at risk.

The time for action is now. As AI capabilities continue to advance rapidly, we cannot afford to wait for perfect solutions or complete consensus. Each of us must commit to continuous learning, ethical practice, and proactive security measures. We must engage in public discourse, contribute to standards development, and work to build trust in AI technologies through responsible security practices. Your role in this journey is crucial. Whether you're just beginning to explore AI security or you're an experienced practitioner, your contributions matter. Share your knowledge, challenge conventional thinking, and advocate for responsible practices in your sphere of influence. Together, we can build a future where AI technology enhances human capabilities while maintaining robust security and protecting societal interests.

Take the first step today. Evaluate your organization's AI security practices, engage with the security community, and commit to continuous improvement. The future of AI security depends on the actions we take now, and every contribution moves us closer to a more secure and ethical AI-enabled world. The path forward requires courage, commitment, and collaboration. So, let's embrace this challenge together, working to ensure that AI technology serves as a force for positive change while maintaining the security and trust that our digital future demands! Go out there and make a safer tomorrow!

Chapter 10 Summary

This concluding chapter examines the transformative intersection of AI and cybersecurity, highlighting how security professionals' roles are evolving in response to AI advancements. The chapter introduces the GAI Security Triad Framework (GSTF), a comprehensive approach that analyzes generative AI through three critical dimensions: as a tool for enhanced defense capabilities, a potential weapon in malicious hands, and a vulnerable target requiring protection. The framework provides structured methodologies for assessment, analysis, and action phases, with implementation strategies that vary between large organizations and small-to-medium businesses based on available resources and complexity requirements. AI-driven incident response emerges as a transformative force, offering capabilities for automated threat containment, enhanced recovery processes, and predictive analytics that enable proactive defense mechanisms.

The chapter emphasizes the importance of preparing for future challenges through dynamic governance structures, ethical AI considerations, collaborative threat intelligence sharing, and continuous investment in R&D. Throughout, the discussion maintains focus on human–AI collaboration rather than replacement, stressing that while AI can excel at data processing and pattern recognition, human expertise remains crucial for strategic thinking, ethical judgment, and stakeholder communication in complex security scenarios.

Key Takeaways:

Security professionals must evolve to become AI-literate while maintaining traditional security expertise, developing skills in AI model validation, system monitoring, and data analysis to effectively work with AI-enhanced security operations. The GAI Security Triad Framework provides organizations with a structured approach to comprehensively evaluate AI security risks by examining systems as tools, weapons, and targets simultaneously, with implementation strategies that can be adapted to organizational size and resource constraints. AI-driven incident response represents a paradigm shift toward proactive and predictive defense mechanisms, enabling automated threat containment, enhanced recovery processes, and sophisticated scenario planning that strengthens overall organizational resilience. Preparing for future AI security challenges requires organizations to invest in dynamic governance structures, ethical AI frameworks, collaborative threat intelligence sharing, and continuous R&D, while fostering a culture of responsible AI implementation that considers societal impacts and maintains human oversight in critical security decisions.

Practice Quiz: AI Security Triangular Framework

Instructions

This comprehensive practice quiz covers all the chapters of this book. Answer all questions to test your understanding of the triangular framework (AI as tool, weapon, and target) and its practical applications across different organizational contexts.

Questions

1 **Integration and Strategy (Chapters 1 and 9)**
Which of the following best demonstrates why GFSC's initial dual-lens approach to AI security was insufficient for modern threats?
a) It failed to consider the computational costs of AI implementation

b) It overlooked the interconnected nature of AI systems as potential attack vectors
c) It focused too heavily on regulatory compliance rather than practical security
d) It required too many specialized personnel to implement effectively

2 **Technical Foundations (Chapter 2)**
In TechSecure's implementation, why was their understanding of different neural network architectures crucial for both offensive and defensive AI security strategies?
a) It allowed them to minimize hardware requirements for AI deployment
b) It enabled them to choose appropriate architectures for specific security tasks while anticipating vulnerabilities
c) It simplified the integration process with existing legacy systems
d) It reduced the training time required for new security personnel

3 **Generative AI Applications (Chapter 3)**
How did FinSecure Bank's use of generative AI for penetration testing exemplify the triangular framework's "AI as a tool" perspective?
a) By creating realistic attack scenarios that exposed vulnerabilities before they could be exploited
b) By automating all security decisions without human intervention
c) By replacing traditional security measures with AI-only solutions
d) By generating synthetic data to train other AI systems

4 **Advanced Threat Analysis (Chapter 4)**
What made the deepfake attack in Case Study 2 particularly sophisticated compared to traditional phishing attempts?
a) It used quantum computing to enhance processing speed
b) It combined real-time lip-sync technology with voice cloning and behavioral analysis
c) It bypassed all existing security measures through advanced encryption
d) It targeted multiple organizations simultaneously through coordinated attacks

5 **Cross-Case Pattern Recognition (Chapters 3 and 5)**
Both XYZ Bakery (Chapter 5) and FinSecure Bank (Chapter 3) implemented AI systems that required protection. What fundamental security principle applies to both cases?
a) All AI systems should operate independently without human oversight

b) Protecting AI systems as targets is essential regardless of organizational size
c) Small organizations face identical security challenges to large enterprises
d) Generative AI should only be used for noncritical business functions

6 **Technical Implementation (Chapter 6)**
In FinTech Solutions' comprehensive defense strategy, what was the primary advantage of implementing ensemble methods against adversarial attacks?
a) Ensemble methods process data faster than individual models
b) They require less computational resources than single models
c) Adversarial inputs typically cannot manipulate all models in an ensemble simultaneously
d) They automatically generate new training data for improved accuracy

7 **Regulatory and Ethical Considerations (Chapter 7)**
The financial institution's approach to addressing bias in their fraud detection system demonstrates which key principle of ethical AI implementation?
a) AI systems should always prioritize efficiency over fairness
b) Regular auditing and retraining are necessary to ensure equitable treatment across demographic groups
c) Regulatory compliance is more important than system performance
d) Human oversight should be eliminated once AI systems are properly trained

8 **Future-Oriented Strategy (Chapter 8)**
According to the triangular framework analysis in Chapter 8, what makes postquantum cryptography (PQC) particularly important for protecting AI systems?
a) It improves the processing speed of AI training algorithms
b) It protects AI training pipelines against future quantum-enabled attacks and reverse engineering
c) It reduces the computational requirements for AI model deployment
d) It eliminates the need for traditional encryption methods in AI systems

9 **Organizational Transformation (Chapter 9)**
CyberSecure Inc.'s phased implementation approach (pretrained models → custom development → adaptive systems) exemplifies which key principle of organizational AI security adoption?
a) Organizations should implement all AI security measures simultaneously for maximum effectiveness

b) Custom AI development should always precede the use of pretrained models
c) Gradual implementation allows for learning, adaptation, and risk management while achieving quick wins
d) Pretrained models are always inferior to custom-developed solutions

10 **Multichapter Synthesis**
A healthcare organization is considering implementing an AI diagnostic system similar to DEF Corp's (Chapter 5). Based on lessons learned across all case studies, what should be their primary concern regarding the triangular framework?
a) Focusing solely on AI as a tool since healthcare requires maximum accuracy
b) Implementing all three aspects (tool, weapon, target) with particular attention to data poisoning risks in critical healthcare applications
c) Prioritizing AI as a weapon to defend against cyberattacks on medical records
d) Concentrating on regulatory compliance rather than technical security measures

11 **Cross-Organizational Learning**
What common vulnerability pattern appears across small (XYZ Bakery), medium (ABC Solutions), and large (DEF Corp) organizations in the case studies?
a) All organizations lacked sufficient computational resources for AI implementation
b) Each organization underestimated AI-specific security risks unique to their AI systems
c) All organizations faced identical regulatory compliance challenges
d) Every organization had inadequate traditional cybersecurity measures

12 **Advanced Technical Application**
Based on the technical implementations described across chapters, which approach would be most effective for an organization implementing AI security measures across all three aspects of the triangular framework?
a) Deploy separate, isolated systems for each aspect (tool, weapon, target) to minimize interdependencies
b) Implement an integrated approach where security measures for each aspect reinforce and inform the others

c) Focus resources on the aspect most relevant to the organization's primary business function
d) Prioritize AI as a weapon since offensive capabilities provide the strongest defense

13 **Strategic Decision Making**
An organization's leadership is concerned about the cost of implementing comprehensive AI security measures. Based on the case study outcomes, what evidence best supports the investment?
a) AI security measures always provide 100% protection against all cyber threats
b) The financial and operational benefits (fraud reduction, incident response time, customer trust) demonstrate clear ROI
c) Regulatory requirements make AI security implementation legally mandatory in all industries
d) AI security measures eliminate the need for traditional cybersecurity investments

14 **Future Threat Adaptation**
Considering the evolution of threats described across all chapters, what capability is most crucial for organizations to develop for long-term AI security success?
a) The ability to purchase and implement the most advanced AI security tools available
b) Comprehensive documentation and compliance with all current regulatory frameworks
c) Adaptive learning and continuous improvement in response to evolving AI threats and capabilities
d) Complete replacement of human security analysts with AI-powered automation

15 **Practical Implementation Synthesis**
A mid-sized organization wants to apply lessons learned from all the case studies. What implementation sequence would be most effective based on the triangular framework?
a) Implement AI as a weapon first, then as a tool, and finally as a target
b) Begin with a readiness assessment, develop an integrated strategy addressing all three aspects, and implement in phases with continuous monitoring
c) Focus exclusively on one aspect of the triangular framework until mastery is achieved
d) Implement AI as a target protection first since this provides the foundation for other aspects

Answer Key

1. **Correct Answer: b) It overlooked the interconnected nature of AI systems as potential attack vectors**
   Explanation: GFSC's experience demonstrated that the dual-lens approach created "dangerous blind spots" by not considering AI systems themselves as targets. The triangular framework showed how these three aspects are interconnected—compromising AI as a target affects its effectiveness as a tool and can enable its use as a weapon.

2. **Correct Answer: b) It enabled them to choose appropriate architectures for specific security tasks while anticipating vulnerabilities**
   Explanation: The case study explicitly states that TechSecure's "understanding of how different architectures (CNNs, RNNs, transformers) process information helped them choose the right tools for specific security tasks while anticipating potential vulnerabilities."

3. **Correct Answer: a) By creating realistic attack scenarios that exposed vulnerabilities before they could be exploited**
   Explanation: The case study describes how FinSecure Bank used generative AI to discover "a misconfigured API endpoint that could have allowed unauthorized access to sensitive customer data," demonstrating proactive vulnerability identification.

4. **Correct Answer: b) It combined real-time lip-sync technology with voice cloning and behavioral analysis**
   Explanation: Case Study 2 specifically mentions the attack used "real-time lip-sync and voice cloning to enhance believability" along with analysis of communication patterns, making it far more sophisticated than traditional phishing.

5. **Correct Answer: b) Protecting AI systems as targets is essential regardless of organizational size**
   Explanation: Both cases demonstrate that AI systems require protection from manipulation and attack regardless of organization size—XYZ Bakery faced prompt injection attacks, while FinSecure Bank needed protection during training and operation.

6. **Correct Answer: c) Adversarial inputs typically cannot manipulate all models in an ensemble simultaneously**
   Explanation: The case study states that "Ensemble voting mechanisms ensured robustness, as adversarial inputs failed to manipulate all models simultaneously."

7 **Correct Answer: b) Regular auditing and retraining are necessary to ensure equitable treatment across demographic groups**
Explanation: The case study describes how the institution "introduced fairness metrics" and used "regular updates and diverse datasets" to minimize bias, emphasizing ongoing effort rather than one-time fixes.

8 **Correct Answer: b) It protects AI training pipelines against future quantum-enabled attacks and reverse engineering**
Explanation: Chapter 8 specifically mentions using PQC to "protect AI training pipelines with post-quantum cryptography to mitigate risks posed by future quantum computing attacks."

9 **Correct Answer: c) Gradual implementation allows for learning, adaptation, and risk management while achieving quick wins**
Explanation: The case study explicitly states the phased approach "emphasized quick wins, such as deploying pre-trained models, while planning for long-term enhancements."

10 **Correct Answer: b) Implementing all three aspects (tool, weapon, target) with particular attention to data poisoning risks in critical healthcare applications**
Explanation: Healthcare systems like DEF Corp's face all three aspects of the triangular framework, with particular vulnerability to data poisoning attacks that could compromise patient safety.

11 **Correct Answer: b) Each organization underestimated AI-specific security risks unique to their AI systems**
Explanation: Across all case studies, organizations faced novel AI-specific vulnerabilities (prompt injection, model extraction, data poisoning) that differed from traditional cybersecurity threats.

12 **Correct Answer: b) Implement an integrated approach where security measures for each aspect reinforce and inform the others**
Explanation: The triangular framework emphasizes interconnection—GFSC's experience showed that "enhancements in one area often strengthened the others."

13 **Correct Answer: b) The financial and operational benefits (fraud reduction, incident response time, customer trust) demonstrate clear ROI**
Explanation: Multiple case studies provide specific metrics: FinSecure Bank saw "40% reduction in financial losses," CyberSecure achieved "40% decrease in incident response time," demonstrating measurable ROI.

14 **Correct Answer: c) Adaptive learning and continuous improvement in response to evolving AI threats and capabilities**
Explanation: All case studies emphasize the need for continuous adaptation—GFSC developed "a sustainable approach that could adapt to emerging threats," and other organizations implemented continuous monitoring and updating.

15 **Correct Answer: b) Begin with readiness assessment, develop an integrated strategy addressing all three aspects, and implement in phases with continuous monitoring**
Explanation: This sequence reflects CyberSecure's successful approach and incorporates lessons from all case studies: assessment first, integrated strategy, phased implementation, and ongoing adaptation.

References

Habbal, A., Ali, M. K., & Abuzaraida, M. A. (2024). Artificial intelligence trust, risk and security management (AI trism): Frameworks, applications, challenges and future research directions. *Expert Systems with Applications, 240*, 122442.

Manoharan, A., & Sarker, M. (2023). Revolutionizing cybersecurity: Unleashing the power of artificial intelligence and machine learning for next-generation threat detection. *International Research Journal of Modernization in Engineering Technology and Science, 4*(12), 1. https://doi.org/10.56726/IRJMETS32644.

Rana, S., & Chicone, R. (2025). *Fortifying the future: Harnessing AI for transformative cybersecurity training*. Springer Nature.

Index

Generative AI Security: Defense, Threats, and Vulnerabilities, First Edition. Shaila Rana and Rhonda Chicone.

d

e

f

i

m